Crime and Justice

Crime and Justice
A Review of Research

Edited by Michael Tonry

VOLUME 34

The University of Chicago Press, Chicago and London

The University of Chicago Press, Chicago 60637
The University of Chicago Press, Ltd., London

© 2006 by The University of Chicago
All rights reserved.
Printed in the United States of America

ISSN: 0192-3234

ISBN: 0-226-80859-9

LCN: 80-642217

The paper used in this publication meets the minimum requirements of American
National Standard for Information Sciences—Permanence of Paper for Printed
Library Materials, ANSI Z39.48-1984. ⊛

Contents

Preface

Part of the fun of editing *Crime and Justice* for three decades has been the opportunity it provides for observing changes over time in crime patterns and policies, and in the scholarly enterprises that attempt to understand and explain them.

American crime patterns and policies have been out of synch for most of the last forty years. Policies became steadily more punitive from the early seventies through the late nineties, after which they stabilized at historically severe levels. The number of prison inmates quintupled and continues to increase. Official crime rates rose from the late sixties through the early eighties, fell through 1986, climbed again through 1991, and have declined substantially since.

Anyone predisposed (many are) to believe that severe crime control policies caused the declines in crime rates or that the rising crime rates produced rising prison populations need look no further than across the border to Canada to see it isn't so. Rises and falls in Canada's crime rate have closely paralleled America's for thirty years, but its imprisonment rate has remained stable. A look across the Atlantic Ocean is similarly chastening. Crime rates everywhere rose steeply from the late sixties through the early to mid-nineties and have since fallen steadily. Imprisonment rates display every pattern imaginable, from steady increase (the Netherlands) through broad stability (Germany, most of Scandinavia, and Switzerland) and up-and-down gyrations (France and Italy) to steady decline (Finland). Go figure.

In the 1970s when *Crime and Justice* began, reasonable people believed, and it was reasonable to believe, that changes in crime control policies and prison use could substantially affect crime rates and patterns. In the early twenty-first century we know beyond peradventure of doubt that imprisonment rates result from policy decisions but that crime rates result from the operation of deep social, cultural, and economic changes that affect all Western countries and that in the aggregate are largely impervious to anything done in the name of crime control or prevention. Changes in policy and practice can affect crime rates and patterns at the margin, but the heavy lifting is done by social and structural forces over which policy makers have no control and little influence.

Astonishingly little serious effort has been made to explain why crime rates in Western countries followed the trajectory they did, and particularly why they fell so steeply after the early nineties. A slightly larger literature, though still a small one, has tried to explain changes in punishment, especially imprisonment, patterns. It is clearly established that changes in punishment patterns result primarily from deliberate policy decisions, but little is understood about why particular policies are adopted in some places and times and not in others.

On many other subjects relating to crime and punishment, however, knowledge has steadily advanced since 1977. Criminology and criminal justice were fledgling subjects then but now are taught in hundreds of colleges and universities; PhDs are offered in dozens. Research on kindred topics occurs in many other university departments. The number of specialist English-language journals has grown from a handful to several dozen. The number of participants in meetings of the American Society of Criminology has grown from hundreds to thousands, a large fraction of whom come from other countries.

Research and the research community have changed substantially. The world has become smaller. Research subjects and research communities have become less parochial. Topics of inquiry have shifted (terrorism, genocide, crimes against humanity, international criminal courts, money laundering, and human trafficking, e.g., appeared only recently on social scientists' agendas).

Changes in *Crime and Justice* over time reflect those changes. Seven of nine writers in volume 1 (1979) were Americans and the other two were English. In volume 34, five of ten are American (one born in Australia); the others are Danish, English, and Finnish. Five of the eight topics covered in volume 1 were distinctly American in focus (policing, etiological theories, violence, race relations in prison, and juvenile justice), none mentioning work published outside the United States. Two, both methodological (ecological and longitudinal studies), had broader ambits. Only one, on policing, was broadly comparative.

Only two of the essays in this volume—mine on sentencing purposes and functions and Daniel Rich's on the broadening federal reach into state and local criminal law systems—are narrowly American. The rest are variously transnational (money laundering), international (human trafficking), cross-national (victimization studies), or multinational in scope and coverage (experiments and solitary confinement).

A volume like this inevitably reflects the efforts of many people. The authors to a person (at least seemingly) cheerfully endured a lengthy process of initial drafts, readers' reports, the editor's comment letters, more drafts, and source and cite checks, and all this before the essays were delivered to Chicago for professional editing. This book was worked on by, besides the authors, Kate Blake, Sara Harrop, Julie Moylan, Dee Gibbons, and Hayley Hontos. I am enormously grateful to them all.

Like most recent *Crime and Justice* volumes, this one is a mix of new subjects and previous subjects revisited. Essays by Peter Reuter and Mike Levi on money laundering and by Martti Lehti and Kauko Aromaa on human trafficking address entirely new subjects. Essays by Jim Lynch on victimization research and by me on sentencing continue long series of essays on related topics extending over a quarter century. The others have each a single distinguished predecessor. David Farrington and Brandon Welsh's on experiments updates Farrington's classic and much-cited essay in volume 4 (1983). Peter Scharff Smith's on the use and effects of solitary confinement builds on Leena Kurki and Norval Morris's volume 28 essay (2001) on supermax prisons. Daniel Richman's on federal influence on local law enforcement builds on Norval Morris and Bill Geller's volume 15 essay (1992) on relations between federal and state police. Norval would have liked this volume. Readers will decide for themselves whether they do.

Michael Tonry
Deer Isle, Maine, July 2006

Michael Tonry

Purposes and Functions of Sentencing

ABSTRACT

American sentencing systems have fragmented since the modern sentencing reform movement began in the 1970s and predominant retributive theories of punishment have become obsolete. Indeterminate sentencing was ubiquitous, but when it lost credibility, no single approach replaced it. Every American jurisdiction has a crazy quilt of diverse and, in principle if not practice, irreconcilable elements. Influential retributive theories of punishment were a 1970s response to 1970s problems that no longer galvanize opinion or reform. They are incompatible with the recent growth of restorative and community justice, therapeutic jurisprudence, prisoner reentry programs, and knowledge about the effectiveness of treatment programs. Theories of punishment can provide normative criteria by which policies and practices can be measured, but to be used in that way they must speak to their own times. New sentencing systems more effective and more just than current fragmented systems can be developed, and they will be better if new normative theories germane to them develop in tandem.

Sentencing policy in the United States has fragmented. There is no overriding theory or model. There are no widely shared understandings about what sentencing can or should accomplish or about conceptions of justice it should incorporate or reflect. Painting with a broad brush, utilitarian ideas held sway in the United States from 1900 through the mid-1970s (evidenced most strongly by indeterminate sentencing and extensive parole release), followed in succession by retributive ideas (evidenced most strongly by desert-based guidelines systems

Michael Tonry is Sonosky Professor of Law and Public Policy and director of the Institute on Crime and Public Policy at the University of Minnesota Law School, and senior fellow in the Netherlands Institute for the Study of Crime and Law Enforcement, Leiden. I am grateful to Marc Miller, who first proposed I write on the subjects of this essay. An earlier version of this essay appeared in the *Stanford Law Review* (Tonry 2005*a*).

1

in Minnesota, Oregon, and Washington) in the 1970s and 1980s, deterrent ideas (evidenced most strongly by federal and state mandatory minimum sentence and truth-in-sentencing laws) in the 1980s, incapacitative ideas (evidenced most strongly by three-strikes, dangerous offender/sexual psychopath, and sex offender registration and notification laws) in the 1990s, and a muddle in the early years of the twenty-first century. The muddle is exemplified by greatly reinvigorated interest in rehabilitative programs, such as drug, mental health, and domestic violence courts, reentry programs, and a plethora of new community-based and institutional treatment programs, combined with the continuing operation of laws enacted in all the earlier periods but especially the 1980s and 1990s. Ideas about restorative and community justice and therapeutic jurisprudence percolate through many of these initiatives.

Muddles are not necessarily bad. The absence of a stifling orthodoxy and a limiting conventional wisdom allows for creativity and experimentation, both of which have been evident for a decade. In the longer term, though, new practices and prevailing views will emerge and they will be incorporated into new sentencing systems and laws. As that begins to happen, it will be done better or worse. Thinking through the purposes and functions of sentencing in liberal democratic societies may improve chances it will be done better.

American governments did not do a very good job responding to the collapse of indeterminate sentencing. The developments underlying the collapse—declining confidence in rehabilitative programs, concerns about disparities and racial bias, and lack of procedural fairness—are well known (Blumstein, Cohen, Martin, and Tonry 1983, chap. 1). For a short time sentencing policy changes in the forms of sentencing and parole guidelines and abolition of parole release addressed those problems in some places. From the early 1980s through the late 1990s, though, policy makers lost their way. Some of the policies they adopted, notably mandatory minimums for drug and violent crimes, truth-in-sentencing laws, and three-strikes laws, worsened the problems the sentencing reform movement initially sought to address. Sentencing disparities generally and racial disparities in particular worsened, and proportionality links between the seriousness of crimes and the severity of punishment were broken (Tonry 2005*b*).

The winds, however, began changing direction again in the mid-1990s. Renewed possibilities exist for resuming the original efforts to achieve fair and effective systems of punishment while taking account of changing conceptions of justice. Recent Supreme Court decisions and changes in political and public attitudes toward punishment have focused attention on sentencing policy to a degree not matched since the 1980s. The Court decisions fundamentally altered the federal sentencing guidelines, changed the legal context in which state guidelines operate, and led some states to reconsider the desirability of major elements of their sentencing systems. Evolving attitudes have produced significant policy changes in many jurisdictions.

Two decisions of the U.S. Supreme Court significantly altered the legal environment for guidelines systems. *Blakely* (124 S. Ct. 2531 [2004]) held that Washington State's system of presumptive sentencing guidelines was unconstitutional to the extent that it gave judges discretion to impose prison sentences longer than the maximum authorized by the applicable guidelines. Such "upward departures" may be imposed, the Court asserted, only following a determination, beyond a reasonable doubt, of the facts on which the longer sentence was predicated. The Court's rationale was that the upper limits of the ranges of presumptive sentencing guidelines are equivalent to statutory sentence maximums; just as a person cannot be sentenced more severely than the maximum authorized by statute for the offense of which he was convicted, a person cannot be sentenced more severely than the maximum provided in the applicable guidelines range for that offense. State sentencing commissions had to figure out how best to comply with *Blakely*. It was in some ways a harder problem in theory than in practice;[1] upward departures are rare in every guidelines system.[2]

Booker (125 S. Ct. 738 [2005]) applied *Blakely* to the federal guidelines. *Booker*'s implications were substantially more radical than *Blakely*'s because the federal guidelines are much more detailed and prescriptive than any state's and because their central feature is the "relevant conduct" provision that bases sentences not on the offense of which the defendant was convicted but on the "actual offense be-

---

[1] One option is to apply it literally and compel prosecutors to charge and prove aggravating factors that might justify a harsher than normal sentence; prosecutorial failure to do so would preclude an above-guidelines sentence. A second is to create a postconviction mechanism for jury consideration of aggravating factors at the sentencing stage. A third is to replace presumptive guidelines with voluntary ones. Most states with presumptive guidelines adopted the second option (Reitz 2005*b*).

[2] In Washington State in 2005, e.g., only 0.6 percent of standard cases involved upward departures (Washington State Sentencing Guidelines Commission 2005, table 10).

havior" determined by the judge to be present on the basis of a civil-law "preponderance of the evidence" standard. *Booker* in practice applied to most sentences imposed in federal courts. The Supreme Court had to decide whether its decision required that the entire guidelines system be struck down. It elected to leave the guidelines in effect but with "advisory" rather than "presumptive" or "mandatory" force. Judges must calculate the advisory sentence post-*Booker* exactly as they would have earlier but may reject the guidelines' "advice" and impose some other sentence as long as they give reasons for doing so. By making the guidelines advisory, the Court empowered judges more often and more easily to impose sentences less harsh than those prescribed by the pre-*Booker* guidelines.

Independently of the guidelines developments, public and political attitudes toward criminal justice policy have been changing for a decade. The Supreme Court decisions themselves, prohibiting sentencing policies in effect for two decades, are one sign of this. So is an earlier decision of the California Supreme Court, *the People v. Alvarez* (60 Cal. Rep. 2d 93 [1997]), which greatly weakened California's fearsome three-strikes law.[3] Another is the proliferation of drug, gun, domestic violence, and mental health courts, all premised on taking problem-solving rather than solely punitive approaches to offending (Nolan 2001; Casey and Rottman 2003; Redlich et al. 2005). A third is the passage of California's Proposition 36, and similar referenda in other states and the District of Columbia, mandating diversion from prosecution and into treatment of many drug-abusing offenders (Tonry 2004*b*, chap. 1). A fourth is the adoption of laws in many states intended to reduce prison populations and costs by altering mandatory minimum sentencing laws, creating new alternatives to imprisonment, and authorizing new and broader programs of early release (Butterfield 2003). A fifth is the proliferation of new programs, usually at grassroots levels, based on ideas about restorative and community justice (Clear and Karp 1999; Braithwaite 2002). A sixth is the rapid expansion of the "prisoner reentry" movement predicated on the belief that we know

[3] At least some California and U.S. Supreme Court justices would deny that the decisions occurred because the elected branches of government were politically immobilized from repealing or fundamentally altering sentencing systems that nearly all informed people considered deeply unjust and the courts decided they had to step in; it is hard, however, to imagine that the justices were unaware of the systems' fundamental problems and of the intractable political difficulties that precluded legislative solutions and that their decisions would address the problems while sidestepping the politics.

Many initiatives of the past two decades failed to address purposes coherently. The best examples are broad three-strikes laws such as California's (Zimring, Hawkins, and Kamin 2001), the federal 100-to-one crack/powder cocaine sentencing differential (McDonald and Carlson 1993), and many mandatory minimum sentence laws for drug offenses (Tonry 2006). These all resulted in individual sentences that those obliged to apply them often found unjustly severe, and all violated commonsense notions of the relative seriousness of the crimes they affected and other more serious crimes that they did not.

Some misconceived laws resulted from policy makers' overreaction to emotional incidents, such as the death of college basketball star Len Bias, apparently from a crack cocaine overdose, commonly credited as driving the enactment of the federal 100-to-one law (Kennedy 1997). Others may have resulted from simple failures to understand the implications of seemingly straightforward changes. Many, however, resulted not from confused purposes or failures to forecast a law's effects but from the use of sentencing "reforms" to achieve personal, partisan, and ideological goals. Put differently, illegitimate latent goals displaced legitimate primary and ancillary goals. The inevitable result is that individual human beings, like the hypothetical defendant sentenced more severely to help the judge get reelected, received unjust punishments.

Doing better requires two things: first, that both purposes and functions be considered in setting sentencing policy, so that primary and ancillary functions can be taken into account in ways that do not produce individual injustices; second, that illegitimate latent functions be recognized for what they are and eschewed. The second of these can never be completely successful since that would require that human nature be changed. Policy makers may be able, however, to do better than they recently have done if they come to understand that sentencing has multiple functions, that ethical policy making requires that they be recognized, and that many of the latent functions cannot be openly and honestly acknowledged without embarrassment.

The rest of this essay provides the analysis on which the preceding observations rest. Section I sets out a fuller framework for thinking about purposes and functions of sentencing. Sections II and III, applying that framework, examine current knowledge concerning the primary and ancillary functions. Section IV examines latent functions.

The last distills lessons honest policy makers might wish to consider as they devise the sentencing systems of the twenty-first century.

If only legitimate primary and ancillary functions were to be sought to be performed and account were taken of what has been learned from the last thirty years of changes in sentencing laws, here is what a rational, just, and effective sentencing system would look like:

- Only normative purposes and legitimate primary and ancillary functions of sentencing would be taken into account in setting sentencing policy or setting sentences in individual cases, and illegitimate latent functions would be eschewed in both contexts.
- Limiting retributivism, the idea that retributive concerns can set meaningful upper and lower bounds within which other considerations may validly be taken into account in setting sentences in ordinary cases, would be adopted as the system's primary normative rationale, and its scope would be extended to encompass both purposes and functions.
- Subject to that premise, guidelines would set out ranges of presumptive sentences from within which judges would normally select sentences in ordinary cases; but judges would have authority, subject to observance of the requirements of *Booker* and *Blakely*, to depart from guidelines to impose other sentences as long as they specified for the record their reasons for doing so.
- In setting presumptive sentencing ranges, policy makers would not take into account evidence on deterrent and incapacitative effects of sentencing but would authorize judges to take such evidence into account in setting individual sentences within (but not above) presumptive ranges.
- In promulgating sentencing guidelines, policy makers would authorize judges to take account of rehabilitative and restorative programs and possibilities to individualize sentences both within and below (but not above) presumptive ranges, in the latter case as long as they specified for the record their reasons for doing so.
- All mandatory minimum, including three-strikes, laws would be repealed.

I. A Framework

The fundamental purposes and primary functions of sentencing are clear, and are the same: to punish criminals and prevent crimes. There tence in order to help his reelection prospects. A parallel example for policy making is the legislator or governor who proposes policy changes he knows will not achieve their purported primary aims and will, if enacted, cause new injustices, because he hopes their enactment will help him get reelected (e.g., California Governor Pete Wilson's three-strikes proposal: Zimring, Hawkins, and Kamin [2001]).

In the preceding paragraphs, I identified a number of purposes and functions:

A. Purposes (belaboredly, these could be called normative functions)
B. Primary functions
   1. Distribution (consistency, evenhandedness, fairness)
   2. Prevention (crime, fear of crime, costs and consequences of both)
   3. Communication (threat communication, denunciation of wrongful behavior, reinforcement of basic social norms)
C. Ancillary functions
   1. Management (efficiency, cost-effectiveness, resource management)
   2. Communication (procedural justice, legitimacy, public confidence)
D. Latent functions
   1. Self-interest
   2. Ideology
   3. Partisanship
   4. Communication

Normative purposes provide the ultimate criteria by which the justness of a punishment system is assessed. The most important of the remaining functions are the distributive functions of doing justice and the preventive functions of minimizing crime and its consequences. These can be pursued effectively only if account is taken of the implications and constraints associated with the ancillary functions and if ways can be devised to limit pernicious influences of the latent functions.

II. Purposes and Primary Functions

The pre-*Booker* federal sentencing guidelines are a case study in what can happen when policy makers fail to be clear about their purposes and functional goals. Here are four examples. First, the U.S. Sentencing Commission did not make the guidelines' normative purposes clear. It could have; the exceedingly detailed guidelines fine-tuned sentencing to circumstances (e.g., weapons, victim injury, property loss, role in the offense) that relate closely to culpability and thus were largely consonant with retributive purposes. Instead, the commission chose not to make the "profoundly difficult" choice of adopting explicit purposes, electing instead "an empirical approach that uses data estimating the existing sentencing system as the starting point" (1987, pp. 1.3–1.4). Guidelines for drug crimes were a major exception to the "empirical approach," with the result that the guidelines prescribed much harsher punishments for drug crimes than for violent crimes that most people consider more serious and thereby violated widely held proportionality notions. Probably the single most recurrent criticism by practitioners was that the guidelines sentences for drug cases were unjustly severe.[5] This led to widespread circumvention, which increased as time passed (Bowman and Heise 2001). Adopting explicit purposes, and then being guided by them, would have produced guidelines that were more internally consistent and normatively acceptable to practitioners and would more effectively have performed their distributive functions.

Second, the commission was worried that lawyers would manipulate the guidelines by means of charging and plea bargaining decisions and adopted the "relevant conduct" policy as a countermeasure. The logic was that if judges were required to impose sentences on the basis of the defendant's "actual offense behavior," charges to which the defendant pled guilty would generally not much matter (U.S. Sentencing Commission 1987, pp. 1.5–1.6).[6] In practice, the system did not work that way. The sentencing guidelines were widely circumvented by prosecutors, defense lawyers, and judges (Nagel and Schulhofer 1992; Schulhofer and Nagel 1997; Bowman and Heise 2001). The notion that offenders are to be punished for what the judge believed they did, as opposed to what they were convicted of, offended widely held notions of procedural fairness and produced such unjust results that the Supreme Court intervened in *Booker* and demoted the guidelines from

[5] A survey of federal appellate and trial judges conducted by the commission found that 73.7 percent of district court judges and 82.7 percent of circuit court judges reported that drug-trafficking sentences were "greater than appropriate" (U.S. Sentencing Commission 2003, exhibits II-4, III-4).

[6] The major exception is that guidelines are trumped by plea bargains to offenses bearing lower statutory maximums than guidelines prescribe.

16–17), cannot be converted into practicable policy. Killing a murderer fits the model, but what about the punishment for an attempted murderer? How can a rape be punished in like kind or, harder, an attempted rape? Would anyone really want to torture or maim an assailant who caused serious pain or disfigurement? How can deserved punishments for property crimes be calculated, or "victimless" crimes, or inchoate crimes (conspiracy, attempts, aiding and abetting)?

People have tried to solve these problems, but the solutions necessarily are imperfect. Andrew von Hirsch devised a system of ordinal proportionality in which punishment in absolute like kind is not sought but punishment proportionate to the blameworthiness expressed in the crime (von Hirsch 1993). "Proportionality" here, however, is not relative to the nature of the crime but to punishments for other more, less, and comparably blameworthy crimes. The difficulties here, though less well known than those affecting a purer Kantian model, are also considerable (Tonry 2005b). There are three principal ones. First, the principled call for comparable punishments for comparably situated offenders is illusory. Widely divergent practices concerning charging, plea bargaining, and sentencing discounts for guilty pleas make seemingly comparable offenses of conviction widely diverse and seemingly comparable offenders substantially different in their blameworthiness.

Second, definitions of offenses in U.S. law are typically broad: "robbery" encompasses behavior ranging from gangland holdups to takings of basketballs on school playgrounds. Punishing every person convicted of robbery the same way would produce what Arie Freiberg (2001) called "unjustifiable parity." The example I just gave is extreme, of course, but the problem is a general one. Most guidelines systems divide all felonies into a small number of categories of severity, and they inevitably include widely diverse kinds of crimes. Because of wide differences in any jurisdiction in charging and plea bargaining practices, substantially similar crimes result in convictions for different crimes, and conviction offenses obscure wide differences in underlying culpable behavior.

Third, most important, von Hirsch's desert theory is subject to the "punishment of the innocents" charge that retributivists classically toss at utilitarians. The logic of the system requires that all offenders who fall within a category receive the same penalty, including when the severity of punishment for that category is increased for preventive reasons relating to some but not all members of the category. What this means is that some, perhaps many or most, offenders in a category will be punished more severely than their offense warrants because the architecture of the system requires it.[12] In the words of the classic retributive critique of utilitarian punishment theories, the offenders being punished more severely than they otherwise would be are being "used" as means to the end of maintaining the formal structure of the sentencing theory (Pincoffs 1991). As an ethical matter, it is difficult to distinguish between knowingly punishing an innocent person and knowingly punishing a guilty person more than he or she deserves.

A pure utilitarian model also has well-known practical limits, over and above the punishment of the innocents problem. The overriding one is that the necessary "felicific calculus," as Bentham called it, is impossible. Fundamentally contested literatures on economic costs of crime, especially pain and suffering (McDougall et al. 2006), deterrent and incapacitative effects (Nagin 1998), and crime prevention more broadly demonstrate that we are far away from a time when we know enough to take the Benthamite model seriously. Any decisions about the utilitarian gains and pains associated with punishment in an individual case or within broad-based general policies can be little better than guesswork.

On a continuum between those Kantian and Benthamite poles lie hybrid punishment theories that combine retributive and preventive considerations in diverse ways. One, proposed by Andrew von Hirsch (1993), is that culpability concerns predominate heavily but that deterrent or incapacitative concerns may be taken into account in setting the penalty scale. If longer sentences are wanted, they may be imposed collectively on all equally culpable people, by moving that offense up the scale or by extending the scale, and thereby punishing all offenders more severely, but they may not be imposed on an individualized basis. This is unsatisfactory because it forces a choice between forgoing

---

[12] This sentence conflates two separate problems. First, insofar as overbroad offense definitions or charging and plea bargaining practices result in substantially different crimes bearing the same label, sentencing all bearing that label in the same way punishes those whose crimes were less serious more severely than they deserve. Second, as I explain below in the text, von Hirsch would forbid the use of crime preventive considerations (e.g., deterrence or incapacitation) to increase sentences for individuals and would instead allow them to be taken into account only to increase sentences for the entire category of offenses in which target individuals fall (von Hirsch and Ashworth 2005). The effect would be to increase sentences for all in the category so that some can be punished more severely for instrumental reasons.

seemingly realizable preventive goals and gratuitously punishing some, or many, in a class more severely than their crime would otherwise merit. The former is politically and possibly ethically impracticable. The latter violates the parsimony principle's injunction against imposition of gratuitous suffering.[13]

A second hybrid theory, associated with Andrew von Hirsch and Martin Wasik (Wasik and von Hirsch 1988), would permit preventive considerations to influence the type but not the severity of punishment. Punishments must be apportioned to blameworthiness; but if two punishments (e.g., X days of imprisonment versus Y days of community service) have a comparable punitive bite, a choice may be made between them on preventive bases. Their proposal assumes, however, that few penalties can be made comparably punitive and accordingly specifies that imprisonment is more severe than community-based punishments; they in turn are more severe than fines, allowing for interchangeability only at the margins between types of punishments. This is unsatisfactory generally because it is primarily a variation of the preceding hybrid theory and because it consigns preventive considerations to the narrowest margins.

A third hybrid theory, proposed by Paul Robinson (1987), calls for strict observance of culpability standards except in a small number of cases for which disproportionate punishments would prevent really serious harms. This is unsatisfactory for conceptual (how in principle justify the abandonment of retributive premises?), definitional (what harms count as really serious?), and empirical reasons (how can we know we're additionally punishing the correct people? We're not very good at predicting really serious future harms).

A fourth hybrid, proposed by former English civil servant John Halliday (2001, app. 8), is described as being a form of limiting retributivism concerned with "consistency of approach rather than uniformity of outcome" (p. 20). The notion is that the same set of punitive and preventive considerations should be taken into account in every case, but the seriousness of the offense would limit the maximum sentence that should be imposed. This is at best obscure and implies something closer to a theory of procedural than to a theory of substantive justice.

---

[13] Von Hirsch's response (1993) would be that parsimony should be sought at collective levels by setting the overall penalty scale as low as possible while furthering the aim of treating like cases alike. General parsimony-based objections could be raised to this position, but, importantly for the point made in the text, it does not speak to the special problems involved in raising the overall scale to pursue preventive goals.

It is in any case a very weak form of limiting retributivism in that the upper limits of aggregate punishment that may be imposed are vaguely expressed and are subject to major exceptions for serious offenses, re-peat offenders, and offenders who fit into a very broad definition of dangerousness (Tonry 2004*a*).

The fifth and sixth hybrids are other versions of limiting retributiv-ism. In "asymmetric proportionality," culpability sets strict upper limits on the sentence that may be imposed, but there are no lower limits (Lappi-Seppälä 2001). Finnish law sets out fairly detailed statutory principles that govern sentencing; they give pride of place to culpability considerations but allow on a case-by-case basis for the operation of other considerations including preventive considerations in a narrowly defined set of cases. The Finnish system, however, operates in a coun-try in which most sentences are measured in days or weeks, sentences longer than a year are uncommon, and the total imprisonment rate including pretrial detainees fluctuates between sixty and seventy per 100,000 population, less than a tenth the American rate. Finland has no sentencing guidelines as Americans understand the term because the latitude for unwarranted disparities is incomparably lower. Asym-metric proportionality on the Finnish model is probably unsatisfactory for American adoption because it depends on Finland's very different punishment practices and penal culture and its application by career cadres of judges and prosecutors who subscribe to its values.

In Norval Morris's limiting retributivism (1974), culpability sets up-per limits and for some but not all crimes sets lower limits. Compared with von Hirsch's proportionality doctrine, in which desert limits are artificial, set relative to sentences for lesser and greater crimes, Morris's are cultural. He famously urged that "not undeserved" was a more useful conception of culpability constraints on punishment than "de-served" because it is far easier for people to agree that a sentence is undeservedly harsh or unduly lenient than that it is just right. Within those bounds, however, for Morris, Bentham's parsimony principle, cause no unnecessary or gratuitous pain, required that the least severe "not undeserved" punishment be imposed.

Morris first set out his limiting retributivism argument in the early 1950s (Morris 1953), and it took its fullest form in his *Future of Im-prisonment* (1974), before modern sentencing guidelines were more than a gleam in anyone's eyes. There is no reason in Morris's argument why the upper and lower bounds of allowable punishments cannot derive from policy decisions that grid-style guidelines made possible (as long as they respect cultural limits), as his later writings showed (e.g., Morris and Tonry 1990, chap. 3).

It appeared clear to Morris in 1974 that preventive considerations would seldom justify imposition of sentences more severe than the parsimonious minimum. The most successful predictions of dangerousness were wrong at least two times out of three, too often to justify confining people longer because they were purportedly dangerous, and the research evidence concerning deterrence and rehabilitation gave no grounds that either was sufficiently often effective[14] to justify deprivations of liberty on their basis.

The world has changed since 1974 in ways germane to Morris's analysis. Though the evidence concerning the effectiveness of deterrent and incapacitative penalties is not much stronger now than it was then, doubts about basing sentencing laws on them are much less influential. More significantly, the research evidence on rehabilitative programs has reversed, and both conventional wisdom and many meta-analyses and literature reviews agree that well-run, well-targeted programs can reduce reoffending rates (and drug abuse) (e.g., U.S. Surgeon General 2001; Farrington and Welsh, in this volume; Welsh and Farrington 2006).

This discussion of purposes supports two conclusions. First, as the discussion of the federal guidelines at this subsection's beginning showed, purposes have consequences and provide guidance that is necessary if policies are to be coherent, internally consistent, and perceived as just. Second, any coherent and practicable set of purposes will be embodied in a hybrid model.

In the sections that follow, and in the conclusion, I propose that both sentences imposed and legitimate functional goals pursued should be consistent with whatever normative purposes are set. For myself, and for most modern sentencing systems (Frase 1997, 2004, 2005a), something like Morris's limiting retributivism appears best to express the optimal balance of competing moral intuitions about punishment and crime prevention, but reasonable people disagree about that.

[14] In these views he was ahead of his time; Martinson's "What Works?" article, suggesting that existing evidence gave little basis for confidence in rehabilitative programs, did not appear until 1974. The National Academy of Sciences report on deterrence and incapacitation, whose conclusions Morris anticipated, did not appear until 1978 (Blumstein, Cohen, and Nagin 1978).

B. Distribution

Whatever the applicable normative purposes of a sentencing system may be, the principal distributive aims are consistency, evenhandedness, and fairness relative to those purposes. Imposition of punishment for crime is a paradigmatic instance of the conflict between individual liberty and collective interests. Sentencing is a process in which government actors are empowered to intrude on individuals' liberty and autonomy in order to prevent crimes and sanction wrongdoing. To be consistent with core values underlying constitutional notions of due process and equal protection, sentencing needs to respect offenders' rights to be treated as equals, to have decisions about them made deliberately and impartially, and to be dealt with under fair procedures.

I would be surprised if many people disagree. A major challenge for sentencing policy, however, is that consistency, evenhandedness, and fairness look different when viewed from different places. To legislators, a ten-year mandatory minimum sentence, three-strikes, or 100-to-one law is not necessarily inconsistent with those values. Nor, presumably, to members of the U.S. Sentencing Commission were the "actual-offense behavior" policies, drug-trafficking guidelines, or a decision to forbid judges to take account in sentencing of ethically important differences in individual offenders' circumstances.[15] From the perspective of policy making at the wholesale level, the policies were for Congress and the commission to set and for judges and prosecutors, equably, evenhandedly, and fairly, to implement.

If literally applied in every case, however, those policies would have made practitioners complicit in imposing sentences in many cases that everyone directly involved believed to be substantively or procedurally unjust. Practitioners see cases firsthand. Problems appear simpler the farther away the point from which they are observed. District court judges, whether liberal or conservative, or appointed by Republican or Democratic administrations, for example, who see living, breathing defendants, are more hostile to the federal guidelines than are appellate judges who see only written appellate briefs. The same generalization applies to laypeople. The more detailed the information people are given about particular criminal cases, the less harsh and stereotyped

---

[15] From the outset, the guidelines provided that such commonsense considerations as family responsibilities, drug dependence, and mental health problems were not "ordinarily relevant in determining whether the sentence should be outside the guidelines" (U.S. Sentencing Commission 1987, secs. 5H1.1–6).

the sentences they would impose become. As a result, as surveys in a number of countries show, the sentences laypeople would impose for particular kinds of cases are often less severe than the sentences judges do impose (Roberts et al. 2002).

Legislators and senior executive branch officials, by contrast, deal in stereotypes. Often, like citizens responding to survey questions, they think in terms of extreme cases, even when setting policies that will mostly be applied to run-of-the-mill ones. They are also more likely to think of sentencing policy in terms of its latent functions of self-interest, ideology, and partisanship, considerations that are much less likely to move practitioners when pondering an individual's fate. Nearly all judges and prosecutors—"officers of the court" in American legal systems—take their ethical obligation to do justice seriously. Policies that substantially obstruct their ability to do justice are likely to be resisted or undermined.

The federal guidelines often directed judges to impose sentences they believed to be unjustly severe (Zlotnick 2004).[16] In such circumstances, judges had three options: compliance, resignation, and circumvention. They could apply the guidelines as written, but at the cost of behaving unjustly; most did this much of the time, occasionally after announcing that they felt they had no alternative but to impose an unjust sentence. They could announce that the guidelines required them to impose an unjust sentence and, refusing to do so, resign. A few did this. They could resolve neither to impose an unjust sentence nor to defy the law openly nor to resign, but together with counsel circumvent the guidelines to produce a sentence everyone involved considered appropriate. Many did this, and increasing numbers did so as time passed (Bowman and Heise 2001).

J. Lawrence Irving, the first federal district court judge to resign in protest over the federal guidelines, was appointed by President Ronald Reagan. On resigning in 1990, he said: "If I remain on the bench I have no choice but to follow the law. I just can't, in good conscience, continue to do this" (*New York Times* 1990, p. 2). Federal district court judge John S. Martin resigned in 2003 over what he called "a sentencing system that is unnecessarily cruel and rigid" (Martin 2004, p.

[16] A U.S. Sentencing Commission survey in 2003 showed that 73.7 percent of district judges and 82.7 percent of circuit judges said that federal drug-trafficking sentences are inappropriately severe, which necessarily means that many judges appointed by Presidents Reagan, Bush I, and Bush II held this view (U.S. Sentencing Commission 2003, exhibits II-4, III-4).

A31). Richard Boylan's statistical analyses concluded that the guidelines' unpopularity led judges on average to retire earlier than they otherwise would have (Boylan 2004).

My personal experience working with judges and prosecutors is that most practitioners most of the time want to do justice in individual cases, to do the right thing, to achieve a just and appropriate sentence. When applicable laws make that difficult or impossible, they still feel powerfully moved to do so anyway.

This is human nature, and there is a lot of evidence for it, going back centuries. Between 1714 and 1830, the British Parliament created 156 new capital crimes punishable by death, many of them property offenses, but the number of executions fell by three-fourths. Why? Because juries refused to convict offenders or convicted them for offenses not punishable by death, and judges created and narrowly interpreted technical rules that had to be followed if death was to be imposed, but seldom were (Stephen [1883] 1977; Select Committee on Capital Punishment 1930; Hay 1975).

The American Bar Foundation in the 1950s and 1960s carried out major studies of criminal court operations in several states (Newman 1966; Dawson 1969; Miller 1969). Prosecutorial and judicial circumvention of mandatory sentences was common in each court studied. Exemplifying this, Donald Newman described the application in Michigan of a fifteen-year maximum sentence for nighttime burglary (compared with a five-year maximum for daytime burglary): "The frequency of altering nighttime burglary to breaking and entering in the daytime led one prosecutor to remark: 'You'd think all our burglaries occur at high noon'" (Newman 1966, p. 182). The maximum mattered so much then and there because, taking time off for good behavior into account, it set the date by which the parole board had to release a prisoner. A lower maximum was insurance against a much longer stay in prison.

As Frank Remington, executive director of the nearly two-decades-long series of projects, summarized, "Legislative prescription of a high mandatory sentence for certain offenders is likely to result in a reduction of charges at the prosecution stage, or if this is not done, by a refusal of the judge to convict at the adjudication stage. The issue . . . thus is not solely whether certain offenders should be dealt with severely, but also how the criminal justice system will accommodate to the legislative change" (Remington 1969, p. xvii).

Evaluations of the effects of mandatory minimums enacted in the

1970s in Massachusetts (Rossman et al. 1979), Michigan (Heumann and Loftin 1979), and New York (Joint Committee 1978) reached the same conclusions. So did an evaluation of Oregon's Measure 11, enacted by referendum in 1994 and requiring lengthy mandatory sentences for people convicted of sixteen serious crimes (Merritt, Fain, and Turner 2003, 2006). An evaluation of New Jersey's 1994 "No Early Release Act," requiring offenders to serve 85 percent of their sentences before release, hypothesized that changes in plea bargaining would largely nullify the act and result in times served little different from before the law took effect. That is what was found (McCoy and McManimon 2003).

Experience with the federal guidelines was the same. During their first decade, a host of studies, some sponsored by the U.S. Sentencing Commission, showed that circumvention of the guidelines' harshest and most rigid provisions was commonplace (Nagel and Schulhofer 1992; Schulhofer and Nagel 1997). In recent years, Frank Bowman and Michael Heise (2001) showed that a wide range of circumvention techniques by prosecutors and judges resulted throughout the 1990s in continuously decreasing average sentence lengths in the federal courts.

The consistent evidence that practitioners often circumvent sentencing laws mandating sentences they believe to be unjust should not be surprising. James Eisenstein and his colleagues, reporting on research on how practitioners in felony courts in nine counties reached sentencing decisions, observe that sentences result from "accommodations among competing values and interests that support these values, accommodations that are superimposed on a common basic structure supported by broad consensus." Of reforms imposed from outside, they conclude that "the more radical a proposed change, the less likely is its adoption" (Eisenstein, Flemming, and Nardulli 1988, p. 294).

C. Prevention

The preventive functions focus on crime, fear of crime, and reduction in their costs and consequences. For purposes of this essay, I assume that efforts to prevent crime will also lessen fear and reduce crime's costs and consequences; that is a reasonable assumption, even though a finer-tuned analysis would discuss different policy mechanisms for achieving each outcome.[17]

---

[17] A harm-reduction approach to drug policy, e.g., might imply different drug policy

The preventive functions center on the collective interest in domestic tranquility, on enabling citizens to get on with their lives in security. These are core functions of the state and basic goals of criminal law and punishment. If they are to be pursued effectively, policy makers need to take account of the considerable body of knowledge on the effectiveness of sanctions.

Precisely how crime prevention, fear reduction, and cost savings should be sought involves policy decisions about which reasonable people differ and depends in part on what normative purposes are deemed applicable. I assume though that most policy makers regard crime prevention as among the justifiable normative purposes even if some sets of normative purposes that might be adopted might constrain the policy options available to pursue them. That being so, knowledge of what works, and what doesn't, is essential.

Writing on this subject is a ticklish business because it is probably generally assumed that the writer has axes to grind that shape how the evidence is summarized. Perhaps surprisingly, however, there is broad agreement among academics of liberal (e.g., Ruth and Reitz 2003) and conservative (e.g., Wilson 2002) political inclinations about conclusions to be drawn from research on the preventive effects of criminal sanctions and criminal justice interventions.

1. *Deterrence.* Current knowledge concerning deterrence is little different than eighteenth-century theorists such as Beccaria ([1764] 1995) supposed it to be: certainty and promptness of punishment are more powerful deterrents than severity. This does not mean that punishments do not deter. No one doubts that having a system of punishment has crime-preventive effects. The important question is whether changes in punishments have marginal deterrent effects, that is, whether a new policy causes crime rates to fall from whatever level they would otherwise have been at. Modern deterrent strategies, through sentencing law changes, take two forms: increases in punishments for particular offenses and mandatory minimum sentence (including "three-strikes") laws.

Imaginable increases in severity of punishments do not yield significant (if any) marginal deterrent effects. Three National Academy of

---

approaches than are now common in the United States. Fear of crime can be addressed by things such as increased visible police presence on the streets and improved neighborhood conditions (e.g., more street lighting, prompt repair of vandalized public property, altered traffic patterns) that lie far beyond the reach of the sentencing judge.

Sciences panels, all appointed by Republican presidents, reached that conclusion (Blumstein, Cohen, and Nagin 1978; Blumstein, Cohen, Roth, and Visher 1986; Reiss and Roth 1993), as has every major survey of the evidence (Cook 1980; Nagin 1998, 1999; von Hirsch et al. 1999; Doob and Webster 2003). This is also the belief, in my experience, of most experienced judges and prosecutors.

There are a number of good practical reasons why this widely reached conclusion makes sense. First, serious sexual and violent crimes are generally committed under circumstances of extreme emotion, often exacerbated by the influence of alcohol or drugs. Detached reflection on possible penalties or recent changes in penalties seldom if ever occurs in such circumstances. Second, most minor and middling and many serious crimes do not result in arrests or prosecutions; most offenders committing them, naïvely but realistically, do not expect to be caught. Third, those who are caught and prosecuted almost always are offered plea bargains that break the link between the crime and the prescribed punishment. Fourth, when penalties are especially severe, they are often, albeit inconsistently, circumvented by prosecutors and judges. Fifth, for many crimes including drug trafficking, prostitution, and much gang-related activity, removing individual offenders does not alter the structural circumstances conducing to the crime. Sixth, even when one ignores all those considerations, the idea that increased penalties have sizable marginal deterrent effects requires heroic and unrealistic assumptions about "threat communication," the process by which would-be offenders learn that penalty increases have been legislated or are being implemented.

Mandatory minimum penalties including three-strikes laws are nothing more than efforts to deter crime through penalty increases. The clear weight of the evidence, not surprisingly given what we know about severity increases generally, is that they are seldom if ever crime preventatives (e.g., Tonry 1996, chap. 4; Zimring, Hawkins, and Kamin 2001). Besides the not inconsiderable problem that mandatory minimums often are circumvented by practitioners, and always will be, the best evidence suggests that they have no marginal deterrent effects or have only modest effects that quickly waste away.

There is no good evidence that justifies fine-tuning sentences in individual cases, or enacting mandatory minimum sentence laws, for deterrent reasons. Having a system of punishments has deterrent effects. Having punishments scaled to the severity of offenses should provide rational incentives, as Beccaria and Bentham urged, to commit fewer rather than more serious crimes and, as Durkheim urged, to reinforce basic social norms.

The principal implications of current knowledge about deterrence are that certainty of punishment is more important than severity, that penalties that are too rigid or too severe result in widespread circumvention, and accordingly that mandatory minimums and three-strikes laws are ineffective, cause foreseeable injustices including gross disparities, and should be repealed.

2. *Incapacitation.*   Incapacitative crime control strategies have some potential if used discriminatingly for people who commit very serious crimes at high rates (Monahan 2004). Offenders in confinement necessarily are disabled from committing offenses in the free community. We know a good bit more about incapacitation than we did thirty years ago. For a time, policies referred to as "collective incapacitation" were in vogue, influenced or at least evidenced by proposals in James Q. Wilson's *Thinking about Crime* (1976): extend all sentences of people convicted of violent crimes such as robbery by several years. This was soon shown to be impracticable. Large numbers of people are convicted of such crimes, but the average likelihood of recidivism is too low for the resulting huge increases in imprisonment to be justified (Blumstein, Cohen, and Nagin 1978; Cohen 1983).

This was followed by proposals for "selective incapacitation," catalyzed by a RAND Corporation report purporting to show the feasibility of such policies (Greenwood and Abrahamse 1982). This was soon discredited by a National Academy of Sciences report that showed that RAND's proposals worked with hindsight—it was based on self-reported past crimes of imprisoned violent offenders and in retrospect seemed to characterize those prisoners—but not prospectively (Blumstein et al. 1986). The prediction methods proposed were so over-inclusive, producing so many "false positives," that selective incapacitation was dismissed as impracticable.

After that, the theoretical writing and related empirical research on incapacitation pretty much came to a halt (Nagin 1998), but policy makers kept increasing lengths of sentences and accepted the imprisonment numbers that in the 1970s and early 1980s appeared unimaginable (Blumstein 1988). Collective incapacitation, in effect, became national policy, though not under that name. Studies in the late 1990s (Spelman 2000) and early in this century (Blumstein and Wallman

2000) concluded that mass imprisonment had reduced crime rates by 10–25 percent.

That last conclusion needs to be taken with a grain of salt for two reasons. First, comparable declines in crime rates occurred throughout the Western world, and no country other than the United States quintupled its imprisonment rate and experimented with mass imprisonment (Tonry 2004*b*, chap. 2). There is a reasonably good chance that American crime rates would have fallen like every other Western country's. The contrast with Canada—a flat imprisonment rate of 100 per 100,000 population for forty years but crime rate trends closely paralleling those in the United States (Doob and Webster 2006)—is especially cautionary. Second, and no less important, the studies concluding that incapacitation caused significant declines in crime rates are based on exceedingly complex modeling, which like all such modeling is highly vulnerable to the assumptions on which it is based and the modeling technique used; even highly sophisticated modelers seldom agree about either (viz., compare Webster, Doob, and Zimring [2006] with Kessler and Levitt [1999] and Rosenfeld, Fornango, and Baumer [2005*a*, 2005*b*] with Berk [2005]).

Incapacitative considerations have little legitimate place in decisions about individual offenders. The principal difficulty is that current incapacitation policies often, and expensively, target the wrong people. There are five main problems. First, incapacitation strategies targeted on repeat serious offenders generally result in long sentences for older offenders, most of whom in any case would soon desist from crime. This is known as the problem of residual career length; most thirty- or forty-year-old offenders are unlikely to continue as active offenders for long. There may be other justifications for confining such offenders for extended periods; but from an incapacitative perspective, such sentences are expensive, inefficient, and largely ineffective.

Second, strategies that target repeat offenders, in earlier times generally called "habitual-offender" laws and now called "three-strikes" laws, tend to ensnare socially inadequate, high-volume property offenders for whose prevented crimes lengthy prison sentences costing $40,000–$50,000 per year are not a sensible investment of public resources.

Third, for many offenses, including particularly drug sales, drug trafficking, and some gang-related crime, there is the "replacement" problem: offenders taken off the streets are quickly replaced by willing successors. Removing a seventeen-year-old drug dealer from an inner-city street corner is seldom likely to stop drug dealing at that corner; plenty of willing volunteers are usually waiting in the wings to step into what looks to be a lucrative opportunity. Similarly, unless the gang itself is completely destroyed, locking up one or several of its members will not stop its illegal activities. Other, and new, members will step in to replace their fallen comrades.

Fourth, there is the "false-positive" problem. For crimes of any significant seriousness, we are not very good at predicting which offenders will commit them in the future. For every "true positive" who will, three or four others predicted to do so will not. From a cost-benefit perspective, locking up all those people is not an obviously good investment of public resources. From a moral perspective, many people are troubled by the thought of lengthy confinement of individuals not because of their current crime but because they might commit another, especially when we know most will not.

Fifth, there is the "true-but-trifling-positive" problem. We are pretty good at predicting petty reoffending. David Farrington (1979) long ago demonstrated that an offender who has been arrested nine times has an 80 percent likelihood of being arrested again. This raises the cost-benefit question already mentioned: Is it worth $40,000–$50,000 per year to prevent shoplifting, minor thefts, acts of prostitution, or low-level drug dealing? It also raises the moral question whether the disproportionate character of a multiyear prison sentence for a person convicted of such crimes can be justified.

As with deterrence, the answer is not to forgo efforts to incapacitate offenders, but to do so intelligently. This means working hard at the policy level to develop strategies targeting particular kinds of serious offenders whose future behavior we can reasonably confidently predict and whose averted crimes save substantial suffering. At the individual level, however, it means limiting judges' authority to predicate sentencing decisions on incapacitative ambitions.

3. *Rehabilitation.*   Prevention through rehabilitation looks to be a considerably more viable strategy in the early twenty-first century than it did during the closing decades of the twentieth. The view that "nothing works" was an important backdrop to the shift toward determinate sentencing, the abolition of parole, and adoption of incapacitative and deterrent crime control strategies. If we do not know how to reduce

offenders' prospects for later offending, it is hard to justify giving judges and parole boards broad discretion to individualize sentencing.

The prospects for rehabilitation, however, have changed radically. Evidence is accumulating from many sources—individual evaluations, meta-analyses (e.g., Lipsey and Landenberger 2006; Mitchell, Mac-Kenzie, and Wilson 2006), literature reviews (e.g., Gaes et al. 1999; U.S. Surgeon General 2001), and practical experience—that well-managed, well-targeted programs can reduce participants' probability of reoffending. A wide range of programs, including drug treatment, anger management, cognitive-skills programs, sex offender treatment, and various educational- and vocational-skills programs have been shown to reduce reoffending (Gaes et al. 1999). A report from the English Home Office, which underpinned a massive reorganization of the English criminal justice system mandated by the Criminal Justice Act of 2003, concluded that "a reasonable estimate at this stage is that, if the [treatment] programmes are developed and applied as intended, to the maximum extent possible, reconviction rates might be reduced by 5–25 percentage points (i.e. from the present level of 56 percent within two years to (perhaps) 40 percent)" (Halliday 2001, p. 7). The most recent meta-analysis of the effects of cognitive-behavioral programs concluded that, on average, they reduced reoffending by 27 percent (Lipsey and Landenberger 2006). The proliferation of drug courts and prisoner reentry programs in the United States bears witness to the widely shared perception that some things work.

That litany of positive findings does not mean that reducing reoffending rates is easy. The results obtained from a well-funded pilot project, led by motivated people, cannot automatically be obtained by institutionalizing a new program model throughout a jurisdiction. A recent survey of violence prevention programs by the U.S. Surgeon General (2001) concluded that many programs can reduce violent offending but that the challenge is broad-based implementation. This is nonetheless much better news than the state of the evidence twenty-five years ago. We now know what we do; we need to figure out how to do it on a large scale.

An important implication is that rigid sentencing policies obstruct efforts to prevent crime through rehabilitation of offenders. For drug and other treatment programs to work, they must be targeted to the characteristics and needs of particular offenders, and this requires sentences to be individualized. With the fall of the nothing works psychology goes much of the case for rigid sentencing standards.

4. *Moral Education.* Deterrence, incapacitation, and rehabilitation are not needed to restrain most adults from selling drugs, burglarizing houses, holding up convenience stores, or mugging passersby. Most people's personal norms and values make predatory crime almost unthinkable. European scholars and theorists have long observed that the criminal law's main function is "general prevention": reinforcement of basic social norms that are learned in the home, the church, the school, and the neighborhood (Lappi-Seppälä 2001). These primary socializing institutions must do the heavy lifting—what the criminal courts can do is too little and too late for the criminal justice system to serve as a primary socializing institution—but it is important that law and the legal system reinforce those norms and not undermine them.

One implication, consistent with research findings on deterrence, is that it is more important that crimes have consequences than that the consequences be severe. Another, consistent with the research findings on rehabilitation, is that the choice of sanctions should be tailored to the circumstances of particular cases.

The evidence on the preventive effects of punishment all points in the same direction. A sentencing system that sets firm upper limits on punishments, scaled to offenders' culpability or the severity of their crimes, but allows substantial individualization below those limits, promises greater preventive effectiveness than current laws in the federal system or most states.

III. Ancillary Functions

The criminal justice system has limited material and manpower resources. Prosecutors, presiding judges, and corrections managers need to organize their offices, courtrooms, and programs to get the job done as efficiently and cost-effectively as possible while trying to achieve appropriate outcomes in individual cases.

Sentencing guidelines in some states have proved to be useful tools in reconciling distributive, preventive, and management functions. These guidelines have achieved reasonable consistency in sentences imposed and have proved an effective tool for projecting the effects of alternate policy proposals and thereby managing corrections resources and controlling corrections budgets at a systems level. Although plea

bargaining occurs everywhere, in the states with well-designed guidelines, bargaining takes place in the shadow of the guidelines and has
not been characterized by the widespread circumvention, and resulting
disparities, that characterized the federal system (Tonry 1996; Reitz
2001, 2005*a*; Frase 2005*c*).

A. *Efficiency and Cost-Effectiveness*

Court dockets are crowded, treatment resources are scarce, and correctional programs including prisons are overcrowded and underre-
sourced. Managers have to figure out how to juggle their budgets and
manpower to keep cases flowing, hold backlogs down, and prioritize
their resource allocations so that the most serious and important cases
receive the attention they warrant. Most courts and prosecutors' offices
have monthly case disposition and backlog targets; failure to meet them
is interpreted as laziness or ineffectiveness. This is generally understood to mean that most cases must be resolved as quickly as possible.
Trials should be avoided whenever possible, and bench trials are preferable to jury trials.

Plea bargaining is the mechanism for achieving most of those goals
and requires that the state have something to offer the defendant to
induce cooperation and that prosecutors, defense counsel, and judges
get along. Generally, the parties do get along because many criminal
court practitioners work for extended periods in the same setting and
soon learn the prevailing conventions ("going rates") and get to know
the relatively small number of people in the courtroom in which they
work.

Peter Nardulli and his collaborators in the most extensive study to
date of courtroom communities put it like this: "The web of interper-
sonal ties and mutual need that holds the [courtroom community] together also creates norms and understandings that guide and restrict
behavior. In a sense court communities emerge because of the need to
establish these understandings, as well as to meet other human needs
. . . . It is in the interest of all to establish, abide by, and enforce a
common set of understandings about how normal cases should be handled and how defendants should be punished" (Nardulli, Eisenstein,
and Flemming 1988, p. 306).

People who are oppositional or uncooperative soon find that they
receive little cooperation back and that they are felt by their colleagues
to be unreasonable. Those are pretty effective sanctions for uncoop-

erative behavior: "The importance attached to conflict avoidance and conflict management is another important component of the court community's court culture. In some communities, a great deal of emphasis was placed upon going along and getting along, upon not rocking the boat" (Nardulli, Eisenstein, and Flemming 1988, p. 125).

Lawyers and judges become socialized into the local courtroom culture, which, given that felony courts are usually staffed by people from the communities they serve, generally reflects prevailing community notions about right and wrong and the severity of punishment. People working in big-city courts tend to have somewhat different local cultures than people working in suburban and small-town courts. Legal cultures vary from city to city and region to region (Eisenstein, Flemming, and Nardulli 1988). A U.S. Sentencing Commission–sponsored study of prosecutorial circumvention of guidelines documented wide variations in legal culture in different federal district courts (Nagel and Schulhofer 1992).

What practitioners do largely depends on the prevailing courtroom culture. If sentencing statutes and guidelines set standards that are incompatible with local traditions and beliefs, local traditions often win out, with the acquiescence of everyone involved. Practitioners' needs to achieve management goals and the importance of local courtroom cultures together mean that local courts will do what is needed to operate efficiently and cost-effectively and to achieve outcomes that those involved consider appropriate and just. Sentencing standards that are too harsh, too lenient, or too mechanistic often will be circumvented.

B. Resource Management

Governments and individual agencies need to get their business done within the resource constraints presented by their budgets. They need to be able to predict changes in their likely flow of work and to plan for resources they will need in the future. These things inevitably entail choices.

One of the great advantages of sentencing guidelines is that they are a proven tool for effective resource management (Boerner and Lieb 2001; Wright 2002; Frase 2005b). States that adopted sentencing guidelines as a resource management tool have successfully tailored their sentencing policies to their correctional budgets and programs. By making sentencing decisions predictable in the aggregate, guidelines enable policy makers to project likely future resource needs. If, for example, a jurisdiction contemplates doubling sentence lengths for sex crimes, it can project how many more prison beds will be needed. If current and planned facilities cannot accommodate the increased numbers, policy makers can respond in a number of ways. They can appropriate funds to build new facilities, revise sentences for other offenses downward to free up the needed spaces, reconsider whether the sex offender proposal is a good idea, or do some combination of these things.

Sound resource management is a necessary characteristic of effective government and a primary rationale for sentencing guidelines systems. Its scope should extend to needs for nonincarcerative sanctions, availability of appropriately targeted rehabilitative programs, and effectuation of appropriately targeted incapacitation policies.

C. Communication

Communicative functions are described briefly, not because they are less important than the other functions but because the basic propositions can be simply stated. Communicative functions interact with normative, distributive, and preventive functions. Legitimacy and public confidence depend in part on whether the law is seen to operate reasonably and in ways that are consonant with widely held ideas about justice (including, e.g., that claims be fairly considered and that penalties be proportionate to the severity of crimes).

1. *Legitimacy.* Legitimacy is increasingly recognized as a key element in how people relate to government (Tyler 2003). Whether people have confidence in, support, and cooperate with public institutions is influenced by the institution's legitimacy in their eyes. People are more likely to react positively when the police stop them, or to accept an adverse decision by a court, if they believe that they have been treated fairly, that decisions about them have been evenhanded and impartial, and that they have had a chance to have their say. Sentencing policies that respect offenders' rights to be treated as equals, to have decisions about them made deliberately and impartially, and to be dealt with under fair procedures are more likely to be perceived as legitimate than policies that do not satisfy these requirements of procedural justice.

2. *Public Reassurance.* Sometimes laws are enacted or policies are adopted to "send a message" that the public's views have been noted

or that their anxiety, apprehension, or unhappiness has been noted. Sociologist David Garland (2001) argues that much recent crime control policy in the United States and England was adopted primarily for "expressive" reasons, not because policy makers necessarily thought that new, tougher policies would reduce crime rates but because they wanted to reassure an anxious public that was fearful of rising crime rates and troubled by the uncertainties of a rapidly changing world.

Legislators have long adopted symbolic policies meant primarily to acknowledge public anxiety. Senator Alfonse D'Amato of New York, for example, according to the *New York Times*, conceded that two amendments he successfully offered to federal crime legislation, "which Justice Department officials sa[id] would have little practical effect on the prosecution of crimes, might not solve the problem. 'But,' he said, 'it does bring about a sense that we're serious'" (Ifill 1991, p. A6). The seeming eighteenth-century English paradox that many more crimes were made punishable by death during a century in which the number of executions rapidly and substantially declined is generally explained in expressive terms; legislators were trying to stress the seriousness of the new death-eligible offenses, generally property crimes, even though there was little appetite for executing property offenders (Hay 1975).

3. *Public Confidence.* For nearly a decade the English government has explained major changes in criminal justice policy as parts of a larger effort to increase public confidence in the legal system (e.g., Home Office 2002). The criminal justice system is believed by the English government to lack credibility in the eyes of voters, and measures meant to make punishments harsher and more certain and convictions more likely are portrayed as parts of a larger campaign to increase public confidence in the legal system and generally. This is in effect a collective, bystander's parallel to legitimacy. Public confidence in the legal system is likely to increase if it is seen to be addressing problems that trouble citizens effectively.

4. *Reinforcement of Basic Social Norms.* This is the corollary of the preventive function of "moral education." That is why Scandinavian countries attach great significance to proportionality in punishment (so that the severity of sanctions acknowledges the comparative seriousness of crimes) and more frequently impose prison sentences (though shorter ones) and their equivalents than most other countries do (so criminal behavior has consequences) (Lappi-Seppälä 2001).

Conversely, if the law's treatment of crimes is incompatible with basic social norms, the effect will be to undermine the legitimacy of the legal system. At times, for example, when cannabis is treated as a dangerous drug on par with heroin or crack cocaine, enforcement becomes lax and inconsistent, and the legal system is seen by many as being out of step with prevailing behavioral norms. Or when drug trafficking in small amounts is treated as being more serious than rape, manslaughter, or serious assault, it is clear that the legislature is out of step. Recent prosecutions and severe punishments in white-collar crime cases offer an example of the system responding to a widespread public perception that it was unjust that corporate malefactors in crimes involving hundreds of millions of dollars often received milder punishments than less privileged citizens convicted of much less serious crimes.

A few strong inferences can be drawn from these observations about communicative functions. First, they fit together: people expect legal institutions to be fair, consistent, rational, and in step with prevailing social norms. Second, public confidence and reassurance are likelier to be achieved by fair, consistent, and rational policies and practices than by expressive and symbolic policies that lack those qualities. It is hard to imagine, for example, that statutes that call for five-, ten-, and twenty-year minimum sentences for drug crimes, which are routinely circumvented and thereby lack legitimacy and fail to mirror prevailing social norms, have greater positive effects on public reassurance and confidence than more moderate laws would.

IV. Latent Functions

The latent functions of sentencing and sentencing policy—using sentencing to achieve personal, ideological, or partisan political goals—sometimes fundamentally obstruct performance of sentencing's primary and ancillary functions. Many practitioners and policy makers hanker for more lucrative or powerful jobs. Elected officials want to be reelected and aspirants want to be elected for the first time. Prosecutors and judges sometimes call for or impose unusually severe punishments to win favor with voters or party leaders. Legislators propose and vote for new laws for those reasons. Many practitioners and policy makers have strong ideological beliefs and want to bear witness to their beliefs. Policy makers sometimes want to posture before ideological soul mates and make symbolic statements. Policy makers sometimes subordinate their personal beliefs to achievement of partisan political goals.

A. Self-Interest

Purely personal ambitions and self-serving motives are illegitimate considerations in decision making by prosecutors and judges about individual cases. Performance of the distributive, preventive, and communicative functions is undermined when cases are dealt with in a particular way because a practitioner believes she is likelier to gain a nomination, win an election, or obtain a new job. Retributive theories of punishment call for punishments to reflect the personal culpability and harm associated with an offense. Utilitarian and mixed theories call for punishments to be based at least in part on good-faith assessments of their likely crime-preventive effects. No theory justifies punishments based on substantively unrelated ulterior considerations. Decisions based on practitioners' personal self-interest are in effect whimsical or arbitrary and irreconcilable with any prevailing theory of punishment.

The analysis is somewhat more complicated for legislators and other policy makers, primarily because the issues of self-interest are sometimes more opaque. When a prosecutor or judge treats an offender in a particular way to realize a purely personal goal, there is no arguable public benefit that can be said to outweigh or counterbalance the harm done the offender. When an entirely self-motivated legislator votes to support a particular policy for which there is little substantive justification, but claims in good faith to be trying to reassure the public or, more complicatedly, claims a need to vote in a particular way on this subject in order to win others' support for a vote on a more important subject, it is almost impossible to assess what the real motives are. The governing ethical premise, however, should be the same as for a prosecutor or a judge: only disinterested motives are legitimate. Observers may have difficulty knowing policy makers' motives, but they themselves know whether their motives are legitimate or ignoble. A good ethical litmus test is whether a legislator at a press conference could comfortably and completely truthfully explain his or her motives.

In the introduction I described a judge up for a vigorously contested reelection who in a particular case, to win favorable publicity, might impose a much harsher sentence than in his own mind can be justified, and I suggested that few observers who knew why he had done so would approve. The analysis of policy making predicated on pursuit of instrumental latent goals is the same as that which applies to a judge who bases the sentence he imposes on his electoral hopes. A legislator or governor who proposes or enacts policy changes he knows will not achieve their purported aims and will, if enacted, cause new injustices, because he hopes his support for the new policy will help him get reelected, is behaving unethically.

The entanglement of sentencing policy in individuals' self-interest has been especially acute at the federal level. Repeatedly in this essay I have used examples from the federal sentencing guidelines. A major reason why they were so inadequate and disliked was that the U.S. Sentencing Commission's policy making in its formative years became entangled in the personal ambitions of William Wilkins, the first chair (initially, unsuccessfully, to become FBI director, then successfully to become a federal court of appeals judge), and Stephen Breyer (successfully, to get to the Supreme Court). Wilkins had been a senior staffer to Senator Strom Thurmond and Breyer had been chief of staff to Senator Edward Kennedy when the two senators were successively chairmen of the Senate Judiciary Committee. Breyer's cross-aisle political credibility was such that Senate confirmation of his appointment as a federal court of appeals judge occurred in October 1980, just before the presidential election, at a time when Republicans otherwise were refusing to act on President Carter's judicial nominations. Wilkins's and Breyer's judicial ambitions meant that a major function of the guidelines was to win favor with Strom Thurmond and his personal staff in the Senate in particular, with congressional Republicans more generally, and with Ed Meese's Justice Department (von Hirsch 1988; Tonry 1996, p. 84). Tens of thousands of federal defendants paid a high price for Wilkins's and Breyer's judicial appointments.

Sometimes penal policies are proposed for reasons having nothing to do with the goals of punishment per se. The prison guards union in California, for example, is often said to promote harsher policies as means to the ends of job creation and maintenance (Petersilia 2003, pp. 237–38). Many communities have sought placement of prisons within their boundaries and, implicitly, increased use of imprisonment, as a form of economic development (p. 239). On the face of it these considerations are entirely unrelated to punishment and prevention.

All the things I have described and decried happen and no doubt will continue to. Anyone who reads newspapers knows that. That is the world we will continue to live in, but practitioners and policy makers can be more self-aware, intellectually honest, and transparent, and the rest of us can try to hold them to account.

B. *Ideological Expression*

Crime control policy in our time has become entangled in ideological conflict. Recent conflicts over medical use of marijuana and Oregon's assisted-suicide law offer front-page examples. Voters initially in California and eventually in more than a half dozen states approved referenda authorizing medical use of marijuana. Voters in Oregon, initially by a narrow margin and later by a wide margin, approved a law allowing physicians in narrowly defined circumstances to provide drugs to mentally competent, terminally ill patients who want to die. In general under American constitutional doctrines of federalism, criminal justice policy is within the purview of the states (Richman, in this volume).

Public health and the regulation of medical practice also are generally recognized as matters of state law, but that has not stopped ideologically motivated federal officials from trying to control state policies. Successive U.S. Attorneys General John Ashcroft and Alberto Gonzales have attempted to use tortured readings of federal drug laws to overrule the decisions by Oregon voters to allow doctors to assist suicides and by California voters to allow doctors to prescribe marijuana for health care reasons. In each case, the federal government threatened to act under federal drug laws against doctors who complied with the state laws. The U.S. Supreme Court repudiated the effort in the Oregon case, in *Gonzales v. Oregon* (126 S. Ct. 904 [2006]), but, in *Gonzales v. Raich* (125 Supreme Court 2195 [2005]), supported the federal government's position concerning medical use of marijuana.

Ideology is at least as powerful an influence on sentencing policy. Drug policy offers stark examples. The federal 100-to-one law punishes people, mostly black, convicted of crack cocaine offenses as severely as people, many white, convicted of powder cocaine offenses involving amounts that are 100 times larger. The law was enacted in 1986, after the much-publicized death, generally attributed to a crack overdose, of Len Bias, a University of Maryland basketball player forecast to become a National Basketball Association superstar (Kennedy 1997). The law's role in exacerbating racial disparities in federal prisons soon became clear (McDonald and Carlson 1993), and the U.S. Sentencing

Commission proposed that the differential be eliminated. Both the Clinton White House and the Congress opposed any change, and none was made. In later years Attorney General Janet Reno, Drug Czar Barry McCaffrey, and the U.S. Sentencing Commission proposed that the differential be reduced. The Clinton and Bush II White Houses opposed all changes, and the differential remains. No one presumably wants federal sentencing laws to worsen racial disparities, but neither successive administration nor congressional leaders have been willing to risk being accused of condoning drug use or trafficking (Tonry 2004*b*, chap. 1).

Mandatory minimum and three-strikes laws, for other examples, often are primarily based on ideology. Research findings discussed in earlier sections make it clear, and for at least a century have made it clear, that such laws seldom achieve their putative goals and always produce undesirable and unwanted consequences. Ideological posturing is no better an explanation for why an offender is punished unjustly than is a judge's hope for reelection.

C. Partisan Advantage

Pursuit of partisan advantage is the most cynical of the latent functions. Ideological influences grow out of deeply held beliefs; those beliefs may sometimes be blinding. Self-interested acts can, of course, be criticized, but as long as men aren't angels they will remain at least psychologically understandable. Decisions made for partisan reasons, by contrast, are made in cold calculation. Partisan influences often result in the passage of laws that cannot be justified on the substantive merits and foreseeably produce unjust results. Republican Senator Orrin Hatch, according to a member of his staff, for example, long believed reducing sentences for drug offenders "was the right thing to do, but he couldn't do it for political reasons" (Gest 2001, p. 214).

California's three-strikes law, according to Frank Zimring's account, resulted from politicians' competing attempts to use punishment policies to pursue partisan advantage. It was enacted not because thoughtful policy makers really believed that people who stole pizza slices in schoolyards or handfuls of compact discs from Wal-Mart deserved decades-long prison sentences, but because Republican Governor Pete Wilson and California Assembly leader Willie Brown played a game of chicken in which, in the end, neither backed down. Democratic legislators agreed among themselves to pass any proposal Governor

Wilson offered, in hopes "that he would back down from an unquali-
fied 'get tough' stand or be politically neutralized if he persisted." Wilson did not blink. Nor did the Democrats. The law was passed as
proposed because both sides were "unwilling to concede the ground
on 'getting tough' to the other side in the political campaign to come."
Neither Wilson nor Brown was willing to propose refinements to Wilson's extreme initial proposal and thereby expose himself and his party
to the other's accusation of softness. As a result California adopted the
most far-reaching, rigid, and unjust three-strikes law in the country
(Zimring, Hawkins, and Kamin 2001, p. 6).

Former president Bill Clinton famously decided in the 1980s never
to let the Republicans get to his right on controversial crime control
issues, no matter how unjust, wasteful, or ineffective the policies under
consideration (Edsall and Edsall 1991; Friedman 1993). Clinton himself in 1994 admitted that "I can be nicked on a lot but nobody can
say I'm soft on crime" (Tonry 2004*b*, p. 8). It worked for Clinton but
not for the tens of thousands of people whose lives were changed for
the worse.

Britain's Labour Party, after a trip to Washington by Tony Blair to
meet with Clinton's political advisors, did the same thing in 1993
(Downes and Morgan 2002). Since then England has adopted sentencing laws of unprecedented severity, and the prison population has
reached historic highs and has increased more rapidly since 1994 than
in any other Western country (Tonry 2004*a*).

Latent functions and to a lesser extent communicative functions pose
a formidable problem for principled policy making. They are not primarily aimed at what goes on in courtrooms or on punishments imposed, crimes prevented, or efficiency enhanced, but on reputations
developed, political goals achieved, and elections won.

V. Reconciling Purposes and Functions

In principle, only normative purposes and primary and ancillary functions should count. Thought of as machinery meant to produce something of value, a sentencing system's most important functions, most
people would agree, are the imposition of deserved punishments and
the prevention of crime. Political maneuvers and passions sometimes
result in the passage of laws that produce injustices, and practitioners
may sometimes impose unjust sentences for idiosyncratic (e.g., an emo-

tional reaction to a particular offense or offender) or corrupt (e.g., to gain reelection or curry favor) reasons. But it is hard to imagine that many people think that is a good way to make policy or that unjust outcomes in individual cases are a good thing. Some of the main ancillary functions—addressing administrative concerns for efficiency, cost-effectiveness, and resource management—are regularly challenged on normative or policy grounds. In practice, though, the latent functions always powerfully shape policy and sometimes shape practice.

I do not kid myself that my or any other academic's disparagement of policy makers' motives is important or likely to influence policy makers to behave differently. It does, however, seem to me important that academics describe what they see and speak truth to power when opportunity arises.

Researchers and theorists can, however, work to develop better ways of understanding sentencing and sentencing policy. We need, for example, to devise new normative theories to encompass ways the world has changed since desert theories took shape in the 1970s (Tonry 2005b). In the early years of the twenty-first century, many people believe that efforts should be made to rehabilitate offenders, and a substantial body of credible evidence shows that sometimes, in well-targeted, well-run programs, this can be done. New restorative and communitarian conceptions of justice are taking shape and programs based on them are proliferating. Recent initiatives such as drug, family violence, and mental health courts are being established across the country as are new programs to divert many offenders from prosecution or prison into treatment. Most of these developments are happening and will continue to happen even though they are hard to reconcile with prevailing retributive theories of punishment. If theorists want to try to influence policy for the good and to be able at least to offer models and ways of thinking that will help policy makers make better choices, the work of developing new theories needs to be done.

That theorizing needs, however, to take account of all normative purposes and primary and ancillary functions. Practitioners want to act justly and to prevent crime effectively, if they can, but they also need to manage their offices efficiently, work within resource constraints, and allocate their efforts among multiple objectives. Most sentencing theories address the primary distributive and preventive functions of punishment, but I know of none that attempt also to encompass the major ancillary functions.

Ignoring the ancillary functions forces their influence into the shadows and often, as happened with the federal guidelines, produces outcomes of the sort Judge Marvin Frankel (1972) referred to as "lawless." By that he meant that sentencing in the 1970s was not subject to rules and was vulnerable to idiosyncratic and arbitrary decision making, and the resulting sentences often said more about the judge than about the offender. Bringing the ancillary functions within the frameworks for thinking about principles governing punishment and prevention will make explicit much that has been invisible and, maybe, achieve greater fairness and justice overall.

Much empirical evidence shows that well-managed guidelines systems can make sentencing more predictable and consistent. A quarter century's experience shows how guidelines' multiple functions can be reconciled in ways that achieve broad support from practitioners and reasonably consistent patterns of sentences imposed while allowing jurisdictions to take account of valid management concerns including resource allocation. The key elements are the development of guidelines that classify offenses and offenders in reasonable ways, that authorize sentences that accord with the sensibilities of the judges and prosecutors charged to apply them, and that allow sufficient flexibility for the individualization of sentences to take account of special circumstances.

The goal is a sentencing system that is fair, evenhanded, and consistent, that takes realistic account of key management interests, and that optimizes legitimacy, public reassurance, and public confidence. We know how to do that.

REFERENCES

Anderson, David. 1995. *Crime and the Politics of Hysteria: How the Willie Horton Story Changed American Justice*. New York: Times Books.
Beccaria, Cesare. 1995. *"On Crimes and Punishments" and Other Writings*. Trans. Richard Davies. Cambridge: Cambridge University Press. (Originally published 1764.)
Bentham, Jeremy. 1970. *An Introduction to the Principles of Morals and Legislation*, edited by J. H. Burns, H. L. A. Hart, and F. Rosen. Oxford: Oxford University Press. (Originally published 1789.)
Berk, Richard. 2005. "Knowing When to Fold 'em: An Essay on Evaluating

the Impact of Ceasefire, Compstat, and Exile." *Criminology and Public Policy* 4:451–66.

Blumstein, Alfred. 1988. "Prison Population: A System Out of Control?" In *Crime and Justice: A Review of Research*, vol. 10, edited by Michael Tonry and Norval Morris. Chicago: University of Chicago Press.

Blumstein, Alfred, Jacqueline Cohen, Susan Martin, and Michael Tonry, eds. 1983. *Research on Sentencing—the Search for Reform*. Washington, DC: National Academy Press.

Blumstein, Alfred, Jacqueline Cohen, and Daniel S. Nagin, eds. 1978. *Deterrence and Incapacitation: Estimating the Effects of Criminal Sanctions on Crime Rates*. Washington, DC: National Academy Press.

Blumstein, Alfred, Jacqueline Cohen, Jeffrey Roth, and Christy Visher, eds. 1986. *Criminal Careers and "Career Criminals."* Washington, DC: National Academy Press.

Blumstein, Alfred, and Joel Wallman, eds. 2000. *The Crime Drop in America*. New York: Cambridge University Press.

Boerner, David, and Roxanne Lieb. 2001. "Sentencing Reform in the Other Washington." In *Crime and Justice: A Review of Research*, vol. 28, edited by Michael Tonry. Chicago: University of Chicago Press.

Bowman, Frank O., and Michael Heise. 2001. "Quiet Rebellion? Explaining Nearly a Decade of Declining Federal Drug Sentences." *Iowa Law Review* 86:1043–1136.

Boylan, Richard T. 2004. "Do the Sentencing Guidelines Influence the Retirement Decisions of Judges?" *Journal of Legal Studies* 33:231–53.

Braithwaite, John. 2002. *Restorative Justice and Responsive Regulation*. New York: Oxford University Press.

Butterfield, Fox. 2003. "With Cash Tight, States Reassess Long Jail Terms." *New York Times* (November 10), p. A1.

Casey, Pamela M., and David Rottman. 2003. *Problem-Solving Courts: Models and Trends*. Williamsburg, VA: National Center for State Courts.

Clear, Todd, and David Karp. 1999. *The Community Justice Ideal: Preventing Crime and Achieving Justice*. Boulder, CO: Westview.

Cohen, Jacqueline. 1983. "Incapacitation as a Strategy for Crime Control: Possibilities and Pitfalls." In *Crime and Justice: An Annual Review of Research*, vol. 5, edited by Michael Tonry and Norval Morris. Chicago: University of Chicago Press.

Cook, Philip. 1980. "Research in Criminal Deterrence: Laying the Groundwork for the Second Decade." In *Crime and Justice: An Annual Review of Research*, vol. 2, edited by Norval Morris and Michael Tonry. Chicago: University of Chicago Press.

Dawson, Robert. 1969. *Sentencing: The Decision as to Type, Length, and Conditions of Sentence*. Boston: Little, Brown.

Doob, Anthony N., and Cheryl Marie Webster. 2003. "Sentence Severity and Crime: Accepting the Null Hypothesis." In *Crime and Justice: A Review of Research*, vol. 30, edited by Michael Tonry. Chicago: University of Chicago Press.

———. 2006. "Countering Punitiveness: Understanding Stability in Canada's Imprisonment Rate." *Law and Society Review* 40(2):325–67.

Downes, David, and Rod Morgan. 2002. "The Skeletons in the Cupboard: The Politics of Law and Order at the Turn of the Millennium." In *The Oxford Handbook of Criminology*, 3rd ed., edited by M. Maguire, R. Morgan, and R. Reiner. Oxford: Oxford University Press.

Durkheim, Emile. 1933. *The Division of Labour in Society*. Trans. George Simpson. New York: Free Press. (Originally published 1893.)

Edsall, Thomas, and Mary Edsall. 1991. *Chain Reaction: The Impact of Race, Rights, and Taxes on American Politics*. New York: Norton.

Eisenstein, James, Roy Flemming, and Peter Nardulli. 1988. *The Contours of Justice: Communities and Their Courts*. Boston: Little Brown.

Farrington, David. 1979. "Longitudinal Research on Crime and Delinquency." In *Crime and Justice: An Annual Review of Research*, vol. 1, edited by Norval Morris and Michael Tonry. Chicago: University of Chicago Press.

Farrington, David, and Brandon C. Welsh. In this volume. "A Half Century of Randomized Experiments."

Frankel, Marvin E. 1972. *Criminal Sentences: Law without Order*. New York: Hill & Wang.

Frase, Richard. 1997. "Sentencing Principles in Theory and Practice." In *Crime and Justice: A Review of Research*, vol. 22, edited by Michael Tonry. Chicago: University of Chicago Press.

———. 2004. "Limiting Retributivism." In *The Future of Imprisonment*, edited by Michael Tonry. New York: Oxford University Press.

———. 2005*a*. "Punishment Purposes." *Stanford Law Review* 58:67–83.

———. 2005*b*. "Sentencing Guidelines in Minnesota, 1978–2003." In *Crime and Justice: A Review of Research*, vol. 32, edited by Michael Tonry. Chicago: University of Chicago Press.

———. 2005*c*. "State Sentencing Guidelines: Diversity, Consensus, and Unresolved Policy Issues." *Columbia Law Review* 105:1190–1232.

Freiberg, Arie. 2001. "Three Strikes and You're Out—It's Not Cricket: Colonization and Resistance in Australian Sentencing." In *Sentencing and Sanctions in Western Countries*, edited by Michael Tonry and Richard Frase. New York: Oxford University Press.

Friedman, Lawrence. 1993. *Crime and Punishment in American History*. New York: Basic Books.

Gaes, Gerald G., Timothy J. Flanagan, Lawrence L. Motiuk, and Lynn Stewart. 1999. "Adult Correctional Treatment." In *Prisons*, edited by Michael Tonry and Joan Petersilia. Chicago: University of Chicago Press.

Garland, David. 2001. *The Culture of Control*. Chicago: University of Chicago Press.

Gest, Ted. 2001. *Crime and Politics: Big Government's Erratic Campaign for Law and Order*. New York: Oxford University Press.

Greenwood, Peter W., and Allan Abrahamse. 1982. *Selective Incapacitation*. Santa Monica, CA: RAND.

Halliday, John. 2001. *Making Punishments Work: Report of a Review of the Sentencing Framework for England and Wales.* London: Home Office.

Hart, H. L. A. 1968. *Punishment and Responsibility.* Oxford: Oxford University Press.

Hay, Douglas. 1975. "Property, Authority, and the Criminal Law." In *Albion's Fatal Tree: Crime and Society in Eighteenth Century England,* edited by Douglas Hay, Peter Linebaugh, and E. P. Thompson. New York: Pantheon.

Heumann, Milton, and Colin Loftin. 1979. "Mandatory Sentencing and the Abolition of Plea Bargaining: The Michigan Felony Firearms Statute." *Law and Society Review* 13:393–430.

Home Office. 2002. *Justice for All.* CM5563. London: H.M. Stationery Office.

Ifill, Gwen. 1991. "Senate's Rule for Its Anti-crime Bill: The Tougher the Provision, the Better." *New York Times* (July 8), p. A6.

Joint Committee on New York Drug Law Evaluation. 1978. *The Nation's Toughest Drug Law: Evaluating the New York Experience.* A Project of the Association of the Bar of the City of New York and the Drug Abuse Council. Washington, DC: U.S. Government Printing Office.

Kant, Immanuel. 1887. *The Philosophy of Law: An Exposition of the Fundamental Principles of Jurisprudence as a Science of Right.* Trans. W. Hastie. Edinburgh: T. and T. Clark. (Originally published 1796.)

Kennedy, Randall. 1997. *Race, Crime, and the Law.* New York: Pantheon.

Kessler, Daniel, and Steve Levitt. 1999. "Using Sentence Enhancements to Distinguish between Deterrence and Incapacitation." *Journal of Law and Economics* 42:343–63.

Lappi-Seppälä, Tapio. 2001. "Sentencing and Punishment in Finland: The Decline of the Repressive Ideal." In *Sentencing and Sanctions in Western Countries,* edited by Michael Tonry and Richard S. Frase. New York: Oxford University Press.

Lipsey, Mark W., and Nana Landenberger. 2006. "Cognitive-Behavioral Interventions." In *Preventing Crime: What Works for Children, Offenders, Victims, and Places,* edited by Brandon C. Welsh and David P. Farrington. Dordrecht, Netherlands: Springer.

Martin, John S., Jr. 2004. "Let Judges Do Their Jobs." *New York Times* (June 23), p. A31.

Martinson, Robert. 1974. "What Works? Questions and Answers about Prison Reform." *Public Interest* 10:22–54.

McCoy, Candace, and Patrick McManimon Jr. 2003. *Final Report: New Jersey's "No Early Release Act": Its Impact on Prosecution, Sentencing, Corrections, and Victim Satisfaction.* Newark, NJ: Rutgers University, School of Criminal Justice.

McDonald, Douglas, and Ken Carlson. 1993. *Sentencing in the Federal Courts: Does Race Matter?* Washington, DC: U.S. Bureau of Justice Statistics.

McDougall, Cynthia, Mark A. Cohen, Amanda Perry, and Raymond Swaray. 2006. "Costs and Benefits of Sentencing." In *Preventing Crime: What Works for Children, Offenders, Victims, and Places,* edited by Brandon C. Welsh and David P. Farrington. Dordrecht, Netherlands: Springer.

Merritt, Nancy, Terry Fain, and Susan Turner. 2003. *Oregon's Measure 11 Sentencing Reform: Implementation and System Impact*. Santa Monica, CA: RAND.

———. 2006. "Oregon's Get Tough Sentencing Reform: A Lesson in Justice System Adaptation." *Criminology and Public Policy* 5(1):5–36.

Messinger, Sheldon, and Philip Johnson. 1978. "California's Determinate Sentence Statute: History and Issues." In *Determinate Sentencing: Reform or Regression*. Washington, DC: U.S. Department of Justice, National Institute of Law Enforcement and Criminal Justice.

Miller, Frank W. 1969. *Prosecution*. Boston: Little, Brown.

Mitchell, Ojamarrh, Doris L. MacKenzie, and David B. Wilson. 2006. "Incarceration-Based Drug Treatment." In *Preventing Crime: What Works for Children, Offenders, Victims, and Places*, edited by Brandon C. Welsh and David P. Farrington. Dordrecht, Netherlands: Springer.

Monahan, John. 2004. "The Future of Violence Risk Management." In *The Future of Imprisonment*, edited by Michael Tonry. New York: Oxford University Press.

Morris, Norval. 1953. "Sentencing Convicted Criminals." *Australian Law Review* 27:186–208.

———. 1974. *The Future of Imprisonment*. Chicago: University of Chicago Press.

Morris, Norval, and Michael Tonry. 1990. *Between Prison and Probation*. New York: Oxford University Press.

Nagel, Ilene H., and Stephen J. Schulhofer. 1992. "A Tale of Three Cities: An Empirical Study of Charging and Bargaining Practices under the Federal Sentencing Guidelines." *Southern California Law Review* 66:501–66.

Nagin, Daniel S. 1998. "Deterrence and Incapacitation." In *The Handbook of Crime and Punishment*, edited by Michael Tonry. New York: Oxford University Press.

———. 1999. "Criminal Deterrence Research at the Outset of the Twenty-First Century." In *Crime and Justice: A Review of Research*, vol. 23, edited by Michael Tonry. Chicago: University of Chicago Press.

Nardulli, Peter, James Eisenstein, and Ron Flemming. 1988. *The Tenor of Justice: Criminal Courts and the Guilty Plea Process*. Champaign: University of Illinois Press.

Newman, Donald J. 1966. *Conviction: The Determination of Guilt or Innocence without Trial*. Boston: Little, Brown.

New York Times. 1990. "Criticizing Sentencing Rules, U.S. Judge Resigns." September 30, sec. 1, p. 2.

Nolan, James L., Jr. 2001. *Reinventing Justice: The American Drug Court Movement*. Princeton, NJ: Princeton University Press.

Petersilia, Joan. 2003. *When Prisoners Come Home*. New York: Oxford University Press.

Pincoffs, Edmund L. 1991. *Philosophy of Law: A Brief Introduction*. Belmont, CA: Wadsworth.

Redlich, Allison D., Henry J. Steadman, John Monahan, John Petrila, and

Patricia A. Griffin. 2005. "The Second Generation of Mental Health Courts." *Psychology, Public Policy, and Law* 11:527–38.

Reiss, Albert J., Jr., and Jeffrey Roth, eds. 1993. *Understanding and Controlling Violence*. Washington, DC: National Academy Press.

Reitz, Kevin R. 2001. "The Disassembly and Reassembly of U.S. Sentencing Practices." In *Sentencing and Sanctions in Western Countries*, edited by Michael Tonry and Richard S. Frase. New York: Oxford University Press.

———. 2005a. "The Enforcement of Sentencing Guidelines." *Stanford Law Review* 58:155–73.

———. 2005b. "The New Sentencing Conundrum: Policy and Constitutional Law at Cross-Purposes." *Columbia Law Review* 105:1082–1123.

Remington, Frank. 1969. "Foreword" to *Sentencing: The Decision as to Type, Length, and Conditions of Sentence*, by Robert Dawson. Boston: Little, Brown.

Richman, Daniel. In this volume. "The Past, Present, and Future of Violent Crime Federalism."

Roberts, Julian, Loretta Stalans, David Indermaur, and Mike Hough. 2002. *Penal Populism and Public Opinion*. New York: Oxford University Press.

Robinson, Paul H. 1987. "Hybrid Principles for the Distribution of Criminal Sentences." *Northwestern University Law Review* 82:19–42.

Rosenfeld, Richard, Robert Fornango, and Eric Baumer. 2005a. "Did Cease-fire, Compstat, and Exile Reduce Homicide?" *Criminology and Public Policy* 4:419–50.

———. 2005b. "The Straw Man Bluff: A Reply to Berk." *Criminology and Public Policy* 4:467–70.

Rosett, Arthur, and Donald R. Cressey. 1976. *Justice by Consent: Plea Bargains in the American Courthouse*. New York: Lippincott Williams and Wilkins.

Rossman, David, Paul Froyd, Glen Pierce, John McDevitt, and William Bowers. 1979. *The Impact of the Mandatory Gun Law in Massachusetts*. Report to the National Institute of Law Enforcement and Criminal Justice. Washington, DC: U.S. Government Printing Office.

Rothman, David. 1980. *Conscience and Convenience*. Boston: Little, Brown.

Ruth, Henry, and Kevin R. Reitz. 2003. *The Challenge of Crime: Rethinking Our Response*. Cambridge, MA: Harvard University Press.

Schulhofer, Stephen J., and Ilene H. Nagel. 1997. "Plea Negotiations under the Federal Sentencing Guidelines: Guideline Circumvention and Its Dynamics in the Post-Mistretta Period." *Northwestern University Law Review* 91:1284–1316.

Select Committee on Capital Punishment. 1930. *Report*. London: H.M. Stationery Office.

Spelman, William. 2000. "What Recent Studies Do (and Don't) Tell Us about Imprisonment and Crime." In *Crime and Justice: A Review of Research*, vol. 27, edited by Michael Tonry. Chicago: University of Chicago Press.

Stephen, James Fitzjames. 1977. *A History of the Criminal Law of England*. New York: B. Franklin. (Originally published 1883.)

Tonry, Michael. 1996. *Sentencing Matters*. New York: Oxford University Press.

———. 2004a. *Punishment and Politics*. Cullompton, Devonshire: Willian.

———. 2004b. *Thinking about Crime: Sense and Sensibility in American Penal Culture*. New York: Oxford University Press.

———. 2005a. "The Functions of Sentencing and Sentencing Reform." *Stanford Law Review* 58:37–66.

———. 2005b. "Obsolescence and Immanence in Penal Theory and Policy." *Columbia Law Review* 105:1233–75.

———. 2006. "Criminology, Mandatory Minimums, and Public Policy." *Criminology and Public Policy* 5(1):45–56.

Travis, Jeremy. 2005. *But They All Come Back: Facing the Challenges of Prisoner Reentry*. Washington, DC: Urban Institute Press.

Travis, Jeremy, and Christy Visher, eds. 2005. *Prisoner Reentry and Crime in America*. Cambridge: Cambridge University Press.

Tyler, Tom R. 2003. "Procedural Justice, Legitimacy, and the Effective Rule of Law." In *Crime and Justice: A Review of Research*, vol. 30, edited by Michael Tonry. Chicago: University of Chicago Press.

U.S. Sentencing Commission. 1987. *Guidelines Manual*. Washington, DC: U.S. Sentencing Commission.

———. 2003. *Survey of Article III Judges on the Federal Sentencing Guidelines*. Washington, DC: U.S. Sentencing Commission.

U.S. Surgeon General. 2001. *Youth Violence: A Report of the Surgeon General*. Washington, DC: U.S. Public Health Service.

von Hirsch, Andrew. 1976. *Doing Justice*. New York: Hill & Wang.

———. 1988. "Federal Sentencing Guidelines: The United States and Canadian Schemes Compared." Occasional Paper no. 4. New York: New York University, Law School, Center for Research in Crime and Justice.

———. 1993. *Censure and Sanctions*. Oxford: Oxford University Press.

von Hirsch, Andrew, and Andrew Ashworth. 2005. *Proportionate Sentencing: Exploring the Principles*. Oxford: Oxford University Press.

von Hirsch, Andrew, Anthony E. Bottoms, P.-O. Wikström, and Elizabeth Burney. 1999. *Criminal Deterrence and Sentence Severity: An Analysis of Recent Research*. Oxford: Hart.

Wacquant, Loïc. 2001. "Deadly Symbiosis: When Ghetto and Prison Meet and Mesh." *Punishment and Society* 3:95–134.

Washington State Sentencing Guidelines Commission. 2005. *Statistical Summary of Adult Felony Sentencing*. Olympia: Washington State Sentencing Guidelines Commission.

Wasik, Martin, and Andrew von Hirsch. 1988. "Non-custodial Penalties and the Principles of Desert." *Criminal Law Review* 1988:555–72.

Webster, Cheryl, Anthony Doob, and Franklin Zimring. 2006. "Proposition 8 and Crime Rates in California: The Case of the Missing Deterrent." Unpublished paper. Toronto: University of Toronto, Department of Criminology.

Welsh, Brandon C., and David P. Farrington, eds. 2006. *Preventing Crime: What Works for Children, Offenders, Victims, and Places*. Dordrecht, Netherlands: Springer.

Wilson, James Q. 1976. *Thinking about Crime*. New York: Basic Books.

———. 2002. "Crime and Public Policy." In *Crime: Public Policies for Crime Control*, edited by James Q. Wilson and Joan Petersilia. Oakland, CA: Institute for Contemporary Studies.

Winick, Bruce J., and David B. Wexler. 2003. *Judging in a Therapeutic Key: Therapeutic Jurisprudence and the Courts*. Durham, NC: Carolina Academic Press.

Wright, Ronald F. 2002. "The Cost of Sentencing in North Carolina, 1980–2000." In *Crime and Justice: A Review of Research*, vol. 29, edited by Michael Tonry. Chicago: University of Chicago Press.

Zimring, Franklin E., Gordon Hawkins, and Sam Kamin. 2001. *Punishment and Democracy—Three Strikes and You're Out in California*. New York: Oxford University Press.

Zlotnick, David M. 2004. "Shouting into the Wind: District Court Judges and Federal Sentencing Policy." *Roger Williams University Law Review* 9:645–84.

David P. Farrington and Brandon C. Welsh

A Half Century of Randomized Experiments on Crime and Justice

ABSTRACT

The number of randomized experiments on crime and justice with a minimum of 100 participants more than doubled between 1957 and 1981,
when there were thirty-seven, and between 1982 and 2004, when there
were eighty-five. There was an increase in very large, multisite replication
experiments and in experiments in which the unit of randomization was
the area. Results in the second period were generally more encouraging,
showing that some interventions reduced offending. The main advantage
of a randomized experiment is its high internal validity. Randomization
ensures that the average person or place in one condition is equivalent on
all measured and unmeasured variables to the average in another condition, within the limits of statistical fluctuation. Observed differences in
outcomes can be attributed to differences in interventions rather than to
pre-existing differences. Randomized experiments have formidable practical and ethical problems but are often feasible and should be used to test
causal hypotheses and evaluate well-defined technologies wherever
possible.

More than twenty years ago, the first detailed review of randomized
experiments on crime and justice was published in volume 4 of *Crime
and Justice* (Farrington 1983). This revealed that large-scale experiments involving 100 or more participants were infrequent. Only thirty-
five had been published between 1957 and 1981 that investigated the
effect of some kind of intervention on measures of offending or reof-

David P. Farrington is professor of psychological criminology at the Institute of Criminology, Cambridge University. Brandon C. Welsh is associate professor in the Department of Criminal Justice and Criminology, University of Massachusetts–Lowell.

fending.[1] Disappointingly, twenty-five of the thirty-five found no significant effect of the intervention. Most (twenty-five) were carried out in the United States, with seven in the United Kingdom, two in Canada, and one in Denmark.

This essay updates that earlier review to the present day and thus summarizes the first half century of criminological experiments. Its main aim is to investigate whether, after another two decades, there have been changes in the uses, methods, conclusions, and challenges of such experiments. We set out to explore a number of key questions. Has the nature of experiments changed? For example, do more modern experiments include larger numbers of participants? Are there more multisite experiments nowadays? Are there more efforts to replicate experiments? Have their numbers increased? Have their uses changed? Are they still largely carried out in the United States? Are the findings more encouraging today? What methodological advances have taken place? Are the challenges the same today? What has been done to address these challenges?

We conclude that the case for using randomized experiments is as strong as ever. Encouragingly, the number of randomized experiments has increased over time, although they remain relatively uncommon. They are still used mainly in the United States rather than in other Western industrialized countries. While results obtained in correctional, court, and community settings indicate few significant effects of interventions on offending, prevention and policing experiments have been more successful. Experiments show that some interventions work, especially developmental prevention, policing "hot spots," correctional therapy, court-mandated domestic violence programs, drug courts, and juvenile restitution. Experiments also show that other interventions—notably, Scared Straight, boot camps, and intensive supervision—do not work.

The essay is organized as follows. Section I defines terms, contrasts experimentation with other possible methods, and describes the techniques, searches, and analyses used in our review. Sections II and III examine, respectively, the major randomized experiments on crime and justice conducted during the two time periods (1957–81 and 1982–2004), organized in five areas: policing, prevention, corrections, courts, and community. Section IV examines changes in randomized

---

[1] In the present essay we review thirty-seven experiments during this time period (see below).

experiments on crime and justice over the two periods. Section V reviews major methodological, practical, and ethical challenges facing randomized experiments. Section VI offers a number of conclusions and recommendations.

I. Introduction

The word "experiment" is often used loosely to refer to any social action (especially if innovative) whose ultimate effects are uncertain. Following this definition, most methods of dealing with crime are experimental in nature. The word "experiment," however, has a more precise and more technical meaning in this essay. It refers to a systematic attempt to investigate the effect of variations in one factor (the independent variable) on a second (the dependent variable).

It is easiest to explain the nature of experimentation by discussing a specific example. Sherman and Berk (1984) wanted to investigate the relative effectiveness of three police methods of dealing with domestic violence: arrest the offender, separate the offender from the victim, and mediate between the offender and the victim. All three methods were being used and advocated at the time their research was conducted in 1981–82.

With the support of the mayor and police chief of Minneapolis, Sherman and Berk carried out an experiment in which misdemeanor domestic violence cases were randomly assigned to arrest, separation, or mediation conditions. The best way to ensure that people receiving one treatment are equivalent to those receiving another is to assign them at random to the treatments. If a reasonably large number of people are randomly assigned, those receiving one treatment will be equivalent, within the limits of statistical fluctuation, to those receiving another. It is then possible to disentangle the effects of the treatments from the effects of extraneous variables (uncontrolled differences between the groups). Sherman and Berk found, during a six-month follow-up period, that the arrested offenders were less likely to reoffend than those in the separation or mediation conditions, suggesting that arrest was the most effective method of dealing with these cases.

In this example, the independent variable was the method of dealing with offenders, and the major dependent variable was reoffending (measured in police records and in interviews with victims). The random assignment meant that offenders in the three conditions were equivalent in extraneous factors that might have been related to reoffending (e.g., age, race, prior record, unemployment) and that might have been used as a basis for dealing with offenders in the uncontrolled (naturalistic) situation. Therefore, in some way the subsequent differences in reoffending must have been produced by the different methods of dealing with offenders (see also Sherman 1992, chap. 3).

The defining feature of an *experiment* is control of the independent variable. Sherman and Berk assigned each offender to one of the three conditions. Thus the experimenters controlled which offender was in which condition. This essay is concerned with *randomized* experiments. In the Minneapolis experiment, offenders were assigned to conditions by reference to a table of random numbers. This meant that extraneous variables were controlled (i.e., made equivalent in each condition). Unlike statistical control of variables, randomization controls for unknown and unmeasured variables as well as known and measured variables (Weisburd, Lum, and Petrosino 2001). In randomized experiments, there is control of both independent and extraneous variables.

The control of extraneous variables by randomization is similar to, but not exactly the same as, control of extraneous variables in the physical sciences by holding physical conditions (e.g., temperature, pressure) constant. Randomization ensures that the average unit in one treatment group is approximately equivalent to the average unit in another before the treatment is applied. Holding physical conditions constant ensures a more exact equivalence of experimental units, but the theory of experimental control is the same in both cases.

A. Advantages of Randomized Experiments

An experiment is designed to test a causal hypothesis about the effect of variations in one variable on variations in another. A hypothesis cannot be tested experimentally unless it can be expressed in these terms. In the classic model of scientific progress, a series of testable causal hypotheses is derived from each theory. If each hypothesis is tested in an experiment, the pattern of results can be compared with the pattern of theoretical predictions. On the basis of this comparison, and taking into account other considerations such as the complexity of a theory, one can conclude that one theory is preferable to another. Ideally, each experiment should be one link in a chain of cumulative knowledge, guided by theory. In practice, well-developed, explicitly specified, falsifiable theories are rare in criminology, and the hypotheses tested by experiments are usually isolated rather than systematic tests of a larger theory.

Following Campbell and Stanley (1966), Cook and Campbell (1979), and Shadish, Cook, and Campbell (2002), the methodological adequacy of any test of a causal hypothesis can be assessed on four major criteria. *Statistical conclusion validity* refers to whether the two variables of interest really are related. *Internal validity* refers to whether a change in one variable really did produce a change in another. *Construct validity* refers to the theoretical constructs that underlie the measured variables; and *external validity* refers to how far the results can be generalized to different persons, settings, and times.

The unique advantages of randomized experiments over other methods are high internal validity and no ambiguity about the direction of causal influence. Many threats to internal validity that are eliminated in randomized experiments are serious in nonexperimental research. The main threats to internal validity are well known (see, e.g., Farrington 2003*b*):

1. Selection: the effect reflects pre-existing differences between experimental and control conditions.
2. History: the effect is caused by some event occurring at the same time as the intervention.
3. Maturation: the effect reflects a continuation of pre-existing trends.
4. Instrumentation: the effect is caused by a change in the method of measuring the outcome.
5. Testing: the pretest measurement causes a change in the posttest measure.
6. Regression to the mean: where an intervention is implemented on units with unusually high scores (e.g., areas with high crime rates), natural fluctuation will cause a decrease in these scores on the posttest, which may be mistakenly interpreted as an effect of the intervention.
7. Differential attrition: the effect is caused by differential loss of units (e.g., people) from experimental compared to control conditions.
8. Causal order: it is unclear whether the intervention preceded the outcome.

The best way of overcoming these threats to internal validity is to

carry out a randomized experiment. The next best way is to carry out
a quasi-experimental evaluation. Quasi-experimental techniques are described in detail in Shadish, Cook, and Campbell (2002). Unfortunately, experimental and quasi-experimental methods do not always
give the same results. For example, after reviewing over 300 evaluations
described in the University of Maryland report *Preventing Crime* (Sherman et al. 1997), Weisburd, Lum, and Petrosino (2001) found that the
weaker an evaluation design, as indicated by internal validity, the more
likely a study was to report a result in favor of treatment. Even when
randomized experiments were compared with strong quasi-experimental designs, systematic and statistically significant differences were observed. The implication is that randomized experiments are necessary
to produce the most valid and unbiased estimates of the effects of
criminological interventions.

B. *Selection of Randomized Experiments*

The criteria for including experiments in the present essay were essentially the same as in the 1983 review, with the additional requirement that the outcomes should include some measure of offending.
Experiments were included in this essay on the basis of four criteria.

First, units (persons or places) were randomly assigned to conditions.
We included experiments in which persons were assigned alternately
to conditions (Britt, Gottfredson, and Goldkamp 1992), but not studies
in which persons were assigned to one condition during one time period and to another condition during another (McDonald, Greene, and
Worzella 1992).

Second, at least fifty units were initially assigned to each condition,
or at least 100 units were initially assigned to two experimental conditions. We set this minimum sample size because, with smaller numbers, randomization was unlikely to achieve its main aim of equating
the conditions on extraneous variables.[2] Unfortunately, there was often

[2] To understand why randomization ensures closer equivalence with larger samples,
imagine tossing samples of 20, 50, 100, or 200 unbiased coins. With a sample size of N
and a probability of a head of $p = 0.5$, the expected number of heads is Np and the
standard deviation is the square root of $Np(1 - p)$. For example, in a sample of fifty coins,
the expected number of heads is twenty-five and the standard deviation is 3.5. Almost
always (95 percent of the time), the number of heads in a sample of fifty coins will be
between eighteen and thirty-two.

If two samples of fifty coins are tossed, the standard deviation of the difference between
the number of heads in the first sample and the number of heads in the second sample
is $2Np(1 - p)$, or 5. Hence, almost always (95 percent of the time), the difference between

a considerable dropout between persons initially assigned and persons finally assessed (e.g., in follow-up interviews), and differential dropout was one of the most important threats to internal validity. We report results for initially assigned units ("intent-to-treat") rather than for those who completed or actually received the treatment ("treatment-of-treated").

Third, there was an outcome measure of offending (e.g., as opposed to self-reported drug use, childhood antisocial behavior, or inmate misconduct). Criminological experiments focusing on other outcomes, such as court dispositions (Greenwood and Turner 1993b), were excluded. There were often many outcome measures, and in our summary tables we have reported only one (because of space limitations). We chose to report rearrests or reconvictions rather than self-reported offending because of the differential attrition problem with self-reports (e.g., Greenwood and Turner 1993a). We chose to report rearrests or reconvictions rather than parole revocations or returns to prison because the latter measures are more dependent on agency decision makers. We chose measures of crime in general rather than specific types of offending such as violent or property offenses. Where information was given for several follow-up periods, we chose the longest one.

Fourth, the experiment was published in English. There is a problem of defining what is meant by "published." We did not limit our review to books and journals but also included agency reports (e.g., California Youth Authority 1997).

---

the two numbers will be ten or less. Almost always, the two percentages of heads will not differ by more than 20 percent of the total (e.g., twenty heads in one sample, or 40 percent, versus thirty heads in the other, or 60 percent).

With two samples of twenty coins, the number of heads will rarely differ by more than 6, or by 30 percent of the total. With two samples of 100 coins, the number of heads will rarely differ by more than fourteen, or by 14 percent of the total. With two samples of 200 coins, the number of heads will rarely differ by more than twenty, or by 10 percent of the total. Hence, as the two sample sizes increase, the two percentages of heads will become more and more similar in general.

As the sizes of experimental and control samples increase, they will in general become more similar on all extraneous measured and unmeasured variables. The above coin-tossing example shows that two samples of twenty could be very different by chance, with the percentage of heads possibly fluctuating from 35 to 65 percent. With two samples of fifty, the possible fluctuation reduces to 40–60 percent; with two samples of 100, it reduces to 43–57 percent; and with two samples of 200, it reduces to 45–55 percent. The choice of any minimum sample size to achieve reasonable equivalence on extraneous variables depends on the definition of reasonable equivalence. We felt that the likelihood of large nonequivalence would be too great with samples of fewer than fifty. A minimum size of 100 in each sample might have been preferable, but this criterion would have caused the exclusion of too many experiments. Hence, we set a minimum size for inclusion of fifty in each sample, or 100 in total.

Where an experiment was conducted in several sites, we report results for each site where possible (i.e., if the results were presented separately for each site and if the initial sample size in a site was at least 100).

There can of course be several independent variables, several dependent variables, and complex experimental designs. For example, a *factorial* design might include two independent variables, each investigated at three levels (high, medium, and low). If each level of one variable was studied in combination with ("crossed" with) each level of the other, people would be assigned to one of nine conditions.

Matching and randomization can be combined in a design. For example, in the classic Cambridge-Somerville study (Powers and Witmer 1951), 325 pairs of boys were matched on rated delinquency potential, and one member of each pair was chosen at random to receive the special treatment. This design reduces the number of sources of variation and so makes it more possible to detect any effect of the treatment. However, it can create problems in statistical analysis. Many statistical tests are based on an underlying assumption of independent random samples, and matched groups are clearly not independent.

It might be thought that another method of ensuring equivalent groups would be to give all treatments to the same people in a random order; this is the method favored in behavior modification research (see, e.g., Farrington 1979). However, in these "within-individual" designs, people who receive one treatment second are not necessarily the same as those who receive the other treatment second, because of the different effects of the treatments received first. It is possible to estimate the effects of prior treatments by comparing treated and untreated groups, but this requires a "between-individual" design. Pure within-individual designs are not discussed in this essay because they are likely to have lower internal validity than between-individual designs.

The dependent variable can be measured after the manipulation of the independent variable or both before and after, as in a pretest-posttest design. An advantage of pretest measurement is that it can help to verify that the random assignment was successful in producing equivalent groups. A disadvantage is that the pretest may affect the posttest in some way, although it is possible to control for this in more complex designs.

C. Other Methods

An experiment is especially suitable for testing a hypothesis about the influence of one factor on another. Remember that Sherman and Berk were interested in testing the hypothesis that arrest, separation, and mediation had different effects on domestic violence offenders. The experimental method is unsuitable in the absence of such causal hypotheses. Hypothesis-testing research should ideally be preceded by hypothesis-generating research, which need not be experimental. Indeed, unstructured interviews or participant observation may be more effective than experiments in generating hypotheses, although experiments are usually more effective in testing hypotheses.

Experiments are usually more suitable to establish whether changes in an independent variable produce changes in a dependent variable than to determine the relative importance of or interactions between many independent variables. Sherman and Berk demonstrated that arrest led to a decrease in reoffending (compared with other methods) but did not establish the relative influence of the police method and other variables such as age, race, prior record, and unemployment. Many factors such as age and race could not be manipulated as independent variables, except in simulation experiments. Correlational research may be more suitable for establishing relative importance. Similarly, experimentation, with its static independent variable/dependent variable design, is not very suitable for investigating reciprocal influences between variables.[3] Interestingly, Sherman (1992) discovered an interaction effect, since arrest for domestic violence seemed most effective for offenders with a "high stake in conformity" (e.g., employed or married).

While a given experiment can demonstrate whether a change in A produces a change in B, it will not usually establish the variables or processes that intervene between A and B. For example, Sherman and Berk did not demonstrate *why* arrest was more effective than separation or mediation, although a deterrent effect was clearly more plausible than a labeling or deviance amplification effect. Any experiment is likely to leave loose ends of this kind, often generating further testable hypotheses. The interpretation of any experiment is easier if it includes interviews and observations.

---

[3] A reciprocal influence between two variables, A and B, occurs if a change in A produces a change in B and a change in B produces a change in A.

D. Searching for Experiments

We did not have the resources to carry out an exhaustive systematic review of randomized experiments on crime and justice to update the 1983 review. Searching all the major abstracting systems would produce many thousands of references that would need to be obtained and read for possible inclusion. However, we searched key books (e.g., Sherman et al. 2002), key systematic reviews (e.g., Braga 2001; MacKenzie, Wilson, and Kider 2001; Tong and Farrington 2006), key journals (e.g., *Criminal Justice and Behavior, Justice Quarterly*), and selected online databases such as NCJRS Abstracts and SPECTR (Petrosino et al. 2000), and we consulted leading researchers.

Petrosino and his colleagues (2003) reported that there were 267 distinct criminological experiments published or available in English between 1945 and 1993. The annual average number of experiments increased sharply from 1.8 in 1961–65 to 9.4 in 1971–75 but then leveled off to 9.4 in 1986–90 and 11.6 in 1991–93. This research suggests that, since 1982 (the 1983 review covered experiments between 1957 and 1981), there have been about ten experiments per year reported in English, but some of them would not meet our inclusion criteria (e.g., because there were small numbers or they were not published).

Weisburd, Lum, and Petrosino (2001) analyzed the Maryland report on the effectiveness of criminological interventions (Sherman et al. 1997). They excluded school-based interventions, few of which had offending outcomes. They found 308 studies with offending outcomes, of which forty-six scored 5 on the Maryland Scientific Methods Scale (Farrington et al. 2002*b*) because they were randomized controlled trials. However, there were also some randomized experiments among the twenty-eight evaluations that scored 4 ("quasi experiments") that had been downgraded from 5 to 4 because of differential dropout, for example.

Of the forty-six studies coded as randomized experiments, twenty-two reported a nonsignificant effect, seventeen found a desirable effect, and seven found an undesirable effect of the intervention. Some of these forty-six experiments would not meet our inclusion criteria because they were based on small numbers. Nevertheless, the two reviews by Petrosino and his colleagues (2003) and Weisburd, Lum, and Petrosino (2001) suggest that the number of criminological experiments conducted since 1982 that would meet our inclusion criteria is probably between forty and 150.

Despite this surprisingly large number of randomized experiments, only a small fraction of criminological evaluations use the experimental method. For example, only five out of forty-four evaluations of boot camps (MacKenzie, Wilson, and Kider 2001), only three out of thirty-two evaluations of prison-based drug treatment (Mitchell, MacKenzie, and Wilson 2005), and only four out of forty-two evaluations of drug courts (Wilson, Mitchell, and MacKenzie 2006) used randomized experiments.

E. Summarizing the Experiments

We classified experiments into five categories: policing, prevention, corrections, courts, and community. This is to some extent an arbitrary classification system, and some experiments could perhaps be placed in more than one category (e.g., the experiment by Killias, Aebi, and Ribeaud [2000] comparing community and institutional sentences, which we placed in the "community" category). Nevertheless, we thought it useful to organize the experiments according to their main focus. Because of space limitations, it is possible to provide only brief details of each experiment in this essay. For more details, the original reports should be consulted.

Our tables summarize:

- Author, publication date, and location of research.
- Description and initial size of sample.
- Experimental and control conditions: In order to simplify the presentation, we have sometimes combined or eliminated conditions in order to reveal the key contrast.
- Results: We report the percentage who became offenders in the different conditions, where this was given. In other cases, we report offending rates. We do not report the results of multivariate analyses.
- Effect size: A major development since 1983 has been the emphasis on effect size as well as statistical significance. In the interests of simplicity and understanding, we report the percentage offending in the experimental condition compared with the control condition. This is the relative difference rather than the absolute difference in percentages. For example, if 50 percent of the control group and 20 percent of the experimental group reoffended, the

percentage decrease would be 60 percent ($[50 - 20]/50$). Positive values of the percentage difference indicate that there was a higher offending rate in the experimental condition than in the control condition.[4] Another development since 1983 has been the use of meta-analysis to summarize a set of effect sizes. We do not use meta-analysis here, but we did use meta-analysis (and Cohen's d as a measure of effect size) in a paper that summarizes experiments in 1982–2004 (Farrington and Welsh 2005), which interested readers can consult.

II. The Uses of Randomized Experiments, 1957–81

A total of thirty-seven experiments carried out between 1957 and 1981 met our criteria for inclusion. This period of time is not arbitrary. The beginning date marks the first published report of a randomized experiment on crime and justice that we included, and the ending date represents the last year in which studies could be included in Farrington (1983).[5] Reassuringly, our later searches revealed only one experiment (Maynard 1980) that might have been included in the earlier review, although it was arguably "published" in a project report. The number of experiments increased from thirty-five to thirty-seven partly because of the addition of this study and partly because we have counted two separate experiments by Rossi, Berk, and Lenihan (1980); these were amalgamated into one experiment in the 1983 essay. This section provides more detailed information about these studies than was contained in the 1983 essay.

Disappointingly, few of these experiments concluded that interventions were effective. Offending was significantly lower for the experimental group in only nine out of thirty-seven experiments. In most cases, the nonsignificant results revealed the ineffectiveness of counseling. However, there were some encouraging findings.

---

[4] Where pretest offending was reported as well as posttest offending, we took both into account. In this case,

$$\text{percent decrease} = 100 \times [1 - (EA \times CB)/(EB \times CA)],$$

where EA is the percent offending after in the experimental condition, EB is the percent offending before in the experimental condition, CA is the percent offending after in the control condition, and CB is the percent offending before in the control condition.

[5] The first published experiment was by Powers and Witmer (1951), but we included the later follow-up report on this experiment by McCord (1978); see later.

A. Policing Experiments

Table 1 summarizes four policing experiments. Two showed significant reductions in offending. The first is Binder and Newkirk's (1977) study of juvenile diversion through the Youth Services Program in Orange County, California. An unknown number of juvenile offenders who were referred by police were randomly assigned to receive either diversion, which included a behavioral component (e.g., contingency contracting), or no treatment. Six months after the program ended, it was found that the rearrest rate of the experimentals was significantly lower than that of the controls, for a reduction in offending of 62 percent. However, Binder and Newkirk's positive results are complicated by a later unpublished report indicating that their program had the desired effects in one town but not in another.

The other policing experiment that showed desirable results was carried out by Quay and Love (1977). This too was a test of the effects of a juvenile diversion program on subsequent criminal activity. Participants in the program group were diverted from formal processing in the juvenile justice system and received various forms of counseling (i.e., vocational, academic, and personal), whereas control group participants were "treated by whatever other means were available to the juvenile justice system" (p. 377). A one-year follow-up found that the program group had significantly lower rearrest rates compared to their control counterparts.

Rose and Hamilton (1970) evaluated a police juvenile liaison scheme in Blackburn, England, using a randomized experiment. Juveniles could be diverted into this scheme if they were minor offenders, if they admitted guilt, if their families were willing to cooperate and accept supervision from the police, and if the complainant was agreeable that the police not prosecute. The police supervision lasted six months. All eligible arrested male juveniles (394) were randomly assigned either to be cautioned only or to be cautioned and supervised. A thirty-month follow-up showed that the recidivism percentages of these two groups were very similar (26 and 27 percent, respectively), and hence it was concluded that police supervision was ineffective. This was a convenient conclusion for the government of the day, which believed that supervision of juveniles should be given by social workers, not by police.

In the final policing experiment, Byles and Maurice (1979) evaluated the success of the police-run Juvenile Services Project, which provided

TABLE 1
Policing Experiments (4)

Publication, Location	Initial Sample	Conditions	Results (N)	% Change
Rose and Hamilton (1970), Blackburn, UK	394 male arrested juveniles	E = cautioned and supervised C = cautioned	30 months recidivism E 26.8% (194) C 25.5% (200)	+5%
Binder and Newkirk (1977), Orange County, CA	juveniles referred by police (n.a.)	E = diversion with behavioral component C = no treatment	6 months rearrests EM 0.14 (n.a.) CM 0.37 (n.a.)	−62%*
Quay and Love (1977), Pinellas County, FL	568 male and female referred juveniles	E = diversion with counseling C = control	1 year rearrests E 31.2% (436) C 44.7% (132)	−30%*
Byles and Maurice (1979), Hamilton, Canada	305 male and female youths referred by police	E = family therapy C = traditional youth bureau	2 years rearrests E 62.3% (154) C 55.0% (151)	+13%

NOTE.—E = experimental; C = control; EM = experimental mean; CM = control mean; n.a. = not available.
* $p < .05$.

family therapy for "higher-risk" juveniles and their parents in Hamilton, Ontario, Canada. This therapeutic approach was crisis-oriented, providing immediate assistance to address the problems that the family believed were contributing to the child's delinquency. The intervention began with a meeting involving the police, therapist (a social worker or nurse), and family and was administered in the participant's home by a therapist, lasting about six sessions. Three hundred and five male and female juveniles (under fourteen years of age) with prior police contacts (but not previously charged to appear in court) were randomly assigned to receive either the program or traditional investigation by Youth Bureau officers. A two-year follow-up showed that the experimentals had (13 percent) lower arrest rates than their control counterparts, but the difference was nonsignificant.

B. Prevention Experiments

Table 2 summarizes six prevention experiments that met our inclusion criteria.[6] They are roughly ordered according to the age of the children, from the youngest upward. Only one (Maynard 1980) found that the intervention had a significantly desirable effect in reducing later offending.

According to Weisburd and Petrosino (2004), the Cambridge-Somerville Youth Study (Powers and Witmer 1951) was the first randomized experiment on crime and justice. McCord (1978) followed up 506 men in this experiment who at age ten (on average) had been randomly allocated either to a group that received individual counseling and home visiting or to a control group. The counselors talked to the boys, took them on trips and to recreational activities, tutored them in reading and arithmetic, encouraged them to participate in the YMCA and summer camps, played games with them at the project's center, encouraged them to attend church, kept in close touch with the police, and gave advice and general support to families (McCord and McCord 1959). The treatment lasted five years on average, and the follow-up occurred at an average age of forty-five.

Unfortunately, the treatment seemed to have undesirable effects. Slightly more from the treatment group were convicted of serious crimes as adults (19 percent compared with 17 percent), and significantly more treatment group offenders than control offenders com-

[6] Many other prevention experiments were based on fewer than 100 participants.

TABLE 2
Prevention Experiments (6)

Publication, Location	Initial Sample	Conditions	Results (N)	% Change
McCord (1978), Cambridge and Somerville, MA	650 schoolboys	E = counseled C = no treatment	30 years adult serious convictions E 19.4% (253) C 16.6% (253)	+17%
Meyer, Borgatta, and Jones (1965), New York City	381 schoolgirls	E = counseled C = control	3 years court appearances E 6.9% (188) C 4.7% (191)	+47%
Reckless and Dinitz (1972), Columbus, OH	1,094 schoolboys	E = classes to improve self-concept C = control classes	3 years police contacts EB 19.8% (632) EA 37.7% (632) CB 19.0% (462) CA 36.4% (462)	−1%

Study	Sample	Treatment	Measure	Effect
Hackler and Hagan (1975), Seattle, WA	353 male youths in 4 public housing projects	E = supervised work C = teaching machine testing	4 years delinquency EB 38.4% (85) EA 32.6% (85) CB 43.3% (67) CA 25.4% (67)	+45%
O'Donnell, Lydgate, and Fo (1979), Hawaii	553 male and female referred youths	E = mentoring C = control	3 years rearrests E 27.5% (335) C 22.9% (218)	+20%
Maynard (1980), 5 sites, US	1,252 unemployed high school dropouts	E = supported work C = no treatment	27 months police arrests E 30.5% (n.a.) C 39.3% (n.a.)	−22%**

NOTE.—E = experimental; C = control; EB = experimental before; CB = control before; EA = experimental after; CA = control after; n.a. = not available.

* $p < .05$.
** $p < .10$.

mitted two or more crimes. More from the treatment group died early, had stress-related diseases, or showed symptoms of alcoholism, and fewer of them were married. McCord speculated that the treatment might have caused high expectations and dependency, so that there were negative effects when it was withdrawn.

Meyer and his colleagues (1965) evaluated the impact of social work services (i.e., casework or group counseling) provided to high school girls judged to be at higher risk for deviance. A three-year follow-up found that those girls who received the services, compared to their control counterparts, showed no significant difference in delinquency rates, as measured by court appearances (the numbers were exceedingly low), but were less likely to be truant from school (almost significant).

In another experiment on school-based delinquency prevention, Reckless and Dinitz (1972) evaluated the success of classes to improve the self-concept of seventh-grade boys judged to be at risk for delinquency and dropping out of school. They found no differences in delinquency rates or in a number of school outcomes (e.g., academic achievement or attendance) between the experimental and control groups.

Hackler and Hagan (1975) evaluated the Opportunities for Youth Project in Seattle, Washington, which involved two different delinquency prevention modalities: a program of supervised work and a teaching-machine testing program, the latter being used "not for remedial education" but for "confidence-building" (1975, pp. 92, 95). A four-year follow-up of the program found no significant difference in delinquency rates between the two conditions, although the experimental group improved less than the control group.

O'Donnell, Lydgate, and Fo (1979) evaluated a Hawaii mentoring program called the "Buddy System" in which nonprofessionals were employed as "buddies" of youngsters referred by public schools for behavior and academic problems and were trained to use contingency management techniques (behavior therapy). Youths were randomly assigned to the program or to an untreated control group, and both groups were followed up in arrest records for three years. Unfortunately, the program was not notably successful: 28 percent of treated youngsters, compared with 23 percent of control youths, were arrested. The researchers concluded that the program was more effective with previously arrested youths and less effective with previously nonarrested youths.

The final prevention experiment by Maynard (1980) evaluated a large-scale, multisite community-based intervention carried out in the United States and operated by the Manpower Demonstration Research Corporation. More than 1,200 unemployed high school dropouts were randomly assigned to a program of supported work or to an untreated control group. Supported work offers a highly structured work experience for those suffering from "severe employment disabilities," and it is distinguished from other employment or training programs by its emphasis on three programmatic techniques: "peer group support, graduated stress, and close supervision" (1980, p. v). Job placement assistance was also provided toward the end of the program, which lasted twelve to eighteen months depending on the site.

A twenty-seven-month follow-up found that the program group had a significantly lower arrest rate than the control group (31 percent compared with 39 percent). A slightly longer follow-up period (i.e., thirty-six months) found no significant differences between the program and control groups on employment, earnings, income, or public assistance, although an earlier follow-up (ten to eighteen months after the program) found significant desirable effects in these areas favoring the program group.

C. Correctional Experiments

Table 3 summarizes twelve experiments carried out in correctional facilities. Three reported significant reductions in offending, and one other reported a reduction in offending that approached significance.

In an innovative experiment on the amenability of offenders to correctional treatment, Adams (1970) randomly assigned 400 institutionalized delinquents (rated amenable or nonamenable) to four conditions: two treatment conditions involving individual counseling and two control conditions involving the usual correctional services. Offenders' amenability to treatment was based on clinical assessments. Individual counseling was provided once to twice weekly for nine months for both treated amenables and nonamenables. A thirty-three-month follow-up found that the treated amenables (E1) had the lowest rate of return to custody—57 percent lower than their control counterparts—and the treated nonamenables (E2) had the highest rate of return to custody.

In an another experiment to test the effectiveness of counseling (largely done on an individual basis), Berntsen and Christiansen (1965) randomly assigned 252 male offenders sentenced to short-term prison

TABLE 3
Correctional Experiments (12)

Publication, Location	Initial Sample	Conditions	Results (N)	% Change
Adams (1970), CA	400 institutionalized delinquents rated amenable or nonamenable	E1 = individual counseling (amenable) E2 = individual counseling (nonamenable) C1 = control (amenable) C2 = control (nonamenable)	33 months return to custody E1 6.2% (100) C1 14.5% (100) E2 16.7% (100) C2 14.6% (100)	E1 v. C1: −57%* E2 v. C2: +14%
Berntsen and Christiansen (1965), Copenhagen, Denmark	252 male prisoners	E = counseled C = control	6 years (min.) reconvictions E 41.3% (126) C 58.0% (126)	−28%*
Annis (1979), Ontario, Canada	150 male prisoners	E = group therapy C = control	1 year reconvictions EM .9 (99) CM 1.0 (50)	−10%
Kassebaum, Ward, and Wilner (1971), CA	512 male prisoners	E1 = small-group counseling E2 = large-group counseling C = control	3 years rearrests E1 57% (171) E2 70% (68) C 58% (269)	E1 vs. C: −2% E2 vs. C: +21%
Shaw (1974), UK	176 male prisoners	E = counseled C = control	2 years reconvictions E 57.3% (75) C 78.1% (73)	−27%*
Fowles (1978), Liverpool, UK	304 male prisoners	E = counseled C = control	1 year reconvictions E 39.4% (142) C 43.1% (144)	−9%

Study	Sample	Conditions	Outcome	Effect
Cornish and Clarke (1975), Bristol, UK	173 institutionalized delinquents	E = therapeutic community C = traditional training	2 years reconvictions E 69.8% (86) C 69.0% (87)	+1%
Williams (1970), UK	610 male institutionalized youths	E1 = casework institution E2 = group counseling institution C = traditional institution	2 years reconvictions E1 51% (150) E2 63% (187) C 63% (164)	E1 vs. C: −19%** E2 vs. C: 0%
Waldo and Chiricos (1977), FL	281 prisoners	E = work release C = control	46 months arrests SR: E 70.4% (98) C 66.7% (48) police: E 48.9% (188) C 53.8% (93)	SR: +5% police: −9%
Jesness (1971a), CA	281 male institutionalized delinquents	E = 20-bed unit C = 50-bed unit	5 years revocations E 81.9% (77) C 89.7% (166)	−9%
Jesness (1971b), CA	1,173 male institutionalized delinquents	E = treated according to I level C = regular living units	2 years revocations E 64.6% (655) C 64.7% (518)	−0.2%
Jesness (1975), CA	913 male institutionalized delinquents	E1 = psychodynamic institution E2 = behavioral institution	2 years parole violations E1 47.6% (487) E2 48.1% (426)	−1%

NOTE.—E = experimental; C = control, SR = self-report; EB = experimental before; CB = control before; EA = experimental after; CA = control after; EM = experimental mean; CM = control mean.

* $p < .05$.
** $p < .10$.

sentences in Copenhagen, Denmark, to receive either counseling or the usual correctional services. The counseling services were wide-ranging, including assistance in finding employment upon release and help with family problems. A long-term follow-up lasting a minimum of six years showed that the experimental group, compared to the con-trol group, had significantly lower reconviction rates, for a 28 percent reduction in offending.

The next two experiments examined the success of group therapy/counseling compared to the usual correctional services. In a Canadian experiment involving 150 male prisoners in a minimum-security insti-tution, a one-year follow-up found that those who received group ther-apy, compared to their control counterparts, had slightly lower recon-viction rates (Annis 1979). Kassebaum, Ward, and Wilner (1971) examined the impact of two different forms of group counseling (small and large) for adult male prisoners in a California prison. A three-year follow-up found that neither intervention, compared to the control group, was effective in reducing recidivism. Rates of return to prison were relatively high, with over one-half of the participants back in prison at the end of the follow-up period.

The next four correctional experiments were carried out in the United Kingdom in the 1970s. Shaw (1974) randomly assigned 176 male prisoners to receive special casework assistance from welfare of-ficers during the last six months of their sentences or to a control condition in two prisons (Ashwell and Gartree). The experimental pris-oners had more contacts, on average, with welfare officers (thirteen as opposed to six) and were significantly less likely to be reconvicted in a two-year follow-up period (57 percent versus 78 percent). Shaw thought that the active ingredient of this treatment might have been the increased interest of the welfare officers. There was an interaction between types of offenders and types of treatment, because introverted inmates did much better in the experimental condition, whereas extro-verted inmates did better in the control condition.

Unfortunately, in a replication of this experiment by Fowles (1978) in one prison (Liverpool) with 304 male short-term prisoners, the ex-perimental inmates were not significantly less likely to be reconvicted in a one-year follow-up period (39 percent versus 43 percent). The experimental inmates had more contacts with welfare officers (average ten contacts, compared with two for the control inmates). There was some suggestion that the control inmates were reconvicted more quickly: 65 percent of them (compared with 46 percent of the experimentals) were reconvicted within six months. Shaw and Fowles justified these experiments ethically by pointing out that control prisoners could seek welfare help and were not refused, whereas the welfare officers actively sought out the experimental prisoners to try to help them.

Cornish and Clarke (1975) randomly assigned 173 Kingswood training school boys to one of two houses, respectively, operating a therapeutic community and a traditional paternalistic regime. Reconviction probabilities in a two-year follow-up period did not vary according to the regime (70 percent therapeutic community, 69 percent traditional). Possibly because of these negative results, Clarke and Cornish (1972) became disillusioned with the randomized experimental method and concluded that "it is particularly unlikely that its widespread use at present would significantly advance our knowledge about institutional treatment in ways that could not be otherwise achieved" (p. 21). The Clarke-Cornish critique was very influential in ending Home Office–funded randomized experiments for a quarter century (Nuttall 2003).

Williams (1970, 1975) randomly allocated 610 male borstal inmates to one of three open borstals, differing in their regimes (traditional, group counseling, or casework). The experimental analysis did not begin until these borstals were full of randomly allocated inmates. The inmates treated in the casework borstal were significantly less likely to be reconvicted in a two-year follow-up period (51 percent, compared with 63 percent in the other two conditions, and a 63 percent probability for all borstal boys at that time).

One methodological problem was that only inmates who were not transferred out of the borstals were followed up. Since more of the casework inmates had been transferred out (23 percent, compared with 15 percent of group counseling and 16 percent of traditional inmates), it was possible that the followed-up casework inmates were a better group to start with than the other followed-up inmates. This may account for at least part of their lower reconviction rates. Contrary to the psychologists' predictions, the most disturbed boys did best and the least disturbed boys did worst in the traditional borstal.

Waldo and Chiricos (1977) evaluated the success of a work release program for prison inmates in Florida that lasted between two and six months. A forty-six-month follow-up found no appreciable differences between treatment and control participants on any of the recidivism measures.

Similarly disappointing results were found in a group of experiments conducted by Jesness (1971a, 1971b, 1975), which were designed to test the effectiveness of different correctional interventions with male delinquents in California Youth Authority institutions. In each case, no significant difference was found between experimental and control participants on the reoffending outcomes of revocations or parole violations. Jesness (1971b) did, however, find significantly greater gains by experimentals on various psychological and behavioral measures (i.e., alienation and aggression).

D. Court Experiments

Table 4 summarizes three experiments carried out in the courts, one of which reported a significant reduction in offending. This experiment, conducted by Berg and his colleagues (1978), was the first ever to be carried out on sentencing in England (see also Berg, Hullin, and McGuire 1979). They aimed to investigate the relative effectiveness of two court dispositions for truants, adjournment (continuance) versus supervision by social workers. Both dispositions were being used by the juvenile court in Leeds. A retrospective study (Berg et al. 1977) suggested that adjournment was more effective than supervision in reducing subsequent truancy. However, the juveniles chosen for adjournment may have been different in some way from those chosen for supervision, and these pre-existing differences may have caused the difference in outcome.

With the cooperation of the Leeds juvenile court, ninety-six truants were randomly assigned either to adjournment or to supervision.[7] The drive and enthusiasm of the chairman of the juvenile magistrates (Hullin), who was a biochemist at Leeds University, was critical in getting this experiment off the ground (Berg, Brown, and Hullin 1988, p. 113). During a six-month follow-up period, the supervised juveniles were more often truants and committed more offenses (33 percent of supervised compared with 13 percent of adjourned were convicted), suggesting that adjournment was the more effective disposition in preventing truancy and delinquency. The reason was probably that adjourned cases were dealt with by educational welfare officers, who

---

[7] We did not slavishly adhere to our minimum sample size of 100, but included this study since the numbers were close to 100.

TABLE 4
Court Experiments (3)

Publication, Location	Initial Sample	Conditions	Results (N)	% Change
Berg et al. (1978), Leeds, UK	96 male and female truants	E = adjourned C = supervised	6 months reoffending E 13.3% (45) C 33.3% (51)	-60%*
Ditman et al. (1967), San Diego, CA	301 male and female drunk offenders	E1 = alcoholic clinic E2 = Alcoholics Anonymous C = no treatment	1 year (min.) rearrests E1 68.3% (82) E2 68.6% (86) C 56.2% (73)	E1 vs. C: +21.5% E2 vs. C: +22.1%
Baker and Sadd (1981), New York City	666 male defendants in felony cases	E = helped in court, given job counseling C = processed normally by court	1 year rearrests E 30% (271) C 33% (170)	-9%

NOTE.—E = experimental; C = control.
* p < .05

were very concerned to get them back to school, whereas the supervising social workers gave more priority to dealing with family problems.

In the next experiment, Ditman and his colleagues (1967) investigated the differential effects of randomly assigning 301 male and female chronic drunk offenders sentenced to probation in the San Diego Municipal Court to one of three conditions: a community alcohol treatment clinic with a psychiatric orientation, Alcoholics Anonymous, or no treatment. Chronic drunk offenders were those who had either two drunk arrests in the last three months or three drunk arrests in the last year. Disappointingly, a one-year follow-up found that participants in the no-treatment condition had lower (but not significantly so) rearrest rates than those in the two treatment conditions. Put another way, offending increased by about 22 percent in both treatment groups compared to the control group. The authors speculated that this iatrogenic effect was caused by too few mandated treatment sessions or anxiety in the offenders over the court-imposed referral to treatment.

In the final court experiment, Baker and Sadd (1981) evaluated the Vera Institute of Justice's Court Employment Project in New York City, the first pretrial diversion program in the United States. Program participants were diverted before trial; spent four months in the program in which they received remedial education, counseling, and help finding work; and, upon successful completion, had their cases dismissed; those in the control group were processed in the usual fashion. The experiment randomly assigned more than 600 male felony offenders to one of the two conditions. A one-year follow-up found that, compared to the controls, program group participants were more likely to have their cases dismissed, but the two groups were equally likely to be rearrested.

E. *Community Experiments*

Table 5 summarizes twelve community experiments. Only one reported a significant reduction in offending; one other claimed a significant reduction in offending, but tests of significance were not reported, and we could not investigate this because numbers were not provided.

In the first two experiments, Empey and Lubeck (1971) and Empey and Erickson (1972) evaluated the success of an alternative residential

TABLE 5
Community Experiments (12)

Publication, Location	Initial Sample	Conditions	Results (N)	% Change
Empey and Lubeck (1971), CA	261 male recidivists	E = community program including guided group interaction C = institution	1 year mean offenses EB 2.71 (140) EA .73 (140) CB 2.66 (121) CA .74 (121)	−3%
Empey and Erickson (1972), Utah County, UT	150 male recidivists	E = community program including guided group interaction C = probation	4 years rearrests EM 3.31 (62) CM 2.83 (69)	+17%
Folkard, Smith, and Smith (1976), 4 sites in UK	900 male and female probationers	E = intensive probation C = regular probation	1 year reconvictions E 32.2% (475) C 29.6% (425)	+9%
Lichtman and Smock (1981), Wayne County, MI	503 male probationers	E = intensive probation C = regular probation	2–3 years reconvictions E 36.5% (233) C 35.0% (197)	+4%
Lamb and Goertzel (1974), San Mateo, CA	110 male offenders sentenced to jail	E = community program C = jail	1 year parole revocations E 35.5% (31) C 29.0% (31)	+22%
Palmer (1974), CTP1, CA	802 male delinquents	E = community treatment C = institution	2 years reoffending E 44% (n.a.) C 63% (n.a.)	−30%[a]

TABLE 5 (*Continued*)

Publication, Location	Initial Sample	Conditions	Results (N)	% Change
Palmer (1974), CTP2, CA	106 male delinquents needing/not needing institutionalization	E = community treatment C = institution	18 months reoffending (if needing institution) E 94% (n.a.) C 58% (n.a.) 18 months reoffending (if not needing institution) EM 1.5 (n.a.) CM 1.2 (n.a.)	+62%[a] for needing +25% for not needing
Reimer and Warren (1957), CA	3,793 male parolees	E = low caseload C = high caseload	23 months major arrests E 14.2% (1,479) C 15.7% (2,314)	−10%
Venezia (1972), Woodland, CA	123 male and female delinquents	E = unofficial probation C = counsel and release	6 months probation re-referrals E 18.5% (65) C 27.6% (58)	−33%
Rossi, Berk, and Lenihan (1980), LIFE, Baltimore, MD	432 male former prisoners	E1 = job placement and financial aid E2 = financial aid E3 = job placement C = no treatment	1 year (total) rearrests E1+E2 49.5% (216) E3+C 56.9% (216)	−13%*

82

Study	Sample	Groups	Outcome	Results
Rossi, Berk, and Lenihan (1980), TARP, GA	2,007 male and female former prisoners	E1, E2, E3 = unemployment benefit E4 = job counseling C1, C2 = control	1 year rearrests E1 49.9% (176) E2 49.2% (199) E3 49.2% (199) E4 49.1% (201) C1 48.4% (201) C2 48.7% (1,031)	E1, E2, E3 vs. 2Cs: +2% E4 vs. 2Cs: +1%
Rossi, Berk, and Lenihan (1980), TARP, TX	1,975 male and female former prisoners	E1, E2, E3 = unemployment benefit E4 = job counseling C1, C2 = control	1 year rearrests E1 37.7% (175) E2 38.0% (200) E3 42.5% (200) E4 34.0% (200) C1 36.5% (200) C2 35.5% (1,000)	E1, E2, E3 vs. 2Cs: +9% E4 vs. 2Cs: −6%

NOTE.—E = experimental; C = control; SR = self-report; EB = experimental before; CB = control before; EA = experimental after; CA = control after; EM = experimental mean; CM = control mean; CTP = Community Treatment Project; LIFE = Living Insurance for Ex-Prisoners Project; TARP = Transitional Aid Research Project; n.a. = not available.

[a] Significance claimed but not reported.

* $p < .05$

community control program that involved daily group meetings and followed the social learning technique of Guided Group Interaction, attendance at school, and limited work and tutorial activities. In the Silverlake, California, experiment (Empey and Lubeck 1971), offenders were randomly allocated to receive the program or institutional treatment, whereas in the Provo (Utah) Experiment (Empey and Erickson 1972), offenders were randomly allocated to receive the program or probation. Follow-ups of one and four years, respectively, found that neither program significantly reduced reoffending.

In the next two experiments, intensive probation versus regular probation was the subject of investigation. In the IMPACT study (Intensive Matched Probation and After-Care Treatment), 900 offenders placed on probation in four sites across England were randomly assigned either to regular probation (with an average caseload of forty to forty-five per officer) or to intensive probation (where officers had a caseload of a maximum of twenty offenders and had no court work or social inquiry reports to prepare). On average, experimental offenders had about twice as many contacts per month with their probation officer (three compared with 1.5 for the control group). However, there was little difference in the percentage reconvicted (30 versus 32 percent) after one year (Folkard et al. 1974; Folkard, Smith, and Smith 1976). Similar results were obtained in a Wayne County, Michigan, experiment by Lichtman and Smock (1981) that included only male probationers.

In the next three experiments, general community programming versus institutional confinement was the subject of investigation. In San Mateo, California, Lamb and Goertzel (1974) randomly assigned 110 male offenders sentenced to jail either to a community rehabilitation program known as Ellsworth House or to jail. House residents were expected to seek employment in the community and take part in group meetings and individual counseling sessions. A one-year follow-up found no significant difference in offending rates between the two groups, as measured by parole revocations, although the experimental group fared 22 percent worse.

Also in California, Palmer (1974), in two separate experiments, evaluated the effectiveness of the Community Treatment Project (CTP), an intensive community supervision and treatment alternative to institutional placement. In the first experiment (CTP1), Palmer claimed a significant reduction in reoffending in a two-year follow-up (44 percent in the experimental group versus 63 percent in the control group). In the second experiment (CTP2), he claimed a significant increase in reoffending among those offenders in need of institutionalization in an eighteen-month follow-up.

In the earliest known community experiment to have been published, Reimer and Warren (1957) randomly assigned almost 3,800 male parolees to either a small (fifteen cases per parole officer), intensively supervised caseload or a large (ninety cases per parole officer), regular caseload. A twenty-three-month follow-up found no significant difference in reoffending rates between the two conditions, as measured by arrests for major crimes.

In the next experiment, Venezia (1972) evaluated the success of unofficial probation, which is comparable to formal probation supervision but does not require that allegations be filed or court proceedings be initiated. About 120 male and female delinquents were randomly assigned either to receive unofficial probation or to receive counseling and be released (control group). A six-month follow-up found no significant difference between the experimental and control groups on the rate of probation re-referrals, although they were one-third less in the experimental group.

The last three experiments evaluated the effectiveness of transitional aid for former prisoners to help them to reintegrate into the community. Transitional aid took the form of modest levels of financial support or unemployment benefits offered over a short period of time (between thirteen and twenty-six weeks). In the first of these experiments, known as Living Insurance for Ex-Prisoners (LIFE), carried out in Baltimore, Rossi, Berk, and Lenihan (1980) randomly allocated more than 400 male former prisoners to one of three experimental groups that received financial aid, intensive job counseling and placement services, or both, or to a control group that received no payments or counseling. A one-year follow-up found a significant 13 percent reduction in reoffending, as measured by rearrest rates. Two replication experiments, known as the Transitional Aid Research Project (TARP), carried out with much larger sample sizes in Georgia and Texas, failed to reproduce the results achieved by the LIFE experiment. Rossi, Berk, and Lenihan (1980) speculated that the TARP payments might have produced two opposing effects that balanced each other out: "On the one hand, for a given level of employment TARP payments lowered the number of arrests experienced by persons receiving the payments.

On the other hand, because TARP payments increased unemployment, and unemployment increased arrests, the payments produced a side-effect that wiped out the direct arrest-averting effects" (pp. 16–17).

F. Overall

The results in these thirty-seven experiments published between 1957 and 1981 are not very encouraging. Only nine produced significantly desirable results, one produced a significantly undesirable result, and twenty-seven reported nonsignificant effects. With regard to the effect sizes (percentage differences), twenty-one were negative (desirable), whereas sixteen were positive (undesirable). When a higher criterion is set, thirteen effect sizes showed that the experimental group offended less than the control group by at least 10 percent, whereas eleven effect sizes showed that the control group offended less than the experimental group by at least 10 percent. In light of these results, we can perhaps understand why Martinson (1974) and Brody (1976) reached generally negative conclusions about the effectiveness of correctional treatment. The results indicate that providing nonspecific help, general counseling, and "intensive" supervision for offenders was not effective in reducing their offending. Were the results any different in the next two decades?

III. The Uses of Randomized Experiments, 1982–2004

A total of eighty-five experiments meeting our criteria were published between 1982 and 2004. While results obtained in correctional, court, and community settings indicate few significant effects of interventions on offending, prevention and policing experiments have been more successful. In general, experiments show that some interventions work, especially developmental prevention, policing "hot spots," correctional therapy, court-mandated domestic violence programs, drug courts, and juvenile restitution. Experiments also show that other interventions do not work, notably Scared Straight, boot camps, and intensive supervision.

A. Policing Experiments

Table 6 summarizes twelve experiments on policing for crime reduction. We begin with these because of the great historical importance of the Minneapolis Domestic Violence Experiment (Sherman and

Berk 1984). This showed that arresting male perpetrators for misdemeanor domestic assaults caused fewer repeat incidents of this crime (against the same victim) than ordering the offender to leave the premises for eight hours or offering advice and mediation. These results were welcomed by the U.S. Department of Justice and used to encourage police forces to arrest male perpetrators of domestic violence rather than deal with them in other ways (Sherman and Cohn 1989; Meeker and Binder 1990). In short, this study's findings, against the recommendation of Sherman and Berk (1984), were used to support mandatory arrest laws across the nation (Bayley 1998). Furthermore, according to Sherman (1992, p. 103), "the publicity helped to gain acceptance for the idea of randomized experiments."

The results of the original Minneapolis experiment encouraged the National Institute of Justice to fund an ambitious program of research to see whether the findings could be replicated in different settings. The results from published evaluations in Milwaukee (Sherman et al. 1992), Charlotte, North Carolina (Hirschel, Hutchison, and Dean 1992), Colorado Springs (Berk et al. 1992), Miami (Pate and Hamilton 1992), and Omaha (offender absent: Dunford [1990]; offender present: Dunford, Huizinga, and Elliott [1990]) are shown in table 6. In some cases, the percentages of offenders in experimental and control conditions who were rearrested were taken from Garner, Fagan, and Maxwell (1995), because they were not published in the original reports. (For a more recent research synthesis of these experiments, see Maxwell, Garner, and Fagan [2002].)

Table 6 shows that the results of these seven experiments on the effects of arrest on spouse assault were quite variable. Only the original Minneapolis experiment and the offender-absent experiment in Omaha found that arrest had significantly desirable effects. Rearrests decreased by 56 percent in Minneapolis and by 48 percent in Omaha. In attempting to reconcile all these results, Sherman (1992) concluded that male offenders with a lower stake in conformity (e.g., unemployed or unmarried) tended to get worse after arrest, whereas those with a greater stake in conformity tended to improve (i.e., offend less).

The next two experiments in table 6 investigated the effects of deterrent police activity in "hot spots," that is, high-crime places. These experiments are noteworthy because the unit that was randomized was an area, not an individual. No experiments in the 1983 review randomized 100 or more areas. Sherman and Weisburd (1995) found that in-

TABLE 6
Policing Experiments (12)

Publication, Location	Initial Sample	Conditions	Results (N)	% Change
Sherman and Berk (1984), Minneapolis, MN	330 domestic violence suspects	E = arrest C = advise or separate	6 months rearrests E 6.5% (93) C 14.8% (237)	−56%*
Sherman et al. (1992), Milwaukee, WI	1,200 domestic violence suspects	E = arrest C = warning	7–9 months rearrests E 20.5% (624) C 23.2% (297)	−12%
Hirschel, Hutchison, and Dean (1992), Charlotte, NC	686 domestic violence suspects	E = arrest C = citation, advise or separate	6 months rearrests E 18.2% (214) C 15.6% (436)	+17%
Berk et al. (1992) Colorado Springs, CO	1,658 domestic violence suspects	E = arrest C = protection order, counseling, restore order	6 months rearrests E 19.2% (421) C 19.3% (1,158)	−1%
Pate and Hamilton (1992), Miami, FL	907 domestic violence suspects	E = arrest C = no arrest	6 months rearrests E 19.1% (465) C 20.6% (442)	−7%
Dunford (1990), Omaha, NE	247 domestic violence suspects (offender absent)	E = arrest C = no arrest	12 months rearrests E 10.8% (111) C 20.6% (136)	−48%*
Dunford, Huizinga, and Elliott (1990), Omaha, NE	330 domestic violence suspects (offender present)	E = arrest C = mediate or separate	6 months rearrests E 11.9% (109) C 10.0% (221)	+20%

Study	Sample	Treatment	Measure	Effect
Sherman and Weisburd (1995), Minneapolis, MN	110 hot spots	E = increased patrol C = normal patrol	12 months crime calls EB 6,531 (55) EA 6,931 (55) CB 6,491 (55) CA 7,702 (55)	−11%*
Sherman and Rogan (1995), Kansas City, KS	207 hot spots	E = crack house raid C = no raid	30 days calls for service EB 1,059 (104) EA 865 (104) CB 1037 (103) CA 929 (103)	−9%
Eck and Wartell (1998), San Diego, CA	121 rental properties	E = police letter or meeting C = no police action	30 months crimes EM 3.2 (79) CM 5.1 (42)	−37%*
Mazerolle, Roehl, and Kadleck (1998), Oakland, CA	100 high-risk places	E = civil remedies C = police response	Observed drug selling EB 6% (50) EA 4% (50) CB 10% (50) CA 44% (50)	−85%*
Abrahamse et al. (1991), Phoenix, AZ	480 repeat offenders	E = police targeting C = no targeting	6 months convictions E 82.6% (270) C 75.4% (253)	−10%**

NOTE.—E = experimental; C = control; EB = experimental before; CB = control before; EA = experimental after; CA = control after; EM = experimental mean; CM = control mean.

* $p < .05$.
** $p < .10$.

creased police patroling in hot spots caused a significant (11 percent) decrease in crime calls for service, whereas Sherman and Rogan (1995) reported that police raids on crack houses caused some decrease (9 percent) in calls for service. Several other randomized experiments based on places and targeted at crime hot spots have been conducted but were excluded from this review because the number of units randomized was less than 100 (e.g., Weisburd and Green 1995; Braga et al. 1999).[8]

Braga's (2001) systematic review of policing of hot spots, which included these randomized studies, concluded that targeted police actions such as problem-oriented policing (compared to routine levels and types of traditional police services, e.g., random patrol) do reduce crime and disorder in high-activity crime locations. The review also found some evidence that spatial crime displacement is rare and that crime control benefits associated with the focused police interventions can be diffused to neighboring areas that did not receive the treatment.

Two more randomized experiments targeted on places focus on the threat of civil law to curtail drug dealing and related crime problems in private residential premises, known as nuisance abatement laws. In San Diego, Eck and Wartell (1998) randomly assigned 121 rental properties to receive either a letter or a visit from the police or no treatment. The police actions were intended to reduce drug dealing, and there were indeed 37 percent fewer crimes reported in the experimental places during the thirty-month follow-up period. In the other nuisance abatement experiment, Mazerolle, Roehl, and Kadleck (1998) compared the impact in controlling social disorder of civil remedies (police working with city agency representatives to inspect drug nuisance properties, coerce landlords to clean up blighted properties, post "no trespassing" signs, enforce civil law codes and municipal regulatory rules, and initiate court proceedings against property owners who failed to comply with civil-law citations) versus traditional police tactics (surveillance, arrests, and field interrogations). Observations of street blocks showed that conditions improved in the experimental places compared with the control places. In the most direct measure of offending, observed drug selling, there was a significant reduction in prevalence in experimental blocks compared to control blocks.

---

[8] A recent issue of the *Annals of the American Academy of Political and Social Science*, edited by Robert Boruch (vol. 599, 2005), is devoted to randomized experiments on places.

Finally, Abrahamse and his colleagues (1991) investigated the impact of a Repeat Offender Program that gave special attention to certain offenders to try to increase their probability of being convicted. The results were desirable, since the experimental offenders were 10 percent more likely to be convicted. This is the only example in table 6 in which a higher conviction rate is considered a desirable outcome.

B. Prevention Experiments

Table 7 summarizes fourteen developmental prevention experiments that met our inclusion criteria. They are roughly ordered according to the age of the children, from the youngest upward. Five found that the intervention had significantly desirable effects in reducing later offending.

Olds and his colleagues (1998) investigated the effects of a home visiting program for pregnant women in Elmira, New York. The home visitors (nurses) gave the women advice about child rearing, infant development, nutrition, and the need to avoid alcohol and drugs. Hence, this was a general parent education program. A fifteen-year follow-up of the program, which lasted two years, showed that the children of visited mothers were arrested at a significantly (54 percent) lower rate than the children of nonvisited mothers. Like almost all the prevention experiments reviewed here, the effects of the home visiting program on other outcomes were investigated. For example, at program completion, a substantial reduction in child abuse and neglect was found for higher-risk visited mothers compared to their control counterparts (4 percent versus 19 percent; see Olds et al. [1986]), and the fifteen-year follow-up showed that fewer visited than nonvisited mothers in the sample as a whole were identified as perpetrators of child abuse and neglect (29 percent versus 15 percent; see Olds et al. [1997]).

Schweinhart and his colleagues (2005) carried out the longest follow-up of the effects of an intervention. In the famous Perry Preschool Project, experimental children attended a cognitively oriented preschool program designed to increase their thinking and reasoning abilities and school achievement. The experimental and control children were followed up to age forty, with a retention rate of 91 percent (112 of the original 123 participants interviewed). Compared to the control group participants, those in the experimental group had 35 percent fewer arrests, were more likely to graduate from high school (79 percent versus 60 percent) and obtain a college degree (18 percent versus

TABLE 7

Prevention Experiments (14)

Publication, Location	Initial Sample	Conditions	Results (N)	% Change
Olds et al. (1998), Elmira, NY	400 pregnant women	E = home visits C = no home visits	15 years arrests E 16.6% (176) C 36.0% (148)	−54%*
Schweinhart et al. (2005), Ypsilanti, MI	123 children	E = preschool C = no preschool	Felony arrests up to age 40 E 31% (58) C 48% (65)	−35%**
Campbell et al. (2002), SC	111 children	E = intensive preschool C = usual preschool	Felony conviction up to age 21 E 8% (53) C 12% (51)	−33%
Mills et al. (2002), WA	206 children	E = cognitive preschool C = usual preschool	SR offending up to age 15 EM 12.62 (90) CM 11.05 (81)	+14%
Tremblay et al. (1996), Montreal, Canada	319 boys	E = child skills training plus parent training C = no treatment or just attention	SR arrest up to age 15 E 14.0% (43) C 30.1% (123)	−53%*
Harrell, Cavanagh, and Sridharan (1999), US	671 adolescents	E = risk focused prevention C = no treatment	12 months recorded crime E 28.0% (264) C 34.3% (236)	−18%
Borduin et al. (1995), Columbia, MO	176 delinquents	E = MST C = individual therapy	4-year arrests E 26.1% (92) C 71.4% (84)	−63%**

Study	Sample	Conditions	Outcome	Effect
Henggeler et al. (1997), SC	155 delinquents	E=MST C=probation	1.7-year arrest rate EM .89 (70) CM 1.20 (70)	−26%
Henggeler et al. (1999), Charleston, SC	116 psychiatric adolescents	E=MST C=hospitalization	4 months arrest rate EB .46 (57) EA .33 (57) CB .30 (56) CA .27 (56)	−20%
Henggeler et al. (2002), Charleston, SC	118 delinquents	E=MST C=usual community services	4-year conviction rate EM .34 (43) CM .77 (37)	−56%*
Leschied and Cunningham (2002), London, Canada	409 delinquents	E=MST C=probation	12 months criminal convictions E 41.2% (211) C 37.6% (198)	+10%
Grossman and Tierney (1998), US	1,138 youths	E=Big Brothers Big Sisters C=no treatment	12 months SR violence E 41% (487) C 41% (472)	0%
Schochet, Burghardt, and Glazerman (2001), US	15,386 youths	E=Job Corps C=no Job Corps	40 months arrests E 28.8% (6,828) C 32.6% (4,485)	−12%**
Kling, Ludwig, and Katz (2005), 5 sites in US	3,079 persons	E=move to better area C=no vouchers	5 years arrests E 32.9% (1233) C 31.8% (943)	+3%

NOTE.—E = experimental; C = control; SR = self-report; MST = multisystemic therapy; EB = experimental before; CB = control before; EA = experimental after; CA = control after; EM = experimental mean; CM = control mean.

* $p < .05$.
** $p < .10$.

6 percent), and earned significantly higher annual incomes. Because of small numbers, the difference in arrest rates was significant only at $p = .10$.

Similarly, in the Abercedarian project, Campbell and her colleagues (2002) found that an intensive cognitively oriented preschool curriculum led to 33 percent fewer convictions up to age twenty-one (compared with a regular preschool program), but that the difference was not statistically significant. Desirable results were also found in other areas for the experimental compared to the control group, including a slightly better high school graduation rate, a significantly higher enrollment in college, and a higher employment rate. However, encouraging results for offending (the only outcome measured) were not obtained in the preschool experiment of Mills and her colleagues (2002).

Tremblay and his colleagues (1996) evaluated the success of a multimodal program including child skills training and parent management training targeted at disruptive boys from low socioeconomic status neighborhoods in Montreal. The program, which ran for two years, reduced arrests up to age eighteen (by 53 percent), and the desirable effects increased over time. The program also improved school achievement and reduced alcohol use.

Another multimodal program, termed Children at Risk, was evaluated by Harrell, Cavanagh, and Sridharan (1999) in five sites across the United States. The intervention was designed to reduce the number of risk factors to which adolescents were exposed through family services, skills training, mentoring, education, and after-school activities. The program was effective in reducing offending (by a nonsignificant 18 percent), and the researchers concluded that the main effects arose through reducing peer risk factors: experimental youths associated less often with delinquent peers, felt less pressure to engage in delinquency, and had more positive peer support. In contrast, there were few changes in individual, family, or community risk factors, possibly linked to the low participation of parents in parent training and of youths in mentoring and tutoring.

The next five experiments in table 7 evaluated multisystemic therapy (MST), which is a multimodal intervention designed for serious juvenile offenders. The particular type of treatment is chosen according to the needs of the young person, and it may include individual, family, peer, school, and community interventions (including parent training and skills training). Four of the five trials of MST, all carried out by

Henggeler (the originator of this treatment) and his colleagues, found that the intervention was effective in reducing later offending (Borduin et al. 1995; Henggeler et al. 1997, 1999, 2002). The results obtained by Borduin and his colleagues (1995) showed a 63 percent reduction in the prevalence of arrests, whereas the reduction was 56 percent in the Henggeler et al. (2002) study. For two of these programs (Borduin et al. 1995; Henggeler et al. 1999), improvements were also found in the functioning of the family unit as a whole, as measured by the outcome of family cohesion. However, the one large-scale independent evaluation of MST, by Leschied and Cunningham (2002) in Ontario, did not find it effective in reducing later convictions (compared with the usual community services, which typically involved probation supervision); those in the MST group were 10 percent more likely to be convicted within twelve months. Unfortunately, two meta-analyses of the effectiveness of MST came to diametrically opposite conclusions. Curtis, Ronan, and Borduin (2004) found that it was effective, and Littell (2005) found that it was not.

The final three experiments evaluated large-scale community-based interventions in multisite studies. Grossman and Tierney (1998) found that the mentoring program Big Brothers Big Sisters had some beneficial effects, for example, in decreasing the onset of illegal drugs and alcohol use. However, it had no effect according to the only prevalence measure (of self-reported violence). Schochet, Burghardt, and Glazerman (2001) studied the impact of Job Corps, a nationwide program in the United States designed to improve the employability of at-risk young people (ages sixteen to twenty-four) by offering a comprehensive set of services, including vocational skills training, basic education (the ability to obtain graduate equivalent degrees), and health care. The program resulted in statistically significant reductions in the arrest rate, as well as higher employment rates and greater earnings for those who received it.

Kling, Ludwig, and Katz (2005) evaluated the impact of the Moving to Opportunity program in five cities in the United States; low–socioeconomic status (often minority) families were given vouchers to enable them to move to better areas. The effects of this move on the offending of their children were investigated. There was little effect on the prevalence of arrests overall, but there were desirable effects on the number of arrests of girls for violent and property crimes and undesirable effects on the number of arrests of boys for property crimes.

The authors speculated that brothers and sisters might have responded differently to new neighborhood environments; possibly, girls reacted to their more affluent schoolmates by trying harder in school, whereas boys reacted with resentment, stealing from their classmates and not trying in school.

C. Correctional Experiments

Table 8 summarizes fourteen experiments carried out in correctional facilities. The first two, by Lewis (1983) and Cook and Spirrison (1992), evaluated the Scared Straight program, in which adult prisoners harangue young delinquents about the terrors of imprisonment in an attempt to deter them from offending. Both experiments found negative effects; the percentage convicted in Lewis (1983) was 21 percent greater in the Scared Straight condition, whereas the decrease in offending rates (after versus before) in Cook and Spirrison (1992) was 7 percent less in the Scared Straight condition. These results are quite typical. A systematic review by Petrosino, Turpin-Petrosino, and Buehler (2003) found that reoffending was greater after Scared Straight in every one of seven evaluations. They concluded that "doing nothing would have been better than exposing juveniles to the program" (p. 58). The only positive finding to emerge from these studies was a significant decrease in school dropout rates, as reported in Cook and Spirrison (1992).

The next four experiments, three by Peters, Thomas, and Zamberlan (1997) and one by the California Youth Authority (1997), evaluated the effectiveness of juvenile boot camps, which were also intended to deter juveniles from offending. Started in the late 1980s, juvenile boot camps were introduced as a way to get tough on youthful offenders through rigorous military-style training, while at the same time providing them with treatment programs. None of these four experiments found a significant desirable effect of a boot camp, and one (Peters, Thomas, and Zamberlan 1997 [Cleveland]) concluded that it led to a significantly increased prevalence (44 percent) of offending compared with confinement in youth services facilities. Again, these results are not untypical. A systematic review of twenty-nine evaluations of boot camps by MacKenzie, Wilson, and Kider (2001) reported that boot camp participants had lower recidivism in nine studies, had higher recidivism in eight studies, and were no different in twelve studies. They concluded that "a meta-analysis found no overall significant differences in recidivism between boot camp participants and comparison samples" (p. 126).

The next four experiments, by Greenwood and Turner (1993*a*), Robinson (1995), Ortmann (2000), and Armstrong (2003), evaluated therapeutic programs for inmates. Paint Creek and Reasoning and Rehabilitation were both cognitive-behavioral programs, whereas social therapy and moral reconation therapy were more akin to psychotherapy. None of the four evaluations found significant desirable effects on offending, although the results were encouraging in the first three cases. No noncrime outcomes were assessed in these four experiments.

A systematic review of twenty-six evaluations of the Reasoning and Rehabilitation program by Tong and Farrington (2006) concluded that it was effective in reducing reconvictions, with a weighted mean odds ratio of 1.16, corresponding to a 14 percent reduction in offending. Also, Wilson, Allen, and MacKenzie (2005) concluded that Reasoning and Rehabilitation, moral reconation therapy, and other cognitive-behavioral programs were all effective according to "higher-quality" evaluations. Similarly, Lipsey and Landenberger (2006) in a more narrowly focused systematic review of cognitive-behavioral therapy found a significant desirable effect on recidivism. Interestingly, Lipsey and Landenberger found that the most important factor was whether the intervention was carried out as part of a research or demonstration project or routine criminal justice practice. A comparison of the treatment-control differences for the two types of studies revealed that the research and demonstration projects were four times more effective than the routine practice projects, with a reduction in recidivism rates of 49 percent versus 11 percent.

The next three experiments in table 8 evaluated prison-based therapeutic community programs for drug-involved inmates. Inciardi and his colleagues (1997) found that therapeutic community treatment had significantly desirable effects on offending (a 20 percent decrease) and drug use (a 25 percent decrease), whereas Wexler and his colleagues (1999) also obtained encouraging but nonsignificant results on offending (an 8 percent decrease). Arrest rates were 32 percent higher for experimental inmates in the Dugan and Everett (1998) evaluation, but the difference was nonsignificant. No other outcomes were assessed.

A systematic review of thirty-two evaluations of prison-based drug treatment by Mitchell, MacKenzie, and Wilson (2006) concluded that it was effective in reducing arrests, with a weighted mean odds ratio

TABLE 8
Correctional Experiments (14)

Publication, Location	Initial Sample	Conditions	Results (N)	% Change
Lewis (1983), CA	108 male delinquents	E = Scared Straight C = no treatment	12 months arrests E 81.1% (53) C 67.3% (55)	+21%
Cook and Spirrison (1992), MS	176 male delinquents	E = Scared Straight C = no treatment	12 months mean offenses EB 1.32 (97) EA .43 (97) CB 1.25 (79) CA .38 (79)	+7%
Peters, Thomas, and Zamberlan (1997), Cleveland, OH	About 354 male delinquents	E = boot camp C = confinement	9 months convictions E 72% (182) C 50% (172)	+44%*
Peters, Thomas, and Zamberlan (1997), Denver, CO	About 230 male delinquents	E = boot camp C = confinement or probation	9 months convictions E 39% (124) C 36% (106)	+8%
Peters, Thomas, and Zamberlan (1997), Mobile, AL	About 526 male delinquents	E = boot camp C = probation (mostly)	9 months convictions E 28% (187) C 31% (339)	−10%
California Youth Authority (1997), CA	632 male delinquents	E = boot camp C = confinement	12 months arrests E 60.7% (313) C 58.0% (243)	+5%
Greenwood and Turner (1993a), OH	150 male delinquents	E = Paint Creek C = usual training school	12 months arrests E 50.7% (73) C 61.3% (75)	−17%

Study	Sample	Treatment	Outcome	Effect
Robinson (1995), Canada	4,072 male offenders	E = Reasoning and Rehabilitation C = Other	12 months convictions E 21.3% (1,673) C 24.8% (369)	−14%
Ortmann (2000), Germany	228 male prisoners	E = social therapy prison C = usual prison	5 years convictions E 60.4% (111) C 67.9% (112)	−11%
Armstrong (2003), Prince George's County, MD	256 male inmates	E = moral reconation therapy C = no treatment	2.3 years convictions E 64.5% (110) C 64.7% (102)	0%
Inciardi et al. (1997), DE	367 drug-involved inmates	E = therapeutic community C = no treatment	18 months arrests E 43% (179) C 53.9% (180)	−20%*
Dugan and Everett (1998), WA	145 drug-involved inmates	E = therapeutic community C = no treatment	2 years arrests EM 4.5 (61) CM 3.4 (56)	+32%
Wexler et al. (1999), San Diego, CA	715 drug-involved inmates	E = therapeutic community C = no treatment	3 years reincarceration E 68.9% (289) C 75.1% (189)	−8%
Marques et al. (1994), CA	229 volunteer male sex offenders	E = cognitive behavioral treatment C = no treatment	34 months sex arrests E 10.4% (106) C 13.4% (97)	−22%

NOTE.—E = experimental; C = control; EB = experimental before; EA = experimental after; CB = control before; CA = control after; EM = experimental mean; CM = control mean.
* $p < .05$.
** $p < .10$.

of 1.29, corresponding to a 22 percent reduction in offending. On the basis of a smaller number of comparisons ($n = 11$), the intervention seemed to be even more effective in reducing drug use.

The final experiment in table 8, by Marques and her colleagues (1994), evaluated a cognitive-behavioral treatment program for sex offenders. Those who volunteered for the treatment were placed in pairs matched on age, offense type, and previous criminal history, and the members of each pair were randomly assigned to experimental or control conditions. However, it seems that only offenders who were actually transferred to the treatment program had a matched control offender. The treated group had a nonsignificantly lower reoffending rate (for sex crimes) than the controls. No other outcomes were assessed.

Only one of these experiments found a significantly desirable effect of the correctional treatment, and conversely only one found a significantly undesirable effect.

D. Court Experiments

Table 9 summarizes results obtained in twenty-two court experiments. We begin with three experiments on court-mandated treatment of male domestic violence offenders. The first experiment, by Feder and Dugan (2002), is historically important because of the battle involved in implementing it. The local prosecutor's office sought an injunction against the experiment on legal and ethical grounds, namely that judicial discretion was misused (a legal issue) and that it was unethical to deny treatment on the basis of chance. In response, Feder (1998) argued that it was unethical to mandate an intervention (counseling) that had not been rigorously tested to establish its possible positive and negative consequences.

Feder (1998, p. 7) noted that "though many associations were supportive of our research, only one—the American Society of Criminology (ASC)—stepped forward and agreed to serve as a friend of the court." The three ASC presidents who were involved in this issue argued that "scholarly societies have an obligation to uphold and promulgate the principle that random assignment to treatment options is the best scientific method for determining the effectiveness of options such as those proposed in this case" (Short, Zahn, and Farrington 2000, p. 295). Eventually, the prosecutor withdrew the injunction and the experiment was completed.

TABLE 9
Court Experiments (22)

Publication, Location	Initial Sample	Conditions	Results (N)	% Change
Feder and Dugan (2002), Broward County, FL	404 domestic violence defendants	E = counseling plus probation C = probation	12 months arrests E 24% (230) C 24% (174)	0%
Davis, Taylor, and Maxwell (2000), Brooklyn, NY	380 convicted male spouse abusers	E = psychotherapy C = community service	12 months arrests E 14.4% (194) C 25.8% (186)	−44%*
Dunford (2000), San Diego, CA	861 Navy spouse assaulters	E = cognitive behavioral C = no treatment	12 months arrests E 3.1% (321) C 4% (150)	−22%
Britt, Gottfredson, and Goldkamp (1992), Pima County, AZ	231 pretrial defendants	E = drug testing C = usual supervision	Pretrial arrests EM .04 (153) CM .12 (78)	−67%*
Britt, Gottfredson, and Goldkamp (1992), Maricopa County, AZ	234 pretrial defendants	E = drug testing C = release	Pretrial arrests EM .25 (118) CM .24 (116)	+4%
Britt, Gottfredson, and Goldkamp (1992), Maricopa County, AZ	890 pretrial defendants	E = drug testing C = usual supervision/ release	Pretrial arrests EM .45 (425) CM .37 (465)	+22%*
Goldkamp and Jones (1992), Milwaukee, WI	737 pretrial defendants	E = drug testing C = usual supervision	3 months arrests E 13.6% (382) C 18.4% (332)	−26%
Goldkamp and Jones (1992), MD	596 pretrial defendants	E = drug testing C = usual supervision	4 months arrests E 10.4% (298) C 11.8% (289)	−12%

TABLE 9 (*Continued*)

Publication, Location	Initial Sample	Conditions	Results (N)	% Change
Deschenes, Turner, and Greenwood (1995), Maricopa County, AZ	639 drug offenders	E = drug court C = probation	12 months arrests E 31.3% (176) C 32.6% (454)	−4%
Gottfredson, Najaka, and Kearley (2003), Baltimore, MD	235 drug arrestees	E = drug court C = usual court	2 years arrests E 66.2% (139) C 81.3% (96)	−19%*
Marlowe et al. (2003), Wilmington, DE	197 drug offenders	E = frequent hearings C = as needed	12 months SR arrests E 17.6% (68) C 36.5% (52)	−52%*
Klein (1986), US	306 juvenile arrestees	E = release C = court petition	27 months arrests E 48.8% (82) C 72.8% (81)	−33%*
Schneider (1986), Boise, ID	181 adjudicated juveniles	E = restitution C = weekend detention	22 months court referrals E 53% (86) C 59% (95)	−10%
Schneider (1986), Washington, DC	411 adjudicated juveniles	E = mediation C = probation	32 months court referrals E 54% (274) C 63% (137)	−14%
Schneider (1986), GA	257 adjudicated juveniles	E = restitution C = probation or incarceration	36 months court referrals E 47.6% (147) C 56.4% (110)	−16%
Schneider (1986), OK	298 adjudicated juveniles	E = restitution C = probation or incarceration	24 months court referrals E 49.5% (220) C 52% (78)	−5%

Strang and Sherman (2006), Canberra, Australia	269 juvenile property offenders	E = restorative conference C = usual court	12 months arrests E 32.3% (127) C 31.1% (122)	+4%
Strang and Sherman (2006), Canberra, Australia	143 juvenile shoplifters	E = restorative conference C = usual court	12 months arrests E 28.6% (77) C 42.4% (66)	−33%
Strang and Sherman (2006), Canberra, Australia	121 violent offenders	E = restorative conference C = usual court	12 months arrests E 32.3% (62) C 37.3% (59)	−13%
Strang and Sherman (2006), Canberra, Australia	900 drunk drivers	E = restorative conference C = usual court	12 months arrests E 16.2% (450) C 14.0% (450)	+16%
McGarrell et al. (2000), Indianapolis, IN	261 juvenile offenders	E = restorative conference C = diversion	12 months arrests E 30.8% (130) C 41.2% (131)	−25%
McCold and Wachtel (1998), Bethlehem, PA	143 juvenile property offenders	E = restorative conference C = usual court	12 months arrests E 33.3% (90) C 20.8% (53)	+60%

NOTE.—E = experimental; C = control; EM = experimental mean; CM = control mean; SR = self-reported.
* $p < .05$.
** $p < .10$.

In the three experiments, Davis, Taylor, and Maxwell (2000) found that court-mandated psycho-educational treatment of male batterers caused a significant 44 percent decrease in reoffending against the same victim, whereas Dunford (2000) reported an encouraging 22 percent decrease in repeat assaults. (Only results obtained with Dunford's cognitive-behavioral interventions are shown in table 9.) However, Feder and Dugan (2002) found that counseling had no effect on rearrests.

In a systematic review of court-mandated batterer treatment programs, Feder and Wilson (2006) found differential program impacts on reoffending depending on the source of the outcome measure. In the case of official reports, there was evidence that batterer intervention programs caused a reduction in reoffending, whereas victim reports suggested that the intervention caused no overall reduction in reoffending. The authors cautioned that the beneficial effects might apply only to a select and motivated group of convicted batterers.

The next five experiments evaluated the impact of frequent pretrial drug testing on arrests while on bail. Britt, Gottfredson, and Goldkamp (1992) found significantly desirable effects (a 67 percent reduction) in one experiment, significantly undesirable effects (a 22 percent increase) in another, and no effect in a third. In another wave of randomized experiments on pretrial drug testing, Goldkamp and Jones (1992) reported encouraging but nonsignificant results in Milwaukee (a 26 percent reduction in arrests) and in Prince George's County, Maryland (a 12 percent reduction).

The next three experiments evaluated the effectiveness of drug courts. In a comparison with the usual court treatment, Gottfredson, Najaka, and Kearley (2003) found that drug courts caused a significant decrease in rearrests (66 percent versus 81 percent) over a two-year follow-up period. The numbers of new arrests (1.6 versus 2.3) and new charges (3.1 versus 4.6) were also significantly lower for the drug court participants than for the controls. Interestingly, upon rearrest, drug court participants were almost as likely as controls to be reconvicted (49 percent versus 53 percent). Further analyses of this drug court experiment by Banks and Gottfredson (2004) found that those in the program group had a significantly longer time to rearrest than the control group.

An earlier drug court experiment by Deschenes, Turner, and Greenwood (1995) found no significant effect of drug courts, compared with routine probation, on rearrests over a twelve-month follow-up period, but did find a desirable effect on technical violations, specifically, drug violations. Marlowe and his colleagues (2003) evaluated the impact of frequent judicial status hearings for drug court clients compared with hearings as needed. Rearrests were significantly (52 percent) fewer in the frequent hearing group, but these results were based on self-reports in interviews with about two-thirds of the offenders. In a systematic review of forty-two drug court evaluations, Wilson, Mitchell, and MacKenzie (2006) concluded that drug court programs were effective in reducing offending.

The next experiment, by Klein (1986), evaluated the effectiveness of diversion programs compared with court petitions for juveniles. Table 9 shows only the comparison of the most extreme conditions, that is, release compared with court petition. The reoffending rate was significantly (33 percent) less for the released cases, in agreement with labeling theory rather than deterrence.

The remaining ten experiments evaluated restitution and restorative justice programs. Schneider (1986) carried out four experiments on restitution in four communities: Boise, Idaho; Washington, DC; Clayton County, Georgia; and Oklahoma County, Oklahoma. In all four cases, restitution (compared with probation or incarceration) caused a nonsignificant decrease in reoffending over a follow-up period that ranged from twenty-two to thirty-six months.

Strang and Sherman (2006) carried out four experiments on restorative justice conferences compared with the usual court appearances in Canberra, Australia. The experiments showed mixed results, with a substantial decrease in reoffending for juvenile shoplifters, a small decrease for violent offenders under age thirty, no effect on juvenile property offenders, and a small increase in reoffending for drunk drivers.

Conflicting results were also obtained in two other evaluations of restorative conferences that were reviewed by Strang and Sherman (2006). McGarrell and his colleagues (2000) reported a desirable 25 percent reduction in reoffending by juvenile offenders, but McCold and Wachtel (1998) found an undesirable 60 percent increase in reoffending by juvenile property offenders. However, many cases were not treated as assigned in this last experiment, and the results were not significant.

E. Community Experiments

Table 10 summarizes results obtained in twenty-three community supervision experiments. The first eight entries are drawn from a nationwide, fourteen-site evaluation of intensive supervision probation/parole (ISP) conducted by Petersilia and Turner (1993*a*, 1993*b*). ISP is a form of early release into the community that mandates close monitoring of offenders and the imposition of rigorous release conditions, such as random and unannounced drug testing and participation in relevant treatment programs (Petersilia and Turner 1993*a*, p. 1). The initial sample size was greater than 100 in seven sites, and so these are included in table 10 as separate experiments. Intensive supervision had desirable effects on recidivism (a 40 percent decrease) in only one of these sites (Ventura, California) over a twelve-month follow-up period. The initial sample size was about 50 in the other seven sites, and so they are amalgamated into one experiment. Intensive supervision had undesirable effects on recidivism (a 94 percent increase) in these seven sites. Over all fourteen sites, 37 percent of experimentals and 33 percent of controls were rearrested, a nonsignificant difference. Petersilia and Turner (1993*a*, p. 5) speculated that the increased surveillance in the experimental condition might have increased the probability that crimes would be detected and arrests made.

In Minnesota, Deschenes, Turner, and Petersilia (1995) evaluated two experiments on intensive supervision and found that it did not significantly reduce arrest rates compared with either prison or the usual supervision over a two-year follow-up period. No differences were found for drug use, but among offenders who tested positive, those in the experimental group were more likely than their control counterparts to be arrested and detained in jail.

In Portland, Oregon, and Washington, DC, Rhodes and Gross (1997) evaluated an intensive program for substance-using arrestees, in which case managers coordinated drug treatment programs, employment and job-training agencies, housing programs, and community health services in trying to help clients in a nonjudgmental way. In Washington, the program had significant results, with self-reported arrests reduced from 16 percent to 10 percent; in Portland, the program had hopeful (but not significant) results, with self-reported arrests reduced from 27 percent to 22 percent, both over a six-month follow-up period. Significant reductions in heavy drug use were also reported

TABLE 10
Community Experiments (23)

Publication, Location	Initial Sample	Conditions	Results (N)	% Change
Petersilia and Turner (1993*a*), Seattle, WA	173 drug-involved offenders	E = intensive supervision C = usual supervision	12 months arrests E 46.1% (89) C 35.7% (84)	+29%
Petersilia and Turner (1993*a*), Des Moines, IA	115 drug-involved offenders	E = intensive supervision C = usual supervision	12 months arrests E 23.7% (59) C 28.6% (56)	−17%
Petersilia and Turner (1993*a*), Dallas, TX	221 parolees	E = intensive supervision C = usual supervision	12 months arrests E 39.2% (130) C 29.7% (91)	+32%
Petersilia and Turner (1993*a*), Houston, TX	458 parolees	E = intensive supervision C = usual supervision	12 months arrests E 43.9% (239) C 40.2% (219)	+9%
Petersilia and Turner (1993*a*), Contra Costra, CA	170 drug offenders	E = intensive supervision C = usual supervision	12 months arrests E 29% (85) C 27% (85)	+7%
Petersilia and Turner (1993*a*), Ventura, CA	168 probationers	E = intensive supervision C = usual supervision	12 months arrests E 32% (82) C 53% (86)	−40%*
Petersilia and Turner (1993*a*), Los Angeles, CA	100 probationers	E = intensive supervision C = usual supervision	12 months arrests E 32% (51) C 30% (49)	+7%
Petersilia and Turner (1993*a*), 7 other sites in US	357 adult offenders	E = intensive supervision C = usual supervision	12 months arrests E 35% (182) C 18% (175)	+94%*

TABLE 10 (*Continued*)

Publication, Location	Initial Sample	Conditions	Results (N)	% Change
Deschenes, Turner, and Petersilia (1995), MN	124 adult offenders	E = intensive supervision C = prison	2 years arrests E 50% (76) C 50% (48)	0%
Deschenes, Turner, and Petersilia (1995), MN	176 adult offenders	E = intensive supervision C = usual supervision	12 months arrests E 15% (95) C 21% (81)	−29%
Rhodes and Gross (1997), Portland, OR	696 substance-using arrestees	E = intensive supervision C = no supervision	6 months SR arrests E 22% (185) C 26.5% (376)	−17%
Rhodes and Gross (1997), Washington, DC	673 substance-using arrestees	E = intensive supervision C = no supervision	6 months SR arrests E 10% (193) C 16% (375)	−38%*
Barton and Butts (1990), Detroit, MI	511 committed juveniles	E = intensive supervision C = placement	2 years arrests EM 3.69 (326) CM 3.58 (160)	+3%
Fagan (1990), 4 sites in US	229 violent delinquents	E = reintegration C = usual program	3 years felony rearrests E 40.4% (104) C 38.5% (91)	+5%
Greenwood, Deschenes, and Adams (1993), Detroit + Pittsburgh	187 delinquents	E = intensive aftercare C = usual supervision	12 months arrests E 34.4% (96) C 32.2% (90)	+7%
Land, McCall, and Williams (1990), NC	174 status offenders	E = intensive supervision C = usual supervision	12 months court referrals E 20.4% (49) C 28.1% (57)	−27%

Study	Sample	Conditions	Outcome	Effect
Sontheimer and Goodstein (1993), Philadelphia, PA	106 male juvenile offenders	E = intensive aftercare C = usual aftercare	3 months arrests E 20.5% (44) C 34.8% (46)	−41%
Taxman and Byrne (1994), Maricopa County, AZ	415 probation absconders (warrants issued)	E = office and field apprehension strategy C = office only apprehension strategy	3 months new arrest E 53.8% (130) C 63.4% (104)	−15%*
van Voorhis et al. (2004), GA	468 male parolees	E = Reasoning and Rehabilitation C = no Reasoning and Rehabilitation	9 months arrests E 37.8% (229) C 42.4% (232)	−11%
Killias, Aebi, and Ribeaud (2000), Switzerland	123 convicted offenders	E = community service C = prison	2 years convictions EB 92.9% (84) EA 21.4% (84) CB 84.6% (39) CA 25.6% (39)	−24%**
Swanson et al. (2001), NC	216 mentally ill persons	E = outpatient commitment C = community release	12 months arrests E 18.6% (102) C 19.3% (114)	−4%
McAuliffe (1990), US, Hong Kong	168 opioid addicts	E = relapse prevention C = no program	12 months SR arrests E 23.1% (91) C 28.4% (74)	−19%
Latessa and Moon (1992), US	271 drug-involved offenders	E = outpatient acupuncture C = no acupuncture	n.a. arrests E 20.1% (184) C 20.7% (87)	−3%

NOTE.—E = experimental; C = control; EM = experimental mean; CM = control mean; EB = experimental before; EA = experimental after; CB = control before; CA = control after; SR = self-reported; n.a. = not available.

* $p < .05$.
** $p < .10$.

109

in Washington, whereas Portland reported nonsignificant increases in heavy drug use, also over a six-month follow-up period.

The next five experiments evaluated intensive supervision, community reintegration, or aftercare for juvenile offenders. The effects on recidivism were small in the experiments by Barton and Butts (1990), Fagan (1990), and Greenwood, Deschenes, and Adams (1993). They were substantial—a 27 percent reduction—in the study by Land, McCall, and Williams (1990) and also—a 41 percent reduction—in the study by Sontheimer and Goodstein (1993), but neither of these differences was statistically significant. In the Land, McCall, and Williams study, which involved intensive supervision (compared to usual supervision) for youths referred to juvenile court for status offenses, the positive results were confined to delinquent rather than status offenses. In the Sontheimer and Goodstein study, which involved intensive aftercare probation (compared to usual aftercare) for serious male juvenile offenders, experimental offenders also had lower conviction and incarceration rates.

The final six experiments are quite heterogeneous. Taxman and Byrne (1994) evaluated an innovative program to improve the location and apprehension of probation absconders. It was found that a combination of office- and field-based location strategies, compared to office only, significantly increased the apprehension rate of probation absconders and resulted in significantly fewer new arrests prior to apprehension.

Van Voorhis and her colleagues (2004) evaluated the impact of the Reasoning and Rehabilitation program on parolees and found little effect. There was also little effect of involuntary outpatient commitment (requiring patients to comply with recommended treatment) compared with community release in the experiment by Swanson and his colleagues (2001), of a relapse prevention program for drug addicts in the evaluation by McAuliffe (1990), or of acupuncture in a study by Latessa and Moon (1992).

Killias, Aebi, and Ribeaud (2000) reported that community service in Switzerland, compared with short-term imprisonment (sentences up to fourteen days), caused a near-significant 24 percent decrease in convictions over a two-year follow-up period. However, no differences were found between experimental and control groups for employment and social and private life circumstances.

IV. Trends in Randomized Experiments over the Last
Fifty Years

How have randomized experiments on crime and justice changed over
the last half century? The most obvious change is an increased number
of experiments, doubling from thirty-seven in 1957–81 to eighty-five
in 1982–2004. Policing experiments increased from four to twelve, prevention experiments from six to fourteen, correctional experiments
from twelve to fourteen, court experiments from three to twenty-two,
and community experiments from twelve to twenty-three. Hence, the
largest increase occurred in court experiments and the smallest in correctional experiments. Historically, many of the pioneering experiments in criminology were concerned with the effectiveness of correctional treatment (i.e., correctional and community experiments), but
other types of experiments—on policing, prevention, and courts—have
particularly increased in the last two decades.

Are the findings obtained in randomized experiments more encouraging nowadays? Recall that, in the first half of our time period, only
nine experiments produced significantly desirable results, one produced
a significantly undesirable result, and twenty-seven reported nonsignificant effects. In the second half of the time period, the distribution
of these three possible outcomes was broadly similar: twenty experiments produced significantly desirable results, three produced significantly undesirable results, and sixty-two reported nonsignificant effects.
Most of the significant desirable effects were found in policing (six out
of twelve) and prevention (five out of fourteen) experiments.

When one looks at effect sizes, however, the conclusions become
more optimistic in the second half of the time period. Recall that, in
the first half, twenty-one effect sizes (percentage differences) were negative (desirable), whereas sixteen were positive (undesirable). In the
second half, fifty-six effect sizes were negative (desirable), whereas
twenty-five were positive (undesirable) and the other four were zero.
Whereas twenty-one out of thirty-seven was not significantly greater
than chance expectation, fifty-six out of eighty-one is ($z = 3.44$, $p =$
.0006).

We can therefore conclude that experiments in the second half of
the time period were significantly likely to produce desirable results.
This was most true of policing (ten out of twelve desirable), prevention
(ten out of thirteen desirable, with one zero effect), and court (sixteen
out of twenty-one desirable, with one zero effect) experiments and least

true of correctional (seven out of thirteen desirable, with one zero effect) and community (thirteen out of twenty-two desirable, with one zero effect) experiments. When one sets a higher criterion, in the second half of the time period forty-eight effect sizes showed that the experimental group offended less than the control group by at least 10 percent, whereas thirteen effect sizes showed that the control group offended less than the experimental group by at least 10 percent. Again, forty-eight out of sixty-one is significantly greater than chance expectation ($z = 4.49$, $p = .0001$).

In the last two decades, there have been great advances in the use of meta-analysis to summarize effect sizes (see, e.g., Lipsey and Wilson 2001). Farrington and Welsh (2005) carried out meta-analyses and concluded that criminological experiments in the last twenty years showed that prevention methods in general, and multisystemic therapy in particular, were effective in reducing offending. Also, correctional therapy, batterer treatment programs, drug courts, juvenile restitution, and police targeting of "hot spots" were effective. However, Scared Straight and boot camps were ineffective or harmful. Hence, conclusions from experiments about "what works" were more optimistic in the second half of the time period than in the first half.

How did the nature of experiments change between the first half and the second half of the time period? There was clearly an increase in the number of large-scale, multisite replication experiments, which of course are highly desirable on scientific grounds. In the first half of the time period, Folkard, Smith, and Smith (1976) and Maynard (1980) carried out large-scale, multisite experiments; Palmer (1974) conducted a replication study; and Rossi, Berk, and Lenihan (1980) did both. In the second half, there were seven replication experiments on the effect of arrest on domestic violence offenders and five on multisystemic therapy. Numerous large-scale, multisite experiments were conducted, on Children at Risk (Harrell, Cavanagh, and Sridharan 1999), Big Brothers Big Sisters (Grossman and Tierney 1998), Job Corps (Schochet, Burghardt, and Glazerman 2001), Moving to Opportunity (Kling, Ludwig, and Katz 2005), boot camps (Peters, Thomas, and Zamberlan 1997), pretrial drug testing (Britt, Gottfredson, and Goldkamp 1992; Goldkamp and Jones 1992), juvenile restitution (Schneider 1986), restorative justice (Strang and Sherman 2006), and intensive supervision (Petersilia and Turner 1993a; Rhodes and Gross 1997).

Randomized experiments on crime and justice continued overwhelmingly to be carried out in the United States in the second half of the time period (seventy-five in the United States, four in Australia, three in Canada, one in Germany, one in Switzerland, and one partly in Hong Kong), as they had been in the first half (twenty-seven in the United States, seven in the United Kingdom, two in Canada, and one in Denmark).

The reduction in the number of British experiments is noteworthy. Farrington (2003a) and Nuttall (2003) have put forward reasons for this, largely centering on the influence of the report by Clarke and Cornish (1972), which argued against the usefulness of randomized experiments. However, there have been "feast" and "famine" periods in the United States as well, which often depended on the influence of a few key individuals. For example, Farrington (2003c, p. 220) stated that "the tenure of James K. 'Chips' Stewart as Director of the National Institute of Justice between 1981 and 1988 ushered in a new golden age of randomized experiments in American criminology." In England, Strang and Sherman (2006) are currently conducting eight randomized experiments on restorative conferencing.

The most noteworthy methodological advance in the second half of the time period has been an increase in the number of experiments in which places were randomly assigned, especially to study policing initiatives. Weisburd (2005) reviewed such experiments in a special issue of the *Annals of the American Academy of Political and Social Science* on place-based randomized trials. He pointed out that it was useful (in order to maximize the equivalence of experimental and control conditions) to divide places into four or five "blocks" equated on crime rates and to randomize places within blocks. The Minneapolis Hot Spots experiment (Sherman and Weisburd 1995) and the Jersey City drug market analysis experiment (Weisburd and Green 1995) were the first experiments in crime and justice to use block randomization. Block randomization has been used in experiments in which the unit is the school (e.g., Mason et al. 2003), but we were unable to find any criminological experiments in which 100 or more schools were randomly assigned. The related technique of randomizing within matched pairs of individuals (e.g., McCord 1978; Marques et al. 1994) is also uncommon.

There have been other methodological advances in the second half of the time period. Most noteworthy are the increased number of experiments (especially on prevention) with long-term follow-ups and the increased tendency to interview participants as well as follow them up in records. Methodological, practical, and ethical challenges facing randomized experiments on crime and justice are briefly reviewed in the next section.

V. Challenges Facing Randomized Experiments

Randomized experiments are not without their challenges. Among the most formidable are practical and ethical. The most common objection focuses on the denial of treatment to members of the control group. The greatest threat to internal validity is the differential attrition of participants from experimental and control groups.

A. The Independent Variable

Ideally, experiments should test causal hypotheses derived from theories, but it is more usual for experiments to test some kind of technology that is considered likely to be effective. Multimodal interventions are common because researchers wish to maximize their chances of finding an effect (Wasserman and Miller 1998), but it is often difficult to disentangle the different elements of a complex intervention package to identify the "active ingredients." Ideally, the demonstration that a package "works" should be followed by experiments studying the elements, but this is uncommon.

Information given about interventions is sometimes insufficient to permit replication. However, some treatments (e.g., multisystemic therapy) are fully described in a manual. It is important to establish "treatment integrity," or the extent to which a treatment was implemented as intended. If an intervention does not work, this may reflect implementation failure rather than treatment failure. It is common to find that interventions work better in small-scale demonstration projects than in large-scale routine implementation. Lipsey (2003) found that effect sizes were reduced by between one-third and one-half in routine implementation compared with demonstration projects.

It is important to monitor interventions to ensure that they do not vary over time and place. The existence of a randomized experiment may cause official policies to change, and it is usually found that the flow of eligible cases decreases over time. It is also common to find that not all members of an experimental group receive the treatment, whereas some members of a control group may receive it. In the Minneapolis Domestic Violence Experiment, 99 percent of those assigned to the arrest condition were arrested, but only 73 percent of those assigned to separation were separated (23 percent were arrested), and 78 percent of those assigned to mediation were mediated (18 percent were arrested). It may be possible to adjust the effect size upward to estimate what would have been found if there had been no treatment crossovers.

Differential attrition from intervention and control groups is a major problem in criminological experiments, especially those including interviews. In order to maintain the benefits of randomization, it is important to analyze those originally assigned to conditions (in an "intention-to-treat" analysis) rather than to analyze those who complete the treatment (in a "treatment-of-treated" analysis). It is common to find that treatment completers do better than controls, whereas treatment noncompleters do worse. These differences could reflect selection effects (pre-existing differences between completers and noncompleters) rather than effects of completion or noncompletion of the treatment. An advantage of randomizing within matched pairs is that, if the experimental person fails to complete the treatment, both members of the matched pair can be dropped from the analysis, thus avoiding the problem of differential attrition.

All experiments determine the effect of an intervention compared to whatever the control group received. If there is no difference in outcome between experimental and control conditions, it may be that both were equally effective. Hence, it is important to document what happened to the controls as fully as what happened to the experimentals. For example, in the evaluation of "intensive" probation by Folkard, Smith, and Smith (1976), the "intensive" group had an average of three contacts per month with a probation officer, compared with one and a half per month for the control group. It seems likely that the magnitude of the intervention (the difference between one and a half and three contacts per month) was not large enough to have any effect.

Experimenters have rarely investigated interactions between types of interventions and types of individuals. Where this has been done, it has often been done retrospectively rather than prospectively. For example, Kling, Ludwig, and Katz (2005) found that Moving to Opportunity had different effects on boys and girls. Ideally, participants should be stratified on the basis of a prior theory, and interventions should be assigned at random within blocks of individuals, but this has rarely been done (see, e.g., Adams 1970).

B. The Dependent Variable

As with the independent variable, the choice of the dependent variable should be guided by theory. For example, some interventions may have a primarily rehabilitative effect, whereas others may have a primarily deterrent effect. A follow-up measure of arrests or convictions could not distinguish between these effects. Follow-up interviews are needed to test hypotheses about causal mechanisms intervening between treatments and outcomes. It is important to investigate not only mediators but also moderators: boundary conditions that influence the effects of the treatment (see, e.g., Baron and Kenny 1986). For example, treatments may work better in some settings than in others.

Outcome measures such as parole revocation or recall to prison reflect not only offending behavior but also the behavior of agency personnel. In some cases, interventions may change the behavior of agency personnel rather than the behavior of offenders. For example, offenders who received an innovative program may be treated more leniently. It is useful to have pretest and posttest measures of offending in order to investigate changes over time. However, if samples are selected on the basis of their unusually high rate of offending, "regression to the mean" may occur in the posttest. In a classic exchange, Murray and Cox (1979) found that youths' arrest rates were significantly lower after intervention than before it, but Maltz and his colleagues (1980) pointed out that this could be caused by regression to the mean.

How long should the follow-up period be and when should it start? It might be expected that any effects of an intervention would be strongest immediately afterward and would then decrease over time. However, as mentioned, Tremblay and his colleagues (1996) found that the desirable effects of their treatment increased over time. Long-term follow-ups are needed to investigate the persistence of treatment effects. One problem in choosing the follow-up period is whether it should start when treatment is assigned or when treatment is completed. For example, if the follow-up period began on release for an institutional group and on sentencing for a community group, the groups would be at risk during different age ranges and time periods, so that the benefits of randomization in equating the groups on extraneous variables might be lost. Similarly, if the number of offenses committed per time at risk is calculated for each group, the time periods at risk may not be comparable. Nevertheless, measures based on numbers and costs of crimes (see, e.g., Farrington et al. 2002*a*) are more sensitive and are preferable to the simple recidivist/nonrecidivist dichotomy.

C. Practical, Ethical, and Legal Problems

Since many randomized experiments have now been conducted, are they now easier to mount than they used to be? Unfortunately, this seems doubtful. Farrington and Jolliffe (2002) carried out a study of the feasibility of evaluating the treatment of dangerous, severely personality-disordered offenders using a randomized controlled trial. They found that all the clinicians involved were opposed to a randomized controlled trial because they thought that everyone should be treated and no one should be denied treatment. However, where the number of persons who want treatment greatly exceeds the number who can be treated, random assignment may be the fairest way to select people for treatment (Wortman and Rabinowitz 1979).

Program administrators may be unwilling to relinquish control of the assignment to an experimenter, even when randomization has been accepted. There are many examples in the literature of randomization designs that have broken down, for example, because exceptions were allowed and the assignment procedure was not controlled by the research staff. Ideally, program administrators and participants should be kept ignorant of the experimental conditions and hypotheses. However, this is usually difficult to achieve, although Berg and his colleagues (1978) kept their experiment secret from the juveniles and the treatment staff (educational welfare officers and social workers). Of course, the methodological desirability of keeping participants "blind" to conditions conflicts with the ethical requirements of informed consent.

Ultimately, it is important to weigh the likely benefits of an experiment against its likely costs. According to Weisburd (2003), the key question is why a randomized experiment should *not* be used: "The burden here is on the researcher to explain why a less valid method should be the basis for coming to conclusions about treatment and practice" (p. 352). Other researchers have also attempted to outline and answer objections to randomized experiments (e.g., Cook and Payne 2002). Boruch (1997) has provided detailed practical advice about how to mount such experiments successfully.

VI. Conclusions

Randomized experiments are especially useful for testing causal hypotheses (e.g., derived from theories) and evaluating well-defined technologies. Their unique advantage over other methods is their high internal validity, or high ability to demonstrate the effect of one factor on another. This is not just a theoretical advantage. Several reviews have found that effect sizes are typically (misleadingly) larger in non-experimental research than in randomized experiments (e.g., Weisburd, Lum, and Petrosino 2001). Such experiments have been carried out to investigate the crime-reducing effects of policing, prevention, correctional, court, and community programs.

Despite their advantages, relatively few randomized experiments have been carried out because of their formidable methodological, practical, and ethical problems. No researcher should embark on such an experiment without being aware of these problems. The challenge is to identify where randomized experiments are feasible and to demonstrate that their theoretical and practical benefits outweigh their costs.

There are some causal hypotheses, such as the role of broken homes in producing delinquency, which could never be tested in randomized experiments, at least in Western society at present. Some variables, such as age and gender, cannot be manipulated realistically. Events that have already happened, such as changes in the law, cannot be investigated experimentally, since experiments must be prospective. Randomized experiments are most feasible when the effects of a treatment are unknown and when it is impossible to treat everyone. It would be economical to evaluate social and penal policies in small-scale experiments before a great deal of money was spent implementing them on a large scale, but this has rarely happened. Against this, it should be pointed out that effect sizes are often greater in demonstration projects than in routine implementation.

While we cannot claim to have carried out an exhaustive systematic review, our survey of the first half century of randomized experiments on crime and justice shows that the number of reasonably large-scale experiments with offending outcomes has more than doubled between the first half and the second half of this time period. Furthermore, there has been an increase in very large, multisite replication experiments and in experiments in which the unit of randomization is the area rather than the individual. Also, there have been longer follow-up periods and more use of interview data as well as official records of offending. However, there are still relatively few experiments conducted outside the United States.

Perhaps most important, the results of randomized experiments in the second half of our time period are generally more encouraging than in the first half, in suggesting that some interventions are effective (i.e., early developmental prevention, correctional therapy, batterer treatment programs, drug courts, juvenile restitution, and police targeting of "hot spots"), partly because of the greater emphasis nowadays on effect sizes rather than on statistical significance. Many experiments have large effect sizes but do not find statistically significant results because of small numbers. Clearly, power analysis is needed in planning an experiment to determine what sample sizes are needed (Weisburd, Petrosino, and Mason 1993).

There are differing views about the usefulness of randomized experiments. Clarke and Cornish (1972) essentially argued in favor of correlational research, using methods such as retrospective matching and statistical control of variables, on the grounds that the decrease in internal validity was outweighed by the increase in external validity and the decrease in ethical and practical problems (compared with experiments). Farrington (2003a) set out and attempted to answer his criticisms. There is nowadays more of an organized movement advocating randomized experiments, including the Campbell Collaboration (see, e.g., Farrington and Petrosino 2001), the Academy of Experimental Criminology, and the new *Journal of Experimental Criminology*.

Randomized experiments still present many challenges. There are often problems of getting permission and cooperation from policy makers and practitioners, leading to case flow problems and difficulties in carrying through the randomization successfully. There are often serious differences between treatments assigned and treatments delivered. Differential attrition is a great problem, although it might be overcome by randomizing within matched pairs and dropping both members of a pair if one member cannot be followed up. There is a great need for better specification of the nature of the intervention and of how the controls were treated so that causal conclusions can be drawn. Better measures of offending are required, including the number, seriousness, and cost of crimes per time at risk (before and after the intervention), so that comparable measures of effect size can be calculated in different experiments. "Scaling-up" factors, from official crimes to self-reported crimes, should be used (e.g., Farrington et al. 2003).

One of the frustrations in writing the earlier essay (Farrington 1983) was that the reporting of experiments was often poor, with even basic information about the number and gender of participants missing. Hence, a checklist of nineteen questions that should be answered in each report of an experiment was presented. Since then, the CONSORT statement has been developed for medical experiments (Moher, Schulz, and Altman 2001) and adopted for American Psychological Association journals. A similar statement needs to be agreed on to enhance the reporting of criminological experiments.

We should not dwell too much on the difficulties of carrying out randomized experiments on crime and justice. Well over 100 such experiments have been conducted in the last half century and are described in this essay. It is clear that such experiments are often feasible, and we hope that our essay shows how they can be conducted better in the future. Our own view is that, because of high internal validity, attempts should be made to test causal hypotheses using randomized experiments wherever possible. We end with and endorse conclusions from Weisburd and Petrosino (2004, p. 883):

> There is a growing consensus among scholars, practitioners, and policy makers that crime control practices and policies should be rooted as much as possible in scientific research. This would suggest that randomized experiments, sometimes termed the "gold standard" of evaluation design, will become an ever more important component of criminological study.

REFERENCES

Abrahamse, Allan F., Patricia A. Ebener, Peter W. Greenwood, Nora Fitzgerald, and Thomas E. Kosin. 1991. "An Experimental Evaluation of the Phoenix Repeat Offender Program." *Justice Quarterly* 8:141–68.
Adams, Stuart. 1970. "The PICO Project." In *The Sociology of Punishment and Correction*, edited by Norman Johnston, Leonard Savitz, and Marvin E. Wolfgang. New York: Wiley.
Annis, Helen M. 1979. "Group Treatment of Incarcerated Offenders with Al-

cohol and Drug Problems: A Controlled Evaluation." *Canadian Journal of Criminology* 21:3–15.

Armstrong, Todd A. 2003. "The Effect of Moral Reconation Therapy on the Recidivism of Youthful Offenders: A Randomized Experiment." *Criminal Justice and Behavior* 30:668–87.

Baker, Sally H., and Susan Sadd. 1981. *Diversion of Felony Arrests: An Experiment in Pretrial Intervention*. Washington, DC: U.S. Department of Justice, National Institute of Justice.

Banks, Duren, and Denise C. Gottfredson. 2004. "Participation in Drug Treatment Court and Time to Rearrest." *Justice Quarterly* 21:637–58.

Baron, Reuben M., and David A. Kenny. 1986. "The Moderator-Mediator Variable Distinction in Social Psychology Research: Conceptual, Strategic, and Statistical Considerations." *Journal of Personality and Social Psychology* 51: 1173–82.

Barton, William H., and Jeffrey A. Butts. 1990. "Viable Options: Intensive Supervision Programs for Juvenile Delinquents." *Crime and Delinquency* 36: 238–56.

Bayley, David H. 1998. "Introduction: Spouse Assault." In *What Works in Policing*, edited by David H. Bayley. New York: Oxford University Press.

Berg, Ian, Imogen Brown, and Roy Hullin. 1988. *Off School, in Court: An Experimental and Psychiatric Investigation of Severe School Attendance Problems*. New York: Springer-Verlag.

Berg, Ian, Margaret Consterdine, Roy Hullin, Ralph McGuire, and Stephen Tyrer. 1978. "The Effect of Two Randomly Allocated Court Procedures on Truancy." *British Journal of Criminology* 18:232–44.

Berg, Ian, Roy Hullin, and Ralph McGuire. 1979. "A Randomly Controlled Trial of Two Court Procedures in Truancy." In *Psychology, Law and Legal Processes*, edited by David P. Farrington, Keith Hawkins, and Sally M. Lloyd-Bostock. London: Macmillan.

Berg, Ian, Roy Hullin, Ralph McGuire, and Stephen Tyrer. 1977. "Truancy and the Courts: Research Note." *Journal of Child Psychology and Psychiatry* 18:359–65.

Berk, Richard A., Alec Campbell, Ruth Klap, and Bruce Western. 1992. "A Bayesian Analysis of the Colorado Springs Spouse Abuse Experiment." *Journal of Criminal Law and Criminology* 83:170–200.

Berntsen, Karen, and Karl O. Christiansen. 1965. "A Resocialization Experiment with Short-Term Offenders." In *Scandinavian Studies in Criminology*, vol. 1, edited by Karl O. Christiansen. London: Tavistock.

Binder, Arnold, and Martha Newkirk. 1977. "A Program to Extend Police Service Capability." *Crime Prevention Review* 4:26–32.

Borduin, Charles M., Barton J. Mann, Lynn T. Cone, Scott W. Henggeler, Bethany R. Fucci, David M. Blaske, and Robert A. Williams. 1995. "Multisystemic Treatment of Serious Juvenile Offenders: Long-Term Prevention of Criminality and Violence." *Journal of Consulting and Clinical Psychology* 63: 569–78.

Boruch, Robert F. 1997. *Randomized Experiments for Planning and Evaluation: A Practical Guide.* Thousand Oaks, CA: Sage.

Braga, Anthony A. 2001. "The Effects of Hot Spots Policing on Crime." *Annals of the American Academy of Political and Social Science* 578:104–25.

Braga, Anthony A., David L. Weisburd, Elin J. Waring, Lorraine G. Mazerolle, William Spelman, and Francis Gajewski. 1999. "Problem-Oriented Policing in Violent Crime Places: A Randomized Controlled Experiment." *Criminology* 37:541–80.

Britt, Chester L., Michael R. Gottfredson, and John S. Goldkamp. 1992. "Drug Testing and Pretrial Misconduct: An Experiment on the Specific Deterrent Effects of Drug Monitoring Defendants on Pretrial Release." *Journal of Research in Crime and Delinquency* 29:62–78.

Brody, Stephen R. 1976. *The Effectiveness of Sentencing.* Home Office Research Study no. 35. London: H.M. Stationery Office.

Byles, John A., and A. Maurice. 1979. "The Juvenile Services Project: An Experiment in Delinquency Control." *Canadian Journal of Criminology* 21: 155–65.

California Youth Authority. 1997. *LEAD: A Boot Camp and Intensive Parole Program: The Final Impact Evaluation.* Sacramento, CA: Department of the Youth Authority.

Campbell, Donald T., and Julian C. Stanley. 1966. *Experimental and Quasi-Experimental Designs for Research.* Chicago: Rand McNally.

Campbell, Frances A., Craig T. Ramey, Elizabeth Pungello, Joseph Sparling, and Shari Miller-Johnson. 2002. "Early Childhood Education: Young Adult Outcomes from the Abercedarian Project." *Applied Developmental Science* 6: 42–57.

Clarke, Ronald V. G., and Derek B. Cornish. 1972. *The Controlled Trial in Institutional Research.* London: H.M. Stationery Office.

Cook, David D., and Charles L. Spirrison. 1992. "Effects of a Prisoner-Operated Delinquency Deterrence Program: Mississippi's Project Aware." *Journal of Offender Rehabilitation* 17:89–99.

Cook, Thomas D., and Donald T. Campbell. 1979. *Quasi-Experimentation: Design and Analysis Issues for Field Settings.* Chicago: Rand McNally.

Cook, Thomas D., and Monique R. Payne. 2002. "Objecting to the Objectives to Using Random Assignment in Educational Research." In *Evidence Matters: Randomized Trials in Education Research*, edited by Frederick Mosteller and Robert F. Boruch. Washington, DC: Brookings Institution Press.

Cornish, Derek B., and Ronald V. G. Clarke. 1975. *Residential Treatment and Its Effects on Delinquency.* London: H.M. Stationery Office.

Curtis, Nicola M., Kevin R. Ronan, and Charles M. Borduin. 2004. "Multi-systemic Treatment: A Meta-Analysis of Outcome Studies." *Journal of Family Psychology* 18:411–19.

Davis, Robert C., Bruce G. Taylor, and Christopher D. Maxwell. 2000. *Does Batterer Treatment Reduce Violence? A Randomized Experiment in Brooklyn.* Washington, DC: U.S. Department of Justice, National Institute of Justice.

Deschenes, Elizabeth P., Susan Turner, and Peter W. Greenwood. 1995. "Drug

Court or Probation? An Experimental Evaluation of Maricopa County's Drug Court." *Justice System Journal* 18:55–73.

Deschenes, Elizabeth P., Susan Turner, and Joan Petersilia. 1995. "A Dual Experiment in Intensive Community Supervision: Minnesota's Prison Diversion and Enhanced Supervised Release Programs." *Prison Journal* 75: 330–56.

Ditman, Keith S., George G. Crawford, Edward W. Forgy, Herbert Moskowitz, and Craig Macandrew. 1967. "A Controlled Experiment on the Use of Court Probation for Drunk Arrests." *American Journal of Psychiatry* 124: 160–63.

Dugan, John R., and Ronald S. Everett. 1998. "An Experimental Test of Chemical Dependency Therapy for Jail Inmates." *International Journal of Offender Therapy and Comparative Criminology* 42:360–68.

Dunford, Franklyn W. 1990. "System-Initiated Warrants for Suspects of Misdemeanor Domestic Assault: A Pilot Study." *Justice Quarterly* 7:631–53.

———. 2000. "The San Diego Navy Experiment: An Assessment of Interventions for Men Who Assault Their Wives." *Journal of Consulting and Clinical Psychology* 68:468–76.

Dunford, Franklyn W., David Huizinga, and Delbert S. Elliott. 1990. "The Role of Arrest in Domestic Assault: The Omaha Police Experiment." *Criminology* 28:183–206.

Eck, John E., and Julie Wartell. 1998. "Improving the Management of Rental Properties with Drug Problems: A Randomized Experiment." In *Civil Remedies and Crime Prevention*, Crime Prevention Studies, vol. 9, edited by Lorraine G. Mazerolle and Jan Roehl. Monsey, NY: Criminal Justice Press.

Empey, LaMar T., and Maynard L. Erickson. 1972. *The Provo Experiment: Evaluating Community Control of Delinquency*. Lexington, MA: Heath.

Empey, LaMar T., and Steven G. Lubeck. 1971. *The Silverlake Experiment: Testing Delinquency Theory and Community Intervention*. Chicago: Aldine.

Fagan, Jeffrey A. 1990. "Treatment and Reintegration of Violent Juvenile Offenders: Experimental Results." *Justice Quarterly* 7:233–63.

Farrington, David P. 1979. "Delinquent Behaviour Modification in the Natural Environment." *British Journal of Criminology* 19:353–72.

———.1983. "Randomized Experiments on Crime and Justice." In *Crime and Justice: A Review of Research*, vol. 4, edited by Michael Tonry. Chicago: University of Chicago Press.

———. 2003*a*. "British Randomized Experiments on Crime and Justice." *Annals of the American Academy of Political and Social Science* 589:150–67.

———. 2003*b*. "Methodological Quality Standards for Evaluation Research." *Annals of the American Academy of Political and Social Science* 587:49–68.

———. 2003*c*. "A Short History of Randomized Experiments in Criminology: A Meager Feast." *Evaluation Review* 27:218–27.

Farrington, David P., John Ditchfield, Gareth Hancock, Philip Howard, Darrick Jolliffe, Mark S. Livingston, and Kate A. Painter. 2002*a*. *Evaluation of Two Intensive Regimes for Young Offenders*. Home Office Research Study no. 239. London: Home Office.

Farrington, David P., Denise C. Gottfredson, Lawrence W. Sherman, and Brandon C. Welsh. 2002*b*. "The Maryland Scientific Methods Scale." In *Evidence-Based Crime Prevention*, edited by Lawrence W. Sherman, David P. Farrington, Brandon C. Welsh, and Doris L. MacKenzie. New York: Routledge.

Farrington, David P., and Darrick Jolliffe. 2002. *A Feasibility Study into Using a Randomized Controlled Trial to Evaluate Treatment Pilots at HMP Whitemoor.* Online report no. 14/02. London: Home Office. http://www.homeoffice.gov.uk/rds/pdfs2/rdsolr1402.pdf.

Farrington, David P., Darrick Jolliffe, J. David Hawkins, Richard F. Catalano, Karl G. Hill, and Rick Kosterman. 2003. "Comparing Delinquency Careers in Court Records and Self-Reports." *Criminology* 41:933–58.

Farrington, David P., and Anthony Petrosino. 2001. "The Campbell Collaboration Crime and Justice Group." *Annals of the American Academy of Political and Social Science* 578:35–49.

Farrington, David P., and Brandon C. Welsh. 2005. "Randomized Experiments in Criminology: What Have We Learned in the Last Two Decades?" *Journal of Experimental Criminology* 1:9–38.

Feder, Lynette. 1998. "Using Random Assignment in Social Science Settings." *Professional Ethics Report* 11(1):1–7.

Feder, Lynette, and Laura Dugan. 2002. "A Test of the Efficacy of Court-Mandated Counselling for Domestic Violence Offenders: The Broward Experiment." *Justice Quarterly* 19:343–75.

Feder, Lynette, and David B. Wilson. 2006. "Mandated Batterer Programs to Reduce Domestic Violence." In *Preventing Crime: What Works for Children, Offenders, Victims, and Places*, edited by Brandon C. Welsh and David P. Farrington. New York: Springer.

Folkard, M. Steven, Anthony J. Fowles, Brenda C. McWilliams, William McWilliams, David D. Smith, David E. Smith, and G. Roy Walmsley. 1974. *IMPACT (Intensive Matched Probation and After-Care Treatment).* Vol. 1, *The Design of the Probation Experiment and an Interim Evaluation.* Home Office Research Study no. 24. London: H.M. Stationery Office.

Folkard, M. Steven, David E. Smith, and David D. Smith. 1976. *IMPACT.* Vol. 2. London: H.M. Stationery Office.

Fowles, A. J. 1978. *Prison Welfare.* London: H.M. Stationery Office.

Garner, Joel H., Jeffrey A. Fagan, and Christopher D. Maxwell. 1995. "Published Findings from the Spouse Assault Replication Program: A Critical Review." *Journal of Quantitative Criminology* 11:3–28.

Goldkamp, John S., and Peter R. Jones. 1992. "Pretrial Drug-Testing Experiments in Milwaukee and Prince George's County: The Context of Implementation." *Journal of Research in Crime and Delinquency* 29:430–65.

Gottfredson, Denise C., Stacy S. Najaka, and Brook Kearley. 2003. "Effectiveness of Drug Treatment Courts: Evidence from a Randomized Trial." *Criminology and Public Policy* 2:171–96.

Greenwood, Peter W., Elizabeth P. Deschenes, and John Adams. 1993. *Chronic*

Juvenile Offenders: Final Results from the Skillman Aftercare Experiment. Santa Monica, CA: Rand.

Greenwood, Peter W., and Susan Turner. 1993*a*. "Evaluation of the Paint Creek Youth Center: A Residential Program for Serious Delinquents." *Criminology* 31:263–79.

———. 1993*b*. "Private Presentence Reports for Serious Juvenile Offenders: Implementation Issues and Impacts." *Justice Quarterly* 10:229–43.

Grossman, Jean B., and Joseph P. Tierney. 1998. "Does Mentoring Work? An Impact Study of the Big Brothers Big Sisters Program." *Evaluation Review* 22:403–26.

Hackler, James C., and John L. Hagan. 1975. "Work and Teaching Machines as Delinquency Prevention Tools: A Four-Year Follow-up." *Social Service Review* 49:92–106.

Harrell, Adele V., Shannon E. Cavanagh, and Sanjeev Sridharan. 1999. *Evaluation of the Children at Risk Program: Results 1 Year after the End of the Program.* Research in Brief. Washington, DC: U.S. Department of Justice, National Institute of Justice.

Henggeler, Scott W., W. Glenn Clingempeel, Michael J. Brondino, and Susan G. Pickrel. 2002. "Four-Year Follow-up of Multisystemic Therapy with Substance-Abusing and Substance-Dependent Juvenile Offenders." *Journal of the American Academy of Child and Adolescent Psychiatry* 41:868–74.

Henggeler, Scott W., Gary B. Melton, Michael J. Brondino, David G. Scherer, and Jerome H. Hanley. 1997. "Multisystemic Therapy with Violent and Chronic Juvenile Offenders and Their Families: The Role of Treatment Fidelity in Successful Dissemination." *Journal of Consulting and Clinical Psychology* 65:821–33.

Henggeler, Scott W., Melisa D. Rowland, Jeff Randall, David M. Ward, Susan G. Pickrel, Phillippe B. Cunningham, Stacey L. Miller, James Edwards, Joseph J. Zealberg, Lisa D. Hand, and Alberto B. Santos. 1999. "Home-Based Multisystemic Therapy as an Alternative to the Hospitalization of Youths in Psychiatric Crisis: Clinical Outcomes." *Journal of the American Academy of Child and Adolescent Psychiatry* 38:1331–39.

Hirschel, J. David, Ira W. Hutchison, and Charles W. Dean. 1992. "The Failure of Arrest to Deter Spouse Abuse." *Journal of Research in Crime and Delinquency* 29:7–33.

Inciardi, James A., Steven S. Martin, Clifford A. Butzin, Robert M. Hopper, and Lana D. Harrison. 1997. "An Effective Model of Prison-Based Treatment for Drug-Involved Offenders." *Journal of Drug Issues* 27:261–78.

Jesness, Carl F. 1971*a*. "Comparative Effectiveness of Two Institutional Treatment Programs for Delinquents." *Child Care Quarterly* 1:119–30.

———. 1971*b*. "The Preston Typology Study." *Journal of Research in Crime and Delinquency* 8:38–52.

———. 1975. "Comparative Effectiveness of Behavior Modification and Transactional Analysis Programs for Delinquents." *Journal of Consulting and Clinical Psychology* 43:758–79.

Kassebaum, Gene, David Ward, and Daniel Wilner. 1971. *Prison Treatment and Parole Survival: An Empirical Assessment.* New York: Wiley.

Killias, Martin, Marcelo Aebi, and Denis Ribeaud. 2000. "Does Community Service Rehabilitate Better than Short-Term Imprisonment? Results of a Controlled Experiment." *Howard Journal* 39:40–57.

Klein, Malcolm W. 1986. "Labeling Theory and Delinquency Policy: An Experimental Test." *Criminal Justice and Behavior* 13:47–79.

Kling, Jeffrey R., Jens Ludwig, and Lawrence F. Katz. 2005. "Neighborhood Effects on Crime for Female and Male Youth: Evidence from a Randomized Housing Voucher Experiment." *Quarterly Journal of Economics* 120:87–130.

Lamb, H. Richard, and Victor Goertzel. 1974. "Ellsworth House: A Community Alternative to Jail." *American Journal of Psychiatry* 131:64–68.

Land, Kenneth C., Patricia L. McCall, and Jay R. Williams. 1990. "Something That Works in Juvenile Justice: An Evaluation of the North Carolina Court Counselors' Intensive Protective Supervision Randomized Experimental Project, 1987–1989." *Evaluation Review* 14:574–606.

Latessa, Edward J., and Melissa M. Moon. 1992. "The Effectiveness of Acupuncture in an Outpatient Drug Treatment Program." *Journal of Contemporary Criminal Justice* 8:317–31.

Leschied, Alan, and Alison Cunningham. 2002. *Seeking Effective Interventions for Serious Young Offenders: Interim Results of a Four-Year Randomized Study of Multisystemic Therapy in Ontario, Canada.* London, Canada: London Family Court Clinic.

Lewis, Roy V. 1983. "Scared Straight—California Style: Evaluation of the San Quentin Squires Program." *Criminal Justice and Behavior* 10:209–26.

Lichtman, Cary M., and Sue M. Smock. 1981. "The Effects of Social Services on Probationer Recidivism: A Field Experiment." *Journal of Research in Crime and Delinquency* 18:81–100.

Lipsey, Mark W. 2003. "Those Confounded Moderators in Meta-Analysis: Good, Bad, and Ugly." *Annals of the American Academy of Political and Social Science* 587:69–81.

Lipsey, Mark W., and Nana A. Landenberger. 2006. "Cognitive-Behavioral Interventions." In *Preventing Crime: What Works for Children, Offenders, Victims, and Places,* edited by Brandon C. Welsh and David P. Farrington. New York: Springer.

Lipsey, Mark W., and David B. Wilson. 2001. *Practical Meta-Analysis.* Thousand Oaks, CA: Sage.

Littell, Julia H. 2005. "Lessons from a Systematic Review of Effects of Multisystemic Therapy." *Children and Youth Services Review* 27:445–63.

MacKenzie, Doris L., David B. Wilson, and Suzanne B. Kider. 2001. "Effects of Correctional Boot Camps on Offending." *Annals of the American Academy of Political and Social Science* 578:126–43.

Maltz, Michael D., Andrew C. Gordon, David McDowall, and Richard McCleary. 1980. "An Artifact in Pretest-Posttest Designs: How It Can Mistakenly Make Delinquency Programs Look Effective." *Evaluation Review* 4:225–40.

Marlowe, Douglas B., David S. Festinger, Patricia A. Lee, Maria M. Schepise, Julie E. R. Hazzard, Jeffrey C. Merrill, Francis D. Mulvaney, and Thomas A. McLellan. 2003. "Are Judicial Status Hearings a Key Component of Drug Court? During-Treatment Data from a Randomized Trial." *Criminal Justice and Behavior* 30:141–62.

Marques, Janice K., David M. Day, Craig Nelson, and Mary A. West. 1994. "Effects of Cognitive-Behavioral Treatment on Sex Offender Recidivism: Preliminary Results from a Longitudinal Study." *Criminal Justice and Behavior* 21:28–54.

Martinson, Robert. 1974. "What Works? Questions and Answers about Prison Reform." *Public Interest* 35:22–54.

Mason, W. Alex, Rick Kosterman, J. David Hawkins, Kevin P. Haggerty, and Richard L. Spoth. 2003. "Reducing Adolescents' Growth in Substance Use and Delinquency: Randomized Trial Effects of a Parent-Training Prevention Intervention." *Prevention Science* 4:203–12.

Maxwell, Christopher D., Joel H. Garner, and Jeffrey A. Fagan. 2002. "The Preventive Effects of Arrest on Intimate Partner Violence: Research, Policy, and Theory." *Criminology and Public Policy* 2:51–79.

Maynard, Rebecca. 1980. *The Impact of Supported Work on Young School Dropouts.* New York: Manpower Demonstration Research Corp.

Mazerolle, Lorraine G., Jan Roehl, and Colleen Kadleck. 1998. "Controlling Social Disorder Using Civil Remedies: Results from a Randomized Field Experiment in Oakland, California." In *Civil Remedies and Crime Prevention*, Crime Prevention Studies, vol. 9, edited by Lorraine G. Mazerolle and Jan Roehl. Monsey, NY: Criminal Justice Press.

McAuliffe, William E. 1990. "A Randomized Controlled Trial of Recovery Training and Self-Help for Opioid Addicts in New England and Hong Kong." *Journal of Psychoactive Drugs* 22:197–209.

McCold, Peter, and Ted Wachtel. 1998. *Restorative Policing Experiment: The Bethlehem Pennsylvania Police Family Group Conferencing Project.* Pipersville, PA: Community Service Foundation.

McCord, Joan. 1978. "A Thirty-Year Follow-up Report on the Cambridge-Somerville Youth Study." *American Psychologist* 33:284–89.

McCord, Joan, and William McCord. 1959. "A Follow-up Report on the Cambridge-Somerville Youth Study." *Annals of the American Academy of Political and Social Science* 322:89–96.

McDonald, Douglas C., Judith Greene, and Charles Worzella. 1992. *Day Fines in American Courts: The Staten Island and Milwaukee Experiments.* Washington, DC: U.S. Department of Justice, National Institute of Justice.

McGarrell, Edmund, Kathleen Olivares, Kay Crawford, and Natalie Kroovand. 2000. *Returning Justice to the Community: The Indianapolis Restorative Justice Experiment.* Indianapolis: Hudson Institute Crime Control Policy Center.

Meeker, James W., and Arnold Binder. 1990. "Experiments as Reforms: The Impact of the 'Minneapolis Experiment' on Police Policy." *Journal of Police Science and Administration* 17:147–53.

Meyer, Henry J., Edgar F. Borgatta, and Wyatt C. Jones. 1965. *Girls at Voca-*

tional High: An Experiment in Social Work Intervention. New York: Russell Sage Foundation.

Mills, Paulette E., Kevin N. Cole, Joseph R. Jenkins, and Philip S. Dale. 2002. "Early Exposure to Direct Instruction and Subsequent Juvenile Delinquency: A Prospective Examination." *Exceptional Children* 69:85–96.

Mitchell, Ojmarrh, Doris L. MacKenzie, and David B. Wilson. 2006. "Incarceration-Based Drug Treatment." In *Preventing Crime: What Works for Children, Offenders, Victims, and Places*, edited by Brandon C. Welsh and David P. Farrington. New York: Springer.

Moher, David, Kenneth F. Schulz, and Douglas Altman. 2001. "The CONSORT Statement: Revised Recommendations for Improving the Quality of Reports of Parallel-Group Randomized Trials." *Journal of the American Medical Association* 280:1987–91.

Murray, Charles A., and Louis A. Cox. 1979. *Beyond Probation.* Beverly Hills, CA: Sage.

Nuttall, Christopher. 2003. "The Home Office and Random Allocation Experiments." *Evaluation Review* 27:267–89.

O'Donnell, Clifford R., Tony Lydgate, and Walter S. O. Fo. 1979. "The Buddy System: Review and Follow-up." *Child Behavior Therapy* 1:161–69.

Olds, David L., John Eckenrode, Charles R. Henderson, Harriet Kitzman, Jane Powers, Robert Cole, Kimberly Sidora, Pamela Morris, Lisa M. Pettitt, and Dennis Luckey. 1997. "Long-Term Effects of Home Visitation on Maternal Life Course and Child Abuse and Neglect: Fifteen-Year Follow-up of a Randomized Trial." *Journal of the American Medical Association* 278:637–43.

Olds, David L., Charles R. Henderson, Robert Chamberlin, and Robert Tatelbaum. 1986. "Preventing Child Abuse and Neglect: A Randomized Trial of Nurse Home Visitation." *Pediatrics* 78:65–78.

Olds, David L., Charles R. Henderson, Robert Cole, John Eckenrode, Harriet Kitzman, Dennis Luckey, Lisa Pettitt, Kimberley Sidora, Pamela Morris, and Jane Powers. 1998. "Long-Term Effects of Nurse Home Visitation on Children's Criminal and Antisocial Behavior: 15-Year Follow-up of a Randomized Controlled Trial." *Journal of the American Medical Association* 280:1238–44.

Ortmann, Rudiger. 2000. "The Effectiveness of Social Therapy in Prison: A Randomized Experiment." *Crime and Delinquency* 46:214–32.

Palmer, Ted B. 1974. "The Youth Authority's Community Treatment Project." *Federal Probation* 38(1):3–14.

Pate, Anthony, and Edwin E. Hamilton. 1992. "Formal and Informal Deterrents to Domestic Violence: The Dade County Spouse Assault Experiment." *American Sociological Review* 57:691–97.

Peters, Michael, David Thomas, and Christopher Zamberlan. 1997. *Boot Camps for Juvenile Offenders.* Program summary. Washington, DC: U.S. Department of Justice, Office of Juvenile Justice and Delinquency Prevention.

Petersilia, Joan, and Susan Turner. 1993a. *Evaluating Intensive Supervision Probation/Parole: Results of a Nationwide Experiment.* Research in Brief. Washington, DC: U.S. Department of Justice, National Institute of Justice.

————. 1993*b*. "Intensive Probation and Parole." In *Crime and Justice: A Review of Research*, vol. 17, edited by Michael Tonry. Chicago: University of Chicago Press.

Petrosino, Anthony, Robert F. Boruch, David P. Farrington, Lawrence W. Sherman, and David Weisburd. 2003. "Toward Evidence-Based Criminology and Criminal Justice: Systematic Reviews, the Campbell Collaboration, and the Crime and Justice Group." *International Journal of Comparative Criminology* 3:42–61.

Petrosino, Anthony, Robert F. Boruch, Catherine Rounding, Steve McDonald, and Iain Chalmers. 2000. "The Campbell Collaboration Social, Psychological, Educational and Criminological Trials Register (C2-SPECTR) to Facilitate the Preparation and Maintenance of Systematic Reviews of Social and Educational Interventions." *Evaluation Research in Education* 14:293–307.

Petrosino, Anthony, Carolyn Turpin-Petrosino, and John Buehler. 2003. "Scared Straight and Other Juvenile Awareness Programs for Preventing Juvenile Delinquency: A Systematic Review of the Randomized Experimental Evidence." *Annals of the American Academy of Political and Social Science* 589:41–62.

Powers, Edwin, and Helen Witmer. 1951. *An Experiment in the Prevention of Delinquency*. New York: Columbia University Press.

Quay, Herbert C., and Craig T. Love. 1977. "The Effects of a Juvenile Diversion Program on Rearrests." *Criminal Justice and Behavior* 4:377–96.

Reckless, Walter C., and Simon Dinitz. 1972. *The Prevention of Juvenile Delinquency: An Experiment*. Columbus: Ohio State University Press.

Reimer, Ernest, and Martin Warren. 1957. "Special Intensive Parole Unit." *NPPA Journal* 3:222–29.

Rhodes, William, and Michael Gross. 1997. *Case Management Reduces Drug Use and Criminality among Drug-Involved Arrestees: An Experimental Study of an HIV Prevention Intervention*. Washington, DC: U.S. Department of Justice, National Institute of Justice.

Robinson, David. 1995. *The Impact of Cognitive Skills Training on Post-release Recidivism among Canadian Federal Offenders*. Research Report no. R-41. Ottawa: Correctional Service of Canada.

Rose, Gordon, and R. A. Hamilton. 1970. "Effects of a Juvenile Liaison Scheme." *British Journal of Criminology* 10:2–20.

Rossi, Peter H., Richard A. Berk, and Kenneth J. Lenihan. 1980. *Money, Work, and Crime: Experimental Evidence*. New York: Academic Press.

Schneider, Anne L. 1986. "Restitution and Recidivism Rates of Juvenile Offenders: Results from Four Experimental Studies." *Criminology* 24:533–52.

Schochet, Peter Z., John Burghardt, and Steven Glazerman. 2001. *National Job Corps Study: The Impacts of Job Corps on Participants' Employment and Related Outcomes*. Princeton, NJ: Mathematica Policy Research.

Schweinhart, Lawrence J., Jeanne Montie, Xiang Zongping, W. Steven Barnett, Clive R. Belfield, and Milagros Nores. 2005. *Lifetime Effects: The High/Scope Perry Preschool Study through Age 40*. Ypsilanti, MI: High/Scope Press.

Shadish, William R., Thomas D. Cook, and Donald T. Campbell. 2002. *Ex-*

perimental and Quasi-Experimental Designs for Generalized Causal Inference. Boston: Houghton Mifflin.

Shaw, Margaret. 1974. *Social Work in Prison.* London: H.M. Stationery Office.

Sherman, Lawrence W. 1992. *Policing Domestic Violence: Experiments and Dilemmas.* New York: Free Press.

Sherman, Lawrence W., and Richard A. Berk. 1984. "The Specific Deterrent Effects of Arrest for Domestic Assault." *American Sociological Review* 49: 261–72.

Sherman, Lawrence W., and Ellen G. Cohn. 1989. "The Impact of Research on Legal Policy: The Minneapolis Domestic Violence Experiment." *Law and Society Review* 23:117–44.

Sherman, Lawrence W., David P. Farrington, Brandon C. Welsh, and Doris L. MacKenzie, eds. 2002. *Evidence-Based Crime Prevention.* New York: Routledge.

Sherman, Lawrence W., Denise C. Gottfredson, Doris L. MacKenzie, John E. Eck, Peter Reuter, and Shawn D. Bushway. 1997. *Preventing Crime: What Works, What Doesn't, What's Promising.* Washington, DC: U.S. Department of Justice, National Institute of Justice.

Sherman, Lawrence W., and Dennis P. Rogan. 1995. "Deterrent Effects of Police Raids on Crack Houses: A Randomized Controlled Experiment." *Justice Quarterly* 12:755–81.

Sherman, Lawrence W., Janell D. Schmidt, Dennis P. Rogan, Douglas A. Smith, Patrick R. Gartin, Ellen G. Cohn, Dean J. Collins, and Anthony R. Bacich. 1992. "The Variable Effects of Arrest on Criminal Careers: The Milwaukee Domestic Violence Experiment." *Journal of Criminal Law and Criminology* 83:137–69.

Sherman, Lawrence W., and David Weisburd. 1995. "General Deterrent Effects of Police Patrol in Crime 'Hot Spots': A Randomized Controlled Trial." *Justice Quarterly* 12:625–48.

Short, James F., Margaret A. Zahn, and David P. Farrington. 2000. "Experimental Research in Criminal Justice Settings: Is There a Role for Scholarly Societies?" *Crime and Delinquency* 46:295–98.

Sontheimer, Henry, and Lynne Goodstein. 1993. "An Evaluation of Juvenile Intensive Aftercare Probation: Aftercare versus System Response Effects." *Justice Quarterly* 10:197–227.

Strang, Heather, and Lawrence W. Sherman. 2006. "Restorative Justice to Reduce Victimization." In *Preventing Crime: What Works for Children, Offenders, Victims, and Places,* edited by Brandon C. Welsh and David P. Farrington. New York: Springer.

Swanson, Jeffrey W., Randy Borum, Marvin S. Swartz, Virginia A. Hiday, H. Ryan Wagner, and Barbara J. Burns. 2001. "Can Involuntary Outpatient Commitment Reduce Arrests among Persons with Severe Mental Illness?" *Criminal Justice and Behavior* 28:156–89.

Taxman, Faye S., and James M. Byrne. 1994. "Punishment, Probation, and the Problem of Community Control: A Randomized Field Experiment on Absconder Location Strategies." In *Innovative Trends and Specialized Strategies in Community-Based Corrections*, edited by Charles B. Fields. New York: Garland.

Tong, L. S. Joy, and David P. Farrington. 2006. "How Effective Is the 'Reasoning and Rehabilitation' Programme in Reducing Reoffending? A Meta-Analysis of Evaluations in Four Countries." *Psychology, Crime and Law* 12: 3–24.

Tremblay, Richard E., Louise C. Masse, Linda Pagani, and Frank Vitaro. 1996. "From Childhood Physical Aggression to Adolescent Maladjustment: The Montreal Prevention Experiment." In *Preventing Childhood Disorders, Substance Use, and Delinquency*, edited by Ray D. Peters and Robert J. McMahon. Thousand Oaks, CA: Sage.

van Voorhis, Patricia, Lisa M. Spruance, Neal P. Ritchey, Shelley J. Listwan, and Renita Seabrook. 2004. "The Georgia Cognitive Skills Experiment: A Replication of Reasoning and Rehabilitation." *Criminal Justice and Behavior* 31:282–305.

Venezia, Peter S. 1972. "Unofficial Probation: An Evaluation of Its Effectiveness." *Journal of Research in Crime and Delinquency* 9:149–70.

Waldo, Gordon P., and Theodore G. Chiricos. 1977. "Work Release and Recidivism: An Empirical Evaluation of a Social Policy." *Evaluation Quarterly* 1:87–108.

Wasserman, Gail A., and Laurie S. Miller. 1998. "The Prevention of Serious and Violent Juvenile Offending." In *Serious and Violent Juvenile Offenders: Risk Factors and Successful Interventions*, edited by Rolf Loeber and David P. Farrington. Thousand Oaks, CA: Sage.

Weisburd, David. 2003. "Ethical Practice and Evaluation of Interventions in Crime and Justice: The Moral Imperative for Randomized Trials." *Evaluation Review* 27:336–54.

———. 2005. "Hot Spots Policing Experiments and Criminal Justice Research: Lessons from the Field." *Annals of the American Academy of Political and Social Science* 599:220–45.

Weisburd, David, and Lorraine Green. 1995. "Policing Drug Hot Spots: The Jersey City Drug Market Analysis Experiment." *Justice Quarterly* 12:711–35.

Weisburd, David, Cynthia M. Lum, and Anthony Petrosino. 2001. "Does Research Design Affect Study Outcomes in Criminal Justice?" *Annals of the American Academy of Political and Social Science* 578:50–70.

Weisburd, David, and Anthony Petrosino. 2004. "Experiments, Criminology." In *Encyclopedia of Social Measurement*, edited by Kimberly Kempf-Leonard. San Diego, CA: Academic Press.

Weisburd, David, with Anthony Petrosino and Gail Mason. 1993. "Design Sensitivity in Criminal Justice Experiments." In *Crime and Justice: A Review of Research*, vol. 17, edited by Michael Tonry. Chicago: University of Chicago Press.

Wexler, Harry K., Gerald Melnick, Lois Lowe, and Jean Peters. 1999. "Three-Year Reincarceration Outcomes for Amity In-Prison Therapeutic Community and Aftercare in California." *Prison Journal* 79:321–36.

Williams, Mark. 1970. *A Study of Some Aspects of Borstal Allocation*. London: Home Office Prison Department, Office of the Chief Psychologist.

———. 1975. "Aspects of the Psychology of Imprisonment." In *The Use of Imprisonment*, edited by Sean McConville. London: Routledge.

Wilson, David B., Leana C. Allen, and Doris L. MacKenzie. 2005. "Quantitative Review of Structured, Group-Oriented, Cognitive-Behavioral Programs for Offenders." *Criminal Justice and Behavior* 32:172–204.

Wilson, David B., Ojmarrh Mitchell, and Doris L. MacKenzie. 2006. "A Systematic Review of Drug Court Effects on Recidivism." Unpublished manuscript. Alexandria, VA: George Mason University, Department of Administration of Justice.

Wortman, Camille B., and Vita C. Rabinowitz. 1979. "Random Assignment: The Fairest of Them All." In *Evaluation Studies Review Annual*, vol. 4, edited by Lee Sechrest, Stephen G. West, Melinda A. Phillips, Robin Redner, and William Yeaton. Beverly Hills, CA: Sage.

Martti Lehti and Kauko Aromaa

Trafficking for Sexual Exploitation

ABSTRACT

Current estimates of human trafficking for sexual exploitation underestimate rather than overestimate the volume. They exaggerate the role of trafficking in international prostitution of adults but underestimate trafficking in minors. About 60–80 percent of the crime is domestic, and the bulk of cross-border trafficking is regional. The major flows run from rural areas to cities and from economically depressed regions to affluent ones. Traffic to industrialized countries is 10–20 percent of the whole; most takes place within and between third-world countries. Prevention should concentrate on the main source countries and the most important junctions. This requires efficient police and intelligence cooperation both regionally and internationally. It is also crucial to harmonize national legislation.

International regulation of trafficking in persons is historically linked closely to the regulation of prostitution as a whole. The two phenomena are also linked closely in everyday life, so intertwined that it is difficult to study or discuss them separately. According to some statistics, between 70 and 90 percent of contemporary traffic in women and children in Europe and Asia is related to prostitution and other forms of sexual exploitation (mainly the pornography industry) (Hajdinjak 2002, p. 51; Omelaniuk 2002; "Trafficking in Persons Report" 2004, p. 23). The real percentages are probably lower because other forms of trafficking, especially those related to private housework, are less visible, and interest action groups and authorities are less interested (Ghijs 2004). However, there exists a general consensus that a majority of female victims of trafficking are trafficked for prostitution.

Martti Lehti is a researcher in the National Research Institute of Legal Policy in Helsinki, Finland. Kauko Aromaa is the director of the European Institute for Crime Prevention and Control affiliated with the United Nations (HEUNI).

133

The prevailing model of regulation of prostitution in Western countries distinguishes three legal frameworks: prohibition, legalization, and decriminalization. A system based on prohibition bans prostitution as a whole, whereas its modified form, abolition, allows the sale and purchase of sex while banning all other prostitution-related activities (e.g., exploitation of the prostitution of others). In a system based on legalization, prostitution is legal but subject to special legislation and close regulation through licensing, registration, and health checks. Prostitutes working outside the system are usually subject to criminal penalties. In a system based on decriminalization, prostitution and other forms of sex work are officially considered comparable to other lines of business and are subject to general regulation by civil employment law (West 2003, p. 533).

During the last 150 years, Western countries' policies toward prostitution have vacillated. During the first wave of increasing local and migratory prostitution from the 1840s to the 1890s, policies in Europe, North America, and their overseas colonies were mainly based on legalization. The focus was on public order and prevention of the spread of sexually transmitted diseases. The method to achieve these goals was the tightening up of the control of prostitutes.

After the emergence of the antitrafficking movement in the 1890s, prohibition began gradually to supersede legalization as the dominant model in both national and international (intra-European) policies. All the international treaties of the twentieth century regulating prostitution were based on an abolitionist ideology, which found its culmination in the 1949 Convention for the Suppression of Traffic in Persons and of the Exploitation of the Prostitution of Others. Abolitionist views have dominated U.N. policies and actions since then[1] and to a large extent dominate current international debates.

In Western countries, however, prohibitionist policies began to lose their grip in the second half of the century, especially since the 1960s, when decriminalization began to gain ground, first in policy debates and later in legislation. General changes in ideology and moral attitudes were important; so were the prostitutes' rights movement and the growth of sex worker collectives in North America, western Eu-

[1] Some scholars think, however, that the earlier abolitionist policies underwent a profound change during the 1990s: the focus in U.N. policies shifted from combating prostitution as a whole to combating organized crime–related prostitution and consequently to forced prostitution only (Niemi-Kiesiläinen 2004, p. 455).

rope, and Australia. The collectives' goals were the full decriminalization of prostitution and establishment of employment rights for prostitutes comparable to those in other businesses. The movement so far has failed to produce radical law reforms but has influenced legislation in many Western countries and contributed to more balanced prostitution discussions and policies. However, its influence on international legislation has been marginal (West 2003, pp. 533–45).

Regulation of prostitution is changing rapidly in Western countries, but the direction of change is not clear. Prostitution policies in Western countries have never been internally homogeneous and have usually included elements of more than one, often all, of the main legal frameworks. For example, in many countries with strict prohibitive or abolitionist legislation, prostitution (or at least some forms) has been de facto tolerated. This has led to a situation in which the legal status of prostitutes is vague at best, a situation conducive to corruption and arbitrary harassment. The general trend is to define the legal status of prostitution more clearly than before. However, measures to do this have been contradictory: control of some forms of prostitution (especially street prostitution) has tightened as control of others has been loosened. In Western countries, licensing, decriminalization, and recriminalization are pursued simultaneously and with equal vigor, although usually by different interest groups (West 2003).

In the ideological context, prostitution is usually portrayed as a moral, gender, sexual equality, or human rights question. Niemi-Kiesiläinen (2004) sees three major ideological bases: the sexual moralist, the libertarian, and the feminist. None is internally coherent. Each is represented in prostitution debates and influences policy and practice. The extreme positions characterize prostitution as immoral or violative of gender or human rights (the view of many moral-majority groups, religious movements, and the feminist mainstream), or as one form of economic activity among others, with no special ethical or other connotations (the view, e.g., by the sex workers' rights movement).

Not only does this ideological chasm divide people at the ideological poles, but the sharpest divisions are found inside each, including the feminist movement. The feminist mainstream regards female prostitution as a form of slavery, an expression of structural inequalities of modern patriarchal society, and a form of exploitation of women. The distinction between free and forced prostitution is seen as a distraction only. Prostitution can never result from free will, but is always a result of a lack of other forms of livelihood for women. From this perspective the idea of prostitution by free choice is absurd; the prostitute is always an object and a victim, never an individual acting of her own free will. Types of prostitution that are hard to fit into this frame, such as, for example, male prostitution, are usually ignored (West 2003, p. 539; Niemi-Kiesiläinen 2004, pp. 453–55; Jahic and Finckenauer 2005, pp. 33–34).

The other ideological pole in the feminist movement is the prostitutes' rights movement, which see prostitutes as independent actors making their own choices. It aims at the normalization of prostitution and at ending social stigmatization and exclusion. Problems concerning power relations in prostitution between employees, employers, and clients compared with other service industries, the diverse forms of prostitution, and conflicting interests of representatives of different types of prostitution are often underplayed (West 2003).

Between these two extremes fall a wide variety of opinions approaching prostitution on a pragmatic basis, as advocated by many groups and nongovernmental organizations (NGOs) engaged in work among prostitutes and victims of trafficking. The ideological differences are often explainable at least partly by the differences in how different groups and persons meet and see prostitution in their everyday lives (West 2003).

During the last 150 years, the most restrictive prostitution policies in Western countries have coincided with periods of rapid growth in the volume of international prostitution. These periods were characterized by an increase in all forms of migration, deepening inequalities in living standards between and within continents, and lax border controls.

The first wave of growth in international prostitution and related legislation extended from the 1840s to the First World War. The simultaneous growth of migratory prostitution and prostitution-related trafficking was caused by the industrial revolution and modern colonialism, which led to global growth in the demand for and supply of prostitution. According to Scully (2001, pp. 75–78), the growth in demand resulted from three developments: the large-scale deployment of African and Asian indentured labor to replace slaves in agriculture and in industry and large infrastructure construction projects in industrial countries and their colonies; mobilization and migration flows of non-

Western males within the Western colonies; and large-scale, long-distance movements of men from Europe and North America to colonies and frontiers. These developments were linked to deepening inequalities in living standards throughout the world (and within Europe between the fast-growing western part and stagnant eastern and southern peripheries) and the revolution in transportation, with railroads and steamboats making mass travel easier, faster, and cheaper. These developments generated an international traffic in sex workers and intensified local prostitution. The main flows were within and between colonies. However, in Europe and North America both migratory prostitution and related trafficking increased rapidly during the second half of the nineteenth century. Especially in Europe and the European colonies, these developments interacted with practically non-existent border controls (Scully 2001, p. 87).

After the First World War, border controls tightened substantially, especially in Europe and North America, which caused a significant decrease in international migratory prostitution. This period of decreasing numbers continued from the 1920s to the second half of the century. The decreasing trend did not change the basic policy lines in international legislation, but it began to affect national policies in Western countries after the Second World War, when decriminalization began to displace abolition as the main policy model. Prostitution and prostitution-related trafficking disappeared to a large extent from the public agenda (Scully 2001).

The second wave of international migratory prostitution began in Asia in the 1960s and in Europe in the 1970s and 1980s. In Asia the growth was connected with wars and large foreign armies in the area, especially the Vietnam War, which lasted from the early 1950s through the mid-1970s. Large prostitution industries emerged in several Southeast Asian countries to serve U.S. troops and military bases. After the Vietnam War, these industries were restructured to serve European, Australian, North American, and Japanese sex tourism, often with the consent and open support of local governments. In Europe, the volume of migratory prostitution began to grow in the western European big cities during the 1970s. At this phase the growth occured mainly in immigrant sex workers from Africa, Latin America, and Southeast Asia.

The second wave of rapid increase in migratory prostitution in the last two decades was to a large extent the result of the collapse of the Soviet Union and its empire. Strict border controls that had prevented free travel between western and eastern Europe disappeared almost overnight in the late 1980s, but the legacy of social misery and economic underdevelopment left behind by the decades-long Soviet occupation of eastern Europe has been much slower to disappear. An ideal situation for large-scale migrant prostitution inside Europe came into existence.

The current growth in migratory prostitution and related trafficking is also connected with rapidly increasing economic and social inequalities between industrialized and third-world countries (Scully 2001; Jahic and Finckenauer 2005, pp. 24–27). These developments have brought trafficking and prostitution into the international public debate and onto legislative agendas. Especially in the Western countries, they have produced a substantial tightening up of prostitution policies.

Prostitution and related trafficking have historically been closely linked to organized crime. Both are lucrative enterprises with relatively high profits and low risks. Many criminal activities, for example, drug trafficking and human smuggling, are easy to combine with them. For international drug trafficking networks, pandering is an alluring side business, in which profits equal those from the wholesale trade in mild drugs, but the risks are almost nonexistent. Trafficking, pandering, and retail sale of drugs complement one another well. Drug distribution can be concentrated on the premises where prostitutes work, and prostitutes can be used as dealers and couriers. At the same time prostitutes can effectively be brought under the control of pimps as accomplices and through drug abuse. All kinds of smuggling enterprises can easily be combined with trafficking in prostitutes (NCIS 2002, pp. 35, 38–39; see also Junninen 2005).

The link between prostitution, trafficking, and organized crime exists also in the prostitution debate today and is used as a rationale for both more liberal prostitution policies and tighter control measures. Advocates of liberal policies see decriminalization and licensing as a way to cut the links. If prostitution is given a legal status equal to that of other legitimate businesses, prostitutes' needs for services and protection provided by organized crime will disappear as will the potential of criminal groups to control and exploit prostitutes.

Those pursuing more prohibitive policies see the links as justification for total abolition. Prostitution is seen as integral to activities and financing of organized crime and as corrupting society and creating a favorable ground for the spread of all forms of vice and criminality and for general social disintegration. In Europe, during the last decade, the debate has especially concerned the growth of eastern European migrant prostitution in western Europe and its role in the infiltration of eastern European criminal groups into western markets. The real and alleged connections between these phenomena have been used by the authorities and community action groups to justify more prohibitive policies and legislation (e.g., in the United Kingdom and the Nordic countries).

Prostitution, trafficking, and organized crime are also linked in current international agreements. While the roots of the international regulation of prostitution-related trafficking lie in the treaties created for the regulation and combating of prostitution as a whole, the focus in the United Nations 2000 Protocol to Prevent, Supress, and Punish Trafficking in Persons, Especially Women and Children (the Palermo Protocol) has shifted to the combat and prevention of organized crime. According to Niemi-Kiesiläinen (2004, p. 455), this mirrors not only the central roles that prostitution and prostitution-related trafficking have acquired in the international control of organized crime, but also a more general change in U.N. prostitution policies during the nineties, a shift from an aim of total abolition to one of prohibition only of forced prostitution.

Public health had a central role in the prostitution policies and licensing systems of the nineteenth and early twentieth centuries. Most systems required regular medical examinations for licensed prostitutes, the objective being to prevent the spread of syphilis and other sexually transmitted diseases. This became less important after the Second World War, when antibiotics and other drugs made treatment of venereal diseases easier, cheaper, and more effective, a medical revolution that influenced the moral revolution in Western countries and the liberalization of prostitution policies in the second half of the century.

However, the 1980s and HIV/AIDS brought prostitution again back onto the public health agenda. The impact of HIV/AIDS on prostitution, the prostitution debate, and prostitution policies has been manifold, but the general tendency has been a strengthening of prohibitionist and abolitionist attitudes, and a shift away from civil rights and prostitutes' rights toward control and regulation (if not recriminalization). This shift has been partly a direct consequence of concerns about the spread of HIV/AIDS for both public and prostitutes' health, but HIV/AIDS has also provided a suitable front for more generally motivated abolitionist policies (Scully 2001, pp. 75–83; McKeganey and Barnard 2003, pp. 573–85).

All in all, two major changes have taken place in international prostitution during the last two decades. First, the volume of migrant cross-border prostitution (and related trafficking) has increased rapidly. In Europe this increase has been a consequence of the increase in the demand for prostitution and other sexual services in western Europe and the economic and social problems in the former socialist countries in eastern Europe that created a source area from which migrant prostitution and prostitution-related trafficking can travel far more easily and more economically than from Southeast Asia, West Africa, and Latin America. In Southeast Asia and some parts of Latin America, an important factor has been growing Western sex tourism, but there are also several other contributing factors. Growth in the volume of prostitution and the increase in the number of foreign prostitutes have made prostitution more visible in many countries and increased prostitution-related disturbances.

The increase in international prostitution has yielded increasing revenues for international organized crime and has contributed to the infiltration of eastern European and other criminal groups into western markets. Prostitution thus has increasingly been brought into the focus of law enforcement authorities (*Organized Crime Situation Report* 2001, p. 41; Hajdinjak 2002, p. 51).

The emergence of HIV/AIDS as an incurable sexually transmitted, serious disease since the 1980s has meant that prostitution has increasingly (again) become a major public health concern. Both of these developments, the increase in the volume of international prostitution and the emergence of HIV/AIDS, have strengthened abolitionist and moralist tendencies in international prostitution debates and policies and tightened control of prostitution in many countries.

The general trend in Western legislation seems to be to define the legal status of prostitution more precisely. The result has been a mix of legalization, decriminalization, and recriminalization. In Europe, the most liberal policies have been pursued in the Netherlands and Germany. In Germany, the new prostitution law of 2002 legalized both prostitution and brothels and gave prostitutes the legal status and social benefits of other service sector employees. It also recognized the prostitute's right to compensation for her or his sexual services if agreed on beforehand. The compensation cannot, however, be transferred to another person, a restriction aimed at preventing pandering.

In the Netherlands, brothels have been legal since 2000. The legal status of prostitutes as employees is the same as that of other service sector workers. In both countries attempts are also being made to protect prostitutes' independence and working conditions with extensive criminalization covering, among other things, prostitution-related trafficking, buying sexual services from minors, and profiting from forced or underage prostitution (West 2003, pp. 533–45).

In the Scandinavian countries (except Sweden), in the United Kingdom, in many southern European countries, and in the former socialist countries, prostitution (both selling and buying) is decriminalized, but the civil and labor law status of prostitutes has been left undefined and is thus much weaker than in Germany or the Netherlands. Pandering and all forms of promoting prostitution of others are usually criminalized. In some countries, for example, in Scandinavia and the United Kingdom, there has been a strong recent tendency to tighten prostitution policies. Street prostitution and some other forms of prostitution in public places have been recriminalized, and control measures against foreigners engaged in prostitution have been tightened (Lehti and Aromaa 2002, pp. 10–16; West 2003, pp. 533–45).

The new trend to recriminalize prostitution has manifested itself in the last few years most strongly in Sweden, where, since 1999, all purchase of sexual services has been criminalized. Pandering and other forms of profiting from prostitution of others were criminalized earlier. The selling of sexual services remains legal, but the legal status of prostitutes is undefined and vague. Recent Swedish prostitution policies have been guided by mainstream feminist ideology, which regards prostitution as an expression of structural inequality between genders and all women engaged in prostitution as victims of a patriarchal society. Against this background, a situation in which buying sex is criminalized but selling it is legal is not seen as a problem. The Swedish policies basically return to the roots of the abolitionist policies of the beginning of the twentieth century. The idea that women engaged in prostitution are passive victims with no choices and no will is not a new one, but had a strong influence on the international antiprostitution treaty system created between 1904 and 1949 (Scully 2001; Lehti and Aromaa 2002, pp. 10–16).

In this essay we discuss current international approaches to regulation of trafficking for prostitution and other sexual exploitation. Trafficking for prostitution and other forms of sexual exploitation (trafficking in women)[2] dominates current trafficking discussions and policy planning, especially in Western countries. Hard data and scientific research remain scarce, although the situation is improving. This essay analyzes and synthesizes existing data. We begin in Section I by assessing the existing information sources. In Section II we discuss basic characteristics of the crime, its victims, and its organizers. Section III deals with the development of the concept of trafficking in women in international legislation, discussion, and research; Section IV with the crime's volume and geography; and Section V with prevention and control. Section VI synthesizes the findings and proposes steps that need to be taken if we are to know more about human trafficking for sexual exploitation and how it can better be prevented and controlled.

I. Information Sources

The major problem in studying and combating trafficking in persons is the scarcity, unreliability, and noncomparability of existing national and international data. Accurate information on the volume of the crime does not exist. Some major reasons are the absence of comparable statistics on reported crimes, indictments, court cases, and victims; the diverse ways the crime of trafficking in women is criminalized in the legislation of nation-states; the characteristics of trafficking (as organized—in part, transnational—crime), which result in a high level of uncounted crimes (i.e., because such crime is not readily reported to the police) and make trafficking hard to identify, control, and prevent; the weak legal status of victims in most countries, which contributes to their reluctance to report crimes or to cooperate with investigations and court proceedings; and the inconsistent uses of the concept of trafficking in women and persons in international and national contexts.

The main sources of quantitative data are statistics kept by national governments and criminal justice and immigration authorities on reported crimes, indicted offenders, and irregular migrants; statistics kept

[2] The terms *trafficking in women* and *prostitution-related trafficking* are used in this essay as synonyms for trafficking for sexual exploitation regardless of the sex and age of the victims; *traffic in women* refers to trafficking in female victims and *traffic in children* to trafficking in minors.

by NGOs and associations assisting victims of trafficking and prostitutes; statistics kept by various international and regional organizations, for example, the International Organization for Migration (IOM), the International Police Organization (Interpol), and the United Nations on crime and migration trends; and information available from surveys and publications produced by national and international research projects.

The most extensive global database is that of the U.N. Global Program against Trafficking in Human Beings (GPAT) comprising 161 countries and special administrative territories. It includes data on trafficking flows between 1996 and 2003 and is based on 473 reports and statistics from 190 international and national institutions. However, the database has important limitations. The quality of the data is no better than that of the original sources, which is highly variable, and North American and western European organizations are vastly overrepresented among the source institutions, which distorts regional comparability. The database does not provide global or regional estimates of the annual numbers of trafficking victims, but the country profiles are publicly available on the Internet and comprise assessments of the intensity of the crime and information on the countries of origin of the victims, together with short victim profiles (GPAT 2005; see also www.unodc.org/unodc/en/trafficking_human_beings.html). Despite improvements in recent years, national statistics are highly unsatisfactory even inside the European Union, and also on the international level. Very little is known about numbers of irregular migrants or migrating prostitutes who may have used the services of traffickers or about numbers of individuals working for criminal groups involved in trafficking. The problem becomes worse concerning statistics on numbers and characteristics of various categories of trafficked persons (Mon-Eu-Traf II 2004).

According to a study conducted by the IOM in Europe in 1998, the main sources of data were statistics from police, border guard, and migration authorities. The situation has changed little in the last seven years. According to a second Mon-Eu-Traf study conducted in 2004, information on trafficking in the E.U. member countries is mainly found in general crime statistics or in general migration statistics and is usually scattered in several different (often noncomparable) national databases. Of the twenty-five surveyed countries, eighteen had no data on traffic in children, thirteen none on trafficking in women, and eleven none on trafficking in general. Only eleven countries had statistics on the number of convictions for trafficking (IOM 1998). In several countries the existing databases are at least partly confidential, and their information cannot be used for other than investigative purposes (Mon-Eu-Traf II 2004). Because the databases are created to meet administrative needs of criminal justice and immigration authorities, and not for criminological or trafficking research, the data are usually overly general. The same data forms are used for every offense, which means that crime-specific data are seldom collected. The other major shortcoming is that the main focus is on offenses and offenders; information on victims is rarely collected. However, the numbers and characteristics of victims are crucial not only for understanding trends in trafficking but also for producing reliable estimates of the total number of trafficked persons and for hindering the trafficking process. These data are practically nonexistent (IOM 1998; Mon-Eu-Traf II 2004).

Systematized databases kept by NGOs are rare. In many countries (e.g., Finland, Italy, the Netherlands, Spain), NGOs possess significant information, but the challenge is to make this information available for research and to coordinate it with data from other sources. If this could be done, the result would be more and better information on numbers, characteristics, and needs of victims.

NGOs could provide highly detailed qualitative information on victims but also quantitative data on the number of trafficked women who come into contact with NGOs each year, the ratio between trafficked women and foreign prostitutes, and the number of trafficked women granted stay permits under social protection programs. This knowledge should be preserved, and data should be gathered by NGOs, on the basis of common standards, and disseminated for research and policy purposes. Current data collection and storage systems of most NGOs in Europe are unsatisfactory. Outside Europe the problems are identical: differing definitions; noncomparable, poor, and scattered data sources; and many estimates whose origins are obscure (Mon-Eu-Traf II 2004).

Grave problems also characterize the available qualitative data. The most detailed information on the characteristics of trafficked persons is to be found in IOM and U.N. Interregional Crime and Justice Institute (UNICRI) surveys on the situation in the former socialist countries and in some African and Asian countries (IOM 2000–2004; *Traf-*

ficking of Nigerian Girls to Italy 2004; Travnickova 2004), as well as in
the two Mon-Eu-Traf studies (2002, 2004), the later of which comprises most of the old E.U. member countries.[3] However, even at its
best this information is based on a relatively small number of cases and
victims and covers only short periods. Some authors have criticized the
studies for the uncritical way many treat their sources. The narratives
of interviewed victims are usually accepted at face value, and their stories and claims are not validated in any way (Legget 2004, p. 3). Most
focus on the former socialist countries. It is not self-evident that information and research concerning these countries can be generalized
to the world as a whole. However, despite their shortcomings, the IOM
and UNICRI studies are the most reliable current overviews available.

Another source widely used is the annual "Trafficking in Persons
Report" of the U.S. State Department. It is put together using local
contacts and sources in each country, and data are thus of uneven quality. The report estimates global, regional, and national numbers and
assessments of the crime prevention activities of nation-state governments. It is published annually and can also be found on the Internet
(www.state.gov/g/tip/rls/tiprpt).

As long as information is scarce, unreliable, and noncomparable, it
will be difficult to develop effective and efficient counterstrategies, even
regionally, much less internationally. The current emphasis in the fight
against organized crime is on reducing legal and illegal opportunities
for criminal activities. This will require knowledge of how illegal activities develop. In the case of trafficking in persons, this requires accessible, up-to-date, comparable qualitative information on recruitment, transportation, exploitation, organizations, clients, and victims
(Mon-Eu-Traf II 2004).

The Netherlands has adopted a data collection model that could be
used with minor adjustments as a basis for a comparable inter-Euro-

---

[3] The reports of IOM and UNICRI are based on surveys of former victims (contacted
by NGOs or government officials), traffickers, and police and migration officers. The
two Mon-Eu-Traf studies were carried out by TRANSCRIME (Italy), the Finnish National Research Institute of Legal Policy, and the European Institute for Crime Prevention
and Control, affiliated with the United Nations (HEUNI) (Finland) and the Research
Centre on Criminology at the University of Castilla–La Mancha (Spain) under the E.U.
2002 Stop II Programme in 2001–4 in the old E.U. member countries. The aim was to
create standardized research methods for trafficking in women and use them to collect
information on criminal legislation, on the availability and adequacy of existing statistical
data, and on quantitative and qualitative indicators of the crime situation in the studied
countries.

pean and international database. An official confidential database called the central registration of victims of trafficking is kept by the Foundation against Trafficking in Women (STV), an NGO. Police must report every victim they encounter to the STV, which maintains a computerized database on the gender, age, country of origin, language, children, traveling documents, place of residence, form of prostitution, age of recruitment, number of promises, amount of legal assistance, and number of asylum requests and grants of the victims. Also recorded are a request for financial compensation if the victim is in the Netherlands and, if not, the reason for return and return assistance. These and other data are reported in annual reports of the Dutch National Rapporteur on Trafficking in Human Beings (Mon-Eu-Traf II 2004; see also www.fo-stvkennisnet.nl/kr_fo; Dutch National Rapporteur 2004).

II. Characteristics of Trafficking, Traffickers, and Victims
In this section we discuss the main characteristics of victims and organizers and the modi operandi of the crime. The data discussed derive mainly from information on Europe and from IOM and UNICRI reports on selected African and Asian countries.

A. Types of Trafficking
Trafficking for sexual exploitation dominates the Western trafficking discussion. The reason is partly that information is even scarcer and concepts more confused concerning other forms of trafficking in persons. The sex industry, however, is more visible than other forms of exploitation (domestic servitude, sweatshop industries, etc.) and arouses stronger moral responses. The sex industry is also economically less important and thus has fewer and less powerful interest groups to defend its interests (IOM 2004, p. 12).

This does not mean that trafficking for sexual exploitation is not a major problem. According to some estimates, as many as 70–90 percent of the traffic in women and children in Europe and Asia, and a substantial percentage in other regions, serves organized prostitution and other forms of sex business (Omelaniuk 2002). Concerning the traffic in adult men, sexual exploitation has only a marginal role. As most of the total volume of global trafficking involves men, sexual exploitation–related trafficking makes up less than half the volume of global trafficking in persons (see Sec. IV).

Estimates of the volume of trafficking for economic exploitation in Europe are scarce, but it appears that traffic of workers for the underground economy mainly involves men and serves mostly agriculture, the construction industry, and other related business sectors that employ unskilled workers and experience a high turnover of labor. The destination for laborers in Europe is the old E.U. member countries. Women are trafficked into western Europe mainly to work as domestic servants and nannies. The main source areas for economic exploitation-related trafficking in Europe are the Balkans and eastern Europe, but workers are also smuggled from North Africa and East and South Asia (Ehrenreich and Hochschild 2003).

North America and the Persian Gulf are other main destinations for trafficking for economic exploitation. In both areas, the volume of trafficking related to economic exploitation is estimated to be larger than the volume of trafficking for sexual exploitation. Traffic in children and adults for economic exploitation is also rampant in Latin America, Africa, and Asia. The question of when terms of employment and working conditions meet the criteria of trafficking in persons is not clear or easy to answer. Terms and conditions as a rule are considerably worse than in the legal labor market, and various abusive practices are general. The workers (in the case of adults), however, usually know this when they are recruited and voluntarily contract with the traffickers. Drawing a line between economic and sexual exploitation also is often difficult, because many women and children who are trafficked for work as domestic servants are also exploited sexually (Plant 2002; www.globalmarch.org).

Evidence of trafficking associated with the international trade in human organs is almost nonexistent in Europe, and evidence from other continents is scarce. Adult victims in this trade seem to be fairly rare (www.globalmarch.org; see, however, Travaini et al. 2003).

B. Victims

There appear to be substantial differences between different forms of trafficking and between different source and destination countries. In Belgium, according to Vermeulen and van der Beken (2004), trafficked women are on average younger than those smuggled as illegal immigrants, although in both categories most are under thirty (about

90 percent of those trafficked and two-thirds of those smuggled). Women trafficked for sexual exploitation are on average younger than those trafficked for labor exploitation.[4]

The situation in other European countries seems to be similar. Most of those trafficked for prostitution are between eighteen and twenty-five years of age and are on average younger than those exploited as domestic servants or in sweatshops (Travnickova 2004). The age structure of domestic prostitution and of independent migrant prostitution is usually older than that of forced prostitution. For example, in Finland, over 60 percent of Russian migrant prostitutes are over twenty-five, whereas in Italy the bulk of Russian women forced into prostitution are under twenty-five years (Lehti and Aromaa 2002, pp. 52–55; Leskinen 2003, pp. 13–14; Bopp and Cauduro 2004).[5] Young girls are easier to recruit, control, and resell than older women and thus are preferred by traffickers. They usually also have fewer possibilities, connections, and resources for seeking employment independently abroad and for this reason easily fall prey to the traffickers (Mon-Eu-Traf II 2004).

Data on the proportion of minors among victims are scattered, but the percentage appears to vary considerably between regions. Two recent studies concerning the Balkans estimate that minors make up 10–30 percent of the victims of prostitution-related trafficking from the area. Most are fifteen- to seventeen-year-old girls, but some younger children are also involved (Hajdinjak 2002, p. 51; Omelaniuk 2002). A survey based on twenty-nine victims trafficked to Europe from the Edo State in southwestern Nigeria gave the percentage of minors as 15 percent; none of the interviewed victims was under fifteen at the time of recruitment (Trafficking of Nigerian Girls to Italy 2004, p. 62). The percentage of minors is probably considerably lower in Europe, North America, and other industrialized countries than in other regions (because of harsher criminalization, higher standards of living, compulsory school attendance, and effective social security systems). In South and Southeast Asia and in some regions of Latin America,

---

[4] In the studied group, 72 percent of those trafficked for prostitution were under twenty-five years of age; among those trafficked for other reasons the corresponding percentage was 61 percent (Vermeulen and van der Beken 2004).

[5] The same difference exists in other forms of trafficking. In Belgium, Ecuadorian girls trafficked as nannies and domestic servants are usually young, between eighteen and twenty-five, whereas the (illegal) migrant women employed in the same markets are on average older, many in their thirties or forties (Ghijs 2004).

the majority of victims of prostitution-related trafficking are assumed to be minors (Muhonen 2005; www.globalmarch.org).

The family backgrounds of women trafficked for sexual exploitation in western Europe differ substantially from those of other trafficking victims. In Belgium, only about 10 percent of those trafficked for prostitution are married or have lived with a partner in their native country; the corresponding percentage for victims of other forms of trafficking is about 30 percent and for illegal migrants over 50 percent (Vermeulen and van der Beken 2004). This difference in family status is not explainable by differing age structures only. The victims of prostitution-related trafficking in Europe and the former Soviet Union typically come from worse economic circumstances than victims of other types of trafficking, and a large number are single mothers. According to the IOM, almost 90 percent of victims of prostitution-related trafficking in Tajikistan have at least one child, and almost 80 percent are unmarried, divorced, or widowed. The corresponding figures for Moldovan victims are 45 percent and 85 percent (IOM 2001a, 2003a).

The situation in West Africa is different. According to a UNICRI survey of Nigerian women trafficked to Europe, practically all are single and fewer than 10 percent have children. However, most of the Nigerian victims are the eldest or next-eldest daughters in their families and (like eastern European victims) typically not only support themselves but also have economic responsibility for supporting their near relatives (IOM 2003a; *Trafficking of Nigerian Girls to Italy* 2004). A disproportionately high percentage of victims of sexual exploitation also come from broken or abusive family relations: of the victims in the Netherlands, about 40 percent have grown up without a father; of those with a father, more than half had a nonexistent, poor, or shallow relationship with him (Dutch National Rapporteur 2004). Of the Moldovan victims in Bosnia, over 80 percent have been subjected to domestic violence in their home country. Two-thirds of Nigerians trafficked to Europe come from polygamous families.[6] In fact, according to a Bosnian study, dysfunctional family relations (usually caused by alcoholism, drug abuse, and physical and sexual abuse) are the most

---

[6] It should be noted, however, that no data are available on the prevalence of polygamy in their home regions. Thus it is not known if the high percentage reflects only the general rate of polygamy in those regions or if the offspring of polygamous families are overrepresented among victims (as the study mentioned suggests).

significant factor explaining victimization (*Trafficking of Nigerian Girls to Italy* 2004; Maljevic 2005).

The bulk of victims of trafficking usually come from the most economically depressed and politically most unstable areas in the world and from the most disadvantaged social and ethnic groups in those areas. Information from the European countries shows, however, that there are major differences in social and educational backgrounds of victims from different recruitment areas.

Victims trafficked for sexual exploitation into Europe from Africa, Latin America, and South and Southeast Asia come almost without exception from low or very low social classes, usually from the countryside, and have elementary educations at best (e.g., of Nigerian women trafficked to Italy, more than 95 percent have only basic education at the highest [*Trafficking of Nigerian Girls to Italy* 2004]). This partly reflects the overall social and educational situation in these countries, especially for the rural female population.

The backgrounds of victims from eastern Europe, however, are substantially different. Data from Austria, Finland, Italy, the Netherlands, and Portugal show that the educational and professional backgrounds of victims of trafficking, and migrant prostitutes, from Russia and the central European countries are heterogeneous and that the number of middle-class women with university degrees is substantial (Mon-Eu-Traf II 2004). In Austria, about a third of eastern European victims of trafficking who take refuge with the NGOs have university degrees or are university students (Kaufmann and Zwettler 2004). In Finland, the corresponding percentage among Russian migrant prostitutes in Helsinki is about 40 percent (Hollmen and Jyrkinen 1999, p. 41). It is probable that women with higher education are overrepresented among those fleeing exploitative situations and contacting the NGOs, but the figures indicate that the educational backgrounds of the eastern European victims are not only substantially different from those of third-world victims but also substantially higher than the average of the population in their native countries. There is, however, a considerable number of women with very poor social and educational backgrounds among the eastern European victims, too, especially among those from the Balkan countries (Mon-Eu-Traf II 2004). In the Netherlands, at the time of recruitment, the average standard of living of nearly three-quarters of all victims of prostitution-related trafficking, regardless of ethnic background, was very low (Dutch National Rapporteur 2004).

Information on the number of professional prostitutes among victims of trafficking in Europe is inconsistent. In Russia, many local researchers and authorities believe that most women trafficked for prostitution abroad are recruited from among persons already engaged in prostitution in their home countries (Kleimenov and Shamkov 2004, p. 40). In Estonia and the other Baltic countries, authorities estimate that the number of professional prostitutes among women emigrating abroad for prostitution is very high. The Finnish police authorities estimate that almost all Russian and Estonian migrant prostitutes operating in their country have also engaged in professional prostitution in their native countries (Leskinen 2003, pp. 12–16).

There is, however, very little information on how and why these women were recruited into prostitution in the first place. That they are engaged in prostitution in their native countries before emigrating or that they engage in prostitution simultaneously in their own country and in its neighboring countries may say more about how prostitution is organized and operated than about the backgrounds of those who engage in it. Research among Russian prostitutes in Finland shows that the majority have been engaged in prostitution only for a short time (55 percent less than two years). Only a third have been prostitutes for five years or longer (Hollmen and Jyrkinen 1999, p. 41). The Finnish figures do not refer to trafficked women but to migrant prostitutes, and it is probable that among women *trafficked* for prostitution from Russia, the percentage of those previously engaged in prostitution (especially professionally) would be substantially lower. According to data on victims of trafficking in the Netherlands (regardless of ethnic background), only about 20 percent have been engaged in prostitution at the time of their recruitment (Dutch National Rapporteur 2004). A study of the victims trafficked from and through the Czech Republic gives an identical picture: one-fifth have earned their livings as prostitutes at the time of recruitment (Travnickova 2004, p. 83).[7] The situation is probably more or less similar throughout Europe. The European data refer to adult victims. Where the bulk of victims are minors, the percentage is certainly even smaller (*Trafficking of Nigerian Girls to Italy* 2004; Muhonen 2005).

---

[7] The study was based on data concerning thirty-nine victims in crimes reported to the Czech police.

According to data from the Netherlands, only about 60 percent of victims of prostitution-related trafficking had a job at the time of their recruitment; of those, a third were prostitutes, and the others worked mainly in the hotel and catering industry, in factories, or in the entertainment industry. A survey of Nigerian victims trafficked to Italy gives a fairly similar picture: only about half had a job when recruited. Most were engaged in small-scale subsistence trading or were hairdressers. Thus a very large percentage of victims (at least in Europe and West Africa) were unemployed, and many had no earlier working experience. The bulk of those with a job worked in prostitution or in the kinds of industries (hotel, catering, or entertainment) in which the use of international and illegal labor is common and that are often used as fronts for organized prostitution (Dutch National Rapporteur 2004; *Trafficking of Nigerian Girls to Italy* 2004, p. 63).

Victims' reasons to accept recruiters' offers are fairly similar regardless of the type of trafficking. Both women trafficked for prostitution and women trafficked for economic exploitation are moved mainly by economic motives (e.g., 93 percent of the surveyed victims in Bosnia). There seem to be significant differences between the promises made to those trafficked for prostitution and to those trafficked for economic exploitation: the victims of prostitution-related trafficking have usually agreed on a much vaguer basis (Maljevic 2005). Half of victims of economic exploitation in Belgium received a promise of a specific job. For victims of sexual exploitation, only one-fourth did (Vermeulen and van der Beken 2004). For both groups, most of those promised a specific job were promised work in the hotel and catering industry (according to the Netherlands data, a large proportion before their recruitment worked in these industries).

Considering the publicity that trafficking has recently received in many source countries, it could be asked how victims can be so naive that they believe traffickers' promises (especially when the promises usually seem to be vague). One explanation is that recruiting is increasingly done through acquaintances, relatives, and others who have the victim's trust. Despite this, many victims have serious doubts about the reliability of the promises, but their domestic situations make the risk seem worth taking. According to Nigerian data, as many as 80–90 percent of repatriated victims of prostitution-related trafficking admit that they knew when recruited that they might end up as prostitutes. However, they had little choice other than to accept, since they could not find employment and lacked funds to continue their educations at home (*Trafficking of Nigerian Girls to Italy* 2004, p. 73).

The number of those in Europe who have other than economic motives or who have been abducted is small. In Belgium, 8 percent of victims say that they were mainly looking for adventure, and 7 percent say they were kidnapped. In the Netherlands, the percentage kidnapped has been 10–15 percent in the last few years. In Belgium less than 5 percent fled political instability or wars (Dutch National Rapporteur 2004; Vermeulen and van der Beken 2004).[8]

The European data refer mainly to adult victims; the situation concerning minors, who make up a large percentage of the victims outside the industrialized countries, is different. Very few had any previous working experience, and almost all were recruited by force or sold by their families. Thus they were passive bystanders even at the point of recruitment (Mon-Eu-Traf II 2004; Muhonen 2005).

To sum up, the victims of sexual exploitation–related trafficking in Europe and other industrialized countries are usually older than in third-world countries, where a large proportion are minors. Even in the industrialized countries, the victims of prostitution-related trafficking are typically younger than those of other forms of trafficking and come from more depressed economic circumstances. In Europe, over 40 percent of victims of prostitution-related trafficking are unemployed at the time of recruitment, and many have no previous working experience. Of those with a job, for about a third it is prostitution. A large percentage of victims are single mothers with economic responsibility for their children and often for other relatives. The European data indicate that the victims of prostitution-related trafficking have, on average, fewer choices than the victims of other types of trafficking when deciding whether to accept the offer made. This is even more evident in Asia, Africa, and Latin America, where the bulk of victims are minors recruited by force or sold by their families and have not even in theory any capacity to influence their fate (Mon-Eu-Traf II 2004; Muhonen 2005).

Women become victims of prostitution-related trafficking mainly because of the economic and social circumstances of their lives rather

[8] Low figures are not intended to trivialize the problem; it may indeed be conceived as very high if as many as 5–20 percent of all trafficked women have been forcibly abducted! This would also indicate that it is not always overly easy to recruit women to this trade, considering that abduction/kidnapping is a demanding and risky method.

than because of their personal characteristics. Some data, however, indicate that economic and social circumstances are not the only explanation for victimization. According to Dutch, Bosnian, and Nigerian
data, the risk of victimization increases significantly if economic and
social deprivation is combined with dysfunctional and abusive family
relations. Among Bosnian victims, family relations explain victimization better than economic or social factors (Dutch National Rapporteur 2004; Vermeulen and van der Beken 2004; Maljevic 2005). Some
data indicate that personal characteristics have some role to play in
victimization at least in Europe. According to a recent IOM study from
Romania, victims of prostitution-related trafficking are more independent and keener to take risks than their age-mates. Most come from
broken families, but they also usually have more materialistic values
than their age-mates and do not value education as the means to
achieve success. They also have an above-average propensity to break
official and informal rules.[9] Thus the general profile of an adult victim
of prostitution-related trafficking in Europe in many respects is similar
to that of victims of other types of sexual and violent crime (IOM
2003*e*).

C. Organizers and Forms of Organization

Trafficking operations inside and to Europe are usually carried out
in cooperation with several relatively small local criminal groups. Vermeulen and van der Beken (2004) classify the organizers into three
main categories: loners who operate as individuals; isolated groups consisting of two or more persons accounting for recruitment, transport,
and exploitation; and clusters of persons operating as criminal networks. According to them, the last category is responsible for 50–80
percent of the volume of trafficking in western Europe. The clusters
consist mainly of smaller networks of pimps with a common contact
point where the victims arrive and the profits leave. The contact point
operates directly or through go-betweens. The networks have a flexible
composition rather than a strong hierarchical structure, and the elimination of one cluster does not usually affect the activity of the whole
network. The deleted link is replaced by another. The relations between groups are normally pure business relations, and each group or
individual can act in several networks simultaneously. The structure

---

[9] Whether such characteristics are produced or at least reinforced by their status is not
indicated.

allows a painless assimilation of competing independent operators, either loners or smaller groups, into the network. In this way, the independent smaller groups dealing with trafficking often become entangled in the long run in major (organized) crime groups or networks (NCIS 2002, pp. 34–36; Mon-Eu-Traf II 2004).

According to the Belgian data, about 40 percent of the victims of sexual exploitation are trafficked by large networks with five or more mediators, and about 45 percent by smaller networks with two to four mediators. The networks trafficking humans for other purposes are smaller: only about 20 percent of victims of economic exploitation are trafficked by large networks (about 50 percent are trafficked by smaller networks). The significance of loners is substantially higher in economic exploitation than in sexual exploitation: only about 15 percent of victims of prostitution-related trafficking in Belgium are trafficked by loners. The corresponding percentage in other fields of trafficking is about 30 percent. Small networks and loners also dominate the smuggling of illegal immigrants to Belgium (Vermeulen and van der Beken 2004). Thus, in western Europe the organization of trafficking seems to differ significantly depending on the type. The networks specialized in trafficking for sexual exploitation are larger and have more complicated structures (Mon-Eu-Traf II 2004).

The ethnic backgrounds of the networks differ depending on the type of exploitation. The available data refer usually to the backgrounds of the exploiters operating in the countries of destination, who are easiest to indict and bring to court. In Belgium, about 40 percent of offenders in cleared trafficking crimes linked with prostitution have been ethnic Albanians, whereas the bulk of offenders in illegal labor-related trafficking have been Belgian citizens. Groups of mixed nationalities make up about a third of offenders in all forms of trafficking and human smuggling (Vermeulen and van der Beken 2004). The situation seems to be the same in most European countries. Organized prostitution and related trafficking are often in the hands of ethnic or foreign criminal groups and networks, whereas other forms of trafficking are usually perpetrated by native citizens. However, regardless of the type of trafficking, both recruiters and transporters are usually of the same nationality as the victim (Mon-Eu-Traf II 2004).

The gender structure of trafficking networks varies from region to region. In the Baltic countries, in parts of Russia, and in central Asia, the majority of recruiters are women, often former prostitutes. However, the networks are usually led by men, and the majority of those who handle the transport, control, and pandering of victims in the destination countries are men, although some women are involved (IOM 2001*a*; Lehti and Aromaa 2002, pp. 60–64). In western Europe the networks seem to be dominated even more by men than in the Baltics. In the Netherlands, to which prostitutes are mainly trafficked from the Balkans and central Europe, female recruiters are involved only in about 20 percent of the cleared cases of prostitution-related trafficking (Dutch National Rapporteur 2004).

There are also examples of networks run to a large extent by women. From central Asia, several cases of networks recruiting, trafficking, and exploiting women for prostitution have been reported that have been operated by women only (IOM 2001*a*). Organized Nigerian prostitution in Italy is largely controlled by women (although recruiting and transportation of victims are often handled by men) (Bopp and Cauduro 2004). In some other parts of Africa, for example, in Malawi, prostitution-related trafficking is mainly operated by female-led and operated networks. The same applies to the large-scale trafficking in domestic servants from Ecuador to Belgium, which is organized (both recruiting in Ecuador and running the business in Belgium) mainly by women (many of them earlier victims) (IOM 2003*d*; Ghijs 2004, pp. 57–82; Mon-Eu-Traf II 2004).

Although trafficking in western Europe and the Balkans is mainly controlled and organized by men, prostitution-related trafficking, either in Europe or elsewhere, is not organized and run solely by men. Women work in large numbers as recruiters and in the control activities in most trafficking networks, but there are also a large number of networks organized and run by women only. This reality is often overlooked by those who see trafficking for sexual exploitation as a crime solely perpetrated by men against women.

D. Modi Operandi

Victims are recruited by individual recruiters, through newspaper and Internet advertisements, or by front agencies offering employment opportunities abroad. The current trend, at least in Europe and in West Africa, is toward personal recruiting rather than general advertising; the recruiting is also increasingly done by people the victims know and trust. According to Nigerian data from Edo State, the majority of interviewed victims were recruited through family members or close friends; only one-fourth were recruited by strangers or through Internet or newspaper advertisements. The current situation in Europe is similar: according to Bosnian, Czech, and Dutch data, the majority of victims are recruited through acquaintances, friends, or relatives. The majority of victims in West Africa were actively searching for job opportunities abroad at the time of their recruitment. In Europe, contacts with unknown recruiters are usually made in places of entertainment: discos, bars, hotels, and restaurants (Hajdinjak 2002, p. 51; NCIS 2002, p. 35; Sipaviciene 2002, p. 14; Dutch National Rapporteur 2004; *Trafficking of Nigerian Girls to Italy* 2004, pp. 67, 73; Travnickova 2004, p. 91; Maljevic 2005).

The most common recruiting method for adults throughout the world consists of promises of employment opportunities, often in hotel, catering, and entertainment industries or as domestic servants and nannies. Some victims are recruited knowingly into prostitution, and a large percentage of others know that there exists a substantial risk that they may end up in prostitution.

However, even these cases satisfy the criteria for trafficking if the recruitment or the conditions of employment include deception, coercion, or violence. Women and especially children are recruited by abduction or sold to traffickers by their families. In western Europe the percentage of identified victims who have been outright kidnapped or sold into prostitution is altogether less than 20 percent; most of these cases are from the Balkans, especially Albania and Kosovo. Outside the industrialized countries, recruiting by force is more common. Especially where a large percentage of victims are minors, both abduction and selling by relatives are prevalent. For example, in Cambodia, where minors make up the majority of victims of organized prostitution, they have almost without exception been sold to traffickers by their parents, who also receive a share of the income. The situation is similar in parts of Africa, South and Southeast Asia, and Latin America (Mon-Eu-Traf II 2004; *Trafficking of Nigerian Girls to Italy* 2004; Muhonen 2005).

The departure usually takes place quickly (in the Netherlands in nearly 70 percent of investigated cases the departure was within a week after recruitment [Dutch National Rapporteur 2004]). The women either are transported directly to the ultimate destination country, and engaged in prostitution upon arrival, or are moved in stages, in which case they often are exploited at each stage (NCIS 2002, pp. 34–36; *Trafficking of Nigerian Girls to Italy* 2004).

Once recruited, victims are controlled in various ways, but violence (implied and actual) is common and ever-present. Often there is first an initiation period, lasting for a couple of weeks, during which the victim's resistance and will are broken by a combination of psychological and physical pressure and violence. After the victim submits to the wishes of her or his traffickers, open violence usually becomes less common. There are, however, in this respect substantial differences among the trafficking networks in how they operate.

In Europe, trafficking from and through the Balkans was earlier exceptionally violent. However, the working methods of the Balkan groups seem to have become less violent lately, and open violence seems to be becoming less common among other networks operating in Europe. Traffickers have become aware that the business can be organized and run more effectively and profitably when the victims are engaged on a relatively voluntary basis. Earlier victims are increasingly used as recruiters (Laczko, Klekowski von Koppenfels, and Barthel 2002, p. 15; Lehti and Aromaa 2002, pp. 87–92; NCIS 2002, pp. 35, 38–39; Maljevic 2005).

Traffickers also exploit the economic, social, and cultural vulnerabilities of victims. Debt is one of the most common means of control. The women usually agree to pay recruiting expenses from future earnings. This debt is passed from one trafficker to the next until it ends up in the hands of the exploiter in the destination country. Combined with inflated housing and living expenses charged to victims, repayment usually takes months, even years, and in many cases becomes impossible to handle. The earnings of the victims are directed to the pockets of the exploiters, and the women have no financial means to escape. In regions of Africa, Asia, and Latin America in which the prostitution of minors is common and victims are often sold to traffickers by parents or near relatives, it is not uncommon for a share of the victim's earnings to be paid directly to their families monthly or annually.

Another globally used control method, especially in transborder trafficking, is to confiscate passports and other identity documents and to threaten victims with local authorities, detention, and deportation. The threats are effective because they are at least partly real: in industrialized and third-world countries, it is almost impossible for victims to avoid deportation even in the most aggravated cases of abuse (NCIS 2002, p. 36; Muhonen 2005).

In some regions the religious beliefs of the victims can be used as a control method. In Nigeria and other parts of West Africa, victims are often obliged to make an oath before traditional shrines or spiritualists before they depart, agreeing to repay a certain sum of money to their *mamans* after they have arrived at their destination. This kind of psychological bondage is said to be even more effective than violence or economic bondage (*Trafficking of Nigerian Girls to Italy* 2004, pp. 75–76).

Relatives and families are used in several ways as a control method. Especially in the trafficking of minors, families are sometimes co-exploiters. In these cases the victim often sees prostitution as her or his social obligation and submits without resistance to the wishes of the traffickers. The victims can also be controlled through economic or violent threats to the relatives and through the (actual or imagined) shame that public knowledge about her or his situation would cause them (*Trafficking of Nigerian Girls to Italy* 2004, pp. 75–76; Muhonen 2005).

Victims of sexual exploitation are usually significantly worse treated and more threatened and deprived of their freedom than victims of economic exploitation or human smuggling. According to Belgian data, 50–60 percent of victims of sexual exploitation are assaulted, raped, or subjected to aggravated mental abuse during transportation or exploitation; the corresponding percentage among victims of other forms of trafficking is about 10 percent and among smuggled illegal immigrants about 5 percent. Victims of sexual exploitation are also usually subjected to much graver economic abuse than other victims of trafficking,[10] and they are more strictly controlled.[11] All kinds of threats are also more common in sexual exploitation[12] (Vermeulen and van der Beken 2004).

[10] In Belgium, 40 percent of the victims of sexual exploitation receive no pay at all from their exploiters, compared with under 20 percent of other victims of trafficking.

[11] In Belgium, about 45 percent are allowed no personal freedom, compared with 10 percent for those trafficked for labor exploitation; among those exploited sexually, 35 percent are subjected to continuous control, compared with 5 percent of those exploited economically.

[12] In Belgium, of victims exploited sexually, 45 percent are subjected to personal threats and 23 percent have been intimidated indirectly, by threats to harm their families; the corresponding percentages for victims of other types of trafficking are 15 percent and 5 percent.

The Belgian figures are aggregates. Italian, Russian, and Chinese data show that there are substantial differences in the treatment of victims and in the ways the activity is organized not only between but also inside different forms of trafficking. These differences depend mainly on the ethnic backgrounds and traditions of the organizers.

According to Bopp and Cauduro (2004), in Italy the organization of prostitution-related trafficking in the main recruiting areas (Nigeria, Albania, and eastern Europe) varies substantially. The Nigerian networks have loose structures and operate mainly in and from Nigeria; they have bases in Europe through which women are transported before arriving in Italy. Exploitation in Italy is handled by resident Nigerian women, *mamans*, often former victims themselves. The Albanian networks consist of small and autonomous groups (based on shared ethnicity and bonds of clan membership) with an internal hierarchical organization. Open violence is the standard method to reinforce the hierarchy and to control and subjugate victims. The networks usually handle the whole operation from recruitment to exploitation. The groups that control the trafficking of eastern European women are less structured, and the process is highly fragmented. The victims are usually repeatedly bought and sold during the journey from their countries of origin, and their exploitation in Italy is often handled by local criminals.

Differences in the organization of trafficking are reflected in the exploitation process. Nigerian women must work for the networks until they have repaid their transfer costs, which usually takes two years. Many who survive the period (which is not inevitable because of the harsh living and working conditions) join the network and continue working as *mamans*. Albanian women are forced to work as prostitutes for an indeterminate period, sometimes their entire lives. The rules imposed on them and the modes of recruitment (deceit or abduction) imply unconditional exploitation. Eastern European women in principle have the least restricted working conditions and usually arrive with the intention of prostituting themselves only for a couple of months: the time needed to save enough to live for the rest of the year. Their prostitution is to a large extent based on contracts for a fixed period. However, their working conditions are often worse than is agreed on in advance, and the periods of work become longer than planned (Bopp and Cauduro 2004).

Shelley shows important differences between the organization of trafficking in Russia and China and explains the differences by reference to cultural traditions. Chinese organized crime groups operate as integrated networks, running and controlling all phases of trafficking from recruitment to exploitation. The groups run their operations like businesses, and the victims are treated as valuable commodities to be taken care of. Although conditions are often harsh and the payments the victims obtain for their work are small, aggravated cases of abuse are few, agreements are kept, and victims are free after they have paid their debts. Honoring of agreements is necessary and advantageous because groups usually use former victims to recruit new ones, often among their relatives and families. The operations are thus based on long-term business and profit interests, and the groups invest most of their profits into the Chinese economy. These characteristics guarantee a fairly humane operations model, although violence and abuse are not unknown (Shelley 2004).

The methods of the Russian groups are radically different. While the Chinese groups traffic persons mainly for labor and operate on a long-term profit basis, the Russians have specialized in trafficking for prostitution and aim to maximize short-term profits. Victims are hunted all over the country, often recruited with violent intimidation or abduction, and are sold abroad to foreign exploiters who pay the best prices. The survival or destiny of the victims does not concern the traffickers, since they act only as recruiters and deliverers of commodities and are not involved in the exploitation. Aggravated violence, rape, coercion, and other forms of serious abuse are common, and only a few victims can leave prostitution later or profit financially from their exploitation. The profits are rarely reinvested and almost never repatriated to Russia (Shelley 2004).

Shelley attributes the differences to national cultures. Chinese organized crime operates according to old Chinese business traditions, whereas the Russian criminal groups act like ancient trappers: operating within a short time frame and spending earnings on a luxurious life. The differences are also probably influenced by the differences in the types of trafficking the Chinese and Russian groups are involved in. Chinese organized crime traffics mainly in human labor, whereas the Russian groups mostly traffic women for prostitution. Trafficking related to prostitution at least in Europe is generally more violent and operates with shorter time frames than trafficking in illegal labor.

To sum up, at least in Europe, the organizational and operational models of different types of trafficking differ significantly, and there also exist substantial differences related to the ethnic background and traditions of the perpetrators. Trafficking for prostitution is infested to a much larger extent with aggravated human rights abuses than are other forms of trafficking. Victims of sexual exploitation are subjected to aggravated violence and intimidation, rape, and other forms of gross abuse more often than victims of labor exploitation. They are also more tightly controlled than other victims and often receive no financial compensation.

There are, however, significant differences between different ethnic trafficking networks. In Europe the victims in the worst position are those trafficked by Balkan networks. The situations of central and eastern European victims are somewhat better, partly because they are, on average, better educated and have higher social backgrounds and thus have better abilities to defend themselves and seek help. Central and eastern European trafficking networks are more fragmented and control their victims less tightly than do the Balkan groups. This does not mean that all eastern European victims are better off than those from other source areas, and the differences are relative, since the eastern European women also are subjected to abuse and coercion.

The social and economic functions and consequences of trafficking differ from country to country. In eastern Europe and the Balkans, trafficking is to a very large extent focused only on prostitution and has no positive effects whatsoever. Large-scale export of women of fertile age to practical slavery abroad worsens the demographic distortions in these areas and leads to more rapid demographic and social decline. As the operations are based on short-term profit maximization and the profits are usually neither reinvested nor repatriated, the crime does not financially benefit local communities.

In some other regions, even large-scale trafficking despite its abusive characteristics has some positive social and economic functions. In these cases it is a matter of long-established traditions of trafficking and smuggling of human labor abroad. Although prostitution-related trafficking is an important part of local economies in some parts of the world, the human rights abuses and socially corruptive influences it involves are so grave that it can scarcely be considered anywhere to have positive functions (Shelley 2004).

III. International Agreements and Practices

Use of the concepts "trafficking in women"and "trafficking in persons" is inconsistent and confused, partly because of the diversity of the phenomena and the national laws regulating them, and divergent ideological and moral attitudes toward prostitution, the commercial sex trade, and (irregular) migration. Trafficking in women and trafficking in persons are social phenomena with multiple dimensions, and it is impossible to encapsulate them into one definition or framework. The confused use of the concepts also relates to the history and changing objectives of international legislation. In this section we describe the evolution of the concepts in international legislation over the past century and their use in modern American and European legislation.

A. Trafficking in International Legislation

Modern international agreements on trafficking go back to early twentieth-century treaties on the slave trade, the white slave trade, and prostitution. Until the 1990s, trafficking related to commercial sex was regulated separately from other forms of trafficking in persons. Since 2000, the two have been joined in the Palermo Protocol.[13] The context has changed from combating slavery or prostitution to the international fight against organized crime.

1. *The Regulation of Slave Trade.*   The international regulations concerning trafficking relating to the exploitation of human labor have their roots in the treaty system created to prevent slavery and the slave trade,[14] culminating in the Geneva Convention of 1926.[15] The original convention had a fairly restricted scope comprising only slavery and the slave trade. Slavery was defined as "a status or condition of a person over whom any or all of the powers attaching to the right of ownership

---

[13] United Nations 2000 Protocol to Prevent, Suppress and Punish Trafficking in Persons, Especially Women and Children, Supplementing the United Nations Convention against Transnational Organized Crime (Palermo Protocol; A/RES/55/25).

[14] Including the General Act of Berlin of 1885, the General Act of the Brussels Conference of 1889–90 concerning the African Slave Trade (between Great Britain, Austria-Hungary, Belgium, Congo, Denmark, France, Germany, Italy, the Netherlands, Persia, Portugal, Russia, Spain, Sweden, Norway, Turkey, the United States, and Zanzibar), and the Convention of Saint-Germain-en-Laye of 1919, to revise the General Act of Berlin of 1885, and the General Act and Declaration of Brussels of 1890.

[15] The signatories of the 1926 convention were Albania, Australia, Austria, Belgium, the British Empire, Bulgaria, Canada, China, Colombia, Cuba, Czechoslovakia, Denmark, Estonia, Abyssinia, Finland, France, Germany, Greece, India, Italy, Latvia, Liberia, Lithuania, New Zealand, the Netherlands, Norway, Panama, Persia, Poland, Portugal, Romania, the Kingdom of the Serbs, Croats, and Slovenes, Spain, Sweden, the Union of South Africa, and Uruguay.

were exercised." The slave trade included "all acts involved in the capture, acquisition, or disposal of a person with intent to reduce him to slavery; all acts involved in the acquisition of a slave with a view to selling or exchanging him; all acts of disposal by sale or exchange of a slave acquired with a view to being sold or exchanged, and, in general, every act of trade or transport in slaves" (article 1). The signatories were obliged to suppress the slave trade, to abolish slavery in all its forms, and to criminalize the slave trade and slavery in their territories and colonies. The convention also included stipulations concerning other forms of forced labor. It was allowed only for public purposes and on the responsibility of the competent central authorities of the territory concerned, always had to involve adequate remuneration, and could not involve removal of laborers from their places of residence. All forms of forced or compulsory labor were to be abolished progressively.

The scope of the Geneva Convention was enlarged substantially in the Supplementary Convention of 1956. The definition of slavery (and its criminalization) was broadened to include debt bondage and serfdom. Some forms of trade in women and children were included in the list of banned practices. From the viewpoint of traffic in women and children, the most important new stipulations were paragraphs *c* and *d* of the first article, which obliged the parties to abolish forced paid marriages, some forms of trade in women by relatives, and all forms of trade in children under eighteen years of age by relatives or guardians:

> Each of the States Parties to this Convention shall take all practicable and necessary legislative and other measures to bring about progressively and as soon as possible the complete abolition or abandonment of . . .

> (c) any institution or practice whereby:
> (i) A woman, without the right to refuse, is promised or given in marriage on payment of a consideration in money or in kind to her parents, guardian, family or any other person or group; or
> (ii) The husband of a woman, his family, or his clan, has the right to transfer her to another person for value received or otherwise; or
> (iii) A woman on the death of her husband is liable to be inherited by another person.
> (d) Any institution or practice whereby a child or young person

under the age of eighteen years is delivered by either or both of his natural parents or by his guardian to another person, whether for reward or not, with a view to the exploitation of the child or young person or of his labour.

In the second paragraph of the sixth article, committing, encouraging, and aiding the named acts were criminalized. The 1926 convention and the 1956 supplementary convention prohibited both international and intranational trade and transfers.

The 1926 and 1956 conventions focused on the slave trade and related forms of servitude and forced labor. The conventions continue to exist and remain in effect today and are germane especially to the prevention and combat of trafficking related to exploitation of human labor and to trafficking for domestic servants. The antislavery treaties have had and today have, however, only limited significance to trafficking for sexual exploitation (although slavery and related institutions have always included various forms of sexual exploitation and abuse).

2. *The Regulation of Prostitution.*   Modern international conventions on trafficking related to sexual exploitation have their basis in the international regulation of prostitution, with roots in treaties of the first half of the twentieth century[16] culminating in the 1949 Convention for the Suppression of the Traffic in Persons and of the Exploitation of the Prostitution of Others.

The first modern wave of rapid increase in migratory prostitution and related trafficking took place between the 1840s and the First World War and was closely connected with the industrial revolution, urbanization, and European colonialism, and the migration flows and social and economic changes these processes caused all over the world. The growth of international and local prostitution was mainly seen and discussed as a question of immigration policies, colonial management, and public health. Governments in Europe and North America tried to regulate the increase by tightening the control of prostitutes, especially foreign and non-European ones (Scully 2001, pp. 75–83).

The beginnings of the international antitrafficking movement oc-

---

[16] That is, the International Agreement of 18 May 1904 for the Suppression of the White Slave Traffic, the International Convention of 4 May 1910 for the Suppression of the White Slave Traffic, the 1921 Convention for the Suppression of the Traffic in Women and Children, the 1933 Convention for the Suppression of the Traffic in Women of Full Age, and the 1947 Protocol to Amend the Convention for the Suppression of the Traffic in Women and Children of 30 September 1921, and the Convention for the Suppression of the Traffic in Women of Full Age of 11 October 1933.

curred in Britain in the last few decades of the nineteenth century. In the 1890s, various British abolitionist groups formed the National Vigilance Association (NVA), which became the nucleus of a European antitrafficking coalition. National committees were soon created under NVA supervision in various European countries (including Austria, Belgium, Denmark, France, Germany, the Netherlands, Russia, Sweden, and Switzerland). In 1899 these committees organized an international conference in London, which became the starting point for the international campaign against the "white slave trade" that culminated in the 1904 Paris Conference and Convention. The focus was on abolition of the traffic in European women for prostitution. Non-European native and colonial prostitution came within the scope of the antitrafficking movement only after the First World War (Scully 2001, pp. 84–85).

The 1904 Paris Convention among the major European powers[17] was the first of six international treaties on prostitution and prostitution-related trafficking in the twentieth century. It recognized the white slave trade as a juridical concept in international law and had high objectives: "being desirous of securing to women of full age who have suffered abuse or compulsion, as also to women and girls under age, effective protection against the criminal traffic known as the 'White Slave Traffic,' [the signatories] have decided to conclude an Agreement with a view to concerting measures calculated to attain this object." In practice the measures taken were restricted to recommendations on collecting information on international cross-border prostitution and harmonization of procedures used in the repatriation of foreign prostitutes to their native countries. The criminalization of traffic in women and children and related activities was left exclusively to regulation by internal legislation of the contracting states.

The next convention in 1910 was substantially more ambitious. It criminalized all forms of exploitation by third parties of minors' prostitution (persons under twenty years of age) and forced prostitution of adults (articles 1 and 2). Criminalization was restricted to female prostitution but included both international cross-border prostitution and national prostitution. There was one important exception: prostitution in brothels, even forced prostitution, and regardless of the age of the

[17] The signatories were the United Kingdom, Germany, Denmark, Belgium, Spain, France, Italy, the Netherlands, Portugal, Russia, Sweden, Norway, and Switzerland.

prostitutes, was not regulated by the convention but left exclusively to national legislation.

The 1910 convention provided:

Article 1: Whoever, in order to gratify the passions of another person, has procured, enticed, or led away, even with her consent, a woman or girl under age, for immoral purposes, shall be punished, notwithstanding that the various acts constituting the offense may have been committed in different countries.

Article 2: Whoever, in order to gratify the passions of another person, has, by fraud, or by means of violence, threats, abuse of authority, or any other method of compulsion, procured, enticed, or led away a woman or girl over age, for immoral purposes, shall also be punished, notwithstanding that the various acts constituting the offense may have been committed in different countries.

A separate final protocol of the treaty stated that the stipulations of articles 1 and 2 were to be considered minimums, and the contracting states were free to punish other analogous offenses, such as, for example, procurement of adult women, even when neither fraud nor compulsion was involved. It also included stipulations concerning punishments and aggravating circumstances (those referred to in article 2).

In 1913, a broad coalition of antitrafficking groups agreed in Madrid on a joint agenda of future action, which focused on eight main points: abolition of licensed brothels, creation of a global data bank on victims of trafficking, creation of programs for assisted repatriation and rehabilitation of victims, creation of methods to protect female emigrants en route, uniform legislation on regulation of employment agencies offering jobs abroad, total criminalization of trafficking of minors for prostitution regardless of the consent of the victims, full suppression of colonial prostitution, and more effective punishment of procurers and third parties involved in the exploitation of the prostitution of others (Scully 2001, p. 87).

The First World War caused a break of several years in development of new antitrafficking legislation (and at the same time led to a major increase in organized and unorganized prostitution in all war theaters). After the war, the main responsibility for antitrafficking efforts and legislation was transferred to the new League of Nations, which began its work with optimistic spirits and expansive proclamations. The factual achievements of the league in its antitrafficking and prostitution policies during its short existence, however, were modest, although not insignificant (Scully 2001, pp. 87–88).

No international data bank was ever created (no such data bank exists today), and the gathering of information remained sporadic. Data collection was based mainly on self-reporting by the signatories of the treaties, annual conferences of enthusiasts and specialists, and traveling commissions of inquiry (Scully 2001, p. 88).

The 1921 convention[18] mainly reinforced the stipulations and obligations agreed on in the earlier prostitution treaties. The influence of the Madrid agenda of 1913 was seen in some changes in the earlier criminalizations. The emphasis of the new treaty was on the suppression of traffic in children, and in contrast to the convention of 1910, traffic in boys also was now criminalized (article 2). The age of majority was raised by one year to twenty-one years of age (article 5).

The treaty also included new stipulations concerning the protection of immigrant women and children and regulations concerning licensing and supervision of employment agencies and offices to ensure the protection of women and children seeking employment abroad (article 6):

> Article 6. The High Contracting Parties undertake in connection with immigration and emigration to adopt such administrative and legislative measures as are required to check the traffic in women and children. In particular, they undertake to make such regulations as are required for the protection of women and children travelling on emigrant ships, not only at the points of departure and arrival, but also during the journey, and to arrange for the exhibition, in railway stations and in ports, of notices warning women and children of the danger of the traffic and indicating the places where they can obtain accommodation and assistance (article 7).

The criminalizations of the 1910 treaty were broadened further in the 1933 Convention for the Suppression of the Traffic in Women of Full Age,[19] in which all forms of exploitation of female prostitution by third

---

[18] Between Albania, Germany, Austria, Belgium, Brazil, the British Empire (with Canada, the Commonwealth of Australia, the Union of South Africa, New Zealand, and India), Chile, China, Colombia, Costa Rica, Cuba, Estonia, Greece, Hungary, Italy, Japan, Latvia, Lithuania, Norway, the Netherlands, Persia, Poland (with Danzig), Portugal, Romania, Siam, Sweden, Switzerland, and Czechoslovakia.

[19] The signatories included Albania, Austria, Belgium, the British Empire (with Canada, the Commonwealth of Australia, the Union of South Africa, New Zealand, and India), Bulgaria, Chile, the Republic of China, the Free City of Danzig, France, Germany,

parties were criminalized. This general criminalization for the first time included cases in which exploitation was based on mutual consent. However, the stipulation concerned only international cross-border prostitution:

> Article 1. Whoever, in order to gratify the passions of another person, has procured, enticed or led away even with her consent, a woman or girl of full age for immoral purposes *to be carried out in another country*, shall be punished, notwithstanding that the various acts constituting the offense may have been committed in different countries. (Emphasis added)

The treaty in article 3 also tightened up earlier stipulations concerning the prevention and control of prostitution-related trafficking and organized pandering by including new regulations on international data exchange and police cooperation (article 3).

After the dissolution of the League of Nations, the prostitution treaties were incorporated in the U.N. treaty system in 1947 by the Protocol to Amend the Convention for the Suppression of the Traffic in Women and Children of 30 September 1921 and the Convention for the Suppression of the Traffic in Women of Full Age of 11 October 1933. The substance of the treaties was left unchanged.

A new broader treaty on prostitution and trafficking was agreed on in 1949 when the Convention for the Suppression of the Traffic in Persons and of the Exploitation of the Prostitution of Others was signed. For the first time, the abolitionist ideology that had inspired and dominated international prostitution policies since the 1890s was expressed in clear words in the preamble: "Prostitution and the accompanying evil of the traffic in persons for the purpose of prostitution are incompatible with the dignity and worth of the human person and endanger the welfare of the individual, the family and the community." The ideology was most clearly expressed in articles 6 and 16, in which all forms of licensing of prostitutes were prohibited. Signatory states were obliged to take and encourage measures for the prevention of prostitution as a whole through public and private educational, health, social, economic, and other services.

The changes in the earlier criminalizations were also substantial. The criminalizations of the earlier prostitution treaties were united in

---

Greece, Hungary, Latvia, Lithuania, Monaco, the Netherlands, Norway, Panama, Poland, Portugal, Spain, Sweden, Switzerland, Czechoslovakia, and Yugoslavia.

article 1 of the 1949 convention, which prohibited all forms of exploitation of prostitution (regardless of the age or sex of the prostitutes) by third parties. As in the criminalization in the 1933 convention, article 1 of the 1949 convention also included cases in which exploitation was based on mutual consent. However, application of the criminalization was much broader than in 1933. It now included all prostitution and trafficking, whether international borders were crossed or not, and regardless of the nationality of the prostitutes.

The current international regulation of trafficking in women has ensued to a large extent as a by-product of the general regulation of prostitution, and for a long time its criminalization has been part of a far more extensive criminalization of exploitation of prostitution of others. It is not surprising that the borderline between trafficking and prostitution in international discussion has been and remains obscure, because the setting of this border is new and exists only in the international treaties of the last decade.

The terms "white slave traffic" and "trafficking" have had varying definitions in international legislation. The term white slave traffic was used in the 1904 and 1910 conventions as a synonym for organized, illegal prostitution, both international and national. The term "traffic in women and children" made its first appearance in international treaties in the 1921 convention, where it was used as a synonym for the white slave traffic of the earlier treaties. Although the treaty, like the two previous ones, emphasized international cross-border prostitution and trafficking,[20] the criminalizations included all prohibited activity, whether or not international borders were crossed. This was, however, not the case in the 1933 treaty, which concerned only international, cross-border prostitution.

The regulatory system created by the treaties of 1904–47 criminalized all forms of exploitation of the prostitution of minors (except buying) and the prostitution-related trafficking in children regardless of sex or of whether international borders were crossed. The age of majority in these treaties was initially twenty and then later twenty-one years of age.

Regulations concerning prostitution of adults were more ambiguous. Under the 1910 and 1921 treaties, the forced prostitution of females and trafficking in women were criminalized whether or not interna-

---

[20] See articles 6 and 7, which regulated cross-border trafficking only.

tional borders were crossed. However, the criminalization of the 1933 convention concerning the exploitation by third parties of female prostitution on mutual consent was applicable only to international cross-border prostitution. The concept of trafficking in all of them can be seen to have included at minimum all forms of exploitation of child prostitution by others (except buying), forced female prostitution of adults, and trafficking inside national borders and over international borders.

In the 1949 convention, in which "traffic in persons" was mentioned in the preamble separately from prostitution, in the text of the treaty the term was used only in article 17, which mainly referred to international cross-border prostitution and its supportive services:

Article 17. The parties to the present convention undertake, in connection with immigration and emigration, to adopt or maintain such measures as are required in terms of their obligations under the present convention, to check the traffic in persons of either sex for the purpose of prostitution. In particular they undertake:

1. To make such regulations as are necessary for the protection of immigrants or emigrants, and in particular, women and children, both at the place of arrival and departure and while en route;
2. To arrange for appropriate publicity warning the public of the dangers of the aforesaid traffic;
3. To take appropriate measures to ensure supervision of railway stations, airports, seaports and en route, and of other public places, in order to prevent international traffic in persons for the purpose of prostitution;
4. To take appropriate measures in order that the appropriate authorities be informed of the arrival of persons, who appear, prima facie, to be the principals and accomplices in or victims of such a traffic.

Although the term "traffic in persons" was used more restricted than in the earlier treaties, the convention broadened the concept's scope. Unlike the 1910 or the 1933 treaties, articles 1 and 17 of the 1949 convention included all forms of prostitution, including prostitution by mutual consent of the parties, and regardless of whether international borders had been crossed.

The 1949 convention had been joined by the end of the 1990s by sixty-eight states, including twenty European countries.[21] It has not been ratified by the United States, the United Kingdom, Canada, Germany,[22] the Netherlands, Sweden, or Australia. Most, however, are parties to the 1921 and 1933 conventions.

In a more general way, but with the same substance, the prohibition of all forms of trafficking in women and exploitation of prostitution of women were included in the sixth article of the 1979 Convention on the Elimination of All Forms of Discrimination against Women: "States Parties shall take all appropriate measures, including legislation, to suppress all forms of traffic in women and exploitation of prostitution of women."

3. *The Regulation of Organized Crime.* The two lines of regulating trafficking in persons in international legislation were joined in 2000 in the Palermo Protocol. The context of the regulation changed substantially from the earlier ones. The primary objective of the Palermo Protocol is the regulation of neither the slave trade nor prostitution, but international cooperation in the prevention and control of organized crime. This can also be seen in the formulation of the articles criminalizing trafficking, in which prostitution has no special status (although particular attention is paid to crimes against women and children). Trafficking in persons is defined as in article 3, subparagraph *a*: "the recruitment, transportation, transfer, harbouring or receipt of persons, by means of the threat or use of force or other forms of coercion, of abduction, of fraud, of deception, of the abuse of power or of a position of vulnerability or of the giving or receiving of payments or benefits to achieve the consent of a person having control over another person, for the purpose of exploitation."

The criteria of the crime, thus, include three main elements, all critical: the act of the perpetrator, the intentional recruitment (see article 5), transportation, transfer, harboring, or receipt of persons; the means by which this act is perpetrated (threat, use of force, other forms of coercion, etc.); and the goal of the act: exploitation. According to article 3, exploitation includes, among other things, "the exploitation of the prostitution of others or other forms of sexual exploitation, forced labour or services, slavery or practices similar to slavery, servi-

---

[21] The European countries that were parties of the convention in 1992 were Albania, Belarus, Belgium, Bulgaria, Cyprus, Czechoslovakia, Denmark, Finland, France, Hungary, Italy, Latvia, Luxembourg, Norway, Poland, Romania, Russia, Spain, Ukraine, and Yugoslavia.

[22] The German Democratic Republic was part of the convention in 1974–90.

tude or the removal of organs." The definition and criminalization of trafficking in the Palermo Protocol include both cross-border and intraborder acts. The consent of a victim is irrelevant if any of the means mentioned above was used. Acts perpetrated against persons under eighteen years of age are considered trafficking regardless of the means used, even in cases in which none of the listed means was used. Attempting to traffic in persons, to organize or direct other persons to commit the crime, or to participate as an accomplice are also criminalized.

The protocol is not limited to criminalizing trafficking in persons only, but also includes stipulations on victim protection and repatriation and general regulations concerning crime prevention and information exchange.

The Palermo Protocol is an organic continuation of the international regulation of trafficking in persons, which started in the early 1900s. At the same time it brings together the two separate lines of regulation. For the first time, all forms of trafficking are regulated in the same treaty by similar stipulations.

It is also the first major international treaty in which "trafficking in persons" is defined in detail. This definition varies in some substantial ways from how "trafficking" was used in earlier international treaties, especially the 1949 convention. The scope of criminalization in the protocol is similar to those in the 1910 and 1921 conventions, although the use of the concept is more restricted. As in the earlier treaties on prostitution and in the treaties on slave trade, trafficking in the Palermo Protocol includes both international (cross-border) and national (intraborder) activity. However, whereas the 1904, 1910, and 1921 conventions used trafficking as a synonym for all organized prostitution (although in the case of adults they criminalized only forced prostitution) and the 1949 convention criminalized all forms of the exploitation of prostitution of others, regardless of how it was perpetrated and organized, the Palermo Protocol considers and criminalizes as trafficking only those forms of exploitation of prostitution in which the free will of the prostitute has been violated by force, coercion, or fraud. The objective is not to regulate prostitution, but to combat organized crime, and prostitution is only one among the many forms of exploitation mentioned in the third article of the treaty as constituting the illegal purpose in trafficking.

B. Trafficking in Current U.S. and E.U. Legislation

The stipulations of the Palermo Protocol form the basis for both the U.S. and the E.U. legislation regulating crimes of trafficking. However, some differences can be observed.

In the United States the regulation of trafficking is based on the Trafficking Victims Protection Act (TVPA; 22 U.S.C. 7101 et seq.), passed by the Congress in 2000, and amended in 2003 by the Trafficking Victims Protection Reauthorization Act ("Trafficking in Persons Report" 2004, pp. 24–27). Severe forms of trafficking in persons are defined as:

a) sex trafficking in which a commercial sex act is induced by force, fraud, or coercion, or in which the person induced to perform such an act has not attained 18 years of age; or

b) the recruitment, harbouring, transportation, provision, or obtaining of a person for labour or services, through the use of force, fraud, or coercion for the purpose of subjection to involuntary servitude, peonage, debt bondage, or slavery.

The U.S. legislation includes traces of the former dichotomy separating trafficking for commercial sex from other forms of trafficking. "Sex trafficking" comprises the recruitment, harboring, transportation, provision, or obtaining of a person for the purpose of a commercial sex act. The concept "commercial sex act" is defined to mean any sex act on account of which anything of value is given to or received by any person. It should be noted that neither "prostitution" nor "commercial sex act" has so far been defined in the international treaties.

The definition in U.S. legislation is fairly broad. It is, however, much simpler than many other attempts to define prostitution found in national legislation.[23] "Coercion" is defined in American law in more detailed terms than in the Palermo Protocol. It comprises not only threats of serious harm or physical restraint against a person, but also "any scheme, plan or pattern intended to cause a person to believe that failure to perform an act would result in serious harm to or physical restraint against any person, and the abuse or threatened abuse of the legal process."

[23] So far, there exists no generally accepted international definition of prostitution that would cover the whole phenomenon and meet the needs of both research and legislation. One reason for this is that the creation of such a definition is very difficult if not outright impossible. This is also why the international treaties regulating prostitution have never tried to define the phenomenon they regulate (Turunen 1996, p. 10).

In the same way as in the Palermo Protocol, the criteria of trafficking in the TVPA do not require that a trafficking victim be physically transported from one location to another. The criteria can be met by any recruitment, harboring, transportation, provision, or obtaining of a person for the enumerated purposes.

In E.U. legislation the central stipulation is the framework decision 2002/629/JHA:

1. Each Member State shall take the necessary measures to ensure that the following acts are punishable: the recruitment, transportation, transfer, harbouring, subsequent reception of a person, including exchange or transfer of control over that person, where:
   (a) use is made of coercion, force or threat, including abduction, or
   (b) use is made of deceit or fraud, or
   (c) there is an abuse of authority or of a position of vulnerability, which is such that the person has no real and acceptable alternative but to submit to the abuse involved, or
   (d) payments or benefits are given or received to achieve the consent of a person having control over another person for the purpose of exploitation of that person's labour or services, including at least forced or compulsory labour or services, slavery or practices similar to slavery or servitude, or for the purpose of the exploitation of the prostitution of others or other forms of sexual exploitation, including in pornography.

2. The consent of a victim of trafficking in human beings to the exploitation, intended or actual, shall be irrelevant where any of the means set forth in paragraph 1 have been used.
3. When the conduct referred to in paragraph 1 involves a child, it shall be a punishable trafficking offense even if none of the means set forth in paragraph 1 have been used.
4. For the purpose of this Framework Decision, "child" shall mean any person below 18 years of age.

Article 1 obligates the member states to ensure that trafficking in human beings is punishable. The commission stressed trafficking especially as a gender problem: "In particular, women and children are vulnerable to become victims of trafficking due to inter alia lack of education and professional opportunities . . . a comprehensive policy therefore needs to include a clear gender perspective" (Document COM 2000, p. 854). The definition adopted is, however, gender-neutral and reflects the key elements in the Palermo Protocol. The act of the perpetrator is defined identically, but the exchange or transfer of control over a person is added. In addition, the offense includes a requirement that the act be perpetrated by coercion, fraud, or other criminal means listed in the article and that the purpose of the act is to exploit the victim in forced labor, in prostitution, or in other ways. Trade in organs was left out of the forms of exploitation listed in the decision. In the original proposal, trafficking for sexual exploitation and for other forms of exploitation was regulated in separate articles. According to that proposal, "sexual exploitation" includes the purposes to exploit a person in prostitution, in pornographic performances, or in production of pornographic material (COM 2000, p. 854).

The criteria of the criminal offense do not include a requirement that the victim cross a border. The stipulation in this respect follows both the Palermo Protocol and the Europol Convention. Moreover, it is stressed that the key elements of the offense should focus on the exploitative purpose, rather than on the "movement" (COM 2000, p. 854).

As in the Palermo Protocol, the consent of a victim is always irrelevant if any of the means mentioned were used. Acts perpetrated against persons under age eighteen are to be considered as trafficking regardless of the means used, even when none of the listed means was used.

Article 2 criminalizes instigation of, aiding, abetting, and attempting to commit trafficking for the purpose of labor or sexual exploitation. Article 3 concerns the aggravated circumstances of trafficking. Four circumstances that typically should qualify trafficking as aggravated are listed. These circumstances represent a minimum list; additional definitions are possible in the legislation of the member states. Trafficking is considered as aggravated if the offense deliberately or by gross negligence endangered the life of the victim, the offense was committed against a victim who was particularly vulnerable, or the offense was committed by use of serious violence or caused particularly serious harm to the victim. Trafficking is also considered aggravated when it is committed within the framework of a criminal organization. This stipulation is to be applied in accordance with article 1 of the 98/733/ JHA Joint Action, which makes it a criminal offense to participate in a criminal organization in the member countries of the European Union.

C. Trafficking and Human Smuggling

According to the Palermo Protocol, "smuggling of migrants" means "the procurement, in order to obtain, directly or indirectly, a financial or other material benefit, of the illegal entry of a person into a state of which the person is not a national or a permanent resident." According to the protocol, "illegal entry" means crossing borders without complying with the necessary requirements for legal entry into the receiving state. The key component in human smuggling is always the crossing of international borders, a requirement that does not apply in trafficking.

Trafficking as defined in the Palermo Protocol has as a legal concept no links at all to human smuggling or illegal migration. Trafficking concerns forced or fraudulent trade and exploitation of humans; whether an illegal crossing of international borders has taken place during this trade or exploitation is irrelevant. However, in everyday life, trafficking, human smuggling, and illegal migration are closely related and hard to distinguish.

Distinguishing the two phenomena not only has theoretical interest but is of utmost importance in terms of the rights of the individuals involved. The definition of an act as smuggling or as trafficking has a direct effect on the situation of the objects of the action. In trafficking in persons, the objects are treated as victims of crime and often are entitled to various special protective measures. In human smuggling, the objects are usually treated as accomplices in crime, or at least as illegal immigrants, and their legal status is considerably weaker (Pärssinen 2003, pp. 13–15).

In principle, human smuggling is always based on free mutual consent of the parties; trafficking, by contrast, is based on fraud, force, or coercion. In the "Trafficking in Persons Report" of 2004 of the U.S. State Department, this is seen as the distinction between trafficking and smuggling. According to the report, victims of trafficking may have initially consented, but their consent has been negated (i.e., should be seen as negated) by the coercive, deceptive, or abusive actions of the traffickers. It may be questioned how clear a definition this is when applied to everyday smuggling and trafficking. It is often difficult to find out whether the persons involved have consented and to what they have consented. In practice, fraud and coercion, at least to some degree, are involved in almost all human smuggling actions.

A clearer distinguishing element between trafficking and human smuggling is the trafficker's purpose of exploitation in the destination country; this is always an elementary part of trafficking but should be lacking in human smuggling. Although many smuggled migrants end up in exploitative situations, if the future exploitation is implied in the process of smuggling, the activity should always be considered as human trafficking. If there exists no evidence of such a purpose, it may be mere human smuggling (Pärssinen 2003, pp. 13–15; "Trafficking in Persons Report" 2004, p. 18).

According to the current stipulations of the United Nation, the United States, and the European Union, the mere facilitation of illegal entry into or through a country is never trafficking, even though it be undertaken in dangerous or degrading conditions, if the smuggled persons have consented, and if a purpose of exploitation is lacking.

D. *Victims and Victim Protection*

International legislation concerning the rights and legal status of victims of trafficking was for a long time substantially different in the activities covered by the antislavery treaties and in those coming under the antiprostitition treaties.

The antislavery treaties included almost no general victim protection stipulations. The only provision that could be seen as such was article 4 of the 1956 convention, which stated that any slave taking refuge on board any vessel of the signatory states was ipso facto free. However, as slave trade, slavery, and related forms of servitude were criminalized, the objects of the activities usually had the full rights and status of a victim of crime in national courts and authorities.

The number of victim protection mechanisms in the antiprostitution treaties was substantially larger. The 1904 convention included two such stipulations. In article 3 the signatories were obliged to provide temporary protection for victims of white slave traffic, when such protection was not available from NGOs or private individuals. Article 4, again, included regulations concerning repatriation costs. The costs were to be shared between the country of origin and the country of residence (if the repatriated prostitute or her relatives could not pay the costs themselves).

In the 1949 convention, victim protection provisions were greatly increased. Article 5 guaranteed foreigners and nationals equal rights in the courts and in the authorities as injured parties. Article 6 obliged the signatories to repeal or abolish laws, regulations, or administrative provisions that subjected prostitutes to special registration or other special requirements for supervision or notification. Significant, at least in principle, was a stipulation in article 16 that obliged the signatories not only to general prevention of prostitution but also to rehabilitation and social adjustment of the victims of prostitution and related trafficking. The stipulation was, however, only a declaration of principle that did not give rise to concrete obligations. The stipulations of the 1904 convention (concerning the temporary care and maintenance of the victims before repatriation and the sharing of the repatriation costs) were included in article 19:

> Article 19. The Parties to the present Convention undertake, in accordance with the conditions laid down by domestic law without prejudice to prosecution or other action for violations thereunder and so far as possible:
>   1. Pending the completion of arrangements for the repatriation of destitute victims of international traffic in persons for the purpose of prostitution, to make suitable provision for their temporary care and maintenance;
>   2. To repatriate persons referred to in article 18 [alien prostitutes] who desire to be repatriated or who may be claimed by persons exercising authority over them or whose expulsion is ordered in conformity with the law. Repatriation shall take place only after agreement is reached with the State of destination as to identity and nationality as well as to the place and date of arrival at frontiers. Each Party to the present Convention shall facilitate the passage of such persons through its territory.
> Where the persons referred to in the preceding paragraph cannot themselves repay the cost of repatriation and have neither spouse, relatives nor guardian to pay for them, the cost of repatriation as far as the nearest frontier or port of embarkation or airport in the direction of the State of origin shall be borne by the State where they are in residence, and the cost of the remainder of the journey shall be borne by the State of origin.

The main objective was the security and well-being of the state, society, and law-abiding citizens (their protection from costs caused by international prostitution). The needs of victims of trafficking came second. However, the main problem (considering the rights of the victims) was that there were very few injured parties in the activities regulated and criminalized by the treaties who could enjoy the guaranteed rights. Most of the crimes (e.g., pandering) defined by the 1949 convention and its predecessors were crimes against the state. Although the aim of the treaty system created in 1904–49 was to a large extent to protect women against prostitution and related trafficking, the legal status of those engaged in prostitution and those who were victims of related trafficking was left mostly undefined, and the victim protection stipulations could not replace this major defect. Consequently, the status of the objects of pandering and other forms of exploitation of prostitution was much weaker than that of the victims of slavery or the slave trade. As the treaties criminalized only the supportive services of prostitution but did not take any clear stand on prostitution itself, neither legalizing nor criminalizing it, they contributed to creating and maintaining a legal limbo for prostitution and prostitutes in many countries and consequently facilitated the exploitation of persons engaged in prostitution.

The Palermo Protocol and the consequent shift to consideration of trafficking in the context of combating and prevention of organized crime has standardized the legal status of the victims of different forms of trafficking and has substantially improved the situation concerning the victims of prostitution-related trafficking, at least in principle. The protocol is the first international treaty concerning trafficking that includes extensive victim protection mechanisms.

The victims are guaranteed not only the full legal status and rights of a victim of crime in the courts and authorities of the signatory states, but article 7 also includes stipulations that aim to improve victims' chances of obtaining residence permits in the country to which they have been trafficked.

Under article 6, victims are entitled to the protection of their physical safety and privacy; adequate legal assistance and counseling; interpreting services; appropriate housing; medical, psychological, and material assistance; employment; and educational and training opportunities. In application of the rights, the age, gender, and special needs of the victims must be taken into account. Article 8 regulates procedures and conditions of repatriation of victims. Although the framework remains state-centered, the needs of victims are in a more central position than in the prostitution treaties of 1904–49. Repatriation must take place with due regard to the safety of the victim and preferably be voluntary.

The Palermo Protocol has been criticized because the aim of abolition of prostitution in the 1904–49 treaties has been replaced by the prohibition only of forced prostitution (Niemi-Kiesiläinen 2004, p. 455). This is no doubt true, but when considered from the perspective of the status and the rights of victims, the protocol represents substantial improvement. Victims whom the antiprostitition treaties dealt with as vague "victims of conditions" with no defined legal rights have obtained a defined legal status as victims of crime with consequent legal rights.

This does not mean that the situation in individual countries and their legislation is satisfactory. Enactment of the provisions of the Palermo Protocol in national legislation remains incomplete in several signatories, and obligations imposed by the treaty have been interpreted in diverse ways, often very narrowly. It is to be hoped that efforts will continue to define more explicitly the legal status of prostitution and persons engaged in it and to clarify the present indeterminate state of affairs in many countries.

E. The Diverse Definitions of Trafficking in Persons

The international treaties, and the U.S. and E.U. legislation, today define trafficking in persons almost identically. This is not surprising because current U.S. and E.U. legislation are, to a large extent, based on the Palermo Protocol. The crime of trafficking in persons, whether prostitution-related or not, comprises three elements, all of which are crucial: the act of the perpetrator, how the act is committed, and the purpose of exploitation. If any element is missing, the activity is not trafficking.

The situation is not equally clear in scientific or social debate, since different organizations, individuals, and scholars have preferences of their own and laudable enthusiasm to develop their own concepts and definitions.[24] For example, only activities crossing international borders are regarded as trafficking by some researchers and NGOs, whereas all forms of organized prostitution are included in the phenomenon by

---

[24] See, e.g., the recent article by Kleimenov and Shamkov (2004), which includes altogether three substantially differing definitions, all different from the Palermo definition.

others (Kleimenov and Shamkov 2004). The diverse uses of the concept are due to the heterogeneity of the phenomenon itself; definitions depend on the dimensions of the phenomenon under consideration and the context. It is probably impossible to create a definition of trafficking in persons that satisfactorily encapsulates all its aspects.

The current definition in international legislation is criticized mainly for concentrating too much on pre-exploitation activities and for not addressing the outcome of the trafficking (the situation the victim is placed into) or the abuses victims experience (IOM 2004, p. 10). For example, the Bangladesh report of the IOM interprets "for the purpose of exploitation" in the definition of the Palermo Protocol to exclude the actual exploitation process itself and thus leads to a focus on recruitment, movement, and transport at the expense of the exploitation phase.

To change this, it proposes a new paradigm that addresses the phenomenon from the perspective of the harm caused by trafficking itself. The factors that should be incorporated are loss of control (whether a person can leave the situation if he or she wishes to), third-party involvement (are third parties benefiting or participating in placing or maintaining a person in an exploitative situation?), commercial nature (the exploitation must produce some kind of commercial gains for a third party), time (trafficking usually has a clear beginning and ending), violation of human rights and national laws, and mobility (within or across borders) (IOM 2004, pp. 10, 23–27).

The definition in the Palermo Protocol has its own defects, nor is it ideologically acceptable to everyone. However, to make it possible to study, discuss, and combat trafficking in persons internationally, a homogeneous, clear, and short definition is needed. The definition in the Palermo Protocol is the best solution so far.

IV. Numbers and Geography

There are several ways to measure the volume of trafficking in women, the most common being numbers of victims and financial amounts involved. As hard data about victims are scarce, most estimates are based on either reported crimes or the number of active prostitutes. In the first case, there usually exists some link to reality even if police information in many countries suffers from reliability problems. In the latter case, estimates are often based only on other estimates. When the number of reported crimes is used as the base figure, it is typically multiplied by a factor correcting for the dark number of unknown and unreported crimes, which is often purely theoretical (80 or 90 percent of cases missing seems to be the most common assumption). When the estimates are based on the number of people engaged in prostitution, the methods are more varied. Some are based on the assumption that the percentage of prostitutes who are victims of trafficking is the same all over the world. Others treat all migrant and underage prostitutes as victims and add a suitable percentage of domestic adult prostitutes to the total (see, e.g., Aromaa 2005, p. 9; Poulin 2005).

The economic aspects of the crime are usually measured as total turnover or total profits in the local or some other currency, or as a percentage of gross domestic product. These estimates are normally based on scattered national information on the profits per victim of separate trafficking or pandering operations, multiplied by the estimated annual total number of the victims (see Jahic and Finckenauer 2005, p. 29).

Here we discuss mainly information concerning the numbers of victims. This information is more abundant than that on economic aspects of trafficking, but it is also the basis for most of the economic volume calculations. Thus the problems of the victim estimates are usually multiplied in the latter.

In spite of the difficulties, it is not impossible to measure the volume of global trafficking. This would require, however, considerable basic research work in all the major nation-states involved. A good example of how this kind of research could be carried out is provided by Kelly and Regan (2000) for the United Kingdom; they combined diverse data from police, NGOs, media, immigration, and other sources (pp. 6–8, 16–22). Similar projects have been carried out in Spain and Italy (Mon-Eu-Traf 2002).

A. Global Volume

Estimates of the number of people trafficked each year worldwide for sexual or economic exploitation vary between 600,000 and more than 4 million (Flam 2003; "Trafficking in Persons Report" 2004, pp. 46, 54). Table 1 shows recent estimates, drawn from a wide range of sources that we discuss in this section.

The U.S. State Department estimates that 600,000–800,000 persons are trafficked across international borders annually, 80 percent of

TABLE 1
Global Trafficking Volumes for Sexual Exploitation, Prostitution

Area Given Assistance	Identified Victims in Reported Crimes or Assisted by NGOs/Authorities (Year)	Estimated Number				
		Victims Trafficked within Region (Year)	Victims Trafficked to/through Region (Year)	Victims Trafficked from Region (Year)	People Engaged in Prostitution, Region	Child Prostitutes
Nordic	0–50	0	100–1,000	0	<10,000	<100
Baltic	50–500	1,000–10,000	1,000–10,000	1,000–10,000	<25,000	>1,000
Western Europe	3,000–5,000		50,000–100,000		260,000–500,000	>20,000
Central Europe	500–2,000		100,000[a]		60,000–70,000	<5,000
Balkans	1,500–2,000		>70,000	200,000[a]	>200,000	>60,000
Mediterranean			10,000–50,000		100,000–140,000	>5,000
Eastern Europe	>300			5,000–100,000	>200,000	>100,000

North America	50,000–120,000		>1,000,000	200,000
Central America	10,000–20,000[b]		>100,000	>10,000
Caribbean	10,000–20,000[c]		>300,000	>30,000
South America	300,000–2,000,000[b]		<10,000,000	<3,000,000
East Asia	300,000–1,500,000[b]	>110,000	>3,000,000	>1,000,000
Southeast Asia	200,000–3,000,000[b]		>2,500,000	>1,000,000
South Asia	250,000–500,000[b]		<10,000,000	<3,000,000
Central Asia			>10,000	>10,000
Middle East	10,000–50,000[b]	1,000–15,000[a]	>20,000	>20,000
Oceania	<10,000		>30,000	>30,000
North Africa	>10,000[b]		>500,000	5,000
West Africa		50,000–100,000[b]	>500,000	<100,000
Central Africa		10,000–100,000[b]	>500,000	>100,000
East Africa		10,000–50,000[b]	>500,000	>100,000
Southern Africa	50,000–100,000[b]		>500,000	>50,000

[a] Trafficked through and out.
[b] Trafficked within, to, through, and out.
[c] Trafficked within, to, and through.

whom are women and 50 percent children. The number of female victims would thus be 400,000–650,000 each year. The IOM gives a fairly similar figure: 700,000 women and children trafficked across international borders annually. Both estimates include all forms of trafficking (IOM 2001a; "Trafficking in Persons Report" 2004, pp. 46, 53). If we use the data from Europe and Asia, according to which 70–90 percent of female and child victims are trafficked for sexual exploitation, as the basis for global estimates, the annual maximum volume of this kind of trafficking would be between 500,000 and 650,000. This does not include intraborder trafficking.

The U.S. State Department estimates 2 million to 4 million people are victims each year in global domestic trafficking. Under the assumption that the percentage of victims of prostitution-related trafficking is the same as in the cross-border traffic, this would mean 1 million to 3 million victims annually. The total number of victims of prostitution-related trafficking would thus be 1.5 and 3.7 million a year. According to the IOM, the number of women trafficked annually for prostitution to and within Europe only is about 500,000 ("Trafficking in Persons Report" 2004, pp. 46, 54).

The estimates are fairly high if compared with similar estimates of the number of migrant prostitutes in the world, which vary between 500,000 and 800,000 (De Tapia 2003, p. 29). They are fairly low, however, compared with estimates of the number of child prostitutes around the world (according to the Palermo definitions, most child prostitutes fulfill the criteria of victims of trafficking). The number of minors in prostitution in Europe and North America (where the estimates can be considered fairly reliable) is about 400,000.

According to the national and regional estimates referred to in the following pages, the annual volume of trafficking for sexual exploitation would be several millions. The number of minors engaged in organized child prostitution around the world according to these estimates is somewhere between 5 and 10 million.

A major problem when analyzing the existing estimates is not only that neither the definition of trafficking nor the sources of data that have been used are usually mentioned, but it is also rarely said to what the figures actually refer. Do they refer to persons or border crossings? Do they comprise only those trafficked across international borders or also the victims trafficked within countries? Do they include only new recruits or also victims of earlier years whose exploitation continues?

There are additional problems with regional estimates. The same persons in principle can and even should appear in the estimates of several countries at the same time. For example, a victim abducted in Ukraine and transferred through the Balkan route to Belgium in theory should be included in the figures of six to ten countries and, thus, would appear as six to ten victims in joint European statistics (which do not exist). A victim can also appear several times in the estimates of a single country. For example, a foreigner who is trafficked into a country, exploited there in several different towns, and then again trafficked out of the country should be counted in the statistics of those trafficked into, out of, and within that single country and thus count as at least three different victims. Considering these problems, only data concerning native victims trafficked out of and within each country should be used as the basis of the international estimates. This rule, however, is impossible to apply. For many countries, only estimates concerning the aggregate numbers of victims are available, the use of which (even considering their gaps) inevitably inflates regional and global numbers. The fact is that currently there exist no data to serve as bases for reliable estimates on the global volume of prostitution-related trafficking (defined on the basis of the Palermo criteria).

According to the minimum figures in table 1 concerning people trafficked out of or within each region, the estimated numbers of victims are 300,000 for Europe and Russia, 50,000 for North America, 500,000 for East Asia, 250,000 for South Asia, 200,000 for Southeast Asia, 300,000 for Latin America, and 120,000 for Africa, making together 1.7 million people. The corresponding number of persons trafficked out of the major geographical regions is about 400,000.[25]

These figures correspond fairly well with those given by the U.S. State Department: 1.5 million as the annual minimum figure for the victims of global cross- and intraborder trafficking and 500,000 for cross-border trafficking only ("Trafficking in Persons Report" 2004, pp. 53–54). This, however, says nothing of their reliability: the figures correspond mainly because the sources have probably been to a large extent the same.

The World Bank recently reported the global total of legal immigrants and refugees in the early 1980s to be about 100 million and to

---

[25] According to these figures the victim rates per 100,000 population would be Europe and Russia, 37; North America, 15; East Asia, 34; Southeast Asia, 39; South Asia, 19; Latin America, 73; and Africa, 15.

have increased considerably since then (Russell 2005, pp. 2–3). The IOM estimates the current global volume of labor migration at about 150 million (*Labour Migration* 2005). A Council of Europe report estimates the global number of irregular immigrants as over 30 million (De Tapia 2003, p. 29). For the annual volume of human smuggling, Babha (2005) estimates some 800,000 (his sources are not indicated). All these estimates, referring either to the total volume of migrants at a given time or to annual migration flows, are as hazy as those concerning the estimates of trafficking. They are, however, as a rule much more moderate. The minimum estimate referred to above of 400,000–500,000 victims of prostitution-related cross-border trafficking annually, compared with the estimates concerning the annual flows of irregular migration, suggests that the bulk of irregular migration in the world consists of prostitution-related trafficking. As this cannot be true, either the current estimates concerning global irregular migration are much too low or those concerning global prostitution-related cross-border trafficking are much too high.

The regional estimates in the following pages suggest that about 30 million people are engaged in prostitution around the world. This estimate should be treated with caution because in some countries the figures we use refer to registered prostitutes, in other countries to estimated professional prostitutes, and in yet other countries to the joint number of professional and part-time prostitutes. For countries for which official or NGO estimates have not been available, we have estimated the number on the basis of the numbers of professional prostitutes given for neighboring countries and the total population. If the estimate of 30 million is, however, more or less right, the minimum estimate of 1.7 million victims of prostitution-related trafficking would make up about 6 percent of the total of people engaged in prostitution around the world. Many of the national estimates do not include domestic organized child prostitution and also omit victims trafficked in earlier years whose exploitation is continuing, so the real minimum estimate is very likely higher than 1.7 million. Maybe even the U.S. State Department maximum of 3.7 million is not high enough. This means that as many as 10–15 percent of those involved in prostitution globally are victims of trafficking—an average percentage not too unlikely, even if large fluctuations across regions may be observed.

In the following pages we try to give the most recent figures and estimates concerning the annual minimum and maximum numbers of

victims of trafficking, people engaged in prostitution, and children engaged in prostitution from each major geographic area and compare
them with the estimates given by the international organizations. The
estimates have been collected mainly from the Web sites of global-
march and protectionproject and from the IOM and Mon-Eu-Traf reports. One should treat all these figures with caution.

B. Europe and Russia

The highest estimates of prostitution-related trafficking in Europe
come from Human Rights Watch, the Swedish NGO "Kvinna till
kvinna," and from Maltzahn in the Australian Women Conference
(2001) (it is probable that they all are based on a common unmentioned
source), which give 500,000 women and children as the annual volume
of trafficking *to the E.U. old member countries* (E.U. 15) (or, alternatively,
to "western Europe"). According to the latest IOM estimate, the volume of trafficking *to and within the whole continent* is 500,000 annually
(whether this is based on the same source as those above is not clear,
but it is significantly more moderate, since it also includes the countries
outside the pre-2004 E.U. borders). Trafficking to the European
Union[26] from and through the Balkans would be 120,000 women and
children a year, and from the whole of eastern Europe about 200,000
women and children. According to the latest estimate of the U.S. Drug
Enforcement Administration (DEA), 200,000 women and children are
trafficked through the Balkans each year (a figure fairly similar to that
of IOM) (*Organized Crime Situation Report* 2001, p. 41; Hajdinjak 2002,
p. 51; Laczko, Klekowski von Koppenfels, and Barthel 2002, p. 4;
"Trafficking in Persons Report" 2004, p. 46; *Trafficking of Nigerian Girls
to Italy* 2004; fpmail.friends-partners.org; www.janes.com; www1.umn
.edu/humanrts/usdocs).

The volume of trafficking for prostitution has been increasing in
Europe for the last fifteen years. Table 2 presents recent estimates,
drawn from sources discussed in this subsection. The demand for prostitution and other sexual services has been increasing in western Europe, and the former socialist countries in central and eastern Europe
with their current economic and social problems offer a source area
from which trafficking to western Europe can be organized far more
easily and more economically than from the old source areas (Southeast

---

[26] These estimates refer to the pre-2004 member countries only.

TABLE 2

Estimates, Trafficking for Sexual Exploitation, Prostitution, Europe

Country	Role	Full-Time Prostitutes	Foreign Prostitutes	Annual Trafficking Victims	Proportion European Victims
Albania	s, t	?	?	>10,000	Majority
Armenia	s, t	?	?	500–700	Majority
Austria	d, t	6,000–12,000	5,000–10,000	?	80–90%
Azerbaijan	s, t	?	?	?	Majority
Belarus	s,t	?	?	?	Majority
Belgium	d	30,000	>15,000	1,000–3,000	>50%
Bosnia	d, s, t	15,000	10,000	>10,000	Majority
Bulgaria	s, t	?	?	3,000–4,000	Majority
Croatia	t	?	?	100–200	90–100%
Czech Republic	d, s, t	?	?	>100	Majority
Denmark	d	6,000	2,000	10–50	90–100%
Eire	d, t	?	>10%	?	Majority
Estonia	s	2,000–5,000	<1,000	?	100%
Finland	d	3,000–7,000	3,000–6,000	10–100	100%
France	d	20,000–40,000	12,000–25,000	?	Majority
Georgia	s, t	?	?	Thousands	Majority
Germany	d	60,000–300,000	30,000–150,000	2,000–20,000	80%
Great Britain	d, t	80,000	20,000	1,500	>50%
Greece	d, t	>20,000	16,000–20,000	<40,000	90%
Hungary	d, s, t	10,000	3,000–4,000	?	Majority
Iceland	d	<500	<500	A few	Significant part
Italy	d, t	50,000–70,000	30,000–40,000	2,500–5,500	Majority
Kosovo	d, s, t	Thousands	Thousands	<30,000	Majority
Latvia	s	2,500–9,000	?	<1,500	100%
Lithuania	s	3,000–10,000	500–3,000	<10,000	100%
Luxemburg	d	300	300	<300	?
Macedonia	d, s, t	>2,500	1,500–2,500	8,000–18,000	90–100%
Moldova	s, t	?	?	>10,000	Majority
Netherlands	d	20,000–30,000	13,000–20,000	1,000–3,000	>50%
Norway	d	3,000	600–1,000	10–50	90–100%
Poland	d, s, t	30,000–35,000	>15,000	>15,000	Majority
Portugal	d, t	Lisbon 6,500	Half	Thousands	Significant part
Romania	s, t	?	?	>10,000	90–100%
Russia	d, s, t	?	Thousands	10,000–100,000	Majority
Serbia and Montenegro	d, s, t	?	?	Thousands	Majority
Slovakia	s, t	?	?	>25	Majority
Slovenia	t	?	?	?	Majority
Spain	d, t	45,000	>27,000	4,000–8,500	20%
Sweden	d	1,200–2,500	200–700	10–100	90–100%
Switzerland	d	7,000–8,000	2,000–4,000	?	<50%

TABLE 2 (*Continued*)

Country	Role	Full-Time Prostitutes	Foreign Prostitutes	Annual Trafficking Victims	Proportion European Victims
Turkey	d, t	?	>60,000	>1,000	Majority
Ukraine	s, t	?	?	10,000–100,000	Majority

NOTE.—d = destination, s = source, and t = transit.

Asia, West Africa, and Latin America). Estimates of the annual turnover vary from 100 million euros to several milliards of euros (*Organized Crime Situation Report* 2001, p. 41; Hajdinjak 2002, p. 51; fpmail.friends-partners.org).

The majority of victims come from Albania, Lithuania, Moldova, Romania, Russia, and Ukraine. Of the victims of coerced prostitution assisted by the IOM in the last few years, about half have been Moldovians, a quarter Romanians, and a tenth Ukrainian. Trafficking in women to Europe from other continents has significance mainly in the Mediterranean countries and in western Europe. The main source areas are Southeast Asia (Thailand), Latin America (Colombia, Brazil, and the Dominican Republic), and North and West Africa (Morocco, Nigeria, and Sierra Leone). According to Europol, the extent of this trade has remained about the same in recent years. The increase in Europe is due to trafficking from eastern Europe (*Organized Crime Situation Report* 2001, p. 41; fpmail.friends-partners.org/pipermail/stop-traffic).

Concerning trafficking in women, Europe is divided into two parts: the old member countries of the European Union serve as a destination area, and central Europe, the Balkans, and the Confederation of Independent States (CIS) countries serve as source and transit areas. Irregular immigration as a whole has six main routes to and inside Europe: from Moscow through Lithuania, Poland, or the Czech Republic to Germany and Austria; from Ukraine through Slovakia, Hungary, the Czech Republic, or Poland to Austria and Germany; from the Middle East and Turkey to Greece and Italy; from North Africa to Spain and Italy; from Turkey through the Balkans to Italy and Austria; and from South and Central America to Portugal and Spain. These routes also serve as the main routes of trafficking in persons (NCIS 2002, p. 34).

Tables 1 and 2 show the volume of victims of prostitution-related trafficking and numbers of persons engaged in prostitution in the major geographic regions of Europe based on the latest data and estimates available in different European countries. The main sources are the reports of the IOM and STOP-project (Hollmen and Jyrkinen 1999; *A Study: Trafficking in Women* 2001; Laczko, Klekowski von Koppenfels, and Barthel 2002), and some national summaries (Mon-Eu-Traf 2002; Mon-Eu-Traf II 2004). The data mainly describe the situation in 1999–2001.

1. *Northern Europe (Denmark, Estonia, Finland, Iceland, Latvia, Lithuania, Norway, Sweden).* Trafficking in northern Europe is regionally internal to a large extent. The main destination area is the Nordic countries: Denmark, Finland, Norway, and Sweden, the source area being the Baltic countries and northwestern Russia. A secondary destination area consists of the Baltic countries, to which women are trafficked from Russia, Ukraine, and other CIS countries. Prostitution from Lithuania and Latvia is mainly directed to Germany, Sweden, and Denmark; and prostitution from Estonia and northwestern Russia to Finland, northern Norway, and western Europe. A significant number of Baltic and Russian prostitutes are also active outside Europe in North America, the Middle East, and the Far East (*Kännedom om prostitution* 2000, pp. 27–29; *Norwegian Report on Anti-trafficking Activities* 2000; *Trafficking in Women* 2001, pp. 71, 110–11, 123–28, 210–26; *EU Organized Crime Report* 2002, pp. 45, 76; Lehti and Aromaa 2002, pp. 50–69; Moustgaard 2002, pp. 4–9; Leskinen 2003, pp. 9–28).

Prostitution from Russia and the Baltic countries to Scandinavia is mostly mobile; prostitutes come as tourists and work for a few days or a couple of weeks. Organization seems usually to be fairly loose. The recent entry of the Baltic countries into the European Union (and the consequent relaxing of border controls) has further loosened the grips of panderers of Baltic prostitution in Scandinavia (Kontula 2005, p. 39).

The volume of foreign prostitution in the Nordic countries increased rapidly in the 1990s, but the number of cases of coerced prostitution reported to the police remained almost nonexistent. The number of women from Russia and the Baltic countries who work in Nordic prostitution is estimated to be 5,000–10,000. The annual number of victims is probably a couple of hundred at the highest, although much higher figures have occasionally been referred to in public discussion. The low number of reported crimes and the overall loose organization of prostitution do not, however, support these claims.

Internal prostitution in the Baltic countries and northwestern Russia is likely to employ full-time 30,000–50,000 persons. The number involved in part-time prostitution is considerably higher. Most prostitutes working in the Nordic countries also work in prostitution in their home countries. No estimates are available of the number of victims of trafficking in the internal prostitution of the Baltic countries or northwestern Russia, but it is probably higher than in the Scandinavian countries (Lehti and Aromaa 2002, pp. 50–69; Lehti 2003, pp. 9–14; Leskinen 2003, pp. 13–14).

In all three Baltic countries, most workers in the sex business are natives, especially members of the Russian-speaking minority formed by immigrants of the Soviet era. The core of Baltic prostitutes in western Europe and Scandinavia consists of local professional prostitutes, whose numbers are estimated at 2,000–3,000 in Estonia, 2,500–9,000 in Latvia, and 3,000–10,000 in Lithuania. The number of foreign prostitutes is largest in Lithuania: 20–30 percent of all full-time prostitutes in the country. Most come from the Kaliningrad enclave of Russia, Ukraine, and Belarus. In Estonia and Latvia, the source areas are the same: Russia, Ukraine, and other CIS countries; the number of foreign prostitutes is estimated to be considerably smaller. Local prostitution, the import of foreign prostitutes, and the export of local prostitutes are partly controlled by organized crime in all three Baltic countries.

The number of minors in prostitution directed to the Nordic countries is almost nonexistent. In the Baltic countries and the St. Petersburg region the volume of underage prostitution is, however, considerable. The number is estimated to be hundreds in the Baltic countries and thousands in the St. Petersburg region. Their customers include many Scandinavian sex tourists (*Trafficking in Women* 2001, pp. 71, 110–11, 123–28, 210–26).

2. *Western Europe (Austria, the Benelux Countries, the British Isles, France, Germany, Liechtenstein, Monaco, Switzerland).* Western Europe is the most important destination area in Europe for prostitution-related trafficking. The victims come mainly from central Europe, the Balkans, the Baltic countries, and the CIS countries, but women and children are trafficked to the area from other continents (Latin America, Africa, and Southeast Asia), too. Table 3 shows recent estimates for selected countries.

TABLE 3

Trafficking Volumes, Source Areas, Western Europe

Country	Identified Victims Trafficked into Country, Reported Crimes (Year)	Estimated Annual Victims Trafficked into Country	Source Areas
Austria	150 (2000)	?	IE and CIS 81%; LA 10%; other 9%
Belgium	270 (2000)	1,000–3,000	IE 23%; CIS 21%; EU 1%; AF 26%; LA 8%; AS 20%
France	700–900 (2000–2003)	?	NT 23%; IE and CIS 43%; AF 27%
Germany	926 (2000)	2,000–20,000	IE 54%; CIS 28%; AF 3%; AS 5%; other 10%
Netherlands	289 (1999), 203 (2000)	3,500	IE 25%; CIS 17%; EU 7%; AF 28%; LA 5%; AS 10%; other 9%
United Kingdom	71 (1998)	142–1,420	IE and CIS 50%; AS 25%; AF and LA 25%

NOTE.—IE = new E.U. member countries and the Balkans; CIS = the CIS countries; EU = E.U. member countries; AF = Africa; LA = Latin America; AS = Asia; NT = native (source: Fijnaut et al. 1998; Laczko, Klekowski von Koppenfels, and Barthel 2002; Mon-Eu-Traf II 2004).

The number of identified victims in reported crimes or assisted annually by NGOs is 3,000–5,000. It is usually assumed that they make up only a small proportion of the total. When the estimates given by the national authorities of each individual country are added together, the annual total is at least 50,000–60,000. According to some international organizations (e.g., the IOM), it is considerably higher, even 100,000–150,000 women and children (Fijnaut et al. 1998, pp. 102–6; Hollmen and Jyrkinen 1999, pp. 12–15; Kelly and Regan 2000, pp. 18, 22; *Organised Crime Situation Report* 2001, p. 41; *Trafficking in Women* 2001, pp. 111, 226; *EU Organized Crime Report* 2002, pp. 38, 65; Laczko, Klekowski von Koppenfels, and Barthel 2002, pp. 9–13; NCIS 2002, pp. 38–39; Lehti 2003, pp. 15–20; Mon-Eu-Traf II 2004).

The number of people engaged in prostitution in the region is estimated to be 270,000–500,000, of whom over 20,000 are minors (www.globalmarch.org).

3. *Central Europe (the Czech Republic, Hungary, Poland, Slovakia, Slovenia).* The central European countries are an important transit

and secondary destination area from the Balkans and the CIS countries to western Europe. They also form a major source area for trafficking in women to Germany, Austria, the Netherlands, and Belgium (IOM 2000; Laczko, Klekowski von Koppenfels, and Barthel 2002, pp. 9–15; Travnickova 2004).

Data concerning the annual number of identified victims in reported crimes have been available only from Poland, Hungary, and the Czech Republic and mainly refer to cases, not individuals. However, when these figures are multiplied by the average numbers of victims in known cases mentioned in the literature, we get the following *annual* average numbers: Poland, 50–300; Hungary, 20–150; and the Czech Republic, 90–250. If we assume that the situation is more or less the same in Slovakia and Slovenia, this would mean 1,000–1,500 identified victims a year for the whole area (Travnickova 2004, p. 72; www.globalmarch.org).

According to the IOM, the annual volume of trafficking *from and through* central Europe is much higher, about 100,000 women and children. Poland is the main route between western Europe and eastern Europe, and a recent UNICRI report estimates the number of victims transported *through* the country to be as high as 50,000 annually. The number of women trafficked *from* central Europe has been decreasing over the course of the last decade (e.g., in the mid-1990s more than half of the foreign prostitutes assisted in Austria were from central Europe; the proportion more recently was only 15 percent). However, the volume of trafficking through the area and to the area has not decreased (Laczko, Klekowski von Koppenfels, and Barthel 2002, p. 13; Travnickova 2004, p. 39).

There are 30,000–35,000 active prostitutes in Poland, more than half of whom are foreigners. In Hungary, the number of prostitutes is estimated to be 10,000, a third of whom are foreigners, mainly Ukrainians, Russians, and Romanians. If the volume of prostitution in the Czech Republic, Slovakia, and Slovenia is about the same, there would be 60,000–70,000 people engaged in prostitution in the area (*Country Report of the Republic of Slovenia* 2000; Laczko, Klekowski von Koppenfels, and Barthel 2002, p. 9; www.globalmarch.org; www.undcp.org).

4. *The Balkans (Albania, Bosnia, Bulgaria, Croatia, Cyprus, Greece, Kosovo, Macedonia, Romania, Serbia and Montenegro, Turkey).* In the 1990s, the Balkans became the main source and transit area for trafficking in women for sexual exploitation in Europe. The primary

source countries are Albania, Bulgaria, and Romania. Bosnia, Macedonia, Montenegro, Kosovo, Serbia, and Turkey are the key transit areas. The main destinations are Greece, Turkey, and the successor states of the former Yugoslavia. Most victims trafficked into and through the Balkans come from inside the area or from Ukraine, Moldova, and Russia. The main junctions of the trade are Belgrade, Budapest, Bucharest, and Istanbul (IOM 2001*b*, 2003*a*, pp. 9–18; *Organised Crime Situation Report* 2001, p. 41; Hajdinjak 2002, pp. 52–56).

It is not possible to give exact estimates in the Balkans for individual countries. According to the DEA, the total number of victims (trafficked into, through, and from the Balkans) is about 200,000. The number of identified victims assisted by NGOs between January 2000 and June 2003 according to the IOM was 4,072 (thus an average of 1,163 a year), about 70 percent of whom originated in the area. Most of the rest (29 percent) were from Moldova, Ukraine, Russia, or Belarus.[27] In Bosnia, there were 691 victims in reported crimes or assisted by NGOs in 1999–2003; their annual numbers varied between fourteen and 255, the majority (81 percent) being Moldovans or Romanians. However, according to IOM, it is not possible to assess even the minimum number of women trafficked from the area to the European Union, Russia, or elsewhere outside the Balkans because of the absence of consolidated data (IOM 2001*b*, 2003*a*, pp. 10–11; Maljevic 2005).

The number of Balkan prostitutes working abroad is estimated to be 250,000–800,000, the majority coming from Romania, Albania, and Kosovo (www.globalmarch.org).

The Balkans are also an important destination for trafficking in women. Bosnia, Kosovo, and Macedonia alone are estimated to have about 30,000 prostitutes, a considerable number of whom work in conditions that meet the criteria of coerced prostitution. A notable part of the customers (in Bosnia, about a fifth) consists of the personnel of the international peacekeeping operations. Other major destination countries are Greece, Serbia, and Turkey. The number of victims in Greece is estimated to be up to 40,000, although the annual numbers of identified victims in the last few years have been only a few hundred (Maljevic 2005; www.globalmarch.org).

5. *The Mediterranean Countries (Andorra, Italy, Malta, Portugal, San*

---

[27] The largest single groups were Albanians (43 percent), Moldovans (22 percent), Romanians (15 percent), Bulgarians (7 percent), Ukrainians (6 percent), and Kosovars (5 percent).

TABLE 4
Trafficking Volumes, Sources Areas, Southern Europe

Country	Identified Victims Trafficked into Country, Reported Crimes (Year)	Estimated Annual Victims Trafficked into Country	Source Areas
Italy	?	2,500–5,500	IE 28%; CIS 12%; AF 52%; LA 2%; other 7%
Portugal	?	?	LA and IE
Spain	?	4,000–8,500	LA 65%; IE and CIS 20%; AF 10%; EU 5%

NOTE.—IE = new E.U. member countries and the Balkans; CIS = the CIS countries; EU = E.U. member countries; AF = Africa; LA = Latin America (source: Laczko, Klekowski von Koppenfels, and Barthel 2002; Mon-Eu-Traf 2002, pp. 50–55; Mon-Eu-Traf II 2004).

Marino, Spain). The Mediterranean countries form a major destination and transit area. In the Iberian peninsula the majority of victims come from outside of Europe (the main source area is Latin America: Colombia, Brazil, and the Dominican Republic), and trafficking for prostitution is closely connected with drug trafficking. In Italy the main source area is eastern Europe, but the proportion of victims from other continents (especially from West Africa) is substantial (*Organised Crime Situation Report* 2001, p. 41; *Trafficking in Women* 2001, p. 70; Laczko, Klekowski von Koppenfels, and Barthel 2002, p. 14; Mon-Eu-Traf 2002, pp. 41–55; Mon-Eu-Traf II 2004). Table 4 shows recent estimates for the three large countries in the region.

Statistics concerning the number of identified victims are not available, but the annual volume into and through the Mediterranean countries is estimated at 10,000–50,000 women and children.

The number of people engaged in prostitution in the area is estimated to be between 100,000 and 140,000 (Spain, 45,000; Italy, 50,000–70,000; and Portugal, 10,000–20,000). The percentage of foreigners is about 60 percent in Spain and Italy and 50 percent in Portugal (www.globalmarch.org; www.portcult.com).

6. *Eastern Europe (Moldova, Ukraine, Belarus, Russia).* Moldova, Ukraine, and Russia form one of the two main source areas for traf-

ficking in women to western Europe. The volume of Russian internal trafficking is significant, and from Russia and Ukraine great numbers of women are also recruited as prostitutes for markets outside Europe.

Recent estimates suggest that 50,000–100,000 Moldovans, over 100,000 Ukrainians, and as many as 500,000 Russians are active in international prostitution outside their home countries. Moreover, a considerable number of Russians not included in the above numbers take part in mobile prostitution in neighboring countries. The majority of Moldovan, Ukrainian, and Russian prostitutes work in Europe. Other major destinations are the Middle East, Southeast Asia, North America, China, and Japan (fpmail.friends-partners.org; Hollmen and Jyrkinen 1999, pp. 34–36, 42–43; *Organised Crime Situation Report* 2001, p. 41; www.globalmarch.org; www.uri.edu).

How many of the sex workers are victims of trafficking and coerced prostitution is impossible to estimate. The highest estimates are around 80 percent; however, Russian authorities believe that the majority of prostitutes who emigrate or work abroad do so voluntarily (Lehti 2003, p. 29; Leskinen 2003, pp. 9–28). According to the IOM, all estimates given by the authorities or the local NGOs should be treated with caution because they systematically exaggerate the problem. Trafficking in women for prostitution and prostitution are perceived as closely interrelated, and the two terms tend to be used interchangeably in the numbers received. Thus the numbers concerning "trafficking" in women often reflect the rapid expansion of prostitution as such, rather than actual trafficking activities, since networking is common and necessary to both (IOM 2000, 2003*b*).

Reliable data concerning identified victims have been available only from Moldova. The number of Moldovan victims assisted by the NGOs in the Balkans between January 2000 and June 2003 was 1,131 (thus a little over 300 a year). Applying the tenfold rule of the IOM would make about 3,000–4,000 victims a year, many fewer than the wildest estimates claiming tens of thousands of victims annually, but still a significant number for a country with a population of only a little over 4 million (IOM 2003*a*, p. 10).

7. *The Caucasus (Georgia, Armenia, Azerbaijan).* The Caucasian countries are a major transit and source area for trafficking in women to the Middle East, Europe, and North America. The annual number of local victims is estimated to be several hundred. Armenian and Azerbaijanian women normally end up as prostitutes or domestic servants

TABLE 5

Trafficking Volumes, Source Areas, North America

Country	Identified Victims Trafficked into Country, Reported Crimes (Year)	Estimated Annual Victims Trafficked into Country	Source Areas
Canada	?	8,000–16,000	AS; IE and CIS; LA
Mexico	?	?	
United States	?	14,500–50,000	IE and CIS; AS; LA

NOTE.—IE = new E.U. member countries and the Balkans; CIS = the CIS countries; LA = Latin America; AS = Asia; NT = native (www.globalmarch.org).

in Turkey or in the Persian Gulf states, whereas the destinations of the Georgian trafficking networks are more various (*A Study* 2001; www.rferl.org).

C. North and South America

The total volume of trafficking for sexual exploitation in the Americas is estimated at 400,000–2,500,000 victims annually. Most takes place inside or out of Brazil, other main source countries being the Dominican Republic and Colombia. The trafficking routes inside the Americas go mainly south to north, although a considerable proportion takes place in South and Central America and between neighboring states. Brazil and the Dominican Republic are main recruiting areas for migrant prostitution and prostitution-related trafficking for Europe and to a lesser extent for the sex industry centers in Asia, the Middle East, and South Africa.

1. *North America (Canada, Mexico, the United States).* North America is a major destination and transit area, but there is also large-scale internal trafficking. Table 5 shows recent estimates. The main destination is the United States. According to official estimates, 14,500–50,000 people, primarily women and children, are trafficked to the country annually. These estimates have decreased substantially in recent years. There is also significant trafficking inside the country, and a small number of U.S. citizens are trafficked annually to Canada and Mexico. Canada is the other major destination area; the annual number of victims is estimated at 8,000–16,000. Canada is an important transit area and a minor source country for trafficking to the United States. The main source areas for trafficking to the United

States and Canada are eastern Europe (the Balkans, Russia, and Ukraine), East Asia (China), Southeast Asia (Thailand and the Philippines), and Latin America (Mexico, Brazil, Honduras, and the Dominican Republic) (www.globalmarch.org; "Trafficking in Persons Report" 2004, p. 54).

The situation in Mexico differs considerably from that in Canada and the United States. Although Mexico is also a major destination country (especially from Central America, China, and the Caribbean), it is a more important transit and source area. The main trafficking routes from eastern Europe, Latin America, and Asia to the United States go through Mexico, and Mexican women are trafficked in significant numbers to its northern neighbor. There have been no estimates available of the volume of trafficking into, from, or through Mexico, but the annual number of victims is probably over 10,000. The annual number of victims in the whole area is somewhere between 50,000 and 120,000 (www.globalmarch.org).

In Canada, an estimated 50,000–100,000 people are engaged in prostitution. In the United States, the North American Task Force on Prostitution suggests that over 1 million people work as part-time or professional prostitutes; the number of minors in prostitution is estimated to be 100,000 at least. The number of prostitutes in Mexico is believed to be larger than in Canada and smaller than in the United States (archives.econ.utah.edu/archives/marxism/2004w28/msg00164.htm).

2. *Central America.*   Central America is a transit, source, and destination area. Table 6 shows recent estimates. Most takes place between and within the Central American countries. The main destinations outside the area are Mexico and the United States. The major source countries are Guatemala and Honduras (GPAT 2005, p. 6).

The minimum number of victims is estimated to be about 2,000 for each country except Belize and Costa Rica. Trafficking in Belize seems to be very rare. Costa Rica is mainly a destination for trafficking from eastern Europe and Southeast Asia (serving the European and North American sex tourism in the country), and the number of victims is estimated to be smaller than that in the neighboring countries. The total of annual victims is probably between 10,000 and 20,000. The number of people engaged in prostitution in the area is substantially higher (www.globalmarch.org).

3. *The Caribbean (Antigua-Barbuda, Bahamas, Barbados, Cuba, Dominica, the Dominican Republic, Grenada, Haiti, Jamaica, Puerto Rico, St.*

TABLE 6
Trafficking Volumes, Source Areas, Central America

Country	Identified Victims Trafficked into Country, Reported Crimes (Year)	Estimated Annual Victims Trafficked into Country	Source Areas
Belize	?	<100	LA
Costa Rica	?	100–500	LA; IE and CIS; AS
El Salvador	?	>2,000	LA
Guatemala	?	>2,000	LA
Honduras	?	>2,500	LA
Nicaragua	?	?	LA
Panama	?	?	?

NOTE.—IE = new E.U. member countries and the Balkans; CIS = the CIS countries; LA = Latin America; AS = Asia (www.globalmarch.org).

Kitts and Nevis, St. Lucia, St. Vincent, Trinidad and Tobago). From the Caribbean region, information is available only for the major islands and states. The Dominican Republic is the main source country and also one of the major source areas for the whole world. At least 50,000 women from the Dominican Republic are estimated to be engaged in the sex industry overseas. How many are victims of trafficking is not known, but the number is not insignificant. The main concentrations are in western and southern Europe and in the Caribbean area, but Dominican women are also engaged in prostitution in South America (Argentina), the Middle East (Israel), and the United States. A large-scale domestic sex industry serves European and North American sex tourism. It is estimated that more than 25,000 minors and a much higher number of adults are involved in prostitution in the Dominican Republic (Ehrenreich and Hochschild 2003; www.globalmarch.org).

Other major destinations of large-scale sex tourism (and thus also main destinations for trafficking) are Cuba (with about 100,000–160,000 prostitutes) and Jamaica (at least the same number). Many prostitutes are minors, both girls and boys (archives.econ .utah.edu/archives/marxism/2004w28/msg00164.htm).

The annual number of victims of prostitution-related trafficking in the area is probably about the same as in the Central American countries, 10,000–20,000.

4. *South America (Argentina, Bolivia, Brazil, Chile, Colombia, Ecuador, Guyana, Paraguay, Peru, Surinam, Uruguay, Venezuela).* South Amer-

ica is a major source area, but also a destination and transit area. According to the United Nations, Brazil is the largest exporter of women in South America and one of the most important globally. Brazil is also a major destination country, and there is large-scale trafficking for prostitution within the country. The majority of victims trafficked from Brazil end up in the commercial sex industry in Europe (Germany, Italy, Portugal, and Spain), Japan, Israel, and the United States. According to the United Nations and the Helsinki International Federation of Human Rights, the number of Brazilians forced into prostitution within the boundaries of the European Union[28] is about 75,000 (it is not clear if these estimates refer to annual new recruits or to a cumulative total, presumably the latter). Most victims come from the states of Goiás, Rio de Janeiro, and São Paulo. Brazil has one of the worst child prostitution problems in the world and is a favored destination for sex tourists from Europe and North America. NGOs estimate that every year between 200,000 and 2 million women and children are trafficked *within* the country or *to* the country for the sex tourism business only. The main centers of sex tourism are the cities along the northeastern coast (www.protectionproject.org/human_rights/countryreport/brazil.htm).

Another major source country is Colombia, whose citizens are trafficked mainly to Asia (Japan, Singapore, and Hong Kong), western Europe (Britain, Belgium, Germany, the Netherlands, and Spain), and the United States. There is also large-scale trafficking within the country and to its neighbors. The annual number of repatriated victims has been around 100 in recent years. Estimates of the total annual volume are much higher: 20,000–35,000 at the lowest. Lesser source areas for prostitution-related trafficking in the region are Bolivia, Ecuador, Guyana, and Uruguay (www.globalmarch.org).

The other major destination for trafficking is Argentina, whose sex industry imports prostitutes from the neighboring countries (Chile, Bolivia, and Brazil) and from the Caribbean (the Dominican Republic). Lesser destinations for intraregional trafficking are Surinam and Venezuela. Chile is mainly a transit country for trafficking from Asia to South and North America (www.globalmarch.org).

If the estimates concerning each country are summed up, the total of annual victims is between 300,000 and 3 million, most of whom are

[28] The estimates were made before the 2004 enlargement of the European Union and refer to the old member countries only.

victims of trafficking inside Brazil. The real figure is probably nearer the minimum end estimates.

D. Asia and Oceania

The total volume of trafficking for sexual exploitation within, to, and out of Asia is estimated to be somewhere between 500,000 and 5 million. The United Nations Children's Fund (UNICEF) estimates that trafficking of women and children in Asia for sexual exploitation has victimized over 30 million people in the past thirty years, which would mean more than 1 million per year (Flam 2003).

The continent (excluding Russia) is divided into three main regions: the Middle East, South Asia, and the Asian Pacific Rim (East and Southeast Asia and Oceania). The Middle East imports commercial sex workers from all over the world, mainly from eastern Europe, central Asia, South Asia, Southeast Asia, and East Africa. Prostitution-related trafficking to the region mainly takes place from the same source areas. In South Asia and the Asian Pacific Rim region, trafficking for sexual exploitation is mainly internal: the main destinations and source areas are found inside the regions, and most countries in both regions act simultaneously as source, destination, and transit areas. Both regions are major sources for international long-distance trafficking. South Asia supplies commercial sex workers to Europe, the Middle East, and North America and the Asian Pacific Rim region to all over the world. The Pacific Rim region also imports commercial sex workers in large numbers from all over the world, especially from Russia, eastern Europe, and the Balkans. The main centers of long-distance trafficking are Sri Lanka, Thailand, the Philippines, and China.

The total profits of the trade in the area are estimated to be between US$6 billion and $7 billion annually (Flam 2003).

1. *East Asia (China, Hong Kong, Japan, the Koreas, Macao, Mongolia, Taiwan).*   East Asia is an important source, destination, and transit area, and large-scale trafficking exists within the area. Table 7 shows recent estimates. The major key point is China. It is estimated that annually about 250,000 women are trafficked *within* the country for prostitution and about the same number *out of* the country. The main destinations outside China for Chinese women are Southeast Asia, North and Latin America, and Europe, but the trafficking networks cover the whole world. Large numbers of foreign women are trafficked each year to the sex industry in China, many from Burma, Vietnam,

TABLE 7
Estimated Trafficking Volumes, Source Areas, East Asia

Country	Annual Victims Trafficked within Country	Annual Victims Trafficked to/through Country	Annual Victims Trafficked from Country	Source Areas
China	250,000	>15,000	50,000–250,000	AS; CIS
Hong Kong		1–100[a]		AS; CIS
Macao				AS; CIS
Japan		50,000–250,000		AS; CIS
Mongolia				
North Korea				
South Korea		>1,000	>100	AS
Taiwan				AS; IE and CIS

NOTE.—IE = the new E.U. member countries and the Balkans; CIS = the CIS countries; EU = the E.U. member countries; AF = Africa; LA = Latin America; AS = Asia; NT = native (www.globalmarch.org).

[a] Annual number of cases reported to the police in 1990–99 (www.hku.hk/ccpl/pub/occasionalpapers/paper3/paper3-part5.htm).

and Russia, and ethnic Chinese from Southeast Asia. Russian authorities estimate that about 15,000 Russians are engaged in prostitution in China (Erokhina 2004; www.globalmarch.org).

Other source areas for prostitution-related trafficking in the region are Mongolia, Taiwan, and the Koreas. Mongolian women are trafficked mainly to Russia and Korean women to China. Taiwanese women are trafficked to the sex markets in Thailand and Malaysia. Aboriginal Malayo-Polynesians make up a large percentage of the victims (www.globalmarch.org).

Besides China, the other main destination is Japan. The annual number of victims is estimated at between 50,000 and 250,000, most from the Philippines, Thailand, and Russia. Hong Kong, Macao, Taiwan, and the Republic of Korea are lesser destination areas. Hong Kong is a major transit point for trafficking to Europe and North America (www.globalmarch.org).

The annual total of victims in the region (according to the above estimates) would be somewhere between 300,000 and 1.5 million.

According to official estimates, some 1 million women and children are engaged in prostitution in China (www.indianngos.com/issue/child/sexual/statistics/statistics11.htm). However, other estimates give 200,000–600,000 for the number of children involved in

TABLE 8
Estimated Trafficking Volume, Source Areas, Southeast Asia

Country	Annual Victims Trafficked within Country	Annual Victims Trafficked to/ through Country	Annual Victims Trafficked from Country	Source Areas
Brunei				Philippines
Burma		>1,000	10,000–50,000	China
Cambodia		>3,000	10,000–15,000	Vietnam
East Timor				Indonesia
Indonesia			500–1,000,000	AS
Malaysia		>3,000	4,000	AS
Philippines	>60,000		50,000–150,000	
Thailand		200,000–1,000,000	200,000–1,000,000	AS; IE and CIS
Vietnam			3,000	

NOTE.—IE = new E.U. member countries and the Balkans; CIS = the CIS countries; countries; AS = Asia (www.globalmarch.org).

prostitution only (www.unicef.org/vietnam/childse.pdf). The total number of persons engaged in prostitution is probably several millions. In Japan, the number of professional and part-time prostitutes is estimated to be somewhere between 500,000 and 1 million. The number of prostitutes in the Republic of Korea is also hundreds of thousands. In the other countries of the region the numbers are smaller (www.globalmarch.org).

2. *Southeast Asia (Brunei, Burma, Cambodia, East Timor, Indonesia, Laos, Malaysia, the Philippines, Singapore, Thailand, Vietnam)*. According to the U.S. State Department, the annual number of victims of *transborder* trafficking for sexual exploitation in Southeast Asia is about 225,000. Table 8 shows recent estimates. In addition, there exists large-scale domestic trafficking related to the sex industry in Burma, Cambodia, Thailand, Vietnam, the Philippines, and Indonesia (Flam 2003).

Thailand is the entry point. It is a major source, destination, and transit country and the main destination for European and North American sex tourism in Asia. The main sources for trafficking are Laos, Burma, China, Russia, and Vietnam. Thai women are trafficked all over the world, the main destinations being Japan, western Europe, and North America. Estimates of the volume of trafficking *into* Thailand vary wildly, between 200,000 and a million women annually. Estimates of trafficking *from* Thailand abroad are on the same scale (www.globalmarch.org).

According to the Thai authorities, there are approximately 75,000 active prostitutes. NGOs estimate the number at close to 2 million (the highest available estimate puts the number at 2.8 million), about a third of whom are minors (www.catw-ap.org/facts.htm). The main concentrations are Chiang Mai, Bangkok, Pattaya, and Phuket. The largest groups of foreigners in prostitution according to Thai officials are from Burma (20,000–50,000), Russia and the CIS countries (10,000), and China (5,000) (www.stickman bangkok.com/reader/reader291.html). The largest concentration of Thai prostitution abroad, 40,000–60,000 women, is in Japan (www.globalmarch.org).

Cambodia is another important source, transit, and destination country. The centers of the sex industry are Phnom Penh and other cities. Victims come mainly from the surrounding countryside, and Cambodians are also trafficked to neighboring countries in Southeast Asia. There is little reliable data on the volume of trafficking, but some estimates are that as many as 10,000–15,000 women and girls are trafficked *out of* the country annually. There is also large-scale trafficking from abroad. Many of the estimated 15,000–20,000 prostitutes in Phnom Penh are Vietnamese, with as many as 3,000 trafficked to Cambodia each year. A large percentage are minors, and many of their clients are foreign sex tourists (Muhonen 2005; www.globalmarch.org).

The other main source areas are the Philippines and Burma. Estimates of the volume of trafficking from the Philippines are vague. In Japan, there are 60,000–150,000 Filipinos engaged in prostitution, and in South Korea about 1,000–2,000; how many are victims of trafficking is not known. However, the Philippines is one of the main source countries of female migration, legal and illegal, in Asia, and the migration networks out of the country extend throughout the whole world. The number of victims of trafficking is high, and they are to be found on every continent. The number of women and children in prostitution in the Philippines is estimated at between 300,000 and 500,000. The country has a significant child prostitution problem, with 60,000–100,000 children involved (Ehrenreich and Hochschild 2003).

The main destinations for Burmese victims are the other countries in the region, especially Thailand, China, and Pakistan. There is also large-scale internal trafficking from rural areas to major cities. Estimates of the annual number of victims in Burma vary between 10,000 and 50,000. At least 50,000 Burmese women are believed to be engaged

in prostitution in Thailand and about 200,000 in Pakistan (www
.globalmarch.org).

Source countries of lesser importance are Indonesia and Vietnam.
Malaysia is mainly a destination, and the volumes to and from the
country are substantially smaller than in its neighbors. Singapore is an
important transit point for trafficking networks connecting India,
Thailand, Malaysia, China, Sri Lanka, and Indonesia.

3. *Central Asia (Afghanistan, Kazakhstan, Kyrgyzstan, Tajikistan, Tur-
kestan, Uzbekistan).* According to IOM estimates, central Asia is becoming an important source area for Asia. The economic difficulties
that the central Asian countries are currently facing are fostering a
favorable environment for the recruitment of potential victims (IOM
2001*a*).

The number of Kyrgyz women working as commercial sex workers
abroad is estimated at somewhere between 500 and 2,000, and that of
Tajik women at between 2,000 and 3,000. Estimates are not available
from the other central Asian countries. The main destination is Russia.
Secondary destinations are the United Arab Emirates, other Persian
Gulf states, and Turkey (IOM 2001*a*).

In Afghanistan, trafficking in women is usually linked to ancient local
traditions. Women and young girls are abducted in significant numbers
for forced marriages. The number of reported crimes was twenty-four
in 2002–3. The real figure, however, is believed to be high, partly
because the abductors are often armed groups under local military control. Women and girls are also used in substantial numbers as a tradable
sexual commodity in the settling of disputes between families and communities[29] (IOM 2003*c*).

A third form of trafficking for sexual exploitation common in Afghanistan is sexual servitude. It is a specific form of servitude with a
sexual violence component and is often difficult to distinguish from
rape. The victims are abducted by armed groups, or by individuals, and
held captive for a period from some days to several months. During
captivity, they are subjected to repeated rapes and forced to perform

---

[29] For example, in cases of homicide the family of the perpetrator must offer one or
more girls to the victim's family to restore its honor. The girl is engaged or married to
a member of the victim's family. Occasionally, the victim's family will also offer a daughter
to the perpetrator's family, especially if members on both sides have been killed through
retribution attacks. The marriages agreed on this way are tainted, however, since the
stigma of the crime remains with the girl for life, and many of the girls commit suicide
(IOM 2003*c*).

domestic labor (the latter pertains primarily to women and girls) (IOM 2003*c*).

Information on the volume of trafficking to, within, and from the region is scarce, but on the basis of data from Tajikistan and Kyrgyzstan, a reasonable estimate is 1,000–15,000 victims a year.

4. *Middle East (Bahrain, Iran, Iraq, Israel, Jordan, Kuwait, Lebanon, Oman, Palestine, Qatar, Saudi Arabia, Syria, the United Arab Emirates, Yemen).* The Middle East is mainly a destination and transit area. The main destination countries are Israel and the Persian Gulf states (especially the United Arab Emirates).

To the Israeli sex industry, women are brought mainly from Moldova, Russia, and Ukraine and in lesser numbers from Brazil, Turkey, South Africa, and Southeast Asia. According to local NGOs, thousands of women are trafficked into the country annually. During 1995–97, 1,500 Russian and Ukrainian trafficked women were deported (500 per year on average) (www.globalmarch.org).

In the United Arab Emirates the main source areas are Russia, Ukraine, central Asia, South Asia, and Southeast Asia. Estimates of the volume of trafficking are scarce, but it is believed to have slightly decreased after the country tightened its entry visa requirements for young women.

Prostitution is largely taboo in the region, and information on prostitution-related trafficking is even scarcer than elsewhere. The annual number of victims is likely to be several thousands in Israel and the United Arab Emirates. The total number of victims in the whole region is somewhere between 10,000 and 50,000.

5. *South Asia (Bangladesh, Bhutan, India, Maldives, Nepal, Pakistan, Sri Lanka).* South Asia is one of the main source and destination areas in the world. Table 9 shows recent estimates. The major trafficking flows go from Bangladesh and Nepal to India and Pakistan. About 10,000 Nepalese and 20,000 Bangladeshi women and girls (most of the victims in this region are minors) are estimated to be trafficked to neighboring countries annually. In addition, about 20,000 Burmese women are trafficked to Pakistan annually and an unknown number to India. There is also large-scale domestic trafficking in both India and Pakistan. In smaller numbers, Indian and Pakistani women are trafficked abroad to neighboring countries, the Middle East, Europe, Southeast Asia, and North America (www.globalmarch.org).

Estimates of people engaged in prostitution vary significantly.

TABLE 9

Estimated Trafficking Volumes, Source Areas, South Asia

Country	Annual Victims Trafficked within Country	Annual Victims Trafficked to/ through Country	Estimated Annual Victims Trafficked from Country	Source Areas
Bangladesh			20,000	Pakistan
Bhutan				
India	>150,000	12,000–50,000		Bangladesh/Nepal
Nepal			5,000–10,000	India
Sri Lanka	18,000–30,000			EU; AS; NA
Pakistan	>20,000	40,000–100,000		Bangladesh/Burma

NOTE.—EU = the E.U. member countries; AS = Asia; NA = North America (www.globalmarch.org).

About 200,000 Bangladeshi women and girls are estimated to be engaged in prostitution abroad (Pakistan and India) and from 60,000 to 100,000 in Bangladesh. In India, estimates of the number of people engaged in prostitution vary from 1 million to 9 million, some 15–30 percent of whom are children. The Indian Social Welfare Board estimates that there are 500,000 foreign prostitutes in India, of whom 160,000–200,000 are Nepalese. Another 25,000 Nepalese are engaged in prostitution in their home country (mainly in Kathmandu), 20 percent of them under age sixteen. In Pakistan it is estimated that 200,000 to 1 million Bangladeshi women and 200,000 Burmese women are engaged in prostitution in addition to an unknown number of natives. There are between 20,000 and 250,000 children in prostitution in Pakistan, about 40,000 of them of Bangladeshi origin (www.globalmarch.org).

The total of annual victims according to the above estimates lies somewhere between 250,000 and 500,000.

6. *Oceania (Australia, Fiji, Kiribati, Nauru, New Zealand, Papua New Guinea, Samoa, Tonga, Vanuatu).* Oceania is mainly a destination and transit area. The main destination is Australia; the victims come mainly from Thailand and Malaysia. Australia is also a major source for organized sex tourism abroad (the primary destinations are Indonesia, the Philippines, Thailand, South Korea, Sri Lanka, Taiwan, and Hong Kong).

In New Zealand, prostitution-related trafficking is rare. There are an estimated 6,000–8,000 prostitutes active in the country, 25 percent of whom are of Thai or other Asian origin (www.globalmarch.org).

The total number of annual victims is likely to be between a few hundred and 10,000.

E. Africa

In Africa economic exploitation makes up a much larger percentage of trafficking than sexual exploitation does; however, the continent is also an important source area for prostitution-related trafficking to Europe and the Middle East. It is not possible to categorize the individual African countries as clear source, destination, or transit countries since almost all are all three. The destinations of large-scale prostitution-related trafficking and migrant prostitution inside Africa are mainly the South African Republic and Kenya, where the sex industries also recruit employees from outside the continent, from Asia and eastern Europe (the main source areas are Thailand and the Russian Federation). According to the GPAT database, Nigeria, Benin, Ghana, and Morocco are the main countries of origin of all types of trafficking in humans in the region. Trafficking inside the region originates mainly from other African countries (GPAT 2005, p. 1).

Estimates of the total volume of trafficking are even more vague than elsewhere. The annual figure is perhaps between 100,000 and 500,000.

1. *North Africa (Algeria, Egypt, Libya, Mauritania, Morocco, Tunisia).* Little information is available on the volume of trafficking. Algeria and Morocco are countries of origin for prostitution-related trafficking to Europe, especially to Italy and other southern European countries. Morocco is also an important transit country for trafficking from West Africa to Europe (www.protectionproject.org/human_rights/country report/algeria.htm; morocco.htm).

Libya is mainly a transit country for trafficking from inner Africa to Europe. Egypt is a destination for Eastern European prostitutes, many of whom are trafficked further to Israel. In Mauritania, the problem is mainly domestic and related to sexual slavery common in the country (www.protectionproject.org/human_rights/countryreport/egypt.htm; libya.htm; mauritania.htm).

No estimates are available of the volume of trafficking, but the number of victims is probably at least 10,000 annually. In Morocco the estimated number of women and children engaged in (illegal) prostitution is over 200,000. In Algeria it is likely to be in the same range. In Egypt, the number is probably higher (www.protectionproject.org/human_rights/countryreport/algeria.htm/morocco.htm).

2. *West Africa (Benin, Burkina Faso, Cape Verde, Gambia, Ghana, Guinea, Guinea-Bissau, the Ivory Coast, Liberia, Mali, Niger, Nigeria, Senegal, São Tomé and Príncipe, Sierra Leone, Togo).* In West Africa, the main trafficking flows occur inside the region and aim mostly at economic exploitation. Prostitution-related trafficking abroad goes mostly to Europe, but also to the Middle East, North Africa, and North America. The main source areas are Nigeria, Benin, Gambia, Ghana, and Senegal, and the major destinations are Belgium, France, Germany, Italy, the Netherlands, and Spain. Nigerian women are trafficked in larger numbers to North America (GPAT 2005, p. 1).

The dual legal system in many of the countries contributes to trafficking. In practice, customary laws derived from precolonial legal traditions govern the majority of the population. Under these laws, both legally and culturally, women and children are viewed as objects owned by their family, and as individuals they have few rights other than those granted by the heads of their families. This cultural context fosters the silence of abused women and children (www.protectionproject.org/human_rights/countryreport/benin.htm; togo.htm).

Estimates of the numbers of victims or people engaged in prostitution are few. UNICEF estimates that 200,000 children in West Africa are enslaved annually by cross-border trafficking rings; however, most are victims of economic exploitation. According to Nigerian authorities, 45,000 Nigerian women are trafficked for prostitution to Europe annually. The crime recruits its victims to a large extent in the Edo State in southwestern Nigeria (*Trafficking of Nigerian Girls to Italy* 2004; www.ipsnews.net/interna.asp?idnews = 19418). The annual number of repatriated victims in Nigeria in recent years has been between 1,000 and 2,000 annually (*Trafficking of Nigerian Girls to Italy* 2004; www .protectionproject.org/human_rights/countryreport/nigeria.htm). The total number of deported illegal prostitutes from Niger and Mali in Algeria was 1,400 in the late 1990s (www.protectionproject.org/human _rights/countryreport/mali.htm). In Niger, 262 victims of trafficking were repatriated in 2001 (www.protectionproject.org/human_rights/countryreport/niger.htm).

The number of victims of prostitution-related trafficking in the region is probably considerable, perhaps 50,000–100,000 annually.

3. *Central Africa (Burundi, Cameroon, Central African Republic, Chad, the Congos, Equatorial Guinea, Gabon, Rwanda).* Information on trafficking is scarce. Cameroon is reported to be a country of transit, origin, and destination. According to a report of the International Labour Organization, the volume of traffic of minors out of Cameroon is several thousands every year; most are transported for exploitative labor in neighboring countries, but many victims of economic exploitation are also sexually abused. The destination for prostitution-related trafficking from Cameroon is mainly western Europe (www.protectionproject.org/human_rights/countryreport/cameroon.htm).

Gabon again is mainly a destination country. Trafficking mostly involves the economic exploitation of children, but many victims of economic exploitation are also exploited sexually. Prostitution-related trafficking to Gabon takes place mainly from West Africa (www.protectionproject.org/human_rights/countryreport/gabon.htm). One of the main transit points in the region is reported to be Rwanda.

The main regional source country is the Democratic Republic of Congo (Kinshasa). Women and children are trafficked in large numbers to sex industries in western Europe, particularly Belgium. Prostitution flourishes in refugee camps in the country and in Tanzania, where more than 70,000 refugees from Burundi and Congo have moved because of civil wars (www.protectionproject.org/human_rights/countryreport/congo.htm).

No estimates of the total number of victims exist. A reasonable guess is between 10,000 and 100,000 annually.

4. *East Africa (Djibouti, Eritrea, Ethiopia, Kenya, Somalia, Sudan, Tanzania, Uganda).* The main destination areas are Djibouti (French military bases) and Kenya. The other countries act mostly as recruiting areas. The main routes run within the area (to Kenya and Djibouti) and to the Middle East (Saudi Arabia, Bahrain, and Lebanon) and southern Africa (Malawi and South Africa). Ethiopian women are also reported to be trafficked in larger numbers to Europe (England) and Canada. The Kenyan sex industry imports employees from outside the region, mainly South Asia (India and Pakistan) (www.protectionproject.org/human_rights/countryreport/kenya.htm; eritrea.htm; ethiopia.htm; uganda.htm; tanzania.htm).

Estimates of numbers of victims are few. There is a documented case of the repatriation of the bodies of sixty-seven Ethiopian women sold for prostitution in the Arab countries. According to the Women's Affairs Department in the Ethiopian Ministry of Labour, about 90,000 women work as prostitutes in Ethiopia, of whom 20 percent are minors. There is information on a case of 200 Kenyans trafficked for prostitution to Saudi Arabia. In Sudan, according to various reports, human slavery (including sexual slavery) is rampant, and U.S. government figures show that some 14,000 women and children from southern Sudan have been abducted in recent years (www.protectionproject.org/human_rights/countryreport/kenya.htm; eritrea.htm; ethiopia.htm; uganda.htm; tanzania.htm; sudan.htm).

The annual number of victims in the region is well over 10,000. The volume of prostitution-related trafficking into and out of the region seems, however, to be smaller than in West Africa or in Central Africa.

5. *Southern Africa (Angola, Botswana, the Comoro Islands, Lesotho, Madagascar, Malawi, Mauritius, Mozambique, Seychelles, South Africa, Swaziland, Zambia, Zimbabwe).* In southern Africa the situation varies substantially depending on the country. Trafficking is rampant in Angola, Malawi, Mozambique, South Africa, and Zambia, whereas Botswana and Namibia seem fairly free of it.

Angola, Malawi, Mozambique, and Zambia are the main source countries. Angolan and Mozambican women and children are trafficked mainly to South Africa or within their native countries. Zambian women are trafficked mainly to South Africa but also in large numbers to the Far East. Malawi is characterized by three different trafficking flows. Malawian-Nigerian female networks traffic women and girls to Europe by air. The main destinations are the sex industries in the Netherlands, Belgium, Germany, and Italy. Another type of trafficking takes place along major transportation routes, where long-distance truckers recruit women with promises of marriage, jobs, or educational opportunities in South Africa. Once in Johannesburg, the victims are held as the traffickers' sex slaves in private flats or sold further. Female Malawian trafficking networks also traffic victims directly to brothels in Johannesburg. Malawi also has a large-scale domestic sex industry mainly serving European sex tourism (IOM 2003*d*).

South Africa is a major country of origin, destination, and transit. The country's sex industry recruits employees within the country and from the neighboring countries and West Africa, but also from eastern

Europe, the Balkans, and Asia (India, Pakistan, China, Taiwan, and Thailand). South Africa is a major transit point for trafficking networks between developing countries and Europe, the United States, and Canada (IOM 2003d).

Volume estimates are few. According to Angolan officials, there are at least 38,000 Angolan victims of trafficking in South Africa alone. In Angola, the number of children in prostitution is at least 10,000. Namibian officials estimate that more than 4,000 Namibians may have been trafficked and forced into labor or prostitution during the last decade. In 2000, a Zambian government study found that an estimated 563,000 children between the ages of five and seventeen were involved in some form of domestic labor or prostitution. More than 75,000 children live in the streets in Zambia's major cities (www.protectionproject.org/human_rights/country report/angola.htm; namibia.htm; zambia.htm).

The numbers of victims in the region are probably similar to those in West and Central Africa (e.g., 50,000–100,000).

F. The Regional Distribution of Trafficking for Sexual Exploitation

Most of the global traffic for sexual exploitation is short-distance. In Europe, South Asia, the Asian Pacific Rim region, and West Africa, most of the trafficking takes place inside each region, from rural areas to cities and from economically depressed regions to affluent ones.

The main source areas of large-scale, long-distance trafficking are Brazil and the Dominican Republic in Latin America, Russia in Europe, Sri Lanka in South Asia, China in East Asia, Thailand and the Philippines in Southeast Asia, and Nigeria in West Africa.

The industrialized countries in Europe, North America, and the Asia-Pacific region are major destinations for international trafficking for prostitution as well as migrant prostitution. The trafficking to these countries constitutes only about 15 percent of the estimated global total minimum volume of 1.7 million victims, but their share of cross-border trafficking is considerably higher, maybe even over 30 percent.

The bulk of the prostitution-related cross-border trafficking takes place, however, between the third-world countries. This has been the case during the whole history of modern prostitution-related trafficking. It is estimated that in the first half of the twentieth century, 90 percent of all victims of global trafficking for prostitution were non-white women. The main roads of the trade ran between and inside the

European colonies in Africa and Asia (Scully 2001, pp. 86–87). Although the rapidly growing impact of European, Australian, Japanese, and North American sex tourism should not be underestimated, legislative and preventive measures taken in the E.U. member countries or North America only (especially if they do not effectively cover sex tourism elsewhere) have but a modest impact. Any effective preventive measures should be carried out globally.

V. Prevention, Crime Control, and Witness Protection

The factors that create, motivate, and direct global flows of trafficking are the same as those that direct the global migration flows as a whole: deep differences in standards of living between and within different geographic regions of the world. It is unlikely that fundamental changes can be achieved until global differences in living standards become less acute.

The most effective means of preventing trafficking is to support more equal global social and economic development and to remove obstacles to it. In Europe, the enlargement of the European Union can be expected to produce significant positive results in the future, although the most troubled countries (Albania, Moldova, and Ukraine) have so far not been included.

Measures taken in Europe or North America, however, can have only a minor effect on the global situation, since most trafficking takes place elsewhere. Thus all crime control and prevention policies ought to be global to be effective. The most crucial objectives are creating extensive and reliable global data-collecting systems; criminalizing trafficking in women globally with relatively uniform criteria and sanctions; developing and increasing cooperation in crime prevention internationally and interregionally (e.g., using as a model the experiences collected of the cooperation between the European countries); improvement of the status and rights of the victims in national legislation; creating efficient witness protection legislation and programs for victims of trafficking; and creating effective social and economic shelter programs for victims globally.

No reliable, comparative information is available anywhere on the extent of any type of trafficking or on the numbers and the nationality of the victims, not even concerning reported and prosecuted crimes. International efforts should be made (e.g., by the United Nations) to create and harmonize national statistics concerning reported trafficking crimes, using relatively unifom criteria and compiled according to relatively consistent standards. NGOs are an important source of information, and means should be created to facilitate efficient and extensive collection of their information in each country and internationally. Mere statistics, however, produce only indicative information at best. To obtain better information and to create a basis for more efficient data collection systems, basic research concerning trafficking and organized prostitution should be increased all over the world. Plenty of valuable knowledge has already been produced within the research projects of the IOM and UNICRI, the STOP projects in Europe, and national research programs. The need for additional research is, however, urgent and great.

Legislation concerning trafficking in women is highly diverse, although attempts to unify it have been progressing. The international community should aim to harmonize national legislation and to improve the legal status of victims of trafficking. Trafficking should be made a special offense. Courts should have the right to seize assets belonging to convicted traffickers. Victims should receive help and protection when necessary. Governments should set up agreements to facilitate victims' return to their native countries if they so wish. Victims should be granted, if necessary, temporary residence status on humanitarian grounds. Extensive ratification of the Palermo Protocol and rapid application of its obligations in national legislation would hasten harmonization and should be a primary goal.

Special witness protection legislation for victims of trafficking exists mainly in some European countries. The laws are relatively recent, and there is not yet much experience with how they will work. All include the possibility of issuing temporary residence permits. In Belgium and the Netherlands, the consent of the victim to cooperate in the investigation and prosecution is required. In Italy, all victims have similar rights whether they cooperate or not. In Spain, the general witness protection law applies to victims of trafficking. Only Italy and Spain offer victims active police protection, which continues after court proceedings have ended (e.g., including the possibility of a new identity), but even in those countries the right to this kind of protection is largely theoretical. It is questionable how effectively victims' willingness to cooperate with the authorities (which is crucial for combating trafficking in persons) can be improved by granting only temporary residence permits. Most European countries and countries elsewhere have no efficient witness protection programs (Pearson 2001, pp. 10–13).

Trafficking in persons is a transnational crime, and it is necessary to have effective international and regional police cooperation to combat and prevent it. Bilateral police and intelligence cooperation between different countries and international cooperation should be promoted in all possible ways.

VI. Conclusions

Trafficking and migration have historically been closely linked. This is also true today. The globalization of the international economy and the consequent transformation of local economies and societies, and deepening disparities in wealth and living standards, have led to a simultaneous increase in international migration (both legal and irregular) and in trafficking in persons related to both illegal labor markets and commercial sex markets. Trafficking networks exploit both the increasing economic and social misery in the countries on the losing side of globalization and the disintegration of the old nation-state structures in the industrialized world.

The current global extent of trafficking for prostitution is subject to rough estimates only, and in most cases it is unclear how these estimates have been reached. Despite widespread political and media publicity, trafficking for prostitution is not among the priorities of everyday crime prevention work in any country. Hence, accurate data are scarce, and information and studies are to a large extent based on the same few original sources and usually repeat the same stories. The topic (and consequently also data collection) is loaded both ideologically and moralistically, which does not help interpretation of data or research results. The needs to collect and exchange comparative information on trafficking throughout the world, allocate sufficient funds to monitor it, create databases, and carry out further research are great.

It is usually assumed that prostitution-related trafficking makes up 70–80 percent of all global trafficking in persons when measured by the numbers of victims. It is also assumed that the volume of this kind of trafficking and forced prostitution is much larger than the available sources show.

If we use the Palermo criteria as the definition of trafficking in persons, it is highly probable that the first assumption is false. Although

TABLE 10

Estimates, Trafficking, Child Prostitution, Industrialized
Countries

	Annual Victims, Adults and Minors	Minors in Prostitution
Western Europe[a]	60,000–150,000	>25,000
Central Europe	<50,000[b]	<5,000
Israel	<5,000	
Canada	8,000–16,000	>1,000
United States	14,500–50,000	>100,000
Japan	50,000–250,000	<100,000
Australia and New Zealand	<10,000	5,000
Total	200,000–550,000	>235,000

[a] Western Europe, the Mediterranean, and the Nordic countries.
[b] Estimated victims trafficked to the region and from the region other than western Europe.

available data are sporadic and full of gaps, it is likely that other forms of trafficking, especially traffic for economic exploitation as domestic servants and as workers in agriculture, construction, and sweatshop industries, are at least as common as trafficking for sexual exploitation. In some regions, for example in Africa and North America, they are more numerous.

In spite of this, however, it is probably true that current estimates of the absolute volume of prostitution-related trafficking are underestimated rather than overestimated. Although the police authorities and the NGOs have a tendency to *exaggerate* rather than underestimate the role of trafficking and organized crime in *international prostitution of adults* (the new paradigm of organized crime can easily lead to this kind of exaggeration, and many NGOs have an ideological tendency to see all prostitution as trafficking-related), most of the existing estimates *underestimate the volume of domestic prostitution of minors*, or at least do not include it in the numbers concerning victims of trafficking (table 10 shows recent estimates). In order to obtain better knowledge and to create a basis for more efficient data collection systems, it is important to harmonize the definitions of trafficking in persons used in national legislations and statistics. The creation of an international database (an idea presented for the first time at the 1913 Madrid Conference) would improve the present situation considerably.

Most global trafficking for sexual exploitation is short-distance. According to the available estimates, about 60–80 percent of the trade takes place *within* countries. The percentage of cross-border trafficking is only 25–30 percent of the total global volume, and the bulk is regional, taking place between neighboring countries. The major flows run from rural areas to cities and from economically depressed regions to affluent ones. The proportion of the traffic to the major industrialized countries (Australia, Canada, the E.U. member countries, Israel, Japan, and the United States) is only 10–20 percent of the global volume. Most prostitution-related trafficking takes place within and between the third-world and eastern European countries. However, industrial countries have an important indirect role in trafficking outside their borders, since Western and Japanese sex tourism forms a substantial part of the clientele of local prostitution in several third-world countries and in parts of Russia.

The main source areas of large-scale long-distance trafficking are Brazil, the Dominican Republic, Russia, Sri Lanka, China, Thailand, the Philippines, and Nigeria. Common to all of them is that they have an exceptionally good infrastructure for such trafficking: either strong domestic organized crime with wide global connections or long-standing traditions of female economic emigration with established global migration networks and immigrant communities (Ehrenreich and Hochschild 2003; Shelley 2004).

Although available data very likely overestimate the importance of prostitution-related trafficking relative to all global trafficking in persons, there are good reasons for keeping a focus on it. Aggravated abuses of human rights are substantially more common in trafficking for sexual exploitation than in other types of trafficking. The victims are submitted to violence and intimidation more often than victims of economic exploitation, their living and working conditions are worse, and their economic exploitation is more blatant. The victims are also usually younger and less capable of defending themselves or escaping abuse without outside help.

Whether prostitution as such should be allowed or abolished is a moral and ideological question and is beyond the scope of this essay. However, there is indisputable evidence that the criminalization of prostitution, and current policies in many countries (based to a large extent on the prostitution treaties of the twentieth century) that criminalize the exploitation of prostitution by third parties but leave the status of prostitutes unclear, create favorable circumstances for all forms of abuse of individual prostitutes (including trafficking). It is important for the prevention of prostitution-related trafficking that the rights and the status of prostitution and prostitutes be defined clearly and that prostitutes be given the same economic, civil, and social rights as other citizens and foreigners.

It is also important to harmonize legislation concerning trafficking globally, as regards the criteria of crime, sanctions, and the status and the rights of the victims. Trafficking in persons should be made a special offense, and the victims of trafficking should be given legal rights to help and protection. Governments should also set up agreements to facilitate victims' return to their native countries if they wish, and victims should be granted, if necessary, temporary residence status on humanitarian grounds. The ratification of the Palermo Protocol as extensively as possible and the rapid application of its obligations in national legislation would hasten the harmonization process and should be a primary goal for the international community.

Even the most effective legislation is not enough if the will and resources for implementation are lacking. The volume of prostitution-related trafficking is so large, the routes used for trafficking so manifold, and the organization of the crime so flexible that it is not possible to close all the routes and eliminate all the networks. It is more practicable to concentrate on the main regional source countries and the most important junctions of the trafficking routes. This will require more efficient police and intelligence cooperation regionally and internationally. It is also crucial to continue and to invigorate efforts against corruption in border controls and police forces and on all levels of government (NCIS 2002, pp. 34–36).

Efforts against the crime networks should be combined with developing and strengthening effective protection and assistance mechanisms for victims of trafficking and with strengthening socioeconomic support programs and awareness-raising activities in both source and destination countries.

In the long run, the best ways to prevent prostitution-related trafficking and prostitution as a whole are to support and facilitate general social and economic development in the countries on the losing side of the current globalization process and work to achieve a more equal and balanced global economic and social development.

APPENDIX

International Treaties and Conventions

General Act of the Brussels Conference relative to the African Slave Trade (Great Britain, Austria-Hungary, Belgium, Congo, Denmark, France, Germany, Italy, Netherlands, Persia, Portugal, Russia, Spain, Sweden and Norway, Turkey, United States, and Zanzibar), with Annexed Declaration of the same date (Brussels, 2 July 1890; Australian Treaty Series no. 82/1892: C 6557).

International Agreement for the Suppression of the White Slave Traffic (Paris, 18 May 1904; Australian Treaty Series no. 024/1905: Cd 2689).

International Convention for the Suppression of the White Slave Traffic (Paris, 4 May 1910; Australian Treaty Series no. 020/1912: Cd 6326).

International Convention for the Suppression of the Traffic in Women and Children (Geneva, 30 September 1921; Australian Treaty Series no. 010/1922).

International Convention with (the) Object of Securing the Abolition of Slavery and the Slave Trade (Geneva, 25 September 1926; Australian Treaty Series no. 016/1927: Cmd 2910).

International Convention for the Suppression of the Traffic in Women of Full Age (Geneva, 11 October 1933; Australian Treaty Series no. 012/1936).

Protocol to Amend the Convention for the Suppression of the Traffic in Women and Children of 30 September 1921, and the Convention for the Suppression of the Traffic in Women of Full Age of 11 October 1933 (Lake Success, 12 November 1947; Australian Treaty Series no. 017/1947).

Protocol Amending the International Agreement for the Suppression of the White Slave Traffic of the 18th May 1904 and the International Convention for the Suppression of the White Slave Traffic of 4th May 1910 (Lake Success, 4 May 1949; Australian Treaty Series no. 085/1953: Cmd 9042).

Convention for the Suppression of the Traffic in Persons and of the Exploitation of the Prostitution of Others (Geneva, 1949; www.unhchr.ch/html/menu3/b/33.htm).

Slavery Convention signed at Geneva on the 25th September 1926, as amended by the Protocol agreed at New York on 7th December 1953 (together with the Protocol of 7th December 1953 and the Annex to that Protocol) (New York, 7 December 1953; Australian Treaty Series no. 24/1956: Cmd 9797).

Convention on the Abolition of Slavery, the Slave Trade and Institutions and Practices Similar to Slavery, Supplementary to the International Convention signed at Geneva on 25 September 1926 (Geneva, 7 September 1956; Australian Treaty Series no. 059/1957: Cmnd 257).

Convention on the Elimination of All Forms of Discrimination against Women (New York, 18 December 1979; Australian Treaty Series no. 009/1983).

United Nations 2000 Protocol to Prevent, Suppress and Punish Trafficking in Persons, Especially Women and Children, Supplementing the United

Nations Convention against Transnational Organized Crime (Palermo Protocol; A/RES/55/25).

E.U. Legislation
Council Framework Decision of 19 July 2002 on Combating Trafficking in Human Beings (2002/629/JHA; Official Journal L 203, 01/08/2002 P. 0001–0004).
Document COM (2000)854 final du 21.12.2000.

U.S. Legislation
Trafficking Victims Protection Act (22 U.S.C. 7101 et seq.).

Web Sites
allserv.rug.ac.be/~rmak/europap/rappor.html
   archives.econ.utah.edu/archives/marxism/2004w28/msg00164.htm
   fpmail.friends-partners.org: fpmail.friends-partners.org/pipermail/stop-trafficmigration.ucdavis.edu/mn/
more_entireissue.php?idate = 1999_11&number = 11
   missions.itu.int/~romania
   news.bbc.co.uk/1/hi/world/europe/2293947.stm
   stangoff.com/?p = 70
   209.190.246.239: 209.190.246.239/ver2/cr/COUNTRY.pdf[30]
   web.pdx.edu/~leopoldo/ncsexwork.pdf
   www.althingi.is/go/raedur/safn/000241.html
   www.balticseataskforce.dk/Trafficking/Traffickingreport.htm
   www.brama.com
   www.erieri.com
   www.europap.net/pdf/bu_question_1.pdf
   www.ex.ac.uk: www.ex.ac.uk/politics/pol_data/undergrad/aac/COUNTRY
.htm
   www.fo-stvkennisnet.nl/kr_fo
   www.georgia-gateway.org
   www.globalmarch.org: www.globalmarch.org/worstformsreport/world/
COUNTRY.html
   www.greekhelsinki.gr: www.greekhelsinki.gr/english/reports/ihf-wit-july-2000-COUNTRY.html
   www.hrw.org/wr2k1/europe/macedonia.html
   www.indianngos.com/issue/child/sexual/statistics/statistics11.htm
   www.inet.co.th
   www.interpol.int
   www.ipsnews.net/interna.asp?idnews = 19418
   www.janes.com
   www.osce.org: www.osce.org/odihr/attf/pdf/nap_COUNTRY.pdf

---

[30] To access information on a specific country for this and other Web sites, replace the word COUNTRY in the URL with the name of that country.

www.portcult.com
www.protectionproject.org/human_rights/countryreport/COUNTRY.htm
www.rferl.org
www.sexwork.com: www.sexwork.com/coalition/englandwales.html
www.state.gov: www.state.gov/g/drl/rls/hrrpt/2001/eur/COUNTRY.htm
www.state.gov/g/tip/rls/tiprpt
www.stickmanbangkok.com/reader/reader291.html
www.un.org/News/Press/docs/2001/WOM1294.doc.htm
www.undcp.org: www.undcp.org/odccp/trafficking_projects_COUNTRY
.html
www.unhchr.ch/html/menu3/b/33.htm
www.unicef.org/vietnam/childse/pdf
www.unodc.org/unodc/en/trafficking_human_beings.html
www.uri.edu: www.uri.edu/artsci/wms/hugnes/COUNTRY.htm
www.worldsexguide.org: www.worldsexguide.org/COUNTRY.html
www1.umn.edu/humanrts/usdocs

REFERENCES

Aromaa, Kauko. 2005. "Trafficking in Human Beings: Uniform Definitions for Better Measuring and for Effective Counter-measures." Paper presented at the International Scientific and Professional Advisory Council International Conference on Measuring Human Trafficking, Courmayeur Mont Blanc, December 2–4.

Babha, J. 2005. *Trafficking, Smuggling and Human Rights*. Migration Information Source of Migration Policy Institute. http://www.migration information.org.

Bopp, Vanessa, and Andrea Cauduro. 2004. "Italy." In *A Study for Monitoring the Trafficking of Human Beings for the Purpose of Sexual Exploitation in the EU Member States*. Unpublished final draft. Helsinki: HEUNI.

Country Report of the Republic of Slovenia: Trafficking in Human Beings. 2000. Permanent Mission of the Republic of Slovenia to the OSCE (Organization for Security and Cooperation in Europe). OSCE/ODIHR Country Reports. http://www.osce.org/odihr/attf/pdf/nap_slovenia.pdf.

De Tapia, Stéphane. 2003. *New Patterns of Irregular Migration in Europe*. Strasbourg: Council of Europe.

Dutch National Rapporteur on Trafficking in Human Beings. 2004. "The Netherlands." In *A Study for Monitoring the Trafficking of Human Beings for the Purpose of Sexual Exploitation in the EU Member States*. Unpublished final draft. Helsinki: HEUNI.

Ehrenreich, Barbara, and Arlie Russell Hochschild. 2003. *Global Woman: Nannies, Maids and Sex Workers in the New Economy*. London: Granta Books.

Erokhina, Liudmila. 2004. "Trafficking in Women in the Russian Far East."

In *Human Traffic and Transnational Crime: Eurasian and American Perspectives*, edited by Sally Stoecker and Louise Shelley. Lanham, MD: Rowman & Littlefield.

EU Organized Crime Report 2002. 2002. The Hague: EUROPOL.

Fijnaut, Cyrille, Frank Bovenkerk, Gerben Bruinsma, and Henk van de Bunt. 1998. *Organized Crime in the Netherlands.* The Hague: Kluwer Law International.

Flam, Mikel. 2003. "UN Chronicle June–August 2003." http://www.findarticles.com/p/articles/mi_m1309/is_2_40/ai_105657548.

Ghijs, Inge. 2004. *Vernederd, verkracht, verborgen. Huisslaven in België.* Antwerp: Manteau.

GPAT (Global Programme against Trafficking in Human Beings). 2005. *Regional Patterns of Trafficking in Human Beings.* http://www.unodc.org.

Hajdinjak, Marko. 2002. *Smuggling in Southeast Europe.* CSD (Center for the Study of Democracy) Reports no. 10. Sofia: Center for the Study of Democracy.

Hollmen, Lauri, and Marjut Jyrkinen, eds. 1999. *Building up a Network for Monitoring, Analysing and Combatting Trafficking in Women and Children.* Helsinki: Ministry of the Interior.

IOM (International Organization for Migration). 1998. *Analysis of Data and Statistical Resources Available in the EU Member States on Trafficking in Humans, Particularly in Women and Children for Purposes of Sexual Exploitation.* Project of the IOM for the European Commission's STOP Programme. Final Report. Geneva: IOM.

———. 2000. *Migrant Trafficking in Europe: A Review of the Evidence with Case Studies from Hungary, Poland and Ukraine.* Geneva: IOM.

———. 2001a. *Deceived Migrants from Tajikistan: A Study in Trafficking in Women and Children.* Geneva: IOM.

———. 2001b. *Victims of Trafficking in the Balkans: A Study of Trafficking in Women and Children for Sexual Exploitation to, through and from the Balkan Region.* Geneva: IOM.

———. 2003a. *First Annual Report on Victims of Trafficking in Southeastern Europe.* Geneva: IOM.

———. 2003b. *Irregular Migration and the Trafficking in Women: The Case of Turkey.* Geneva: IOM.

———. 2003c. *Trafficking in Persons: An Analysis of Afghanistan.* Geneva: IOM.

———. 2003d. *The Trafficking of Women and Children in the Southern African Region: Presentation of Research Findings.* Geneva: IOM.

———. 2003e. *Who Is the Next Victim? Vulnerability of Young Romanian Women to Trafficking in Human Beings.* Geneva: IOM.

———. 2004. *Revisiting the Human Trafficking Paradigm: The Bangladesh Experience. Part I: Trafficking of Adults.* Geneva: IOM.

Jahic, Galma, and James O. Finckenauer. 2005. "Representations and Misrepresentations of Human Trafficking." *Trends in Organized Crime* 8(3):24–40.

Junninen, Mika. 2005. *Finnish Professional Criminals and Their Organisations.* Helsinki: HEUNI.

Kännedom om Prostitution 1998–1999. 2000. SoS-rapport 2000:5. Linköping: Socialstyrelsen.

Kaufmann, Eva, and Erich Zwettler. 2004. "Austria." In *A Study for Monitoring the Trafficking of Human Beings for the Purpose of Sexual Exploitation in the EU Member States*. Unpublished final draft. Helsinki: HEUNI.

Kelly, Liz, and Linda Regan. 2000. *Stopping Traffic: Exploring the Extent of, and Responses to, Trafficking in Women for Sexual Exploitation in the UK*. Police Research Series Paper no. 125. London: Home Office.

Kleimenov, Mikhail, and Stanislav Shamkov. 2004. "Criminal Transportation of Persons: Trends and Recommendations." In *Human Traffic and Transnational Crime: Eurasian and American Perspectives*, edited by Sally Stoecker and Louise Shelley. Lanham, MD: Rowman & Littlefield.

Kontula, Anna. 2005. *Prostituutio Suomessa*. Helsinki: Sexpo.

Labour Migration. 2005. http://www.iom.int/en/who/main_service_areas_labour.shtml.

Laczko, Frank, Amanda Klekowski von Koppenfels, and Jana Barthel. 2002. "Trafficking in Women from Central and Eastern Europe: A Review of Statistical Data." Paper presented at the European Conference on Preventing and Combating Trafficking in Human Beings, Brussels, September 18–20.

Legget, Ted. 2004. "Hidden Agendas." *SA Crime Quarterly* 9:1–6.

Lehti, Martti. 2003. *Trafficking in Women and Children in Europe*. HEUNI Papers no. 18. Helsinki: HEUNI.

Lehti, Martti, and Kauko Aromaa. 2002. *Trafficking in Human Beings, Illegal Immigration and Finland*. Helsinki: HEUNI.

Leskinen, Jari. 2003. "Organisoitu paritus ja prostituutio Suomessa." In *Rikostutkimus 2002*. Helsinki: Keskusrikospoliisi.

Maljevic, Almir. 2005. "Trafficking in Women in Bosnia and Herzegovina." In *The Organized Crime Economy: Managing Crime Markets in Europe*, edited by Petrus C. van Duyne, Klaus von Lampe, Maarten van Dijck, and James L. Newell. Nijmegen: Wolf Legal Publishers.

McKeganey, Neil, and Marina Barnard. 2003. "Prostitution and HIV/AIDS." In *Prostitution*, edited by Roger Matthews and Maggie O'Neill. Wiltshire: Ashgate.

Mon-Eu-Traf. 2002. *A Pilot Study on Three European Union Key Immigration Points for Monitoring the Trafficking of Human Beings for the Purpose of Sexual Exploitation across the European Union*. Final Report. Brussels: European Commission.

Mon-Eu-Traf II. 2004. *A Study for Monitoring the Trafficking of Human Beings for the Purpose of Sexual Exploitation in the EU Member States*. Unpublished final draft. Helsinki: HEUNI.

Moustgaard, Ulrikke. 2002. "Bodies across Borders." *NIKK magasin* 1:16–17.

Muhonen, Pihla. 2005. "Interview in Ajankohtainen kakkonen." YLE TV2, July 26.

NCIS (National Criminal Intelligence Service). 2002. *UK Threat Assessment 2002*. http://www.ncis.co.uk/ukta.

Niemi-Kiesiläinen, Johanna. 2004. "Naiskauppa, paritus ja seksin osto." *Lakimies* 3:451–65.

Norwegian Report on Anti-trafficking Activities. 2000. Royal Ministry of Foreign Affairs. OSCE/ODIRH Country Reports. http://www.osce.org/odihr/attf/pdf/nap_norway.pdf.

Omelaniuk, Irena. 2002. "Trafficking in Persons: Nature and Logistics." Paper presented at the conference on Trafficking: Networks and Logistics of Transnational Crime and International Terrorism, Courmayeur, Italy, December 6–8.

Organized Crime Situation Report 2001. 2003. Strasbourg: Council of Europe.

Pärssinen, Venla. 2003. *Ihmiskauppa rikoksena Suomen lainsäädäntömaisemassa. Ehdotus hallituksen esitykseksi rikoslain 25 luvun ja oikeudenkäynnistä rikosasioissa annetun lain muuttamisesta.* Turku: Turun yliopisto.

Pearson, E. 2001. "The Need for Effective Witness Protection in the Prosecution of Traffickers: A Human Rights Framework for Witness Protection." Paper presented at the First Pan-African Regional Conference on Trafficking in Persons, Abuja, Nigeria, February 19–23.

Plant, Roger. 2002. "Trafficking for Labour Exploitation. The Role and Activities of the ILO." Paper presented at the conference on Trafficking: Networks and Logistics of Transnational Crime and International Terrorism, Courmayeur, Italy, December 6–8.

Poulin, Richard. 2005. "The Legalization of Prostitution and Its Impact on Trafficking in Women and Children." http://stangoff.com/?p=70.

Russell, Sharon Stanton. 2005. *International Migration: Implications for the World Bank.* Human Capital Development and Operations Policy Working Papers no. 54. World Bank. http://www.worldbank.org/html/extdr/hnp/hddflash/workp/wp_00054.html.

Scully, Eileen. 2001. "Pre–Cold War Traffic in Sexual Labour and Its Foes: Some Contemporary Lessons." In *Global Human Smuggling*, edited by David Kyle and Rey Koslowski. London: Johns Hopkins University Press.

Shelley, Louise. 2004. "Russian and Chinese Trafficking: A Comparative Perspective." In *Human Traffic and Transnational Crime: Eurasian and American Perspectives*, edited by Sally Stoecker and Louise Shelley. Lanham, MD: Rowman & Littlefield.

Sipaviciene, Audra. 2002. "You Will Be Sold like a Doll." *NIKK magasin* 1: 10–15.

A Study: Trafficking in Women and Children from the Republic of Armenia. 2001. http://www.iom.int/documents/publication/en/Armenia_traff_report.pdf.

"Trafficking in Persons Report Office to Monitor and Combat Trafficking in Persons June 14, 2004." *Trends in Organized Crime* 8(1):38–45.

Trafficking in Women and Prostitution in the Baltic States: Social and Legal Aspects. 2001. Helsinki: IOM.

Trafficking of Nigerian Girls to Italy. 2004. Turin: UNICRI.

Travaini, G. V., S. Garibaldo, V. Arcari, and R. Molteni. 2003. "International Trafficking in Human Organs." In *Organised Crime, Trafficking, Drugs: Selected Papers Presented at the Annual Conference of the European Society of Crim-*

inology, Helsinki 2003, edited by Sami Nevala and Kauko Aromaa. HEUNI Publication no. 42. Helsinki: HEUNI.

Travnickova, Ivana. 2004. *Trafficking in Women: The Czech Republic Perspective.* Prague: UNICRI.

Turunen, Merja-Maaria. 1996. *Kun kaikki on kaupan . . . Prostituution asiantuntijatyöryhmän raportti.* Stakesin raportteja 190. Helsinki: Stakes.

West, Jackie. 2003. "Prostitution: Collectives and the Politics of Regulation." In *Prostitution*, edited by Roger Matthews and Maggie O'Neill. Wiltshire: Ashgate.

Vermeulen, Gert, and Tom van der Beken. 2004. "Belgium." In *A Study for Monitoring the Trafficking of Human Beings for the Purpose of Sexual Exploitation in the EU Member States*. Unpublished final draft. Helsinki: HEUNI.

James P. Lynch

Problems and Promise of Victimization Surveys for Cross-National Research

ABSTRACT

In the late 1960s self-report surveys of criminal victimization were controversial and new. Now, they are common, a mainstay of statistical systems
and a familiar research tool. More complex questions have arisen concerning the validity and reliability of victim survey data, including whether
they can be used in cross-national comparisons of crime and criminal justice issues. Victim survey data are sufficiently valid and reliable for use in
cross-national comparisons. Victim surveys can tell us a great deal about
crime cross-nationally that police administrative data cannot. While surveys in principle should be more comparable across nations than police
administrative data, in practice this comparability cannot be assumed. Self-
consciously comparative surveys, such as the International Crime Victimization Survey (ICVS) produce more comparable data across nations than
nation-specific surveys do. Nation-specific surveys produce higher-quality
data on their specific nation than the ICVS does. Steps should be taken to
enhance the quality of ICVS data and the cross-national comparability of
nation-specific surveys.

The practice of asking crime victims to report their victimization experience in sample surveys was rare until the late 1960s. At that time
a number of factors encouraged intense interest in the idea of using
victim reports to estimate the volume of crime in the United States.
The impetus for a victimization survey came largely from the level of
crime and urban unrest at the time in the United States and efforts of
the federal government to improve the criminal justice system. The

I thank Michael Tonry for encouraging me to write this essay and, with David P.
Farrington and Patrick Langan, organizing meetings at Cambridge University on cross-
national comparisons. Lynn Addington, Paul Nieuwbeerta, and William Sabol offered
useful suggestions, for which I am grateful.

229

President's Commission on Law Enforcement and Administration of Justice was charged with developing a strategy to reduce crime by improving the administration of justice. One of the commission's major goals was to reduce the amount of crime that eluded the attention of the police. Commission members realized that their success in achieving this goal would be perceived as failure unless there was an indicator of crime that was independent of the police (Cantor and Lynch 2000). At the same time, police statistics were coming under fire for understating the crime problem, as exposés of several police departments showed evidence of "killing crime on the books." The time was ripe for instituting a victimization survey as an indicator of the level of crime.

While the climate in the United States was favorable for victimization surveys, there were a number of unknowns that had to be resolved before this idea could be put into practice on a large scale. The first of these unknowns was whether respondents could accurately identify criminal acts, recall them, and report them to interviewers. The second unknown was whether the "dark figure" of unreported crime was large enough to be detected in a sample survey of reasonable size. If most crime was already reported to the police, then the additional volume of crime in society would not be large enough to be detected efficiently in a sample of households. If that were the case, then it would be better to improve police recording of crime than to begin an entirely new system of crime statistics.

To resolve these questions, the commission sponsored a number of small-scale victimization surveys. One of these was conducted by the Bureau of Social Science Research, Inc. (Biderman et al. 1967) in Washington, DC, another, by the University of Michigan (Reiss 1967) in Boston and Chicago, and a third, a national survey done by the National Opinion Research Center (Ennis 1967). These surveys demonstrated that respondents could report on their victimization experience, that the volume of crime in the United States was substantial enough to warrant an alternative to police-based crime statistics, and that a sample of reasonable size could be used to estimate the level and change in level of crime. These field tests conducted by private survey firms were followed by a number of studies by the U.S. Census Bureau in which different survey design features were tested, including the appropriate reference period and the number of respondents per household. Most of these features had to do with easily accommodating the victimization survey within the environment of the Census Bureau rather than with the general feasibility of the victim survey method. In 1972, the National Crime Survey (NCS) was fielded by the Census Bureau, and it has been a component of the crime statistics system in the United States ever since.

Since 1972, victimization surveys have spread to other nations. The Netherlands fielded its first national victimization survey in 1973 and has had some type of national survey ever since (Bijleveld and Smit 2004). Other nations waited some time and approached the task more gradually. The British Crime Survey (BCS) was first fielded in 1982, although it was preceded by smaller-scale surveys conducted by academics (Sparks, Genn, and Dodd 1977). From 1982 until 2001, the BCS was typically conducted every other year. Over that period the sample size grew from 14,000 in 1982 (Hough and Mayhew 1982) to 23,000 in 2000 (Clancy et al. 2001), and the survey became an important part of the crime statistics system in the United Kingdom. In 2001, the BCS sample was increased to 40,000 and moved to continuous data collection that would permit annual estimates (Kershaw et al. 2001).

Still other nations have chosen less extensive and less expensive ways of including self-report victimization surveys in their systems of crime statistics. Some, such as Canada, have added victimization supplements to general social surveys or labor force surveys (Statistics Canada 2004). Other nations, such as Switzerland, have maintained a freestanding victimization survey but have conducted it more episodically (Killias, Lamond, and Aebi 2004). Whatever the particular format of the survey, there has been a steady increase in the availability of national victimization surveys worldwide since the late sixties.

The development of the International Crime Victimization Survey (ICVS) has done the most to increase the availability of nationally representative victim survey data worldwide. Through the efforts of the Dutch Ministry of Justice and the United Nations, victim surveys with reasonably uniform methodology have been conducted in a large number of nations throughout the world (Van Dijk, Mayhew, and Killias 1990; Alvazzi del Frate, Zvekic, and Van Dijk 1993; Van Kesteren, Mayhew, and Nieuwbeerta 2001). The first ICVS was fielded in 1989 and included seventeen industrialized nations, mostly in Western Europe. There have been three sweeps of the survey since, with the last administration in 2000 involving seventeen industrialized nations and a number of city surveys in nonindustrial nations. In all, the ICVS has been the umbrella for 140 separate victim surveys in twenty-six different nations (some being surveyed numerous times) and forty-six cities.

The availability of high-quality victimization surveys has thus increased substantially over the last two decades, and they have become a common means of describing crime and criminal justice policy both within and across nations (Van Dijk, Mayhew, and Killias 1990; Van Dijk and Mayhew 1993; Kershaw et al. 2000; Rennison 2001; Van Kesteren, Mayhew, and Nieuwbeerta 2001). As with police-based data on crime, however, questions have arisen concerning the quality and appropriate use of these data for cross-national comparisons. Given the limitations of these data, can they be used for cross-national comparisons, and if so, how should they be used?

Existing victimization surveys can be used for various types of cross-national studies. They are useful for cross-national comparisons because they provide incident-level data on crime and a great deal of information on issues related to victimization and the criminal justice system. This provides flexibility and context that police administrative data do not. Moreover, victim surveys in principle are not as bound to legal and political institutions as police administrative data and can be made more comparable across nations than police data can be. Existing victim surveys, however, differ in design in ways that can affect cross-national comparisons of crime and victimization rates. Studies that compare victim surveys across nations must take account of these design differences.

The ICVS, which is designed explicitly for cross-national comparisons, is more uniform than nation-specific surveys and can therefore be used more easily for cross-national comparisons of all sorts. Small sample sizes in the ICVS and the need to keep costs to a minimum, however, limit the types of crime that can be compared to gross classes of violence or very prevalent property crime. Nation-specific surveys have larger samples and employ more expensive and sophisticated techniques, but they differ considerably in the survey designs employed, and these design differences must be taken into account when cross-national comparisons are made.

These caveats are not restricted to simple comparisons of rates at a specific time. Design differences affect both change estimates and multivariate models of victimization risk estimated with victim survey data. We should not assume that these analyses are immune from the effects of design differences across surveys.

I reach these conclusions by examining the ways in which victim survey data have been used in cross-national comparisons. The essay begins with a review of the evidence as to whether self-report surveys generally provide a reasonable measure of some component of the crime problem. Section II describes various types of cross-national studies and assesses the usefulness of crime surveys (as opposed to the most commonly used alternative—police administrative series data) for conducting these types of inquiries. Section III focuses on comparability and on sources of noncomparability in cross-national comparisons of data from victim surveys and assesses two different strategies for maximizing comparability in cross-national comparisons of victim survey data. The conclusion (Sec. IV) sets out recommendations for improving victim surveys and ways of using the data to minimize the negative impact of known methodological problems on cross-national comparisons.

I. Do Victimization Surveys Measure Crime?

In spite of the growing popularity of victimization surveys, some suspicion still exists that they are simply "polls" and do not provide an accurate count of crime events. Some of this skepticism is warranted in that victim survey data are only as good as the memory, cognitive capacity, and forthrightness of respondents. At the same time, survey researchers have learned a great deal about making the recall and reporting tasks in retrospective surveys easier to perform and less subject to the frailties of individual respondents (Sudman, Bradburn, and Schwarz 1996). The empirical data that we have on the validity and reliability of victim surveys support the contention that self-report surveys of victimization do accurately measure some component of the crime problem.

A. Test of Convergent Validity

Validating crime statistics is not easy. There is no gold standard for victimization that is comparable to the testing of urine or hair samples in self-report surveys of drug use, for example (Fendrich and Vaughn 1994; Magura and Kang 1994). Police administrative data have been used to validate survey estimates, but it is clear that the social organization of these two methods of data collection is very different, and we should not expect 100 percent congruence (Biderman 1966). Nonetheless, Biderman and Lynch (1991) found a high degree of congruence in the United States between annual change estimates from the Uniform Crime Reports (UCRs) and those from the National Crime Victimization Survey (NCVS). In a review of a number of comparisons of national trends generated from police and survey data, McDowall and Loftin (forthcoming) find a high degree of convergence in the trends when obvious differences in scope and definitions are taken into account.[1] Rosenfeld (forthcoming) finds similar levels of congruence in "unambiguous" types of crime, for example, gun assaults, and somewhat less congruence in less well-defined crimes, for example, nongun assaults. The few studies that find negative correlations between police and survey data are those involving ambiguous types of crime such as aggravated assault in which the variability in both police and survey data is substantial (Decker 1977; Nelson 1979; Mennard and Covey 1988; Smith et al. 1999).

At the incident level, reverse record checks (RRCs) have also been employed to validate victim surveys, and they find that a substantial proportion of the crimes reported and recorded by the police are not reported subsequently in the survey. The complexity of matching target events, however, and the highly selected nature of the population of persons and events included make these studies highly suspect for validation purposes. The RRCs begin with a sample of incidents drawn from police records. Interviewers contact victims and ask them about their recent victimization experience in an effort to elicit a report of the target incident (Dodge 1970; Law Enforcement Assistance Administration 1972). If the target incident is mentioned, then this is taken as evidence of the validity of the self-report method. While all of this seems straightforward in concept, it is not that easy to accomplish in practice. One of the biggest problems in conducting RRC studies is ensuring that the event reported by the respondent is, indeed, the target event. Persons reporting crimes to the police are more heavily victimized than the general population (Biderman et al. 1967; Biderman and Lynch 1981), and they are much more likely to have multiple events occur in a given span of time. This complicates the matching of target events with events reported by the respondent. Miller and

---

[1] The scope of crime in the UCR, e.g., includes crimes against commercial victims that are not included in the NCVS. Conversely, the NCVS includes crimes not reported to the police, and the UCR does not. The two series track better when these noncommon components are omitted.

Groves (1985) encountered substantial difficulty in matching reported and target events. In many cases, several attributes of the event would be the same, while other attributes would differ across the two reports. It was very difficult to know if the respondent had mentioned the target event. Their conclusion was, in effect, that RRC studies of crime reporting could not be done well enough to be used as a means of validating survey responses.

The RRC studies also suffer from substantial selectivity such that the sample of victims eligible to report target events is quite different from the general public responding to victimization surveys. First, victims reporting to the police are different from victims who do not report to the police. Second, even among those victims reporting to the police, there is considerable attrition in RRC studies because the victim simply cannot be found. The reverse record surveys had a nonresponse rate of 35 percent compared to about 11 percent in the NCVS generally (Biderman and Lynch 1981). This selectivity raises questions about generalizing the results of RRC studies to the population of survey respondents, even if there were no problems with the matching.

B. Tests of Construct Validity

Construct validity offers another approach to validating victim survey data. According to construct validity, if victimization as measured by the survey is correlated with attributes of victims, offenders, and crimes in a manner consistent with theory, then the survey data are valid. One of the most consistent findings in criminology is the negative relationships between age and offending rate and age and victimization rate. If victim survey data show consistently that age is negatively related to victimization rate, then this would be additional evidence that victim surveys are accurately measuring crime. When data on the proportion of persons victimized from the ICVS are plotted by age of the victim across sixteen nations, the probability of victimization declines with age in every nation except one (see fig. 1). The same distribution is found with country-specific surveys such as the NCVS and the BCS (see fig. 2).

Criminological theory would also lead us to expect that estimates of victimization will vary across gender and specifically that men should have higher rates of violent victimization than women. In an analysis of the ICVS in eighteen nations, Verweij and Nieuwbeerta (2001)

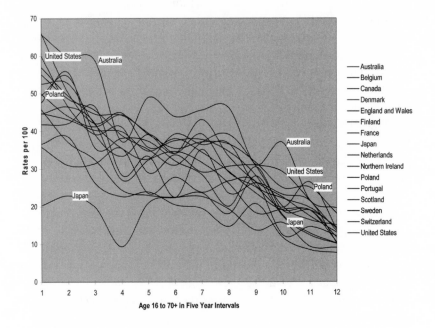

FIG. 1.—Prevalence rates for total victimization by age and nation. Source: Lynch (2002).

found that violent victimization rates for men were higher than those for women in all but one of the nations. On average, men had violent victimization rates that were 20 percent higher than those of women. In the BCS, men report being victims of violence at a rate 60 percent higher than that for women (Kershaw et al. 2000), and in the NCVS, males have violent victimization rates 38 percent higher than those of women (Rennison 2001).

While the results from victimization surveys are consistent with expectations from criminological theory, there are also a number of inconsistencies, the best known of which is the "education effect" (Taylor 1983). In a number of victim surveys, highly educated respondents report more minor assaults than less educated respondents. This is contrary to criminological theory that maintains a negative relationship between socioeconomic status and violence. This inconsistency is often attributed to the greater cognitive capacity of more highly educated respondents, but it could as easily be due to differential cuing in victim

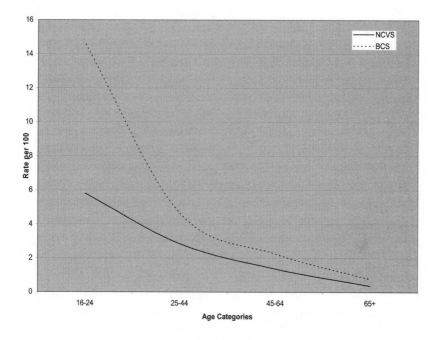

FIG. 2.—Age of victim by survey, 2000. Sources: Kershaw et al. 2000, p. 88; Trends in Violent Crime by Age of Victim, 1973–2003 at http://www.ojp.usdoj.gov/bjs/glance/tables/vagetab.htm.

surveys or differential encoding of events in memory. Since the effect has been observed across a number of survey designs with different cuing strategies, the cuing explanation seems less plausible. The encoding explanation assumes that minor violence is so ubiquitous among less educated respondents that they simply do not encode it in memory, whereas the infrequency of minor violence for higher-status respondents encourages them to encode these events. This same education effect is not observed for more clearly defined criminal events such as robbery or assaults with weapons (Cantor and Lynch 2005). Consequently, while the education effect is not consistent with theory, it is a fairly localized problem for victimization surveys (restricted to minor assaults) and does not raise fundamental questions about the method more generally.

While establishing the validity of crime statistics is difficult, the evidence that we have from police administrative series trends indicates that surveys and administrative series trends are generally very consistent. Moreover, in terms of construct validity, victimization surveys show that the risk of victimization is correlated with attributes of victims in the way that theory dictates. Both of these results give us confidence that victim surveys provide a reasonable measure of the crime problem generally.

II. How Useful Are Victim Surveys for Cross-National Comparisons of Crime and Justice?

While the foregoing suggests that victim surveys are useful measures of crime generally, the central question in this essay is whether victim surveys are specifically useful for cross-national studies of crime and justice issues. Good cross-national research has three requirements: data that are comparable, data that are available, and data that are used in a manner that makes them interpretable. Meeting these requirements is more or less important, depending on the type of comparative research being done.

A. Data Requirements for Cross-National Research

Getting data that are comparable across nations has always been the most challenging aspect of cross-national research (Council of Europe 1999; Farrington, Langan, and Tonry 2004). Cross-national research is done because we suspect that the nation-state is a relevant and distinctive unit for the study of differences in crime and justice. Unfortunately, this can also mean that nations differ in the ways they define crime, respond to crime, or collect information on crime. It is important that the differences across nations in crime and justice are not masked or distorted by these differences in definitions and procedures.

"Availability" refers to the range of nations for which comparable data are available. While any cross-national comparison can be enlightening, the greater the variability in nations included, the more enlightening these comparisons will be. Since most cross-national studies employ convenience samples based on the availability of data, it is difficult to generalize findings with any certainty (Bennett and Basiotis 1991; Fajnzylber, Lederman, and Loayza 1998; Schaefer and Lynch 2003). The more nations included in the study, the more likely the results are to be applicable to the populations of nation-states. For multivariate models of crime at the national level, having a large number of nations is essential. The more nations in the study, the more complex explanatory models can be. The goals of availability and comparability are often at odds, since the number of nations for which comparable data can be obtained is small and highly selected (Council of Europe 1999; Farrington, Langan, and Tonry 2004; Tonry and Farrington 2005).

"Interpretability" refers to the ability of a broad range of consumers to understand the results of cross-national comparisons. Simple comparisons of rates are the most easily understood cross-national comparisons. These comparisons, however, are often too simple for drawing conclusions about the ways that nation-states differ in relation to crime and justice policies and about the underlying causes or explanations for those differences. Multivariate analyses of cross-national data on crime are much more powerful in holding constant factors that vary across nations and that could explain variability in crime rates. These models go beyond establishing differences across nations and begin to test explanations for these differences. Unfortunately, these analyses are not easily understood, and not just by lay audiences. Interpreting the meaning of a coefficient in a multivariate model must go beyond whether the coefficient for a nation is statistically significant. Size of the effect is often not evaluated in these multivariate analyses, where differences in the variance in predictor variables can influence the magnitude of the effect. Variables excluded from the model as well as the selectivity in the group of nations included in the sample can complicate the interpretation of results.[2]

Satisfying these often competing demands of comparability, availability, and interpretability can be more or less important and more or less difficult depending on the type of cross-national study. No single source of data will be ideal for every type of cross-national analysis. In the next subsection, I distinguish various approaches to cross-national analyses that put different demands on sources of cross-national data and compare the relative advantages of police administrative series and victim surveys for meeting those demands.

[2] This problem of interpretability increases with the use of pooled cross-sectional time series, where data from nations are pooled over time (Bennett and Basiotis 1991; Bennett and Lynch 1991). Dummy variables are introduced into these models to control for both nation and time. This technique is often used in cross-national studies to increase the sample size, since a case becomes the nation-year rather than simply the nation. These pooled data are treated essentially as a cross section when they are not. It is difficult to say how these pooled analyses relate to either cross-sectional analyses or time series (Forst and Lynch 2003).

B. Varieties of Cross-National Comparisons

For purposes of this essay, cross-national research is empirical research that includes data from more than one nation and in which the nation-state is an important variable in the model being tested. The purpose of the research is to describe or understand the effects of the nation on the level, change, or distribution of crime and victimization or on responses to crime. Cross-national research typically focuses on comparisons of the level and changes in level of crime, and this tends to be the yardstick used to evaluate the utility of cross-national data on crime and justice issues (Van Dijk and Mayhew 1993; Farrington, Langan, and Tonry 2004; Tonry and Farrington 2005). It is important in evaluating various statistical data and specifically victim surveys to use a wider array of yardsticks, since the demands of cross-national comparisons of crime rates can be excessively stringent and not appropriate for other types of analyses.

1. *Comparing Crime Rates across Nations.* Perhaps the most prevalent form of cross-national comparisons involves annual crime or victimization rates (Van Dijk, Mayhew, and Killias 1990; Farrington, Langan, and Wikstrom 1993; Lynch 1995; Farrington and Langan 1998). Here the incidence or prevalence of crime is divided by the resident population to obtain a crime rate, and nations are compared on these rates. In many ways this may be the most demanding use of crime and justice statistics.

Crime rates are very sensitive to any sources of noncomparability in the surveys or administrative records being used to compare nations. The omission of any eligible crime event from the numerator of the rates will affect these rates and their comparison across nations, unless we can make the heroic, and generally unwarranted, assumption that these omissions are constant across nations. Nations can differ a great deal in terms of their culture and social structure. The cultural and legal definitions of what a crime is can vary, as well as the institutions and organizations responsible for applying those definitions in the context of a statistical system. The definition of assault within families, for example, can differ across cultures and legal systems, with the result that what would be considered assault in one nation would not be so defined in another. Even small differences in agency rules concerning crime classification, for example, can affect crime rates (Mayhew 1987). To assume that statistics on crime are similar across nations without adjustments for these differences would be unwise.

2. *Comparing Changes in Crime Rates across Nations over Time.*   Here, crime rates are calculated for a given year and compared to the same rate calculated for a subsequent year. The use of crime statistics to compare the change in crime over time is a little more forgiving than the comparison of level estimates. If errors within nations are constant over time, then they will not affect comparisons of change. So flawed estimates of level in two nations can still produce accurate change estimates for those nations (Farrington and Langan 1998; Farrington, Langan, and Tonry 2004; Tonry and Farrington 2005).

3. *Modeling Crime Rates across Nations.*   As cross-national data become more prevalent, exploring the differences in crime rates using multivariate nation-level models has become more popular. These studies estimate aggregate crime rates in a large group of nations using other aggregated data on those nations, such as unemployment rates, gross national product, and the like (Stack 1984; Messner 1989; Bennett and Basiotis 1991; Fajnzylber, Lederman, and Loayza 1998). This method is robust with regard to noncomparability of procedures for collecting data on crime across nations, as long as these sources of noncomparability are not correlated with predictor variables in the model. So, for example, if one nation collects data on children under sixteen and another nation does not, then the cross-sectional crime rates could be significantly off. But in a correlational analysis, as long as younger people commit more crime than older people, the correlation between age and crime will be negative.

4. *Nation as Context.*   With the availability of incident-level data on crimes across nations, nested data analyses are becoming more popular (Verweij and Nieuwbeerta 2001; Raudenbush and Bryk 2003; Goudrian, Lynch, and Nieuwbeerta 2004). In these studies, the dependent variable is measured at the individual level, and the predictor variables are both attributes of individuals and attributes of aggregates such as cities and nations. When data are nested like this, it is easier, among other things, to assess the relative influence on crime of the attributes of individuals who live in a country as opposed to the social organization of the nation. Characteristics of individuals can be held constant while assessing the effects of living in a particular nation on the risk of crime or victimization. In this type of analysis, noncomparable measurement across nations could overstate the effects of nations on victimization risk when characteristics of individuals are held constant.

They should not affect estimates of the influence of individual-level variables.

5. *Estimating Crime versus Estimating Other Things of Interest.* There are cross-national comparisons that are relevant for crime and justice policies but are not themselves comparisons of crime or victimization. Issues such as why victims mobilize the police or the role of public preferences in the determination of sentencing policy are important questions, the answers to which can differ substantially across nations (Kury, Obergfell-Fuchs, and Wurger 2001; Goudrian, Lynch, and Nieuwbeerta 2004). For example, there is good reason to believe that political institutions and other institutions of accountability that vary substantially across nations can affect citizens' perceptions of the legitimacy of the police. Perceived legitimacy, in turn, can influence the decision to call the police in response to criminal victimization. Cross-national research can shed some light on this topic and others related to crime. Often, studies of these subjects do not put the same kind of demands on data that comparative studies of crime and victimization do. In the case of perceived legitimacy, for example, every respondent can have an opinion, whereas only a very small number of respondents will have experienced a serious violent crime. The sample size required to make a reliable estimate of perceived legitimacy will be much less than that required to estimate the rate of serious violent crime.

C. *Assessing Relative Value of Victim Survey Data for Types of Cross-National Research*

Victim surveys are different from administrative series of official records in ways that make them more or less appropriate for the uses of the data outlined in the foregoing subsection. Victim surveys are collected on a person or incident basis, whereas police administrative data are often aggregated counts of crime incidents. Victim surveys generally record a great deal of detailed information on crime events. Police administrative data often rely on much more aggregated information such that most of the relevant information on a crime incident is reduced to a crime class or type, for example, aggravated assault. Surveys rely on samples, whereas police administrative data are often a census or something quite close to a census. Virtually every police agency is required to keep statistics on crime reported and actions taken in response to crime, so police administrative data are available in a large number of nations. Victim surveys are usually freestanding data collections that are not required by the provision of police service and are therefore available in fewer nations.

1. *Advantages of Victim Surveys.*   One of the major advantages of victim survey data is that they are collected on an incident or individual basis. So, instead of simply producing a crime rate for a jurisdiction, victimization rates can be produced for subgroups of victims, offenders, and crimes. This disaggregation of national crime rates can be very illuminating with regard to the sources of cross-national differences in crime rates or their change over time.[3] If, for example, cross-national differences in crime rates were simply due to the greater abundance of young persons, then calculating age-specific victimization or offending rates by nation would make that apparent in a readily interpretable way.[4]

In addition to the advantages that flow from incident-level data, victim surveys also have greater potential for disaggregating crime incidents, which has repercussions for achieving greater comparability across nations. Information that describes crime incidents can be aggregated at the time of collection or left as attributes that can be aggregated in various ways after collection. Crime classification, for example, can be done at the time of data collection when someone examines the available information and, on the basis of that information, places the event into a crime category. In police administrative data, police officers at the scene may make a coding decision that a specific event is a burglary.[5] This is an aggregation of information. Once it is done, it cannot be done differently without access to the original information. In some victimization surveys, a substantial amount of information is collected on the incident, and that information is retained in the data in a highly disaggregated form. This is extremely useful in defining comparable crime classes across countries.

---

[3] For an illustration of the power of disaggregating national trends, see Blumstein and Wallman (2005).

[4] It is possible to do this type of analysis with multivariate modeling of nation-level data simply by introducing median age into the model predicting crime. This method is more difficult to use when investigating complex subgroups, e.g., young black males, largely because aggregate data for these specific subgroups are not readily available on a large number of nations. Moreover, multivariate models would evaluate this effect across the entire sample of countries and not in specific comparisons. So, if this effect of population composition does not affect the entire sample of a nation, it will not be detectable in this type of analysis.

[5] In some cases this decision is reviewed by supervisors who read the field reports and sometimes not.

For example, if one nation includes commercial burglary in its burglary classification and another does not, then, if commercial victims are identified in the interview, they can be excluded from one nation's classification to make it comparable with the other.[6]

Incident-level data also let analysts employ nested data techniques that are more powerful and more appropriate for separating individual-level effects from nation-level effects. Multivariate modeling with nation-level data provides a distorted picture of cross-national differences in crime risk. They examine only the variation in crime across nations and ignore the substantial variation of crime within nations. They answer the question, "What accounts for cross-national differences in crime or victimization risk?" This is the question asked because we have been largely limited to national-level data coming from police administrative series. The question that should be asked is, "How much of the variation in crime risk among individuals is attributable to the nation in which they live?" Much of the variation in crime or victimization risk comes from one's place in the social structure and not from the nation-state that one happens to live in. Young people, for example, are everywhere more at risk of crime and victimization than older people. Nested data techniques let us decompose the variation in victimization risk into that due to the individual and that due to membership in some cluster, including the nation. In order to use nested data, person-level data nested within nations are needed. Victimization surveys provide such data, and police administrative series customarily do not.

Indeed, police administrative data cannot easily support this type of nested data analysis, but not because they cannot provide incident-level data within nations. This is conceivable, although not routinely done. The larger problem with doing nested analyses of victimization risk with police data is that they do not include information on nonvictims. There is no variation on the dependent variable, victimization risk. Researchers have skirted this problem by doing jurisdiction-level analyses and modeling crime rates in which the numerators were taken from police data and the denominators were taken from census data or some other source (Stack 1984; Messner 1989; Bennett and Basiotis 1991; Fajnzylber, Lederman, and Loayza 1998). These census data in-

---

[6] This can be done with police administrative data, but only if the records contain very fine-grained charges by specific statute, and this is seldom available.

clude the entire at-risk population, victims, and nonvictims. This approach still does not permit nested data analysis.

Victim surveys also have the advantage of having more information on their error structure than police administrative data, which again has implications for comparability. Nonuniformities in measurement in victimization surveys occur usually as the result of a design decision and not as the result of discretion in the application of rules (Biderman and Lynch 1991). So, for example, that researchers in one nation employ in-person interviews and in another telephone interviews could affect the level of crime reported in each nation. Researchers know who has gotten which type of interview, and as long as there is sufficient variability in the use of the two methods, adjustments can be made to take account of the effects of mode differences. Since most of the nonuniformities in measurement in administrative series are not the result of design but discretion in the application of rules, it is more difficult to identify and adjust for these factors. Moreover, there is a substantial amount of research done on survey methodology that can be used to identify the effects of survey design on response. The same is not the case for police administrative series.

Finally, victim surveys offer an opportunity to study crime-related issues in addition to crime or victimization itself. Respondents who report on their victimization can also report on a variety of crime-related behaviors and sentiments relevant for crime and responses to crime. Police administrative data do not typically include this type of information.

2. *Disadvantages of Victim Surveys.* Victim survey data suffer from three major disadvantages relative to police administrative data for the study of crime cross-nationally. First, because the surveys use samples, they are affected by sampling error. Second, it is difficult for samples to provide representative data efficiently for both national and subnational units. Third, surveys are freestanding data collection efforts not associated with the provision of a specific service, so they are less prevalent than police administrative data.

Sampling error occurs when a sample is not representative of the population from which it is chosen. Sampling error is not a great problem for the study of prevalent forms of crime because it will not be that great and it can be estimated. For relatively rare events, such as serious violence, however, the effects of sampling error can be substantial, with the result that estimates of rates for these crimes will not be reliable. The typical response to this problem is to collapse crime classes to get more reliable estimates, but this has the unfortunate effect of creating a less internally homogeneous class of crime (Lynch 1987). The use of sexual assault rather than rape, for example, results in a much more heterogeneous class of crime. This, in turn, masks enlightening differences in rates across nations. It also suppresses the correlation between victimization and predictor variables because some variables are highly correlated with some subcomponent of the aggregated crime class but not with another.

A more troubling aspect of the nonrepresentativeness of samples is the effect of undercoverage and nonresponse. The former refers to the situation in which certain persons or groups are excluded from the sample because they are excluded from the lists or frame from which the sample is chosen. Homeless persons, for example, are excluded from address lists that serve as the sampling frame for household surveys and are therefore underrepresented in the sample. Nonresponse occurs when persons selected into the sample cannot be interviewed. If these nonresponses occur in a nonrandom fashion, which they undoubtedly do, then this makes the sample less representative of the populations. Surveys generally attempt to lessen the effects of undercoverage and nonresponse by weighting or imputing the data. Both of these strategies rest on the assumption that persons in the sample have the same victimization experience as demographically similar persons omitted from the sample. These strategies are clearly superior to ignoring this missing information, but the assumption remains largely untested. Given the relative size of the undercovered and nonresponding populations, it would seem that nonresponse is much more likely to affect national crime rates than the undercovered population.[7]

A second problem resulting from sampling is the inability to get reliable estimates for subnational jurisdictions. Usually samples are drawn to produce national estimates of crime rates, which means that selection of respondents should be random within the nation. Making estimates for subnational units such as counties or cities, however, requires clustering the selection of respondents in those jurisdictions so

---

[7] In the United States, less than 1 percent of the population is believed to be omitted from the Census Bureau address frame. Even among the most undercovered demographic group, young black males, the undercoverage rate is only 9 percent (Robinson et al. 2002). In contrast, the individual-level nonresponse rate for the NCVS is 11 percent and 28 percent for young black males (per personal communication with author Michael Rand on November 15, 2005).

that there are sufficient samples to make reliable estimates for the unit.[8] Clustering samples in subnational jurisdictions will reduce the efficiency of the sample for national estimates purposes. Consequently, the sample design for most national surveys will not support subnational estimates. Since national surveys are the norm, this is a real problem currently.[9]

Victimization surveys are not yet institutionalized to the point at which they are used to monitor the provision of specific public services in many nations. Police administrative data, in contrast, are routinely used to document the delivery of police services. Consequently, wherever police services are provided, police administrative data will be available. This means that victim surveys are not as widely available as police administrative data. While national victimization surveys are much more prevalent than they were twenty years ago, they are still relatively rare compared to the availability of police administrative statistics on crime. The ICVS has fielded victim surveys of some sort at least once in twenty-four industrialized nations and forty-six cities (Van Kesteren, Mayhew, and Nieuwbeerta 2001). In contrast, INTERPOL includes administrative data on more than seventy-two nations over a twenty-year period (Bennett and Lynch 1991).[10]

Victimization surveys, in principle then, should be preferred to police administrative data for most types of cross-national research because of their greater potential for achieving comparability in crime definitions across nations. Because these data are incident-based, they can be disaggregated by population subgroups, and this disaggregation provides a readily interpretable way to identify and understand cross-national differences in crime. These advantages exist in comparisons of prevalent classes of crime such as burglary and less so for rare crimes, such as serious violence, because of the sampling error in-

---

[8] Many nation-specific surveys employ multistage cluster samples to reduce interviewing costs and particularly travel costs. While these clusters are meaningful for interviewing purposes, they are not necessarily meaningful for crime. Moreover, the amount of sample in a specific cluster is not sufficient to make reliable estimates for that geographical area.

[9] This need not be the case, however. As more subnational jurisdictions conduct their own victimization surveys, it may be possible to have multiple city surveys within several countries so that the effects of nation-level, jurisdiction-level, and person-level characteristics on crime risk can be estimated with sample-based data.

[10] INTERPOL currently makes its crime statistics available to members and not the general public. Similar police data are offered for a large number of nations through the *United Nations Survey on Crime Trends and the Operations of Criminal Justice Systems*. In the latest wave of the survey, ninety-two nations participated (see http://www.uncjin.org/Statistics/WCTS/WCTS6/wcts6.html).

volved. The real advantage of victim survey data comes in nested analyses in which the incident-level data from the surveys can be combined with nation-level data from other sources to disentangle the role of the nation-state in the production of crime risk. Victimization data are not as useful for nation-level modeling of crime rates because of the sampling error in survey estimates and the relatively limited availability of victim survey data.

III. Do Differences in Survey Designs Affect Reporting in Victim Surveys across Nations?

While victim surveys can, theoretically, be made more comparable across nations than administrative series, it is not at all clear that this is so easily achieved in practice. Most surveys are not designed with comparability in mind, so design decisions are made differently in different nations. Even when there is forethought about comparability and an intention to make surveys comparable, it is possible that the political, logistical, and financial constraints of fielding surveys will inhibit comparability. At the same time, however, it could be that prevalent design differences across national surveys have very little effect on cross-national comparisons. At this point, we simply do not know if the potential for comparability in victimization has been or can be achieved. In this section, I examine two strategies for achieving comparability in victim surveys cross-nationally and evaluate them in terms of their ability to provide comparable data for different types of cross-national comparisons.

The most extensive effort for achieving comparable victim survey data comes from the ICVS (Van Kesteren, Mayhew, and Nieuwbeerta 2001). The goal of the ICVS is to field surveys with very comparable information content and procedures across a large number of nations. Another less often used strategy for making comparisons involves simply taking whatever survey data are available in the nations of interest and comparing the resulting estimates. The ICVS strategy begins with the aim to achieve comparability and then makes compromises in terms of data quality and comparability to achieve the greatest availability possible. The latter strategy assumes that whatever design differences there are among nation-specific surveys can be safely ignored for comparative purposes (Farrington, Langan, and Tonry 2004; Tonry and Farrington 2005).

In this section, I assess these various strategies in terms of their assumptions. I look to see whether the definitions and procedures used in the ICVS are, indeed, uniform across nations. I also examine several country-specific surveys to see how different they are in terms of definitions and procedures and speculate as to whether these differences can affect various types of cross-national comparisons. Before exploring the specific strategies for achieving comparability in victim surveys cross-nationally, I use the victim survey literature to identify important design differences between surveys that could affect crime rates across nations.

A. Important Design Differences in Self-Report Surveys of Victimization

Victimization surveys differ in terms of their substantive scope, their sample design, instrumentation, and procedures. "Substantive scope" refers to the classes of crime that are the subject of the survey. The "sample design" refers to the population of interest, the methods for identifying members of that population, and the method for selecting them for interviewing. "Instrumentation" refers to the interrogation that respondents are subjected to in order to identify victims and to describe their victimization and its social context. "Procedures" include all the rules that prescribe how interviewers should behave and how the data should be used after the interview is over, for example, respondent selection, callbacks to nonresponding households, type of crime classification, and rate estimation.

While survey designs can differ in many ways, not all of them are consequential for crime and victimization rates and specifically for comparisons of crime across nations. Methodological research on retrospective surveys generally, and on victimization surveys specifically, suggests that some design differences are more consequential than others. Computer-assisted interviewing, for example, has been shown to have a large effect on reporting (Hubble and Wilder 1988; Percy and Mayhew 1992). Strategies for screening the population to find victims have also had big effects on the reporting of victimization (Persley 1995). These and other of the more consequential design features are described below.

1. *Sample Design.* Most victim surveys employ a cross-sectional design in which a sample is drawn at a given time and those selected are interviewed once. The NCVS employs a rotating panel design in which respondents are selected at a given time, rotated into the sample

throughout the year, interviewed up to seven times over a three-and-one-half-year period, and then rotated out of the sample. The BCS interviews respondents only once, but the interviews are conducted continuously throughout the year and not at one time.

Many of the country-specific surveys that have cross-sectional designs use address or phone list sampling frames. In contrast, most of the ICVS surveys employ random digit dialing (RDD) designs. In general, phone lists and RDD exclude nontelephone households, which traditionally have rates of victimization that are multiples higher than those of households with telephones. The RDD designs usually have higher nonresponse rates than other sample designs because nothing is known about the households contacted and they cannot be solicited by mail before the interview.[11] These "cold contact" surveys have the lowest response rates. While the differences between cross-sectional designs from address lists or phone lists may not differ much, differences could be expected between list frames and RDD designs, with the latter producing lower rates due to the exclusion of nontelephone households and highly selective nonresponse.

Differences might also be expected between cross-sectional designs and rotating panel designs. Part of this will come from the greater stability of the rotating panel designs over time. The first time a household is contacted for an interview, a great number of things can go wrong. Telephone numbers may have changed or housing units been destroyed. Once someone in the household is contacted and has cooperated, however, it is much easier to get cooperation in subsequent contacts. The rotating panel design may underrepresent marginal populations relative to cross-sectional designs, but it will have higher response rates generally. This may result in rotating panel designs underestimating annual crime rates but providing more reliable change estimates.

Perhaps more important than the sampling issues are the effects of rotating panel designs on the dating of reported crime events. Respondents in retrospective surveys have trouble dating events and tend

---

[11] To illustrate the potential magnitude of the difference in response rate, the response rate for "cold contact" RDD surveys conducted in twelve cities with an NCVS-like instrument averaged around 50 percent (Smith et al. 1999), whereas the person response rate in the NCVS nationally is 89 percent (per personal communication with author Michael Rand on November 15, 2005). The NCVS employs an address sample and contacts respondents prior to the interview: i.e., a letter or a phone call to arrange an appointment.

to "telescope" events that occur out of the reference period into that period. So, a person interviewed in January 2005 and asked about her victimization experience in 2004 will report on events that occurred beyond the far bound of the reference period in 2003. Rotating panel designs reduce this telescoping by using the previous interview to bound the reference period (Neter and Waksberg 1964).[12] Cross-sectional designs should produce higher rates than rotating panel designs because of greater telescoping.

2. *Instrumentation*.   The massive literature in survey research indicates that the questions asked, how they are asked, and in what context can make a big difference in responses (Tourengeau 1984; Strack and Martin 1987; Schwarz 1995; Sudman, Bradburn, and Schwarz 1996). In victimization surveys, the strategy used to screen the population to find potential victims has a substantial effect on the resulting responses (Hubble 1995; Persley 1995; Rand and Taylor 1995; Koss 1996). The reference period for which the respondent is asked to report is another important feature of instrumentation that could affect cross-national comparisons. Generally, the longer the reference period, the less complete the reporting of crime events (Lepkowski 1981; Kobelarcik et al. 1983). Finally, various bounding procedures used in cross-sectional surveys in an attempt to reduce telescoping can substantially affect the amount of telescoping that occurs (Sudman, Finn, and Lammon 1984).

a. Screening Strategies.   One important characteristic of screening strategies is whether screening and classification of victimizations into crime classes are done in the same step (Biderman et al. 1986; Cantor and Lynch 2000). Another important distinction is the density of cues given to respondents in the screening interview to elicit mention of victimization (Biderman et al. 1986).

Strategies that unify the screening and classification functions assume a one-to-one correspondence between the cues given to the respondent in the screening interview and the type of event that these cues will elicit. If the respondent is asked, "Has anyone entered your home by force and taken something?" an answer of yes to this question indicates that the respondent has been the victim of a burglary. Similar questions are asked about assaults and robberies, and an affirmative answer will indicate victimization by that type of crime. Each screen

---

[12] This serves as both a cognitive and mechanical bound. Reference is made to the prior interview to give respondents a benchmark, and interviewers have lists of events reported in previous interviews that can be used to exclude previously mentioned events.

question contains all the attributes that define that particular crime, and presumably, the respondent searches her memory for events with all these attributes and on finding them responds affirmatively. Since classification is accomplished in the screening interview, there is little reason to collect additional information on the incident, and subsequent questioning about the event is relatively brief.

Strategies that separate out the screening and classification processes do not assume a one-to-one correspondence between affirmative answers to screening questions and a particular type of crime (Biderman et al. 1967; Cantor and Lynch 2000). The sole purpose of the screening interview is to elicit mention of a potential victimization event. If an affirmative response is given to a specific question, the interviewer continues on with the rest of the questions in the screening interview. Any affirmative response requires the administration of an incident form that elicits detailed information on the alleged victimization. This information is used to determine whether the incident was a crime within the scope of the survey and, if so, what particular type of crime it was.

Fisher and Cullen (2000) demonstrate quite convincingly that using the screener/incident form strategy eliminates a large number of events mentioned in response to screening questions. When the details are provided, it becomes clear that the events mentioned do not have the characteristics of the crimes of interest. For example, of the 314 events mentioned in response to a screening question on rape asked by Fisher and Cullen, only seventy-nine were actually classified as rape on the basis of the information provided in the incident form. One hundred and fifty-five were determined to be sexual assaults, and eighty were not found to be crimes within the scope of the survey.

Within these two screening strategies, victimization surveys can differ in terms of the number and explicitness of cues given to convey the cognitive task of searching memory for the target events and reporting the events found. Research has shown that crime events are not stored in memory in uniform ways across individuals. Traditional cuing assumes that crime events are stored according to the behaviors that make the act a crime (e.g., hitting or taking), but they can be stored under the activities being pursued at the time (e.g., at work), by the persons involved (e.g., a brother), or by some other attribute of the event. Consequently, more and varied cues will result in greater recall and reporting (Biderman et al. 1986).

The results from the early field tests of the victim survey methodology in the United States suggested that screening strategies separating the screening task from the classification task get more complete reporting of victimization events (Biderman et al. 1967). The methodological work surrounding the redesign of the NCVS indicates that the same is true for the density of cues—the more cues, the greater the reporting (Hubble 1990). However, the incident form questions will result in "unfounding" events that do not meet the threshold requirements to be called a crime within the scope of the survey.[13]

b. Reference Period.   "Reference period" refers to the amount of time over which the respondent is asked to search for and report victimization events within the scope of the survey. Reference period is important because of the extreme recency bias in retrospective surveys (Biderman and Lynch 1981). As time passes between the event of interest and the interview, respondents forget events. The longer the reference period, the less complete the reporting of victimization events. However, short reference periods give respondents less opportunity for victimization and result in covering less of the calendar period in each interview, which effectively reduces sample size. A reference period of three months, for example, will require four times as many interviews to describe a calendar year as a survey with a twelve-month reference period. It is basically a trade-off between measurement error and sampling error. Most victim surveys choose in favor of sampling error and opt for a twelve-month reference period that also comports with annual reporting requirements.

In considering the reference period used in the surveys, it is important to take account of the differences between the reference period and the recounting period. The reference period is that period of time for which the respondent is asked to search his memory for eligible crime events. So a respondent may be asked to report events occurring in the last twelve months, for example, between January 2004 and December 2004. The recounting period is the reference period plus the

---

[13] Comparisons of different approaches to identifying violence against women also demonstrate the effects of cuing. The National Violence against Woman Survey (NVAWS) cued extensively for violence among intimates as compared to the NCVS. Comparisons of violence rates from the two surveys showed that rates of intimate violence were much higher in the NVAWS than in the NCVS, but the rates of nonintimate violence were higher in the NCVS. The NVAWS used its cuing resources to identify intimate violence exhaustively with less attention paid to nonintimate violence. The cuing density affected the resulting rates. Fisher and Cullen (2000) also demonstrated that extensive and explicit cuing will substantially increase the number of victimizations reported in victim surveys.

time between the near bound of the reference period and the interview date. A person interviewed in March of 2005 about events occurring in 2004 will have a fourteen-month recounting period and a twelve-month reference period. Asking respondents to disregard events occurring in January and February 2005 complicates the recall task. Moreover, given the extreme nature of recency bias, allowing long periods between the near bound of the reference period will also contribute to underreporting of events in the reference period.

c. Bounding. The problem of telescoping was discussed earlier in the context of sample designs. While the rotating panel design affords an opportunity to "bound" a reference period with a prior interview, it is also possible to reduce telescoping with special instrumentation. Some surveys employ various forms of temporal anchors that help respondents place events more accurately in time and thereby prevent telescoping. In this procedure respondents are asked to identify and date significant life events such as the birth of children, the opening of school, and so on. Then, these temporal anchors are used to date crime events. Presumably this will reduce the misdating of crime events that results in their being reported as occurring within the reference period when they did not (Loftus et al. 1990). Another more commonly used approach employs a long and a short reference period. Respondents are asked to report victimizations occurring in the last five years, for example, and then they are asked about their experience in the past twelve months (Sudman, Finn, and Lammon 1984; Killias, Lamond, and Aebi 2004). The logic behind this approach is based on the assumption that telescoping comes not from misdating but from the desire of respondents to perform the task they are asked to do. Respondents want to find something that the interviewers are asking about, and to please the interviewers they will report events occurring outside the reference period as occurring in the reference period (Biderman and Cantor 1984). The long reference period gives respondents the opportunity to report something, and the short reference period allows dating of the event with less pressure to misdate it in order to please the interviewer. Surveys that employ these various techniques to reduce telescoping should have lower rates than those that do not, although no head-to-head tests of these methods and the bounding interview method have been conducted.

3. *Procedures.* This covers a wide variety of rules and practices for collecting, processing, and disseminating data as well as rate estimation

with data from victimization surveys. Procedures pertaining to the collection, processing, and dissemination of data affect all users of the information, but procedures affecting estimation affect only those who use the official estimates.

a. Collection Mode. The mode of the interview is, perhaps, the procedure most likely to affect rates across nations. "Mode" refers to the medium used to conduct the interrogation. The traditional modes are in-person, telephone, and mailed self-administered surveys. While there are a number of advantages to in-person interviews, there are no good studies indicating that in-person interviewing will produce victimization rates different from telephone interviewing. The sample repercussions of mode may influence rates because of differences in response rates or the exclusion of nontelephone households, but administering the interview by phone seems to have little effect on reporting compared to in-person interviews. The response rate problems with mailed surveys make comparisons with the other modes fruitless, but the self-administered mode within the context of an in-person interview does affect reporting. The reporting of sensitive matters appears to be better using self-administered procedures than face-to-face interviews (Percy and Mayhew 1992; Mirrlees-Black 1999).

Computers have increased the variety of interviewing modes, and some of these computer-assisted modes have been shown to have large effects on reporting in victimization surveys. Split sample tests of computer-assisted telephone interviewing (CATI) in the NCVS demonstrated substantial differences between CATI and telephone or in-person interviews (Hubble and Wilder 1988). Respondents interviewed by CATI reported more victimization. That these effects were seen primarily with CATI conducted in centralized facilities suggests that the increases in reporting observed with CATI result from increased supervision of interviewers. Whatever the source of the CATI effect, it is clear that it should be taken into account in comparing surveys cross-nationally.

Exactly how it should or can be taken into account will depend on the survey and the use to which the data are put. For rate or change comparisons, adjustments to the rates can be made if CATI has been phased into the survey randomly or if it was randomly administered (or not administered) to a subset of respondents. An adjustment factor can be obtained by comparing those who were randomly assigned CATI to those who were not. This adjustment would be applied to the victimization rates of that portion of the sample not receiving CATI to bring their rates up to what they would have been had they received a CATI interview. If CATI was not randomly assigned to groups in the sample, but not every respondent received CATI, then it may be possible to obtain an adjustment factor by modeling the effect of CATI on reporting to isolate its effect. Modeling is a bit more uncertain because it must account for all the factors that may have caused some person to get a CATI interview and other persons not to. Otherwise, the adjustment will include the effects of the interview mode and the effects of any variables that caused a respondent not to be interviewed by CATI. Absent these two sources of data on the effects of CATI, it will be difficult to adjust rates for differences in mode across nations. In the case of modeling victimization risk, if there is some variability in the mode such that some respondents get CATI and others do not, then it would be sufficient to enter simply a CATI variable into the model to account for its effects.

b. Estimation Procedures.[14]   For researchers who use published estimates from victimization surveys, estimation procedures can affect cross-national comparisons. Estimation procedures include all the steps occurring after the collection of the data that are necessary to produce rates and other statistics that make the data useful. Rate estimation requires generating a numerator and a denominator. Generally there are rules defining the events eligible for inclusion in the numerator and rules for separating eligible events into classes of crime such as robbery, theft, and the like.

Among estimation procedures, the handling of high-volume repeat victimization can differ across surveys and affect cross-national comparisons of crime rates. High-volume repeat victimization can be a problem for victimization surveys because it requires collecting information on a large number of incidents, much of which is redundant because the events are similar (Dodge 1987). This becomes a burden for interviewers and respondents that can affect response rates. Moreover, there is some concern about the quality of the information pro-

---

[14] Many surveys apply weights to the data as part of the estimation process. In most cases the weights simply multiply each case by the inverse of the probability of selection into the sample to obtain the population numbers from the sample data. If that is the case, then comparisons of rates with weighted data will lead to the same conclusions as comparisons with unweighted data. There is a possibility that weighting will affect comparison, if they include adjustments for nonresponse, but this will occur only in specific subgroups with high nonresponse rates.

vided about these events, especially the number of such events occurring in a given period of time. Consequently, most victimization surveys have procedures for handling high-volume repeat victimization. In the NCVS, for example, if a respondent reports six or more incidents that are similar and for which she cannot provide the particulars (and especially the date of the incident), then the interviewer can treat all the events as a series incident (Dodge 1987; Cantor and Lynch 2000). For series incidents, the respondent is asked details about the most recent incident, and then the interviewer simply records the number of this type of event occurring in the reference period. The BCS long capped the number of incidents at three (recently changed to five) for which extensive information is collected and records the number of incidents for the remainder. Up to five incidents are included for each of these high-volume events. Although there are very few high-volume repeat victimizations, they account for a large proportion of all reported crime, when all the incidents in the series are included in victimization rates (Planty, forthcoming). The Bureau of Justice Statistics in the United States chooses to exclude series incidents from their estimates, largely because they are suspicious of the number of events that respondents claim have occurred. Including these estimates in rates at face value substantially increases the rates and makes them unstable over time, with a few events driving the rates (Biderman and Lynch 1991; Planty, forthcoming). Differences between nations in the treatment of high-volume repeat victimization for rate estimation can affect cross-national comparisons.

Crime classification rules can also affect the numerator of crime rates by moving crimes from one category to another. In surveys that employ the unified screening strategy, the rules for crime classification are simple. An affirmative answer to a particular screener question will result in that event being classified as a certain type of crime. In surveys that separate screening from classification, there will be a reasonably complicated procedure in which specific attributes of the event captured in the incident form are used to classify events into crime types. These procedures specify the attributes that must be present to classify an event as a particular class of crime and as part of a hierarchy among resulting crime types. So in the NCVS, an event that includes both breaking and entering and a minor assault will be classified as an assault because the hierarchy gives precedence to assaults over property crime.

Comparisons of the two strategies suggest that the unified strategy can result in substantial misclassification of events.[15]

Estimation procedures may also exclude events from the numerator in other ways. I have discussed procedures for handling high-volume repeat victimization and that these may be excluded from the numerators of the rates. Other classes of crime such as those befalling eligible respondents outside of their country of residence are also routinely excluded from the numerator of crime rates in some nations but not in others (Biderman and Lynch 1991; Bolling et al. 2003).

B. Evidence on the Effects of Design on Reporting from Current Research

The literature on retrospective surveys generally and victimization surveys specifically suggests that some design features of surveys can substantially affect the resulting rates. If surveys in nations differ on these design features, then cross-national comparisons of victimization rates will likely be affected. It is difficult to say exactly how much different design features affect rates and the comparison of rates. Survey methods research usually attempts to isolate the effect of one design feature when most designs include a combination of features that may have offsetting effects on reporting. So a survey with a one-year reference period will have less complete reporting of the respondents' victimization experience occurring during the reference period. If that survey also has no bounding procedure, this will increase the number of incidents reported as a result of telescoping. If the magnitude of these two errors is equal, then they will be offsetting and the victimization counts will not be affected. Nonetheless, one should be wary when comparing estimates of the level of victimization across nations when the surveys differ in one or more of the design features discussed above.

[15] Fisher and Cullen (2000) showed that crimes identified by a screening question designed to elicit mentions of a particular class of crime very often are classified as another. Of the 314 affirmative answers to the rape question in the screener, e.g., 155 of them were classified as sexual assault because they did not satisfy the legal conditions for rape. Other analyses of NCVS data indicate that this problem may be most pronounced in assaults generally (and sexual assaults specifically) because of the ambiguous nature of this crime (Weiss 2004). The correspondence between screener questions and the ultimate classification of crime events is much less problematic for more stereotypic crimes such as robbery. Misclassification is usually to proximate types of crime and not to radically different crime classes. So Fisher and Cullen find that the most frequent misclassification of potential rape events is to the necessarily included subclass of sexual assault. This may not affect rate comparisons of more global crime classes such as violent crime or sexual violence.

To the extent that these design features are constant over time within nations, change estimates should not be as greatly affected by differences in design across nations (Farrington, Langan, and Tonry 2004; Tonry and Farrington 2005). Constancy in design, however, should be investigated and not assumed. Even very good and well-established surveys such as the BCS change procedures in response to financial and political exigencies. Different vendors have been used to field the survey over time, and while the design has remained the same, the implementation of the design has changed in ways that can affect rates. Different vendors have, for example, started and ended the interviews at different times, which effectively extends the reference period from twelve months to fifteen months (Lynch and Tseloni 2003). Even the NCVS, which is one of the more stable designs, changes over time. The survey was massively redesigned in 1992. Even after this break in the series, the allocation of interviews to various modes has changed over time with little fanfare. This should not have much effect on rates, but when the allocation of CATI changes, this can affect rates because of the big effect that CATI has had in split sample tests (Hubble and Wilder 1988).

The evidence on the effects of design differences on multivariate modeling using victim survey data is complicated and difficult to interpret. This occurs in part because not all combinations of design features have been tested, so that we are inferring from designs that have been tested to those that have not. It is also complicated in that some tests have examined only three-way interactions among a predictor variable (Lynch and Cantor 1996; Kindermann, Lynch, and Cantor 1997), victimization, and the design, whereas others have tested much more complex models that included many more predictor variables (Cantor and Lynch 2005). The latter approach provides a much stronger test of the effects of design differences on interrelationships between predictor variables and victimization risk.

The redesign of the NCVS provided one of the more drastic changes in survey design and, therefore, a good opportunity to assess the effects of design on multivariate models of victimization risk. The redesigned NCVS included a radically changed screening procedure that substantially increased the nature and volume of cues given to respondents, the use of CATI in about one-third of the sample, and a series incident procedure that allowed for fewer events to be treated as a series incident (Rand and Taylor 1995). For eighteen months, the old and the new designs were run in parallel with random halves of the sample. Using this "overlap" sample, Lynch and Cantor (1996) found very few significant interactions among design, victimization, and attributes of victims. This test of the effects of design was fairly conservative because the split sample did not provide the statistical power that a full sample would. Hence, only very strong effects would achieve statistical significance. To supplement this initial analysis, Cantor and Lynch (2005) conducted subsequent analyses using full samples from the old and the new designs. The general results were the same: there were relatively few interactions among predictor variables, victimization, and survey design. This suggests some robustness in multivariate models of victimization across survey designs.

C. Do Differences in the Design of Victim Surveys Affect Cross-National Comparisons?

Ability to generalize from the existing literature on victim surveys to their use in cross-national comparisons is limited. Specific packages of design features may have different effects than a single design feature in an experimental study. To supplement this literature, I examine data from the ICVS as well as a number of nation-specific surveys to determine first how variable these designs are across nations and then whether surveys with different designs produce different results in various forms of cross-national studies.

1. *How Much Variability Is There in the Designs of Surveys across Nations?*   To the extent that victim surveys employ different designs across nations, these differences could be expected to affect the resulting crime rates. In this subsection, I examine the ICVS and nation-specific surveys to determine whether survey designs differ in important ways across nations. If these essential design features do not vary across nations, then survey methodology will not affect cross-national comparisons.

The ICVS is explicitly designed to maximize uniformity of design in the surveys across nations. Financial constraints and logistical considerations in specific countries could lead to adopting different procedures in different nations. In general, the screening strategy and the information content of the instrument are fairly consistent across nations in the survey. There are differences in mode and in sample design across nations and over time. Some nations use in-person interviewing, whereas others use telephone interviewing and others

TABLE 1

Identifiable Procedural and Sample Design Differences in the ICVS
by Nation, 1999

Nation	Respondent and Interviewer Same Gender	Item Missing Count = 0	CATI Administration	Sample Design	Response Rate
Australia	NA	74.3	Yes	RDD	58
Belgium	59.4	67.2	Yes	RDD	56
Canada	48.7	67.1	Yes	RDD	57
Denmark	60.8	76.5	Yes	RDD	66
England and Wales	58.4	61.6	Yes	RDD	57
France	98.7	92.0	Yes	RDD	45
Japan	51.3	69.9	Yes	RDD	74
Netherlands	54.8	63.3	Yes	RDD	58
Northern Ireland	64.3	59.2	Yes	RDD	81
Poland	59.8	63.7	No	Address list	78
Portugal	67.3	74.7	Yes	RDD	56
Scotland	60.3	32.5	Yes	RDD	58
Sweden	99.3	68.7	Yes	RDD	66
Switzerland	56.8	81.5	Yes	RDD	65
United States	80.5	76.4	Yes	RDD	60

SOURCE.—Lynch 2002.
NOTE.—NA = not available.

CATI. The sample design employed is generally RDD, but there are
some telephone list frames and address frames in those countries using
in-person interviews. Overall, the survey procedures used in the ICVS
are fairly uniform across nations (see table 1). Nonetheless, even these
relatively minor differences in survey design have been shown to have
some effect on the reporting of victimization (Kury, Obergfell-Fuchs,
and Wurger 2001; Lynch 2002).

It is more difficult to assess differences in design across nation-specific surveys simply because the documentation on many aspects of
these surveys is not readily available. A quick search of readily available
documentation indicates wide variations in major aspects of survey designs across nations. Some nations have freestanding victimization surveys, whereas others obtain their victim survey data through supplements to labor force surveys or some other survey vehicle.
Freestanding surveys should be able to devote more resources to
screening for victimizations than surveys that are supplements to omnibus surveys. Some nations employ a unified screening strategy and

others do not. Many nations interview by telephone whereas others conduct interviews in person. The Australian survey is a self-administered survey that is left with a respondent after the labor force interview is administered. Of the surveys administered by phone, most are computer-assisted. Some nations have procedures for handling high-volume repeat victimizations and others do not.

A few design features are broadly similar across nations. Most nations employ cross-sectional designs, except for the NCVS, which uses a rotating panel design. Among the cross-sectional surveys, some conduct interviews at one point during the year, and others interview throughout the year. The latter strategy eliminates the effects of the seasonality of crime on reporting and lets survey organizations distribute the interviewing burden, eliminating the need to rely on a hastily assembled and temporary interviewing staffs. Virtually every national victimization survey identified employs a one-year reference period, except for the NCVS, which uses a six-month reference period. Most reference periods are unbounded, although the NCVS bounds the reference period with a prior interview, and Switzerland employs the long and short reference period technique used in the ICVS. The ICVS surveys do not differ very much in their major design features across nations, and these surveys are much more similar in their design across nations than nation-specific surveys (see table 2).

2. *How Much Difference Does Survey Design Make in Cross-National Research?*   This review of the victim survey literature suggests that certain differences in the design of victimization surveys make a difference in level estimates within nations. Design differences do not seem to have much effect on multivariate modeling of victimization. The design of the ICVS is relatively invariant across nations, and nation-specific surveys vary considerably in terms of their design. This suggests that differences in survey design are more likely to affect comparisons of nation-specific surveys than comparisons of the ICVS. Because of the need to keep costs of the ICVS to an absolute minimum, however, sample sizes are small and state-of-the-art survey methods are not used. These factors could introduce errors into the ICVS estimates that distort cross-national comparisons. If the victim survey method is robust enough that design differences in surveys do not affect reporting of victimization or the effects of combinations of design features are equal and offsetting, then comparisons of estimates from nation-specific surveys should be similar to those from the ICVS. This conjecture is

TABLE 2

Design Features of Nation-Specific Surveys by Nation

Design Feature	Australia	Canada	England and Wales	United States	Sweden	Netherlands	Scotland	Switzerland	Ireland
Sample:									
Cross section	Yes	Yes (rotated)	Yes (rotated)	No	Yes	Yes	Yes (rotated)	Yes	Yes
RDD	No	Yes	No	No	No	No	No	No	No
Clustered		Yes	No				Yes		Yes
Screening:									
Unified	Yes	Yes	No	No	Yes	Yes	No	Yes	Yes
Dense cuing	No	No	No	Yes	No	No	No	No	No
Bounding	No	No	No	Prior interview	No	No	No	Short/long reference period	No
Reference period (months)	12	12	12	6	12	12	12	12	12
Mode	Self-administered	Phone	In person	Mixed mode	In person	Self-administered	In person	Phone	In person
CATI	No	CATI	CAPI	CATI	No	No	No	CATI	No
Series	No	No	Yes	Yes	Yes	None	Yes	Yes	No
Freestanding survey	No	No	Yes	Yes	No	Yes	Yes	Yes	No

SOURCE.—For Australia, Carcach (2004) and Australian Bureau of Statistics (2002); for Canada, Welch and Irving (2004) and Statistics Canada (2004); for England and Wales, Bolling et al. (2003) and Farrington and Jolliffe (2004); for the United States, Biderman and Lynch (1991); for Sweden, Wikstrom and Dolmén (2004); for the Netherlands, Bijleveld and Smit (2004); for Scotland, MVA (2002) and Smith (2004); for Switzerland, Killias, Lamond, and Aebi (2004); for Ireland, Central Statistics Office (2004).

explored below by comparing estimated crime rates and changes in crime rates for eight nations and four types of crime using both the ICVS and nation-specific victimization surveys. I also estimate multivariate models of victimization risk in three nations.

The ICVS data used in the level and change estimate that follows are taken from appendix A, table 2 in Van Kesteren, Mayhew, and Nieuwbeerta (2001). The victimization rates from nation-specific surveys are taken from the chapters on these particular countries included in Farrington, Langan, and Tonry (2004). This was an ambitious and careful effort to use nation-specific data in a comparable way from the point of offense through imprisonment. Differences in definitions and procedures in victim surveys and police, court, and corrections data were identified, and attempts were made to adjust for these differences or at least take them into account when drawing conclusions from the data. This effort produced a great deal of useful information on differences in crime and criminal justice across nations and over time. Farrington, Langan, and Tonry's (2004) collection emphasized comparisons of change over time across nations. Therefore, they gave more attention to ensuring that definitions and procedures were comparable over time within countries and less attention to identifying and adjusting for definitional and procedural differences across countries. This means that using these data in the following comparisons will provide a particularly liberal test of using nation-specific surveys for comparisons of change over time across nations. The adjustments made in this collection should reduce the effects of changes in definitions and procedures on estimates of change in nation-specific surveys.

a. Level Estimates. The level estimates in the ICVS are substantially higher than estimates from nation-specific surveys in almost every instance (see figs. 3–6). The robbery rate per 100 for Australia in the ICVS is 4 times that reported in the Australian National Victimization Survey, whereas in England and Wales the ICVS estimate is 2.43 times that of the BCS. The differences in the United States and Scotland are less—1.66 and 1.71 times, respectively—and they are least for Canada (1.28) and the Netherlands (1.00). Even larger discrepancies are observed for motor vehicle theft, burglary, and assault. The average ratio of ICVS to nation-specific survey rates for robbery is 1.73, and this increases to 2.23 for motor vehicle theft, 2.55 for burglary, and 5.07 for assault. These differences in level estimates also vary across nations: the United States and England and Wales have the greatest

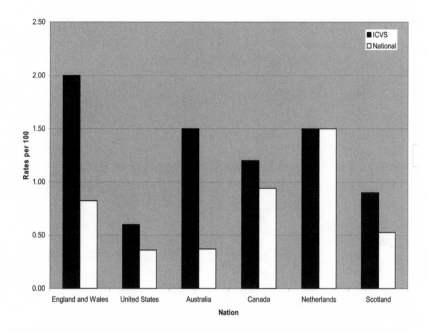

FIG. 3.—Robbery rates per 100 by nation and survey. Sources: The ICVS rates per 100 were taken from Van Kesteren, Mayhew, and Nieuwbeerta 2001, app. A, pp. 180–81. The national rates were calculated from victimization counts and population data presented in the relevant country chapters in Farrington, Langan, and Tonry 2004.

differences across all classes of crimes compared to the ICVS estimates, with ICVS/national survey ratios of 4.48 and 4.52, respectively. They are followed by Australia (3.19), Canada (2.88), and the Netherlands (2.81), and more distantly by Scotland (2.09), Switzerland (1.99), and Sweden (1.08).

These differences in level estimates across designs are large. Moreover, they are so variable across nations that the choice of survey would change the rank ordering of nations in terms of the level of crime (see table 3). England and Wales rank number one in robbery in the ICVS but third according to the nation-specific survey ranking. Australia was tied for second in the ICVS robbery ranking but was in fifth place in the ranking based on nation-specific surveys. Indeed, the correlations between the rankings of nations in terms of crime from the two surveys are not particularly high, with a Spearman's rho of 0.493 for robbery, 0.530 for motor vehicle theft, 0.653 for burglary, and 0.072 for assault.

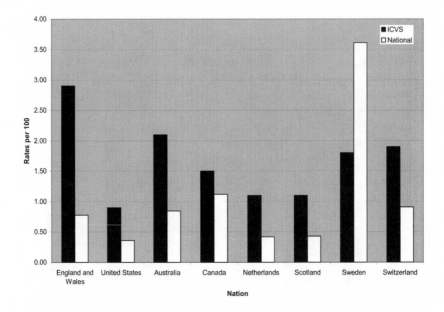

FIG. 4.—Motor vehicle theft rates by nation and survey. Sources: The ICVS rates per 100 were taken from Van Kesteren, Mayhew, and Nieuwbeerta 2001, app. A, pp. 180–81. The national rates were calculated from victimization counts and population data presented in the relevant country chapters in Farrington, Langan, and Tonry 2004.

The pattern of differences across crimes and nations makes some sense in terms of what we know about the response process. Discrepancies between the surveys are least for clearly defined crimes such as robbery or motor vehicle theft and greatest for ambiguous crimes such as assault. Where the cognitive task is ambiguous, the steps taken to define that task—for example, cues—and make it easier—for example, computer-assisted personal interviews (CAPI)—will affect reporting. Nations that take these steps to facilitate reporting will have very different rates than those that do not. Where there is less ambiguity, survey instrumentation and procedure will have less effect. The pattern of differences across nations is also consistent with the rough similarity of nation-specific survey designs to the ICVS. The United States and England and Wales have the survey designs that are most dissimilar to the ICVS, and they also have the rates that are most discrepant from the ICVS. Nations such as Sweden and Switzerland that have designs

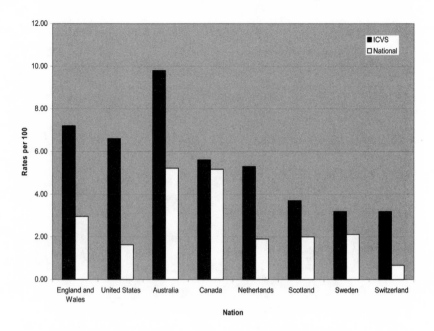

Fig. 5.—Burglary rates by nation and survey. Sources: The ICVS rates per 100 were taken from Van Kesteren, Mayhew, and Nieuwbeerta 2001, app. A, pp. 180–81. The national rates were calculated from victimization counts and population data presented in the relevant country chapters in Farrington, Langan, and Tonry 2004.

in their nation-specific surveys most like the ICVS have the rates most similar to the ICVS.

These patterns of differences in level estimates across designs can be explained by many things, and it will take some detailed analysis to make more definitive statements as to why these patterns exist. These results tell us unambiguously, however, that the design of victimization surveys affects cross-national comparisons of levels of crime. We cannot simply take any survey and compare it to another without knowing whether these surveys are similar in their major design features—screening and classification procedures, reference period, bounding procedures, and use of computer-assisted interviewing. Comparisons of level estimates should adjust for these differences in design, if at all possible.

b. Change Estimates. The comparison of change estimates across nations should be more robust than the comparison of level estimates.

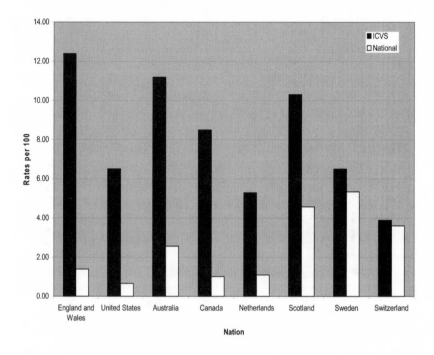

Fig. 6.—Assault rates by nation and survey. Sources: The ICVS rates per 100 were taken from Van Kesteren, Mayhew, and Nieuwbeerta 2001, app. A, pp. 180–81. The national rates were calculated from victimization counts and population data presented in the relevant country chapters in Farrington, Langan, and Tonry 2004.

As long as we can make the assumption that procedures are constant over time within nations, then this form of cross-national comparison should be accurate. We have seen in previous sections, however, that the assumption of constant procedures over time within nations cannot be made. When we compare the change in crime from 1996 to 2000 in the ICVS with that from nation-specific surveys, the results are not as discrepant as those for level estimates, but they are far from uniform across the surveys.

In the case of robbery (fig. 7), the sign of the change is the same across surveys in three nations and different in three nations. When the change estimate has the same sign, the magnitude of the change in the ICVS is about twice that of the national survey in two nations and essentially the same in the third. For motor vehicle theft (fig. 8),

TABLE 3

Rank Ordering of Nations by Level of Crime, Offense, and Survey

	Robbery		Motor Vehicle Theft		Burglary		Assault	
	ICVS	National	ICVS	National	ICVS	National	ICVS	National
England and Wales	1.0	3	1.0	5	2.0	3	1.0	5
United States	6.0	6	8.0	8	3.0	7	5.5	8
Australia	2.5	5	2.0	4	1.0	1	2.0	4
Canada	4.0	2	5.0	2	4.0	2	4.0	7
Netherlands	2.5	1	6.5	7	5.0	5	7.0	6
Scotland	5.0	4	6.5	6	6.0	4	3.0	1
Sweden	NA	NA	4.0	1	7.7	6	5.5	2
Switzerland	NA	NA	3.0	3	7.5	8	8.0	3

SOURCES.—The ICVS ranks were calculated from rates per 100 taken from Van Kesteren, Mayhew, and Nieuwbeerta 2001, app. A, pp. 180–81. The national ranks were calculated from victimization counts and population data presented in the relevant country chapters in Farrington, Langan, and Tonry 2004.

NOTE.—NA = not available.

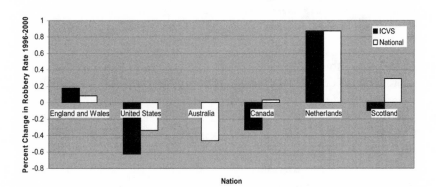

FIG. 7.—Percentage change in robbery rates by nation and survey. Sources: The ICVS change rates were calculated from the rates per 100 in Van Kesteren, Mayhew, and Nieuwbeerta 2001, app. A, pp. 180–81. The national change rates were calculated from victimization counts and population data presented in the relevant country chapters in Farrington, Langan, and Tonry 2004.

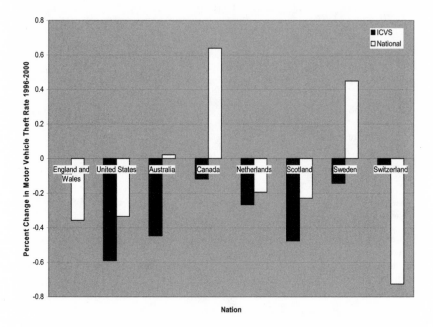

FIG. 8.—Percentage change in motor vehicle theft rate by nation. Sources: The ICVS rates per 100 were taken from Van Kesteren, Mayhew, and Nieuwbeerta 2001, app. A, pp. 180–81. The national rates were calculated from victimization counts and population data presented in the relevant country chapters in Farrington, Langan, and Tonry 2004.

the sign of the change is the same in four nations and different in the other four. The ICVS change estimate is greater in half the nations, and the estimate from the nation-specific survey is greater in the other half. The change estimates for burglary (fig. 9) are more uniform across methods, with six of the eight estimates taking the same sign. The magnitude of the change estimates are reasonably similar for nations in which the sign of the change estimate is the same. The change estimates for assault (fig. 10) take the same sign in four nations and have a different sign in the other four. When the signs are the same, the magnitude estimates are reasonably similar.

c. *Multivariate Modeling of Victimization Risk.*   Earlier in this essay I argued that the results of multivariate analyses across nations would not be affected much by the design of the surveys used, as long as these effects are not correlated with predictor variables in the model.

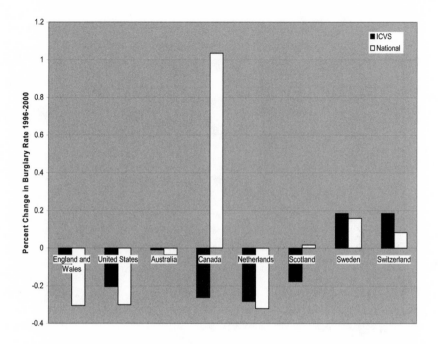

F<small>IG</small>. 9.—Percentage change in burglary by nation in the ICVS and national surveys. Sources: The ICVS rates per 100 were taken from Van Kesteren, Mayhew, and Nieuwbeerta 2001, app. A, pp. 180–81. The national rates were calculated from victimization counts and population data presented in the relevant country chapters in Farrington, Langan, and Tonry 2004.

In order to shed some light on this assertion, I compared a multivariate model of burglary done with country-specific surveys to models estimated with data from the ICVS in the same nations. Tseloni and her colleagues (2004) estimated models of burglary risk using the BCS in England and Wales, the NCVS in the United States, and the Police Monitor Survey (PMS) from the Netherlands. I used all the waves of the ICVS conducted in these nations to estimate very similar models of burglary risk. If survey design makes little difference for multivariate models, the statistical significance and sign of the coefficients in the models estimated with nation-specific surveys will not differ from the ICVS-based results in the same nation. Similarly, comparisons of effects across nations should be similar across the two survey designs.

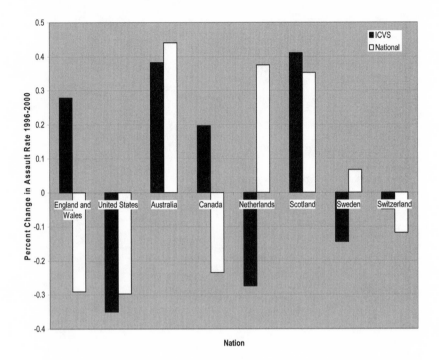

FIG. 10.—Percentage change in the assault rate by nation and survey. Sources: The ICVS rates per 100 were taken from Van Kesteren, Mayhew, and Nieuwbeerta 2001, app. A, pp. 180–81. The national rates were calculated from victimization counts and population data presented in the relevant country chapters in Farrington, Langan, and Tonry 2004.

The cross-national differences in coefficients should be similar in the ICVS analysis and the analyses done with nation-specific surveys.

The data in table 4 indicate that about two-thirds of the relationships between predictor variables and the risk of burglary have the same statistical significance and sign within nations across the two survey designs. This ranges from 75 percent with similar coefficients in England and Wales to 69 percent in the United States and 62 percent in the Netherlands. When the coefficients are considered similar if they take the same sign (regardless of their statistical significance), the correspondence between the two data sets increases to 93 percent, 87 percent, and 88 percent, respectively. While this is a fairly high degree

TABLE 4

Comparisons of Effects of Predictor Variables by Nation and Survey

Predictors	BCS	ICVS	NCVS	ICVS	PMS	ICVS
House type:						
Row	NS	NS	NA	NS	−	−
Flat	NS	−	NA	NS	−	−
Mobile	NS	NS	NS	NS	NS	−
Number of adults	NS	NS	NS	+	−	+
Number of children	NS	NS	+	+	NS	NS
Lone parent	+	NS	NS	+	+	+
Marital status:						
Married	NS	−	NS	−	NA	NS
Divorced	NS	+	+	NS	NA	+
Widowed	NS	NS	+	NS	NA	−
Employed:						
Looking	NS	NS	NS	NS	+	NS
Home	NS	NS	NS	NS	−	NS
Retired	NS	−	NS	NS	NS	NS
Other	NS	NS	NS	NS	NS	NS
Neighbors look in	NA	NS	NA	+	+	+
Go out:						
Greater than once per week	NS	NS	NS	NS	NA	NS
Less than once per week	NS	NS	NS	NS	NA	NS
Neighborhood watch	NS	NS	NS	NS	+	NS
Prevention	+	+	+	+	+	+
Income:						
Poor	NS	NS	+	NS	NA	+
Affluent	+	+	−	NS	NA	+
DK	NA	−	−	NS	NA	+
Education:						
Some college	−		NS		−	
High school	−		NS		−	
Primary	NS		NS		−	
Number of cars	−	NS	NS	+	NS	+
Place size::						
25,000–250,000	NA	+	+	+	NA	+
250,000+	NA	+	+	+	NA	+
Age	NS	−	−	−	−	NS
Male	NS	+	NS	+	NS	NS
Tenure	−	NA	+	NA	NA	NA

SOURCES.—The BCS, NCVS, and PMS data are from Tseloni et al. (2004, pp. 79–80); ICVS data are from the analysis of public use files for the ICVS 2000.

NOTE.—+ = a positive relationship between the variables listed and victimization is positive and statistically significant; − = a negative and significant relationship. NA = not available; NS = not significant. The omitted category for housing type is detached dwelling; for marital status, single; for income, middle income; for education, college graduate or more; for going out, greater than once per week.

of congruence, the understanding of victimization risk that emerges from these different data sources is not exactly the same within nations.

The explanations for burglary risk in each nation show some similarities across designs. In England and Wales, for example, analyses of both surveys find that preventative measures affect the risk of burglary and that the affluent are more at risk than those of more modest means. They also confirm that the frequency of going out at night has little to do with risk. The analyses are not completely consistent with respect to the effects of guardianship variables. In the ICVS analysis, being married has a negative effect on burglary risk and being divorced has a positive effect; in the BCS analysis, neither has a significant effect on risk. Being retired is another proxy for guardianship that influences risk in the ICVS analysis but not in the BCS. In the United States, the picture emerging from the two surveys is more similar, with consistent findings on the effects of housing structure, employment status, evenings out, prevention measures, place size, and the age of the respondent. The analyses differ only in their assessment of the effects of social class and marital status. The ICVS finds that the poor are at greater risk than the affluent, whereas the NCVS finds no class effects. The ICVS finds a reduction in risk for married and cohabiting respondents, but the NCVS does not. In the Netherlands, analyses of the two surveys show consistent results for housing structure, neighbors' assistance, gender, and household composition. The results are not consistent for employment status, presence of neighborhood watch, number of cars, and age of the respondent.

The logic behind the ICVS is not so much to provide the best estimates of victimization for a given nation but to provide estimates of risk that are comparable across nations, that is, the estimates least affected by procedural differences across surveys. If this is the case, then the most appropriate comparisons are not between the ICVS and nation-specific surveys within nations but of differences in models across nations between designs. When coefficients are compared across designs and nations, in some cases the results are reasonably similar across designs, whereas in other cases the results are quite different.

One clear product of the ICVS effort is more similar information content in surveys across nations. In the comparison of England and Wales with the United States using the ICVS, thirteen of the fourteen predictor variables were available in both nations. The same is the case when we compare England with the Netherlands and the United States with the Netherlands using the ICVS. When nation-specific surveys are used, eleven of the fourteen variables in the model are present in both England and the United States, but this similarity decreases to six of fourteen for comparisons between England and the Netherlands; the same is true for comparisons between the United States and the Netherlands.

Models of burglary in the United States and England are reasonably similar. About one-half of the variables in the model have the same statistical significance and sign in the two surveys, and one-half do not. The correspondence is much less between the models in comparisons involving the Netherlands and either the United States or England and Wales across the two survey designs. About twice as many relationships are different across the designs as are similar (see table 5).

The conclusions that one would reach about differences in factors affecting risk across nations would differ depending on the victimization surveys used. Survey design makes a difference in cross-national comparisons. The similarity in the information content of the ICVS surveys makes it easier to estimate similar models across nations. Many of the differences observed across nations and across design may be the result of differences in the models specified. Omitting a variable in one model in one country (because it is not in the survey) and including that variable in another can affect the coefficients that are estimated.

However, the small sample sizes in the ICVS could produce differences in significance of coefficients simply because of the lack of statistical power in such small samples. The NCVS sample includes 49,000 households and the BCS some 40,000 compared to the 1,400 and 2,000 in the respective ICVS surveys. This, however, does not seem to be the case in the comparison made above. The differences in the models across nations and designs do not uniformly occur because of the failure to find statistically significant relationships in the ICVS survey. Nonetheless, small sample sizes are a problem in the ICVS. This is especially the case for rare events such as serious violence. Since the foregoing comparison used burglary, the effects of sample size will not be that great. Indeed, no formal tests of the statistical significance of differences in coefficients were performed here. Since surveys such as the NCVS and BCS use cluster samples, such tests would be difficult to perform, especially since necessary information on clusters was not readily available in all instances.

TABLE 5

Comparisons across Nations Using Nation-Specific Surveys and the ICVS

Predictors	England/United States		England/Netherlands		United States/ Netherlands	
	BCS/NCVS	ICVS	BCS/PMS	ICVS	NCVS/PMS	ICVS
House type:						
Row	NA	NS/NS	NA	NS/−	NA	NS/−
Flat	NA	NS/NS	NA	NS/−	NA	NS/−
Mobile	NS/NS	NS/NS	NS/NS	NS/−	NS/NS	NS/−
Number of adults	NS/NS	NS/NS	NS/−	NS/NS	NS/−	NS/+
Number of children	NS/+	−/NS	NS/NS	−/NS	+/NS	NS/NS
Lone parent	+/NS*	NS/NS	+/+	NS/NS*	NS/+	NS/NS
Marital status:						
Married	NS/NS*	−/−	NA	−/*	NA	−/NS
Divorced	NS/+*	+/NS	NA	+/−	NA	NS/−
Widowed	NS/+	NS/NS	NA	NS/NS	NA	NS/NS
Employed:						
Looking	NS/NS	NS/NS	NS/+	NS/NS	NS/+	NS/NS
Home	NS/NS	NS/NS	NS/−	NS/NS	NA	NS/NS
Retired	NA	−/NS	NS/NS	−/NS	NA	NS/NS
Other	NA	NS/NS	NS/NS	NS/NS	NA	NS/NS
Neighbors look in	NA	NS/+	NA	NS/+	NA	+/+
Go out:						
Greater than once per week	NS/NS	NS/NS	NA	NS/NS	NA	NS/NS
Less than once per week	NS/NS	NS/NS	NA	NS/NS	NA	NS/NS
Neighborhood watch	NS/NS	NS/NS	NS/+	NS/NS	NS/+	NS/NS
Prevention	+/+	+/+	+/+	+/+	+/+	+/+
Income:						
Poor	NS/+*	NS/NS	NA	NS/+	NA	NS/+
Affluent	+/−	+/NS	NA	+/+	NA	NS/+
DK	NA	NS/NS	NA	NS/−	NA	NS/−
Education:						
Some college	−/NS	NA	−/−	NA	NS/−	
High school	−/NS	NA	−/−	NA	NS/−	
Primary	NS/NS	NA	NS/−	NA	NS/−	
Number of cars	−/NS	NS/+	−/+	NS/+	NS/+	+/+
Place size:						
25,000–250,000	NA	+/+	NA	+/+	NA	+/+
250,000+	NA	+/+	NA	+/+	NA	+/+
Age	NS/−	NS/−	NS/−	NS/NS	NS/NS	−/NS
Male	NS/NS	+/+	NS/NS	+/NS	NS/NS	+/NS
Tenure	−/+	NA/NA	NA/NA	NA/NA	NA/NA	NA/NA

NOTE.—NA = not available; NS = not significant; DK = do not know. See also the note to table 4.

At best, this very crude comparison of models across nations and survey designs suggests that we cannot simply assume that the victimization survey method is so robust that any surveys can be used to model victimization risk across nations. Differences in survey design can affect results of multivariate models that would be compared across nations.

IV. Conclusion

The purpose of this essay was to assess the promise and the problems of using victim survey data to study cross-national differences in crime and criminal justice. For many years police administrative data were the only source of data on crime across nations. In the last two decades, however, victimization surveys have come to be accepted as a complementary source of information on crime and justice issues that can tell us things that police data cannot.

Cross-national studies of crime and justice place burdens on data that are similar in kind but different in degree from other types of empirical research. The issues of comparability, availability, and interpretability are always important. For comparison of cities or organizations within a nation, comparable data across these entities are needed. Data will also be needed for a large number of entities to represent the variation across these entities, and the analysis of the data should be able to be understood by a broad audience. All these desirable qualities are more difficult to achieve in the cross-national context. Nations are distinctive, and there is very little incentive to collect data expressly for comparisons with other nations. There are also few incentives to share these data with international bodies so as to make data on a large number of nations easily available.

In principle, victim surveys should have an advantage in terms of comparability over the most prevalently used alternative—police administrative data. These data systems are not tied to service delivery systems that are embedded in institutions unique to nations. The law in England and Wales, for example, will require certain definitions of crime that are dissimilar to those employed by police in the United States. It is unlikely that these definitions will be changed to make comparisons with the United States more accurate. Surveys are less wedded to these wider institutional arrangements and should therefore be more malleable.

Victim surveys provide incident- or person-level data that can be disaggregated. This should facilitate the definition of similar types of crime across nations because traditional crime classes can be subdivided to achieve comparability by referring to additional attributes of the events included in the surveys, for example, with a weapon. Moreover, with incident-level data it is easier to hold constant attributes of persons while testing the effects of national-level characteristics, a major goal of cross-national research. Having incident-level data by nation permits the use of nested data techniques that facilitate estimating the effects of nation-level characteristics and interactions between personal and nation-level factors. All these abilities will help establish comparability and further understanding of why nations differ in their crime problem.

While victim surveys are in principle easier to make comparable across nations, it is not clear that they are in practice. In this essay, I identified differences in the design of victim surveys that are known to affect reporting of victimization and compared nation-specific surveys on these design features. I found that nation-specific surveys differ considerably on important design features. This is not surprising in that there is no incentive to coordinate the design and information content of nation-specific surveys. In recognition of this, I also compared the design of ICVS surveys conducted in various nations. The ICVS is a centrally coordinated effort to field surveys in a large number of nations using comparable designs and instruments. In an examination of these surveys across nations, I found a much higher degree of uniformity in the procedures employed and in the instrumentation. This would suggest that ICVS data should be more comparable than those from nation-specific surveys.

Surveys that differ on individual design features could produce comparable data, if the combination of design features is such that the effects of these design differences are equal and offsetting. In an effort to see if the design differences in nation-specific surveys produce results different from those from the ICVS, I compared analyses across designs within and across nations.

The analyses compared were of three types—level comparisons, change estimates, and multivariate models. This was done because each type of analysis places more or less stringent standards of comparability. Comparisons of the level of crime are the most demanding, followed by estimates of change and multivariate modeling. Since serious issues of comparability are often dismissed by referring to the less demanding requirements of change estimation and modeling, it was important that comparisons included these types of analyses. In each case, the results were quite different across survey designs. The design of a survey makes a difference in level estimates, change estimates, and models of victimization risk. These design differences should not be ignored in cross-national comparisons of survey data.

While self-consciously comparative surveys, such as the ICVS, seem to be more uniform across countries, that uniformity comes at a price. Since these surveys are not the principal source of victimization data in the respective nations, the budget for the survey is limited. As a result, the ICVS surveys have small samples and do not employ state-of-the-art survey techniques to reduce costs. This certainly raises questions about the quality of the data, especially for relatively rare crimes, such as serious violence. Increasing the budgets for surveys within the ICVS would certainly help ameliorate these problems, but it is unlikely to occur. The best we can hope for is to maintain the survey at approximately its current levels and to use these data to investigate prevalent crimes and broad-based responses to crime, such as reporting to the police, where sampling error is less of a concern.

At the same time, greater attention must be given to the comparison of nation-specific surveys if we are to use these data to compare rare crimes and events, such as sexual predation, on which it is difficult to elicit information from respondents. A full accounting of these events requires the large samples and the expensive survey techniques that only ongoing, nation-specific victim surveys can muster. The initial step should be the thorough cataloguing of survey designs, instruments, and procedures, similar to what Killias and his colleagues did in the *European Sourcebook* for crime classification in administrative data (Council of Europe 1999). Currently, there is no place in which this information is readily available. With this information in hand, researchers can find nations that have more comparable surveys for purpose of comparison. The second step involves the development of adjustments that can be used with surveys that have unavoidable differences in survey designs, instrumentation, and procedures. In some instances, this adjustment can be very straightforward, as in the case in which surveys exclude some reported events from official estimates. When these events are included in the data file, the adjustment would simply require adding them back in. For more major and less tractable design differences, research on adjustments is required. If surveys employ different screening strategies, for example, and there are split sample tests of the effect of that difference in a particular nation, this difference can be used to adjust the data across nations. The more complex these adjustments, the more sensitivity analysis should be done in applying them to a specific set of nations. Adjusting data is always risky, but cautious adjustment is preferable to ignoring differences in victim surveys when doing cross-national comparisons.

Finally, the usefulness of victimization surveys for increasing our understanding of the role of the nation-state in generating crime and formulating responses to crime could be improved by supplementing national victimization surveys with more localized surveys in a large number of nations. Here victimization surveys could be conducted in several major cities in a large number of nations. The surveys would not be conducted to make national estimates, per se. Rather, they would represent specific cities or metropolitan areas within a nation. This format would not reduce problems of comparability, necessarily, and some structure for coordinating the content of the surveys would be necessary. This approach would, however, permit analyses of the effects of subnational jurisdictions as well as the nation-state on the risk of victimization while holding constant attributes of respondents. We know that subnational jurisdictions have an effect on crime, but with the current national surveys we cannot investigate this effect. Sample sizes in each nation might increase if, for example, three cities employ samples of 1,200 each compared to national samples of 2,000. Victim surveys and citizen surveys are becoming a more prevalent tool for evaluating public safety by city and police administrators, and these units of government may be willing to supplement funds from national governments to expand local samples. There may be some gains in precision in the estimates of violent crime in city surveys simply because cities generally have higher rates of violence than nonurban places. These local surveys have the additional potential advantage of being linked in meaningful ways to geographical units within the city, which opens the prospect of linking with other sources of crime-relevant data on that geographical unit. So, for example, if samples within jurisdictions are clustered by census tract or postal district, information on these entities can be identified and merged with the survey data to further inform investigation of victimization risk.

It may be useful to test the utility of this proposal by simply assembling local victim survey data that have already been collected.[16] An International Urban Crime Research Consortium could be formed to solicit data and participation from researchers in a large number of nations who have conducted jurisdiction-specific victimization surveys data. Assembling these data would provide some idea of the variability in methodologies used and the quality of these surveys, as well as the availability of geographical identifiers that can be used for linkage purposes. Analyses of these data would indicate whether subnational jurisdictions are consequential in mediating or enhancing the role of the nation-state on the risk of victimization and responses to same. If the variability in survey methodology is substantial, samples are small, geographical links are unavailable, and the effects of subnational jurisdictions are small, then this approach to understanding the role of the nation-state in crime would not be worth pursuing.

REFERENCES

Alvazzi del Frate, Anna, Ugi Zvekic, and Jan Van Dijk. 1993. *Understanding Crime: Experiences of Crime and Crime Control*. Rome: UNICRI.

Australian Bureau of Statistics. 2002. "Measuring Crime Victimization, Australia: The Impact of Different Collection Methodologies." Information paper. Canberra: Australian Bureau of Statistics.

Bennett, Richard R., and Peter Basiotis. 1991. "Structural Correlates of Juvenile Property Crime: A Cross-National Time Series Analysis." *Journal of Research in Crime and Delinquency* 28:262–87.

Bennett, Richard, and James P. Lynch. 1991. "Does a Difference Make a Difference? Comparing Cross-National Crime Indicators." *Criminology* 28: 153–82.

Biderman, Albert D. 1966. "Social Indicators and Goals." In *Social Indicators*, edited by Raymond Bauer. Cambridge, MA: MIT Press.

Biderman, Albert D., and David Cantor. 1984. "A Longitudinal Analysis of Bounding, Respondent Conditioning, and Mobility as a Source of Panel Bias in the National Crime Survey." In *Proceedings of the American Statistical Association: Social Statistics Section*. Washington, DC: American Statistical Association.

Biderman, Albert D., David Cantor, James Lynch, and Elizabeth Martin. 1986. "Final Report of Research and Development for the Redesign of the Na-

---

[16] Farrington, Langan, and Tonry (2004) provide some of this information on survey design, but more detail on instrumentation and procedures would be useful.

tional Crime Survey." Final Report to the Bureau of Justice Statistics. Washington, DC: Bureau of Social Science Research.

Biderman, Albert D., L. A. Johnson, J. McIntryre, and A. W. Weir. 1967. "Report on a Pilot Study in the District of Columbia on Victimization and Attitudes toward Law Enforcement." Field Surveys no. 1 prepared for the President's Commission on Law Enforcement and Administration of Justice. Washington, DC: Government Printing Office.

Biderman, Albert D., and James P. Lynch. 1981. "Recency Bias in Data on Self-Reported Victimization." In *Proceedings of the American Statistical Association, Social Statistics Section*. Washington, DC: American Statistical Association.

————. 1991. *Understanding Crime Incidence Statistics: Why Does the UCR Diverge from the NCS?* New York: Springer.

Bijleveld, Catrien, and Paul Smit. 2004. "Netherlands." In *Cross-National Studies in Crime and Justice*, edited by David Farrington, Patrick A. Langan, and Michael Tonry. Washington, DC: Bureau of Justice Statistics.

Blumstein, Alfred, and Joel Wallman. 2005. *The Crime Drop in America*. New York: Cambridge University Press.

Bolling, Keith, Sam Clemens, Catherine Grant, and Patten Smith. 2003. "2002–03 British Crime Survey: England and Wales ." Technical Report vol. 1 prepared for the Measuring and Analysis of Crime Programme: Research, Development, and Statistics Directorate. London: Home Office.

Cantor, David, and James P. Lynch. 2000. "Self-Report Surveys as Measures of Crime and Criminal Justice." In *Criminal Justice 2000: Measurement and Analysis of Crime and Justice*. Vol. 4. Washington, DC: U.S. Department of Justice.

————. 2005. "Exploring the Effects of Changes in Design on the Analytical Uses of the NCVS Data." *Journal of Quantitative Criminology* 21:293–319.

Carcach, Carlos. 2004. "Australia." In *Cross-National Studies in Crime and Justice*, edited by David P. Farrington, Patrick A. Langan, and Michael Tonry. Washington, DC: Bureau of Justice Statistics.

Central Statistics Office. 2004. *Quarterly National Household Survey: Crime and Victimization*. Dublin: Central Statistics Office.

Clancy, Anna, Mike Hough, Rebbecca Aust, and Chris Kershaw. 2001. *Crime Policing and Justice: The Experience of Ethnic Minorities*. London: Home Office.

Council of Europe. 1999. *European Sourcebook of Crime and Criminal Justice Statistics*. Strasbourg: Council of Europe.

Decker, Scott H. 1977. "Official Crime Rates and Victim Surveys: An Empirical Comparison." *Journal of Criminal Justice* 5:47–54.

Dodge, Richard W. 1970. *Household Survey of Victims Crime: Victim Recall Pretest*. Washington, DC: U.S. Department of Commerce.

————. 1987. *Series Crime: A Report on a Field Test*. Special report. Washington, DC: Bureau of Justice Statistics.

Ennis, Philip H. 1967. "Criminal Victimization in the United States: A Report of a National Survey." Field Surveys 2, a report of a research study submitted to the President's Commission on Law Enforcement and Administration of Justice. Washington, DC: Government Printing Office.

Fajnzylber, Pablo, Daniel Lederman, and Norman Loayza. 1998. *What Causes Violent Crime?* Washington, DC: World Bank.

Farrington, David P., and Derrick Jolliffe. 2004. "England and Wales." In *Cross-National Studies of Crime and Justice*, edited by David P. Farrington, Patrick A. Langan, and Michael Tonry. Washington, DC: Bureau of Justice Statistics.

Farrington, David P., and Patrick A. Langan. 1998. *Changes in Crime and Punishment in England and Wales and America in the 1980s.* Washington, DC: Bureau of Justice Statistics.

Farrington, David P., Patrick A. Langan, and Michael Tonry. 2004. *Cross-National Studies in Crime and Justice.* Washington, DC: Bureau of Justice Statistics.

Farrington, David P., Patrick A. Langan, and P.-O. H. Wikstrom. 1993. "Changes in Crime and Punishment in America, England, and Sweden between the 1980s and the 1990s." *Studies on Crime and Crime Prevention* 20: 104–30.

Fendrich, M., and C. Vaughn. 1994. "Diminished Lifetime Substance Use over Time: An Inquiry into Differential Under-reporting." *Public Opinion Quarterly* 58:96–123.

Fisher, Bonnie S., and Francis T. Cullen. 2000. "Measuring the Sexual Victimization of Women: Evolution, Current Controversies, and Future Research." In *Criminal Justice 2000: Measurement and Analysis of Crime and Justice*, vol. 1. Washington, DC: National Institute of Justice.

Forst, Brian, and James P. Lynch. 2003. "You Must Remember This: A Change Is Not a Difference as Time Goes By." Paper presented at the American Society of Criminology meetings, Denver, November 20.

Goudrian, Heike, James P. Lynch, and Paul Nieuwbeerta. 2004. "Reporting to the Police in Western Nations: The Effects of Country Characteristics." *Justice Quarterly* 21:933–69.

Hough, Mike, and Patricia Mayhew. 1982. *The British Crime Survey: The First Report.* London: Home Office.

Hubble, David. 1990. "National Crime Survey New Questionnaire Phase-in Research: Preliminary Results." Paper presented at the International Conference on Measurement Errors in Surveys, Tucson, November.

———. 1995. "The National Crime Victimization Survey Redesign: New Questionnaire and Procedures Development and Phase-in Methodology." Paper presented at the annual meetings of the American Statistical Association, Orlando, FL, August.

Hubble, David, and B. E. Wilder. 1988. "Preliminary Results from the National Crime Survey CATI Experiment." In *Proceedings of the American Statistical Association: Survey Methods Section.* Washington, DC: American Statistical Association.

Kershaw, Christopher, Tracey Budd, Graham Kinshott, Joanna Mattinson, Pat

Mayhew, and Andy Myhill. 2000. *The 2000 British Crime Survey: England and Wales.* London: Home Office.

Kershaw, Christopher, Natalia Chivite-Matthews, Carys Thomas, and Rebecca Aust. 2001. *The British Crime Survey: First Results England and Wales.* London: Home Office.

Killias, Martin, Philippe Lamond, and Marcelo F. Aebi. 2004. "Switzerland." In *Cross-National Studies in Crime and Justice,* edited by David Farrington, Patrick A. Langan, and Michael Tonry. Washington, DC: Bureau of Justice Statistics.

Kinderman, Charles, James P. Lynch, and David Cantor. 1997. *The Effects of the Redesign on Victimization Estimates: Data Brief.* Washington, DC: Bureau of Justice Statistics.

Kobelarcik, E. L., C. A. Alexander, R. P. Singh, and G. M. Shapiro. 1983. "Alternative Reference Periods for the National Crime Survey." In *Proceedings of the American Statistical Association: Section on Survey Methods.* Washington, DC: American Statistical Association.

Koss, Mary. 1996. "The Measurement of Rape Victimization in Crime Surveys." *Criminal Justice and Behavior* 23:55–69.

Kury, Helmut, Joachim Obergfell-Fuchs, and Michael Wurger. 2001. "Methodological Problems in Victim Surveys: The Example of the ICVS." In *International Comparisons of Crime and Victimization,* edited by Helmut Kury. Freiburg: Max Planck Institute.

Law Enforcement Assistance Administration. 1972. "San Jose Methods Test of Known Victims: Statistical Methods." Technical Report no. 1. Washington, DC: U.S. Department of Justice.

Lepkowski, James. 1981. "Sample Design Issues from the National Crime Survey." Ann Arbor: Survey Research Center, University of Michigan.

Loftus, Elizabeth, Mark Klinger, Kyle Smith, and Judith Fielder. 1990. "A Tale of Two Questions: Benefits of Asking More than One Question." *Public Opinion Quarterly* 54:330–45.

Lynch, James P. 1987. "Routine Activity and Victimization at Work." *Journal of Quantitative Criminology* 3:283–300.

———. 1995. "Crime in International Perspective." In *Crime,* edited by James Q. Wilson and Joan Petersilia. San Francisco: Institute for Contemporary Studies.

———. 2002. "Effects of Design Differences on Rate Comparisons in the ICVS." In *Crime Victimization in Comparative Perspective: Results from the International Crime Victimization Survey, 1989–2000,* edited by Paul Nieuwbeerta. Den Haag: BOOM.

Lynch, James P., and David Cantor. 1996. "Models for Adjusting the NCS Trends to Account for Design Differences between the NCS and the NCVS." Memorandum to the American Statistical Association Committee on Law and Justice Statistics, May 28.

Lynch, James P., and Andromachi Tseloni. 2003. "As Simple as Possible and No Simpler: Cross-National Comparisons of Self-Report Victimization Surveys." Unpublished manuscript. Washington, DC: American University.

Magura, S., and S. Kang. 1994. "The Validity of Self-Reported Cocaine Use in Two High Risk Populations." Paper presented at the National Institute on Drub Abuse Technical Review on the Validity of Self-Reported Drug Use: Improving the Accuracy of Survey Estimates, Rockville, MD.

Mayhew, Patricia. 1987. *Residential Burglary: A Comparison of the United States, Canada, and England and Wales.* Washington DC: National Institute of Justice.

McDowall, David, and Colin Loftin. Forthcoming. "What Is Divergence and What Do We Know about It?" In *Understanding Crime Statistics: Revisiting the Divergence of the NCVS and the UCR,* edited by James P. Lynch and Lynn A. Addington. New York: Cambridge University Press.

Mennard, Scott, and Herbert Covey. 1988. "UCR and NCS: Comparisons over Space and Time." *Journal of Criminal Justice* 16:371–84.

Messner, Steven. 1989. "Economic Discrimination and Societal Homicide Rates: Further Evidence on the Cost of Inequality." *American Sociological Review* 54:597–611.

Miller, Peter V., and Robert M. Groves. 1985. "Matching Survey Responses to Official Records: Validity in Victimization Reporting." *Public Opinion Quarterly* 49:366–80.

Mirrlees-Black, C. 1999. "Domestic Violence: Findings from a New British Crime Survey Self-Completion Questionnaire." Home Office Research Study no. 191. London: Home Office.

MVA. 2002. *The 2000 Scottish Crime Survey: Overview Report.* Edinburgh: Scottish Executive Central Research Unit.

Nelson, James F. 1979. "Implications for the Ecological Study of Crime: A Research Note." In *Perspectives on Victimology,* edited by Willard Parsonage. Newbury Park, CA: Sage.

Neter, J., and Joseph Waksberg. 1964. "A Study of Response Errors in Expenditure Data from Household Surveys." *Journal of the American Statistical Association* 59:18–55.

Percy, A., and Patricia Mayhew. 1992. "Estimating Sexual Victimization in a National Crime Survey: A New Approach." *Studies in Crime and Crime Prevention* 6:125–50.

Persley, Carolyn. 1995. "The National Crime Victimization Survey Redesign: Measuring the Impact of New Methods." Paper presented at the annual meetings of the American Statistical Association, Orlando, FL, August 13.

Planty, Michael. Forthcoming. "Series Victimization and the Divergence of the NCVS and the UCR." In *Understanding Crime Statistics: Revisiting the Divergence of the NCVS and the UCR,* edited by James P. Lynch and Lynn A. Addington. New York: Cambridge University Press.

Rand, Michael, and Bruce Taylor. 1995. "The National Crime Victimization Survey Redesign: New Understandings of Victimization Dynamics and Measurement." Paper presented at the annual meetings of the American Statistical Association, Orlando, FL, August.

Raudenbush, Stephen W., and Anthony C. Bryk. 2003. *Hierarchical Linear Models: Applications and Data Analysis.* Thousand Oaks, CA: Sage.

286   James P. Lynch

Reiss, Albert J., Jr. 1967. "Studies in Crime and Law Enforcement in Major Metropolitan Areas." Field Survey 3, vol. 1, report of a research study submitted to the U.S. President's Commission on Law Enforcement and Administration of Justice. Washington, DC: Government Printing Office.

Rennison, Callie M. 2001. *Criminal Victimization 2000: Changes 1999–2000 with Trends 1993–2000.* Washington, DC: Bureau of Justice Statistics.

Robinson, J. Gregory, Arjun Adlakha, and Kirsten K. West. 2002. "Coverage of Population in Census 2000: Results from Demographic Analysis." Paper presented at the 2002 annual meeting of the Population Association of America, Atlanta, May 8–11.

Rosenfeld, Richard. Forthcoming. "Exploring the Divergence between the UCR and NCVS Aggravated Assault Trends." In *Understanding Crime Statistics: Revisiting the Divergence of the NCVS and the UCR*, edited by James P. Lynch and Lynn A. Addington. New York: Cambridge University Press.

Schaefer, Melissa, and James P. Lynch. 2003. "The Seriousness of Crime: A Cross-National Comparison." *International Journal of Comparative Criminology* 2:90–102.

Schwarz, Norbert. 1995. "What Respondents Learn from Questionnaires: The Survey Interview and the Logic of Conversation." *International Statistical Review* 63:153–77.

Smith, David J. 2004. "Scotland." In *Cross-National Studies in Crime and Justice*, edited by David Farrington, Patrick A. Langan, and Michael Tonry. Washington, DC: Bureau of Justice Statistics.

Smith, Steven, Greg W. Steadman, Todd Minton, and Meg Townsend. 1999. *Criminal Victimization and Perceptions of Public Safety in 12 Cities.* Washington, DC: Bureau of Justice Statistics.

Sparks, Richard F., Hazel G. Genn, and David J. Dodd. 1977. *Surveying Victims: A Study of the Measurement of Criminal Victimization, Perceptions of Crime, and Attitudes toward Criminal Justice.* Chichester: Wiley.

Stack, Steven. 1984. "Income Inequality and Property Crime." *Criminology* 22: 229–57.

Statistics Canada. 2004. *General Social Survey: An Overview.* Ottawa: Statistics Canada.

Strack, F., and L. L. Martin. 1987. "Thinking, Judging, and Communicating: A Process Account of Context Effects in Attitude Surveys. In *Social Information Processing and Survey Methodology*, edited by H. J. Hippler, N. Schwarz, and S. Sudman. New York: Springer.

Sudman, Seymour, Norman M. Bradburn, and Norbert Schwarz. 1996. *Thinking about Answers: The Application of Cognitive Processes to Survey Methodology.* San Francisco: Jossey-Bass.

Sudman, Seymour, A. Finn, and L. Lammon. 1984. "The Use of Bounded Recall Procedures in Single Interviews." *Public Opinion Quarterly* 48:520–24.

Taylor, Bruce. 1983. "Does Higher Socio-economic Status Increase Risk of Violent Victimization or Simply Its Reporting in Crime Surveys?" Paper presented at the annual meetings of the American Society of Criminology, Denver, November.

Tonry, Michael, and David P. Farrington, eds. 2005. *Crime and Punishment in Western Countries, 1980–1999*. Chicago: University of Chicago Press.

Tourengeau, Roger. 1984. "Cognitive Sciences and Survey Methods." In *Cognitive Aspects of Survey Methodology: Building a Bridge between Disciplines*, edited by Tom Jabine, Morton Straf, Judith M. Tanur, and Roger Tourangeau. Washington, DC: National Academy.

Tseloni, Andromachi, Karin Wittebrode, Graham Farrell, and Ken Pease. 2004. "Burglary Victimization in England and Wales, the United States, and the Netherlands: A Cross-National Comparative Test of Routine Activity and Lifestyle Theories." *British Journal of Criminology* 44:66–91.

Van Dijk, Jan, Patricia Mayhew, and Martin Killias. 1990. *Experiences of Crime across the World: Key Findings of the 1989 International Crime Survey*. Deventer, Netherlands: Kluwer.

———. 1993. "Criminal Victimization in the Industrialized World: Key Findings of the 1989 and 1992 International Crime Surveys." In *Understanding Crime: Experiences of Crime and Crime Control*, edited by Anne Alvazzi del Frate, Ugljesa Zvekic, and Jan J. M. Van Dijk. Rome: United Nations Interregional Crime and Justice Institute.

Van Kesteren, John, Patricia Mayhew, and Paul Nieuwbeerta. 2001. *Criminal Victimization in Seventeen Industrialized Nations: Key Findings from the 2000 International Crime Victims Survey*. Leiden, Netherlands: National Institute for the Study of Crime and Law Enforcement.

Verweij, Antonia, and Paul Nieuwbeerta. 2001. "Gender Differences in Violent Victimizations in Eighteen Industrialized Countries: The Role of Emancipation." In *International Comparisons of Crime and Victimization*, edited by Helmut Kury. Freiburg: Max Planck Institute.

Weiss, Karen. 2004. "Using Narrative Descriptions of Incidents in the NCVS to Understand the Classification of Rape Incidents." Paper presented at the ICPSR summer workshop on the Quantitative Analysis of Crime Data, Ann Arbor, MI, July 24.

Welch, Brandon, and Mark J. Irving. 2004. "Canada." In *Cross-National Studies in Crime and Justice*, edited by David Farrington, Patrick A. Langan, and Michael Tonry. Washington, DC: Bureau of Justice Statistics.

Wikstrom, P.-O. H., and Lars Dolmén. 2004 "Sweden." In *Cross-National Studies in Crime and Justice*, edited by David Farrington, Patrick A. Langan, and Michael Tonry. Washington, DC: Bureau of Justice Statistics.

Michael Levi and Peter Reuter

Money Laundering

ABSTRACT

Techniques for hiding proceeds of crime include transporting cash out of the country, purchasing businesses through which funds can be channeled, buying easily transportable valuables, transfer pricing, and using "underground banks." Since the mid-1980s, governments and law enforcement have developed an increasingly global, intrusive, and routinized set of measures to affect criminal revenues passing through the financial system. Except at an anecdotal level, the effects of this system on laundering methods and prices, or on offenders' willingness to engage in various crimes, are unknown. Available data weakly suggest that the anti–money laundering (AML) regime has not had major effects in suppressing crimes. The regime does facilitate investigation and prosecution of some criminal participants who would otherwise evade justice, but fewer than expected by advocates of "follow the money" methods. It also permits the readier recovery of funds from core criminals and from financial intermediaries. However, the volume is very slight compared with income or even profits from crime. Though the regime also targets terrorist finances, modern terrorists need little money for their operations. AML controls are unlikely to cut off their funds but may yield useful intelligence. Money-laundering controls impose costly obligations on businesses and society: they merit better analysis of their effects, both good and bad.

People who commit serious crimes for economic gain want not only to evade imprisonment but also to enjoy the fruits of their crimes. This enjoyment often takes the form of immediate (sometimes conspicuous) consumption. For the more disciplined and those who make vast profits, "enjoyment" may take the form of savings for future economic opportunities. The latter group (plus transnational criminals who have

Michael Levi is a professor in the Cardiff School of Social Sciences, Cardiff University, Wales. Peter Reuter is a professor in the School of Public Policy and the Department of Criminology at the University of Maryland and codirector of the Drug Policy Research Center at RAND. This essay draws significantly on Peter Reuter and Edwin M. Truman, *Chasing Dirty Money* (2004). We are grateful to Dr. Truman Edwin and to the referees for their comments. Jeri Smith-Ready provided valuable research assistance.

to move funds before spending them), how they do their business, and how public and private sectors respond around the world are the focus of this essay.

The conversion of criminal incomes to forms that allow the offender unfettered spending and investment has been an ongoing concern to both criminals and the state since at least the early days of the American Mafia. Meyer Lansky's claim to fame was partly his supposed skill in concealing the origins of funds used to buy real estate and legitimate businesses. His goal was to avoid tax evasion charges, which had famously brought down Al Capone, by making it difficult to trace the connection between wealth and its criminal sources.[1] Laws against handling stolen property traditionally referred only to the physical property obtained in the course of the crime. Only in the last generation has the disguise or concealment of funds obtained from crimes itself become a criminal activity, in a sense created by a new set of laws and regulations aimed at "money laundering."

Developed initially in the United States in the 1970s to combat use of international banks for tax evasion, money-laundering controls became a significant component of the war on drugs. More recently they have grown into an extensive and global set of controls aimed at a wide array of offenses, from cigarette smuggling, through corruption of high-level officials, to terrorist finance. The extent to which money-laundering laws include tax evasion remains an issue of divergence, both in national legislation and in mutual legal assistance.

The array of institutions involved in anti–money laundering (AML) is impressive. The control regime in the United States has extended beyond banks,[2] the original subjects, to a wide range of businesses such as car dealers, casinos, corner shop money transmission businesses, jewelers, pawnbrokers, and certain insurance companies. All these are now required[3] to play an active role in crime control through, inter alia, reporting on those customers whom they suspect of obtaining funds from crime or of using funds (whether from crime or legitimate sources) for terrorist activities. In the United Kingdom, any business handling high-value goods must report a "suspicious transaction."[4] In

---

[1] Mark Haller provided helpful clarifying comments on this matter.

[2] There were also some other regulated retail savings firms.

[3] Garland (1996) offers an inelegant but evocative term, "responsibilized," that might be used for this.

[4] Technically, these should be labeled "*suspected* transactions," since they represent the aftermath of a cognitive process rather than an inherent quality of the act. But as Gold

Canada there have been moves to require accountants to affirmatively report any suspicions of money laundering by their clients, though analogous requirements for lawyers had to be withdrawn following constitutional attack. In Switzerland, long regarded by the media and by anticorruption campaigners as an iconic laundering nation, even hotels that offer money exchange facilities above a modest level are subject to money-laundering regulation and are required to identify customers and record dealings.

The regime aims to be truly global, with both the International Monetary Fund (IMF) and the World Bank playing an active role within a policy framework set by a "temporary body" with a renewable mandate created in 1989—the Financial Action Task Force (FATF). They and a myriad of regional bodies monitor how well each nation complies with at least the formalities (and, increasingly, the substance) of the regime (Levi and Gilmore 2002). Thus, from small beginnings in 1995, by November 2005, the Egmont Group contained 101 National Financial Intelligence Units (FIUs) that meet internally developed criteria for receiving, analyzing, and processing reports (including Suspicious Activity Reports [SARs]) from the regulated institutions mentioned in the previous paragraph. Since 1999, there has been a formal process for imposing economic sanctions on countries that do not play their part, by slowing down their international transactions and making it almost impossible for their banks to clear funds through other countries. There is considerable pressure to expand the regime to other businesses and professions throughout the world, mostly justified since 9/11 as a method for fighting terrorism. Given the small sums involved as direct operational costs in major incidents such as the Madrid bombing of 2004 and the London bombings of July 2005 (not much more than $10,000 in total), it is difficult to predict where this broadening of coverage will end.

Money laundering is difficult to study in part because it is conceptually elusive. Is it a separate activity, like the fencing of stolen goods, or is it better thought of as an element of certain criminal acts, as is conspiracy? There appears to be a disjunction between the legal construct of laundering, which includes acts as modest as the placing of proceeds of crime in a bank account in one's own name, and the an-

---

and Levi (1994) note, it is difficult to shift even misleading terminology once it has entered into routine use. Another example of this might be the continued use of the term "organized crime."

292   Michael Levi and Peter Reuter

alytical construct of laundering, which one would expect to mean the sanitizing of proceeds of crime so that one can spend the funds as though they had been acquired legitimately. Most crimes for significant gain generate more funds than their perpetrators can spend in cash in the short term, and storing large sums creates risks from law enforcement and from other criminal predators. In that sense laundering (or at least "hiding," which has become "laundering" through legal extension of the concept) is an integral part of the serious crime process.

But how distinct is the process from the commission of the underlying "predicate" crimes? There certainly are persons uninvolved in the underlying crime who have laundered money. For example, Lucy Edwards—a senior executive in charge of Eastern European operations at the Bank of New York—and her husband, businessman Peter Berlin, earned large sums by laundering billions of dollars for some Russians who were either evading taxes or concealing the fruits of criminal enterprise. They have no other connection to criminal activities.[5] However, in many instances—especially fraud and tax evasion—the act is built into the underlying criminal offense. In accusations against Enron (Andrew Fastow) and HealthSouth (Richard Scrushy),[6] senior executives were charged with money laundering as well as fraud and embezzlement; but these cases currently involve no person who is charged with having acted as their money launderer. Pragmatically, enforcement authorities may find it useful to be able to charge people with laundering or (in the United States) with structuring payments in order to avoid reporting regulations (discussed later), even where the launderer is in fact the person committing a substantive offense such as drug trafficking or robbery.[7]

Knowing the balance between laundering as a separate activity and as part of the offense is important in judging the likely effectiveness of the AML regime. If the same evidence that might be used to convict people of laundering could also convict them of a substantive offense, there is little marginal benefit from the existence of the offense. There could be a benefit, however, where suspicious transaction reports from institutions point the finger of suspicion or lead to greater asset re-

[5] For a particularly graphic approach to this and other misconduct, see Block and Weaver (2004).

[6] Richard Scrushy was found not guilty of these charges.

[7] These laundering sanctions penalize only savers, since if all proceeds are spent on immediate conspicuous consumption, the principal offenders have not laundered the money.

covery, or where there is court-usable evidence of their connection to the banking or concealment of the proceeds but not of their involvement in the specific offenses that generated the funds. Measuring that benefit is important because the costs of the AML system, in a number of dimensions, are very substantial and are easier to see than the benefits. Indeed, although the costs are normally calculated in terms of the economic costs of implementing the policies, part of the resistance to AML comes from the emotional and practical experiences of ordinary citizens who may find it difficult to open accounts because they lack the identification documents in their own names required by the money-laundering regulations, even though their intended business is small and not remotely connected to the transnational crime activity with which they (and our readers) associate the term "money laundering."[8]

The problem faced by the regime is easily described. By the early twenty-first century (and long before), there was a large and growing range of methods for moving money across international boundaries, yet another facet of globalization. Thus there has evolved a highly differentiated set of financial institutions to meet the needs of various population groups such as low-income migrant workers who repatriate earnings home to poorer countries, very rich investors seeking to find the most politically secure and profitable location for their capital, and a broad array of businesses, from jewelry shops and car dealers to financial services firms themselves.

This makes it difficult to develop regulations that are truly comprehensive across institutions and that also reflect the risk to society that those different sorts of institutions pose through money-laundering activities. Though ultimately banks will almost certainly be involved in handling the proceeds of crimes or (to a far lesser extent) funds that facilitate terrorism, the chains by which the funds reach banks may themselves be complicated enough to make it hard for even well-intentioned banks to identify truly suspect transactions. Not all banks

---

[8] Thus, even when trying to open a new account for children in the same institution in which they already held accounts, one of us (ML) was required to get them to prove their identities by showing passports etc. Bankers we have interviewed have experienced this when trying to open accounts for themselves, even in their own institutions. Little wonder that some senior citizens and married people (usually women) whose utility bills are in their partner's name write to the British press complaining about being treated as money-laundering suspects and denied access to the banking system. This reflects the focus of the authorities on the front end of the due diligence process rather than on the ongoing monitoring of accounts.

are so well intentioned; but the AML regime has increased the reputational, regulatory, and penal risks attached to such commercial myopia or sociopathy.

We cannot dismiss the possibility that the regime's many critics are correct. Whatever their benefits *in theory*, the controls in practice may do little to accomplish crime-fighting goals or to combat terrorism, while imposing a substantial burden on people doing business in those nations—by now the vast majority—that have introduced them. Theoretical arguments suggest the implausibility of large crime suppression effects from AML, and our review of the little available data weakly supports this view, at least given the resources (including their coordination) that have been put into AML so far.[9] The regime does facilitate investigation and prosecution of some criminal participants who would otherwise evade justice, but fewer than expected and hoped for by advocates of "follow the money" methods. It also permits the readier recovery of funds from core criminals and from financial intermediaries and their transfer to victims and law enforcement agencies. However, although this may make communities feel better, the volume is slight compared with total income or even plausible profits from crime.

There is very little empirical research either on the phenomenon of money laundering or on the controls that deal with it. In particular, despite regular intergovernmental reviews of "money-laundering typologies" at FATF and regional gatherings—which at least stimulate some communal thinking about vulnerabilities—there are no systematic studies of how criminal offenders turn their incomes into usable assets or of how AML controls affect this. This essay draws not only on the modest criminological and legal literature but also on a wide array of nonacademic writings, principally from governments, lawyers, and journalists, to describe both money laundering and the regime.

Our emphasis is as much on the regulations as on the offense. The reason is not just that more is known about the regulations but also that the regulations have significant consequences for the architecture of the national and international governance of serious crime and for its flip side—the freedom of citizens from government surveillance.

Section I reviews the evolution of the regime of controls in the United States and summarizes the current global regime. It emphasizes

[9] It is far from certain that additional AML resources would have a significant effect on crime suppression.

the intricacy of the laws and regulations, the institutional complexity, and the multiplicity of goals. Section II describes what is known about money laundering itself. Though the regime has been justified in large part by the claim that money launderers are an important class of criminal offenders who facilitate certain illegal markets, organized crime, and white-collar crime, we offer some indications that self-laundering is the common mode. The section also reviews estimates of the scale of money laundering, since the claim of macroeconomic significance has been an important plank in the construction of the controls. Section III reviews available information on enforcement, which has been given much less policy attention than the laws and regulations themselves. Section IV provides an analytic framework linking the regime to the general goals and analyzes the patchy data available for the United States to suggest that if the volumes of money laundered are of the magnitude conventionally quoted, those involved are at modest risk of being caught. Section V gives our conclusions about how well the system works and briefly lays out a short research agenda, a set of interesting theoretical and policy questions, and some suggestions for how they might be studied.

I. The Anti–Money Laundering Regime

The current AML regime is remarkable for the range of institutions involved and the centrality of international agreements. A World Bank/ IMF guide to the system (World Bank 2003*a*) lists six distinct international bodies in addition to themselves that either set rules or have formal monitoring responsibilities,[10] mostly either for specific industries (such as insurance) or for parts of the process (e.g., FIUs that receive reports from regulated institutions). Alldridge (2003, p. 281)

---

[10] The bodies are the FATF, the Egmont Group of FIUs, the International Organization of Security Commissioners, the United Nations Office of Drugs and Crime, the Basel Committee on Banking Supervision, and the International Association of Insurance Supervisors. These are merely the top layer of standard-setting bodies: there is a myriad of subsidiary public- and private-sector bodies beneath, including the FATF-style regional bodies: Asia/Pacific Group, the Caribbean Financial Action Task Force, ESAAMLG (Eastern and Southern Africa), EAG (Eurasia), GAFISUD (Latin America), MENAFATF (Middle East and North Africa), and Moneyval (Europe). The Offshore Group of Banking Supervisors is also part of this network. In the private sector there are national industry and professional bodies (such as the American Bankers Association and the Law Society of England and Wales), plus the Wolfsberg group of international banks. This collectively constitutes an important component of the governance of crime, though omitted by some recent contributors to discussions of "high policing" (such as O'Reilly and Ellison, forthcoming).

notes that money laundering "is an area in which most jurisdictions' laws are formulated in order to comply with international instruments." However, this international regime has developed only since 1989. How did it begin?

The U.S. Bank Secrecy Act (BSA) of 1970 represents the historic starting point for efforts to detect and sanction money laundering, though the term was not yet commonly used. The irony of the name is frequently noted (e.g., Cuéllar 2003); the statute was intended to limit rather than protect bank secrecy. Banks acquired an affirmative duty to provide information to the Department of the Treasury of transactions involving more than $10,000 in cash (Currency Transaction Reports [CTRs]). In line with its "regulatory" thrust, the BSA criminalized the failure to report, not the provision of the services to facilitate a criminal act.

The BSA was aimed primarily at the use of foreign banks to launder the proceeds of illegal activity and to evade federal income taxes (Villa 1988). Though passed at the beginning of the federal government campaign against the American Mafia (Jacobs and Gouldin 1999), the BSA appears not to have been motivated by that effort. Nor indeed (like RICO[11] itself) was it much used until the 1980s, when the powers of the Department of Treasury were clarified and extended by passage of the Money Laundering Control Act of 1986, whose key provisions (18 CFR 1956 and 1957) remain the principal statutory authorities for prosecutions.

The Money Laundering Control Act of 1986 was explicitly a component of the federal war on drugs, stimulated in part by the findings of a high-profile undercover investigation in the center of the drug trade, southern Florida. Operation Greenback found numerous instances of couriers for drug dealers carrying cash into banks in quantities just under $10,000 in order to evade the formal requirements of the BSA. Following the prosecution of the Bank of Boston for failure to report such patterns of transactions, many banks voluntarily reported noncompliance with the BSA and implemented much more routinized reporting programs:[12] an early instance of deterrence among those who had much to lose.

---

[11] The Racketeer-Influenced Corrupt Organizations Act of 1970 was passed as part of President Nixon's war on organized crime (see Woodiwiss 2001) to try to put into legal effect the criminal enterprise construct and to permit a range of civil and criminal controls.

[12] This illustrates the power of high-profile enforcement activity to trigger behavioral changes among other institutions that have something to lose. Whether, after the oc-

Even before the terrorist attacks of September 11, the system had expanded to include terrorism finance, though efforts to require bankers to be more diligent in identifying and monitoring their customers had met with severe political setbacks. Following the attack, Congress hastily passed the USA PATRIOT Act,[13] which increased the powers of the Departments of Justice and Treasury to obtain information and to expand the net of regulation. For example, the PATRIOT Act allowed (but did not require) the Treasury Department to regulate those involved in securities transactions, currency exchange, fund transfers, and real estate closings and settlements, among others. The act also imposed new requirements on financial institutions, including stricter customer due diligence and the creation of AML programs within each institution.

It is useful to think of the regime as having two basic pillars, prevention and enforcement. The prevention pillar is designed to deter criminals from using institutions to launder the proceeds of their crimes and to create sufficient transparency to deter institutions from being willing to launder. Enforcement is designed to punish criminals (and their money-laundering associates) when, despite prevention efforts, they have successfully laundered those proceeds.

The prevention pillar has four key elements from bottom to top: customer due diligence (CDD), reporting, regulation and supervision, and sanctions (fig. 1). Prevention may be thought of as describing primarily the role of regulatory agencies. CDD involves the requirements to name not just the nominal account holder but also the beneficial owner on whose behalf she or he is acting;[14] to provide proof of identity and an address; and ongoing monitoring to check whether individual and corporate customer account behavior is consistent with the bank's knowledge of their circumstances and work. This is intended to limit criminal access to the financial system and—latterly—to generate continuous reconsideration of whether customers might be benefiting from crime or financing terrorism. The theory is that the requirement to provide information will deter some offenders and others will be denied access once the information has been checked. Reporting refers

casional symbolic shock, criminal prosecution is always necessary to achieve this is open to question, however.
[13] USA Patriot Act stands for "Uniting and Strengthening America by Providing Appropriate Tools Required to Intercept and Obstruct Terrorism."
[14] Though variably implemented in national legislation and in national regulatory supervision.

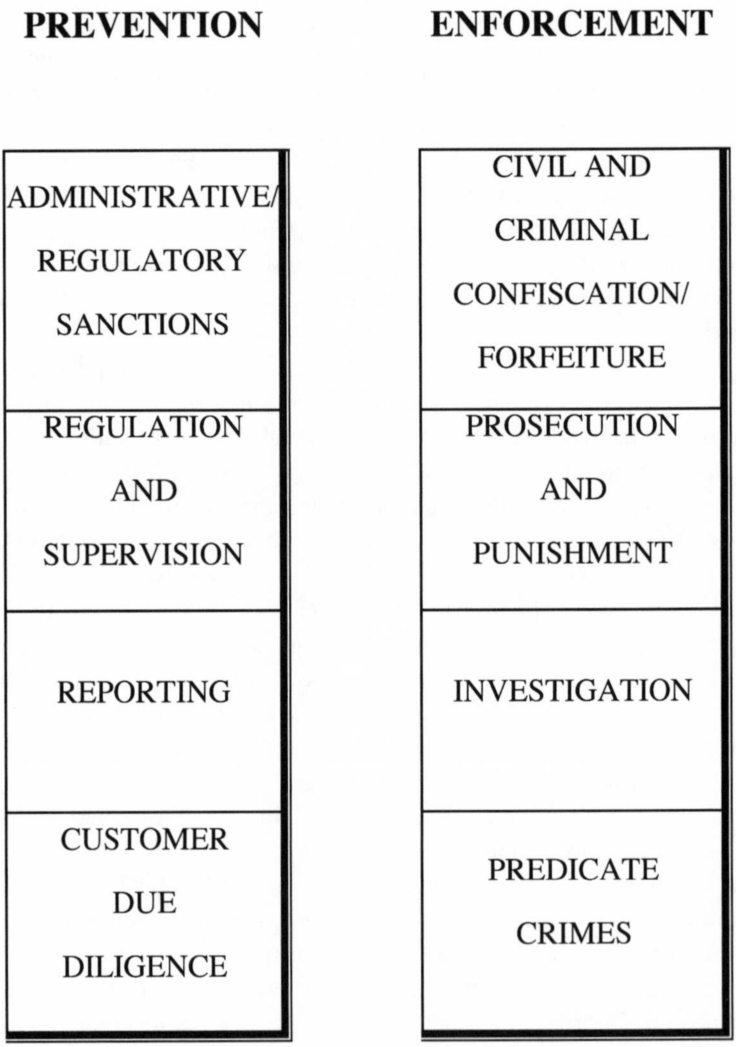

PREVENTION

ENFORCEMENT

ADMINISTRATIVE/ REGULATORY SANCTIONS
REGULATION AND SUPERVISION
REPORTING
CUSTOMER DUE DILIGENCE

CIVIL AND CRIMINAL CONFISCATION/ FORFEITURE
PROSECUTION AND PUNISHMENT
INVESTIGATION
PREDICATE CRIMES

Fig. 1.—The AML regime (source: Reuter and Truman 2004)

to information that the institution or professional must provide to enforcement authorities. External supervision is active monitoring of compliance with CDD and reporting requirements. Finally, sanctions (mostly administrative and civil rather than criminal) punish individuals and institutions that fail to implement the prevention regime, in particular with respect to CDD and reporting requirements.

The enforcement pillar also has four key elements from bottom to top: a list of underlying offenses or predicate crimes, investigation, prosecution and punishment, and confiscation (fig. 1). The list of predicate crimes establishes the legal basis for criminalizing money laundering; only funds from the listed crimes are subject to these laws and regulations. The other three elements are common in the criminal justice system, except for confiscation of proceeds, where often the burden of proof shifts following some early legal elements such as conviction. Enforcement may be triggered or facilitated by information from the prevention apparatus, but it is primarily carried out by criminal investigative agencies.

A. The Current U.S. Anti–Money Laundering Prevention Regime

The U.S. prevention pillar, much imitated because of its pioneering status and because of the U.S. centrality to international finances (e.g., clearing most dollar-denominated trades), is more elaborate and has evolved more than the enforcement pillar. In practice, there may be some tension between the two pillars. For example, financial supervisory authorities are uncomfortable with the delays in changing behavior that arise when institutions (and their lawyers and insurers) shift from "restorative" to defensive criminal justice mode and with the collateral damage to the financial system that may arise from prosecuting major institutions. A criminal indictment of a bank threatens the institution's existence, as happened to the Arthur Andersen accounting firm when it was indicted for obstructing justice in the investigation of Enron.[15] Bank supervisors, while willing to admonish, are interested in the continued existence of the banks they regulate unless the banks are insolvent; they may be fearful that if they hand over information to

---

[15] Though the Arthur Andersen conviction was reversed by the Supreme Court in May 2005, the accounting firm remains a mere shell of its former self, and its staff worldwide mostly moved to other accounting firms. However, the consequences of the Arthur Andersen case are a public warning of how quickly major institutions can unravel—a factor that may deter regulatory as well as criminal intervention and sanctions since they are seen as the "nuclear option."

TABLE 1

Prevention Pillar of the U.S. Anti–Money Laundering Regime

	CDD	Reporting Requirements	Supervision	Sanction
Financial institutions:				
Core financial institutions*	Yes	Yes	Yes	Yes
Other types of financial institutions	Yes	Yes	Some	Limited
Nonfinancial businesses:				
Casinos	Yes	Yes	Some	Yes
Dealers in precious metals and stones	Yes	Yes	No	No
Real estate agents	No	No	No	No
Other[†]	No	Some	No	No
Professions:				
Lawyers and accountants	Limited	Limited	Very limited	Very limited
Trust and company services providers	Limited	Limited	Very limited	Very limited
Other[‡]	Some	Some	Very limited	Very limited

SOURCE.—Reuter and Truman (2004).

* Depository institutions, securities firms, insurance companies, and combinations.

[†] For example, mutual funds and investment advisors.

[‡] For example, travel agencies, commodity trading advisors, and vehicle sellers.

prosecutors, there will be systemic or other "collateral damage," for example, to bank customers.

Table 1 summarizes the prevention pillar of the current U.S. AML regime. The elements are listed across the top of the table, and three broad categories of economic actors (along with some subcategories) are listed down the side. The cells in the table indicate whether or to what extent the elements of the prevention pillar are applied to the various subcategories of economic activities. This heterogeneity is important for understanding the limits of the system.

1. *Core Financial Institutions.* The most stringent requirements apply to core financial institutions such as banks, securities firms, insurance companies, and various combinations of those institutions. All are required to have comprehensive AML compliance programs (a formal set of controls and training programs) and are traditionally subject to

federal as well as state regulation and supervision.[16] These include four different forms.

    a. Customer due diligence. If the institution is unable to satisfy itself that the clients are who they say they are and that their funds are plausibly consistent with what it knows about their inheritance and current sources of income, it is generally expected to decline to open the account or to complete the transaction. The institution is expected to view due diligence as an ongoing process. If an individual suddenly deposits a million dollars in her account, especially in cash, she had better have a verifiable explanation; otherwise the bank will send an SAR to the government.[17]

    b. Reporting requirements. In the United States, institutions are required to submit a variety of reports on transactions to federal agencies.[18] These reports generate an information overload, making it difficult for the recipient agencies to use the information efficiently in law enforcement and related investigatory activities.[19] Interinstitutional variations in reporting behavior are commonplace worldwide, with some engaging in defensive reporting to avoid potential penalties (and reduce internal review staff costs) and others sifting carefully their initial suspicions, thereby risking criticism and even official action for failing to disclose. The U.S. AML regime and core financial institutions have also been criticized for applying more stringent CDD and reporting requirements to foreign than to domestic customers and transactions, possibly on the theory that drug traffickers and other major criminals are likely to be aliens.

    c. Supervision. Core financial institutions such as banks are subject to substantial supervision that normally includes annual on-site

---

[16] Stand-alone U.S. insurance companies are primarily supervised at the state level but are covered by federal AML law and subject to federal AML regulations.

[17] Some economies, e.g., in the Middle East, Asia, and even Switzerland, have much higher rates of cash usage than the United Kingdom and United States; so this sort of "out-of-context" behavior has to be seen in the light of business and social norms—a flexibility that is difficult to reconcile with the pressure for uniform international rules.

[18] SARs go to the U.S. Treasury Department's Financial Crimes Enforcement Network (FinCEN), CTRs to the Internal Revenue Service, and Reports of International Transportation of Currency or Other Monetary Instruments to the Customs Service.

[19] In mid-2004, the American Bankers Association acknowledged that progress had been made in reducing the amount of data generated but recommended that the threshold for banks to file CTRs for corporations and businesses be at least doubled from the $10,000 set in 1970 (Byrne 2004).

examinations to ensure their compliance with a wide array of laws and regulations.

   d. *Sanctions.* Institutions can be subjected to informal or formal administrative actions by the regulator and, potentially, civil and criminal penalties. There have been a few major scandals, such as that concerning the Riggs Bank of Washington in 2004 (U.S. Senate 2004, 2005) after it failed to conduct due diligence inquiries on large flows into accounts connected with ex-President Pinochet of Chile and President Obiang of Equatorial Guinea. Following this, it was fined heavily ($25 million for regulatory violations and $16 million for criminal violations) and placed under a five-year probation.[20] Dutch Bank ABN AMRO was fined $80 million in 2005 for allowing individuals from Russia and other former Soviet republics to move $3.2 billion to shell companies[21] in the United States from August 2002 to September 2003 and for failing to stop Chicago and New York branches from participating in wire transfers and trade transactions from 1997 to 2004 that violated economic sanctions on Libya and Iran (*New York Times* 2005). Israel Discount Bank of New York agreed to pay up to $25 million to settle state and federal claims that it allowed illegal Brazilian money transmitters to move $2.2 billion through its offices over the preceding five years (*Newsday* 2005). The public has not been informed about what JP Morgan Chase has agreed to do in the aftermath of its failure to catch the laundering of $6 billion by the Beacon Hill money service business.

   2. *Noncore Financial Institutions.* A broad range of other types of U.S. financial institutions has been progressively incorporated into the U.S. AML regime. Money service businesses, a major subcategory of "money management activities,"[22] are required to register with FinCEN (Financial Crimes Enforcement Network, a small specialized agency within the Department of Treasury) if they offer such services

---

[20] Pinochet was charged by prosecutors in Chile in November 2005 in relation to accounts allegedly held in Riggs under false names, contrary to Chilean law. Riggs itself subsequently merged with PNC Bank.
   [21] Shell companies are companies that have little or no underlying genuine substantive business but are mainly fronts for hiding or laundering funds.
   [22] FATF's Forty Recommendations (2003) for combating money laundering and terrorist financing finesse this problem by defining a financial institution as any person or entity that conducts as a business activities or operations in one or more of a list of thirteen categories of activities, some with multiple subparts.

as money orders, traveler's checks, money transmission, check cashing, or currency dealing or exchange. These U.S. financial institutions are subject to CDD and reporting requirements that are essentially the same as those applied to core financial institutions, but they are not subject to systematic or comprehensive supervision. In principle, they can be sanctioned either criminally or civilly for not complying with the requirements of AML regulations, but, in practice, the sanctions element of the prevention pillar as it applies to these financial institutions is extremely limited; sanctions will be applied only if suspected offenders are already under surveillance or in the aftermath of an investigation.

3. *Nonfinancial Businesses.* The prevention pillar of the U.S. AML regime is even less rigorous for nonfinancial businesses such as casinos, dealers in precious metals and stones, and real estate agents than it is for noncore financial institutions. With respect to CDD, they are subject to reasonable procedures such as identity checks, record keeping, and determining whether customers are on lists of known or suspected terrorists; but supervision of their compliance and any practical use of sanctions for enforcement are limited because businesses are licensed in state or local jurisdictions. Aside from withdrawing licenses as the result of criminal or civil proceedings against the business, the authorities have little leverage to supervise the CDD or reporting requirements or to punish noncompliance.

Table 1 singles out three categories of nonfinancial businesses (casinos, dealers in precious metals, and real estate brokers) because they are specifically identified in the FATF's 2003 revision of its Forty Recommendations (FATF 2003). Recommendation 20 also states that "countries should consider applying the FATF Recommendations to businesses and professions, other than designated non-financial businesses and professions, that pose a money laundering or terrorist financing risk." Note that it is difficult to find many business and financial activities that pose no risk at all, raising (in our minds) the issue of what might be meant by a risk-based approach to money laundering: there is a danger of confusing the risk of being sanctioned by regulators or prosecutors with the risk of actual laundering.

Other nonfinancial businesses covered to some degree by the U.S. AML regime include travel agents as well as pawnbrokers, telegraph operators, and businesses involved in vehicle, boat, auto, and airplane sales. The regime does not currently cover other businesses sometimes involved in high-value transactions, such as stamp dealers. The line has to be drawn at some point, even if it is moved later.

4. *Professions.* FATF's 2003 revision of its Forty Recommendations called for extending the prevention pillar of the global AML regime to lawyers, notaries, other independent legal professionals, accountants, and trust and company service providers, insofar as they are engaged in specified activities.[23] However, the United States has no preventative CDD or AML reporting requirements that apply to them at present beyond criminal enforcement risks arising from violation of CTR requirements and assisting money laundering. Nor does it have any self-regulatory bodies to which it could delegate preventative responsibilities as per recommendation 24b of the FATF (2003).[24] In their critique of the equality of the international playing field on AML, Pieth and Aiolfi (2003, p. 27) comment that "it would rather stretch the general meaning of the words self-regulation or 'risk-based approach'" to subject attorneys, notaries, and unregulated fiduciaries to this type of regulation.

B. The Global Anti–Money Laundering Regime

The global AML regime has evolved rapidly over the past fifteen years. Despite the push for a "level playing field," there are big differences on a lengthy continuum between, at one extreme, regimes that try to capture vast amounts of financial activity data (most notably Australia, Canada, and the United States) and use them to sift suspicious behavior and at the other extreme, regimes such as Austria, Germany, Liechtenstein, and Switzerland, that see reporting of suspicions as focused on immediate criminal investigation, where the making of a report automatically freezes the account for several days while the prosecutor takes time to decide whether to open a formal money-laundering investigation. Regimes are more similar at the front end (CDD) than at the back end (such as reporting requirements and how reports are handled).

While the current global regime has been shaped and prodded to a considerable extent by U.S. developments and initiatives, national regimes reflect other local influences as well. For example, the principal

---

[23] The recommendations were an outgrowth of the so-called Gatekeepers Initiative agreed to at the Group of Eight Moscow Ministerial Conference in October 1999.

[24] For some European comparisons of lawyer regulation, see the special issue of *Crime, Law and Social Change* (Levi, Nelen, and Lankhorst 2005).

concern that prompted establishment of the Australian AML regime in 1990 was tax evasion rather than drugs. In the United Kingdom, concerns about drugs and Irish terrorism dominated in the 1980s. Influenced by the U.S. focus on coopting the financial services sector, drug trafficking suspicions were required to be reported from 1987, even though comprehensive all-crimes money-laundering regulations did not go into effect until 1994.[25]

Switzerland is an example of a national AML regime that evolved quite differently from the U.S. regime. The Swiss trace their concern with money laundering to adoption of a code of conduct by the Swiss Bankers Association in 1977 in the wake of the Chiasso banking scandals, which began as simple fraud in the early 1960s and ended up a major financial and embarrassment problem for Credit Suisse and much of the rest of the Swiss banking system.[26] The Swiss approach emphasizes deep knowledge of customers, well justified in a banking system heavily oriented toward private banking for high–net worth individuals and toward investment management rather than mass retail banking.

The Swiss system also relies heavily on the integrity and responsibility of financial institutions to ensure compliance with national AML laws and regulations. In contrast, although British and American banks also have significant "wealth management" private banking operations, the U.S. and U.K. AML regimes operate in financial systems in which retail transactions are at least as important as wholesale transactions and asset management relationships.[27] Pieth and Aiolfi (2003) have characterized the U.S. and U.K. AML regimes as emphasizing the collection and submission of data to national authorities as part of an "early warning system" that may produce little more than information

[25] However, it was not until the end of the twentieth century that the U.K. Inland Revenue got access to SARs.

[26] In the early 1960s, the Credit Suisse Chiasso branch manager set up an offshore trustee company, officially managed and controlled by an outside third-party legal office. This provided the Chiasso branch manager with a medium to externalize branch losses and a vehicle to circumvent headquarters controls on loans and investments, reporting continuously high profits while concealing significant losses. It was also acting as a conduit for Italian tax evaders.

[27] So important are retail transactions to the U.K. financial system that the AML regime is sensitive to the charge that the regime itself may impede access to retail financial services by making it too difficult for people without many genuine items (such as utility bills and passports) that might evidence identity to satisfy customer identification requirements. For example, the U.K. CDD regulations contain a subsection providing guidance about application of the regulations to limit financial exclusion.

overload. Though true, this may not reflect sufficiently the origin of the Anglo-American systems in aiming at street- and wholesale-level drug dealing in national markets, rather than the grander corruption and frauds whose primary offenses were usually committed abroad that gave rise to the Swiss reputational risks and control system.

1. *Financial Action Task Force.* Prior to 1989, few countries had explicit AML controls. At the Paris Economic Summit of the Group of Seven (G-7) in 1989, France and the United States proposed an initiative that led to establishment of the FATF, agreeing at this time that it would not address tax issues, thereby enabling the Swiss to join in. For the United States this was an important front in the war on drugs, then at or near its height. Through successive revisions in 1990, 1996, and 2003, the FATF recommendations have been accepted as key global standards for AML.

The FATF has a small secretariat (a budget of only about $3 million in 2005) and limited membership[28] and operates by consensus. It has addressed these latter constraints by ensuring that its standard setting for its members remains dynamic and by directly or indirectly sponsoring a number of semi-autonomous FATF-style regional bodies. Both the FATF and the regional bodies sponsor "mutual evaluations" of national AML regimes. The aim was to get collective bodies to put pressure on member countries to drive standards up. Though there were many successes in generating change, the leading nations in the FATF became impatient with consensus and in 2000 launched a "name and shame" initiative with the publication of twenty-five criteria, based on the Forty Recommendations, for identifying countries falling short in their AML regimes (FATF 2000). While most jurisdictions on the list were small, it included some major nations such as Egypt, Indonesia, Nigeria, the Philippines, and Russia. Most of the twenty-three named countries moved quickly to come into compliance, and as of November 2005, only two countries—Myanmar and Nigeria—remained on the list. The changes almost exclusively addressed prevention, for example, imposing CDD requirements and creating an FIU for receiving reports rather than enforcement.

Dissatisfaction with giving supervisory powers to a self-selected in-

[28] As of November 2005, the FATF comprised thirty-one member jurisdictions (from six continents) and two regional organizations (the European Commission and the Gulf Co-operation Council). The People's Republic of China was granted observer status, but neither it nor India is currently a member; of current FATF members, only one (South Africa) is from Africa.

ternational body led to a change in 2002. The IMF and World Bank agreed to conduct assessments of national AML systems as part of broader financial system reviews that they routinely conduct.

The attempt to institutionalize AML into the routine activities of international bodies came at a price, however. Participation in an IMF/World Bank review is entirely voluntary, and the country being reviewed itself decides whether the resulting report is published, a procedure that has the potential to negate the "name and shame" mechanism used to press countries with shortfalls.[29] The IMF and World Bank have no powers to sanction and limited scope to promote compliance through their lending and technical assistance programs.

2. *The European Union.*   Pressures for AML consistency are particularly strong in the European Union. In 1991, the European Community adopted its first directive on money laundering that sought to establish minimum standards throughout what is now known as the European Union. Stessens (2000) maintains that the action was motivated in part by other global attempts to address money laundering and also by concerns that money launderers or criminals would take advantage of the increasingly free flow of capital and financial services throughout the European Union. The need to establish a level playing field in Europe also was a concern. Nations with tougher AML regimes might lose financial business to those with lax rules. Gilmore (2004) stresses the particular challenge that human rights concerns have posed to establishing an AML regime in Europe, given that both fascism and communism generated concerns about over-mighty central powers and the abuse of intelligence. The Third Money Laundering Directive—which came into force December 2005—builds on and replaces existing E.U. legislation and incorporates into E.U. law the June 2003 revision of the Forty Recommendations of the FATF (including the terrorist finance provisions). Member states have until December 2007 to incorporate this into their national legislation, which will then be evaluated for compliance.

The directive is applicable to the financial sector and to lawyers,

[29] On the other hand, the full reports are normally published, rather than the summaries previously made available. Moreover, nonpublication or even noticeable delay of a report might be taken by the international community that there was something seriously wrong with the jurisdiction's AML system, and this might produce collateral financial and reputational damage. For further details on these reports and other issues, see the FATF Web site (http://www.fatf-gafi.org/pages/0,2987,en_32250379_32235720_1_1_1_1_1,00 .html).

notaries, accountants, real estate agents, casinos, and trust and company service providers. Its scope also encompasses all providers of goods, when payments are made in cash in excess of €15,000. The directive introduces additional requirements and safeguards for situations of higher risk (e.g., trading with correspondent banks[30] situated outside the European Union). From 2005, E.U. member states will also be required to set up controls of cash over €10,000 entering and leaving the European Union and to share financial intelligence about this, implementing FATF recommendations.

C. Geopolitical Context of Money-Laundering Regulation

The international "community" now takes it for granted that the objective of preventing drug trafficking, fraud, and terrorism entitles it to intervene in the laws and practices and criminal justice activities of other states, particularly the less powerful ones. That was not the case when the movement began twenty years ago. A good reason for focusing on the early development of these issues is to tease out how and why all of this international regulatory apparatus of late modernity[31] came to be regarded as self-evident. As an illustration, the annual U.S. State Department International Narcotics Control Strategy Report on Money Laundering and Financial Crimes (State Department 2005, p. 4) reports on the perceived strengths and weaknesses of AML efforts in all countries. It notes a rather lengthy list of fifty-five problematic jurisdictions, including some with small and weak financial systems (where predicate crimes might occur) and others that serve as financial centers, including the United Kingdom and the United States.

AML policy was developed by governments strongly committed to freeing commerce—not just in the United Kingdom and United States, but around the globe—from what they regarded as the oppressive hand

---

[30] Correspondent banks are banks that do not have a local branch or even may not be authorized to operate in the jurisdiction, but that (for a fee) are able to get local banks to clear their transactions for them. Stimulated by the Bank of New York revelations, this is now identified as a high-risk area since those who take on correspondent banking must satisfy themselves that the other bank is itself conducting satisfactory CDD. Following that case and the provisions of the USA PATRIOT Act, most Western banks rigorously reviewed the banks they took on as correspondents, since they thereby took on liability for their counterpart's due diligence standards.

[31] Late modernity is a term used to describe a globalized economic and cultural system in which change is routinized and cultural identity is no longer fixed. Whereas the nation-state was the primary unit of control in classical law, activities that transcend nation-states may call forth different modes of regulation. For an attempt to apply this construct to money laundering, see Sheptycki (2000).

of the state. Compelling the banks to act as the unpaid vanguard of crime prevention represented a challenge to that deregulatory culture, and compelling banks outside direct governmental control to do so *other than for prudential reasons* required a major ideological shift. Such regulation was not in the first instance an attempt to create an international level playing field. Initially, in the United Kingdom and the United States, though foreign banks operating in their jurisdictions were included, AML and allied legislation related to proceeds of crime confiscation were aimed at the domestic market and at domestic crime problems. The notion of international governance over organized crime facilitation developed in the lead up to the 1988 U.N. Vienna Convention and the creation of FATF in 1989; the notion that there was a right—and a mechanism—to impose a global level playing field of minimum standards did not emerge fully formed until the end of the 1990s.

Prior to the creation of the FATF, there was a chasm in the global governance of crime. Despite the growing role of U.S. law enforcement extraterritorially (Nadelmann 1993; Andreas and Nadelmann 2006), there were no international institutions that played or had any mandate to play a strong role in that regard.[32] As the role of the FATF became stronger and the social pressure to become good global citizens through active AML efforts became greater, British officials pushed for greater regulatory efforts by those offshore centers that fell within Britain's sphere of influence, preferably without destroying their economic base entirely. British politicians and officials became increasingly embarrassed at allegations in international fora such as FATF, the United Nations, and the European Union that Britain was allowing its offshore territories to behave like pirates. These allegations were undermining what otherwise was an active leadership of global antilaundering regulation. Thus it was not surprising that the incoming Labour Government was inclined to act. Home Secretary Jack Straw in late 1997 asked a former Treasury civil servant to "review with the Island authorities in Jersey, Guernsey and the Isle of Man their laws, systems and practices for regulation of their international finance centres, the combating of financial crime and co-operation with other Jurisdictions"

---

[32] The key international bodies such as the IMF and World Bank had (and generally still have) no particular interest in crime or even, until the latter part of the 1990s, in governance and anticorruption activities. Crime was not considered to be "macroeconomically relevant" (officials' interviews with ML, August 2001).

(http: // www.archive.official-documents.co.uk/ document/cm41/4109; foreword.htm). Although tax policy was explicitly excluded from the terms of reference (Edwards Report 1998, annex A), far from being a conspiracy to whitewash the islands, the report represented a robust attempt to get the "near islands" in line on those issues that did not bear on differential tax rates.

The inquiry took fifteen months and was politically contentious. Nonetheless, the reforms ended up as something of a political success for the islands, which were pressured not just to change legislation but also to put in place institutional structures and (some increased) re-sources to give effect to those laws and regulations. They gained a reputational advantage at a time when action was being threatened against the "noncooperative."

Consequently, consultants KPMG were appointed to conduct a re-view of the overseas territories (the British Caribbean) plus Bermuda. This review produced a somewhat blander set of recommendations in its published form (KPMG 2000) that brought the islands closer to international legal and institutional standards, reflecting the changed nature of expectations within a changed climate of norm enforcement. However, it has been very difficult not just to reduce the opacity of financial services regimes but also to define and apply sanctions to ensure functional equivalence[33] in how those regimes operate.

It may be surprising to some that economically and politically pow-erful groups such as bankers and accountants have been compelled to act as unpaid deputy sheriffs around the world. That this has happened owes much to the primacy of law and order politics, especially in the aftermath of prominent events related to organized crime, grand cor-ruption, and terrorism. Although there was substantial pressure prior to 9/11, for example, it is less likely that without the attacks, CDD or measures against the financing of terror would have commanded such widespread acceptance, even in the United States, or that the IMF would have taken on responsibility for AML monitoring. These changes (and fears about nontransparent offshore liabilities of large investment funds) have involved international institutions and jurisdic-tions in some very difficult and expensive transformations to enhance

[33] Functional equivalence is an OECD concept applied to compliance, in which different methods of reaching the same objective are permitted. Avoiding the language of impe-rialism is very important in international meetings: hence the use of terms such as this and "approximation" rather than "harmonization" of criminal law within the European Union.

the surveillability of financial movements. However, it is easier to track their impact on the formal financial system than on crimes and their organization. It is to this underlying behavior that the regimes are intended to control that we now turn.

II. Laundering Methods and Volume

We turn now to the targeted activities. We illustrate the diversity of methods used and of the participants involved, which presumably have some interactive relationship with the controls just discussed. We then offer a classification of the offenses that generate laundering and why it is useful to distinguish among them, and conclude by showing that the existing estimates of the volume of money laundered have little credibility.

Money laundering begins with the fruits of a crime—the underlying or "predicate" offense—and ends with funds that can be used safely or at least with minimal risk, for any purpose. Money laundering is usually described as having three sequential elements—placement, layering, and integration. Placement is the introduction of the funds into the financial system, whether through cash deposits or more complex methods. Layering is a set of activities intended to distance the funds from their point of criminal origin. Integration involves converting "illegal proceeds into apparently legitimate business earnings through normal financial or commercial operations" (Board of Governors of the Federal Reserve System 2002, p. 7). In a sense, launderers need to be only as devious as the system of controls requires them to be. Financial secrecy havens as they existed before the 1990s (Blum et al. 1998) required far less skill of large-scale launderers than is the case today, at least for those offenses that are exposed and investigated financially. It would be quite difficult today to find a Caribbean banker willing to accept a known or unknown client flying in by private plane carrying suitcases containing millions of dollars in cash for deposit.

Not all money-laundering transactions involve all three distinct phases, and some may indeed involve more (van Duyne 2003; van Duyne and Levi 2005). Nonetheless, the three-stage classification is a useful decomposition of what can sometimes be a complex process. Investigative attention goes mostly to the placement stage, the point of highest vulnerability.

The paradigm applies awkwardly to terrorist finance. Stage 1 (placement) may not involve any crime at all; it is the ultimate use that is the crime to be prevented. Moreover, integration is turned on its head. The final stage is the financing of the terrorist act rather than the return of the proceeds to the original owner. Whether the same system is proper for both purposes, control of crime and reduction in terrorism, is a fair question. Figure 2 illustrates the flows in the two kinds of cases.

A. Methods

In contrast to most other types of crime, money laundering is notable for the diversity of its forms, participants, and settings. It can involve the most respectable of banks unwittingly providing services to customers with apparently impeccable credentials. The banks through which Andrew Fastow (the chief financial officer of Enron) passed his embezzled moneys from Enron or Robert Maxwell (the U.K. press baron of the 1980s) passed his embezzled funds from the pension funds of British newspaper employees had no basis for suspecting that these were the fruits of crime. No charges have been filed against the banks,[34] though many have settled civil suits, and Fastow was charged with laundering. But money laundering can also involve small nonfinancial businesses knowingly providing similar services to violent criminals, as in the case of truckers smuggling out large bundles of currency for drug traffickers.

Money laundering does not require international transactions; there are many instances of purely domestic laundering.[35] Nonetheless, a large number of cases do involve the movement of funds across national borders. Though governments have unique police powers at the border, those same borders—once crossed—can impede the flow of information.

Money can be laundered in many ways. There is a large and ever-

---

[34] Under controversial post-9/11 fast-track extradition procedures with the United States, which have been applied mainly to white-collar defendants, three U.K. NatWest bankers were ordered (in May 2005, subject to appeal as we write) to be extradited to the United States to face trial. The bank itself has not been charged and is portrayed as the victim of fraud in the Enron case, though it did not press charges against its former employees for their alleged conspiracy with Enron.

[35] For example, in the United States v. Clyde Hood et al., Central District of Illinois, an indictment returned on August 18, 2000, charged the defendant with fraud for collecting checks totaling at least $12,500,000 from investors who were promised a 5,000 percent return. Funds were deposited in checking accounts and used to incorporate and support participants' businesses, as well as to purchase real estate, all within the Mattoon, IL, area.

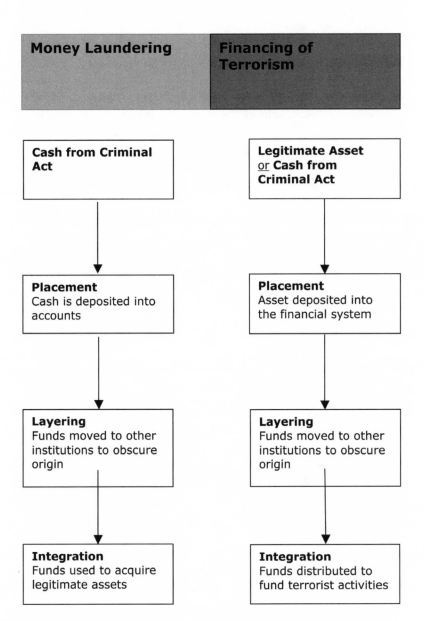

Fig. 2.—The process of money laundering and financing of terrorism (adapted from World Bank [2003a]).

growing literature of a "how to" and "look how awesome and out of control this problem is" nature (e.g., Robinson 1996, 2004; Woods 1998; Blunden 2001; Lilley 2002; Southwell 2002; Mathers 2004; Kochan 2005). The Internet has added to the available set of methods, though most of the e-schemes are arguably more theoretical than real or are very difficult mechanisms through which to launder large sums over a long period. Some of the major mechanisms described below are associated with only one of the three phases of money laundering, whereas others are usable in any phase.

The methods for laundering can be as simple as carrying money in suitcases across borders to jurisdictions that are less diligent in enforcement of global AML rules. The purchase of easily transportable high-value goods, such as rare stamps or diamonds, facilitates this. Insurance and real estate transactions can be used to conceal the origins of funds. More sophisticated schemes involve complex bank transfers and the purchase of businesses that can overstate their takings. Reuter and Truman (2004, pp. 27–32) provide a compact listing and description; further details may be found in the U.S. Money Laundering Threat Assessment (U.S. Department of Justice 2006).

B. The Distribution of Methods across Countries and Crimes

A reasonable conjecture is that different methods are used for laundering the proceeds from different predicate crimes. Using a database of cases summarized in the annual *Typologies* reports from the FATF and Egmont Group (annual, to 2003), Reuter and Truman (2004, chap. 3) found that three offense categories accounted for over 70 percent of entries: drugs (185), fraud (125), and other kinds of smuggling (92). The types of laundering methods were more evenly distributed: wire transfers were involved in 131 cases (22 percent), but no other single method was involved in more than seventy-five cases. For the three major offense categories, the numbers were broadly distributed across methods.

While these findings offer some insights into the laundering methods used for different offenses, the results should not be overgeneralized. Neither the FATF nor the Egmont Group makes any claim to be offering a representative sample of cases in their "money-laundering typology" exercises (which have improved since 2003). However, the information does have some value. For example, the data show that drug traffickers and other smugglers use a wide variety of methods for

TABLE 2

Ways of Disguising and Laundering
Crime Proceeds

Forms of Concealment/ Disguise	Frequency
Export of currency	31
Disguise of ownership	10
False justification:	
Loan back	3
Payroll	2
Speculation	1
Bookkeeping	7
Untraceable	4

SOURCE.—Van Duyne and Levi (2005).

laundering the proceeds of their crimes. More weakly (and perhaps reflecting investigative and forensic difficulties in those areas), the typologies prior to 2003 suggest by omission that some methods are not much used, such as alternative remittance systems and trusts and securities. This seems implausible. Rather than indicating underlying trends in techniques, typologies reflect the shifting focus of financial intelligence within private and public sectors, generating a search for examples of those behaviors on which they have decided to focus.

Van Duyne and Levi (2005) studied the methods used in cases that survived the final appeal stage in the Netherlands over the period 1990–2000. Their findings are summarized in table 2.

Many of these cases brought to justice in Europe and elsewhere pose problems for the AML system. There may be difficulty in finding any substantial assets. This does not necessarily imply a failing in legal powers or forensic skills; the target may simply not own (or may not directly or indirectly control) many assets. The difficulty is remediable only by proactive surveillance before arrest, something that could in principle be dealt with under the current legal regime. There are also policy difficulties over how competent counsel in large complex cases are to be paid for, since for lawyers to accept tainted funds would expose them to money-laundering charges.

Suendorf's (2001) German language study of laundering in Germany (discussed in van Duyne and Levi [2005]) contains forty examples of money laundering in the broad juridical meaning of the word, that is, every subsequent handling of illegal profits aimed at disguising their origins. Two cases can be considered to fall into the category of thoroughly organized money management: the *Bosporus* case and the *Mozart* case. Both cases concerned organizations established to move the crime moneys of heroin wholesalers to their respective home countries.

The *Bosporus* case identified an extensive and complex network of money exchange bureaus directed by an Iranian entrepreneur who served a Kurdish heroin wholesaler. The funds were collected in various cities in Germany and carried to branches of the Iranian or associated independent bureaus. Subsequently the cash was placed in German banks and transferred to bank accounts of allied money change offices in New York. From these accounts the moneys were diverted to Dubai and—if required—back to Germany or Turkey. To allay the potential suspicions of the German police, the *bureau de change* submitted occasional suspicious transaction reports.

The *Mozart* case (which involved $35 million in criminal funds) represents a similar network of money change offices working on behalf of Turkish heroin wholesalers, which were fed with crime money from Italy and Spain. The handling of the crime money appeared to be even better integrated into the legitimate cross-border trade system of Turkey with Europe. Turkish traders, who were in need of E.U. currency, could circumvent the exchange control restrictions by balancing their payments in Germany (made through the exchange office in Germany) by the placement of Turkish money in Istanbul. These legitimate moneys (disregarding the violation of exchange control) could be intertwined with the crime moneys.

In eleven of the forty cases, there was an attempt to make an investment in the upper world, though with variable success and degrees of professionalism. Three examples illustrate this:

- Real estate: three instances of insolvent enterprises; one was a construction firm, which obtained a suspicious Italian infusion of money but nevertheless went bankrupt (208/210). No relationship with drugs is mentioned.
- A greengrocer, whose son was involved in heroin traffic and invested part of the proceeds in his father's firm, which expanded quickly (207).
- A designer bathroom store, whose licit Russian owner was pressured to accept a compatriot as a manager. Money laundering is suspected (208/9). Likewise, no drug relationship is mentioned.

In many cases, it remained unclear whether the moneys had been really "cleansed" sufficiently to defeat courts. Most of the other examples concerned only the placement of suspected moneys rather than its full integration. Overall, the sophistication and professionalism displayed were modest. The same was true in the extensive set of cases discussed by van Duyne and Levi (2005), based on finalized cases.[36]

The Dutch wholesalers discussed in van Duyne and Levi (2005) did not appear to use "financial secrecy havens" for depositing drug money to the extent expected. Most involved neighboring countries: Belgium, Luxembourg, Germany, or countries of the offenders' origins (Morocco and Turkey). Other jurisdictions were very thinly represented. Bank accounts were found in Panama, Gibraltar, Liechtenstein, Jersey, the British Virgin Islands, and Dubai, but in only six out of seventeen cases.

This European finding does not appear to fit the image, conveyed in both the popular money-laundering literature and the laundering nonfiction texts, of transnational criminals spreading their ill-gotten profits worldwide over financial secrecy havens. Instead, it rather seems that the choice of banking jurisdiction is strongly influenced by proximity to the drug entrepreneur's economic home.[37] Even in the global village, most offenders do not venture far from familiar territory.

Terrorist attacks in the twenty-first century have renewed focus on remittances, charities, and other means of both tactical and strategic financing of terror (Passas 2005). The FATF typologies reflect this,[38] even though this may indicate not so much that they are "new trends" as that improvements or shifts in the intelligence collections process have uncovered more about those methods than was previously known.

---

[36] This sample may exclude the most complex cases that were not sufficiently clear-cut to satisfy the courts on a criminal burden of proof and either were not prosecuted or, if prosecuted, did not result in a conviction. These cases might have disproportionately involved financial secrecy havens that frustrated customs and police investigations, but the absence of evidence does not prove that criminals *did* use these havens!

[37] Another factor may be the obstacles that police expected to encounter in trying to track accounts in financial secrecy havens themselves; as a result, they may not have attempted to locate funds there. That would turn this outcome into an artifact of the actual or perceived investigative possibilities. All we can determine is that financial secrecy havens are important, though the frequency of their use was not reflected in the routine practices of the affluent British or Dutch drug entrepreneurs.

[38] The 2002 Typologies Report was devoted entirely to terrorist finance.

C. Who Provides the Laundering Services?

Our understanding of who provides laundering services reflects the intelligence collections process; there is little systematic attention given to aggregate patterns. Much financial investigation is satisfied by "low-hanging fruit," especially outside the United States, where resources are limited. If difficult cases are not pursued, then there are no data to analyze. Thus the following observations about available cases are merely indicative.

It is easiest to launder money with the help of someone inside a financial institution. Bank employees can be coerced or bribed not to file SARs or CTRs. Alternatively, the forms may be filled out, with the government's copy conveniently filed in the trash and the other copy remaining in a drawer in case of an investigation.[39]

Although there may be members of organized crime groups who specialize in money laundering, some professional money-laundering agents are not otherwise involved in criminal activities. Some may not even be aware that they are laundering: in several cases of "negligent money laundering" that resulted in conviction and imprisonment, it was determined that the agent should have suspected that the funds were derived from criminal activities yet demonstrated "willful blindness" in failing to make that observation. This is potentially a major issue. If the business did a risk assessment but nevertheless was used for money laundering without its knowledge, to what extent *should* it be held liable?

Lawyers are thought to be among the most common laundering agents or at least facilitators, though they have been at the center of relatively few cases in the United States; Robinson (1996, chap. 8) provides some interesting descriptions. A lawyer can use his or her own name to acquire bank accounts, credit cards, loan agreements, or other money-laundering tools on behalf of the client. Lawyers can also establish shell corporations, trusts, or partnerships and receive cash deposits and run transactions through their client accounts or even (more riskily) their office accounts. In the event of an investigation, lawyer-client confidentiality privileges can be invoked or attempted, depending on the rules of the jurisdiction. In one case cited by the FATF in its 1997–98 typology report, a lawyer charged a flat fee to

---

[39] Electronic filing, which would eliminate this option, is not currently required in the United States, though it has been standard for years in Australia and is the norm in the United Kingdom, at least for repeat players.

launder money by setting up annuity packages for his clients to hide the laundering. He also arranged for credit cards in false names to be issued to his clients, who could use the cards to make ATM cash withdrawals. The card issuer knew only the identity of the lawyer and had no knowledge of the clients' identities.[40]

Other professionals involved in money laundering include accountants, notaries, financial advisers, stockbrokers, insurance agents, and real estate agents. A British report noted that in 2002, "purchasing property in the UK was the most popular method identified, involving roughly one in three serious and organized crime groups where the method was known" (National Criminal Intelligence Service 2003, chap. 6; however, it is not stated in what proportion of cases it is known). However, as partner, bank, and regulator vigilance over lawyers' client accounts has increased in the United Kingdom—each law firm is required to appoint a money laundering reporting officer who is professionally and criminally responsible for the firm's compliance—it has become harder to wash large amounts of cash in this way. Furthermore, in theory, the purchase of a property does not eliminate the need for explanation of the origins of wealth should such an accounting be required. Hence the importance of the burden of proof, since it is not an offense to have unaccounted wealth.[41] The dependence on conviction at a criminal standard of proof has in turn precipitated the development of civil forfeiture or recovery proceedings in Australia, the Irish Republic, the United Kingdom, and the United States, for example; civil or criminal charges of tax fraud can also be laid.

The most general point is the variety of professions involved. In Europe, among those regulated by money-laundering directives, auto dealers may be used to purchase expensive automobiles for cash, which can then be resold (at significant depreciation); real estate agents may be involved in sale of commercial or private residences, sometimes facilitating under-the-counter cash payments to supplement the recorded price, perhaps "only" to evade property taxes; criminals may purchase holdings in companies or businesses through accountant or

---

[40] It is doubtful that this would occur today.

[41] There is an exception in those (ex–British colony) jurisdictions in which public servants can be prosecuted for living in a manner inconsistent with their known income or wealth. This legislation originated in places such as Hong Kong and Singapore, where the British colonial administration wanted to find easy ways of firing and prosecuting police and civil servants for corruption without having to provide direct evidence of corrupt exchange.

lawyer nominees, or directly; accountants may overstate business takings, understate costs, or otherwise assist the transfer of value by false pricing (or be complicit in such falsifications by criminal businesspeople); art, antiques, and jewelry may be purchased for cash or for other financial instruments.

D. Markets for Laundering Services

Since money laundering is a criminal service offered in return for payment, it is worth considering the "market" for such services. For example, making laundering services more expensive should reduce their volume. It should also lower the volume of predicate crime since the return from crime is reduced. Price might also serve as a performance indicator as to how well the control system works. Unfortunately, law enforcement agencies do not systematically record price information acquired in the process of developing money-laundering cases, since that information is not necessary to obtain a conviction.[42]

Moreover, price is an ambiguous concept in this context. Apart from the fact that some laundering agents provide only partial services (e.g., just placement or layering), there are at least two possible interpretations of price: the fraction of the funds received by the launderer, including what he or she paid to other service providers, and the share of the original total amount that does not return to the owner's control. The latter share could include tax payments, as in the case of a retail proprietor who might charge only 5 percent for allowing the commingling of illegal funds with his or her store's receipts, but then might have to add another 5 percent for the sales tax that would be generated by these fraudulent receipts.

The policy-relevant price is the second of these, the difference between the amount laundered and the amount eventually received by the offender. Pushing offenders to use laundering methods that involve smaller payments to launderers but higher total costs (because of taxes) to the predicate offender is indeed preferable to raising the revenues received by launderers as a group; after all, the difference includes payments to the public sector. Such substitution might occur if the government mounted more sting operations aimed at customers.

The difference is by no means only of theoretical interest. Take, for example, one case cited by the Egmont Group (2000) of high-priced

---

[42] The 2002 U.S. National Money Laundering Strategy noted the importance of collecting such data.

laundering in which most of the price did not accrue to the launderer. A credit manager at a car loan company was suspicious about one of his customers. "Ray" had just bought a luxury sports car worth about $55,000, financing the car through the credit company for $40,000 and paying the balance in cash. Records showed that Ray had taken out several loans over the past few years, all for the same amount of money and with a large portion as a cash deposit. In many cases the loans had been repaid early with cash. The national FIU realized that Ray was laundering for a long-established criminal organization, putting cash from the sale of drugs into the banking system. He would resell the newly bought cars, obtaining checks to deposit into a single bank account, in all totaling over $300,000. The losses made on the loan and the drop in the automobiles' resale values were the cost of obtaining "clean" money.

Information about the price of money-laundering services is scattered and anecdotal. In the money-laundering activity targeted by Operation Polar Cap, a coordinated law enforcement operation (or "sting") during the late 1980s, the drug trafficker would pay only 4.5 percent to the government sting launderer initially, but was willing to go to 5 percent if the laundering were done rapidly (Woolner 1994, p. 43). Later in the operation there were reports of much higher margins. Experienced investigators refer to a general price range of 7–15 percent for laundering for drug dealers, but some reports are inconsistent with such estimates. One National Money Laundering Strategy (U.S. Treasury 2002, p. 12) reported a study that found commission rates varying between 4 and 8 percent but rising as high as 12 percent.

Other criminals pay much less for money-laundering services. For example, John Mathewson, who operated a Cayman Islands bank that laundered money for a number of white-collar offenders (e.g., Medicare fraudsters, recording pirates) and U.S. tax evaders, charged a flat fee of $5,000 for an account, plus a $3,000 per year management fee (Fields and Whitfield 2001). Mathewson, who provided a complete set of services, also kept 1 percent of the float that the clients' money earned when held overnight by other banks (U.S. Senate 2001). Whether Mathewson charged more for drug dealers or refused their business cannot be established from the published materials.

The price paid for a particular money-laundering service apparently is partly a function of the predicate crime and the volume of funds that needs to be laundered. Whereas legitimate, larger financial transactions

generate lower per unit costs, the opposite is true for money laundering: the risk of detection is a major cost (perhaps the principal cost),
and that risk will rise with the quantity being laundered. By contrast,
however, a broker involved in Colombian black-market peso operations
claimed that he charged less for larger volumes of money. Prices may
be affected not just by enforcement risks attached to different predicate
crimes—just as someone on the run for a particular crime involving
heat may have to pay more for counterfeit documents and to be hidden—but even perhaps by moral qualms on the part of potential launderers. One might expect terrorist finance to be expensive by this criterion, though some ideologically sympathetic bankers and business
people might assist freedom fighters from their community for free,
whereas they would not assist drug traffickers at all or would charge
them more. They might also be pressured to assist, as in Colombia
and Ireland as well as in some ethnic diasporas. Despite use of illegal
drugs by financial services personnel, there are very few cases in which
dealers are known to have blackmailed staff, whether prosecuted or
mentioned informally in research: if there is not a "dark figure" of
undetected blackmail, the reason may be that dealers do not wish to
frighten off good clients or that the information does not percolate far
enough upward to those who require laundering services. American
and European banking compliance personnel regularly express concern
about infiltration by organized criminals and—since 9/11—terrorist
sympathizers, and seek to monitor staff for signs of such facilitation as
well as for fraud against banks and customers.[43]

A large number of money-laundering cases appear to involve opportunistic laundering rather than professional services. Where someone apart from the offender provides the service, he may provide it
only to that offender, perhaps because they are related or connected
through some other activity. Drug dealers appear to be more likely to
purchase formal money-laundering services, perhaps because the regular flow of currency makes their needs more acute and less easily met.

E. Classification of Predicate Offenses

For both research and policy it is important to recognize the heterogeneity of money laundering from different criminal activities. Reu-

---

[43] Interviews with Michael Levi, 1990–2005. Periodic background checks (subject to
data protection restrictions) and checks on computer accessing of customer information
are methods used.

TABLE 3

Characteristics of Taxonomy of Money-Laundering Predicate Crimes

	Cash	Scale of Operations	Severity of Harms	Most Affected Populations
Drug dealing	Exclusively	Very large	High	Minority urban groups
Other illegal market	Mostly	Small to medium	Low to modest	?
White-collar	Mix	Mix	Low to modest	Broad
Bribery and corruption	No	Large	Severe	Developing countries
Terrorism	Mix	Small	Very severe	Broad

SOURCE.—Reuter and Truman (2004).

ter and Truman (2004) suggest a preliminary five-part classification of offenses to help understand the effects of specific money-laundering controls: drug distribution, other blue-collar crime, white-collar crime, bribery and corruption, and terrorism. These categories create more homogeneity with respect to the effects of interventions and the seriousness and distribution of the harm caused by particular offenses to society. The categories also differ from each other in these same dimensions. It can be conjectured, for example, that the response to increased scrutiny of, say, casinos on the part of white-collar offenders, whose crimes often generate electronic fund transfers or checks rather than cash, will differ from those who launder money on behalf of drug dealers. Similarly, the benefits from reducing at least some white-collar crimes by $1 billion might be valued substantially less than those associated with a similar reduction in crack cocaine or methamphetamine trafficking. The distribution of benefits from reducing either of the two offenses may also be quite different: those who are harmed by drug trafficking are disproportionately from poor and minority urban populations, whereas the costs of white-collar crimes are borne far more broadly across society, depending on what sorts of frauds they are and in which countries (Levi and Pithouse, forthcoming).

Table 3 provides hypotheses about the differences in the relevant dimensions among the five groups. The entries concerning the "severity of harm" and the "most affected populations" are judgments offered by Reuter and Truman (2004) not as authoritative but simply to identify dimensions that deserve consideration in policy making.

1. *Drug Distribution.*   Major drug traffickers face a unique problem: how to manage large sums of cash regularly and frequently, much of it in small bills. For example, in Operation Polar Cap in the mid-1980s, U.S. agents acting as distributors associated with the Medellín cartel

handled some $1.5 million a week in currency. Few legitimate or criminal establishments operate with such large and steady cash flows.

This distinctive characteristic of drug distribution is particularly important because the current AML regime initially was constructed primarily to control drug trafficking, an aspect of the regime that continues to affect public perceptions of the nature of the money-laundering problem.

2. *Other Illegal Market Crimes.*   Other potential large-scale illegal markets that would seem at first glance as likely candidates for generating a demand for money laundering include gambling and the smuggling of people (both voluntarily as economic migration and involuntarily—by force or fraud—as "people trafficking"). However these markets generate relatively modest demand simply because they have substantially lower revenues than drug markets. That is not a historical constant but an observation about the past two decades in industrial societies, and is independent of the relative seriousness of the behavior, people trafficking being very harmful.

The amounts of money for any individual operation in these other areas appear to be much smaller than for drug distribution, in part because total and unit revenues are smaller and in part because what has to be laundered is net rather than gross revenues. For example, a bookmaker will receive from customers and agents only what they owe at the end of the accounting period (perhaps one or two weeks). A gambler who wagers $10,000 per week on football, where the margin for the bookmaker is less than 3 percent, might make only monthly transfers of $1,000 (see Reuter 1983, chap. 2). In the part of the sex trade that employs trafficked women (as contrasted with locals and voluntary economic migrants), margins would be expected to be much higher; some of the trade may involve credit cards and legitimate front companies, not least so that clients' expenditures can be passed off without embarrassment.

3. *White-Collar Crimes.*   The white-collar crime category covers a heterogeneous range of offenses, including embezzlement, fraud, and tax evasion, some of them confusingly committed by organized crime members involved in racketeering offenses. A distinctive feature of these crimes is that the money laundering is often an integral part of the offense itself. The Enron case demonstrates a complex scheme in which hundreds of shell corporations in the Cayman Islands served not only as questionable tax shelters but also as laundering mechanisms to

obscure a trail of fraudulent behavior. Money-laundering services in such cases often are provided by the offenders themselves, since the offense itself requires skills similar to those involved in money laundering. Indeed, where there are false invoices and other accounting frauds (such as value-added tax frauds in the European Union), such activities often constitute both the predicate and the laundering offense. However, if the underlying transactions are exposed as fraudulent (which is far from automatic), the money may not turn out to have been laundered effectively unless some further steps have taken place to break the money trail and frustrate pursuit. In this sense, as van Duyne and Levi (2005) argue, the funds might be better described as "hidden" rather than "laundered," even though laundering charges may be brought.

4. *Bribery and Corruption.* While bribery and corruption can be classified as white-collar crime, they are distinctive in terms of who benefits (public officials and those who benefit from their decisions), where they occur (primarily though far from exclusively in poor countries[44]), and the nature of their harm (reduced government credibility and public services). The laundering is almost inherently international: those corrupted prefer to keep the proceeds out of local banks unless the banks themselves were complicit or (as in the majority of corrupt acts in poor countries) the amounts were small. Money laundering also is often embedded in the offense itself when the corruption is large-scale. For example, San Diego defense contractor Titan Corporation pleaded guilty to three counts of foreign bribery involving the president of Benin. Among other payments, the company funneled nearly US$1 million to the offshore accounts of the president's reelection campaign. Procurement contracts in construction and defense are particularly prone to such transnational kickbacks.

F. Terrorism

The distinctive feature of terrorism is that it takes money both legitimately and criminally generated and converts it into criminal use. The sums of money involved are said to be modest: tens or hundreds of thousands of dollars rather than millions; see the report of the 9/11

---

[44] Indeed, France, Japan, and Korea, far from being poor nations, have experienced continuing corruption scandals involving the very highest level of government; in the case of Korea, at least one former president has been imprisoned for large-scale bribe taking. Prime Minister Berlusconi of Italy has been prosecuted for corruption and tax offenses.

Commission on the financing of the Twin Towers bombing (National Commission on Terrorist Attacks upon the United States 2004, p. 172). Yet the harm is unique and enormous.

Assessments of the relevant differences between the five types of offenses are just judgments. There will be near consensus that terrorism poses a greater threat to social welfare than any of the other offenses. Many, partly influenced by media coverage, may consider the harm associated with white-collar and blue-collar crimes other than drugs to be relatively modest, although specific offenses may be ranked high in social harm.[45] Yet another offense, major environmental crimes, could well strike some observers as just as harmful as selling cocaine.

The assessment of distributional consequences is intended as a reminder that benefits of interventions are far from uniform, since these offenses affect different parts of society. Indeed, there even are significant differences across nations; kleptocracy is surely more important than any of the other offenses for sub-Saharan Africa and for many parts of South America, but this is not the case in rich nations such as the Netherlands.

Whether this is a useful disaggregation depends in part on the hypothesis presented here that specific interventions will vary in their effects on the money laundering associated with these offenses. For example, elimination of large bills might substantially complicate money laundering for drug smugglers who make extensive use of bulk cash smuggling[46] but have minimal effect on terrorist finance, which (except when funded by drug trafficking) does not use this technique. In making policy, it may be important to identify which kinds of harm are most likely to be reduced by the chosen interventions.

G. How Much Money Is Laundered?

Given the variety of offenses and the diversity of adverse consequences per dollar, estimates of the total volume of money laundered would seem to have limited value. A reduction in the total amount of money laundering that represented a decline in gambling or corporate fraud but hid a smaller increase in terrorist finance would hardly be

---

[45] White-collar and blue-collar crimes are sufficiently heterogeneous that consensus is not likely, and crime seriousness surveys internationally indicate strong public condemnation of a variety of white-collar crimes (Levi and Jones 1985; Levi and Pithouse, forthcoming).

[46] This was a matter of some controversy when the euro was introduced, with the €500 note being the maximum size.

indicative of progress, given the much greater social harm caused by terrorism.

Nonetheless, there is a continuing demand for an estimate of how much money is laundered both in the United States and globally. Numbers are frequently cited, with minimal documentation, becoming "facts by repetition." For example, the IMF estimated a total of $590 billion to $1.5 trillion globally in 1996. In 2005 the United Nations cited the range of $500 billion to $1 trillion (http://www.unodc.org/unodc/en/money_laundering.html, accessed June 2, 2005). A sustained effort between 1996 and 2000 by the FATF to produce a fully documented estimate failed.[47]

There are, however, a few estimates of the potential demand for money laundering that are regularly treated as actual money-laundering estimates. The estimates fall into two categories: macroeconomic and microeconomic. Neither method yields estimates that can be considered as anything more than indicative. The macroeconomic estimates are methodologically flawed: they generate implausibly high figures. The microeconomic estimates lack a credible empirical base. These figures confirm that the phenomenon of money laundering is of sufficient scale to warrant public policy attention, but they are too imprecise to provide guidance for policy.

1. *Macroeconomic Estimates.* The macroeconomic approach is based on a broad definition that assumes that any revenue on which no tax is paid—be it from a legal or illegal activity—will need to be laundered in some way. In this view, the volume of the demand for money laundering is related to the monetary component of the so-called underground economy.

The study of what has been called the underground, shadow, hidden, or black economy first emerged in the late 1970s in response to the observation that, despite the growth of credit cards and other methods of purchase substituting for currency, the ratio of currency to gross domestic product (GDP) had not declined (Gutmann 1977; Feige 1979). More recently, one particular estimation method, the currency-demand approach, has been applied frequently enough to allow for comparison of many different countries over one or two decades.

Schneider and Enste (2000) summarize this research. They present a "reasonable consensus definition" of the underground economy based

---

[47] One of the authors of this study (Peter Reuter) was involved in the latter stages of this effort, which did not result in any official publication.

on an earlier schematization by Mirus and Smith (1997). They provide roughly comparable estimates for many countries based on the currency-demand approach and generate extremely high estimates. The cumulative underground economies of the twenty-one OECD countries since 1997 total over $3 trillion annually, and for single nations the underground economy represented an average of 16–17 percent of GDP. Since 1994 the figure exceeds 10 percent of global GDP for most years.[48] This is substantially above the 2–5 percent of global GDP cited in 1998 by Michel Camdessus, then managing director of the IMF, as a "consensus range" for the scale of money-laundering transactions. Even this lower guesstimate was described by Camdessus in a speech to the FATF (Paris, February 10, 1998) as "beyond imagination." Walker (1999) attempted a heroic global estimation that produced some counterintuitive, if intriguing, estimates for different jurisdictions.

The absolute and percentage estimates are shocking if taken as measures of money laundering. However, they are frail even in their own terms as measures of what evades government taxation and other restrictions, and still more frail as the basis for estimating potential laundering volume. Blades and Roberts (2002) review various estimates. Their main critique is that nonobserved activities are highly concentrated in certain sectors of the economy, such as retail trade, taxis, trucking, and restaurants; whereas other sectors such as power generation, heavy industry, or air transport are intrinsically less vulnerable, simply because the organizations have no incentive to underreport revenues. If one were to take this into account, the high estimates would imply that much larger shares of the susceptible sectors are completely underground, which hardly seems credible. Blades and Roberts (2002) offer a variety of other technical critiques as well.

2. *Microeconomic Estimates.* The microeconomic approach to estimating demand for money laundering is in a sense a complement to the macroeconomic approaches, which pay limited attention to estimating total earnings from criminal activities, aside from tax evasion. The microeconomic approach estimates the incomes from each type of crime. These estimates normally do not include the informal economy or activities that, though legal, are not reported in order to evade taxes. However, in principle it would be possible to graft those esti-

---

[48] On the basis of world GDP in constant 1995 dollars. See World Bank (2003b).

mates onto such measures. The problems associated with the micro-economic approach basically involve the paucity and unreliability of the data.

There have been two systematic efforts to provide estimates of incomes generated by a broad range of criminal activities in the United States. Simon and Witte (1982) cobbled together figures for the late 1970s. Indicative of the uncertainty of their results, which they acknowledge, is the basis for their estimate for income from prostitution. They started with survey-based estimates of the total number of acts of prostitution nationally and the number that a full-time prostitute would commit in the course of a year. This calculation resulted in an estimate of full-time-equivalent prostitutes of 80,000–500,000, disregarding part-time sex work aimed at supplementing low incomes. Add in considerable uncertainty about the annual earnings of a prostitute, and the result is an estimate that spans approximately an order of magnitude.

Under the auspices of the President's Commission on Organized Crime, Wharton Econometrics Forecasting Associates, a U.S. research firm, also developed estimates of incomes from many different criminal activities. In its final report in 1987, the commission stated that organized crime produced an annual net income of approximately $47 billion. Nine of the commission's eighteen members expressed reservations about this estimate.

Reuter and Truman (2004, chap. 2) used estimates of the proceeds from thirty-four crimes in the United States covering one or more years during the period 1965–2000 to estimate total criminal earnings. The thirty sources used included both public agencies and private organizations. For most crimes, estimates were available for only a few years. There were data for ten or fewer crimes for fourteen of the years, for eleven to fifteen crimes for nineteen of the years, and for up to twenty-two crimes for the remaining four years. Sixteen crimes had ten or fewer years of data, whereas only nine crimes had more than twenty-five years' worth. The results are presented in table 4. Simple linear projections were imputed for all the missing years to generate estimates for all crime for all years; some of the projections cover a large number of years.

A glimpse at one of the more complete years in table 5 reveals the general composition of the U.S. criminal economy according to these estimates. In 1990, the most lucrative crime (in aggregate) was fraud

TABLE 4

Estimated Earnings from Criminal Activity in the United States,
1965–2000, Billions of Current U.S. Dollars

Year	Tax Evasion Included		Tax Evasion Excluded	
	Estimated Criminal Income	Percent of GDP	Estimated Criminal Income	Percent of GDP
1965	49	6.8	18	2.5
1970	74	7.1	26	2.5
1975	118	7.2	45	2.7
1980	196	7.0	78	2.8
1985	342	8.1	166	4.0
1990	471	8.1	209	3.6
1995	595	8.0	206	2.8
2000 (estimate)	779	7.9	224	2.3

SOURCE.—Reuter and Truman (2004).
NOTE.—Non–tax evasion crimes included trafficking in illicit drugs, human trafficking, burglary, larceny-theft, motor vehicle theft, robbery, fraud arson, nonarson fraud, counterfeiting, illegal gambling, loan sharking, and prostitution. Tax evasion crimes included federal income, federal profits, and excise tax evasion.

(including tax fraud), producing an estimated $500 billion. Drug trafficking resulted in approximately $70 billion in revenues, and between $5 billion and $20 billion was garnered from illegal gambling. The total for all crimes with available data amounted to roughly $700 billion, approximately 8 percent of U.S. GDP in 1998.[49] A time series of these data shows that criminal income in the United States rose from just under 7 percent of GDP to around 8 percent, with the largest increase occurring in the early 1980s. However, when tax evasion estimates were removed from the totals, the criminal share of U.S. GDP ranged from 2.5 to 4 percent, peaking in the late 1980s before dropping to the levels of the late 1960s.

The fraud estimate, by far the largest single item in most years, is particularly frail. It comes from a report by the Association of Certified Fraud Examiners (2002), which sent survey forms to 10,000 of its members, fewer than 10 percent of whom responded. Respondents provided specific information about cases of which they were aware.

[49] If criminal activities accounted for the same share of GDP of other OECD countries, the global total would be $2.4 trillion. There is no way to validate this assumption, but it appears that the United States has a much larger drug market (in GDP terms) than other nations. However, drugs account for less than 10 percent of the estimated $700 billion in revenues from crime in 1998.

TABLE 5
United States, 1990

Crime	Proceeds in Billions of Current Dollars	Percent of Total
Tax evasion	262.2	55.7
Cocaine trafficking	61.3	13.0
Fraud (nonarson)	59.3	12.6
Heroin trafficking	17.6	3.7
Prostitution	14.7	3.1
Loan sharking	14.0	3.0
Marijuana trafficking	13.5	2.9
Motor vehicle theft	8.0	1.7
Illegal gambling	7.6	1.6
Other drug trafficking	4.8	1.0
Larceny/theft	3.8	.8
Burglary	3.5	.7
Robbery	.5	.2
Human trafficking	.2	.04
Counterfeiting	.1	.02
Fraud arson	.04	.008
Total	471.1	

SOURCE.—Reuter and Truman (2004); ONDCP (2000, 2001); Simon and Witte (1982); GAO (2002); Federal Bureau of Investigation's annual *Uniform Crime Reports*; Internal Revenue Service; International Organization on Migration; Abt, Smith, and Christiansen (1985); Kaplan and Matteis (1968); and Carlson, Weisberg, and Goldstein (1984).

But they also were asked to estimate the percentage of revenues that would be lost in 2002 as a result of occupational fraud and abuse. As the median figure was 6 percent, using an estimate for U.S. GDP of $10.4 trillion in 2002 leads to an estimate of $625 billion. No effort was made to adjust for nonresponse or to ask whether respondents were in fact in a position to make such estimates. Nor did the study consider whether GDP was the correct base for these calculations. If each examiner estimated the share of the flow through his or her corporation, then the right base was much larger, namely the total volume of transactions through corporations.[50]

In advanced economies in which insurance is commonplace, revenues from crimes involving stolen goods (burglary, larceny, and robbery) are probably overestimated, since they are based on the reported value of the stolen property. A victim may inflate the worth of an item

---

[50] See Levi and Pithouse (forthcoming) for a critical review of other fraud survey data.

to receive a higher insurance payment. From the point of view of earnings from crime, even if the claimed amount is accurate, a fence or pawnbroker will not pay a thief the retail value for pilfered goods; indeed, the standard figure used in research studies is that fences pay 20–30 percent of the market value of the good, depending on how easily it can be resold (Muscato 2003).

Even the estimates of revenues from drug sales, by far the most systematically developed, should be seen as having very broad confidence intervals, though the government publishes only point estimates. One can get a sense of the uncertainty of these revenue estimates by examining revisions in the related estimates of the number of drug addicts that are published along with the income estimates. When calculated in 2000, the estimated number of U.S. heroin addicts for 1992 was 630,000; in 2001 this 1992 figure was revised up to 945,000 (Office of National Drug Control Policy 2000, 2001). Estimating the prevalence of a rare behavior, particularly one that leads to erratic lifestyles, is difficult, resulting in a corresponding uncertainty. When one takes into account the range in estimates in the numbers of drug addicts, the $70 billion estimate of revenues from drug sales in 2000 is probably best thought of as somewhere between $35 billion and $105 billion, with no particular central tendency (Office of National Drug Control Policy 2000, 2001).

Outside of the United States, estimates of criminal earnings are sparser and often equally implausible. Blades and Roberts (2002) report a small number of such estimates for OECD and transition economies. Their figures, admittedly partial and essentially guesstimates, are usually in the range of 0.5–1.0 percent of GDP.

Even taken at face value, these numbers are only weakly related to money laundering. Much of this income is earned by people who use the cash to directly purchase legal goods without making use of any financial institution. Small-time thieves earning $25,000 annually are unlikely to make use of a bank or any other means of storing or transferring value.[51] It is impossible to estimate or even guess as to what share of these revenues will require laundering.

3. *Conclusions.* Neither of the two types of broad approaches to

---

[51] In most jurisdictions, the use of money acquired by illegal means to cover living expenses or operating costs is technically considered (self-) money laundering and often can be prosecuted under AML statutes. However, this is not an aspect of the general phenomenon of money laundering that by itself would rise to the level of a public policy problem. Nor do such prosecutions occur frequently.

estimate how much money is laundered—examining incomes in the broadly defined underground economy or incomes from criminal activities—provides numbers that meet minimal standards for policy guidance. The findings can support only the broadest statements about the extent of laundering activities. The underground economy, and even the criminal economy, probably amount to hundreds of billions of dollars each in the United States. However, this statement provides no possible guidance for assessing the effectiveness of money-laundering controls by comparing the volume of money laundered across time or nations. If an estimate rises by 10 percent from one year to the next, it is as likely to be the result of changes in coverage or estimating technique as to be a change in the actual size of the underground economy or of criminal earnings.

Money laundering is a diverse and substantial activity. We examine now the efforts to enforce laws against laundering as a method for reducing crime.

III. Enforcement

One of two pillars of the AML regime is enforcement, consisting of the listing of predicate offenses and the investigation, prosecution, and sanctioning of launderers and their customers. Whereas the prevention pillar can be described through document review, we are now, except for the predicate offense list, into the conventional criminal justice territory of statistics that are meager and difficult to interpret. After discussing the issue of what offenses are listed as predicate crimes, this section describes enforcement in the United States and United Kingdom, for reasons of both parochialism and data availability. We include analysis of the volume of SARS because though produced by the prevention pillar, they are principally used by enforcement agencies. Though only shards of data are available on other nations, the United States appears to be vastly more aggressive in its enforcement activities; in many countries there appears to be minimal use of criminal statutes for AML purposes.

A. Predicate Offenses

The decision about which offenses to list as predicate crimes or whether to opt for the more common approach of criminalizing the laundering of all "serious crimes" is one that has entangled the United

States and other nations in complex and sometimes acrimonious negotiations.[52]

However, consistent with the FATF's original mandate, the list of predicate money-laundering crimes in the 2003 FATF Forty Recommendations does not include tax evasion. This does more than reveal a lack of uniformity in the global AML regime; it can also undercut cooperation and mutual legal assistance under treaties.

Foreign or domestic tax evasion—other than failure to pay U.S. taxes on the proceeds of a crime—does not qualify as a predicate crime in the U.S. AML system. While U.S. prosecutors can work around this lacuna and do not regard it as an impediment to an effective U.S. AML regime, the absence of foreign tax evasion as a predicate offense under U.S. law is often cited as impeding international cooperation.[53] Latin American leaders, for example, often complain privately that while the United States insists on cooperation on issues it considers important, the country itself often fails to cooperate on issues of importance to other countries, such as evasion of taxes on assets held abroad.

B. Investigation

Before we briefly review investigation methods, it may be helpful if we summarize sources of intelligence that may drive them: first, suspicious transaction or activity reports made by bankers and other regulated persons; second, collapses of professional firms or business enterprises that generate information about culpable involvement of intermediaries; third, investigations—sometimes involving criminal and undercover police informants—into major crime networks that throw up suspicions and evidence of active assistance by laundering agents

---

[52] The FATF (2003) definition of "serious offenses" requires a maximum penalty of more than one-year imprisonment or a minimum of more than six months. In some jurisdictions, this would exclude some tax and exchange control offenses, and Switzerland criminalizes tax fraud (falsification on tax returns for those who have to complete them domestically) but not tax evasion. Some countries such as France include tax evasion as a money-laundering offense in their national legislation but undercut the inclusion because the offense is not reportable by financial institutions. The FATF also designates twenty broad categories of offense that include corruption, bribery, market manipulation, and environmental crimes.

[53] Such criticism is not directed only at the United States. Many financial centers are accused of noncooperation on tax matters (and sometimes counter that both tax and other fraud charges—e.g., those coming out of Russia—are politically motivated). For example, an IMF (2001, p. 24) review of Cyprus observed that international cooperation would be strengthened if Cyprus were to clarify that tax evasion is an offense under its money-laundering laws and regulations.

such as bankers and lawyers; and fourth, the boldness and powers of the investigative authorities and their priorities.

In the reactive model, information on suspected customers or transactions is sent by regulated entities (such as banks) to the FIU and then distributed to law enforcement authorities for follow-up. Here the universal message from the modest research that has been conducted is that the proportion of SARs in high-reporting jurisdictions that are actually seriously followed up is low, though the extent to which this is inherent or merely resource-constrained remains unclear (see Gold and Levi [1994], KPMG [2003], and Fleming [2005] for three British studies that try to analyze the financial intelligence process end-to-end).

Many reports are of matters that arouse suspicion in the minds of the bankers or professionals but are difficult to resolve without interviewing the client, which would tip the latter off. So expectations of high prosecution and/or criminal asset yield from SARs may be unrealistic, even without "defensive reporting" by regulated entities to avoid risk of prosecution.[54]

The more that financial intelligence is embedded into the routine investigations of serious crimes for gain and terrorism, the greater the likelihood that such intelligence is used. However, beyond the use of routine and suspicious transaction reports, there is considerable variation across nations in terms of what investigative techniques are allowed. Recommendation 27 of FATF (2003) endorses investigative techniques such as "controlled delivery, undercover operations and other relevant techniques," but not explicitly sting operations, which raise *agent provocateur* issues in several European jurisdictions. Jurisdictions also differ in their standards and procedures to enforce due process, human rights, and privacy. The U.S. Casablanca undercover operation in 1998[55] was regarded as a resounding success in the United States, but the operation's aftermath created tensions with Mexico, in particular. In February 2004, four bankers convicted in Mexican courts

[54] However, from the enforcement perspective, one important trend toward greater use of money-laundering reporting is data sharing both internally (linking databases so that SARs can be matched against intelligence, law enforcement, tax, and social security data) and externally (the European Commission–sponsored FIU.net project within the European Union, with wider potential at least for sharing names within the global Egmont Group of FIUs).

[55] Casablanca was the name of an extensive investigation of Mexican and other foreign banks and bankers by U.S. federal agencies. It resulted in numerous indictments of Mexican citizens for laundering of drug-dealing proceeds.

TABLE 6

Money-Laundering Defendants and Convictions, 1994–2001

Year	ML as Any Charge	ML as Primary or Secondary Charge	Percent with ML as Primary or Secondary Charge	Convictions
1994	1,907	1,341	70	933
1995	2,138	1,487	70	906
1996	1,994	1,457	73	1,080
1997	2,376	1,619	68	1,108
1998	2,719	1,831	67	1,199
1999	2,656	1,885	71	1,371
2000	2,503	1,771	71	1,329
2001	2,110	1,480	70	1,243

SOURCE.—Data from Administrative Office of the Courts, criminal master file.

in connection with the operation were released when the U.S. sting operation was declared unconstitutional under Mexican law. This supported allegations of biased targeting, since no major G-7 jurisdiction-headquartered bank has been selected for this sort of money-laundering sting exercise.

C. Prosecutions and Convictions

Available data on money-laundering charges in the United States—which come from judicial sources for the federal level and from surveys of inmates in federal and state prisons—cover the number of persons charged, convicted, and imprisoned in federal courts.[56] Charges can be brought against both the customer who seeks to have money laundered and the provider of the service; the data do not distinguish between these two types of offenders.

1. *Court Data.* The analysis presented here primarily refers to the Administrative Office of the Court (AOC) data (Bureau of Justice Statistics 2003), although U.S. Sentencing Commission data are also used to provide some additional insights.[57]

Table 6 shows that the total number of defendants charged with

[56] Judicial data on state court convictions are not available, although the inmate survey presented in more detail below reinforces a general impression that there are few convictions in state court on such charges.

[57] The data sets are different because the U.S. Sentencing Commission data reflect only those who were sentenced in a given year, whereas the AOC data reflect all matters related to a criminal charge that were conducted in a given year. For example, some of those convicted in 1999 were not sentenced until 2000.

money laundering rose from 1994 to 1998 and then fell sharply through 2001. Slightly more than 2,100 persons were charged with money-laundering offenses in 2001, compared with more than 2,700 in 1998; only twenty-two businesses were criminally convicted in 2001. For about 30 percent of those charged with money laundering, the offense was not one of the two most serious charges. Table 6 also shows the number of convictions for which money laundering was the lead offense, which is not necessarily the offense with the highest statutory penalty but normally the one that generated the investigation. In the vast majority of these cases (81–88 percent), those charged were convicted.

What predicate crimes generate money-laundering convictions? In this respect, there is a significant difference between those charged with money laundering as the lead offense and those for whom it was a secondary offense. For about 60 percent of the first group (which constitutes two-thirds of the total), a property offense (embezzlement or fraud) was the predicate crime, and for only one in six the predicate crime was a drug offense. However, among the smaller group whose lead charge was not money laundering, about 90 percent were charged with drug trafficking. That is probably the consequence of differences in maximum statutory sentences. Drug offenders face longer sentences than those convicted of money laundering, so drug money launderers are more likely to be charged with the drug offense if they had any involvement beyond pure money laundering.

U.S. Sentencing Commission data in table 6 provide another view on the same matter, since they include other charges that resulted in convictions, such as embezzlement for self in addition to laundering for others.[58] Of the 1,543 defendants sentenced under one or more money-laundering statutes in 2000, 590 were sentenced only for money laundering. If we expand the latter category to include cases involving money-laundering statutes and statutes for conspiracy or being the principal offender, nearly half of those convicted may have been involved only in the laundering and not in other aspects of the crimes, although there is no way to know whether they were customers or providers of money laundering.

Table 6 shows that for both 1995 and 2000, 30 percent of all defendants convicted of money laundering were also convicted of drug of-

[58] Data are not available to compare predicate offenses and these other charges.

fenses. Of 255 cases in which a Title 31 offense[59] was one of the charges, 223 (87 percent) had no non-money-laundering charges.

Interestingly, of all persons convicted of drug offenses in federal court, only 1.5 percent were also convicted of money laundering. This figure was not much different from the proportion of those convicted of fraud who were also convicted of money laundering (1.2 percent). The dominance of drugs among secondary charges for money laundering reflects the dominance of drug offenses in the federal criminal justice system. About 60 percent of federal prison inmates have been convicted of drug offenses.

Money-laundering sentences averaged about thirty-six months, substantially less than the average of approximately forty-eight months for all those convicted in federal court (Bureau of Justice Statistics 2003). Seventeen percent of those sentenced under the guidelines were given longer sentences because they had leadership roles. About 20 percent of the cases involved more than $1 million in funds (U.S. Treasury 2002, p. 5). The mean sentence for cash or monetary instrument smuggling (Title 31) was 19.6 months; for structuring transactions, 13.4 months; and for failure to report a currency transaction, 8.5 months. These results are consistent with the conjecture that most of these cases are pure money laundering, usually with a low-level offender who does nothing else but some illegal legwork for the "predicate criminal." Once again, however, it must be emphasized that the role may be in delivering the funds to the launderer rather than providing the actual service.

The United States stands out in terms of the aggressiveness of its criminal enforcement. Even the United Kingdom, discussed below, has vastly fewer cases per capita.

2. *Prison Data.* The court data have significant limitations because not every successful money-laundering investigation results in a conviction for money laundering, as opposed to some other offense. For example, the prosecutor may drop the money-laundering charge in return for a plea to another charge related to the predicate offense itself. That money-laundering charges usually result from investigations that began with another crime (Joseph 2001) reinforces the concern about the comprehensiveness of the figures. Fortunately, some

---

[59] These Title 31 U.S. Code offenses are mainly monetary reporting/recording offenses such as cash smuggling, structured transactions, and failure to file required reports.

other data throw light on how many money launderers are in prison, regardless of the offense of conviction.

Approximately every five years, the Bureau of Justice Statistics interviews a large sample (about 18,000 in 1997) of inmates in both federal and state prisons. The questionnaire includes items on their criminal activities, not restricted to those for which they were convicted. These data provide an important supplement to the administrative data. Questions in the most recent (1997) survey concerning money laundering have been analyzed by Caulkins and Sevigny (personal communication). Note that although these data are not directly comparable to any year of court data, since most of those incarcerated in 1997 were convicted in an earlier year, table 6 showed little change in the pattern of convictions from 1995 to 2000.

Among federal prison inmates, 3,030 (2.8 percent of the total population) reported that they were serving time for a money-laundering conviction. Two-thirds of those had some drug involvement and another 18 percent reported forgery/fraud convictions.[60] Including those who said that they laundered drug money but were not convicted on that charge, federal prisons in 1997 contained an estimated 4,416 money launderers (5 percent of the total population). Among those who said that they laundered drug money, only about one-sixth (467) were estimated to have had no other involvement with drugs.

None of the state prison inmates reported that they were currently serving time for a money-laundering offense. However, an estimated 6,368 state prison inmates (0.6 percent of the total population) self-reported that they did launder money, and in every case they reported that the money involved came from drug offenses. This latter finding is an artifact of the questionnaire, since only inmates reporting drug convictions were asked about money-laundering activities. Only about 100 reported that they were money launderers exclusively; the others said they were also drug dealers.

Many persons who launder money are in prison for other offenses, particularly for drug offenses. Thus, though there appears to be a neg-

---

[60] Some of the discrepancies between the inmate survey and the court data may reflect the longer sentences of drug offenders; thus the prison population of money launderers will be richer in drug money launderers than the population entering prison. The fact that the inmate survey pertains to 1997, three years earlier than the most recent court data, makes it difficult to integrate all the sources of data, particularly since most of the inmates had been convicted in earlier years. However, the court data suggest relatively modest changes in the level and composition of convictions between 1995 and 2000–2001. Therefore, we ignore here that difference in timing.

ligible number of state-level convictions for money laundering, the self-reported inmate data suggest that there are actually more money launderers in state prison than in federal prison, even if money laundering may have been a minor part of their drug-dealing activities and they may have been customers rather than providers of money-laundering services.

In the federal system, the court statistics (from both the AOC and the U.S. Sentencing Commission) do not suggest a dominant role for drugs. However, the inmate survey suggests that most of those in prison on money-laundering charges were involved in drug dealing. There do not appear to be many stand-alone launderers in the prison system, though the reason may be that involvement in drug dealing creates extra vulnerability to detection and evidence for prosecution.

D. Suspicious Activity Reports

In the United States, SARs have replaced currency transaction reports as the primary source of AML information from financial institutions and other reporting sources. Although CTRs still play a role—more than 13 million of them were filed in 2001, and 1.5 million were at some point identified in the course of a criminal investigation (FinCEN 2002)—SARs at this point are viewed by professionals in the enforcement field as more informative. The number of SAR filings in the United Kingdom is much smaller, but larger per capita and per dollar of gross national product.

1. *The United States.* The number of SARs filed in the United States increased from 52,000 in 1996 to 689,000 in 2004 (FinCEN 2005*a*). Little information is available on the underlying suspected activity. For example, 55 percent of SARs filed by depository institutions between April 1, 1996, and December 31, 2004, were characterized only as "violations of the Bank Secrecy Act (BSA)/Structuring/Money Laundering," which is nonspecific. The only other large category was check fraud, which accounted for 13 percent of the filed reports.

The number of SARs related to terrorism predictably increased sharply following September 11. Whereas, in September 2001, twenty-seven SARs mentioned possible terrorism, another 1,342 terrorism-related SARs were filed in the following six months. The rate of reporting had decreased again within another year. In the six months beginning October 2002, only 290 terrorism SARs were filed. In the second quarter of 2003, however, the number began to rise again in part because of the additional number of financial institutions required to file SARs—for example, money services businesses, casinos, and securities and futures industries—and in part the war in Iraq and the accompanying slight rise in terrorist incidents (FinCEN 2005*b*).

An encouraging trend has emerged with regard to the party initiating terrorism-related SARs. In the six months after September 2001, 85 percent of these SARs were filed because of apparent matches with the names of individuals or entities provided to institutions by government agencies. But from October 2002 onward, most such SARs were a result of due diligence processes of financial institutions themselves, independent of any government-published lists; in fact, during the period April 2003 through June 2004, 80 percent of SARs were proactive. A review of those SARs indicates that several banks created internal watch lists to alert tellers and other employees to customers' previous suspicious behavior.

However, though 177 financial institutions have filed SARs related to terrorism, over a third of the reports from April 2003 to June 2004 came from just two banks. It is unlikely that terrorists rely on such a small number of banks for most of their transactions; it suggests that a few banks are much more alert than others. Sixty-eight terrorism SARs (23.4 percent) were reported directly to law enforcement, meaning that the violation was ongoing and required immediate attention.

The number of SARs filed, like most criminal justice outputs, is an inherently ambiguous indicator of changes in the phenomenon. A rise in the number of SARs may reflect either an increase in money laundering or increased stringency of the AML regime. The rate of increase in recent years is so large that, with a caveat as to quality, there is good reason to believe that it is the stringency of the regime that has intensified. There are no events that would explain a comparable increase in the incidence of money laundering.

SARs are of variable quality. One bank was described as having invested in training its staff to file informative reports only when there was indeed reasonable suspicion. However, sometimes the purpose of filing is primarily to protect the bank against charges of violating reporting requirements, with little focus on assisting the government. If banks and other regulated firms feel a greater need to protect themselves against government sanctions by filing reports, the increase in numbers may not indicate improved diligence. Moreover, the increase may be weakening the effectiveness of the regime in the process, by lowering the signal-to-noise ratio. Such discrepancies in efforts point to the need to examine not merely the number of filings but the extent to which they have resulted in detection and punishment of money-laundering offenses.

For the six and a half–year period ending October 31, 2002, 940,000 SARs produced 70,000 direct referrals to federal law enforcement agencies, of which almost half were to the FBI (FinCEN 2003). Unfortunately, there is no information on how many resulted in criminal cases or contributed to cases.

The U.S. General Accounting Office (GAO) has periodically attempted to ascertain the results of the SAR filings in terms of prosecutions and convictions. An early study (GAO 1998) found that state officials reported "limited or no investigative actions" from materials supplied by FinCEN. Even today, it is unclear what information SARs have produced to make criminal cases. Another GAO study (2002) that examined all SARs involving credit cards during a two-year period from October 1, 1999, to September 30, 2001, found 499 such filings, of which seventy were referred to law enforcement agencies (thirty-nine federal, thirty-one state or local). But the GAO noted that FinCEN was unable to report whether any of these referrals resulted in criminal prosecutions.

The requirement itself to file SARs can indirectly generate useful information. For example, a small community bank in New York City (Broadway National Bank) was identified as problematic because of a lack of filed SARs; it turned out that senior management had allowed the bank to routinely accept deposits from drug dealers.

2. *The United Kingdom.* Concerns about the U.K. AML regime have existed at least since 1992, when Gold and Levi (1994) conducted a review. However, AML activities were not mainstreamed into the law enforcement process until some serious thought was given to proceeds of crime issues during and in the aftermath of the Cabinet Office study (Performance and Innovation Unit 2000). A study of the U.K. system for SARs, funded by the British government (KPMG 2003), found an extraordinary increase in the number of SAR filings since 2000: from 20,000 in 2000 to a projected 100,000 in 2003 (rising subsequently to 154,536 in 2004).[61] According to the study, the increase reflects the

[61] This rise is a fairly universal feature of jurisdictions: e.g., from 2001 to 2004, the number of Dutch SARs doubled to 41,002; in Japan, they quintupled to 95,315 in 2004. There has been a rise (though less marked) also in those jurisdictions in which accounts

extension of AML requirements to lawyers and real estate agents. At least 6 percent of a sample of SARs disseminated by the U.K. National Crime Intelligence Service (NCIS) resulted in "a positive law enforcement outcome (i.e., prosecution, confiscation, cash seizure, etc.)," and another 5 percent were still being used in an active investigation.[62] The study also noted, however, that there was little feedback from law enforcement agencies to the filing institutions.

The NCIS makes some claims about the impact of SARs on enforcement, broadly construed (http://www.ncis.co.uk/financialintelligence.asp, 2005). For example, a fifth of disclosures received by the Inland Revenue from the NCIS identified a new target and a quarter led to new inquiries. In 2002 and 2003, 20–30 percent of the disclosures disseminated to the National Terrorist Financial Investigation Unit were stated either to have led to a longer-term investigation or to have added substantially to an existing investigation.

Fleming (2005, p. v) echoes the findings of the Gold and Levi study over a decade earlier. For example, Fleming found that information technology systems commonly used allow for only limited SARs-related analyses and that SARs may contain unclear reasons for suspicion or may relate to noncriminal activity. Law enforcement agencies receive little guidance, training, or advice on the use of SARs. Along these lines, there is no larger accountability for either law enforcement agencies or the NCIS on the use of SARs; the regime has no real owner to encourage solid performance, to effect change, and to coordinate the SARs-related activity of numerous government departments and agencies. Neither is there a mission statement that clearly sets out the aims of the regime. On the more positive side, smaller-scale studies on metropolitan police data suggest greater potential for linking SARs with existing investigations if field officers use the database (Fleming 2005, pp. 38–42).

Taken together, these reviews amount to a fairly serious indictment of the lack of strategic end-to-end processing in a loose-coupled law enforcement and regulatory system that is both expensive and intrusive of privacy. This is not perhaps quite as critical as the 9/11 Commission

---

are automatically frozen following the making of a report. Jurisdictions that track all wire transfers mostly reflect fluctuations in the economy (see Austrac 2004).

[62] Given that the researchers were unable to track the ultimate use of most of the sample of SARs, this is the least favorable presentation of the data. By the most favorable analysis, one-third of SARs resulted in a law enforcement success, mostly as intelligence rather than as evidence for prosecution.

report but has generated a significant *frisson* in the financial intelligence and enforcement community and a further review in 2005–6 by the chairman of the newly created Serious Organised Crime Agency, which took over responsibility for the dissemination of SARs from NCIS (which it absorbed when it began operations in 2006).

We include here the little data available on criminal enforcement in the United Kingdom. In England and Wales, there were only fifty-four convictions for money laundering in 2004, a rise from 357 prosecutions for violations of money-laundering statutes in the twelve years from 1987 to 1998 (KPMG 2003).[63] Though the U.K. Financial Services Authority has subsequently made AML a major priority, the sense of strategy in criminal investigations and prosecutions was lacking at that time. That view was reinforced by a review of the AML regime in the United Kingdom by the IMF, which found that enforcement was limited even though the structure and laws for it were in place. The report went on to state that "cases are generally considered for enforcement only when there is little likelihood that they will be seriously contested or complicated. . . . The Crown Prosecution Service does not prosecute any matters other than narcotic money laundering" (IMF 2003, p. 100).[64] In 2000 and the first half of 2001, the report continued, there were only eighteen "skilled-person" visits to financial institutions focusing on AML issues (IMF 2003, pp. 100, 102).[65]

E. Seizures and Forfeitures

Given the nature of money laundering as an offense, prosecution of it, unlike prosecution of a violent crime, can be expected to generate substantial financial penalties. The government may seize the laundered money and other assets of those charged and seek forfeiture upon their conviction. In some cases, these seizures and forfeitures can generate very substantial amounts: a prominent case involving a Bank

[63] Data were not available for Scotland and Northern Ireland.

[64] This remains broadly correct even though the IMF may not have considered fully prosecutions for tax fraud by what were then HM Inland Revenue and HM Customs and Excise, and for serious or complex nontax fraud by the Serious Fraud Office. Subsequent to this and in order to implement the Proceeds of Crime Act of 2002—itself a reflection of a major shift in approach by the U.K. government—there have been significant enhancements of investigation, prosecution, and cash seizure regimes in the United Kingdom.

[65] The Financial Services Authority has stepped up its focus on AML since then (see Robinson 2005), but there remain generic problems in applying risk concepts to nonprudential areas.

of New York official in 1999 resulted in criminal forfeitures of $8.1 million (U.S. Treasury 2002, p. A-15).

The total amounts the federal government orders in fines and restitution increased from $100 million in 1996 to $665 million in 2001. The data, provided by the U.S. Sentencing Commission, reflect the growth in the size of the average order rather than the number of orders. The relevant metric to assess this figure is the total volume of funds laundered. If one chooses an estimated total figure toward the lower end of the usual range, such as $300 billion, then the current level of seizures is almost trivial, only 0.2 percent. However, if the total figure is only a few tens of billions—or at least if the forms of money laundering of greatest social concern are only a few tens of billions— then the level of seizures might be 1–3 percent, perhaps enough to have a modest deterrent effect on those tempted to commit the predicate crimes.

A report by the Performance and Innovation Unit (2000) of the U.K. Cabinet Office on the use of confiscation orders also found that the system performed poorly in the United Kingdom. For nondrug crimes in 1998, for example, only 136 confiscations were ordered and £6 million collected—less than half of what was ordered to be confiscated. For drug cases the numbers were larger, but only £10 million were collected in a market estimated to total some billions of pounds in revenues. Since then, the system has been toughened substantially by the Proceeds of Crime Act of 2002, which includes not only joint police-customs Regional Asset Recovery Teams but also a new Asset Recovery Agency (roughly based on the Irish Criminal Assets Bureau) to pursue civilly and via taxation the assets of suspected criminals irrespective of prosecution or conviction. In 2004, there were 709 confiscation orders made in drug-trafficking cases, and additionally, forfeiture orders were made in two-thirds of drug cases on usually modest amounts of property used in the commission of offenses (Home Office 2005). Some £81 million has been confiscated and civilly forfeited in 2004–5, some three-quarters of it via cash seizures under new inland powers (personal communication). There remain very substantial assets (over twice the above figure) on which confiscation orders have been made but not enforced, and reducing this attrition is a prime target of U.K. enforcement bodies.

F. Conclusions

It appears that no other nation prosecutes money-laundering offenses as aggressively as the United States, which is a recurrent complaint of U.S. officials involved in international money-laundering matters. Even with the creation of systems that generate large numbers of
reports, there is little evidence of substantial criminal investigations
that are consistently pursuing substantial cases against violators. The
Netherlands, which has relatively sophisticated capability in criminal
intelligence and investigation of organized crime, may be an exception,
but even there the numbers of major cases remain small.

What might explain this apparent difference in AML efforts between
the United States and other wealthy nations with sophisticated financial and judicial systems? First, drug trafficking, central to the creation
of the AML regime, has been a more significant problem in the United
States than in any other industrial nation, in terms of both politics and
collateral social problems. Second, the United States launched a successful prosecutorial campaign against the Mafia in the 1970s and
1980s that developed many of the legal tools and much of the organizational expertise for money-laundering prosecutions. Only in a very
few other nations (notably Italy) has organized crime prosecution been
prominent. Finally, the United States has a more aggressive law enforcement culture generally than most other nations.

These differences between the United States and the rest of the
world could be either exacerbated or reduced by the relatively new
concern with terrorist financing. The new security agenda that has
developed most dramatically in the United States after 9/11 has received a positive response in the European Union. Although there remain reservations in some E.U. countries about the circumstances that
should give rise to labeling as "terrorism" and about what telecom-
munications data should be kept, for how long, and who should have
access to them, it should be noted that even prior to the bombings in
Spain and England,[66] a 2002 Eurobarometer poll suggested a similarly

[66] The United States did suffer what to date is the largest number of deaths in one
terrorist incident, and the dramaturgy of that awful episode looms large in the collective
psyche. Of course, France, Germany, Italy, Spain, and the United Kingdom (especially
Northern Ireland itself) have experienced a large number of terrorist deaths and incidents
since the 1960s as a result of indigenous non-Islamic armed struggles. In the United
Kingdom, the reduction of funds available to Irish paramilitaries has long been a policy
goal, and though the funds from crime were reduced by significant structural changes
(Levi 2006), charitable donations—principally from the United States via Noraid—were
able to sustain the Irish Republican Army and other groups until the peace agreement
and 9/11 produced a change in American attitudes.

high level of concerns about terrorism in the European Union and the United States, with 82 percent of Western Europe fearing a terrorism incident (European Commission 2003, table 1.13). The London and Madrid bombings have also strengthened the commitment of European states to pursuing terrorist finances, though there is varying commitment and much concern about the negative impact of AML measures on their minority populations and on whether alternative remittance systems make formal AML controls unimportant (Passas 2005).

There remains uncertainty about what the effects are of the differential prosecution and sanctioning levels within Europe and between Europe and the United States. If crime is as globalized as is often believed, one might expect criminals (like licit manufacturers and financial services firms) to shift their centers of operations to foreign countries or to outsource more functions where risks of incrimination or sanctions are lower. There is some anecdotal evidence that in the light of clampdowns on criminal assets in the Irish Republic (arguably, a connected but distinct aspect of AML regimes), drugs traffickers moved to the United Kingdom and to the Netherlands. However, there has been no systematic analysis of what fraction of offenders have *not* moved their operations. This leads us naturally into the next section, assessment of the impact of AML.

IV. Assessing Anti–Money Laundering Efforts

How should the effectiveness of the AML regime be assessed? Money laundering itself is only the intermediate target; the true target is instead the volume of predicate crimes, perhaps weighted in terms of their harmfulness.[67] Reduction in the volume of the money laundered is not a conceptually strong measure of the effectiveness of the regime; subtler outcome measures are needed. This section deals with the problem of finding such measures to reduce crimes other than terrorism and bribery/kleptocracy, since the bulk of AML activities have been

---

[67] A major U.K. Home Office evidence-based review for 2005–6 aims to reweight the objectives of the crime control process in terms of overall harm reduction, developing a common metric for the relative weighting of all crimes. This seems to be analytically defensible, even though very difficult to operationalize in terms that will enable interveners to judge whether one set of policing actions will reduce total harm more than others, whether individually or as part of a basket of controls.

devoted to such criminal activities as drugs, other illegal markets, and white-collar crimes.

A. General Considerations

Writing over ten years ago, Braithwaite (1993) offered the only analysis of this question with a criminological base. At a time when money laundering was almost exclusively concerned with drug revenues, he enumerated the costs and benefits that needed to be considered. For benefits, the central issue was whether money laundering would increase prices enough to make any noticeable difference in drug consumption and whether it would increase the number of serious offenders being punished. On the cost side, in addition to drug-specific issues (e.g., whether drug-related crime and monopolization of drug markets would increase), he identified the costs of enforcement and intrusions as the major considerations. We think that the diversification of AML to other activities also requires a broadening of the evaluative framework.

AML helps reduce crime through two mechanisms. First, CDD and other elements of the prevention pillar can make it more difficult for offenders either to carry out the crime (e.g., pay their suppliers) or to obtain its full benefits. In this respect, the controls have a prospective effect. Second, SARs and other back-end activities can generate evidence of a crime and link individuals to that crime, and SARs can also become evidence for investigations that originate from other sources or were already under way when the reports were made. SARs can also inform the authorities of suspects' assets of which they have no prior knowledge and which, in a system lacking the capacity for centralized information on who directly or indirectly owns specific financial holdings, they have no other obvious means of acquiring.[68] In this sense, SARs act retrospectively in that they not only increase the risk of criminal sanction but also provide the basis for seizure of criminal proceeds.

In terms of crime control, the AML regime may generate two other benefits. First, it produces a form of condign punishment. Part of the social appeal of proceeds of crime confiscation is the satisfaction that offenders do not continue to enjoy the fruits of crime and even are

---

[68] Persons subjected to executive orders, usually in connection with terrorist finance, may have their names circulated. All banks check the list to see whether they have any accounts directly or beneficially owned by those persons, so that they can freeze funds; but this is a tiny proportion of total suspects.

visibly stripped of them. Seizure of funds generates revenue for the government, and the incarceration of those who conspire to make the profits of crime appear legitimate punishes senior offenders. The seizures attack the negative role models offered by offenders living "high on the hog." Research in Europe finds ample illustrations of law enforcement officers stressing the pain that asset confiscation brings to offenders, both in absolute terms and compared with at least European levels of imprisonment (Levi and Osofsky 1995; Nelen 2004);[69] though plausible, this has not been independently verified on a large sample of offenders.

The impact on the ability of others to offend is uncertain, but conviction or professional disqualification of professional intermediaries removes some crime facilitators and may have a disruptive effect on some crime groups (Middleton and Levi 2005; Nelen and Lankhorst 2005). Moreover, given the stakes that financial professionals have in maintaining their employment and licensure, they may be relatively deterrable; that is, unless they are being blackmailed or threatened or unless they or their firms are at serious risk of going bust anyway, modest expected risks of apprehension and punishment may be enough to discourage many from participating.[70] In some instances, the only way to apprehend those principal offenders who separate themselves from the predicate offenses is to convict them of money-laundering offenses associated with predicate crimes that have been committed by others. Such cases show that the law with respect to a wide range of predicate crimes applies to everyone.

Second, AML systems may improve the efficiency of law enforcement, an effect distinct from reducing predicate crime. Even if they do not necessarily result in the government apprehending more offenders, the existence and tools of the AML system may permit the same number of offenders to be captured and convicted at lower cost (at least lower to the government; in this case, the externalities are paid for by the private sector and by users of their services).

---

[69] These are supported by interviews with U.K. law enforcement personnel, 2002–5.

[70] Ironically, the very severity of employment sanctions for any drug taking or viewing Internet pornography at work makes financial services staff readily vulnerable to blackmail; the paucity of public cases revealing actual subornation is evidence of either significant underreporting or underexploitation of crime opportunities. See Levi (2002) and Simpson (2002) for extended discussion of sanctions and corporate offenders.

B. Market Model

A useful starting point to assess the relationship between the AML regime and the reduction in predicate crime quantitatively is to view money laundering as a market, with customers for, and suppliers of, money-laundering services. Specific AML interventions can then be linked to predicate crime reductions by how, through shifting the supply and demand, they affect the money-laundering market, particularly the price of services and, thus, the returns from crime.

For example, if money laundering is more difficult (expensive), then drug dealers will face higher costs and charge higher prices for their services, thus reducing the consumption of drugs. Assume that prior to the creation of an AML regime, a high-level drug dealer charged his customers (themselves lower-level dealers) $10,000 per kilogram of cocaine and received $10 million annually in gross revenues. As a consequence of the barriers imposed by the AML regime, assume that he now has to pay 10 percent of the proceeds to the money launderer and hence receives only $9 million. Under the assumption of competition between drug dealers, which seems a reasonable characterization of such a market (Caulkins and Reuter 1998), the $10 million previously just compensated the dealer for risks (legal and otherwise) and other costs. In the face of reduced net returns, the dealer will raise prices to customers and, thus, increase the retail price of cocaine; numerous studies have shown that even for addictive drugs there is a substantial elasticity of demand (Manski, Pepper, and Petrie 2001 p. 43).

The same logic applies to other income-generating offenses such as fraud and gambling. By creating a higher probability of detection and punishment, the AML regime makes money laundering more risky for both customers and providers. It raises the price of the service or the costs of searching for the service (customers finding suppliers), which in turn reduces the return from the predicate crime and thus the quantity of these offenses. It also brings in a set of different offenders who may be in a position to "trade" information about the primary traffickers in exchange for nonprosecution or reduced sentences. In this framework, the analytic task is to estimate how much AML interventions raise the price of money laundering and the price elasticity of offending with respect to the price of money-laundering services.

What determines the demand for, and supply of, money-laundering services? The demand for money-laundering services can be thought of as a function of two factors. First is the distribution and volume of criminal revenues. Since scrutiny of sources of criminal earnings for low earners is limited (except in the aftermath of divorces and other such transactions in which lawyers may suspect undeclared income and generate SARs, as in the United Kingdom, where the regulations bite) and because low earners do not need to transform (launder) the money they make, it is probably only criminal incomes of more than perhaps $50,000 annually that create a need for concealing the source of the revenues.

The second is the other costs of laundering money, such as the time it takes to find a supplier and the risk of the search. Both are influenced by the intensity of enforcement of the AML regime. Money-laundering customers face a risk of legal and financial penalties if they transact with unreliable suppliers of laundering services. Some potential penalties are derivative of supplier-oriented risk; the launderer can mitigate the penalty by turning in the customer who has committed the predicate offense. In addition, the continuing presence in some jurisdictions of sting operations, in which the government simulates the behavior of a launderer, poses a separate risk to the customer. That risk may be manifested in the time it takes for customers to find a provider to whom they assign a low probability of being a government agent.

The supply of money-laundering services is determined primarily by the stringency of the AML regime. Without the prevention pillar of the AML regime and with only a rudimentary enforcement pillar associated with tracing proceeds of crime back to their source, the cost of laundering those proceeds would surely be low, but not zero. Prior to the 1970 Bank Secrecy Act, criminals could deposit the cash proceeds (no matter how large) from their crimes in local banks with no questions asked by the bank (placement), move them around the world (layering), and enjoy them at their leisure (integration). Criminals and their banks were subject to ex post investigation, but when authorities do not have seizure and confiscation powers and once the proceeds were safely outside the jurisdiction, risks to the "primary offenders" would be minimal, though anyone—including financial facilitators—who remained within the jurisdiction might be indicted as part of a conspiracy such as RICO or Continuing Criminal Enterprise if it could be shown that they had the requisite degree of guilty knowledge.[71]

---

[71] Legislative details vary, but this logic applies to non-U.S. common law and to civil law, e.g., continental European jurisdictions. For example, sanctions against membership of "criminal organizations"—a problematic term—are mandated within the European Union.

Indeed in theory, even without money-laundering legislation, bankers might have been significantly at risk once law enforcement agencies developed this crime reduction model, since they were more likely than primary offenders to be locked into domestic life and therefore less geographically mobile.

Today, it is reasonable to assume that money launderers face no costs other than those posed by law enforcement such as seizure of assets and incarceration and the same kinds of reputational losses associated with any kind of sanction for white-collar offenses. The time involved in actually laundering funds is minimal. Some of the price charged for money-laundering services may reflect skill in the methods used for hiding the origins of money, but one can assume that such skills are in ready supply and that enough of those with the skills can be persuaded to commit this crime for an appropriately high fee. Consequently, incarcerating, say, a few hundred launderers will not reduce the pool of competent labor substantially, though it may raise the price that has to be paid to obtain that labor, redistributing criminal income and inducing entry by new participants as well as, perhaps, taking out of the market those who fear professional stigma or incarceration.

The effective cost of money-laundering services is not fully reflected in the price charged. In addition to search time, there is the risk of sanction by the state(s)[72]—especially in a global enforcement environment marked by FATF pressure to reduce privacy rights—and fraud by the provider. Quality among suppliers may be differentiated, reflecting an institution's or individual's capacity to deliver services reliably, a particularly important consideration in the criminal world. Thus, paradoxically, an observed reduction in prices may reflect a shift from higher- to lower-quality money-laundering services.

C. Multiple Markets

An important analytic complexity is that there may be more than one market for money-laundering services, depending on the predicate offense and the amount that needs to be protected. For example, as was suggested by prior examples, laundering $1 million in drug revenues from the United States to Mexico may require a higher-percentage payment than laundering the same amount in a bankruptcy fraud, simply because the launderer of drug money incurs risks of more likely

---

[72] This can be the jurisdictions in which the primary offenses occurred and also those in which the laundering occurred.

investigation and more serious penalties from law enforcement as well as greater potential physical risks from the customer (violent retaliation for failure to protect assets). If the transaction involves actual cash, it may also be more expensive (per dollar) to launder large sums than small, for the same reasons.

Launderers may also specialize, in terms of either the kinds of funds they accept or the kinds of institutions with which they transact. Money laundering is also differentiated by phase; some launderers may not provide full-service operations. For example, a simple currency exchange bureau may only move money out of the United States (placement) but not provide for the layering of the money so that it can no longer be traced, or bring it back into the United States, where the funds can be freely used with no questions asked (integration). Black-market peso brokers, by contrast, often serve both the supply and the demand ends of the market. They first export the narco-dollars to Colombia (or arrange to purchase them for resale in the United States), then exchange them for pesos for the cartels' domestic use, and finally provide dollars to Colombian importers who wish to avoid the costs and bureaucracy of obtaining dollars legally. Thus the proceeds of drug sales in the United States may resurface, cleaned, in the accounts of U.S. companies that sell their products to Colombian businesses. A similar logic may be involved in the facilitation of cross-border transfers by *hawaladars* (sometimes local shopkeepers) who match currency transfers between jurisdictions, who merely have to "net out" the balances, often in jurisdictions such as the United Arab Emirates (Passas 2005).

One segment of the market for money-laundering services may consist of launderers employing a variety of methods for servicing customers, depending on the customers' specific needs. In this conventional market, the providers have multiple and independent customers and recruit agents (e.g., bank officials, casino employees) to assure that they can provide a range of services. Customers, who know other customers with whom they share information, shift among launderers depending on the price and quality of service. For example, there is anecdotal evidence that drug dealers, circumspect though they may be, do share information about money launderers.

Another segment of the market consists of almost accidental customer-agent relationships. Customers do not find professional money launderers whose principal activity is providing those services, but rather seek out corrupt employees of financial intermediaries who service only one or a small number of clients as a by-product of their legitimate occupations. To the extent that the launderer might have an interest in servicing more than one client, search costs are high for both sides (though more for the customer), reflecting risks of disclosing need or availability and the lack of any organizing focal point for search.

For example, one financier allowed a single drug trafficker to use his company to establish a source of funds. The trafficker gave cash to the financial officer to deposit in a company account, and the funds were then transferred to Monaco for the ostensible purpose of buying Goya paintings. The paintings were fakes and, moreover, were never shipped, and the drug trafficker was the beneficiary of the payments for the fake Goyas, receiving the million dollar transfers. There was no evidence that the financier's business provided money-laundering services for other clients (FATF 1998).

Both types of operations are components of the market. Some customers in high-risk occupations (e.g., cigarette smugglers) with continuing needs in a number of locations may seek out specialized launderers. Others who have a one-time need may be content to find an acquaintance capable and willing to provide the service just to one customer. There is also self-laundering, for example, through acquisition of a small business that does not arouse suspicions or (in the United States) is on the "exempt" list at a bank (i.e., for which it is not necessary to file a CTR for large cash transactions that are consistent with the regular pattern of the business). No one at the bank or any professional except perhaps a forgiving accountant needs to be involved, at least in the placement stage. The Egmont Group (2000) tells of a Western European family of drug traffickers that ran a currency exchange bureau that served as both a cash-intensive front company and a means of laundering money. The rise of artificial tanning and nail parlors in the United Kingdom is an illustration of such a cash-hiding self-laundering potential, especially since tax agencies do not profit from and are not set up to investigate overreporting of taxable income.

Although professional money launderers certainly exist,[73] they are

<hr/>

[73] In Dutch organized crime investigations in 2004, a third of those under investigation were described as having laundering as their primary and another third as a secondary aspect of their criminal work; the significance of laundering to the final third was unknown

surprisingly infrequent in reported cases. A great deal of the revenue from crimes is self-laundered. Robert Maxwell, then a flamboyant press lord and member of Parliament in the United Kingdom, laundered hundreds of millions of dollars from the pension funds of his U.K. company employees through U.S. and other banks (some of which were also defrauded by him) (Bower 1996). Other people may have aided him, but there is no evidence that anyone was an independent provider of laundering services, not least because until after his death, no one in authority knew that he was committing fraud. Terrorist financing cases also seem to involve people who belong very much to the cause rather than being mere commercial launderers; the latter, after all, might be more likely to trade in their sources in exchange for liberal official treatment in relation to other potential criminal liabilities.[74]

This is important for both policy and research purposes. The rationale behind the current AML regime is based in part on the implicit assumption that the regime provides tools to apprehend and punish a set of actors who provide a critical service for the commission of certain kinds of crime and who had previously been beyond the reach of the law—an assumption that makes the market model a useful heuristic device for analyzing the effects of laws and programs.

However, if money laundering is mostly done by predicate offenders or by nonspecialized confederates, then the regime accomplishes much less. There is no new set of offenders, just a new set of charges against the same offenders, and the potential gains from the additional tool represented by the AML regime, while valuable in increasing the efficiency of law enforcement, are likely to be substantially more modest than posited (Cuéllar 2003). The extent to which the modesty of gains is a function of the modesty of enforcement resources would be a matter of much dispute; we present the relevant information in the next section.

For research purposes, the prominence of the amateur launderer implies that the market model concept is a strained analogy. Price may not be well defined to most participants because the service is rarely purchased and the providers are poorly informed. Risk may also be

---

(Council of Europe 2006). We are not in a position to test these ascriptions, but van Duyne and Levi (2005) note the relative lack of sophistication in those laundering schemes that make it through to final conviction after appeals.

[74] In addition, terrorism is often bad for general criminal as well as legitimate business.

hard to observe because it is derivative from participation in other elements of the crime. Assessing how interventions increase risks and prices for those transactions that do involve stand-alone launderers will have only modest value. Finally, stand-alone service providers may be scarce.

Thus the market model may work well for some kinds of predicate offenses and offenders but less well for others. How this element of heterogeneity in the money-laundering underworld affects the research agenda for conceptualizing optimal AML regimes is taken up in the final section.

D. Performance Measures

To what extent does the market framework help assess the effectiveness of an AML regime in reducing predicate crime? While useful for analyzing some of the basic questions, the available data do not permit application for assessing effectiveness. One source of difficulty is that the price of money-laundering services itself is not an adequate indicator. Enforcement aims at both the demand and supply sides. Demand-side efforts such as stings against customers have the effect of lowering observed prices. By raising the nonmoney cost of purchasing money laundering, which now includes some risk of arrest, incarceration, and financial penalties, such stings reduce demand. Supply-side efforts directed at the launderers should raise the price. Both efforts should reduce the quantity of laundering and the net returns from crime, the ultimate goal, but price then can only be interpreted along with estimates of quantity.

An alternative performance measure for assessing the effectiveness of the AML regime in controlling predicate crime is the volume of predicate offenses. Apart from the problem of developing a counterfactual—how much predicate crime would have occurred without the AML regime?—there is a fundamental problem of measuring predicate offense levels.

Consider again illegal drugs, the best-studied of the activities generating a demand for money laundering. While there are a number of possible measures—total revenues, prices, or quantities consumed—none is estimated precisely enough to be useful for analytical purposes, even if we knew more about the volume and cost of drug money laundering. For example, as previously mentioned, the error band around existing drug revenue estimates for the United States is very large, with an official estimate of $70 billion in 2000 (Office of National Drug Control Policy 2001), which should be viewed as the center point of a uniform distribution from $35 billion to $105 billion. A decline of even 25 percent in a five-year period would be hard to detect with confidence.

Alternatively, one might use drug prices, since money-laundering controls are expected to reduce drug use by raising the cost of distribution rather than by reducing demand. A National Research Council report (Manski, Pepper, and Petrie 2001) expressed considerable skepticism that the current system of data collection for prices could detect any but the very largest changes in prices (cf. Caulkins 2001). Moreover, there have been large revisions in the estimated prices for cocaine and heroin for a given year in successive estimation efforts, reinforcing the sense of frailty.[75] Other potential measures such as the number of dependent users or the quantity consumed are similarly estimated with great imprecision.

The performance assessment situation is even less promising for criminal offenses other than drug distribution. Systematic estimates of the volume of these crimes or revenues are often not available or are effectively made up from thin air. It is highly implausible, for example, that one could reliably detect a reduction of 10 percent in the volume of (or revenues from) embezzlement or corporate fraud. Though private-sector data on payment card fraud are fairly reliable, it is far from certain that much of the proceeds from such crimes needs to be laundered; furthermore, as a proportion of all crime costs and benefits to offenders, such frauds are very modest (see Levi and Pithouse, forthcoming). In some countries such as the United Kingdom, regular large-sample victimization surveys for crimes with individual victims have been developed that can be useful at area levels, but there is modest understanding of what offenders get from reselling stolen property or how much of this is laundered: so linkage with AML measures is difficult.

Performance measurement is an increasingly important component of responsive and responsible public policy, so the difficulty in finding credible measures of AML regime performance in reducing crime is a major problem. Perhaps more sophisticated versions of market models

[75] The series produced by Abt Associates in 2001 (ONDCP 2001) differs from that produced by RAND in 2004 (ONDCP 2004). For 1998, e.g., Abt estimated the retail price of cocaine to be $190 (in 2002 dollars); the RAND-estimated price was $132.

will help in this respect, but their utility may remain problematic unless data quality improves, a special problem if one is also trying to measure the wider sociopolitical threat from criminal organizations or networks as well as levels of criminal behavior.

Moreover, it is unlikely that the AML regime itself could have very large effects on the extent of drug use. Low-level drug dealers earn too little to require money-laundering services, yet they account for the bulk of total earnings. Price markups along the distribution system (conservatively estimated at 50 percent at each level) show that more than 60 percent of revenues go to low-level wholesalers and retailers, who are predominantly independent agents rather than employees of larger crime organizations. At the peak of the crack cocaine market in 1988, average annual earnings of retail drug dealers in Washington, DC, were estimated at $28,000 (Reuter, MacCoun, and Murphy 1990). More recent studies report much lower average earnings (Bourgois 1995; Levitt and Venkatesh 2000).

High-level dealers, the only ones who need money-laundering services, account for no more than 25 percent of total drug revenues. Assume that in the current regime money launderers charge customers approximately 10 percent of the amount laundered. Now assume that an improved system raised the price for money-laundering services by half, to 15 percent. The result would be an increase in the price of drugs of only 1.25 percent, far too small to be picked up by existing monitoring systems. This is not an argument that money-laundering controls are neither effective nor cost-effective, but only that their success cannot be empirically assessed by examining prices and quantities in drug markets.

Finally, we review one arena that has provided the most serious analytical difficulties over performance measures: assessing the effectiveness of terrorist finance controls (see Levi 2006). The 9/11 Commission stressed that financing was only a part of the terrorism control issue, but the "War on Terrorist Financing" continues to present a high profile around the world. The effectiveness statistic most often cited is the amounts frozen following E.U., U.N. Security Council, and U.S. designation of persons and organizations (including charities), but these fairly modest sums ($112 million frozen worldwide to the end of 2005) tell us nothing about the size of the denominator. The cost of terrorist finance would vary according to whether it is a gross cost (which would include support during the planning stages, in the case of Islamic bombers perhaps starting with initial transportation to and training in Afghanistan, Bosnia, or Pakistan) or a net cost (which would include only the resources necessary to pull off the job—explosives, backpacks, cell phones, bribes to noncore participants, price paid for inside information, etc.). The operational costs of the 9/11 attacks totaled $400,000–$500,000. A top end estimate for the costs of the Madrid bombings in 2004 (including the Moroccan cannabis partially traded for explosives) is $15,000, with the Bali bombings costing a little more and the "7/7" London bombings of 2005 costing substantially less[76] (*Economist* 2005; interviews with U.K. and U.S. law enforcement sources).

There is some debate in Western government circles as to whether one should include within gross costs the financing of religious intolerance that actively promotes or condones the use of violence against other groups: the financing of terror could then total funding of Wahabi or post-Salafist *madrassas* (religious schools) and mosques around the world (or, as some would counter, the funding of Zionist or fundamentalist Christian or rival Muslim activities that incite violence among their adherents). However, almost none of those who have bombed U.S. or Western European targets attended such places, making direct causal connections and claims of preventative impact difficult to justify. The financing prevention target could range from thousands of dollars to hundreds of millions of dollars, depending on the basis for calculation.[77] Given the modest operational costs, the preventative performance needed to stop $10,000 or even $100,000 from falling into terrorist hands would have to be extraordinary in the context of global incomes from crime, let alone licit income. Rather, performance might best be judged by stopping such sums from getting into the hands of known and suspected terrorists or the leads to terrorists and their logistical supporters provided by the private sector and public financial

---

[76] One of the bombers of humble occupation left over $200,000 net in his estate, suggesting that far more resources could have been available for this and other attacks, and raising the question in our minds of why this was not distributed to other potential terrorists before his death, if planned.

[77] McCulloch and Pickering (2005) allege that the main purpose of controls on terrorist finance is to suppress the charities and nongovernmental organizations in "civil society" in order to reduce opposition to what they view as state crimes and repression. Irrespective of whether or not their interpretation is correct or plausible, this illustrates a radically pluralist approach to measuring performance, depending on judgments about their purpose and as seen through the lenses of various (sometimes diametrically opposed) stakeholders.

investigation. National security considerations make it difficult for outsiders to assess the impact claims made by governments and critics alike, but the acknowledgement that international terrorism is now split up into smaller "Al-Qaeda-inspired" networks or disparate individuals makes financial needs less for terrorist operations. This difficult issue brings us appropriately to the next aspect of AML impact—criminal justice performance.

E. Improving Criminal Justice System Performance

We noted earlier that AML regimes might have two other benefits in addition to controlling crime: improving the efficiency of the system or catching offenders who otherwise would escape. Cuéllar (2003) concedes that such regimes might have improved efficiency in drug control and in reducing a few related criminal activities but argues that they have failed in the second area. The principal use to which the U.S. AML regime has been put has been to increase the penalties with which prosecutors can threaten predicate offenders. The regime has had little success in apprehending professional money launderers or high-level criminals. In Europe, there has been some activity against professionals such as lawyers and bankers—though more by regulatory than criminal sanctions—but the extent to which this has incapacitated crime networks, reduced the variety of their offending, or reduced the scale of their growth as "criminal organizations" remains unknown and largely unanalyzed (Levi and Maguire 2004; Nelen 2004; van Duyne and Levi 2005). There are limits in the extent to which the police (or, for that matter, bankers) can pursue the rationale behind suspected transactions without interviewing suspects. However, improved recording of financial accounts and greater attention to beneficial ownership of assets should logically help with asset recovery compared with post-arrest or even postcharge financial investigations that were commonplace previously; in this sense, AML has an influence on law enforcement methodologies, from drugs to grand corruption. Thus, in the U.K. regime since the Proceeds of Crime Act of 2002, the government has the power to require offenders to provide details of their incomes, expenditures, and assets (for up to twenty years following a conviction) in the Serious Organised Crime and Police Act of 2005, investigators can place monitoring orders on suspected offenders' accounts that prospectively allow them to track funds movements and to require forfeiture of cash over £5,000 inland as well as at borders unless the suspect can convince the court that the funds were legitimately acquired.[78]

The paucity of cases against stand-alone launderers and investigations that have their origin in money-laundering information supports the criticism that the AML regime has brought in few new offenders. There are no systematic data on the origins of cases against major criminals such as principal drug dealers, so it is impossible to tell whether more of them are being captured through money-laundering laws and investigations. Furthermore, where heads of state or their families are involved in grand corruption (including embezzlement and, sometimes, illicit trafficking and other major crimes also), it is far from obvious to whom either domestic or foreign institutions should report without fear of retaliation, or who has sufficient motivation to take serious action. In this respect, the national FIU model, like most national crime investigation and prosecution models, breaks down when confronted with key elites, even where they have no formal immunity for acts performed in office.[79]

F. Costs

Whatever the gains from money-laundering controls, there are also a variety of costs that need to be considered. Reuter and Truman (2004) offer a very rough estimate of $7 billion for the costs of the U.S. AML regime in 2003. That figure includes costs to the government ($3 billion), the private sector ($3 billion), and the general public ($1 billion). However, it does not include two potentially important cost elements: the effect on the international competitive position of business sectors subject to AML rules or the costs of errors. The banking industry has complained substantially about the former from time to time, though less so as FATF has helped increase formal regulation of the financial sector in other money centers. The second is of particular concern for vulnerable populations such as immigrant workers who may be excluded from financial services because of a general suspicion based on their background.

Studies by KPMG (2003) and PriceWaterhouse Coopers (2003) for

---

[78] In December 2005, Prime Minister Blair announced the intention to lower the threshold for this sort of forfeiture to £1,000.

[79] This is not uniquely a problem for the countries of the South, especially Africa: recent scandals have engulfed Prime Minister Berlusconi (Italy), President Chirac (France), and—at a more modest level—former German Chancellor Kohl. In the wealthier as well as some poorer countries, many of these scandals involve campaign finance.

the U.K. NCIS and the Financial Services Authority, respectively, provide a partial cross-check for these estimates. The KPMG study provides a "rough estimate" of the current cost of the U.K. SARs regime
for reporting entities of £90 million: a figure that may be expected to
rise as more sectors are covered by the money-laundering regulations,
though some costs may represent initial start-up rather than recurrent
costs. If we scale this figure by the size of the U.S. economy relative
to the size of the U.K. economy and convert from sterling to dollars,
the corresponding estimate is $1.1 billion. Since reporting of SARs is
an important but not the only element of the AML regime, this rough
estimate suggests that a figure of $3 billion for the entire U.S. regime
is not unreasonable as an upper-bound estimate.[80] Since those reports,
there has been a rise in demand for compliance officers and escalating
use of expensive software that tries to identify "suspicious transactions"
on the basis of pattern analysis.

The two studies for the U.K. authorities also looked at costs to the
government. The KPMG study of the SAR regime estimates these
costs at only about 12 percent of the costs to reporting institutions, to
which we would add that this figure should rise as increasing use is
made of SARs following subsequent legislation and critical performance reviews. However, that figure should not undercut the Reuter
and Truman guesstimate of the rough equality between the overall
costs of the U.S. AML regime to the government and private-sector
institutions. Many government costs with respect to prevention, such
as drafting regulations and conducting examinations, are unrelated to
the actual management of information flows. As already noted, the
United States is also far more active than the United Kingdom in
prosecutions. Moreover, the Reuter and Truman estimate of total U.S.
federal prevention costs is only about one-fifth of the total prevention
plus enforcement costs.[81]

G. How Risky Is Money Laundering?

However crude, an estimate of how risky money laundering in the
United States has become as a result of the AML regime is helpful in

---

[80] The British Bankers Association estimates that British banks spend $400 million
annually on AML compliance (*Economist* 2005).

[81] The PriceWaterhouse Coopers study estimates that the cost to the government of
the expanded retrospective CDD would be a minuscule amount (0.3 percentage points)
of the total cost to firms. This low figure is understandable because the change in the
AML regime applies principally to the reporters and the cost to the government involves
only handling additional reports, and not even, e.g., what might be done with the reports.

assessing regime performance. About 2,000 people are convicted of money-laundering offenses (primary or otherwise) each year in the United States. For the moment, assume that all of those convicted are providers of, rather than customers for, the service. This assumption imparts an upward bias to our risk estimate, since we know that some (perhaps even a majority) of those convicted are not stand-alone providers of money-laundering services.[82]

To estimate risk, a figure for the total number of persons who launder money is also needed. No such estimate is available, so an indicative calculation is all that can be offered. Assume that total U.S. domestic crime money laundered annually is near the low end of conventional estimates, say $300 billion. Only 20 percent of those convicted are reportedly involved with laundering more than $1 million, but that is the amount involved in the specific transactions detected, not an annual flow. If an average money launderer handles $10 million per year (which might generate a gross income of $500,000 to $1 million), then there would be 30,000 money launderers, and the probability of conviction would be about 6.7 percent (2,000/30,000). Of course, some of the launderers will be (or work for) very large financial institutions such as those almost all readers bank with. This institutional size factor should be borne in mind when thinking about violation rates, since different people within the institutions may unconnectedly be doing the laundering. For comparison, there are estimates available that the probability of incarceration for selling cocaine in the late 1980s was approximately 25–30 percent (Reuter, MacCoun, and Murphy 1990). Though dated, these are the only such estimates for an illegal market. There remains, however, a further problem that the enforcement authorities have not highlighted. Even if the probability of conviction is as high as we hypothesize here, the proportion of those assets that are recovered is remarkably low.

This exercise is highly speculative; there are other assumptions that might generate a higher estimate of risk without overly straining plausibility. For example, in addition to those who were convicted of money laundering, there may be substantially more individuals for whom those charges were dropped in exchange for information about the predicate offense or for pleas to some other involvement in the pred-

---

[82] Data on the educational level of those convicted federally for money laundering show that fewer than one-half had more than a high school education. It seems likely that these are customers rather than providers themselves.

icate offense, even though the individual's principal role was money laundering. If only half of those who were caught laundering money were convicted on other charges, then the risk figure might rise to 14 percent. For money launderers with valuable legitimate labor market skills, that risk might generate a very high premium for their services. Compared to street-hardened drug dealers with little education or high social standing to lose, such professionals require a higher incentive to risk the same amount of prison time.

These assumptions generously favor a finding that supports the effectiveness of the AML regime. Most of those convicted of money laundering are also convicted of other offenses, and many are probably customers rather than providers. The assumption that each money launderer handles an average of $10 million per year imparts a similar bias; actual cases point to launderers with much lower volume. That is certainly the case if many of them work for only one client. It is quite plausible that even now, with an elaborate regime in place, money launderers face a less than one in twenty probability of incarceration in the United States.[83] The financial penalties collected by the federal government represent the most modest of taxes, even assuming low-end estimates of money laundering.

However, it must be reemphasized that this is not a complete assessment of the effectiveness of the AML regime. The figures employed cover only those individuals who were themselves involved directly in the money-laundering transaction. It may well be that SARs and other elements of the regime generate useful evidence against larger numbers of drug dealers, but that the final indictments and convictions are for the predicate crime alone. The lack of information on this possibility is a major omission in the current system of data collection.

V. Conclusions and a Research Agenda

Led most prominently by the United States, developed and many less developed nations have now put in place an elaborate set of controls on the financial system that aim to deter a variety of criminal activities by making it difficult to convert illegal proceeds into safely usable

[83] We assume that the set of actual current money launderers is smaller than it would have been if laundering had been subject to a less strict penal and regulatory regime. This estimate is based around those who are actually acting as launderers.

funds. The system has expanded recently with global concerns about terrorism. There is good reason to believe that it will expand still further in the next few years as some kinds of financial transactions that facilitate laundering are still, at best, lightly regulated, and these will be seen as "gaps" that need to be closed.

How well the system works in suppressing crimes and preventing terrorist acts is entirely a matter of speculation. No published papers make any claims to provide an empirical assessment. Nor are we aware of any ongoing research to that end. This is an important gap, given that the controls are expensive, can create problems for individuals falsely identified as involved in laundering, and require private institutions to take on (unpaid) an important and unconventional law enforcement role, for which their customers and shareholders pay.

It is easy to critique the system for its elaborateness and intrusiveness (Naylor 2002); at the same time, for its lack of success in rooting out major criminals or recovering a large percentage of crime proceeds (Naylor 2002; Nelen 2004; van Duyne and Levi 2005); and for its impact on distorting the classical constructions of criminal law (Alldridge 2003). Some critics might choose to have the best of both worlds, simultaneously deriding the lack of serious impact on proclaimed targets and the invasion of privacy, perhaps even suggesting that there may be a wider political motivation for enhancing transparency. This suspicion of Big Government is held by libertarians at either end of the left-right political continuum, especially in North America (Hyde 1995; Levy 1996; Naylor 2002; Alldridge 2003) and in offshore finance centers, whether or not underpinned by economic interests. There are horror stories of both kinds of errors. First are those in which the system unfairly penalizes the apparently innocent, especially before the U.S. Civil Asset Forfeiture Reform Act of 1999. Examples include forfeiture of entire farms on which a small amount of cannabis has been grown or raids on incorrectly suspected persons to generate large asset forfeitures that fund state or federal agencies. In the terrorist finance area, much controversy still exists on the freezing of money transmission businesses run by the Sudanese Al-Barakaat on the basis that they were linked to Bin Laden.[84]

---

[84] The issue of nonjusticiability of decisions to designate (and not to designate) persons and institutions as financiers of terrorism is a broader important issue that we merely flag here. However, given the asset freezing and financial incapacitation consequences of thus designating, say, Hamas or not designating some prominent Saudis, it is easy to see why such decisions are problematic. Is feeding and clothing the families of suicide bombers

Second are those in which it transparently fails to catch the most guilty till long after the money laundering has occurred, if at all. While troubling, these kinds of stories cannot by themselves make an effective case against the regime. They must be weighed against benefits that are much less conspicuous and very difficult to assess.

Defenders of the system offer instances of serious malefactors caught violating AML rules; see, for example, the five *National Money Laundering Strategies* published under U.S. Congressional mandate between 1999 and 2003. Such instances, even when aggregated, also fail to make the case. For example, it is never made clear how many of the offenders would have been caught through their violation of other substantive criminal statutes. Gold and Levi (1994), following up a large sample of SARs to the U.K. NCIS, made an early attempt to analyze the benefits. They concluded that at that time, many reports were made after the banks learned of customs or police interest; that the customs and police usually used the SAR information only when they already were suspicious of the account holder; and that therefore it was impossible to ascertain the potential of the "system" to generate important leads. Moreover, the proportion of reports that generated any significant benefit to prosecutions and conviction-based asset confiscation was under 1 percent of reports made. Despite electronic reporting, given the huge increase in the number of reports made, it seems likely that the current percentage that leads to law enforcement (as contrasted—because of increased resources—with tax) benefits will be substantially lower today.

In light of this, we offer no conclusions about how well the system currently performs. Instead we ask what criteria should enter into decisions about extending the system? That allows us then also to discuss some plausible research activities that would permit better decision making.

The existing system of regulation is driven in part by scandal. The Bank of Credit and Commerce International scandal of the early 1990s led to tougher regulation by the Bank of England and elsewhere in the world. The Chiasso and Marcos scandals led to creative and proactive approaches in Switzerland to both regulation and prosecution of overseas-originating crimes. The revelations about European bank holdings

---

after the fact "financing terrorism"? E.U. member states, e.g., are far from united in such judgments.

of Sani Abacha's fortune, entirely generated by kleptocratic activities as a Nigerian general and unelected head of state, engendered a spate of new rules from various national financial regulatory agencies. The Bank of New York scandal led to a major review of correspondent banking relationships, as banks realized that they were responsible for the due diligence (or lack of diligence) of the banks for which they processed transactions.[85] The Riggs Bank scandal (U.S. Senate 2004, 2005), among others, has led to a sharp tightening of regulatory activities by U.S. bank regulatory agencies since 2004.[86]

It may be true that these changes are aimed at sustaining and legitimating the world financial system, but they also recognize "market failure" in self-regulation. It seems to us that, populist reflexes to egregious wrongdoing apart, the expansion of AML controls to all nations represents an attempt to grapple with the dark side of globalization without "unduly" disturbing the functioning of the world financial services industry, including overseas remittances that totaled $167 billion in 2005 (World Bank 2006, p. 85).[87]

Overreaction can come from the regulated as well. In the United States, the Beacon Hill case, in which JP Morgan Chase handled $6 billion for a money services business (MSB) (the Beacon Hill Corporation), has generated a great concern on the part of New York banks about the business of MSBs. As reported in a Deloitte newsletter (@Regulatory, June 2005), "Fearing that MSBs, who provide a valuable service to the unbanked sector, would themselves lose access to the banking system, FinCEN and the banking agencies attempted to send

[85] Those banks that find it uneconomic to seek formal listing or branches in foreign jurisdictions pay other banks for clearing their transactions, e.g., in U.S. dollars.

[86] A June 2005 newsletter from Deloitte Touche (@Regulatory) states that "the current laser-like focus of the bank regulators has resulted mainly from certain high-profile AML cases which called into question the adequacy of the existing regulatory oversight infrastructure for AML. As a result of these high-profile cases, the U.S. Congress is applying significant pressure on the federal bank regulatory agencies to enhance their supervision of banks' AML programs or risk losing this authority. In turn, the bank regulators are closely scrutinizing the banks' AML programs."

[87] According to the World Bank's review of Global Economic Prospects, "Although there is no universal agreement yet on how to measure international migrants' remittances to developing countries, a comprehensive measure of certain officially recorded flows—workers' remittances, compensation of employees, and migrant transfers—produced an estimate of $167 billion for 2005, up from $160 billion in 2004. Given measurement uncertainties, notably the unknown extent of unrecorded flows through formal and informal channels, the true size of remittance flows may be much higher—perhaps 50 percent or more. Because of their volume and their potential to reduce poverty, remittances are attracting growing attention from policymakers at the highest levels in both developed and developing countries" (2006, p. 85).

the message that banks should not 'throw the baby out with the bath water' but rather establish anti–money laundering (AML) controls commensurate with the higher inherent AML risk with MSB customers, including the varying levels of AML risk within this category of customers." No doubt the problem will be resolved. However, this points to the difficulty of regulators meeting their multiple objectives, even setting aside the more fundamental issue of whether we should opt for a retributive deserts-based model, a "restorative justice" model, or some "mixed economy of sanctions" approach that represents the current spectrum of actual national systems within a global framework that contains equivalent rather than exactly the same laws.[88]

How should decisions be made about the scope and intensity of regulation? Creating a system that is truly comprehensive, that covers all the methods by which the origins of criminal incomes could be hidden or by which funds could be conveyed to terrorists, is too ambitious.[89] It would impose a great burden on societies that place considerable value on the free flow of commerce and on individual and commercial privacy. The system must be risk-based to take account of the relationship between the attractiveness of a channel for these purposes and the costs of subjecting it to monitoring. To do that, though, requires first a knowledge of how drug dealers and embezzlers currently launder funds and of how terrorists move moneys for their operations and, second, how they respond to regulations and controls aimed at specific channels.

Obtaining even the descriptive data for the first task is a major undertaking. The kind of ethnographic research that has led to a better understanding of the lower levels of the drug trade (e.g., Bourgois 1995) is not likely to be so successful for an activity that has involved a much smaller number of high-end offenders. However, there is a small literature on the high end of the drug trade, relying mostly on prison interviews, that has provided some insights (e.g., Reuter and Haaga 1989; Adler 1993; Pearson and Hobbs 2001, 2003). Prison interviews, along with a closer examination of case files, could be helpful in understanding the money-laundering activities of some classes of

---

[88] For some jurisdictions, neither punishment nor firm regulatory monitoring and sanctioning take place.

[89] This is the risk of setting out but not ranking a large number of vulnerabilities to money laundering (U.S. Department of Justice 2006): it seems to make the assumption that all vulnerabilities need to be removed, without undertaking any cost-benefit judgement about them.

offenders. Terrorism finance represents a much greater research challenge since it involves national security considerations that make access to both offenders and files much more limited.

To assess how felons respond to increased regulation and controls requires modeling of counterfactuals. A small literature is starting to emerge on this; for example, de Boyrie, Pak, and Zdanowicz (2001) have shown that Swiss money-laundering controls generated increases in the use of certain trade accounting (underinvoicing of imports, overinvoicing of exports) to conceal the flows of moneys.

Money-laundering controls are now a permanent part of the financial regulatory landscape in Western and most other societies. They impose a new set of obligations on businesses to assist the government in law enforcement and in the reduction of crime. They are worthy of a serious research effort that they have not yet received.

REFERENCES

Abt, Vicki, James F. Smith, and Eugene Martin Christiansen. 1985. *The Business of Risk: Commercial Gambling in Mainstream America*. Lawrence: University of Kansas Press.

Adler, Patricia. 1993. *Wheeling and Dealing*. New York: Columbia University Press.

Alldridge, Peter. 2003. *Money-Laundering Law: A Liberal Critique*. Oxford: Hart.

Andreas, Peter, and Ethan Nadelmann. 2006. *Policing the Globe: Origins and Transformation of International Crime Control*. New York: Oxford University Press.

Association of Certified Fraud Examiners. 2002. "2002 Report to the Nation on Occupational Fraud and Abuse." Austin, TX: Association of Certified Fraud Examiners.

Austrac. 2004. *Annual Report, 2003–4*. http://www.austrac.gov.au/annual_report_2003-04/index.htm.

Blades, Derek, and David Roberts. 2002. *Measuring the Non-observed Economy Statistics*. OECD Brief no. 5. Paris: Organization for Economic Cooperation and Development.

Block, Alan, and Constance Weaver. 2004. *All Is Clouded by Desire*. Westport, CT: Greenwood.

Blum, Jack, Michael Levi, R. Tom Naylor, and Phil Williams. 1998. *Financial Havens, Banking Secrecy, and Money-Laundering*. UNDCP Technical Series, issue 8. New York: United Nations.

Blunden, Brian. 2001. *Money Launderers*. Chalford, Gloucestershire: Management Books.

Board of Governors of the Federal Reserve System. 2002. *Report to Congress in Accordance with §356c of the USA Patriot Act*. Washington, DC: Board of Governors of the Federal Reserve System.

Bourgois, Philip. 1995. *In Search of Respect: Selling Crack in El Barrio*. New York: Cambridge University Press.

Bower, Tom. 1996. *Maxwell: The Final Verdict*. London: HarperCollins.

Braithwaite, John. 1993. "Following the Money Trail to What Destination? An Introduction to the Symposium 1993." *Alabama Law Review* 44:657–68.

Bureau of Justice Statistics. 2003. *Money Laundering Offenders, 1994–2001*. Washington, DC: Bureau of Justice Statistics.

Byrne, John J. 2004. "Improving Financial Oversight: A Private Sector View of Anti–Money Laundering Efforts." Testimony on behalf of the American Bankers Association before the House Financial Services Subcommittee on Oversight and Investigations. May 18. http://financialservices.house.gov/media/pdf/108-87.pdf.

Carlson, Kenneth, Herbert Weisberg, and Naomi Goldstein. 1984. *Unreported Taxable Income from Selected Illegal Activities*. Cambridge, MA: Abt Associates.

Caulkins, Jonathan P. 2001. "Comment on Horowitz 'Should DEA's STRIDE Data Be Used for Economic Analysis of Markets for Illegal Drugs?'" *Journal of the American Statistical Association* 96:1263.

Caulkins, Jonathan P., and Peter Reuter. 1998. "What Can We Learn from Drug Prices?" *Journal of Drug Issues* 28(3):593–612.

Council of Europe. 2006. *Organised Crime Situation Report 2005*. Strasbourg: Council of Europe.

Cuéllar, Mariano-Florentino. 2003. "The Tenuous Relationship between the Fight against Money Laundering and the Disruption of Criminal Finance." *Journal of Criminal Law and Criminology* 93:312–466.

de Boyrie, Maria E., Simon J. Pak,. and John S. Zdanowicz. 2001. "The Impact of Switzerland's Money Laundering Law on Capital Flows through Abnormal Pricing in International Trade." EFMA 2001 Lugano Meetings; CIBER Working Paper. http://papers.ssrn.com/sol3/papers.cfmabstract ?_id=268444.

Economist. 2005. "Financing Terrorism: Looking in the Wrong Places." 377 (October 20): 73–5.

Edwards Report. 1998. *Review of Financial Regulation in the Crown Dependencies*. London: HMSO.

Egmont Group. 2000. *FIUs in Action: 100 Cases from the Egmont Group*. London: Egmont Group.

European Commission. 2003. *Eurobarometer: Public Opinion in the European Union*. Brussels: European Commission.

FATF (Financial Action Task Force). 1998. *1997–1998 Report on Money Laundering Typologies*. Paris: Financial Action Task Force.

———. 2000. *Report on Money Laundering Typologies 1999–2000*. Paris: Financial Action Task Force.

———. 2003. *The Forty Recommendations.* Paris: Financial Action Task Force.

Feige, Edgar L. 1979. "How Big Is the Irregular Economy?" *Challenge* 221: 5–13.

Fields, G., and M. Whitfield. 2001. "Prosecutions Helping Lift the Veil of Secrecy from Offshore Banks." http://www.clevelandtour.com/reyesboard/messages/7.html.

FinCEN (Financial Crimes Enforcement Network). 2002. *Report to Congress: Use of Currency Transaction Reports.* Washington, DC: U.S. Department of the Treasury.

———. 2003. *The SAR Activity Review Report: Tips and Issues.* Bulletin no. 5. Washington, DC: U.S. Department of the Treasury.

———. 2005*a*. *The SAR Activity Review: By the Numbers.* Washington, DC: U.S. Department of the Treasury.

———. 2005*b*. *The SAR Activity Review: Trends, Tips and Issues, #8.* Washington, DC: U.S. Department of the Treasury.

Fleming, Matthew H. 2005. *UK Law Enforcement Agency Use and Management of Suspicious Activity Reports: Towards Determining the Value of the Regime.* http://www.jdi.ucl.ac.uk/downloads/pdf/Fleming_LEA_Use_and_Mgmt_of_SARs_June2005.pdf.

GAO (U.S. General Accounting Office). 1998. *FinCEN's Law Enforcement Support Role Is Evolving.* GAO/GGD 98-117. Washington, DC: U.S. General Accounting Office.

———. 2002. *Money Laundering: Extent of Money Laundering through Credit Cards Is Unknown.* GAO/GGD 02-670. Washington, DC: U.S. General Accounting Office.

Garland, David. 1996. "The Limits of the Sovereign State." *British Journal of Criminology* 36(4):445–71.

Gilmore, William C. 2004. *Dirty Money: The Evolution of Money Laundering Countermeasures.* 3rd ed. Strasbourg, France: Council of Europe.

Gold, Michael, and Michael Levi. 1994. *Money-Laundering in the UK: An Appraisal of Suspicion-Based Reporting.* London: Police Foundation.

Gutmann, Peter M. 1977. "The Subterranean Economy." *Financial Analysts Journal* 34:26–27.

Home Office. 2005. *Sentencing Statistics 2004.* London: Home Office. http://www.homeoffice.gov.uk/rds/pdfs05/hosb1505.pdf.

Hyde, Henry. 1995. *Forfeiting Our Property Rights: Is Your Property Safe from Seizure?* Washington, DC: Cato Institute.

IMF (International Monetary Fund). 2001. *Cyprus: Assessment of the Offshore Financial Sector.* Washington, DC: International Monetary Fund.

———. 2003. *United Kingdom: Financial System Stability Assessment.* Washington, DC: International Monetary Fund.

Jacobs, James B., and Lauryn P. Gouldin. 1999. "Cosa Nostra: The Final Chapter?" In *Crime and Justice,* vol. 25, edited by Michael Tonry. Chicago: University of Chicago Press.

Joseph, Lester M. 2001. "Money Laundering Enforcement: Following the

Money." *Economic Perspectives: An Electronic Journal of the U.S. Department of State*. http://usinfo.state.gov/journals/ites/0501/ijee/justice.htm.

Kaplan, Lawrence J., and Salvatore Matteis. 1968. "The Economics of Loansharking." *American Journal of Economics and Sociology* 27:239–52.

Kochan, Nick. 2005. *The Washing Machine: How Money Laundering and Terrorist Financing Soils Us*. Mason, OH: Thomson Higher Education.

KPMG. 2000. *Review of Financial Regulation in the Overseas Territories*. London: H.M. Stationery Office.

———. 2003. *Money Laundering: Review of the Reporting System*. London: Home Office.

Levi, Michael. 2002. "Suite Justice or Sweet Charity? Some Explorations of Shaming and Incapacitating Business Fraudsters." *Punishment and Society* 42: 147–63.

———. 2006. "Lessons for Countering Terrorist Financing from the War on Serious and Organized Crime." In *Countering the Financing of Global Terrorism*, edited by Thomas Biersteker and Sue Eckert. London: Routledge.

Levi, Michael, and Bill Gilmore. 2002. "Terrorist Finance, Money Laundering and the Rise and Rise of Mutual Evaluation: A New Paradigm for Crime Control?" *European Journal of Law Reform* 4(2):337–64.

Levi, Michael, and Sandra Jones. 1985. "Public and Police Perceptions of Crime Seriousness in England and Wales." *British Journal of Criminology* 25: 234–50.

Levi, Michael, and Mike Maguire. 2004. "Reducing and Preventing Organised Crime: An Evidence-Based Critique." *Crime, Law and Social Change* 41(5): 397–469.

Levi, Michael, Hans Nelen, and Francien Lankhorst. 2005. "Lawyers as Crime Facilitators in Europe: An Introduction and Overview." *Crime, Law and Social Change* 42(2–3):117–21.

Levi, Michael, and Lisa Osofsky. 1995. *Investigating, Seizing, and Confiscating the Proceeds of Crime*. Crime Detection and Prevention Series Paper 61. London: Home Office.

Levi, Michael, and Andrew Pithouse. Forthcoming. *White-Collar Crime and Its Victims*. Oxford: Clarendon.

Levitt, Steven, and Sudhir Alladi Venkatesh. 2000. "An Economic Analysis of a Drug-Selling Gang's Finances." *Quarterly Journal of Economics* 115(3): 755–89.

Levy, Leonard. 1996. *A License to Steal*. Charlotte: University of North Carolina Press.

Lilley, Peter. 2002. *Dirty Dealing: The Untold Truth about Global Money Laundering and International Crime*. London: Kogan Page.

Manski, Charles F., John V. Pepper, and Carol V. Petrie. 2001. *Informing America's Policy on Illegal Drugs: What We Don't Know Keeps Hurting Us*. Washington, DC: National Academy Press.

Mathers, Chris. 2004. *Crime School: Money Laundering: True Crime Meets the World of Business and Finance*. Buffalo, NY: Firefly.

McCulloch, Jude, and Sharon Pickering. 2005. "Suppressing the Financing of

Terrorism: Proliferating State Crime, Eroding Censure and Extending Neo-colonialism." *British Journal of Criminology* 454:470–86.

Middleton, David, and Michael Levi. 2005. "The Role of Solicitors in Facilitating 'Organized Crime': Situational Crime Opportunities and Their Regulation." *Crime, Law and Social Change* 422(2–3):123–61.

Mirus, Rolf, and Roger S. Smith. 1997. "Canada's Underground Economy: Measurement and Implications." In *The Underground Economy: Global Evidence of Its Size and Impact*, edited by Owen Lippert and Michael Walker. Vancouver: Fraser Institute.

Muscato, Frank. 2003. "Testimony before Field Hearing on Organized Retail Theft: Conduit of Money Laundering, House Committee on Government Reform, Subcommittee on Criminal Justice, Drug Policy, and Human Resources." Washington, DC: Congressional Record, 108th Cong., 2nd sess., November 10.

Nadelmann, Ethan. 1993. *Cops across Borders*. State Park: Pennsylvania State University Press.

National Commission on Terrorist Attacks upon the United States. 2004. *9/11 Commission Report*. Washington, DC: Norton.

Naylor, R. Tom. 2002. *Wages of Crime*. Ithaca, NY: Cornell University Press.

NCIS (National Criminal Intelligence Service). 2003. *United Kingdom Threat Assessment of Serious and Organized Crime*. London: National Criminal Intelligence Service.

Nelen, Hans. 2004. "Hit Them Where It Hurts Most? The Proceeds-of-Crime Approach in the Netherlands." *Crime, Law and Social Change* 41: 517–34.

Newsday. 2005. "Israel Discount Bank of New York Settles in Money Laundering Case." December 16. http://www.newsday.com/news/local/wire/newyork/ny-bc-ny--moneylaundering1216dec16,0,1129252.story?coll=ny-region-apnewyor.

New York Times. 2005. "ABN to Pay $80 Million for Violations." December 20, p. C5.

ONDCP (Office of National Drug Control Policy). 2000. *What America's Users Spend on Illicit Drugs, 1988–1998*. Washington, DC: U.S. Government Printing Office.

———. 2001. *What America's Users Spend on Illicit Drugs, 1988–2000*. Washington, DC: U.S. Government Printing Office.

———. 2004. *The Price and Purity of Illicit Drugs: First Quarter 1981 to Second Quarter 2003*. http://www.whitehousedrugpolicy.gov.

O'Reilly, Conor, and Graham Ellison. Forthcoming. "Eye Spy, Private High." *British Journal of Criminology*.

Passas, Nikos. 2005. *IVTS, Terrorism and Money Laundering*. Washington, DC: National Institute of Justice.

Pearson, Geoff, and Dick Hobbs. 2001. *Middle Market Drug Distribution*. Home Office Research Study no. 224. London: Home Office.

———. 2003. "King Pin? A Case Study of a Middle Market Drug Broker." *Howard Journal of Criminal Justice* 42(4):335–47.

Performance and Innovation Unit. 2000. *Recovering the Proceeds of Crime.* London: Cabinet Office.

Pieth, Mark, and Gemma Aiolfi. 2003. "Anti–Money Laundering: Leveling the Playing Field." Manuscript. Basel, Switzerland: Basel Institute of Governance.

President's Commission on Organized Crime. 1987. *The Impact: Organized Crime Today.* Washington, DC: U.S. Government Printing Office.

PriceWaterhouse Coopers. 2003. *Anti–Money Laundering Current Customer Review Cost Benefit Analysis.* London: Financial Services Authority.

Reuter, Peter. 1983. *Disorganized Crime: The Economics of the Visible Hand.* Cambridge, MA: MIT Press.

Reuter, Peter, and John Haaga. 1989. *The Organization of High-Level Drug Markets: An Exploratory Study.* Santa Monica, CA: RAND.

Reuter, Peter, Robert MacCoun, and Patrick Murphy. 1990. *Money from Crime.* Santa Monica, CA: RAND.

Reuter, Peter, and Edwin Truman. 2004. *Chasing Dirty Money: The Fight against Money Laundering.* Washington, DC: Institute for International Economics.

Robinson, Jeffrey. 1996. *The Laundrymen: Inside Money Laundering.* New York: Arcade.

———. 2004. *The Sink: How Banks, Lawyers and Accountants Finance Terrorism and Crime—and Why Governments Can't Stop Them.* London: Constable and Robinson.

Robinson, Phillip. 2005. "Fighting Financial Crime Together." Speech at the Financial Services Authority Financial Crime Conference, London, November 15. http://www.fsa.gov.uk/pages/Library/Communication/Speeches/2005/1115_pr.shtml

Schneider, Friedrich, and Dominik Enste. 2000. "Shadow Economies: Size, Causes, and Consequences." *Journal of Economic Literature* 381:77–114.

Sheptycki, James. 2000. "Policing the Virtual Launderette." In *Issues in Transnational Policing,* edited by James Sheptycki. London: Routledge.

Simon, Carl P., and Ann D. Witte. 1982. *Beating the System: The Underground Economy.* Boston: Auburn House.

Simpson, Sally 2002. *Corporate Crime, Law and Social Control.* Cambridge: Cambridge University Press.

Southwell, David. 2002. *Dirty Cash: Organised Crime in the 21st Century.* London: True Crime.

Stessens, Guy. 2000. *Money Laundering: A New International Law Enforcement Model.* Cambridge: Cambridge University Press.

Suendorf, Ulrike. 2001. *Geldwäsche: Eine Kriminologische Untersuchung.* Neuwied: Luchterhand.

U.S. Department of Justice. 2006. "U.S. Money Laundering Threat Assessment." Press release. http://www.usdoj.gov/dea/pubs/pressrel/011106.pdf.

U.S. Department of State. 2005. *International Narcotics Control Strategy Report INCRS.* Vol. 2. Washington, DC: U.S. Department of State.

U.S. Senate. Minority Staff of the Permanent Subcommittee on Investigations. 2001. "Correspondent Banking: A Gateway for Money Laundering." Feb-

ruary   5.   http://www.senate.gov/~gov_affairs/020501_psi_minority_report
.htm.

———. 2004. *Money Laundering and Foreign Corruption: Enforcement and Effectiveness of the Patriot Act. Case Study Involving Riggs Bank.* Washington, DC: U.S. Department of State.

U.S. Senate. Permanent Subcommittee on Investigations. 2005. *Money Laundering and Foreign Corruption: Enforcement and Effectiveness of the Patriot Act.* Supplemental Staff Report on U.S. Accounts used by Augusto Pinochet. Washington, DC: U.S. Senate

U.S. Treasury. 2002. *The National Money Laundering Strategy NMLS.* Washington, DC: U.S. Department of Treasury.

van Duyne, Petrus C. 2003. "Money Laundering Policy: Fears and Facts." In *Criminal Finance and Organizing Crime in Europe,* edited by Petrus C. van Duyne, Klaus von Lampe, and James L. Newell. Nijmegen, Netherlands: Wolf Legal.

van Duyne, Petrus C., and Michael Levi. 2005. *Drugs and Money: Managing the Drug Trade and Crime-Money in Europe.* Abingdon, U.K.: Routledge.

Villa, John K. 1988. "A Critical View of Bank Secrecy Act Enforcement and the Money Laundering Statutes." *Catholic University Law Review* 37:489–509.

Walker, John. 1999. "How Big Is Global Money Laundering?" *Journal of Money Laundering Control* 3(1):25–37.

Woodiwiss, Michael. 2001. *Organized Crime and American Power.* Toronto: University of Toronto Press.

Woods, Brett F. 1998. *The Art and Science of Money Laundering.* London: Paladin.

Woolner, Ann. 1994. *Washed in Gold: The Story behind the Biggest Money Laundering Investigation in U.S. History.* New York: Simon and Schuster.

World Bank. 2003a. *Reference Guide to Anti–Money Laundering and Combating the Financing of Terrorism.* Washington, DC: World Bank.

———. 2003b. *World Development Indicators.* Washington, DC: World Bank.

———. 2006. *Global Economic Prospects 2006: Economic Implications of Remittances and Migration.* Washington: World Bank.

Daniel Richman

The Past, Present, and Future of Violent Crime Federalism

ABSTRACT

The history of the federal involvement in violent crime frequently is told as one of entrepreneurial or opportunistic action by presidential administrations and Congress. The problem with this story, however, is that it treats state and local governments as objects of federal initiatives, not as independent agents. Appreciating that state and local governments courted and benefited from the federal interest is important for understanding the past two decades, but also for understanding the institutional strains created by the absolute priority the feds have given to counterterrorism since September 11, 2001. Intergovernmental relations are at a crossroads. For two decades, the net costs of the federal interaction with state and local governments on crime have been absorbed nationally, with the benefits felt locally. The federal commitment to terrorism prevention and the roles federal authorities envision for state and local agencies portend a very different dynamic, with reduced federal funding for policing and an inherent tension between domestic intelligence collection and street crime enforcement, particularly in urban areas with a high proportion of immigrants.

It has long been a truism that, in our federal system, episodic violent crime (street crime) is the province of state and local authorities. And usually *local* authorities at that, for very few states have integrated law enforcement hierarchies. State governments provide the preconditions of the system: the penal statutes to be enforced and the prisons to be filled. It is the local police, working with local district attorneys, and county sheriffs, working with county attorneys, who have primary re-

Daniel Richman is professor of law, Fordham University. Portions of this article have been adapted from the author's essay "The Right Fight," which appeared in the December 2004/January 2005 issue of the *Boston Review*.

sponsibility for keeping the streets and roads safe and going after rapists, robbers, and murderers.

This responsibility on the part of states and their instrumentalities has been enshrined in Supreme Court rulings such as *United States v. Morrison* (529 U.S. 598, 618 [2000]), where the Court noted that "we can think of no better example of the police power, which the Founders denied the National Government and reposed in the States, than the suppression of violent crime and vindication of its victims." The point, however, goes far beyond constitutional structure, which has both shaped and been shaped by the expectations of the citizenry. Everybody knows to call the local police when reporting or complaining about violent crime. And those who forget will be reminded by the ever-increasing stream of movies and television programs celebrating the exploits of local police officers and prosecutors.

With this responsibility comes at least the potential for some institutional accountability at the local level (Richman and Stuntz 2005). Not every violent crime is reported to the police, and crime rates are certainly not a simple function of local enforcement efforts. But whether or not a violent crime has occurred is generally undisputable. The conceptual possibility of tracking such crimes, and the nationwide efforts to do so via local and national statistical measures, have put increasing pressure on the police and other local enforcement officials to justify their performance (Stephens 1999).

In contrast, federal law enforcement officials have traditionally faced no such pressure. Few crimes are ineluctably federal. And to the extent that there is a federal "beat," it is one far more elusive than that patrolled by the local cops. Securities frauds, counterfeiting, corruption, tax evasion, or espionage may not even be noticed and, when alleged, may not have even happened. The Federal Bureau of Investigation does yeoman work coordinating the Uniform Crime Reporting (UCR) system. It does not, however, offer any measure of the "federal crime" rate, and few would expect it do so.

One might expect a system that lacks performance measures to revel in its unaccountability and its ability to focus on better-dressed offenders. But like a moth to a flame, the feds have been drawn to street crime (particularly of the urban variety). The operating assumption seemed to be that what citizens can feel and count they will vote on. And so, at least since the 1960s, the UCR crime rate has been a focus of legislative and executive action at the federal level. The drop in the

violent crime rate that began in 1991–92 (FBI 2004*a*) made little difference, and the federal commitment persisted, even intensified (Russell-Einhorn, Ward, and Sheeherman 2000, p. i).

The history of the federal involvement in street crimes has frequently been told as one of entrepreneurial or opportunistic action by
presidential administrations and Congress (Marion 1994; Brickey 1995;
Gest 2001, pp. 63–81). In quest of the political gains to be garnered
by declaring war on "real" crime—the kind that voters actually fear—
federal officials strategically reached into what had always been the
province of state and local authorities. Passing laws meant to be enforced only infrequently, and cherry-picking only the best cases, these
legislative and executive officials, the critique goes, have shown far
more interest in reelection than any rational program of crime reduction (Baker 1999, p. 679).

There is some truth in this. The problem with this story, however,
is that it treats state and local governments as objects of federal initiatives, not as independent agents. This they certainly were not. The
history is not one of intrusion but of codependence. Appreciating the
extent to which state, and particularly local, governments courted and
benefited from federal activity in the violent crime area is important
not just for understanding the past two decades, but also for understanding the institutional strains created by the absolute priority the
feds have given to counterterrorism since the September 11, 2001,
terrorist attacks.

The goal of this essay, which draws on the deft exploration by William Geller and Norval Morris (1992) of the federal-local dynamic, is
to draw on the history of federal, state, and local relations in the law
enforcement sphere as a means of understanding present intergovernmental tensions and considering how those tensions might be resolved.
For most of the twentieth century, the principal role that federal officials envisioned state and local agencies playing in the violent crime
area was that of beneficiary. Sometimes the largesse took the form of
cash. Sometimes it came in kind, through the commitment of federal
enforcement assets such as agents, prosecutors, and judges. This be-
neficence may have been politically motivated and have even occasionally been unwelcome. But the limited federal ambitions and the virtual
monopoly over local knowledge maintained by local police departments ensured that the costs of federal encroachment were small and
the gains to state and local governments substantial.

Since the September 11 attacks, the federal government has been giving less and asking more. Although it is too soon to tell, federal counterterrorism efforts themselves may well be drawing on funds and resources that used to aid local crime-fighting programs. Certainly many localities see it that way. More important, federal counterterrorism efforts threaten to place demands on local police departments that are extraneous to and even inconsistent with their crime-fighting mission. At the heart of advances in policing theory and practice over the past decades has been a recognition that policing will be neither effective nor politically viable without the cultivation of relationships with communities—and especially minority communities. And many local departments have become concerned about the toll that cooperation with federal efforts will place on these relationships.

How these tensions will be resolved remains to be seen, and perhaps they will not be resolved any time soon. It is equally possible that every jurisdiction will arrive at its own peculiar modus vivendi with the federal government. Yet in the desire of the federal government to create an integrated domestic intelligence network lies the seeds of a new, normatively appealing relationship between the feds and state and local governments—one in which the political accountability that comes with local crime fighting becomes a characteristic of the entire network.

What materials does this essay draw on? The legal literature has certainly given considerable (and usually critical) attention to the federal government's movement into the violent crime area over the course of the twentieth century. Yet the attention has generally been restricted to the politics behind the movement and the constitutional issues raised by this extension of federal power into the traditional province of state and local governments. Some scholars with more institutional concerns, such as Geller and Morris and more recently Miller and Eisenstein (2005), have gone beyond the standard speeches, statutes, and judicial decisions, to look at how the feds actually interacted with state and local authorities; but recourse to the broader political science literature and to government and government-sponsored reports is needed for a fuller picture on this score. Some such reports, such as that prepared by Malcolm Russell-Einhorn, Shawn Ward, and Amy Seeherman in 2000, and many by the Government Accountability (formerly General Accounting) Office, are particularly helpful for peering inside agencies and police departments.

The federalization literature rarely intersects with the policing literature, a vast and deep body of scholarship that considers how the local police interact with the communities they protect, how this interaction promotes effective policing, and how one measures police performance. It must, however, if one seeks to understand how the new counterterrorism efforts have strained relations between the feds and local police departments. And to place these counterterrorism efforts in historical context, one also needs to consult the literature on past domestic intelligence programs, and particularly on federal efforts to develop and direct local intelligence capabilities.

One of the challenges, and rewards, of writing a history of the present is watching the story develop and change with daily news accounts. Distinguishing structural change from noise can be quite difficult, especially when one looks from outside at a complex negotiation. When Portland, Oregon, withdraws its police department from the federal Joint Terrorism Task Force, should the move be read as an announcement of local priorities or the opening bid in a bargaining process? Or both? When the FBI promises an unprecedented degree of information sharing with state and local authorities, is it simply pacifying congressional critics? Trying to persuade those authorities to increase a flow that still pretty much goes one way? Or actually moving toward a system that will give state and local officials information that they can use both to secure their communities against terrorism and to fight regular crime? It is too soon to tell. Yet beneath the headlines, the complaints, and the posturing, a new institutional dynamic is emerging in the law enforcement sphere, as intergovernmental relations centered on violent crime are challenged and transformed to meet new threats.

While it is hard for scholars to pin down the underlying realities of a fast-evolving situation, there are some compensating factors with respect to sources. The official actors in this process are well aware of the transformations their world is undergoing and have engaged in wide-ranging conversations about these transformations among themselves and with the legislative and executive authorities that have monitored developments. While the reports, roundtables, legislative advocacy pieces, program guides, and other such publicly available documents sometime need to be read with a grain of salt, they provide valuable windows into the changing world.

Section I of this essay traces the history of the federal government's involvement in violent crime from the founding but gives particular attention to the intensification of this involvement after 1964. Beyond noting the statutory and programmatic milestones of this history, this section examines the allure of violent crime federalism to (almost) all the institutional entities affected by the influx of federal dollars and enforcement personnel into an area traditionally reserved for state and local activity. Section II tells how the attacks of September 11 challenged and disrupted this system of federal, state, and local interaction, with the federal government reconfiguring both its enforcement and funding priorities and placing new demands on its state and local partners. Section III attempts to predict the longer-term effects of the changed federal priorities. It also highlights the normatively appealing aspects of the domestic intelligence network that is being cobbled together from institutions whose previous interactions were centered on violent crime, not terrorism.

I. Federal Involvement in Violent Crime

To the extent that "violent crime" is understood as simply referring to crime that involves violence, the federal government has never been *un*involved in violent crime. From the earliest days of the republic, even the most minimalist visions of federal law enforcement power have included some violent offenses, such as attacks on federal officials. When used (as it is here) to refer to the murders, robberies, and rapes of ordinary citizens, however, the term defines an enforcement sphere that the federal government had little to do with for over a century (except within federal enclaves). Indeed, it was not until 1964 that such street crimes became the subject of sustained federal policy making. Thereafter, however, federal movement into this area quickly went from a trot to a gallop, with each new administration or congress trying to outdo its predecessor in passing new statutes and committing funds and enforcement resources to the War on Crime.

A. A Whirlwind Tour of Federal Involvement in Violent Crime before 1964

The framers of the Constitution did not envision that the federal government would play much of a role in criminal enforcement. To the extent that they contemplated substantive federal criminal law at all, their discussions centered only on piracy, crimes against the law of nations, treason, and counterfeiting (Kurland 1996, pp. 25–26). The document they produced made no effort to give the federal government general police powers of the sort states exercised. The only circumstance the Constitution explicitly envisioned as justifying federal measures against "domestic violence" was when a state certified that federal help was needed (U.S. Constitution, art. IV, sec. 4; Bybee 1997). Otherwise, the only criminal justice interests that government would have were those relating to the powers specifically delegated to it. While the Bill of Rights gave considerable attention to the procedural safeguards that would apply in federal prosecutions, the range of prosecutions envisioned was thus quite small. And few were brought. Between 1789 and 1801, by one count, only 426 criminal cases were brought in federal courts, a great many of which related to the Whiskey Rebellion (Henderson 1985, p. 13; Kurland 1996, p. 59 n. 209).

In its early years, Congress was not even quick to address violent crime in those areas in which it could have used its delegated powers. In 1818, presented with a case in which a marine had murdered a cook's mate while on board the *U.S.S. Independence*, anchored in Boston Harbor, the Supreme Court threw out the conviction (*United States v. Bevans*, 16 U.S. [3 Wheat.] 336 [1818]). Writing for the Court, Chief Justice John Marshall explained that while Congress could have passed a murder statute covering federal warships, it had not, and the matter was left to Massachusetts's exclusive jurisdiction. Indeed, exclusive state jurisdiction over putatively criminal offenses was very much the rule during most of the nineteenth century. Congress took care to target activity that injured or interfered with the federal government itself, its property, or its programs. But "except in those areas where federal jurisdiction was exclusive—the District of Columbia and the federal territories—federal law did not reach crimes against individuals." These "were the exclusive concern of the states" (Beale 1996, p. 40).

By the end of the nineteenth century, Congress had begun to look somewhat beyond direct federal interests to the general welfare of citizens, passing civil rights statutes as part of Reconstruction and exercising its postal powers to address crimes committed through the mails. Yet, save in extraordinary situations in which violence threatened these still relatively narrow interests—as occurred when the protection of the mails was asserted as a basis for federal intervention in turn-of-the-century labor wars—the feds left the arrest of violent bad guys to the states, at least where there were well-developed state governments (Brickey 1995, pp. 1138–41; Richman 2000, pp. 83–84). In the territories, of course, U.S. marshals and their deputies played their now-storied role as keepers of the peace (Traub 1988; Calhoun 1990).

An effect, and a cause, of their limited role was that there were not very many feds during this period. Agents of the postal service protected the mails (Millspaugh 1937, pp. 62–64); U.S. marshals protected judges and performed sundry other duties (Millspaugh 1937, p. 74; Calhoun 1990); Treasury personnel fought smuggling (Millspaugh 1937, pp. 64–68); and after its creation in 1865, the Secret Service targeted counterfeiting (Ansley 1956; Geller and Morris 1992, pp. 241–42; Richman 2002, p. 700). But the federal enforcement establishment was remarkably small. The office of the Attorney General dates back to the founding, but there was no Justice Department until 1870. Until then, the U.S. attorneys brought prosecutions in their respective federal districts, but with little national coordination and with little control over how federal law enforcement personnel were deployed. Even after its creation, the Justice Department had scant resources and had to rely on Treasury's Secret Service agents or Pinkerton Detective Agency operatives for investigative support (Cummings and McFarland 1937, p. 373; Theoharis 1999, pp. 2–3; Powers 2004, pp. 42–61).

In the early part of the twentieth century, Congress's readiness to enlist federal criminal law in the service of national moral crusades—such as those against "white slavery," narcotic drugs, and, in time, alcohol—and its concerns about the challenges that Americans' increased mobility posed to local enforcement efforts (Brickey 1995, p. 1141) led to a substantial extension of federal criminal jurisdiction. The constitutional vehicle of choice for these enactments was the Commerce Clause, and, at least initially, legislators generally paid careful attention to the nexus between interstate commerce and the targeted criminal activity. In 1910, the White Slave Traffic Act (also known as the Mann Act) (ch. 395, 36 Stat. 825) prohibited the transportation of a woman over state lines "for the purpose of prostitution or debauchery, or any other immoral purpose." In 1914, the Harrison Narcotic Drug Act (ch. 1, 38 Stat. 785) established a comprehensive regulatory scheme for narcotic drugs, backed with criminal sanctions. In 1919, the National Motor Vehicle Theft Act (also known as the Dyer Act) (ch. 89, 41 Stat. 324) made it a federal offense to transport a stolen motor vehicle across state lines, and the Volstead Act (National Prohibition Act) (ch. 85, 41 Stat. 305) sent federal agents against bootleggers and moonshiners.

While these enactments, and the agents deployed to enforce them, targeted many of the same bad actors who had hitherto fallen within the exclusive remit of local authorities, the specialized nature of the federal beat, the small size of the federal apparatus, and the alacrity with which locals left morals enforcement (particularly prohibition cases) to the feds kept the friction down (Hoover 1933; Boudin 1943, pp. 261, 273–74; Langum 1994).

The Supreme Court generally accepted these extensions of Commerce Clause authority. Presented with a challenge to the constitutionality of the Mann Act, the Court found no relevant distinction between the long-established ability of the federal government to control the movement of goods over state lines and the ability of the federal government to address criminal conduct that had an interstate dimension. In *Hoke v. United States* (227 U.S. 308 [1913]) the Court noted that "surely if the facility of interstate transportation can be taken away from the demoralization of lotteries, the debasement of obscene literature, the contagion of diseased cattle or persons, the impurity of food and drugs, the like facility can be taken away from the systematic enticement to and the enslavement in prostitution and debauchery of women, and, more insistently, of girls" (Fellman 1945, p. 21; Abrams and Beale 2000, p. 21). This was a critical analytical move. In an age in which railroads and cars were becoming standard tools of ordinary criminal activity, and indeed of ordinary life, such a reading of the Commerce Clause would in time make the limits of federal criminal enforcement more a matter of legislative policy than of constitutional law.

A snapshot of federal enforcement in 1930 is helpful. Of the 87,305 total federal prosecutions in 1930, about 57,000 were for prohibition violations, 8,000 were District of Columbia cases, 7,000 were immigration cases, and 3,500 were drug cases (Rubin 1934). Of the 4,345 convictions obtained in cases investigated by the 400 agents of the Bureau of Investigation in 1930, 2,452 were for violations of the National Motor Theft Act, and 516 were for White Slave Traffic Act (Mann Act) prosecutions (*Annual Report of the Attorney General* 1930, pp. 80–81; Theoharis 1999, p. 4). The real federal activity in the violent crime area that year came in the provision of infrastructure to local authorities. Just months after creating the UCR system as a way of preventing newspapers from "manufacturing 'crime waves' out of thin air," the International Association of Chiefs of Police (IACP) handed it over to be administered by the Bureau of Investigation (Geller and Morris 1992, p. 283; Rosen 1995; Maltz 1999, p. 4). The bureau's chief, J. Edgar Hoover, was quite aware of the limitations of a system that relied on self-reporting. But any supervision, he maintained, would have to come from the IACP, not his or any other federal agency (Hoover 1932, p. 451). The bureau's Identification Division, also established under the "auspices" of the IACP as a clearinghouse for fingerprint and other such data, also took care to play only a supporting role (Hoover 1932, p. 442; Theoharis 1999, p. 12).

In 1930, even as violent gangs were garnering national attention, Attorney General Mitchell was able to say that "dealing with organized crime" was "largely a local problem." "The fact that these criminal gangs incidentally violate some federal statute," he noted, "does not place the primary duty and responsibility of punishing them upon the Federal Government, and until state police and magistrates, stimulated by public opinion, take hold of this problem, it will not be solved" (Cummings and McFarland 1937, p. 478). When defending the targeting of Al Capone (in which he played a significant role), President Herbert Hoover explained on November 25, 1930, that "the Federal Government is assisting local authorities to overcome the hideous gangster and corrupt control of some local governments. But I get no satisfaction from the reflection that the only way this can be done is for the Federal Government to convict men for failing to pay income taxes on the financial product of crime against State laws. What we need is an awakening to the failure of local government to protect its citizens from murder, racketeering, corruption, and a host of other crimes" (Calder 1993, p. 144).

Then came the kidnapping of Charles Lindbergh's son in March 1932, which one newspaper called "a challenge to the whole order of the nation" (Powers 1987, p. 175). Moving gingerly into this new area, President Hoover asked Director Hoover to coordinate federal assistance, but his administration stressed that "it was not in favor of using the case as an excuse for extending Federal authority in the area of law enforcement" (Calder 1993, p. 201). National interest in the case must have been hard to bear, however, for in May 1932, a week after the baby's body was found, Congress passed a federal kidnapping statute, invoking its power under the Commerce Clause (Potter 1998, p. 112). Attorney General Mitchell complained to the president: "If this law had been on the statute books at the time the Lindbergh case arose, there would have been an outcry demanding that the federal government take hold of the case; the local police authorities would have relaxed their activities and been glad to dump the responsibilities on the federal government; we would have spent thousands of dollars with no better results than the state authorities obtained, only to find out at the end that no federal crime had been committed as there had been no interstate transportation" (Cummings and McFarland 1937, p. 479). But the attorney general still recommended that the president not go so far as to veto the bill. And it became law (Cummings and McFarland 1937, p. 479; Calder 1993, p. 203).

The kidnapping statute was just the beginning of what soon became a wave of congressional enactments targeting criminal behavior that had hitherto been the exclusive province of state and local enforcers. As the foreword to a fascinating issue of *Law and Contemporary Problems* devoted to the new federal legislation noted in October 1934:

> So dramatic have been the recent depredations of organized criminal bands, enabled by modern methods of transportation to operate over wide territories, that action has been relatively prompt in forthcoming. The aid of the federal government has first been besought—in part because with respect to certain offenses it alone is competent to act, in part because appeal to Washington affords an outlet for the urge for action without requiring a painstaking—and politically painful—reorganization of state and local law enforcing agencies. (P. 399)

The charge was led by the new president, Franklin Roosevelt, who in his January 3, 1934, address to Congress put crime high on his administration's legislative agenda (O'Reilly 1982, p. 642). "In the short term," Bryan Burrough has noted, this War on Crime "served as powerful evidence of the effectiveness of the Roosevelt administration's New Deal policies, boosting faith in the very idea of an activist central government. On a broader scale, it reassured a demoralized population that American values could overcome anything, even the Depression" (2004, p. 544).

Congress immediately responded, and within six months, 105 crime bills had been introduced (Richman 2000, p. 87). Many passed, including the National Stolen Property Act (ch. 333, 48 Stat. 794) (barring the transportation of stolen property in interstate commerce), the National Firearms Act (ch. 757, 48 Stat. 1236), the Fugitive Felon Act (ch. 302, 48 stat. 782) (prohibiting interstate flight to avoid prosecution for violent felonies), and the Federal Bank Robbery Act (ch. 304, 48 Stat. 783) (Brickey 1995, pp. 1143–44). That same year, Congress also passed the Anti-Racketeering Act of 1934 (ch. 569, 48 Stat. 979), which was intended to allow federal prosecution of the urban gangsters thought to be flourishing around the country but was written to cover a broad range of robberies and extortions.

Under Director Hoover's savvy leadership, the FBI rode the crest of this legislative wave—and of the perceived "crime wave" that occasioned it—to fame and fortune. Its agents "acquired the popular identity of the G-man: the highly professional and apolitical hero who 'always got his man'" (Theoharis 1999, p. 13; see also Potter 1998; Burrough 2004). Yet while the number of these agents more than doubled, from 388 in 1932 to 713 in 1939 (Theoharis 1999, p. 13), the bureau's "war against the underworld" (Whitehead 1956, p. 103) was quite limited, and indeed was intended to be so: The idea was to go only after those roving gangsters who had proved too big for local enforcement, particularly those whose apprehension made (or could be turned into) headlines. State and local officials may have chafed at a justification for federal activity based on their own inadequacies and at grandstanding by their federal counterparts. But they likely saw Hoover more as an entrepreneur creating a new market than as a source of real competition. After all, while the bureau was not above encouraging local police officers (with monetary rewards) to pass information to it about matters of federal interest (Potter 1998, p. 194), the fact was (and continues to be) that the feds could not venture far into local domains without the cooperation of the local enforcement hierarchy. One study in 1945 could observe, perhaps a bit optimistically, that "the police agencies of the central government lean strongly in the direction of cooperation with state and local officials, and in doing so have done much to underscore the possibilities of a cooperative federalism in this country" (Fellman 1945, p. 24). Moreover, the federal law enforcement remained quite small, its numbers in 1936 (excluding the Coast Guard) amounting to about 4 percent of the nation's total police census (Millspaugh 1937, p. 283).

Local authorities got additional assurance from Hoover's oft-repeated opposition to a national police force (Ungar 1976, p. 79; Keller 1989, p. 93)—an opposition born as much from politick modesty as from fear that any move in that direction would impose onerous new responsibilities on his agency. In 1954, Hoover celebrated his restraint in this regard:

> I am unalterably opposed to a national police force. I have consistently opposed any plan leading to a consolidation of police power, regardless of the source from which it originated. I shall continue to do so, for the following reasons . . .:
>
> 1. Centralization of police power represents a distinct danger to democratic self-government.
> 2. Proposals to centralize law enforcement tend to assume that either the state or federal government can and should do for each community what the people of that city or county will not do for themselves.
> 3. The authority of every peace officer in every community would be reduced, if not eventually broken, in favor of a dominating figure or group on the distant state or national level. (1954, p. 40)

Having increased precipitously in the 1930s, the federal role in prosecuting violent crime (organized or other) held steady in the 1940s and 1950s, in large part because "the overwhelming primacy of internal security and counterintelligence matters diverted FBI resources" (Theoharis 1999, p. 35). While it jumped from just over 13,000 inmates in 1930 (when the Federal Bureau of Prisons was created) to 24,360 inmates in 1940, the federal prison population thereafter "did not change significantly between 1940 and 1980 (when the population was 24,252)" (Federal Bureau of Prisons 2001, p. 3). And for a while, "the crime issue largely disappeared from national politics" (Beckett 1997, p. 30).

A conference on organized crime convened by Attorney General J. Howard McGrath in 1950 and the hearings of the Senate Investigating Committee headed by Estes Kefauver in the early 1950s marked the new (or renewed) interest of federal executive and legislative officials in "organized crime"—usually defined in contrast to ordinary crime but with a vagueness allowing considerable overlap. The flames were fanned by hearings that the Senate Select Committee on Improper Activities in the Labor and Management Field, headed by John McClellan (with special counsel Robert Kennedy), held in 1958 and 1959 (Miller 1963, p. 96; Marion 1994, p. 28). These efforts, coupled with the 1957 discovery, by local police, of the high-level mob meeting in Appalachin, New York, put organized crime at the top of the Kennedy administration's (and Attorney General Robert Kennedy's) criminal justice agenda. The only sustained efforts the Kennedy administration made to combat violent crime of the less organized (and more prevalent) variety, however, were directed at preventing and controlling juvenile delinquency (Feeley and Sarat 1980, pp. 39–40; Marion 1994, pp. 28). And even its ambitions in the organized crime area were limited. The head of the Kennedy Justice Department's Criminal Division noted that "optimistically viewed . . . , the federal effort against organized crime is not merely a stopgap remedy for ineffective local law enforcement but can serve as a catalyst in activating local officials and encouraging them to do their share in eliminating this menace to our national institutions" (Miller 1963, p. 103).

B. 1964–1980s: The New Federal Funding Role

Barry Goldwater's acceptance speech at the 1964 Republican convention ushered in a new era of federal interest in violent crime. Attributing the recent rise in crime rates to Democratic administrations, Goldwater made the "violence in our streets" a focus of his presidential campaign (Marion 1994, p. 39; Beckett 1997, p. 31). Goldwater lost big to incumbent Lyndon Johnson, but Johnson noted how much mileage Goldwater had gotten out of the issue and soon made crime a priority in his new administration. One response was the traditional blue-ribbon commission—the President's Commission on Law Enforcement and the Administration of Justice (President's Commission on Law Enforcement 1967). Another was the passage of the Law Enforcement Assistance Act of 1965 and the establishment, under its terms, of the Office of Law Enforcement Assistance to fund state and local anticrime projects. Having "anointed himself Washington's main conduit to local police chiefs," the FBI's Hoover looked askance at the office's efforts, however small, to reach out to local authorities. But members of Congress saw the benefit of a program that allowed them to steer federal money to their constituencies (Gest 2001, pp. 18–19). As Malcolm Feeley and Austin Sarat's study of federal crime policy in 1968–78 explains, the Office of Law Enforcement Assistance "legitimized the view that the federal government should provide financial assistance to state and local law enforcement" (Feeley and Sarat 1980, p. 36). And thereafter, the President's Commission "proposed that the federal government become an active partner in combating crime at the state and local levels" (pp. 36–38).

In 1967, anticipating (quite correctly) that street crime would be a critical issue in the 1968 election, the Johnson administration sought to create a larger-scale grants program, to be run out of the Office of Law Enforcement Assistance. As originally envisioned, the program was to involve direct grants-in-aid to local governments—a form of assistance often used in Great Society programs. "Since crime was perceived as essentially a local and not a state problem, the Administration reasoned that federal assistance should go directly to those units of local government most in need of it" (Feeley and Sarat 1980, p. 41). It was probably not a coincidence that the nation's large urban centers—which would be the biggest aid recipients in this scheme—had given Johnson their overwhelming support in 1964, according to Feeley and Sarat. Local leaders, of course, embraced this proposal. As Charles Rogovin (the administrator of the Law Enforcement Assistance Administration [LEAA] from 1969 to 1970) explained, "Anticrime performance was seen by local officials as an increasingly important factor for attracting voters, and new Federal money with local autonomy could be important in shaping positive political images. Most local officials were also concerned about the prospect of a state government awakened or stimulated to take an increased role in crime control and criminal justice activity through the availability of new Federal money" (1973, p. 11).

The administration's proposal ran into stiff opposition in Congress, however. There, hostility to the idea of a new federal bureaucracy administering direct categorical grants—particularly a bureaucracy headed by an attorney general, Ramsey Clark, perceived by many as overly liberal—combined with enthusiasm for New Federalism, which celebrated states as the primary governmental level for addressing social ills, led to the radical reconfiguration of the program into one of block grants to the states (Feeley and Sarat 1980, pp. 42–46; Cronin, Cronin, and Milakovich 1981, pp. 50–53). This block grant program, enacted as part of the Omnibus Crime Control and Safe Streets Act of 1968 (82 Stat. 197), was to be administered by the new LEAA, also created by the act. Distrust of centralized power generally, and of Attorney General Clark specifically, ran so deep that Congress put a "troika" of three directors in charge of the new agency (Rogovin 1973, pp. 12–13).

Without adequate means to target and monitor expenditures, the new, toothless agency became not a force for crime policy innovation but simply a way of increasing funding to the status quo (Varon 1975). For all the rhetoric of planning and coordination that surrounded the program, the federal government's principal role was simply to write checks (DiIulio, Smith, and Saiger 1995, p. 454).

The LEAA story is usually told as one of policy failure. That it was, from the perspective of those looking for improved crime policies and reduced crime rates (Navasky 1976; Feeley and Sarat 1980, pp. 144–48; Diegelman 1982; DiIuilio, Smith, and Saiger 1995, p. 455). But from the perspective of state and local enforcement agencies eager for federal dollars without federal mandates, the LEAA was a success that only improved with time. Its budget kept increasing, at least until 1977. And the bureaucratic steps that stood between agencies, particularly large police forces, and their money were only reduced over time (Diegelman 1982, pp. 998–99). "Despite the fact that the Safe Streets grant programs were charged with inefficiency, mismanagement, and ineffectiveness, despite the fact that they had not been shown to reduce crime, LEAA monies had become an accepted part of budgets of countless police chiefs, mayors, and governors, who now felt entitled to these funds" (Cronin, Cronin, and Milakovich 1981, pp. 107–8).

The LEAA soon fell out of favor in Washington, attacked by Jimmy Carter for wasting money, and finally phased out by Ronald Reagan in 1982. Reagan's 1983 budget message to Congress noted that "public safety is primarily a state and local responsibility. This administration does not believe that providing criminal assistance in the form of grants or contracts is an appropriate use of federal funds" (DiIulio, Smith, and Saiger 1995, p. 455). Under his administration, "LEAA was declared a failure, its name changed, its authorization narrowed, its appropriations slashed, and its bureaucratic status reduced—the public equivalent of a corporate bankruptcy" (Heymann and Moore 1996, p. 107). Before its demise, the LEAA had spent $8 billion on state and local crime control (McDonald et al. 1999, p. 12). Justice Department components such as the National Institute of Justice, the Bureau of Justice Statistics, and the Office of Justice Assistance, Research, and Statistics—all created in 1979 by the Justice System Improvement Act (93 Stat. 1167)—continued to provide federal support (Diegelman 1982, pp. 999–1000). But the days of large-scale federal funding seemed to be over (Congressional Budget Office 1996, p. 10).

C. 1980s and 1990s—New Operational Role and Continued Funding

Yet President Reagan certaintly did not preside over the withdrawal of the federal government from the war on crime. It would have been hard to do so in 1980, when the homicide rate—10.2 per 100,000—was the highest ever recorded in the UCR system (Fox and Zawitz 2002). During his presidential campaign, he "paid particular attention to the problem of street crime and promised to enhance the federal government's role in combating it" (Beckett 1997, p. 44). Moreover, his administration's readiness to give federal agencies a direct operational role in the area suggested that its opposition to the LEAA had more to do with fiscal policy than federalism concerns.

The idea of federal enforcement agencies playing a direct role in combating local violent crime was hardly uncontroversial. Among the many rocks that caused the massive effort to reform the federal criminal code to founder in the early 1970s was opposition from those who thought it "portended the creation of a vast 'federal police'" (Schwartz 1977, p. 10). Such critics saw in the proposals of the National Commission on Reform of Federal Criminal Laws (known as the Brown Commission, after its chairman, Governor Edmund G. Brown of California) "the wholesale destruction of state responsibility and state autonomy in the preservation of public order and the administration of criminal law" (p. 10 n. 32). Even FBI Director William Webster opined in 1980 that fighting street crime "is not our role, it's not our responsibility" (Beckett 1997, p. 52). Yet the idea received powerful support in the 1981 report of the Task Force on Violent Crime created by Reagan's Attorney General, William French Smith, and chaired by former Attorney General Griffen Bell and Governor James R. Thompson of Illinois. That report called for all available enforcement tools to be deployed against violent crime, particularly against urban youth gangs, and called for the increased use of federal firearms prosecutors against violent offenders (Attorney General's Task Force 1981; Specter and Michel 1982, pp. 65–66).

The primary vehicle for this new federal operational role, at least initially, was the enforcement of the federal narcotics laws. Explaining why his agency needed to "assume a larger role" in the area, FBI Director William Webster—whose volte face on this score was "encourag[ed]" by White House Counselor Edwin Meese (Beckett 1997, p. 53)—declared in 1981 that "when we attack the drug problem head on, . . . we are going to make a major dent in attacking violent street crime" (p. 52). Reflecting this priority, the administration sought and obtained massive increases in funding for the FBI's drug enforcement work and for that of the Drug Enforcement Administration (DEA). J. Edgar Hoover had tried hard to keep the FBI out of the drug enforcement business, for fear of the corrupting influence the work would have on his agents (Theoharis 1999, p. 189). Now the bureau would join the DEA in the fray. And their focus would not be limited to those drug offenders against whom federal enforcement offered a "comparative advantage," such as international traffickers and those involved in multistate operations (Zimring and Hawkins 1992, p. 162). The readiness to target street dealers was in part an inevitable product of investigative tactics that worked up from the most readily arrested offenders, and in part, perhaps, of an also inevitable tendency of all enforcers to go after the most accessible targets (Stuntz 1998). But it also reflected the degree to which drug enforcement priorities intersected with the federal interest in street violence.

Many of the criminal statutes needed to support this new federal operational role were already on the books by 1980: drug trafficking offenses, gun offenses—particularly the statute making it a federal offense for a convicted felon to possess a firearm (18 U.S.C. sec. 922(g))—even racketeering laws such as the Racketeer Influenced and Corrupt Organization (RICO) statute (18 U.S.C. secs. 1961–68), which had been enacted in 1970 (84 Stat. 941). In any event, more were soon passed by legislators eager to show their commitment to the Wars on Crime and Drugs. The primary effect of this legislation, in the drug and violent crime area at least, was to increase the sentences of offenses already covered by federal law (Brickey 1995, p. 1145; Richman 2000). The Comprehensive Crime Control Act of 1984 (98 Stat. 1837) overhauled the federal sentencing system and established a commission to promulgate sentencing guidelines. It also beefed up the RICO forfeiture provisions, increased the penalties for large-scale drug offenses, and established mandatory minimum sentences for the use of a gun during a crime of violence and a fifteen-year mandatory minimum for "armed career criminals." The Firearm Owners' Protection Act of 1986 (100 Stat. 449) extended the mandatory five-year sentence for the use of a gun to uses in the course of narcotics offenses. The Anti–Drug Abuse Act of 1986 (100 Stat. 3207), among other things, established a new regime of nonparolable, mandatory minimum sentences for drug-trafficking offenses that tied the minimum penalty to the amount of drugs involved in the offense (U.S. Sentencing Commission 1991, p. 9). The Anti–Drug Abuse Act of 1988 (102 Stat. 4181) added more mandatory minimums. Both the 1986 and 1988 acts gave special attention to crack cocaine, which was thought to be responsible for increased violent crime rates. The Comprehensive Crime Control Act of 1990 (104 Stat. 4789) also increased drug penalties. And the Violent Crime Control and Law Enforcement Act of 1994 (108 Stat. 1796) increased the number of federal crimes punishable by death, enacted a "three strikes" provision that required life imprisonment for violent three-time federal offenders, and permitted the prosecution as adults of juvenile offenders (thirteen and older) who committed federal crimes of violence or federal crimes involving a firearm (O'Bryant 2003, pp. 3–4).

To this challenge to traditional notions of distinct federal and state enforcement spheres, the Supreme Court's reaction was primarily one of acquiescence. In cases such as *United States v. Culbert* (435 U.S. 371 [1978]), the Court made clear that the fact that criminal activity—in this case an extortion attempt—was also punishable under state law was of no concern, as long as there was some (often quite slim) connection to "commerce" and particularly where Congress intended such a change in the traditional federal-state balance. Indeed, the limits that the Supreme Court put on the expansion of federal criminal jurisdiction during this period tended to be more of form than substance. Interpreting 1968 legislation that made it illegal for a convicted felon to possess a firearm, the Court read in an element that required prosecutors to prove "some interstate commerce nexus" (*United States v. Bass*, 404 U.S. 336 [1971]). But in a subsequent case the Court soon made clear that all that prosecutors need show was that the firearm had *at some time* traveled in commerce—something that could be easily shown for just about any gun (*Scarborough v. United States*, 431 U.S. 563, 575 [1977]; Richman 2000, p. 89).

The existence of federal jurisdiction over a great deal of regular local crime (or at least, through the use of the gun statutes, over regular local criminals) was already clear. What really changed in the 1980s, however, was the readiness of the federal government to exercise its broad jurisdiction under these statutes, to commit investigative and adjudication resources to street crime, and to pay for the incarceration of convicted offenders. It is hard to quantify the degree to which federal enforcers in the 1980s moved into what hitherto had been local cases. The number of drug cases certainly climbed, with the number of suspects prosecuted in federal court for drug offenses going from 9,906 in 1982 to 25,094 in 1990 (Bureau of Justice Statistics 1996, p. 2); but that number includes both higher- and lower-level trafficking offenses. And while federal weapons charges can be used against street criminals, the large number of federal weapons prosecutions brought during this period—which went from 1,970 in 1982 to 12,168 in 1990 (Bureau of Justice Statistics 1996, p. 2)—could have had other targets as well. After all, even an enforcement strategy targeting only organized crime or large-scale narcotics enterprises would involve the use of weapons or low-level drug charges as a means of gaining information or pleading out cases. By the 1990s, however, efforts by both the Bush (I) and Clinton administrations to raise the visibility of federal enforcement operations against street criminals made the extent of federal activity quite clear. One compelling political reason to raise this visibility was that the homicide rate, which had somewhat dropped since 1980—down to 7.9 in 1985—had started climbing again, going back up, to 9.8 in 1991 (Fox and Zawitz 2002).

The nouns fly fast and furious here. Project Triggerlock, announced in 1991 by Attorney General Thornburgh, directed federal prosecutors to work with local police forces to identify repeat and violent offenders who used guns and to prosecute them in federal court, if federal law allowed for a higher sentence. The program's motto was "A gun plus a crime equals hard Federal time" (Richman 2001, p. 374; Russell-Einhorn, Ward, and Seeherman 2000, p. 42). In January 1992, the FBI redeployed 300 of its agents from foreign counterintelligence activities as part of its Safe Street Violent Crimes Initiative targeting violent gangs and crimes of violence (Johnston 1992; FBI 2000; Russell-Einhorn, Ward, and Seeherman 2000, p. 45). During the summer of 1992, the chief of the Criminal Division in the FBI's New York office told some agents that terrorism was dead and tried to move them away from investigating the group later responsible for the 1993 World Trade Center bombing and into urban gang investigations (Miller and Stone 2003, p. 84). In August 1992, the Bureau of Alcohol Tobacco and Firearms (ATF)—which would soon become the federal enforcement agency most focused on violent crime—announced Operation Achilles Heel and pledged to work with state and local authorities to round up 600 "of this nation's most violent criminals" (Russell-Einhorn, Ward, and Seeherman 2000, p. 34; Richman 2001, p. 375).

The change in presidential administrations from Bush (I) to Clinton did not significantly alter the trajectory of federal enforcement policy in this area or the desire to highlight it. While there was sustained debate on Capitol Hill about the Clinton administration's approach to gun crimes, the only real issue was whether the federal interest in pursuing these offenses could be served by federally sponsored state prosecutions as well as federal prosecutions (as the Clinton administration wanted) or whether only federal prosecutions would do (as Republican opponents suggested) (Richman 2001). In any event, the priority given to firearms prosecutions continued unabated. Between 1989 and 1998, the number of federal firearms prosecutions went up 61 percent (Walker and Patrick 2000). The number of arrests by the FBI's violent crimes task forces (in which state and local participants—whose overtime was paid by the feds—outnumbered the federal agents) jumped from over 14,000 in fiscal 1992 to over 25,000 in fiscal 1997 (Russell-Einhorn, Ward, and Seeherman 2000, p. 45; FBI 2000, pp. 2–3).

The most important change in federal-local interaction during the 1990s is not fully captured by these statistics, however, since it came in the institutionalized commitment of federal agencies to take cases that would otherwise have been pursued locally (Glazer 1999, p. 581). The precise structure of these programs varied from district to district; indeed such variation was a hallmark of the Clinton administration's approach (Richman 2001, p. 383). But the trend, particularly in large urban areas such as Richmond, Virginia, and Boston, was to formalize collaborative relationships between federal, state, and local agencies through joint task forces and a variety of special programs (McDonald, Finn, and Hoffman 1999, p. 13; Russell-Einhorn, Ward, and Seeherman 2000).

In the flagship program developed in Richmond, dubbed Project Exile, federal prosecutors made an open commitment of federal resources in February 1997: "When a police officer finds a gun during the officer's duties, the officer pages an ATF agent (twenty-four hours a day). They review the circumstances and determine whether a federal statute applies. If so federal criminal prosecution is initiated" (Richman 2001, p. 379). According to the U.S. Attorney's office, the benefits of taking these cases federally flowed from the federal bail statute, which allows pretrial detention on the ground of dangerousness; the federal system of mandatory minimums and sentencing guidelines, which limited sentencing discretion and resulted in predictable and substantial sentences; and the federal prison system, which made it likely that the sentence would be served far from home (hence the idea of "exile"). By March 1999, 438 federal indictments had been brought, and the U.S. Attorney's office credited the program with helping reduce Richmond's homicide rate by 33 percent. President Clinton extolled Exile's virtues in a radio address, and it was duplicated (in one form or another) around the country (Baker 1999, p. 682; Richman 2001, pp. 379–85). In Boston, a different program, dubbed Operation Ceasefire, targeted youth gangs, getting the message out that violence would no longer be tolerated, backing the deterrent message with prosecutions, and also focusing enforcement attention on gun traffickers (Kennedy et al. 2001).

Lest any violent crime prove beyond the reach of at least one federal statute, Congress was quick to jump in with new ones. Even crimes zealously pursued by local authorities led to new federal legislation. After a widely publicized Maryland case in which Pamela Basu, the victim of an auto theft, was dragged to her death while trying to rescue her daughter from the car, Congress passed a carjacking statute in 1992 (18 U.S.C. sec. 2119). That the Maryland perpetrators were prosecuted in state court and received life prison terms made little difference (Brickey 1995, p. 1162; Zimring and Hawkins 1996, p. 20; Gest 2001, p. 69). Observing the relationship between election years and crime legislation, a former House staffer found especially noteworthy "the amount of floor time spent repeatedly on anecdotal horrific *state* crimes to justify enactment of *federal* law" (Bergman 1998, p. 196).

By the late 1990s, a whole body of scholarly literature condemning the cynical politics behind this tendency to federalize everything had developed (e.g., Scheingold 1984; Marion 1994, 1997; Brickey 1995; Beale 1997; Beckett 1997). Sanford Kadish condemned "creeping and foolish overfederalization," and noted how among its costs were "the needless compromise of the virtues of federalism, the waste of resources with duplicating systems doing much the same thing, and finally, the net increase and nationalization of knee-jerk legislation" (Kadish 1995, pp. 1248, 1251). But it had little or no effect. When, in 1994, a bill was proposed that would have made almost every state crime committed with a gun into a federal offense, it took opposition by FBI Director Louis Freeh and Chief Justice William Rehnquist to block the measure (Richman 1999, p. 767; Gest 2001, pp. 69–70).

The efforts by the Bush (I) and Clinton administrations to deploy federal agents and prosecutors against violent crime (and drug trafficking)—either on their own or in various joint task forces—did not come at the expense of federal grants to state and local governments in this area. Indeed, both in their dollar amounts and in the discretion they gave to state and local enforcers, federal grant programs took off during the 1990s. The LEAA may have been disbanded in 1980, but the Comprehensive Crime Control Act of 1984 reestablished a federal grant program for state anticrime efforts, to be run out of the Office of Justice Programs (Beckett 1997, pp. 94–95). And while federal funding for local crime control in 1986 was only one-fourth of what it had been eight years earlier, it soon took off, quadrupling between 1986 and 1995 in nominal dollars (doubling in real terms) (Congressional Budget Office 1996, p. 36). The Crime Control Act of 1990 (Pub. L. 101–647) authorized $900 million for the Edward Byrne Memorial State and Local Law Enforcement Assistance programs, which funded violence reduction and narcotics enforcement and were administered by the states (Laney 1998; Russell-Einhorn, Ward, and Seeherman 2000, p. 36). Appropriations for these programs ranged from $535 million in fiscal 1996 to $569 million in fiscal 2001 (O'Bryant 2004, p. 3).

With the election of Bill Clinton, and in the wake of his campaign promise to put 100,000 new police officers on the streets, came the Violent Crime Control and Law Enforcement Act of 1994 (Pub. L. 103–322), which "authorized the spending of a staggering $30 billion to help State and local enforcement agencies fight crime over the 6-year life of the bill's coverage" (Roth et al. 2000, p. 41). The big development here was a readiness—in the form of the COPS (Community Oriented Police Services) programs—to put money directly into the hands of local police departments. Actual appropriations to the COPS program were $1.4 billion for each year between 1996 and 1999. They fell to $595 million in 2000 but were back up to over $1 billion in 2001 (O'Bryant 2004, p. 4).

Big cities' police departments did particularly well under the COPS program. Of all the agencies awarded grants under the COPS program by the end of 1997, "only 4% served core city jurisdictions." But they received 40 percent of COPS dollar awards for all programs combined and 62 percent of all COPS MORE (Making Officer Redeployment Effective) funds (which went to technology, civilians, and overtime) (Roth et al. 2000, p. 10). By 1997, local crime prevention took a bigger slice of the Justice Department's budget than the FBI, DEA, or Immigration and Naturalization Service. In fact, among all Justice components, only the Bureau of Prisons got more than the units that funneled money to state and local enforcers (Sherman et al. 1997, pp. 1–11).

D. The Allure of Violent Crime Federalism

The degree to which these federal programs achieved their stated goal of crime reduction is still under study. Figuring out whether or to what extent any policing program or approach has affected crime rates will always be hard (Sherman 1992; Levitt 1997; Blumstein and Wallman 2000), and the limited nature of federal operational interventions makes their assessment particularly difficult. One recent study suggests that Project Exile, whose success in reducing the Richmond homicide rate was celebrated by the Clinton and later the Bush (II) administrations, actually had little or no effect on it (Raphael and Ludwig 2003). An examination of Boston's Operation Ceasefire, however, found that it was "likely responsible for a significant reduction in the city's rates of youth homicide and gun violence" (Kennedy et al. 2001, p. 64).

As for the role of federal funding, this is difficult too, in part because it implicates the long-debated question of whether increasing the size of the police decreases crime, and more particularly whether increases in police size played a role in the crime drop in the 1990s. In 2000, John R. Eck and Edward R. McGuire (2000, p. 209) found "little evidence that changes in the number of police officers are responsible for recent changes (in either direction) in violent crime." Yet others such as Steven Levitt (using nationwide data) and Corman and Mocan (focusing on New York City) maintain that they have found just such evidence (Levitt 1997, 2002; Corman and Mocan 2000; McCrary 2002). In 2004, Levitt broadly asserted that the increase in police between 1991 and 2001 "can explain somewhere between one-fifth and one-tenth of the overall decline in crime" during that period (2004, p. 186).

Even were one to conclude that increases in police forces in the 1990s helped cause the decrease in crime, the question of how much credit for this belongs to federal aid would remain. Certainly the increase in police was coincident with and to some extent was funded by the COPS program. One economist would give President Clinton and the COPS program "credit for engineering more crime reduction through federal policy action than any President since Franklin Roosevelt ushered in the repeal of Prohibition" (Donohue 2004, p. 3). But precisely how much credit should have been given to that program is open to debate (Office of the Inspector General 1999; Roth et al. 2000; Zhao, Scheider, and Thurman 2002; Ekstrand and Kingsbury 2003; Zhao and Thurman 2003; U.S. Government Accountability Office 2005). One needs to figure out how much money localities would independently have spent on a serious crime problem, and how much money actually stuck to the departments it was given to (as opposed to supplanting local funding that ended up being spent outside the criminal justice system [Evans and Owens 2005]). Even in 2005, as the COPS program winds down, the battle about its effectiveness rages (Eisler and Johnson 2005).

From the intergovernmental perspective, however, the important point is that the latter part of the 1990s marked the high-water mark of a federal-state-local relationship based on violent crime enforcement that (surprise, surprise) nicely served the interests of almost all of the governmental actors involved. Presidential administrations of both parties got to tout their commitment to the Fight against Crime and the War on Drugs. Legislators, who readily appropriated large sums of money for these endeavors, could tout their commitment as well, but there was more to it than that. For the essence of the violent crime targeted by the enforcement and funding programs was local. While there was much talk, and perhaps some reality, of coordination, innovation, and "best practices," the thrust of these programs was to dispatch federal dollars and manpower to their constituencies. And with each conspicuous deployment—be it funding grant or enforcement program—a legislator's press release could take some credit. Congressional representatives could also take credit for relieving local enforcers of burdensome grant compliance (Chubb 1985).

The in-kind aid to localities entailed by federal investigations and prosecutions offered certain advantages to the feds over the direct funding alternative: First, in contrast to funding, which all too often had become lost in state bureaucracies or had been diverted to unintended local needs, federal prosecutors and agents could ensure that enforcement assistance reached its intended destination. The long tradition of prosecutorial discretion and the relative opacity of enforcement decision making also allowed federal authorities greater freedom to steer resources to areas of need—far less fettered by the norm of horizontal equity that bedeviled congressional appropriations (Zimring and Hawkins 1992, p. 166). Moreover, lacking any easy ability to predict and measure the extent of this sort of federal aid, state and local policy makers would presumably be less "inclined to offset increased federal aid through decreases in their expenditures" (O'Hear 2004, p. 850).

The interests of federal enforcement agencies were also well served by the new violent crime priorities (which overlapped with the narcotics enforcement priority). The general public was happy to see the "feds" deployed against local bad guys—street gangs, armed robbers, and murderers. And the championship of these cases by local legislative delegations could only redound to the benefit of agencies at funding time and to field offices in their relations with headquarters. The timing for the FBI was particularly propitious, as the end of the Cold War appeared to allow the redeployment of agents from counterintelligence to antiviolence assignments (Johnston 1992). And ATF had its own incentives: By making a specialty of violent crime, the agency whose unpopular gun control mission had almost led to its elimination gained a mission that even the National Rifle Association could not quarrel with and gained valuable allies in the local law enforcement community (Vizzard 1997; Richman 2001, p. 399). Agents and prosecutors also enjoyed the extent of their discretion in this area. There may have been political pressure to do violent crime cases. But there was little pressure to any particular case. Violent crime was still, after all, primarily a local responsibility. Federal enforcers thus could be quite strategic in their case selection decisions and in the neighborhoods they targeted (Glazer 1999).

The only federal branch that did not support federal intrusion into the street crime area was the judiciary (or at least a significant component thereof). Many judges believed that the burgeoning criminal docket impaired the "quality of justice" in criminal cases and also impaired their "ability to perform their core constitutional function in civil cases" (Miner 1992, p. 681; Wilkenson 1994; Beale 1995, p. 983). These particular criminal cases also demanded an unusual expenditure of judicial resources, in part because the high mandatory minimums led many defendants to go to trial. A study by the Administrative Office of the U.S. Courts noted not just a huge increase in federal firearms cases between 1989 and 1998, but also the costs of that increase: "In comparison to 1989, a firearms case filed in 1998 was more likely to involve multiple defendants, more likely to take longer between filing and disposition of the case, more likely than other types of crimes to result in a jury trial, and more likely to result in a longer prison sentence for the defendant(s)" (Walker and Patrick 2000, p. 6). Some judges also complained about efforts to turn "garden-variety state law drug offenses into federal offenses" (*United States v. Aguilar*, 779 F.2d 123, 125 [2d Cir. 1985]) or violent crime prosecutions that turned their dignified setting "into a minor-grade police court" (Campbell 1999, p. 1).

Perhaps because the judiciary bridled at the costs the political branches imposed on it, and certainly because of changes in the Supreme Court's composition that increased the number of justices committed to limiting federal power, the nonchalance with which the Court viewed extensions of federal criminal jurisdiction came to a halt in 1995 (Althouse 2001). In *United States v. Lopez* (514 U.S. 549 [1995]), the Court, by a narrow majority, held that Congress had exceeded its Commerce Clause powers when it enacted the Gun-Free School Zones Act of 1990, which made it a federal offense "for any individual knowingly to possess a firearm" in a school zone. Chief Justice Rehnquist, writing for the majority, stressed the need to judicially enforce the "distinction between what is truly national and what is truly local" (*Lopez*, 514 U.S. 549 [1995]; Moulton 1999). Outside the courtroom, Rehnquist and other luminaries of the bar made the point as well, in testimony to Congress, speeches, and reports (Committee on Long Range Planning 1995; Task Force on the Federalization of Criminal Law 1998; Baker 1999, p. 675; Richman 2003, p. 795 n. 216). In his "1998 Year-End Report of the Federal Judiciary," Rehnquist warned:

> The trend to federalize crimes that traditionally have been handled in state courts not only is taxing the Judiciary's resources and affecting its budget needs, but it also threatens to change entirely the nature of our federal system. The pressure in Congress to appear responsive to every highly publicized societal ill or sensational crime needs to be balanced with an inquiry into whether states are doing an adequate job in these particular areas and, ultimately, whether we want most of our legal relationships decided at the national rather than local level. Federal courts were not created to adjudicate local crimes, no matter how sensational or heinous the crimes may be. State courts do, can, and should handle such problems. While there certainly are areas in criminal law in which the

federal government must act, the vast majority of localized criminal cases should be decided in the state courts which are equipped for such matters. This principle was enunciated by Abraham Lincoln in the 19th century, and Dwight Eisenhower in the 20th century—matters that can be handled adequately by the states should be left to them; matters that cannot be so handled should be undertaken by the federal government. (Rehnquist 1999)

The very intensity of this lobbying effort, however, highlighted the Supreme Court's impotence against the political branches. So did the Court's own case law, which continued to give only light review to statutes that (unlike the one in *Lopez*) made interstate commerce an element of the crime. Once the school gun statute was revised to require a jury to find that a defendant's gun had at some point moved in interstate commerce (18 U.S.C. sec. 922(q)), its constitutionality became unassailable under well-settled precedents, for example, *United States v. Danks*, 221 F.3d 1037, 1038–39 (8th Cir. 1999) (Richman 2000, p. 90; Denning and Reynolds 2003).

For their part, the local officials—particularly police officials—whose sovereign interests the Supreme Court purported to defend against federal encroachment were generally pretty comfortable with federal initiatives (Geller and Morris 1992, pp. 312–13). They liked the direct grants, overtime pay, and the aid-in-kind that federal enforcement activity—and the significant procedural and sentencing advantages flowing therefrom—really amounted to (Geller and Morris 1992, pp. 257–62; Jeffries and Gleeson 1995, pp. 1103–25; GAO 1996; Russell-Einhorn, Ward, and Seeherman 2000, pp. 14–15; Richman 2003, p. 768). In part because of favorable procedural and evidentiary rules, and in part because they had the luxury of lighter dockets, the likelihood of a defendant's conviction was greater in federal court than in state. And because of the federal sentencing scheme—with its high mandatory minimum sentences for certain firearm and narcotics offenses and sentencing guidelines keyed to the facts of the charged conduct (broadly defined) that substantially constrained sentencing judges' ability to consider certain mitigating factors—federal defendants ended up getting more time in prison than they would have in the state system (Clymer 1997; O'Hear 2002; Miller and Eisenstein 2005, p. 248). Not only was each federal street crime defendant someone who otherwise would have been prosecuted in state court, but local enforcers who coordinated their activities with the feds benefited simply from working in the federal shadow: The large difference between federal and state sentences meant that defendants would quickly plead out in state court to avoid (maybe) having their case taken federally (O'Hear 2004, p. 813).

Turf battles between local and federal enforcers happened from time to time. And local officials often perceived cooperation with federal agencies as "a one-way street" (Russell-Einhorn, Ward, and Seeherman 2000, p. 18). But when it came to violent crime, local police officials were generally in the cat-bird's seat. FBI, ATF, DEA, and other federal agents could not patrol the streets. They rarely infiltrated gangs. Calls to 911 were not routed to them. And citizens generally took their complaints to the police. If a federal agency wanted to work the violent crime area, it would have to do it with the acquiescence and probably the full cooperation of the police. And the police knew that. They also gained some bargaining leverage over local prosecutors, on whom they used to be wholly dependant. Explaining how his department determined whether to take a case to federal or state prosecutors, a Richmond, Virginia, police captain noted, in 1998, that "it's like buying a car: we're going to the place we feel we can get the best deal. We shop around" (Bonner 1998, p. 930). Local agencies also were given institutional mechanisms for coordinating and collaborating with federal agencies through the creation of various joint task forces (Russell-Einhorn, Ward, and Seeherman 2000).

From time to time, one would hear local district attorneys complaining about federal incursion. In 1997, the president of the National District Attorneys Association made clear that his organization had "long opposed the unwarranted federalization of crime in the belief that it works to the detriment of the efficient and effective use of our law enforcement and legal resources" (Baker 1999, p. 677 n. 26). And local prosecutors sometimes complained that federal prosecutors "cherry-picked" the best cases (Miller and Eisenstein 2005, p. 259). But even those complaints were rare, since there certainly was enough street violence to go around, and, as one district attorney put it, the increased federal commitment gave local prosecutors "more flexibility" (Richman 2001, p. 405). Indeed, a Justice Department–sponsored study of federal-local collaboration in San Diego, Memphis, and Detroit reported in 2000 that if local prosecutors were bothered by anything, it was more likely to be by the alacrity with which the feds *declined* cases rather than the greed with which they grabbed them (Russell-Einhorn,

Ward, and Seeherman 2000, p. 116). Moreover, the locals benefited even in the cases they kept. As Miller and Eisenstein found in their study of relations between federal and local authorities in an unnamed large city, local prosecutors could "leverage their cooperative relations with the [U.S. Attorney's office] to pressure defendants to plead guilty to higher than average sentences in state court," and they could also send a message to local judges and legislatures about the insufficiency of local sentences (Miller and Eisenstein 2005, p. 262). In addition, local prosecutors also were placated through the system of "cross-designation," in which U.S. Attorneys' offices cross-deputized local assistant DAs as federal prosecutors, allowing the ADAs to follow a case that might have originated locally into a federal court (Miller and Eisenstein 2005, p. 261).

Just because federal authorities depended on the local police to jump-start their violent crime investigations did not mean that information flowed freely between agencies. Indeed, police officers frequently complained that federal agencies—the FBI in particular—were not very good about sharing (Russell-Einhorn, Ward, and Seeherman 2000, p. 120). The advantages flowing from federal activity in the area, however, outweighed this concern, and there was in fact improvement over time, spurred by formal mechanisms such as joint task forces and informal ones such as personal familiarity (Geller and Morris 1992, pp. 266, 272).

At the state level, officials occasionally went on record expressing concern that "some attempts to expand federal criminal law into traditional state functions . . . could undermine state and local anticrime efforts" (Baker 1999, p. 676; see also Richman 2001, p. 249). Their annoyance is particularly understandable when one thinks about the effects that federal activity had on the balance of power between state and local governments. On the funding side, states saw an increased readiness by the federal government to funnel money directly to localities, in contrast to the LEAA model, in which some money and power stuck to state hands on the way. The COPS program was only the most dramatic example of this policy shift. On the enforcement side, state officials saw their local counterparts working directly with field offices and U.S. Attorneys' offices, not just in big cities but in smaller ones as well, rendering state policy making even less relevant than before (Richman 1999, pp. 786–87; O'Hear 2004, p. 852). Overall though, state officials' resistance was muted, perhaps because of their appreciation of the relief that federal activity offered to the state criminal justice budget.

This decade of direct grants, block grants, and enforcement assistance from the federal government to state and local authorities did not come to an end with the election of George W. Bush in 2000. With great fanfare, the new president announced an Initiative to Reduce Gun Violence and, as he had in his campaign, embraced a program of maximal federal involvement in gun violence prosecutions (Bush and Ashcroft 2001). In a May 2001 memo to department heads, Attorney General John Ashcroft included, as two of his seven goals, "reducing drug violence and drug trafficking" and "helping states with anti-crime programs." He did not even mention terrorism (Seper 2001; Clymer 2002). The new administration did announce plans to phase out the COPS program—not that surprising, given that Republicans had long questioned the efficacy of this Clinton program that tended to funnel most of its money to big-city Democratic strongholds. But the plan envisioned a reconfiguring of federal aid in the violent crime area, not a transfer away from it (Oliphant 2001).

Then came the attacks on September 11, 2001.

II. The Post-9/11 Dynamic

We are often told that September 11 "changed everything." Although an obvious overstatement in some contexts, it is quite apt when applied to the federal, state, and local law enforcement dynamic. The new pressures on the system were felt immediately: As the feds made the prevention of future attacks their highest priority, they placed new demands on the police for information and for cooperation in immigration enforcement—quite a shift from the days in which the feds' primary role vis-à-vis the police was as provider of enforcement assistance. Many local authorities saw the role that the feds expected them to play in the counterterrorism effort as inconsistent, or at least in tension, with their local crime-fighting responsibilities. They also saw the federal funding for their local crime fighting diverted to the War on Terror. The intergovernmental tensions stemming from these new pressures continue as this essay is written (in July 2005).

Even as the daily newspapers tell of new flare-ups between state, local, and federal authorities, however, they also show signs of a new modus vivendi emerging—one in which violent crime and terrorism coexist as the focal points of a new domestic intelligence network that is actually the country's first national police system. The cohesiveness and architecture of this network cannot yet be determined. But its emergence as part of the longer-term effects of 9/11 will also be explored here.

A. Immediate Effects of the 9/11 Attacks

The shock that the September 11 attacks gave to the federal enforcement bureaucracy was extraordinary. Before this, there were a few specialized "beats" that the feds had to patrol nationwide—espionage, immigration, federal tax offenses, counterfeiting, maybe organized crime. But the system's defining luxury was the absence of any responsibility to pursue any particular case in most of the areas in which it had jurisdiction (Richman 1999, p. 766). Now, it was suddenly saddled with a politically unavoidable, and all-but-impossible, responsibility: preventing another such attack.

To their credit, federal enforcement officials made a concerted effort to reach out to state and local agencies for intelligence-gathering assistance and diplomatically sought to address long-standing local complaints about the feds' reluctance to share information. FBI Director Mueller made conciliatory speeches and created a new Office of Law Enforcement Coordination, headed by a former police chief, within the FBI (Eggen 2004). Attorney General Ashcroft created new institutional mechanisms for coordinating counterterrorism activities across all levels of government. Prior to September 11, there had been only thirty-five Joint Terrorist Task Forces—operational groups of federal, state, and local agents (912 in all) who conducted field investigations into terrorist activity. After September 11, there would be fifty-six, one for every FBI field office, and, by 2005, 103, with a total of 5,085 members. Ashcroft also created Anti-terrorism Task Forces (later renamed Anti-terrorism Advisory Councils) in every federal district. Their job was to serve as the conduit of information about suspected terrorists between federal and local agencies and to coordinate the district's response to a terrorist attack (U.S. Department of Justice 2002; U.S. Department of Justice. Office of the Inspector General 2005). And the department worked hard to speed up security clearances for state and local officials (GAO 2004c).

These moves all testified to the new intergovernmental intelligence dynamic. Given the nature of the perceived terrorist threat—the sleeper cells waiting to strike again—federal agencies now relied on the intelligence capabilities of local police forces in a way they never did when the primary area of interaction was violent crime. Back then, the feds needed help from the locals; but since they could walk away from any case and could offer many benefits, they had considerable leverage. Now the rush was on to create the semblance of a national intelligence network providing what Philip Heymann has called "untargeted prevention" (1998, p. 82). In this, the participation of local cops was absolutely essential.

What state and local enforcers bring to the counterterrorism intelligence-gathering process is not simply a function of their numbers—708,022 sworn state and local police officers in 2000 (the last count) compared to 93,446 federal law enforcement officers (more than a quarter of whom were in the Federal Bureau of Prisons) in 2002 (Reeves and Bauer 2002, p. 8; Reeves and Hickman 2002, p. 1)—nor even of the many things they learn while on street patrol. It also stems from their involvement in bringing the bulk of serious criminal charges in the United States, because the threat of prosecution (even prosecutions having nothing to do with terrorism) is one of the best tools around for prying loose closely held information. Moreover, their order maintenance and public safety duties give local police a more balanced "portfolio" in dealing with community leaders. The police officer who seeks information from a local Arab-American community leader has probably met and assisted that leader before (Murphy and Plotkin 2003, p. 43; Thacher 2005, pp. 648–49).

The Justice Department quickly went beyond vague talk of "information sharing" and asked for local assistance in a large-scale program to interview thousands of people (mostly young Middle Eastern males) in the country on nonimmigrant visas (GAO 2003b). In the spring of 2002, the department went further and announced its plan to place names of certain aliens who had violated their visa requirements into the national database of wanted suspects. It asked state and local police to arrest these "absconders" and (reversing a position it had taken since 1996) noted that, as a legal matter, such assistance was "within the inherent authority of the states" (Ashcroft 2002; Thompson 2002; National Council of La Raza v. Department of Justice, 411 F.3d 350 [2d Cir. 2005]).

Police departments rushed to help, and the constant drumbeat from them during 2002 and into 2003 was that the feds were not sharing information with the locals, were not putting them "in the game" (Murphy and Plotkin 2003, p. 9). That said, conditions were not altogether propitious for police cooperation. In a number of cities and states, officials took stands (pretty symbolic, to be sure) against the administration's counterterrorism efforts. By July 20, 2005, seven states and 386 local governments had passed resolutions condemning (at least in part) the USA Patriot Act (United and Strengthening America by Providing Appropriate Tools Required to Intercept and Obstruct Terrorism Act of 2001) (115 Stat. 272)—the antiterrorism legislation passed soon after the September 11 attacks—and opposing the involvement of local agencies in federal intelligence initiatives not sanctioned by local law (Bill of Rights Defense Committee 2005) (listing all such resolutions).

Some of this scattered resistance may have arisen from partisan politics or liberal orientation. But there was a historical basis as well, for the federal efforts to recruit local police into a national intelligence network brought back memories of 1968, when, at the behest of the feds, local departments had created intelligence units whose zeal to gather and disseminate information on potential "civil disorders" had led to abuses (Church Committee 1976, pp. 332–33).

Local concerns were not merely partisan, philosophical, or historical. They also grew out of local politics. When the federal-local interaction was centered on violent crime, federal initiatives brought significant positive externalities—credit for local leaders and maybe even improved local safety. To be sure, the feds also claimed credit. But the benefits stayed in the area, and the feds picked up a decent share of the costs. The counterterrorism dynamic has been precisely the reverse, save in some exceptional locations, such as New York City—which, somewhat to the dismay of the FBI, has gone so far as to develop its own overseas intelligence network (Miller 2005; National Academy of Public Administration 2005, p. 39; U.S. Department of Justice. Office of the Inspector General 2005, p. 49). As a general matter, there is no reason to expect that terrorists pose a particular threat to the many places in which they or information about them will be found (Thacher 2005, pp. 637–38). In those areas, the gains from domestic intelligence gathering thus are felt primarily, even exclusively, at the national level. But the costs of gathering fall on the localities—not just the fiscal costs, but the significant negative externalities that attend any large-scale investigations of immigrant activities in communities that have large numbers of immigrants.

Police departments, of course, do not always share the concerns of their political masters. But police officials have had their own pragmatic concerns about federal counterterrorism initiatives, particularly those involving the use of federal immigration statutes. As the International Association of Chiefs of Police has explained:

> Immigration enforcement by state and local police could have a chilling effect in immigrant communities and could limit cooperation with police by members of those communities. Local police agencies depend on the cooperation of immigrants, legal and illegal, in solving all sorts of crimes and in the maintenance of public order. Without assurances that they will not be subject to an immigration investigation and possible deportation, many immigrants with critical information would not come forward, even when heinous crimes are committed against them or their families. Because many families with undocumented family members also include legal immigrant members, this would drive a potential wedge between police and huge portions of the legal immigrant community as well. (IACP 2004b, p. 5; see Badie 2002; Thompson 2002; U.S. House. Judiciary Committee 2003)

(It is worth noting that the FBI may share these concerns. A 2005 report by the National Academy of Public Administration noted that "the FBI is concerned that overly zealous immigration and customs enforcement will undercut its collection operations, which are driven increasingly by prevention, not enforcement" [2005, p. 37]).

The nonfederal officials most disposed to assist in enforcing the immigration laws have come from the state level, not the local. In Maryland, a newspaper reported that "many local police departments . . . , including those in Baltimore and in Anne Arundel and Baltimore counties, generally will not report illegal immigrants unless they have committed crimes." But "state police policy is to inform federal authorities about any suspected of being in the country illegally" (Song 2003, p. 1B). As of June 2005, only Florida and Alabama had formally signed on to the federal initiative, and in Alabama it appears that only state troopers are involved (Orange County, California, may soon sign on too) (U.S. House Judiciary Committee 2003; Swarns 2004; Crummy 2005).

Why the difference between the attitudes of local police departments and their statewide counterparts? Straightforward political differences may play a part here—Republican governors versus more liberal urban local officials. But institutional obligations (or the lack thereof) likely play a role as well. For it is at the local level, and particularly in big cities, that the costs imposed by the federal enforcement initiative on relationships with immigrant communities would hit hardest (Thacher 2005).

Even had nothing else changed in the relationship between federal and local enforcers, the new federal counterterrorism initiatives would have imposed new intelligence-gathering responsibilities on the police and arguably have made it harder to maintain order in areas with significant immigrant populations, including most big cities. But the costs effectively imposed on the police by the federal counterterrorism focus went beyond that, because that focus threatened to come at the expense of federal enforcement activity in the violent crime area. Certainly this was true with respect to the FBI. A September 2004 audit report by the Justice Department's Inspector General's office found that the number of nonsupervisory field agents allocated to "violent crimes and major offenders" had dropped from 2,004 in fiscal 2000 to 1,006 in fiscal 2002 (U.S. Department of Justice. Office of the Inspector General 2004, p. 17). The bureau significantly reduced its narcotics activity as well. Moreover, a March 2004 GAO report noted that "use of field agent staff resources in . . . traditional criminal investigative programs (such as drug enforcement, violent crime, and white collar crime) has continuously dropped below allocated levels as agents from these programs have been temporarily reassigned to work on counterterrorism-related matters" (2004*b*, p. 25). In consequence, the number of FBI violent crime matters opened went from 9,034 in the second quarter of fiscal 2001 to 4,810 in the last quarter of fiscal 2003 (p. 32). Because ATF increased its violent crime activity during this period, the overall number of violent crime referrals in the federal system actually increased by 29 percent between fiscal 2001 and fiscal 2003 (GAO 2004*a*, p. 18). But it is not yet clear whether the DEA will take up the FBI's burden in the narcotics area. As an August 2004 GAO report found, there is not conclusive evidence as to whether shifts in the FBI's priorities have had an effect on overall federal efforts to combat violent and drug crime (pp. 3–4). Nonetheless, local officials might well see the bureau's assertion of the primacy of terrorism prevention as a harbinger of future shifts by all federal agencies away from the areas in which federal activity had eased their load.

Note that the point here is not that the shift in federal resources was a mistake. Indeed, one of the greatest benefits flowing from the federal enforcement bureaucracy's relative lack of political accountability is its flexibility in responding to changing circumstances. However, the duration and apparent stability of federal agencies' commitment to street crime enforcement during the 1980s and 1990s set a new baseline for local expectations of federal enforcement assistance. And, since September 11, these expectations were at obvious risk of being dashed.

Fiscal expectations were certainly being dashed. During a period in which the economic downturn and the political popularity of tax cuts placed new budget pressure on state and local governments (Multistate Tax Commission 2003; Mattoon 2004), local and state governments also found themselves facing massive homeland security expenditures. In January 2002, the U.S. Conference of Mayors estimated the costs of heightened security for cities in the coming year would be $2.1 billion (U.S. Conference of Mayors 2002a). State governments expected their costs would be up to $4 billion (Hobijn 2002, p. 24). Yet particularly in the most populous states, the federal reimbursement formula established by Congress, and reinforced by the new Department of Homeland Security, left these governments bearing a considerable percentage of these costs (U.S. House Select Committee on Homeland Security 2004).

Recapitulating the old debates about how federal crime money was to be distributed, local authorities also complained about the decision to distribute homeland security funds through the states rather than to them directly. One police chief complained in a spring 2003 congressional hearing that homeland security "resources do not go directly to local police departments. They cannot be used to hire new police. They cannot be used to pay overtime expenses that we incur each and every time Secretary Ridge changes the alert level. They can be used to purchase equipment, but not by me. I have to wait for a statewide plan to be developed and then I have to hope that a fair share of those funds will filter to my department" (U.S. Senate. Governmental Affairs Committee 2003a, p. 48 [testimony of Jeffrey Horvath, Police Chief, Dover, Delaware]; see also U.S. Conference of Mayors 2002b).

The response of state governments to the calls of local units for direct federal funding also echoed the state responses in the days of the LEAA. Speaking for the National Governors Association at a spring 2003 congressional hearing, Massachusetts Governor Mitt Romney testified that "we believe it critical that homeland security funding and resources be applied against comprehensive and integrated statewide plans." "Without statewide coordination, there is no check on gaps in coverage, incompatible equipment and communications systems, and wasteful duplication" (U.S. Senate. Governmental Affairs Committee 2003*b*, p. 50). As before, there may have been a degree of self-interest behind these state arguments. But they had considerably more power in the homeland security context, given the geographic scale of the catastrophic attacks that were envisioned (Wise and Nader 2002, p. 49; Kettl 2003).

Because they see cities as bearing the brunt (in both fiscal and political costs) of any nationwide intelligence-gathering and security patrolling effort, local officials, particularly from bigger cities, would likely have complained about the very nature of the Bush administration's embrace of the statewide funding model for homeland security. Their sense of grievance has been intensified, however, by their perception that it is "their" violent crime money that is now going to the states.

The fungibility of money makes the link impossible to prove. And, in the Bush administration's defense, it should be noted that the COPS program has long been a Republican target. Yet urban officials have made much of the coincidence that the COPS program is being phased out, and other crime control grants reduced, just as homeland security funding plans are being made. And they have noted the significant reductions in grants under the Local Law Enforcement Block Grant programs, which went from a total of around $400 million in 2001 to $115 million in 2004 (Bureau of Justice Statistics 2004, p. 1). These are the grants that go directly to local government units, and local officials took it hard. One police chief testified that "there is a concern in the law enforcement community, that new assistance programs are being funded at the expense of traditional law enforcement assistance programs such as the COPS program, the Local Law Enforcement Block Grant Program and the Byrne Grant program" (U.S. Senate. Governmental Affairs Committee 2003*a* [testimony of Jeffrey Horvath, Police Chief, Dover, Delaware]). As a report by the U.S. Conference of Mayors noted in 2002, "The Administration is proposing to cut funding for existing law enforcement programs such as the COPS program (80 percent cut) and the Local Law Enforcement Block Grant (merged and cut 20 percent). If approved by Congress, these cuts would result in a major reduction in the ability of mayors and the police to prevent and respond to both traditional street crime and the new threat of domestic terrorism" (U.S. Conference of Mayors 2002*b*, p. 4).

The fiscal picture remains in flux, as of July 2005 (right after the attacks in London). In November 2004, Congress passed an appropriations bill for fiscal 2005 that cut the three main law enforcement assistance programs by 24.4 percent. And the IACP (2004*a*, p. 1) reported that "the funding levels for these programs have declined by almost $1.24 billion" since 2002, representing "a cut of 50%." In February 2005, the administration's budget request for 2006 proposed further reductions in the COPS program and the elimination of the Justice Assistance Grant Program—the program created in 2005 to replace the Local Law Enforcement Block Grant Program and the Byrne Memorial Grant Program (Reese 2005). The IACP (2005, p. 1) reported that "overall, funding levels for assistance programs that are primarily designed to assist state and local law enforcement agencies were slashed by $1.467 billion when compared to FY 2005." Wrangling continues also over the distribution and designation over homeland security funding as well, with Congress considering cuts in state and local grants, and with representatives from smaller states still preferring pro rata rather than needs-based distribution of federal funds (Gaouette 2005; Mintz 2005).

B. *Longer Term Effects*

It is hard (although not impossible) to imagine that the federal government's new counterterrorist focus will completely displace its decades-old commitment to assisting state and local governments in controlling violent crime. An insightful report completed in 2000 (before the September 11 attacks) for the National Institute of Justice predicted that, although the level of federal activity in the violent crime area would remain high, the reasons for that level might change:

Rather than reflecting the original, predominantly Washington-directed impetus for Federal involvement in urban crime, expanded collaborative activities in the coming decade may demonstrate the influence and support of local politicians and law enforcement authorities who—at least in many areas of the country—have grown accustomed to relying on Federal collaboration as a way of demonstrating heightened commitment to the fight against crime and supplementing what are often scarce local resources in that fight. (Russell-Einhorn, Ward, and Seeherman 2000, p. 125)

These local political influences may lie behind the readiness of the federal government even after September 11 to make conspicuous commitments of resources to the War on Crime. Notwithstanding the continuation of the fall in the national violent crime rate —down 3 percent between 2002 and 2003, down 1.7 percent between 2003 and 2004 (FBI 2004c)—and the shift of FBI agents from violent crime to counterterrorism, the Bush administration still announced the Violent Crime Reduction Initiative in June 2004 (Silver 2004; U.S. Department of Justice 2004) and in December 2004 trumpeted the commitment of FBI agents to the fight against violent gangs (Ragavan and Guttman 2004). In April 2005, Attorney General Alberto Gonzales announced the arrest of more than 10,000 fugitives as part of Operation FALCON (Federal and Local Cops Organized Nationally). He explained that "Operation FALCON is an excellent example of President Bush's direction and the Justice Department's dedication to deal both with the terrorist threat and traditional violent crime" (U.S. Department of Justice 2005).

Nonetheless, the current trajectory of the federal enforcement bureaucracy is toward a reduction in its commitment to fighting violent crime. In December 2003, Massachusetts Public Safety Secretary Edward Flynn called terrorism "the monster that ate criminal justice" (*Law Enforcement News* 2003). Perhaps this is a bit of an overstatement. But it is certainly clear that for the foreseeable future, violent crime will not define the relationship between the federal government and state and local governments with respect to criminal justice. Violent crime remains an indefeasible local obligation. Yet instead of being the focus of coordination between the feds and locals, it now threatens to put them at odds.

It is possible that the developing clash of interests between federal and local enforcers will create a zero-sum game in which any improvements in the emerging domestic intelligence network will come at the expense of local efforts against violent crime. Although overriding national security concerns might be offered to justify the wholesale enlistment of local police forces into a federally directed counterterrorist bureaucracy, the constitutional prohibition against federal "commandeering" would likely prevent the feds from simply ordering the police to cooperate (*Printz v. United States*, 521 U.S. 898 [1997]; *New York v. United States*, 505 U.S. 144 [1992]; Caminker 1995; Hills 1998, 1999). This prohibition, based in part on the Tenth Amendment and more generally on respect for state sovereignty, could be read to preclude Congress from directing state government officials (including law enforcement officers) to implement federal policy. Still, some combination of political pressure and federal conditional funding—which remains largely unregulated by the Supreme Court (Baker 1995)—could push the police in that direction, requiring them to draw down on the community relations capital that they have spent the last decade or more building up.

One could also imagine a scenario in which the police pulled back from cooperating with the federal authorities and the feds tried to develop their own domestic intelligence network that avoided relying too heavily on nonfederal personnel. Any such effort would be hamstrung by the comparative distance of federal agencies from the lives of people in densely populated urban communities. To be sure, federal authorities seem committed to reaching out on their own, and the FBI has worked hard to forge relationships with the Muslim and Arab-American communities (Sullivan 2003; FBI 2004*b*). But one has only to think about the TIPS (Terrorist Information and Prevention System) debacle to recognize how fraught broad-based federal information-gathering initiatives can be. First mentioned by President Bush in his 2002 State of the Union address, the TIPS program was pitched by the Justice Department as a way to enlist the observatory powers of service providers around the nation in the War on Terror. The idea was to create a "national system for reporting suspicious and potentially terrorist-related activity" involving "millions of American workers who, in the daily course of their work, are in a unique position to see potentially unusual or suspicious activity in public places" (Eggen 2002*a*). But reaction from both ends of the political spectrum at this "latest manifestation of Big Brother" was immediate and hostile (Shapiro 2003). Before long, under pressure from Congress and others, the program was reconfigured to "involve only truck workers, dock workers, bus drivers and others who are in positions to monitor places and events that are obviously public" (Eggen 2002*b*, p. 1A). Even this tactical retreat was not enough, and the initiative was soon legislated out of existence (Eggen 2002*a*).

Those who prefer looking further back can recall the American Protective League, with which the Bureau of Investigation (the FBI's predecessor agency) developed an auxiliary relationship during World War I. By June 1917, the league had around 250,000 members, looking for suspicious activity around the nation and inquiring into the loyalty of government and Red Cross personnel (Cummings and McFarland 1937, p. 421). The league's "free-wheeling" operations against alleged "slackers," "spies," and "saboteurs" remain an embarrassment to any who believes in civil liberties, competent domestic security programs, or some combination thereof (Powers 2004, pp. 87–100).

Or moving forward a bit in time, one can look at COINTELPRO (from "counterintelligence program") and other programs in the 1960s, in which the FBI, as well as other intelligence agencies, sometimes with the help of local police intelligence units, launched a broad campaign to determine whether communist infiltration or some other subversive campaign lay behind the urban riots, antiwar protests, the civil rights movement, and other dissenters of all stripes (Cunningham 2003). The agencies quickly moved beyond conventional investigative tactics and resorted to illegal break-ins, warrantless wiretaps, and campaigns to discredit their targets (Keller 1989, pp. 154–89; O'Reilly 1998; Theoharis 1999, pp. 32–35; Kreimer 2004).

The fact is that domestic intelligence operations historically (and perhaps inherently) pose peculiar risks to democratic society. Domestic intelligence operations have even fewer outcome measures than federal law enforcement, have extremely low visibility because of security sensitivities, and often involve political or potentially political judgments about targeting and methods. The more committed an agency is to these operations, the greater its need for political cover from the White House, which has too often been tempted to extract intelligence targeting power in return and to use that power for inappropriate political ends.

These pessimistic scenarios are not the only possible ones, however. A far more optimistic scenario would recognize that improved counterterrorism efforts need not come at the expense of violent crime enforcement at the local level. And it would have the federal government court the assistance of state and local governments by giving them a greater voice in how the federal government interacts with citizens, and particularly with immigrant communities.

The ability of the local police to mediate between federal needs and community sensitivities was highlighted when the Justice Department's call for interviews of certain Middle Eastern immigrants went out in the wake of 9/11. As the police chief of Ann Arbor, Michigan, later recounted, local leaders of the Arab-American community asked that an officer from his force be present during these interviews (George 2001). In Dearborn, local police participated in the interviews, but they made clear to the community that this was primarily a federal effort and saw themselves as monitoring the feds (Thacher 2005, p. 659). Later, in March 2003, the director of the American Arab Chamber of Commerce in Dearborn noted how the local police department had worked to win the Arab community's trust and how the FBI and other federal law enforcement agencies had not done enough. He also noted that after the war with Iraq had broken out, the Wayne County sheriff had dispatched his forces to guard mosques (Gorman 2003). The particulars vary, but the point is universal. As a recent report by the Inspectorate of Constabulary in the United Kingdom noted, "One of the key lessons to emerge from the investigation into the 11th September attacks has been the vital importance of extending the reach of the national security agencies by further utilising the close links between local police and the communities in which they work" (H.M.'s Inspectorate of Constabulary 2003, p. 16).

In our optimistic story, state and local agencies—and particularly local police departments—will exact a toll from federal authorities, as the price of gathering and supplying information. Because of current fiscal constraints, the federal government will not pay in cash, but by giving local police a larger voice in federal domestic intelligence policy and in the architecture of what amounts to a new national police system. And that voice will transform the new national network, giving it a far greater measure of accountability to the citizenry than would otherwise be possible.

The touted benefits of federalism often just reflect the virtues of managerial decentralization, and not necessarily of a genuinely federalist and "polycentric" system in which "leaders of the subordinate units draw their power from sources independent of [the] central authority" (Rubin and Feeley 1994, p. 911). This is partly true here. Even officials in a hypothetical monolithic "national police force" that had prime responsibility for pursuing all violent and street crime would think twice about using tactics that risked alienating chunks of the population in their respective patrol sectors (at least to the extent that they cared about enforcing the law in all neighborhoods). These are crimes that can be and are measured, with police performance judged accordingly. The contribution that local police forces can make to domestic intelligence policy making and collection is thus related to the nature of their "beat."

But the political contribution that police involvement can make to federal counterterrorism efforts stems not just from their "informational accountability"—the obligation to deal with any community from which they will need crime tips. It also reflects their greater electoral accountability. Police chiefs themselves are not generally elected, but the mayors and county executives to whom they report are, as are the chief prosecutors with whom they deal. Scrutiny of police performance by the local electorate, although hardly constant, regularly occurs. Decades of political focus on violent crime, coupled with increasing sophistication in the way crime fighting is assessed have put police departments under an unprecedented degree of pressure to actually achieve results. Although the precise contours of each department's approach will vary, each has made vast strides, with considerable federal encouragement in the 1990s, toward recognizing the essential connection between community relations and effective law enforcement (Kelling 1988; Skolnick and Bayley 1988; Scott 2000; Hickman and Reaves 2001).

To be sure, a lot of the revolution in policing has been rhetorical, and in some departments, "community" or "problem-solving" policing has been more a grants-writing strategy than an operational reality. Still, deployment patterns really have changed, and police commanders now look to community leaders not simply for tips on whom to arrest but increasingly for guidance on how the police can best improve the quality of life within a precinct. In community policing, the emphasis is on establishing partnerships between the police and communities to reduce crime and enhance security; problem-solving policing focuses on the problems that lie behind criminal incidents (Moore 1992). Approaches can vary, with departments that have adopted a community policing style more ready to share decision-making authority with the community than those that, wary of committing themselves to ambitious social objectives, would restrict themselves to problem solving. But either way, the last two decades have seen enormous and accelerating changes in the readiness of urban police forces to solicit and address the concerns of the people they serve (Fridell and Wycoff 2004). And solicitude for the concerns of ethnic or racial minority groups—which are often majorities within a city or precinct—has increasingly become a nonnegotiable part of a police chief's job description.

To some, the notion of police departments as bulwarks of civil liberties against federal encroachment might sound a bit odd. We are accustomed to the idea that the federal government is responsible for monitoring local abuses—stepping in with civil suits or civil rights prosecutions whenever the locals are derelict in their attention to such matters—not local monitoring of the feds (Livingston 1999). The rejoinder, of course, is that while we all have our idiosyncratic estimations of the skills and predilections of each enforcement level, no level has a monopoly of virtue. The obligation of local police departments to combat violent crime and maintain order can push them toward aggressive and even abusive control tactics. Yet that same obligation causes police departments to be especially attentive to the costs imposed by unsettling (or worse) interactions with the local community that have little to do with their ordinary order maintenance or crime-fighting responsibilities.

There have been signs of friction—particularly in the immigration area—as intergovernmental relationships that used to be based on violent crime are pushed to accommodate the threat of terrorism. As a recent white paper by the Police Executive Research Forum noted, there is considerable room for cooperation between the local police and the Bureau of Immigration and Customs Enforcement (Davis and Murphy 2004, p. 18). The dimensions of this interaction, however, need to be a matter of negotiation, not federal fiat. Broadly tasking the police with immigration work—as envisioned by the Bush administration and pending legislative proposals that would condition federal funding for police departments on their commitment to immigration enforcement (Clear Law Enforcement for Criminal Alien Removal [CLEAR] Act of 2005, H.R. 3137, introduced June 23, 2005)—would in all likelihood result in a net intelligence loss. In the neighborhoods that could be the richest source of terrorist tips, it changes the beat cop from peacekeeper to a potential source of personal ruin.

There also have been signs of real progress. Some have simply emerged out of the recognition that what might previously have been characterized as violent crime programs can be labeled counterterrorism programs, at least for funding purposes, without any disingenuity. In May 2005, the Boston Police Commissioner announced her intention to use federal homeland security money to train and fund a neighborhood watch network. "There's no bright line between terrorism and ordinary inner-city crime," she explained. "Whether it's guns, gangs, drugs, or terrorism, we're going to build whatever we do on the backbone of community policing" (Smalley 2005, p. B1). The move probably did not catch Washington by surprise. A recent Guide on Law Enforcement Intelligence for State, Local, and Tribal Law Enforcement Agencies, commissioned by the Justice Department's COPS office, maintained that there did not have to be a trade-off between community policing and counterterrorism responsibilities and exhorted that "it is time to maximize the potential for community-policing efforts to serve as a gateway of locally based information, to prevent terrorism, and all other crimes" (Carter 2004, p. 40). And a former COPS official advised police officials to "reinforce the fact that the gathering and sharing of timely and accurate information depend on strong partnerships between community residents and police. Defeating criminals and defeating terrorists is not an either-or situation" (Scrivner 2004, p. 189).

Perhaps more significant, however, have been developments with respect to intelligence sharing, in particular the National Criminal Intelligence Sharing Plan. This initiative was spearheaded by the IACP as a response to the September 11 attacks. From the start, it received strong federal backing. Yet its orientation was not limited to counterterrorism. Instead, the "vision" was one in which "state and local agencies are not merely adjuncts to a national strategy for improving intelligence communication, but founding partners of and driving participants in any organization that helps coordinate the collection, analysis, dissemination and use of criminal intelligence data in the U.S." (IACP 2002, p. 2). Thereafter, planners sought to create "a nationally coordinated criminal intelligence council that would develop and oversee a national intelligence plan" (National Criminal Intelligence Sharing Plan 2003, p. iii). While it is far too early to assess (or even detail) this initiative, the plan—which for now exists as a collection of separate programs—appears to promise a new era of collaboration among federal, state, and local agencies, and an infrastructure within which the diverse political and operational concerns of local departments can be raised and addressed (National Criminal Intelligence Sharing Plan 2004).

It would be churlish to suggest that the police have extracted aid in their immediate criminal enforcement responsibilities as the price of their counterterrorism efforts. After all, no responsible police official wants to be on the sidelines of the War on Terror. Yet it is also difficult to avoid seeing in this plan an effort by police officials to strategically pivot off the federal interest in counterterrorism to address their own local criminal enforcement responsibilities. Intelligence-led policing is not an abstract concept, just an underdeveloped one, and one that is fast becoming a focus of attention in modern departments (Cope 2004). Even the police commander interested only in drugs and violent crime can appreciate the benefits of sharing intelligence not just within his department (sometimes a challenge enough) but with neighboring departments, and particularly with departments in areas that serious offenders visit, and so on. This is a mammoth job both organizationally and technically, going far beyond the traditional data sharing of criminal records, license plates, and warrants. But the idea marks a return to the federal role in criminal enforcement that a hopeful observer might have envisioned in the early 1930s: as the sponsor, but not the controller, of a platform for broad interjurisdictional cooperation in the service of each participant's respective enforcement priorities.

A pilot program for the new network developed in a way that itself shows the new local role. In late 2003, after the FBI appeared to have pulled out of a counterterrorism information-sharing project in the Puget Sound area, local officials set one up on their own, the Law Enforcement Information Exchange. By May 2005, the Justice Department had thrown its full support behind the project, declaring it a "regional pilot plan" and ordering all its agencies to share their investigative files with local police forces through the Exchange. The goal, according to Deputy Attorney General James Comey, "is to ensure that DOJ [Department of Justice] information is available for users at all levels of government so that they can more effectively investigate, disrupt and deter criminal activity, including terrorism" (Shukovsky and Barber 2003, p. A1; Shukovsky 2005, p. B4).

In another program encompassed by the National Plan (National Criminal Intelligence Sharing Plan 2003, 47), the sequence was quite different, with the feds taking the field first talking terrorism, but soon leaving it for states to pursue under a more general crime-fighting rationale. The Multi-state Anti-terrorism Information Exchange information sharing project (regrettably dubbed Matrix) was funded by the federal government shortly after September 11. Under the aegis of a private contractor, the Florida Department of Law Enforcement, and the nonprofit Florida-based Institute for Intergovernmental Research, the project sought to establish a massive database from a wide variety of official and commercial sources, which participating states could contribute to and draw on for terrorism and criminal investigations. Initially thirteen states signed up. The program soon came under fire, however, by privacy advocates concerned about the use and misuse of a data repository of this magnitude, and it never got off the ground nationwide (Krouse 2004). By May 2005, the project, and the federal funding, had formally come to an end, with only four states remaining in it. Florida and Ohio, however, continued the program, in part with other federal money (Galnor 2005). And the stories that officials offered to justify their continued participation focused on violent crime: Florida officials told how the system had helped identity a Tampa robbery suspect within hours, assisted in kidnapping investigations, and helped crack a hitherto cold murder case. "Although Matrix was designed as a terrorism tool," the Florida official in charge of it noted, "its main value has been for solving more ordinary crimes" (Galnor 2005; Kalfrin 2005; Royse 2005). An Ohio official noted that Matrix had been used in the investigation of a sniper attacking motorists on an interstate highway (Craig 2005). It remains to be seen whether this program will expand to other states and in what form. Yet (barring an escalation in the pace and scope of terrorist attacks), it seems safe to predict that the primary rationale for it will be regular crime fighting—which, at least outside New York City, remains the gold standard of political justifications in this area.

There will be many kinks to work out as the federal interest in a secure intelligence network is squared with demands for accountability at the local level. One such conflict emerged in 2002–3 in Boise, Idaho. There, the community ombudsman invoked his power, under a city ordinance allowing him access to all police files, to look at files created by a new police intelligence unit. This oversight effort, however, ran afoul of federal intelligence-sharing guidelines that barred access to non–law enforcement officers. Backed by Idaho's congressional delegation and the local U.S. attorney, the city unsuccessfully sought a waiver from the Justice Department. The city council was thus left with the choice of either demanding civilian access and precluding membership in the federal intelligence network or giving up its chosen mechanism for promoting civilian oversight (Orr 2002, 2003). Another conflict is playing out in Portland, Oregon, which has pulled its police force out of the joint terrorism task force because federal officials would not give city leaders the oversight powers they demanded. Without more oversight, the mayor asserted, he could not "guarantee that Portland officers [would] obey state laws barring them from investigating people strictly because of their political or religious ties" (Griffin 2005, p. A1). How these sorts of issues will be resolved around the country remains to be seen. One can cautiously expect intergovernmental negotiations to proceed fruitfully, however, between the gains to localities of membership in the national network and the federal interest in nationwide domestic intelligence capability, and as local governments use their congressional representatives to exert influence over the feds under the now-sacred banner of "information sharing" (GAO 2003a).

Even were localities generally eager to participate in a national intelligence network, there would still need to be coordination at the subnational level. One emerging trend is the readiness of state governments to rise to this challenge and to take on operational responsibilities that they never assumed when violent crime alone lay at the heart of federal-local interaction (Farber 2004; Wickham 2004). In some states, for example, state homeland security task forces have merged with, and even supplanted, the local federal Attorney General Antiterrorism Advisory Council (U.S. Department of Justice, Office of the Inspector General 2005, p. 112). And state intelligence centers have begun to "play an intermediary role, connecting state and local law enforcement officers to the FBI's Terrorist Screening Center, CT Watch, and local Joint Terrorism Task Forces" (National Academy of Public Administration 2005, p. 38). An August 2004 survey by the National Governors Association found that "92 percent of responding states [thirty-eight of the fifty-five states and territories responded] either have completed, or are in the process of developing, a statewide capacity to collect, analyze and disseminate intelligence information, most notably in the form of a state intelligence fusion center" (2005, p. 5).

When states defended their control over LEAA or other block grant programs, their claims to be adding value, in the form of coordination and management, could fairly be challenged by the local governments that shouldered most of the responsibility for policing. In the new post-9/11 information-sharing era, however, states have a far more substantial role to play. If the choice for subnational coordinator lies between regional centers run by the Department of Homeland Security and fusion centers managed by state governments, the latter are more attractive. State views will not fully represent those of their urban instrumentalities, since their needs and burdens can be quite different. The recent tension over immigration law enforcement makes that clear enough. Nonetheless, states—which in any event are politically and constitutionally indispensable—may end up providing ready-made politically accountable platforms to support the new architecture, in a way that a new federal construct could not.

III. Conclusion

Perhaps the coming years will see the threat of terrorism recede and violent crime (regardless of the rate at which it actually occurs) reclaim its place at the heart of intergovernmental relationships in the law enforcement area. Perhaps in the wake of future terrorist attacks, the War on Terror will so dominate all government business that officials at all levels will put aside all other concerns. If we continue on our present trajectory, however, the developing equilibrium will fall far short of either extreme. Spearheaded by the federal government, terrorism prevention efforts will continue and will become more institutionalized. Yet the institutions that develop will have to be largely crafted from a system of federal, state, and local agencies that over the past few decades made violent crime (and drugs) the primary focus of their interactions.

There is a deep irony here: It is not at all clear that the federal government had to commit itself to fighting violent crime in the later part of the twentieth century. That commitment was certainly perceived by the congresses and presidential administrations that pursued it as politically advantageous, and it probably was. Yet whether the federal funding programs and operational initiatives that flourished between 1964 and 2001 actually reduced crime or, more precisely, reduced crime more than a very different allocation of money and enforcement resources would have is open to question. So is whether crime reduction actually ought to be a federal goal. Since the September 11 attacks—followed by the 2004 attacks in the Madrid train station and the 2005 attacks in London—federal spending and enforcement priorities have showed signs of shifting away from violent crime in favor of counterterrorism efforts. Yet the federal government's need to court state and local participation in these efforts and the threat that such participation poses to those governments' traditional policing responsibilities may bind the feds to violent crime concerns—or at least defer to state and local interests in this regard—to a far greater, and less optional, extent than before. Now, the feds have less of a choice.

The United States has never had a "national police force" and, one suspects, never will. But it does need a national police system. Sparked by the September 11 attacks, one is indeed emerging. And it is emerging both from the top down and the bottom up. The feds are certainly pushing from above under the rubric of counterterrorism. But the progress from below, though it enhances federal counterterrorism efforts, has primarily been in the name of ordinary crime fighting. There is no blinking the inherent tension between counterterrorism and street crime enforcement strategies. With thoughtful consideration of the demands of each priority, however, this tension need not be destructive and can in fact lead to a national intelligence and enforcement network that is true to the political values of the nation it protects.

REFERENCES

Abrams, Norman, and Sara Sun Beale. 2000. *Federal Criminal Law and Its Enforcement*. 3rd ed. St. Paul, MN: West Group.

Althouse, Ann. 2001. "Inside the Federalism Cases: Concern about the Federal Courts." *Annals of the American Academy of Political and Social Science* 574: 132–43.

Ansley, Norman. 1956. "The United States Secret Service: An Administrative History." *Journal of Criminal Law, Criminology, and Political Science* 47: 93–109.

Ashcroft, John. 2002. "Remarks: National Security Entry-Exit Registration System" (June 6). http://www.immigration.gov/graphics/preparedremarks .htm.

Annual Report of the Attorney General of the United States for the Fiscal Year 1930. 1930. Washington, DC: Government Printing Office.

Attorney General's Task Force on Violent Crime. 1981. *Final Report*. Washington, DC: U.S. Department of Justice.

Badie, Rick. 2002. "Police Uneasy about Helping Arrest Illegals; Ashcroft Favors Local Assistance." *Atlanta Journal-Constitution* (April 10), p. 1JJ.

Baker, A. Lynn. 1995. "Conditional Federal Spending after Lopez." *Columbia Law Review* 95:1911–89.

Baker, John S. 1999. "State Police Powers and the Federalization of Local Crime." *Temple Law Review* 72:673–713.

Beale, Sara Sun. 1995. "Too Many and Yet Too Few: New Principles to Define the Proper Limits for Federal Criminal Jurisdiction." *Hastings Law Journal* 46:979–1018.

———. 1996. "Federalizing Crime: Assessing the Impact on the Federal Courts." *Annals of the American Academy of Political and Social Science* 543: 39–51.

———. 1997. "What's Law Got to Do with It? The Political, Social, Psychological and Other Non-legal Factors Influencing the Development of (Federal) Criminal Law." *Buffalo Criminal Law Review* 1:23–66.

Beckett, Katherine. 1997. *Making Crime Pay: Law and Order in Contemporary American Politics.* New York: Oxford University Press.

Bergman, Carol A. 1998. "The Politics of Federal Sentencing on Cocaine." *Federal Sentencing Reporter* 10:196–99.

Bill of Rights Defense Committee. 2005. *Grassroots Opposition to the USA Patriot Act* (as of June 15, 2005). http://www.bordc.org/resources/Alphalist.pdf.

Blumstein, Alfred, and Joel Wallman, eds. 2000. *The Crime Drop in America.* Cambridge: Cambridge University Press.

Bonner, Charles D. 1998. "The Federalization of Crime: Too Much of a Good Thing?" *University of Richmond Law Review* 32:905–38.

Boudin, Louis B. 1943. "The Place of the Anti-Racketeering Act in Our Constitutional System." *Cornell Law Quarterly* 28:261–85.

Brickey, Kathleen F. 1995. "Criminal Mischief: The Federalization of American Criminal Law." *Hastings Law Journal* 46:1135–74.

Bureau of Justice Statistics. 1996. "Federal Criminal Case Processing, 1982–93." Washington, DC: U.S. Department of Justice. http://www.ojp.usdoj.gov/bjs/pub/pdf/fccp93.pdf.

———. 2004. *Local Law Enforcement Block Grant Program, 1996–2004.* Washington, DC: U.S. Department of Justice.

Burrough, Bryan. 2004. *Public Enemies: America's Greatest Crime Wave and the Birth of the FBI, 1933–34.* New York: Penguin.

Bush, President George W., and U.S. Attorney General John Ashcroft. 2001. "Remarks: Initiative to Reduce Gun Violence." Federal News Service, May 14.

Bybee, Jay S. 1997. "Insuring Domestic Tranquility: *Lopez*, Federalization of Crime, and the Forgotten Role of the Domestic Violence Clause." *George Washington Law Review* 66:1–83.

Calder, James D. 1993. *The Origins and Development of Federal Crime Control Policy: Herbert Hoover's Initiatives.* Westport, CT: Praeger.

Calhoun, Frederick. 1990. *The Lawmen: U.S. Marshals and Their Deputies, 1789–1989.* Washington, DC: Smithsonian Institution Press.

Caminker, Evan H. 1995. "State Sovereignty and Subordination: May Congress Commandeer State Officers to Implement Federal Law?" *Columbia Law Review* 95:1001–89.

Campbell, Tom. 1999. "Bull's Eye or Wasted Shots? Federal Judges Not among Gun Program's Supporters." *Richmond Times-Dispatch* (January 22), p. A1.

Carter, David L. 2004. *Law Enforcement Intelligence: A Guide for State, Local, and Tribal Law Enforcement*. Washington, DC: U.S. Department of Justice, COPS Office. http://www.cops.usdoj.gov/default.asp?Item = 1439.

Chubb, John E. 1985. "The Political Economy of Federalism." *American Political Science Review* 79:994–1015.

Church Committee. 1976. *Intelligence Activities and Rights of Americans*. Bk. 2, Final Report of the Senate Select Committee to Study Governmental Operations with Respect to Intelligence Activities. April 26. http://www.icdc.com/~paulwolf/cointelpro/churchfinalreportIIb.htm.

Clymer, Adam. 2002. "How Sept. 11 Changed Goals of Justice Dept." *New York Times* (February 28), p. A1.

Clymer, Steven D. 1997. "Unequal Justice, the Federalization of Criminal Law." *Southern California Law Review* 70:643–739.

Committee on Long Range Planning. Judicial Conference of the United States. 1995. *Proposed Long Range Plan for the Federal Courts*. Washington, DC: Committee on Long Range Planning.

Congressional Budget Office. 1996. *Trends in Federal Spending for the Administration of Justice*. Washington, DC: Congressional Budget Office. http://www.cbo.gov/ftpdocs/6xx/doc602/justice.pdf.

Cope, Nina. 2004. "Intelligence Led Policing or Policing Led Intelligence." *British Journal of Criminology* 44:188–203.

Corman, Hope, and H. Naci Mocan. 2000. "A Time-Series Analysis of Crime, Deterrence, and Drug Abuse in New York City." *American Economic Review* 90:584–604.

Craig, Jon. 2005. "ACLU Presses State Not to Use Database, Citing Privacy Issues." *Columbus Dispatch* (April 22), p. C5.

Cronin, Thomas E., Tania Z. Cronin, and Michael E. Milakovich. 1981. *U.S. v. Crime in the Streets*. Bloomington: Indiana University Press.

Crummy, Karen E. 2005. "A Reluctant Enforcer Cites Fiscal, Social, Cost of Policing Immigrants." *Denver Post* (May 31), p. A1.

Cummings, Homer, and Carl McFarland. 1937. *Federal Justice: Chapters in the History of Justice and the Federal Executive*. New York: Macmillan.

Cunningham, David. 2003. "The Patterning of Repression: FBI Counterintelligence and the New Left." *Social Forces* 82:209–40.

Davis, Heather J., and Gerard R. Murphy. 2004. *Protecting Your Community from Terrorism*. Vol. 2, *Working with Diverse Communities*. Washington, DC: Police Executive Research Forum.

Denning, Brannon P., and Glen H. Reynolds. 2003. "Rulings and Resistance: The New Commerce Clause Jurisprudence Encounters the Lower Courts." *Arkansas Law Review* 55:1253–1311.

Diegelman, Robert F. 1982. "Federal Financial Assistance for Crime Control: Lessons of the LEAA Experience." *Journal of Criminal Law and Criminology* 73:994–1011.

DiIulio, John J., Jr., Steven K. Smith, and Aaron J. Saiger. 1995. "The Federal

Role in Crime Control." In *Crime*, edited by James Q. Wilson and Joan Petersilia. San Francisco: Institute for Contemporary Studies.

Donohue, John. 2004. "Clinton and Bush's Report Cards on Crime Reduction: The Data Show Bush Policies Are Undermining Clinton Gains." *Economists' Voice* 1 (1): article 4. http://www.bepress.com/ev.

Eck, John E., and Edward R. McGuire. 2000. "Have Changes in Policing Reduced Violent Crime? An Assessment of the Evidence." In *The Crime Drop in America*, edited by Alfred Blumstein and Joel Wallman. Cambridge: Cambridge University Press.

Eggen, Dan. 2002*a*. "Proposal to Enlist Citizens Was Doomed from Start." *Washington Post* (November 24), p. A11.

———. 2002*b*. "Under Fire, Justice Shrinks TIPS Program." *Washington Post* (August 10), p. A1.

———. 2004. "Bridging the Divide between FBI and Police; Assistant Director Works to Improve Relations." *Washington Post* (February 16), p. A25.

Eisler, Peter, and Kevin Johnson, 2005. "10 Years and $10B Later, COPS Drawing Scrutiny." *USA Today* (April 10), p. A1.

Ekstrand, Laurie E., and Nancy Kingsbury. 2003. "Technical Assessment of Zhao and Thurman's 2001 Evaluation of the Effects of COPS Grants on Crime." Letter dated June 13, 2003, to Hon. F. James Sensenbrenner. GAO 03-867R. Washington, DC: General Accounting Office.

Evans, William N., and Emily Owens. 2005. "Flypaper COPS." Unpublished paper. College Park: University of Maryland. http://www.bsos.umd.edu/econ/evans/wpapers/Flypaper%20COPS.pdf.

Farber, Tom. 2004. "Terrorism Intelligence Center Will Connect Local Cops to Feds." *Boston Herald* (September 23), p. 16.

FBI (Federal Bureau of Investigation). 2000. *Safe Street Violent Crime Initiative Report, FY 2000*. Washington, DC: Federal Bureau of Investigation. http://www.fbi.gov/publications/safestreets/ssgu00.pdf

———. 2004*a*. *Crime in the United States B 2003*. Washington, DC: Federal Bureau of Investigation.

———. 2004*b*. "Department of Justice, Federal Bureau of Investigation Reinforce Commitment to Working with Leaders of Muslim, Sikh and Arab-American Communities." Press release. Washington, DC: Federal Bureau of Investigation, July 9.

———. 2004*c*. *Uniform Crime Reports: January–December 2004* (preliminary). Released June 6, 2005. http://www.fbi.gov/ucr/2004/04prelim.pdf.

Federal Bureau of Prisons. 2001. *About the Federal Bureau of Prisons*. Washington, DC: U.S. Department of Justice.

Feeley, Malcolm M., and Austin D. Sarat. 1980. *The Policy Dilemma: Federal Crime Policy and the Law Enforcement Assistance Administration, 1968–1978*. Minneapolis: University of Minnesota Press.

Fellman, David. 1945. "Some Consequences of Increased Federal Activity in Law Enforcement." *Journal of Criminal Law and Criminology* 35:16–33.

Fox, James Alan, and Marianne W. Zawitz. 2002. *Homicide Trends in the United*

States. Washington, DC: U.S. Department of Justice, Bureau of Justice Statistics.

Fridell, Lorie, and Mary Ann Wycoff, eds. 2004. *Community Policing: The Past, Present, and Future.* Washington, DC: Annie E. Casey Foundation and Police Executive Research Forum.

Galnor, Matt. 2005. "FDLE Wants to Cast a Wider Net." *Florida Times-Union* (May 5), p. A1.

GAO (General Accounting Office). 1996. *Violent Crime: Federal Law Enforcement Assistance in Fighting Los Angeles Gang Violence.* Report to the Attorney General. GAO/GGD-96-150. Washington DC: U.S. General Accounting Office.

———. 2003*a. Homeland Security: Efforts to Improve Information Sharing Need to Be Strengthened.* GAO-03-760. Washington, DC: U.S. General Accounting Office.

———. 2003*b. Homeland Security: Justice Department's Project to Interview Aliens after September 11, 2001.* GAO-03-459. Washington, DC: U.S. General Accounting Office.

———. 2004*a. FBI Transformation: Data Inconclusive on Effect of Shift to Counterterrorism-Related Priorities on Traditional Crime Enforcement.* GAO-04-1036. Washington, DC: U.S. General Accounting Office.

———. 2004*b. FBI Transformation: FBI Continues to Make Progress in Its Efforts to Transform and Address Priorities.* GAO-04-578T. Washington, DC: U.S. General Accounting Office.

———. 2004*c. Security Clearances: FBI Has Enhanced Its Process for State and Local Law Enforcement Officials.* Report to the Ranking Minority Member, Subcommittee on Administrative Oversights and the Courts, Senate Judiciary Committee. GAO-04-596. Washington, DC: U.S. General Accounting Office.

Gaouette, Nicole. 2005. "Senate Is Split on Spending Bill for Domestic Security." *Los Angeles Times* (July 12), p. A16.

Geller, William A., and Norval Morris. 1992. "Relations between Federal and Local Police." In *Modern Policing,* edited by Michael Tonry and Norval Morris. Vol. 15 of *Crime and Justice: A Review of Research,* edited by Michael Tonry. Chicago: University of Chicago Press.

George, Maryanne. 2001. "Criticism after Sept. 11: Words from Police Chief in Spotlight." *Detroit Free Press* (December 4).

Gest, Ted. 2001. *Crime and Politics: Big Government's Erratic Campaign for Law and Order.* New York: Oxford University Press.

Glazer, Elizabeth. 1999. "Thinking Strategically: How Federal Prosecutors Can Reduce Violent Crime." *Fordham Urban Law Review* 26:573–606.

Gorman, Siobhan. 2003. "Detroit Finds Some Answers." *National Journal* 35(13) (March 29).

Griffin, Anna. 2005. "Joy in Gallery as Portland Quits FBI Task Force." *Oregonian* (April 29), p. A1.

Henderson, Dwight F. 1985. *Congress, Courts, and Criminals: The Development of Federal Criminal Law, 1801–1829.* Westport, CT: Greenwood.

Heymann, Philip B. 1998. *Terrorism and America: A Commonsense Strategy for a Democratic Society*. Cambridge, MA: MIT Press.

Heymann, Philip B., and Mark H. Moore. 1996. "The Federal Role in Dealing with Violent Street Crime: Principles, Questions, and Cautions." *Annals of the American Academy of Political and Social Science* 543:103–15.

Hickman, Matthew J., and Brian A. Reaves. 2001. *Community Policing in Local Police Departments, 1997 and 1999*. Bureau of Justice Statistics Special Report. Washington, DC: U.S. Department of Justice, Office of Justice Programs. http://www.ojp.usdoj.gov/bjs/pub/pdf/cplpd99.pdf.

Hills, Roderick M., Jr. 1998. "The Political Economy of Cooperative Federalism: Why State Autonomy Makes Sense and 'Dual Sovereignty' Doesn't." *Michigan Law Review* 96:813–944.

———. 1999. "Dissecting the State: The Use of Federal Law to Free State and Local Officials from State Legislatures' Control." *Michigan Law Review* 97:1201–86.

H.M.'s Inspectorate of Constabulary. 2003. *A Need to Know: HMIC Thematic Inspection of Special Branch and Ports Policing*. London: Home Office.

Hobijn, Bart. 2002. "What Will Homeland Security Cost?" *Federal Reserve Bank of New York Economic Policy Review* 8(2) (November): 21–31.

Hoover, J. Edgar. 1932. "The United States Bureau of Investigation in Relation to Law Enforcement." *Journal of Criminal Law and Criminology* 23:439–53.

———. 1933. "Organized Protection against Organized Predatory Crimes." *Journal of Criminal Law and Criminology* 24:475–82.

———. 1954. "The Basis of Sound Law Enforcement." *Annals of the American Academy of Political and Social Science* 291:39–54.

IACP (International Association of Chiefs of Police). 2002. *Criminal Intelligence Sharing: A National Plan for Intelligence-Led Policing at the Local, State and Federal Levels: Recommendations from the IACP Intelligence Summit*. http://www.theiacp.org/documents/pdfs/Publications/intelsharingreport.pdf.

———. 2004a. "Congress Passes Omnibus Appropriations Bill." *IACP Capitol Report* 3(22) (November 24): 1–2.

———. 2004b. *Enforcing Immigration Law: The Role of State, Tribal and Local Law Enforcement*. http://www.theiacp.org/documents/pdfs/Publications/ImmigrationEnforcementconf%2Epdf.

———. 2005. "FY 2006 Budget Released; State and Local Enforcement Assistance Programs Face Massive Cuts, Elimination." *IACP Capital Report* 4(3) (February 9): 1–3.

Jeffries, John C., and John Gleeson. 1995. "The Federalization of Organized Crime: Advantages of Federal Prosecution." *Hastings Law Journal* 46:1095–1134.

Johnston, David. 1992. "F.B.I. to Shift from Cold War to Crime War." *New York Times* (January 9), p. A18.

Kadish, Sanford H. 1995. "The Folly of Overfederalization." *Hastings Law Journal* 46:1247–51.

Kalfrin, Valerie. 2005. "5 Major Jurisdictions Test Network Connection." *Tampa Tribune* (June 1), metro sec., p. 3.

Keller, William W. 1989. *The Liberals and J. Edgar Hoover: Rise and Fall of a Domestic Intelligence State*. Princeton, NJ: Princeton University Press.

Kelling, George. 1988. *Police and Communities: The Quiet Revolution*. Washington, DC: U.S. Department of Justice, National Institute of Justice.

Kennedy, David M., Anthony A. Braga, Anne M. Phihl, and Elin J. Waring. 2001. *Reducing Gun Violence: The Boston Gun Project's Operation Ceasefire*. NCJ 188741. Washington, DC: U.S. Department of Justice, National Institute of Justice.

Kettl, Donald F. 2003. *The Century Foundation's Homeland Security Project, Working Group on Federalism Challenges: The States and Homeland Security: Building the Missing Link*. New York: Century Foundation.

Kreimer, Seth F. 2004. "Watching the Watchers: Surveillance, Transparency, and Political Freedom in the War on Terror." *University of Pennsylvania Journal of Constitutional Law* 7:133–81.

Krouse, William J. 2004. *The Multi-state Anti-terrorism Information Exchange (MATRIX) Pilot Program*. Washington, DC: Library of Congress, Congressional Research Service.

Kurland, Adam H. 1996. "First Principles of American Federalism and the Nature of Federal Criminal Jurisdiction." *Emory Law Journal* 45:1–94.

Laney, Garrine P. 1998. *Crime Control Assistance through the Byrne Programs*. CRS Report no. 97–265 GOV (updated May 20, 1998). Washington, DC: Library of Congress, Congressional Research Service.

Langum, David J. 1994. *Crossing over the Line: Legislating Morality and the Mann Act*. Chicago: University of Chicago Press.

Law and Contemporary Problems. 1934. "Foreword." 1 (October): 399.

Law Enforcement News. 2003. "Can Criminal Justice Tame the 'Monster' That's Eating It?" 29 (December 15/31), nos. 611, 612.

Levitt, Steven D. 1997. "Using Electoral Cycles in Police Hiring to Estimate the Effect of Police on Crime." *American Economic Review* 87 (June): 270–90

———. 2002. "Using Electoral Cycles in Police Hiring to Estimate the Effect of Police on Crime: Reply." *American Economic Review* 92:1244–50.

———. 2004. "Understanding Why Crime Fell in the 1990s: Four Factors That Explain the Decline and Six That Do Not." *Journal of Economic Perspectives* 18 (Winter): 163–90.

Livingston, Debra. 1999. "Police Reform and the Department of Justice: An Essay on Accountability." *Buffalo Criminal Law Review* 2:815–57.

Maltz, Michael D. 1999. *Bridging Gaps in Police Crime Data*. NCJ 176365. Washington, DC: U.S. Department of Justice, Bureau of Justice Statistics.

Marion, Nancy E. 1994. *A History of Federal Crime Control Initiatives, 1960–1993*. Westport, CT: Praeger.

———. 1997. "Symbolic Politics in Clinton's Crime Control Agenda." *Buffalo Criminal Law Review* 1:67–108.

Mattoon, Richard H. 2004. "The State of the State and Local Government Sector: Fiscal Issues in the Seventh District." *Federal Reserve Bank of Chicago Economic Perspectives* 28:2–17. http://www.chicagofed.org/publications/economicperspectives/ep_1qtr2004_part1_mattoon.pdf.

McCrary, Justin. 2002. "Using Electoral Cycles in Police Hiring to Estimate the Effect of Police on Crime: Comment." *American Economic Review* 92: 1236–43.

McDonald, Douglas, Peter Finn, and Norman Hoffman, 1999. *ASP CJ Report (Overview of Criminal Justice in U.S. over Past Three Decades): Chapter for DOJ Strategic Plan 2000–2005.* Cambridge, MA: Abt Associates (prepared for U.S. Department of Justice, National Institute of Justice, Analytical Support Program).

Miller, Herbert J., Jr. 1963. "A Federal Viewpoint on Combating Organized Crime." *Annals of the American Academy of Political and Social Science* 347: 93–103.

Miller, John, and Michael Stone, with Chris Mitchell. 2003. *The Cell: Inside the 9/11 Plot, and Why the FBI and CIA Failed to Stop It.* New York: Hyperion.

Miller, Judith. 2005. "A New York Cop in Israel, Stepping a Bit on F.B.I. Toes." *New York Times* (May 15), sec 1., p. 37.

Miller, Lisa L., and James Eisenstein. 2005. "The Federal/State Criminal Prosecution Nexus: A Case Study in Cooperation and Discretion." *Law and Social Inquiry* 30:239–68.

Millspaugh, Arthur C. 1937. *Crime Control by the National Government.* Washington, DC: Brookings Institution.

Miner, Roger J. 1992. "Crime and Punishment in the Federal Courts." *Syracuse Law Review* 43:681–93.

Mintz, John. 2005. "Security Spending Initiates Disputes." *Washington Post* (April 13), p. A15.

Moore, Mark Harrison. 1992. "Problem-Solving and Community Policing." In *Modern Policing*, edited by Michael Tonry and Norval Morris. Vol. 15 of *Crime and Justice: A Review of Research*, edited by Michael Tonry. Chicago: University of Chicago Press.

Moulton, H. Geoffrey. 1999. "The Quixotic Search for a Judicially Enforceable Federalism." *Minnesota Law Review* 83:849–925.

Multistate Tax Commission. 2003. *Federalism at Risk.* Washington, DC: Multistate Tax Commission. http://www.mtc.gov/Federalism/FedatRisk--FINALREPORT.pdf.

Murphy, Gerald R., and Martha R. Plotkin. 2003. *Protecting Your Community from Terrorism: The Strategies for Local Law Enforcement Series.* Vol. 1, *Improving Local-Federal Partnerships.*Washington, DC: Police Executive Research Forum and U.S. Department of Justice, Office of Community Oriented Policing Services.

National Academy of Public Administration. 2005. *Transforming the FBI: Progress and Challenges.* Washington, DC: National Academy of Public Administration.

National Criminal Intelligence Sharing Plan. 2003. Washington, DC: U.S. Department of Justice, Office of Justice Programs, October.

National Criminal Intelligence Sharing Plan—Executive Summary. 2004. Washington, DC: U.S. Department of Justice, Office of Justice Programs. Revised November.

National Governors Association. Center for Best Practices. 2005. *Homeland Security in the States: Much Progress, More Work*. Issue brief. Washington, DC: National Governors Association. http://www.nga.org/cda/files/0502HOMESEC.pdf.

Navasky, Victor, with Darrell Paster. 1976. *Background Paper for Law Enforcement: The Federal Role*. Report of the Twentieth Century Fund Task Force on the Law Enforcement Assistance Administration. New York: McGraw-Hill.

O'Bryant, Joanne. 2003. *Crime Control: The Federal Response*. Washington, DC: Library of Congress, Congressional Research Service (updated March 5).

———. 2004. *Federal Crime Control Assistance to State and Local Governments*. Washington, DC: Library of Congress, Congressional Research Service (updated May 26).

O'Hear, Michael M. 2002. "National Uniformity/Local Uniformity: Reconsidering the Use of Departures to Reduce Federal-State Sentencing Disparities." *Iowa Law Review* 87:721–73.

———. 2004. "Federalism and Drug Control." *Vanderbilt Law Review* 57:783–882.

Oliphant, Jim. 2001. "DOJ Trims State Funds." *Legal Times* (April 16), p. 18.

O'Reilly, Kenneth. 1982. "A New Deal for the FBI: The Roosevelt Administration, Crime Control, and National Security." *Journal of American History* 69:638–58.

———. 1998. "The FBI and the Politics of the Riots, 1964–1968." *Journal of American History* 75:91–114.

Orr, Patrick. 2002. "Request for Crime-Record Waiver Lost; Feds' OK Needed for Ombudsman to Review Files." *Idaho Statesman* (December 29), p. 1.

———. 2003. "Council Needs to Decide on Ombudsman's Access to CIU Files: Intelligence Team Needs Oversight, Critics Believe." *Idaho Statesman* (April 20), p. 1.

Potter, Claire Bond. 1998. *War on Crime: Bandits, G-Men, and the Politics of Mass Culture*. New Brunswick, NJ: Rutgers University Press.

Powers, Richard Gid. 1987. *Secrecy and Power: The Life of J. Edgar Hoover*. New York: Free Press.

———. 2004. *Broken: The Troubled Past and Uncertain Future of the FBI*. New York: Free Press.

President's Commission on Law Enforcement and Administration of Justice. 1967. *The Challenge of Crime in a Free Society*. Washington, DC: U.S. Government Printing Office.

Ragavan, Chitra, and Monika Guttman. 2004. "Terror on the Streets: The FBI Prepares to Help Beleaguered Police Chiefs Fight a New Brand of Gang Violence That's Spreading like Wildfire." *U.S News & World Report* (December 13).

Raphael, Steven, and Jens Ludwig. 2003. "Prison Sentence Enhancements: The Case of Project Exile." In *Evaluating Gun Policy: Effects on Crime and*

Violence, edited by Jens Ludwig and Philip J. Cook. Washington, DC: Brookings Institution Press.

Reese, Shawn. 2005. *State and Homeland Security: Unresolved Issues for the 109th Congress*. Washington, DC: Library of Congress, Congressional Research Service.

Reeves, Brian A., and Lynn M. Bauer. 2003. *Federal Law Enforcement Officers, 2002*. Washington, DC: U.S. Department of Justice, Bureau of Justice Statistics.

Reeves, Brian A., and Matthew J. Hickman. 2002. *Census of State and Local Law Enforcement Agencies, 2000*. Washington, DC: U.S. Department of Justice, Bureau of Justice Statistics.

Rehnquist, William H. 1999. "The 1998 Year-End Report of the Federal Judiciary." *Third Branch* 31 (1) (January). http://www.uscourts.gov/ttb/jan99ttb/january1999.html.

Richman, Daniel C. 1999. "Federal Criminal Law, Congressional Delegation, and Enforcement Discretion." *UCLA Law Review* 46:757–814.

———. 2000. "The Changing Boundaries between Federal and Local Enforcement." In *Criminal Justice 2000*. Vol. 2, *Boundary Changes in Criminal Justice Organizations*. NCJ 182409. Washington, DC: U.S. Department of Justice, National Institute of Justice.

———. 2001. "'Project Exile' and the Allocation of Federal Law Enforcement Authority." *Arizona Law Review* 43:369–411.

———. 2002. "Federal Criminal Law Enforcement." In *Encyclopedia of Crime and Justice*, vol. 2, edited by Joshua Dressler. 2nd ed. New York. Macmillan Reference.

———. 2003. "Prosecutors and Their Agents, Agents and Their Prosecutors." *Columbia Law Review* 103:749–832.

Richman, Daniel C., and William J. Stuntz. 2005. "The Revenge of Al Capone: An Essay on the Political Economy of Pretextual Prosecution." *Columbia Law Review* 105:583–639.

Rogovin, Charles. 1973. "Genesis of the Law Enforcement Assistance Administration: A Personal Account." *Columbia Human Rights Law Review* 5:9–25.

Rosen, Lawrence. 1995. "The Creation of the Uniform Crime Report: The Role of Social Science." *Social Science History* 19:215–38.

Roth, Jeffrey, et al. 2000. *National Evaluation of the COPS Program—Title I of the 1994 Crime Act*. NCJ 183643. Washington, DC: U.S. Department of Justice, National Institute of Justice.

Royse, David. 2005. "Police Still Using Matrix-Type Database." *Miami Herald* (July 10). http://www.miami.com/mld/miamiherald/news/12101226.htm.

Rubin, Edward. 1934. "A Statistical Study of Federal Criminal Prosecutions." *Law and Contemporary Problems* 1:494–504.

Rubin, Edward L., and Malcolm Feeley. 1994. "Federalism: Some Notes on a National Neurosis." *UCLA Law Review* 41:903–52.

Russell-Einhorn, Malcolm, Shawn Ward, and Amy Seeherman. 2000. *Federal-Local Law Enforcement Collaboration in Investigating and Prosecuting Urban Crime, 1982–1999: Drugs, Weapons, and Gangs*. Report prepared for the National Institute of Justice, U.S. Department of Justice. Washington, DC: Abt Associates.

Scheingold, Stuart S. 1984. *The Politics of Law and Order: Street Crime and Public Policy*. New York: Longman.

Schwartz, Louis B. 1977. "Reform of the Federal Criminal Laws: Issues, Tactics, and Prospects." *Law and Contemporary Problems* 41:1–62.

Scott, Michael S. 2000. *Problem-Oriented Policing: Reflections on the First 20 Years*. Washington, DC: U.S. Department of Justice, Office of Community Oriented Policing Services.

Scrivner, Ellen. 2004. "The Impact of September 11 on Community Policing." In *Community Policing: The Past, Present, and Future*, edited by Lorie Fridell and Mary Ann Wycoff. Washington, DC: Annie E. Casey Foundation and Police Executive Research Forum.

Seper, Jerry. 2001. "Justice Budget Targets Drug Use, Gun Crimes, Attacks on Women." *Washington Times* (April 27), p. A5.

Shapiro, Walter. 2003. "'Awareness' Project Unites Left, Right." *USA Today* (January 17), p. A4.

Sherman, Lawrence, W. 1992. "Attacking Crime: Police and Crime Control." In *Modern Policing*, edited by Michael Tonry and Norval Morris. Vol. 15 of *Crime and Justice: A Review of Research*, edited by Michael Tonry. Chicago: University of Chicago Press.

Sherman, Lawrence W., et al. 1997. *Preventing Crime: What Works, What Doesn't, What's Promising*. Report to the U.S. Congress. Washington, DC: U.S. Department of Justice, National Institute of Justice. http://www.ncjrs.org/works/index.htm.

Shukovsky, Paul. 2005. "State Law Enforcement to Get Feds' Help." *Seattle Post-Intelligencer* (May 13), p. B4.

Shukovsky, Paul, and Mike Barber. 2003. "Data Exchange Critical in Nabbing Terrorists." *Seattle Post-Intelligencer* (November 29), p. A1.

Silver, Jonathan D. 2004. "City Takes Aim at Gun Crimes; Federal Partnership Expected to Result in Stiffer Sentences." *Pittsburgh Post-Gazette* (July 12), p. B4.

Skolnick, Jerome H., and David H. Bayley. 1988. "Theme and Variation in Community Policing." In *Crime and Justice: A Review of Research*, vol. 10, edited by Michael Tonry and Norval Morris. Chicago: University of Chicago Press.

Smalley, Suzanne. 2005. "Terror Plan Relies on Watch Groups." *Boston Globe* (May 30), p. B1.

Song, Jason. 2003. "Local Police May Get Role in Immigrant Law; Federal Bill to Address Disparities among Agencies." *Baltimore Sun* (July 9), p. 1B.

Specter, Arlen, and Paul R. Michel. 1982. "The Need for a New Federalism in Criminal Justice." *Annals of the American Academy of Political and Social Science* 462:59–71.

Stephens, Darryl W. 1999. "Measuring What Matters." In *Measuring What Matters: Proceedings from the Policing Research Institute Meetings*. Washington, DC: U.S. Department of Justice, Office of Justice Programs.

Stuntz, William J. 1998. "Race, Class, and Drugs." *Columbia Law Review*. 98: 1795–1842.

Sullivan, Laura. 2003. "FBI Courts Relations with Arabs, Muslims." *Baltimore Sun* (October 27), p. A1.

Swarns, Rachel L. 2004. "Local Officers Join Search for Illegal Immigrants." *New York Times* (April 12), p. A14.

Task Force on the Federalization of Criminal Law. 1998. *The Federalization of Criminal Law*. Washington, DC: American Bar Association, Criminal Justice Section.

Thacher, David. 2005. "The Local Role in Homeland Security." *Law and Society Review* 39:635–76.

Theoharis, Athan G. 1999. *The FBI: A Comprehensive Reference Guide*. Phoenix: Oryx.

Thompson, Cheryl W. 2002. "INS Role for Police Considered; U.S. Eyes State, Local Help in Enforcing Immigration Laws." *Washington Post* (April 4), p. A15.

Traub, Stuart H. 1988. "Rewards, Bounty Hunting, and Criminal Justice in the West: 1865–1900." *Western Historical Quarterly* 19:287–301.

Ungar, Sanford J. 1976. *FBI*. Boston: Little Brown.

U.S. Conference of Mayors. 2002a. *The Cost of Heightened Security in America's Cities*. Washington, DC: U.S. Conference of Mayors.

———. 2002b. *One Year Later: A Status Report on the Federal-Local Partnership on Homeland Security*. Washington, DC: U.S. Conference of Mayors. http://www.usmayors.org/uscm/us_mayor_newspaper/documents/09_19_02/status_report.asp.

U.S. Department of Justice. 2002. *Fact Sheet 2002: Overview of Information Sharing Initiatives in the War on Terrorism*. Washington, DC: U.S. Department of Justice. http://www.cdt.org/security/usapatriot/020923overview.pdf.

———. 2004. "Justice Department Announces New Violent Crime Reduction Initiative." Press release. Washington, DC: U.S. Department of Justice, June 24.

———. 2005. "Attorney General Alberto R. Gonzalez Announces Arrests of More than 10,000 Fugitives through Operation FALCON. Press release. Washington, DC: U.S. Department of Justice, April 14.

———. Audit Division. 2004. *The Internal Effects of the Federal Bureau of Investigation's Reprioritization*. Washington, DC: Office of the Inspector General.

———. Evaluation and Inspections Division. 2005. *The Department of Justice's Terrorism Task Forces*. Washington, DC: Office of the Inspector General.

———. Office of the Inspector General. 1999. *Management and Administration of the Community Oriented Policing Services Grant Program*. Washington, DC: Office of the Inspector General. http://www.usdoj.gov/oig/au9921/9921toc.htm.

U.S. Government Accountability Office. 2005. *Interim Report on the Effects of COPS Funds on the Decline of Crime during the 1990s*. GAO-05-699R (June 3). Washington: DC: U.S. Government Accountability Office.

U.S. House of Representatives, Judiciary Committee. 2003. *War on Terrorism: Immigration Enforcement since Sept. 11, 2001: Hearing before the Border Security and Claims Subcommittee.* 108th Cong., 1st sess., May 8.

———. Select Committee on Homeland Security. 2004. *An Analysis of First Responder Grant Funding.* Washington, DC: House Select Committee on Homeland Security, April 27.

U.S. Senate. Governmental Affairs Committee. 2003*a. Investing in Homeland Security: Challenges on the Front Line.* 108th Cong., 1st sess., April 9.

———. 2003*b. Hearing on Investing in Homeland Security: Challenges Facing State and Local Governments.* 108th Cong., 1st sess., May 15.

U.S. Sentencing Commission. 1991. *Special Report to Congress: Mandatory Minimum Penalties in the Federal Criminal Justice System.* Washington, DC: U.S. Sentencing Commission.

Varon, Jay N. 1975. "A Reexamination of the Law Enforcement Assistance Administration." *Stanford Law Review* 27:1303–24.

Vizzard, William J. 1997. *In the Cross Fire: A Political History of the Bureau of Alcohol, Tobacco and Firearms.* Boulder, CO: Lynne Rienner Publishers.

Walker, Patrick, and Pragati Patrick. 2000. *Trends in Firearms Cases from Fiscal Year 1989 through 1998, and the Workload Implications for the U.S. District Courts.* Washington, DC: Administrative Office of the U.S. Courts. http://www.uscourts.gov/firearms/firearms00.html.

Whitehead, Don. 1956. *The FBI Story: A Report to the People.* New York: Random House.

Wickham, Shawne K. 2004. "Facing the Terrorist Threat: State's Local-Control Tradition a Factor in Planning." *Manchester (NH) Union Leader* (September 5), p. A15.

Wilkenson, J. Harvie. 1994. "The Drawbacks of Growth in the Federal Judiciary." *Emory Law Journal* 43:1147–88.

Wise, Charles R., and Rania Nader. 2002. "Organizing the Federal System for Homeland Security: Problems, Issue, and Dilemmas." *Public Administration Review* 62:44–57.

Zhao, Jihong, Matthew C. Scheider, and Quint Thurman. 2002. "Funding Community Policing to Reduce Crime: Have COPS Grants Made a Difference?" *Journal of Criminology and Public Policy* 2:7–32.

Zhao, Jihong, and Quint Thurman. 2003. "Reflections and Issues Involved with Our Research Project: The Effect of COPS Funding on Crime Reduction in the U.S." Manuscript. Omaha: University of Nebraska. http://www.unomaha.edu/uac/releases/2003july/zhaopurpose2.pdf.

Zimring, Frank, and Gordon Hawkins. 1992. *The Search for Rational Drug Control.* Cambridge: Cambridge University Press.

———. 1996. "Toward a Principled Basis for Federal Criminal Legislation." *Annals of the American Academy of Political and Social Science* 543:15–26.

Peter Scharff Smith

The Effects of Solitary Confinement on Prison Inmates: A Brief History and Review of the Literature

ABSTRACT

The effects of solitary confinement have been debated since at least the middle of the nineteenth century when both Americans and Europeans began to question the then-widespread use of solitary confinement of convicted offenders. A sizable and impressively sophisticated literature, now largely forgotten, accumulated for more than a half century and documented significant damage to prisoners. More recently the development of supermax prisons in the United States and human rights objections to pretrial solitary confinement in Scandinavia revived interest in the topic and controversy over the findings. The weight of the modern evidence concurs with the findings of earlier research: whether and how isolation damages people depends on duration and circumstances and is mediated by prisoners' individual characteristics; but for many prisoners, the adverse effects are substantial.

The use of solitary confinement can be traced far back[1] but became common with the rise of the modern penitentiary during the first half of the nineteenth century. The practice of isolating individual prisoners has changed significantly since then but has remained a feature of

Peter Scharff Smith is senior researcher at the Danish Institute for Human Rights. He is grateful to Henrik Steen Andersen, Craig Haney, Alison Liebling, Ole Scharff, Annika Snare, Hans Toch, and Michael Tonry for comments on earlier drafts.

[1] Perhaps to the monastic practice of imprisonment during the Middle Ages: so-called *murus strictus* or "close confinement," e.g., seems to indicate imprisonment akin to solitary confinement (Peters 1998, p. 26).

441

Western prison systems. A debate about the effects of solitary confinement was largely settled early in the twentieth century, when the use of large-scale solitary confinement appeared to be on the way out in most Western prison systems. Discussions on the effects of solitary confinement resurfaced in the 1950s when sensory deprivation and perceptual deprivation studies were carried out partly in reaction to stories of brainwashing of U.S. prisoners of war (POWs) during the Korean War. These studies waned by the early 1970s. During the 1980s solitary confinement again regained topicality when supermax prisons caused an explosion in the use of solitary confinement. Probably much less known, pretrial solitary confinement has for many years been an integral part of Scandinavian prison practice and has in recent decades been considered a significant problem. Amnesty International and other human rights organizations regularly report on uses of isolation in prisons elsewhere: for example, in Turkey (Human Rights Watch 2001; Amnesty International 2003), Iran (Human Rights Watch 2004a), and Tunisia (Human Rights Watch 2004b). The use of isolation in connection with interrogations and the current "war on terrorism" is also well known. According to an official U.S. report, "isolation for up to 30 days" has been used at Guantanamo, and isolations "for long periods of time" have been used in Afghanistan (Schlesinger et al. 2004, p. 68; Greenberg and Dratel 2005, p. 227). Use of long-term isolation at Guantanamo has also been reported—eleven months in the case of Salim Ahmed Hamdan (Brief of Amici Curiae Human Rights First et al., *Hamdan v. Rumsfeld*, 546 U.S. 05-184 [2005], p. 15).

Solitary confinement is occasionally used in most prison systems as a means to maintain prison order: as disciplinary punishment or as an administrative measure for inmates who are considered an escape risk or a risk to themselves or to prison order in general. Some inmates, for example, sex offenders, choose voluntary isolation to avoid harassment from other prisoners. Finally, solitary confinement can be used in remand prisons to prevent pretrial detainees from tampering with witnesses or to force out a confession.

The American Supermax. Supermax prisons began with an October 1983 lockdown in Marion Penitentiary in Illinois, following the killing of two prison guards in two different situations on the same day. This happened when the U.S. prison system had been struggling with a rise in prison violence for more than a decade (King 1999, p. 165).[2] In 1979 Marion had become the first level 6 "super–maximum security" prison in the United States (Pizarro and Stenius 2004, p. 250), but this regime was superseded in 1983 when the October lockdown was never lifted: inmates were confined to their cells without access to communal activities, and the use of solitary confinement as a tool used against disruptive prisoners became an ordinary measure.

The Marion lockdown regime (later termed "supermax") inspired similar developments in many U.S. states. By 1997 there were fifty-five supermax facilities in thirty-four states, and in 1998 around 20,000 people were held in supermax facilities, compared to fewer than fifty prisoners held in the very highest security or close supervision centers in England and Wales in 1999 (King 1999, p. 164; Pizarro and Stenius 2004, p. 251). Today there are at least fifty-seven supermax prisons/units in the United States (Brief of Amici Curiae Human Rights Watch et al., *Wilkinson v. Austin*, 545 U.S. 04-495 [2005], p. 8). Rhodes (2004) counts more than sixty U.S. supermax facilities.

Supermax conditions typically include solitary confinement twenty-three hours each day in a barren environment, under constant high-tech surveillance. Inmates are sometimes able to shout to each other but otherwise have no social contact. Most verbal communication with prison staff takes place through intercom systems (Pizarro and Stenius 2004, p. 251). Communication with the outside world is minimal. Visits and phone calls are infrequent and are severely restricted if allowed at all. Visits sometimes take place only via video screens (Kurki and Morris 2001, p. 389). The physical contact available to an inmate in a supermax facility may for several years "be limited to being touched through a security door by a correctional officer while being placed in restraints or having restraints removed" (Riveland 1999, p. 11). These facilities typically claim to operate a regime of behavior modification, but most provide few program activities such as work or education.

A primary rationale for supermax prisons has been to lower the level of violence in prison systems. Recent research, however, suggests that supermax prisons do not fulfill that objective. A study of facilities in three different U.S. states concludes that "the effectiveness of supermax prisons as a mechanism to enhance prison safety remains largely speculative" (Briggs, Sundt, and Castellano 2003, p. 1371). Despite these

---

[2] The term "marionization of American prisons" has been used; see Immarigeon (1992, p. 1).

findings and despite the extreme nature of supermax regimes, "the arguments given on behalf of such facilities are few in number and almost embarrassingly brief" (Lipke 2004, p. 109).

Supermax prisons, their practices and institutional cultures, and the effects of solitary confinement have been the focus of a number of court cases. Recently the way that prisoners are allocated to supermax prisons has been challenged as a violation of due process (*Wilkinson v. Austin*, 545 U.S. 495 [2005]), but most cases have been concerned with the conditions of imprisonment. There has been a "general refusal of courts to find isolated confinement unconstitutional absent aggravating circumstances," although specific conditions in specific facilities have been found to violate the Eighth Amendment of the U.S. Constitution (banning "cruel and unusual punishment") (Boston 2000, p. 4). Several U.S. courts have severely criticized conditions in supermax prisons, but long-term isolation as such has not been declared illegal (*Madrid v. Gomez*, 889 F. Supp. 1146 [N.D. Cal. 1995]; King 1999). According to Hans Toch (2002*b*, p. 16), "courts have hesitated to tell prison administrators that conditions of confinement in their supermax or control units are constitutionally impermissible or unacceptable, even where judicial dicta reek of personal disapproval of such conditions." One reason might be that while the courts feel confident in scrutinizing the physical conditions of imprisonment, they "are hesitant to consider the psychological impact on the prisoner" (Luise 1989, p. 302).

Scandinavian Pretrial Confinement.   Solitary pretrial confinement in Denmark was originally adopted following the Danish 1846 jail regulations, which prescribed the construction of single cells in jails nationwide. By the 1870s, most Danish jails were able to isolate their remand prisoners. This practice continued more or less unchanged during the next 100 years. Since the 1970s the use of solitary confinement in pretrial detention (also called "remand") has declined, but it remains a feature of Danish prison practice. The original rationales were moral (remand prisoners should not be demoralized by each other's company) and practical (to avoid possibilities of collusion, detainees were not allowed to interfere with the investigation), but the moral rationale was abandoned during the twentieth century. Conditions faced by isolated Danish remand prisoners today are very different from those of their U.S. supermax counterparts and would probably be considered much more humane by most observers.[3]

―――――――――
[3] Still, an isolation cell in a typical Danish remand prison is a barren environment of

In 1977 the Danish isolation practice was "rediscovered" after years of unquestioned use; decades of heated debate followed (Koch and Petersen 1988, p. 69). During 1978–79 at least sixty-four articles about solitary confinement appeared in two national newspapers, and during 1980–81 at least sixty articles appeared in three national newspapers. Writers included politicians, lawyers, doctors, psychologists, chaplains, nongovernmental organizations, prisoners, the Danish police, and the Danish Prison Service.[4]

Solitary confinement in Danish remand prisons has received substantial international criticism. In 1980 and 1983 Amnesty International criticized the use of solitary confinement in Denmark (Koch and Petersen 1988, p. 80), and international criticisms grew stronger during the 1990s. Two key actors were the European Committee for the Prevention of Torture (CPT) and the Committee against Torture (CAT). In 1997, CAT recommended that "the use of solitary confinement be abolished, particularly during pre-trial detention, or at least that it should be strictly and specifically regulated by law (maximum duration, etc.) and that judicial supervision should be introduced" (Committee against Torture 1997, paras. 171–88). The CPT visited Denmark in 1990, 1996, and 2002, each time critically raising issues concerning solitary confinement. In 1990 CPT stated that solitary confinement should be used only in "exceptional circumstances." In 1996 CPT called for an increase in meaningful social contact for isolated inmates, and this recommendation was elaborated in 2002 (see visit reports at http://www.cpt.coe.int/en/).

The earlier Danish controversy in 1978 led to a law that subjected solitary confinement of remand prisoners to judicial review. The police, however, simply had to invoke a "reason for the detention in remand" to explain why the detained individual should be isolated (Danish Ministry of Justice 1983, p. 21). In effect, solitary confinement would normally be granted if the police argued that the accused could disturb

---

six to eight square meters, which contains a bed, a chair, a cupboard, a shelf, and a sink. Radio and television can be allowed or disallowed according to the prisoner's circumstances and the wishes of the police. Isolated remand prisoners normally spend around twenty-three hours in their cell each day and are allowed out daily in the exercise yard. This exercise takes place in isolation, e.g., in a six-meter-long triangular space.

[4] On the basis of an archive of newspaper clippings about solitary confinement, 1978–98, originally created by the so-called Isolation Group. The archive is now located at the DCISM library in Copenhagen.

the ongoing investigation. Forty-three percent of all Danish remand prisoners were isolated during 1979–82 (p. 88).

Further revisions in 1984 provided that isolation could be used to keep the detainee from disturbing the ongoing investigation. A proportionality principle was introduced under which the possible length of the period of isolation was connected to the severity of the charges. Remand prisoners could never be isolated for more than eight weeks unless the charges against them could result in imprisonment for six years or more.[5] The intention was to reduce the use of solitary confinement. This was achieved, and 21.5 percent of all remand prisoners were isolated in 1990 compared to 31.4 percent in 1984. But this was still a sizable number involving more than 1,000 imprisonments in isolation.

In 2000 a new law further elaborated the principle of proportionality and called for increased social contacts for inmates in solitary confinement. A so-called maximum limit of three months was introduced— "so-called" because it remains possible to isolate individuals for an unlimited time under special circumstances. It was (and is) possible to subject children under the age of eighteen to pretrial solitary confinement (Koch et al. 2003, p. 321).

During the late 1990s, use of pretrial isolation significantly declined (possibly inspired by the international critique), with 20.1 percent of all remand prisoners isolated in 1995 compared with 12.7 percent in 1999. The decline continued to 8.2 percent in 2002. There were still 501 pretrial imprisonments in a country with a population of 5.4 million and an average prison population of 3,435 inmates in 2002.[6] At the same time, though, the average length of a stay in pretrial solitary confinement has risen from twenty-seven days in 1988 to thirty-seven days in 2003 (Smith 2005, p. 12). The total number of days spent in pretrial solitary confinement has therefore gone up, and during 2003 and 2004 rose to a level beyond the situation in 2000.

Danish use of isolation in remand prisons became topical again during 2004. The European Court of Human Rights (ECHR) accepted a case in which the Danish state was charged with breaching article 3 of

[5] It has been pointed out that it is problematic to apply the principle of proportionality in connection with remand prisoners who are still to be considered not guilty; the question is how pain can be applied and graduated according to a possibly nonexisting offense (Koch et al. 2003, p. 320).

[6] See figures and tables in *Rigsadvokaten Informerer*, no. 21/2003 (http://www .rigsadvokaten.dk/).

the European Convention on Human Rights: "No one shall be sub-jected to torture or to inhuman or degrading treatment or punishment" (1950)—a case that was concerned with the effects of solitary confine-ment. In December 1994 a Danish citizen was arrested at Copenhagen airport, charged with drug trafficking, and sent into solitary confine-ment in Denmark's largest remand prison. There he spent almost a year while the police investigated the matter. In November 1995, the Copenhagen city court lifted the isolation after the accused had sup-plied the police and the court with a version of the story that they believed. The detainee had difficulty leaving solitary confinement and stayed in voluntary isolation for two more weeks, after which he was transferred to communal prison detention. In May 1996 he was ac-quitted of the drug offenses but convicted for tax fraud. It was later discovered that the accused had become insane (paranoid psychotic) during his stay in solitary—a finding on which the Danish Supreme Court, the Danish Legal-Psychiatric Clinic, and the accused concurred. A claim for compensation went through the Danish court system. In the end the Danish Supreme Court offered economic compensation but refused to label his treatment as torture or inhuman or degrading treatment (*Rohde v. Denmark*, the European Court of Human Rights Series A no. 69332/01 [2003]). On July 21, 2005, the ECHR ruled with four votes against three that there had been no violation of article 3. The three dissenting judges argued that the Copenhagen city court (and on appeal the High Court) never explained why it was necessary to isolate the accused and thought it "noteworthy" (*Rohde v. Denmark*, p. 38) that solitary confinement was lifted as soon as the applicant had confessed his involvement in the case. They furthermore pointed out that "no psychological or psychiatric examination was carried out of the applicant" (p. 39) for the last ten months of his isolation, although the effects of solitary confinement were well known, and concluded that Denmark had indeed violated article 3 (*Rohde v. Denmark*, Euro-pean Court of Human Rights Series A no. 69332/01 [2005]).[7] I wrote a report on "The Effects of Solitary Confinement on Prison Inmates" for the prosecution in that case, which formed a starting point for this essay.

Sweden, Norway, and Iceland also have a recent history of extensive

---

[7] This and another recent judgment suggest that the ECHR is finding it difficult to adopt a line in cases concerning the use of solitary confinement in prisons. See Ramirez Sanchez v. France (59450/00), where three out of seven judges also dissented.

use of solitary confinement of remand prisoners—along lines similar to those in Denmark—and have likewise received international criticism from human rights organizations (Smith 2005). As in Denmark, national criticism has been voiced in Norway (although with less intensity). Yngve Hammerlin has described remand imprisonment and isolation in Norway as a "significant ethical problem for the Government services and the rule of law" (2001, p. 19; author's translation) and has found this practice to be in violation of the official principles of the Norwegian Prison Service (p. 20). The Norwegian Prison Service has itself started working seriously toward a better remand practice, but the use of isolation remains a problem (see, e.g., Danielsen and Hansen 2002).

Though several other countries have limited provisions for isolating remand prisoners to avoid collusion, the routine use of pretrial solitary confinement has been termed a Scandinavian phenomenon (Evans and Morgan 1998, p. 247). Rod Morgan has compared this Scandinavian practice with the use of so-called moderate psychological pressure against detained suspects in Israel. He describes how Scandinavian media in 1999 "joyfully published" news of how this practice, which they described as "a euphemism for torture," had been declared illegal by the Israeli Supreme Court. Morgan asked (in a Norwegian journal), "can Scandinavia in general, and Norway in particular, be so self-righteous and complacent? If torture involves the purposive imposition of severe pain in order to gather evidence—confessions, information about accomplices—do you not also torture?" (Morgan 1999, p. 201).

A Definition of Solitary Confinement. Conditions of solitary confinement vary significantly. In this essay the term solitary confinement refers to physical isolation of individuals in which they are confined in their cells for around twenty-three hours each day (typically twenty-two to twenty-four hours). The amount of contact with prison staff can vary and may constitute more than an hour each day, but only rarely will this contact be socially and psychologically meaningful. Contact with prison staff typically takes place in connection with being escorted to the exercise yard or the toilet or through brief encounters when meals are delivered to the cell door. Complete and total isolation is not practiced anywhere. In that sense, solitary confinement constitutes individual social isolation (and perhaps perceptual deprivation) rather than sensory deprivation (Volkart, Dittrich, et al. 1983, p. 27). In many so-called supermax prisons in the United States, it is possible for inmates to communicate by shouting to each other. In many other isolation prisons, various methods can be used such as knocking on walls or lowering strings with messages from cell windows (concerning other definitions of solitary confinement, see Haney and Lynch [1997, p. 496]).

The key factor is that socially and psychologically meaningful contact is reduced to a minimum (Andersen 2004, p. 41). The reduction in stimuli is not only quantitative but also qualitative. The available stimuli and the occasional social contacts are seldom freely chosen, are generally monotonous, and are not typically empathetic.

Sources of Knowledge.   This essay draws on a large number of very diverse sources. They can be grouped into the following categories:

- historical texts of various kinds including nineteenth-century books, articles, and treatises concerning solitary confinement (mainly from the United States, the United Kingdom, and Scandinavia);
- archival materials, principally nineteenth-century material from the Danish Vridsløselille Penitentiary;
- research on sensory deprivation and perceptual deprivation, but this work is treated only briefly;
- post–World War II professional studies of solitary confinement in prisons (and studies of prison health)—ranging from qualitative research with in-depth interviews to randomized medical studies with control groups; and
- a number of related studies concerning isolation of POWs, hostages, and comparable situations, but they are referred to only occasionally.

These sources are based on different and divergent conceptions of history, social science, science, and methodology and can be interpreted in diverse ways. A review of this kind calls for an interdisciplinary approach, which can encompass and use research of many kinds. It is my modest hope that such an approach can help "mend and mind the misconceived gap between science and the humanities," which seems to have played a part in the debate over solitary confinement.[8]

A number of methodological issues are discussed throughout the

---

[8] This is a play on words from Stephen Jay Gould, whose last book after his death in 2002 bears the title *The Hedgehog, the Fox, and the Magister's Pox: Mending and Minding the Misconceived Gap between Science and the Humanities* (2003).

essay, but two issues are preliminarily discussed here: first, study designs and methodology and, second, the establishment of base expectancy rates for mental illness in general prison populations, in remand prisons, and in maximum-security confinement.

Methodological Issues.   In 1995 Bonta and Gendreau stated that "careful empirical evaluations" had "failed to uncover . . . pervasive negative effects of incarceration" in general, and they criticized others for not believing objective quantitative data (1995, p. 76). When dealing specifically with solitary confinement Bonta and Gendreau referred to what they called an "extensive experimental literature," usually involving laboratory research with volunteer college students who were subjected to short periods of solitary confinement or sensory deprivation. This research revealed "few detrimental effects," whereas two studies of solitary confinement in prisons, which did report effects, used no "objective measures or control groups" (p. 85). In 1982 Suedfeld and colleagues voiced similar views and criticized much research on solitary confinement for being politically biased. The authors concluded that "outside observers tend to exhibit sympathy more than empiricism and objectivity" (Suedfeld et al. 1982, pp. 307–8).

Haney and Lynch chose a different approach. "In the absence of a single, definitive piece of research that effectively establishes a causal connection, we rely upon the method of 'triangulation' wherein we systematically review available research from numerous diverse sources, each of which addresses some of the ways in which solitary confinement and punitive segregation may affect prisoners" (Haney and Lynch 1997, p. 498). They argued that crucial information would be lost by narrowing the scope of inquiry as Bonta and Gendreau did (p. 498). Haney and Lynch found, as several had done before them, that the experimental literature on sensory deprivation reported many negative effects (pp. 500–503).

Others have made similar points (e.g., Grassian and Friedman 1986; Jackson 2002). Jackson argued that Bonta and Gendreau lost sight of reality in prisons when defining their "objective" measures, and they concluded that their work on solitary confinement was "quite irrelevant to the real-life experience of prisoners" (sector 4, chap. 3). According to Frank Porporino (2002, p. x), "prisons are real . . . [and] to study reality is bound to be more fruitful than to continue studying the contrived realities of the laboratory."

Morris and Kurki (2001) concluded that the debate over the effects of solitary confinement "seems to have more to do with different research methods, designs, and measures than with the effects of solitary confinement." They emphasized that "when Bonta and Gendreau . . . did not find negative effects of solitary confinement, they referred to studies that used predominantly volunteer substitutes (often college students), limited solitary confinement to ten days or less, and typically excluded from experiments persons with any existing medical, psychiatric, behavioral, or intelligence problems" (p. 413). Jackson (2002) has argued similarly.

In this essay I try to bypass the "old" debate over sensory deprivation studies and experimental studies involving college students and to satisfy the criteria set out by both sides in the debate. Sizable numbers of quantitative research and qualitative studies are available, especially when one deals not only with North American research but also European. Studies that score high on scientific scales have been produced in Denmark.

Base Expectancy Rates.   When one is assessing effects of solitary confinement, especially mental health effects, it is important to include control groups of nonisolated prisoners in study designs; not all studies do. For background, I therefore devote a few pages to the prevalence of psychological suffering and mental disorders in prison populations in general. Such information cannot be easily compared across national borders or incorporated directly into solitary confinement studies, but it provides useful background information. It would be highly anachronistic to use this information, however, when dealing with nineteenth-century prisons, where much lower frequencies of mental disorders and psychological suffering were generally reported in prison populations. This is most likely because understandings and definitions of mental illness were different.

General Prison Populations.   In 2002 a review of sixty-two psychiatric surveys including 22,790 prisoners in twelve different countries concluded that 3.7 percent of all male prisoners and 4 percent of all female prisoners had psychotic illness, and 10 percent of the male and 12 percent of the female prisoners suffered from a major depression. Respectively 65 percent and 42 percent had a personality disorder (Fazel and Danesh 2002). It was concluded "that the risks of having serious psychiatric disorders are substantially higher in prisoners than in the general population" (p. 548).

Another trademark of prison health, which is often treated as psychiatric morbidity, is the very high prevalence of drug and alcohol abuse or dependence (Andersen 2004, p. 27). Alcohol abuse or dependence rates found in eighteen studies ranged from 50 percent to 66 percent in one group, with other studies reporting lower frequencies ranging from 9 percent to 17 percent. This difference might be explained by a gradual shift in abuse or dependence patterns away from alcohol toward drugs. Drug abuse or dependence was reported in eighteen studies with a prevalence rate of 24–61 percent, with one Finnish study reporting 6 percent (Andersen 2004, p. 27).

Not all psychological and psychiatric problems and disorders are significantly more prevalent in prisons. So-called mood disorders (i.e., disorders in the affective spectrum including depression, melancholy, and adjustment disorder) "are generally found with comparable or a little higher frequency in prison studies than in the general population" (Andersen 2004, p. 21), although the differences between studies are quite large, and several found a high prevalence of major depression (Fazel and Danesh 2002).

Andersen (2004) reviewed the recent literature on the prevalence of mental disorders in prison populations in various (primarily Western) countries and found a prevalence of psychiatric morbidity ranging from 46 percent to 88 percent among sentenced prisoners in North America and a prevalence of 37 percent and 57 percent in two European studies. In North American remand populations, two studies reported 70 percent and 94 percent, and European studies reported 62–76 percent (Andersen 2004, pp. 20–21). But these figures counted substance dependence or abuse as disorders, and when studies exclude dependence disorders, the figures drop significantly. In European remand populations, prevalence rates of psychiatric morbidity (excluding dependence) of 26 percent and 29 percent have been reported, and 32 percent was reported among sentenced prisoners in Canada (p. 20). Apart from indirectly confirming the very high degree of substance abuse problems, these figures suggest that there might be some differences between remand populations and sentenced populations. Differences between remand and sentenced populations were also found in Fazel and Danesh's review of sixty-two surveys, but they were apparently not very significant (Fazel and Danesh 2002, p. 545).

Prevalence rates excluding substance abuse or dependence confirm findings from other studies reporting on prison health. According to a Danish study in which data were cross-referenced with the Central

Danish Psychiatric Register, 29 percent of all 8,403 Danish prisoners and criminals under penal supervision on November 3, 1992, had at some point been hospitalized for psychiatric treatment (Kramp 1993). But whether these people still suffered from mental disorders or problems was not assessed. A later Danish study concluded that 15 percent of all 2,689 sentenced inmates in Danish prisons on February 23, 1999, had been treated by or consulted a psychiatrist during their current imprisonment, whereas 24 percent at some point (before or during the imprisonment) had psychological and/or psychiatric problems (Kyvsgaard 1999, vol. 2, pp. 41–42). A Norwegian study of 187 remand and sentenced prisoners reported that 21 percent were in need of psychiatric treatment (Gamman and Linaker 2000).

Research in U.S. prisons generally reveals similar or higher rates than those reported in European prisons. A report on offenders with mental disorders in U.S. correctional institutions in 1998 concluded "that somewhere between 8 and 19 percent of prisoners have significant psychiatric or functional disabilities and another 15 to 20 percent will require some form of psychiatric intervention during their incarceration" (Abramsky and Fellner 2003, p. 17). Two years later the American Psychiatric Association reported estimates that up to 20 percent of all prisoners "were seriously mentally ill" whereas up to 5 percent were "actively psychotic at any given moment" (p. 17). In 2002 the National Commission on Correctional Health Care estimated the prevalence of a number of mental disorders: "On any given day, between 2.3 and 3.9 percent of inmates in state prisons are estimated to have schizophrenia or other psychotic disorder, between 13.1 and 18.6 percent major depression, and between 2.1 and 4.3 percent bipolar disorder (manic episode). A substantial percentage of inmates exhibit symptoms of other disorders as well, including between 8.4 and 13.4 percent with dysthymia, between 22.0 and 30.1 percent with an anxiety disorder, and between 6.2 and 11.7 percent with posttraumatic stress disorder" (quoted from Abramsky and Fellner [2003, p. 17]).

Human Rights Watch furthermore reported that correctional services in individual states themselves report having between 11 percent and 16.5 percent mentally ill offenders in their prisons (Abramsky and Fellner 2003, p. 18).

Remand Prisoners in Solitary Confinement.   When one is looking at the use of solitary confinement in relation to base expectancy rates, it is important to distinguish between remand prisoners (like those in

Scandinavia) and inmates in administrative or disciplinary segregation. There is likely to be a significant average mental health difference between remand prisoners isolated in order to protect an ongoing police investigation and prisoners who are in punitive or administrative segregation because they are considered disruptive or otherwise a danger to prison order. Danish and Norwegian data suggest that remand prisoners in solitary confinement in Denmark and Norway have slightly better base expectancy rates for psychological or psychiatric illnesses (as well as IQ) than average nonisolated remand prisoners (Andersen et al. 1994, p. 56; Gamman 1995, p. 2245; 2001, p. 45; Andersen 2004, p. 11). This difference has to do with the kinds of suspects who are isolated. They are often involved in organized crime (especially involving narcotics) and typically relatively complicated cases, and they have a slightly better psychological profile than the average remand prisoner. When one is studying isolated remand prisoners in Denmark, Norway, and Sweden, a similar or perhaps lower prevalence of psychiatric morbidity would normally be expected than among nonisolated remand prisoners.

Sentenced Prisoners in Punitive or Administrative Segregation.   Segregation of sentenced prisoners is a different matter. When one is dealing with disruptive prisoners, higher rates of psychiatric disorders (and sometimes personality disorders) are found in both North American and European studies. Many prisoners bring psychiatric or psychological problems with them when entering segregation or isolation. Still there might be a difference between inmates in administrative and punitive segregation. A survey of disciplinary segregation in all prisons in England and Wales in fact concluded that there "was no evidence . . . that prisoners with severe mental illness were more likely to experience disciplinary segregation than other prisoners." The "overall impression of segregated prisoners . . . [was] that they tend to be career criminals with personality disorder, together with additional features of emotional instability and impulsivity" (Coid et al. 2003*a*, p. 314). The situation was different among prisoners in so-called "strip" cells (on the basis of the same data as the above survey), which are used for "temporary confinement of a violent or refractory prisoner," and not for punishment (Coid et al. 2003*b*, p. 321). The conclusion was that prisoners "with severe mental disorder, suicidal tendencies, and a history of deliberate self-injury were more likely to report having been placed in special ('strip') cell conditions" (p. 335).

A number of North American studies report different results, including a relatively higher level of psychological distress among inmates in disciplinary segregation than among inmates in the general population. In a correctional institution in Kentucky it was found among thirty-four inmates that "general psychological distress increases with the increase of restriction," and inmates in disciplinary segregation reported more feelings of inadequacy, inferiority, withdrawal, and isolation than the general prison population, and more feelings, thoughts, and actions of rage, anger, and aggression than both the general prison population and those in administrative detention (Miller and Young 1997, pp. 91–92). A Canadian study of two segregation units involving seventy-three inmates reported that the rate of severe mental disorder was higher than in the general prison population. Especially schizophrenia and mania were overrepresented, whereas the rate of major depression was not. The study concluded "that mentally disordered inmates are being isolated within the penitentiaries . . . [without] receiving mental health care" (Hodgins and Coté 1991, p. 181). Abramsky and Fellner concluded that mentally ill prisoners in the United States generally are disproportionately confined in various lockdown, isolation, and segregation units, and they reported different state figures, ranging typically from 30 percent to more than 50 percent of inmates in such settings being mentally ill (2003, pp. 145–49).

While it is often very difficult to compare prison populations, prison conditions (segregation is not necessarily solitary confinement), and health issues across national borders, it is reasonable to conclude that significantly higher rates of psychiatric morbidity should be expected among prisoners in disciplinary or administrative segregation/isolation compared with the general prison population.

Here is how this essay is organized. Section I surveys the history of the use of solitary confinement as a penal measure, beginning with the initiation of the Pennsylvania model at Philadelphia's Cherry Hill Prison early in the nineteenth century. Although adverse effects on prisoners' mental health became evident relatively quickly and American prisons soon moved away from systematic, general use of solitary confinement, prisons in many countries adopted the Pennsylvania model and in a number of European countries continued to follow it well into the twentieth century, despite widespread evidence of its adverse effects. Section I concludes with a brief overview of post–World War II research on the effects of sensory and perceptual deprivation.

Section II examines the modern literature on the mental health effects of isolation. Though a few studies reach discordant findings, the vast majority document significant negative health effects arising from solitary confinement, and several previous literature reviews in the United States and Scandinavia reach that conclusion.

So what are the adverse effects of solitary confinement? Section III surveys the findings concerning physiological, mental health, and personality effects and reviews the evidence on the extent to which the effects appear to be lasting. A wide range of adverse effects have been documented. After release, symptoms appear gradually to diminish for many people, but this like other questions of the long-term effects of imprisonment remains an underresearched subject.

Section IV discusses a number of policy issues isolation raises, including in particular its demonstrated nature as a risk factor in prison suicide and the effects of isolation on criminal prosecution and defendants' efforts to defend themselves. Although rationales for pretrial isolation include preventing defendants from tampering with evidence or witnesses, its effects often include pressuring defendants to plead guilty and impeding their efforts to defend themselves.

Section V, the conclusion, discusses policy implications of current knowledge of the effects of solitary confinement and discusses priority topics for future research.

I. A Brief History of Solitary Confinement and Its Effects on Prison Inmates

The ideology of the modern prison system developed from the 1770s to the 1850s. With the construction of the Auburn and Pennsylvania prison models in the 1820s, the aim of the modern penitentiary system became rehabilitation of criminals through the use of isolation. The Auburn system (developed in the Auburn Prison in New York State) permitted inmates to work together during the day, but under a regime of total silence. No communication was permitted. In Pennsylvania model institutions (first developed in Philadelphia in the Cherry Hill Prison), there was no compromise with the ideal of isolation, and the prisoners spent all their time in the cell, where they also did their work. The inmate was expected to turn his thoughts inward, to meet God, to repent his crimes, and eventually to return to society as a morally cleansed Christian citizen (see, e.g., Rothman 1971; Ignatieff 1978; Foucault 1995; Smith 2003, 2004*b*).

The ideology of the modern penitentiary—and the philosophy of rehabilitation through isolation—had an enormous impact. The American prisons were inspected by numerous visitors from Europe and South America during the 1830s, '40s, and '50s by official state delegations as well as interested experts and curious celebrities, and the vast majority praised the modern and impressive institutions. In the United States, the Auburn model became the more popular, whereas the Europeans favored the Pennsylvania system and therefore solitary confinement. Between 1830 and 1870, several hundred European jails and prisons were constructed (or modernized) on the basis of a system of social isolation. Hundreds of thousands of individuals were subjected to solitary confinement during the nineteenth century (Johnston 2000; Smith 2004*b*; concerning South America, see Salvatore and Aguirre [1996]).

A. Nineteenth-Century Solitary Confinement and Its Effects on the Health of Prisoners

The Auburn system in New York was preceded by a regime put into force in 1821 according to which inmates were completely isolated without work during the day. After eighteen months this system had produced "results so dire" that the governor of New York stopped the experiment after a visit, and 26 inmate "survivors" were immediately set free (Hess 1972, p. xiv). As a result, inmates were allowed to work together during daytime and the Auburn system became a reality.

It soon became apparent that mental health problems were arising in the Pennsylvania model prisons, where isolation was enforced much more strictly. During the initial years of the Cherry Hill Prison in Philadelphia, the resident physician denied the existence of any serious health problems, but later in the 1830s reports materialized[9] about mental disorders—including hallucinating prisoners, "dementia," and "monomania."

The reasons for the numerous cases of mental illness were disputed. Defenders of the Pennsylvania system claimed that solitary confine-

---

[9] See, e.g., the figures, text, and tables concerning mental disorders quoted in *Reports of the Prison Discipline Society of Boston* (1972): fourteenth report (1839, p. 50) and fifteenth report (1840, p. 40). See also Gray (1847, p. 90).

ment did not itself cause the problems. One 1846 report concluded that the disproportionately high number of cases of mental illness in Philadelphia's Cherry Hill Prison were caused by a high proportion of individuals from the "mulatto race" who apparently could not handle the confinement as well as "men of pure Saxon blood." It was considered especially noteworthy that these "mulatto" men were allegedly "very degraded" and "addicted to those sexual excesses which lead particularly to cerebral derangement" (Howe 1846, p. 76). This explanation reflected a widely held nineteenth-century theory that masturbation could cause insanity, as well as common racist views of the period (concerning masturbation and insanity, see Spitz [1952]). A physician at Cherry Hill was of the same opinion and ventured in the late 1830s that "the cases of mental disorder occurring in this Penitentiary are, with a few exceptions . . . caused by masturbation, and are mostly among the colored prisoners" (*Reports of the Prison Discipline Society of Boston* 1972 [fourteenth report, 1839, p. 49]). In Denmark, similar views were expressed during the early 1840s as a way of supporting the use of solitary confinement in Denmark—the argument being that isolation would not cause problems in Denmark since only white men would be incarcerated (Smith 2003, p. 141).

The Pennsylvania model was imported and used in many European nations, including France, England, Germany, Holland, Belgium, Portugal, Norway, Sweden, and Denmark (Morris and Rothman 1998; Nilsson 1999; Johnston 2000; Smith 2003). But the experts who had supported solitary confinement were proved wrong over and over again. When Millbank Prison in England introduced new rules in the 1830s in order to prevent communication between inmates and enforce solitary confinement, "cases of insanity began to appear," and by 1841 separation and isolation had to be limited to the first three months of each sentence (Henriques 1972, p. 76; Toch 2003, p. 225). The inspectors of Millbank complained in a report from 1841 "that a very extraordinary increase has taken place in the number of insane prisoners in the prison" (Laurie 1846, p. 3) and suggested that whenever treatment of insanity was needed the prisoners in question should be placed together and "have the privilege of conversation" (p. 4). In other words, isolation was characterized as the cause of mental illness. According to new 1841 regulations, prisoners after the initial three months were allowed to converse with two or more fellow inmates during exercise hours (Toch 2003, p. 225).

Support for the Pennsylvania model continued, and the ambitious Pentonville Prison in England initially operated in 1842 with a strict regime of solitary confinement during the first eighteen months of incarceration. Each year between five and fifteen inmates were taken away to asylums, and the period of isolation was subsequently reduced (Ignatieff 1978, p. 3). Solitary confinement of remand prisoners was also found in England during the 1840s. In Reading Gaol, Pentonville's regulations were displayed on the walls, and according to a critic, the same system of spirit-breaking solitude was applied (Vyvyan 1845).

Several Pennsylvania model prisons were constructed in Germany. Throughout the later half of the nineteenth century, a number of German psychiatrists described the negative health effects of solitary confinement in great detail (Nitsche and Wilmanns 1912).

Although some U.S. physicians focused on masturbation as the source of the problem, other U.S. physicians—like their German colleagues—described what they saw as a clear connection between solitary confinement and the health of inmates. In 1841, the physician in a New Jersey penitentiary constructed on the Pennsylvania plan concluded that "the opinions expressed heretofore on the effects of solitary confinement are strengthened by every year's experience. The more rigidly the plan is carried out, the more the spirit of the law is observed, the more its effects are visible upon the health of the convicts. A little more intercourse with each other, and a little more air in the yard, have the effects upon mind and body, that warmth has upon the thermometer, almost every degree of indulgence showing a corresponding rise in health of the individual" (*Reports of the Prison Discipline Society of Boston*, seventeenth report [1842, p. 60]).

The New Jersey Penitentiary physician complained about solitary confinement in many reports and described "many cases of insanity," but suddenly problems with mental disorders ceased. This, he said, occurred because when a prisoner showed signs of disease, "if his mind begins to fail, and he shows symptoms of derangement, another convict is put with him in his cell. This invariably restores the patient" (*Reports of the Prison Discipline Society of Boston*, eighteenth report [1843, p. 82]; see also Gray 1847, p. 119). Solitary confinement was simply abandoned when problems arose. A similar conclusion was reached at the state prison in Rhode Island, where "symptoms of insanity" disappeared after convicts were allowed to work together (*Reports of the*

Prison Discipline Society of Boston, nineteenth report [1844, p. 63]; see also Gray 1847, p. 121).

When compared to reports from the Auburn model prison in Charlestown, Massachusetts, the official statistics from Cherry Hill did not aid the cause of solitary confinement. Death rates were significantly higher in Cherry Hill, and cases of regular insanity far outnumbered those in Charlestown (Gray 1847, pp. 106, 109).

In 1842, the English author Charles Dickens famously described and condemned solitary confinement after a visit to Cherry Hill:

> I believe that very few men are capable of estimating the immense amount of torture and agony which this dreadful punishment, pro-longed for years, inflicts upon the sufferers; and in guessing at it myself, and in reasoning from what I have seen written upon their faces, and what to my certain knowledge they feel within, I am only the more convinced that there is a depth of terrible endur-ance in it which none but the sufferers themselves can fathom, and which no man has a right to inflict upon his fellow-creature. I hold this slow and daily tampering with the mysteries of the brain, to be immeasurably worse than any torture of the body. (Dickens 1985, p. 146)

In 1851, the Danish fairy tale author Hans Christian Andersen vis-ited a Swedish Pennsylvania model prison and described how "a silence deep as the grave rests over it. It is as though no one lived there or it was an abandoned house in time of plague. . . . Galleries run along the various storeys and, at the hub, the chaplain has his pulpit; where he holds his Sunday sermons for an invisible congregation. Door upon door of the cells is half-opened to the gallery. The prisoners hear the chaplain, but they cannot see him, nor he them. It is all a well-built machine, a nightmare for the spirit" (Andersen 1851, pp. 29–33; Smith 2004*b*).

The Dutch criminologist Herman Franke observed that the new isolation prisons produced severe problems wherever they were put into use: "Again and again reports of insanity, suicide, and the complete alienation of prisoners from social life seriously discredited the new form of punishment" (1992, p. 128).

Francis C. Gray's impressive study of *Prison Discipline in America* reached the same conclusion in 1847. Gray's study was based on sta-tistical and qualitative evidence of the experiences with both Auburn and Pennsylvania model prisons. Gray concluded "that from the experience of our own country hitherto, it appears that the system of constant separation [solitary confinement according to the Pennsylvania model] as established here, even when administered with the utmost humanity, produces so many cases of insanity and of death as to indicate most clearly, that its general tendency is to enfeeble the body and the mind" (1847, p. 181).

Much of the Western literature on the origins of the modern penitentiary does not deal with the effects of solitary confinement but stresses the capacities of these institutions for controlling and influencing the minds of prisoners (see, e.g., Rothman 1971; Ignatieff 1978; Foucault 1995; Smith 2003, 2004b). Foucault and others have analyzed the new nineteenth-century prisons as examples of a modern technology of power that allowed for a more effective and individualized social control, aimed at controlling not only the bodies and actions of individuals but also their thoughts. Control was to be internalized in the individual. The new prisons therefore reflected a shift "from the body as object to the mind as object" (Spierenburg 1996, p. 31). Contemporaneous observers agreed. In the words of the English nineteenth-century prison chaplain at Preston House of Correction, John Clay, "A few months in the solitary cell renders prisoners strangely impressible. The chaplain can then make the brawny navy cry like a child; he can work on his feelings in any way he pleases. He can . . . photograph his thoughts, wishes, and opinions on his patient's mind, and fill his mouth with his own phrases and language" (Potter 1993, p. 46).

B. Denmark, 1859 to the 1930s

In Denmark, solitary confinement was implemented on a large scale beginning in 1859 when Vridsløselille Penitentiary, based on the Pennsylvania system, opened. During the early 1860s it became apparent that serious health problems had arisen. It quickly became normal procedure to transfer the worst inmates (who became more or less uncontrollable) to insane asylums in different parts of the country, and the prison authorities fought a constant battle to avoid a general state of mental health chaos. The prison staff quickly adopted a strategy, which meant that they broke the rules, by allowing individual prisoners special privileges, such as prolonged yard time or even the chance to work together with other inmates, in order to offset the effects of solitary confinement. The whole point of imprisonment according to the rationale of the modern prisons was to rehabilitate the incarcerated criminals, and this was reflected in the creativity employed by the prison authorities to counter the effects of isolation (Smith 2004a).

Archival studies indicate that at least a third of the inmates reacted to isolation with adverse health effects, and at least a third of these (around 12 percent of the total prison population) might be character-ized as suffering from major psychological and psychiatric problems including hallucinations, paranoia, and different kinds of personal de-generation. Prisoners with adverse health effects were typically de-scribed as healthy upon their entrance to the prison. The archived material allows for a longitudinal analysis of prisoner health, although the inmates still may have brought psychiatric problems with them into the prison (Smith 2004a).[10]

These nineteenth-century figures cannot be compared directly to recent studies of psychiatric morbidity in prisons. Vastly fewer pris-oners were reported as psychiatrically or psychologically ill in nine-teenth-century prisons (in Denmark at any rate) than today. Vrid-sløselille (for male prisoners) originally was considered a near-perfect and very modern prison in a medical and hygienic sense. It had central heating, and each prisoner had running water and a flushing toilet in his cell, which was quite unheard of in those days.

The first governor of Vridsløselille, Frederik Bruun, became a strong opponent of solitary confinement. According to Bruun, more than half of the inmates in long-term isolation (up to three and one-half years) were severely damaged, and the health situation was generally very problematic. Bruun concluded that prisoners in solitary confinement often fell into a state that resulted in "a total lack of energy and will power, in mental and physical laxity . . . which is either cured by means of fortifying medicine, a changed and improved diet, longer exercise spells or light work in the open air, or else gives way to de-pression and thence to higher degrees of mental disorder" (Smith 2004a, p. 18).

Bruun, who was also head of the Danish Prison Service, used statis-tics to describe how mental illness was more widespread in communal

---

[10] Another way of assessing reliability of these historical data is by comparing the situation in Vridsløselille with (the lack of) health problems in prisons without solitary confinement. In Horsens Penitentiary, which was constructed on the Auburn plan six years before Vrisløselille, the health of inmates never became a problem as in Vridsløselille. Some of the diseases found with a high prevalence in Vridløselille were never recorded, or were recorded at much lower frequency, in Horsens. Diseases that appeared clearly related to solitary confinement.

prisons than among the free population, but even more common in cellular prisons than in communal prisons, and more so in cellular prisons in which total isolation was implemented (as in Vridsløselille) than those in which prisoners were allowed to mix in chapel, school, and exercise yards (Bruun 1867, p. 48). Bruun calculated that mentally ill Danes accounted for 0.108 percent of the total population, whereas the proportion of mentally ill in Vridsløselille from April 1863 to 1867 was estimated at 2.28 percent (those were the official figures; the archived material from the prison reveals that many more would be termed mentally ill according to contemporary standards). In addition, cellular prisons, according to Bruun, had higher frequencies of "abnormal states which are generally a precursor of mental illnesses." With reference to data from the penitentiary in Christiania in Norway, it was declared that such states could include cerebral congestion, hypochondria, insomnia with and without anxiety, hallucinations, suspiciousness, despondency, and fixed ideas (Smith 2004a, p. 16).

Following this critique, a psychiatric study was carried out, and the findings were presented in 1871 in a report entitled *Cellestraffens Indvirkning paa Forbrydernes mentelle Sundhedstilstand* (The effect of solitary confinement on the mental health of prisoners), written by Christian Tryde, MD (Tryde 1871). He described a large number of cases of mental illness that had arisen in Vridsløselille and discussed their possible etiology. The cases were divided into three groups: those in which the illness was an element in a different somatic disease, those in which an attack of mental illness in the prison was due to a previous chronic cerebral disorder, and those found in prisoners who had not had any chronic complaint when they came to the penitentiary (Smith 2004a, p. 18).

Tryde was extremely careful about assigning the blame for cases of mental illness to the cellular system and isolation and found support in the biological notions of the time. For example, he stated that the brains of criminals were already encumbered at birth "with a pathological hereditary predisposition from a degenerate family," and like others before him, Tryde cited masturbation as a cause of insanity. He nevertheless concluded that isolation could not be declared to be without blame "for having a harmful effect on the prisoner's mental health" (Smith 2004a, p. 18).

Several of Tryde's colleagues in Danish mental hospitals were more forthright in their conclusions. In those cases in which a transferred prisoner was proclaimed healthy and was to be sent back to serve the rest of his sentence, several doctors advised explicitly against the resumption of isolation. A doctor at the mental hospital in Vordingborg declared of one prisoner, for example, that it was probable that "solitary confinement has been the most significant factor" behind the mental illness. Such discharged prisoners were typically sent to do communal labor at the penitentiary in Christianshavn (Smith 2004*a*, p. 18).

Solitary confinement continued to be used in Denmark, and the numerous mental health problems in Vridsløselille Penitentiary continued. As the discipline of psychiatry developed during the late nineteenth and early twentieth centuries, the mental disorders in Vridsløselille were given new names and old categories of illness disappeared. From 1878 to 1883, official reports concluded that of 1,921 prisoners in Vridsløselille who were healthy on arrival, 5.4 percent suffered from lethargy during their imprisonment, and 1.9 percent became insane; in addition, more than 5 percent suffered from other diseases that according to the Danish Prison Service were caused by the imprisonment, that is, solitary confinement. In Horsens Penitentiary (Denmark's other modern penitentiary from 1853, which operated on the Auburn plan without solitary confinement during daytime), only 0.8 percent suffered from lethargy, and 0.62 percent became insane during imprisonment in the same period (*Beretninger fra Kontoret for Fængselsvæsenet* 1885).

During the late 1880s an illness termed *nervesmerter* ("neurological pains") began to appear in increasing numbers in Vridsløselille, and cases of lethargy diminished (*Beretning fra Overinspektionen for Fængselsvæsenet* 1898). During 1911–12 the so-called *nervesmerter* had disappeared entirely, and only very few cases of lethargy were recorded. But at the same time a new mental disorder, "hysteria," had arrived, which was recorded among more than 3 percent of the inmates. The next financial year around 2 percent of the isolated inmates in Vridsløselille suffered from hysteria, but once again, a new illness appeared. An amazing 9.94 percent of all prisoners in solitary confinement (contrary to 2.17 percent of the prisoners who were not isolated) suffered from *neuralgi* ("neuralgia"[11]). The following year, two new diseases arrived: melancholia and nervousness; but only a few prisoners

[11] Possibly related to "neurasthenia"—a so-called disease of the nervous system that became very "popular" during the late nineteenth century. See Wessely (1995, p. 509) and Køppe (2004).

suffered from these, whereas neuralgia was still reported among 7.64 percent of all isolated inmates. During 1914–15 a massive 13.77 percent of those in solitary confinement were treated for neuralgia (*Beretning om Straffeanstalterne i Danmark* 1913, 1914, 1915, 1916). A study of how nervous diseases, hysteria, neurasthenia, and related disorders were perceived in the late nineteenth century reveals that these disorders were associated with symptoms that today appear related to solitary confinement (Wessely 1995; Køppe 2004).

During the period 1911–15, neither hysteria, melancholia, nervousness, nor neuralgia was reported even once in Horsens Penitentiary. When solitary confinement was finally abandoned in Denmark around 1932–33, the cases of outright insanity in Vridsløselille Penitentiary completely stopped from one year to the other (*Beretning om Straffeanstalterne i Danmark* 1932, 1934, 1939).

C. Solitary Confinement Internationally Condemned

From the 1860s onward a skeptical attitude evolved toward "rehabilitation through isolation," and the ideology of the modern penitentiary faced a serious crisis. The founding nation of the modern prison systems—the United States—was among the first to abandon large-scale solitary confinement.[12] As explained by historian David Rothman, "By the 1860s, and even more obviously by the 1870s and 1880s, the unique arrangements of the Auburn and Pennsylvania plans had disappeared" (1998, p. 112). In France, the Pennsylvania model and solitary confinement "never got off the ground completely," and only a few "cellular" prisons were in operation around 1880 (Franke 1992, p. 137). Other prison regime designs of course emerged, such as the Elmira Reformatory model for younger offenders in the United States, and gradually penitentiary discipline moved "from its earlier emphasis on isolation and work toward a more complex regime that facilitated individualized treatment" (Salvatore and Aguirre 1996, p. 7). Another prison system, which signaled a gradual transition away from the Pennsylvania model, was the so-called progressive system, which typically

[12] According to Johnston (2000, p. 138), all states that tried the Pennsylvania system abandoned this model after a few years—with the exception of Pennsylvania itself. He furthermore writes that "ironically, while Europe and, later, South America and Asia were building radial-plan prisons with cellular isolation, to be used at least in the initial phase of a sentence, the United States did not follow the example of Philadelphia's Eastern State Penitentiary [the Pennsylvania system]" (p. 147). See also Haney and Lynch (1997, p. 487).

combined an initial limited phase of solitary confinement with a number of later stages involving social contact with other prisoners and attainment of different privileges (Bruun 1867, p. 21).

The transformation of the penitentiary had several causes, but one was most certainly the substantial health problems related to isolating inmates. In Germany, for example, a psychiatric literature on "prison psychoses" developed and expanded during the second half of the nineteenth century. One of the pioneers, Delbrück, described how absolute isolation had "a very injurious effect on the body and mind" and gave rise to hallucinations. Delbrück advised "the immediate termination of solitary confinement" (Nitsche and Wilmanns 1912, p. 7). These results were supported by another German psychiatrist, Gutsch, who between 1846 and 1860 studied eighty-four cases of mental disorder that had developed in solitary confinement. These disorders included a wide range of symptoms from emotional and depressive shocks, suicidal tendencies, and manic outbreaks to pathological delusions and hallucinations (p. 8). In 1912 Nitsche and Wilmanns concluded, on the basis of the work of Kirn, that the "acute hallucinatory melancholia" was a psychosis, which related specifically to solitary confinement (p. 74).

In another study, *Problems in Prison Psychiatry*, Wilson and Pescor concluded that the inmates in Pennsylvania model prisons "went insane instead of being reformed." As a result, the authors continued optimistically, solitary confinement during both day and night was no longer practiced by any civilized nation (1939, p. 24).

This matter-of-fact attitude toward the mental health effects of solitary confinement seems to reflect a general consensus in some countries during the late nineteenth century and early twentieth century. This view was expressed by the U.S. Supreme Court in 1890, in a case concerning solitary confinement of a prisoner under sentence of death in the state of Colorado. The Supreme Court ruled that solitary confinement "was an additional punishment of the most important and painful character" and described how inmates had reacted to solitary confinement in U.S. nineteenth-century prisons: "A considerable number of prisoners fell, after even a short confinement, into a semifatuous condition, from which it was next to impossible to arouse them, and others became violently insane; others still, committed suicide; while those who stood the ordeal better were not generally reformed, and in most cases did not recover sufficient mental activity to be of any subsequent service to the community" (*In re Medley*, 134 U.S. 160 [1890]; Boston 2000, p. 1).

Therefore, the Supreme Court continued, different isolation systems were tried out, but finally "some 30 or 40 years ago [the 1850s and 1860s] the whole subject attracted the general public attention, and . . . solitary confinement was found to be too severe" (*Medley*, 134 U.S. 160 [1890]). Other U.S. legal decisions around the turn of the century reflected the same awareness of "the painful psychological effects of solitary confinement" (Haney and Lynch 1997, p. 486).

This development toward condemnation of solitary confinement seems to have been somewhat slower within the international community of prison experts. At a penitentiary congress in London in 1872, solitary confinement was subject to a lively discussion that ended without resolutions being drawn up, and in 1900 at a penitentiary congress in Brussels, some claimed that even prolonged isolation had no health effects. At a penitentiary congress in Prague in 1930, however, international resolutions were drawn up that expressed the troubling aspects of solitary confinement. The congress specified that if solitary confinement was used for a short duration, adequate medical service was to be available. The congress furthermore advised that solitary confinement should not be used in connection with sentences of long duration (Teeters 1949, pp. 38, 110, 172). Solitary confinement before a trial was not discussed.

D. Scandinavia, Holland, and Belgium as Special Cases

From the 1860s onward, the use of solitary confinement declined gradually in the Western world. The Pennsylvania model and the era of large-scale isolation passed sometime in the beginning of the twentieth century. Isolation was, of course, used throughout the nineteenth and twentieth centuries not only in Pennsylvania model institutions, but typically as short-term punishment in most prisons, and on a much lower scale.

In a number of countries, especially Holland, Belgium, Sweden, Norway, and Denmark, the use of large-scale isolation persisted into the twentieth century. In Norway, the Pennsylvania model was still in operation during the late 1920s (Berggrav 1928). In Sweden, 90 percent of all prisoners served their entire sentence in isolation at the beginning of the twentieth century, and solitary confinement of sentenced prisoners was not abandoned until 1946 (Nilsson 1999, p. 443;

2003, p. 9). In Denmark, the Pennsylvania model (including panoptic isolation churches) was used until the early 1930s (Smith 2003, p. 245; 2005). According to one observer, Vridsløselille Penitentiary in Denmark was "one of the last prisons in the world" to give up the characteristics of the Pennsylvania system (Johnston 2000, p. 111). In Belgium, solitary confinement became exceedingly popular in the prison system during the later half of the nineteenth century, and elements of the Pennsylvania system lingered on until after World War II (p. 104). Finally, solitary confinement was used liberally in Holland throughout the first half of the twentieth century (Spierenburg 1996, p. 30).

Possible reasons why the Pennsylvania system persisted in those countries include their relatively small sizes and the fact that they all operated relatively centralized and efficient bureaucracies in the middle of the nineteenth century, which perhaps contributed to a more thorough reformation of their prison systems. In Denmark, for example, the entire prison system, including remand prisons, was reconfigured between 1840 and the 1870s. In larger countries, which experienced more political turmoil or had a more decentralized administration, such as France, Italy, and Germany, the reform process was more blurred, and the philosophy of rehabilitation through isolation passed its heyday before the entire national prison systems were reformed.[13]

The United Kingdom appears to have been a special case. Relatively large-scale use of solitary confinement also survived into the twentieth century, but without the support of the philosophy of rehabilitation. The Pennsylvania system had been modified during the nineteenth century into a progressive system so that only an initial period of the sentence was carried out in isolation. Although the belief in reformation through isolation gradually disappeared and a very harsh and punitive prison practice was adopted from the 1860s onward, this did not put an end to solitary confinement. Isolation was perceived as a contribution to a punitive and deterrent prison system. The first 28 days of a sentence to a local prison were therefore served in isolation from the late nineteenth century until 1921, and a period of solitary confinement remained in use in convict prisons. Still this was a much more modest use of isolation than, for example, in Sweden and Denmark, where several years could be spent in isolation in twentieth-century

---

[13] Concerning other attempts at explaining local isolation practices, see Franke (1992), Spierenburg (1996), Nilsson (1999), and Forsythe (2004).

prisons.[14] In England the period of solitary confinement in convict prisons was gradually reduced between 1842 and 1921 from eighteen months, to twelve months, to nine months, and during Churchill's days as home secretary in 1910 and 1911 to three months for recidivists and one month for first-time offenders (Ignatieff 1978, p. 3; Johnston 2000, p. 90; Forsythe 2004, p. 761). Between 1921 and 1939 this use of isolation was entirely abandoned in England (Forsythe 2004, p. 768).

Contrary to developments in the United Kingdom, Holland, and Belgium, the nineteenth-century Scandinavian approach continued into modern times. Denmark, Sweden, Norway, and Iceland have all been criticized by the CPT during the 1990s for their use of pretrial solitary confinement. Solitary confinement in remand prisons has therefore been termed a "peculiarly Scandinavian phenomenon,"[15] which stands in marked contrast to the traditional image of Scandinavian leniency in the area of penal policy (Evans and Morgan 1998, p. 247). However, this critical view was expressed as early as 1929, when Denmark received international criticism for its use of solitary confinement. In an international journal under the heading "Prisons of Denmark," E. Roy Calvert noted that the Danes still had not learned "the bitter lesson" that solitary confinement damages the health of prisoners (Teeters 1944, p. 89).

E. Post–World War II: New Research

Solitary confinement was more or less rediscovered as a subject for psychological and psychiatric studies during the 1950s. This rediscovery took place largely without reference to the history of the modern penitentiary or the evidence from large-scale isolation in nineteenth-century prisons.

The first wave of post–World War II studies involving different kinds of isolation of individuals became known as experiments in sensory deprivation (SD) and perceptual deprivation (PD) and were initiated at McGill University in Montreal during the early 1950s. The McGill studies—and other SD experiments—were inspired by Donald O. Hebb's theory on behavior and motivation as well as stories about Chinese "brainwashing" of POWs during the Korean War by the use of techniques that involved social isolation (Brownfield 1965; Vernon

---

[14] Up to three years in Sweden by the turn of the century (Nilsson 2003, p. 9) and up to three and one-half years in Denmark (Smith 2003).

[15] See also the official reports from the CPT at http://www.cpt.coe.int/en/.

1965; Suedfeld 1969; Andersen 1992). McGill male volunteers were isolated and subjected to homogeneous sound and light settings. The subjects were told to remain incarcerated as long as they could handle it. Afterward the experimenters described how the volunteers had been affected by the experience. These studies inspired a wide range of psychological experiments with sensory deprivation, and a wave of SD and PD studies followed in universities and hospitals in different parts of the world, especially during the 1950s and 1960s. The results were widely discussed by biological and behavioral scientists, in psychological textbooks, in studies about brainwashing and space travel, and by interested laymen (Suedfeld 1969; Zubek 1973). Generally speaking, these experiments were not about recreating a prison experience, they used volunteers, and they did not last very long—typically from less than an hour to a couple of weeks. Still, many of these studies described and dealt with possible effects of solitary confinement.

A wide range of experimental conditions were used that in different ways deprived the subject of his or her normal range of sensory input (Rossi 1969). Volunteers were incarcerated in boxes or small rooms, confined to a bed throughout the experiment, or submerged into water in various ways. It was often reported that subjects fantasized or hallucinated during these experiments (Smith 2003, p. 212). In the McGill studies, virtually all subjects reported hallucinations. Some witnessed geometric forms, bizarre architecture, and various landscapes and scenes. Hearing and physical senses were also affected in several cases. One subject reported hearing people speak, and another suddenly saw a door handle and experienced an electrical shock when he grabbed it. Hearing music was also reported (Vernon 1965, pp. 119–20; Zuckerman 1969a, pp. 95–97; Zubek 1973, pp. 13–15).

During an experiment at Princeton University, volunteers were isolated in dark soundproof rooms, and once again hallucinations were reported, although with less frequency and intensity. Both minor hallucinations and relatively complex ones such as seeing a window or a ventilator were reported. One subject saw a coin on the floor, which disappeared as he tried to pick it up. As the SD conditions were made more severe during additional experiments, more (and more complex) hallucinations were reported (Vernon 1965, pp. 124–34).

Other symptoms repeatedly reported in SD and PD research include cognitive effects, such as disturbed thought processes, concentration problems, and impaired memory (Andersen 1992, p. 2666). A drop in

EEG (electroencephalography) frequency has also been recorded in isolated volunteers (Scott and Gendreau 1969; Zuckerman 1969*b*, p. 60; Andersen 1992), as have drowsiness and prolonged periods of sleep (Vernon 1965, pp. 11–14; Andersen 1992).

Positive effects of SD and PD have also been reported (although with much lower frequency than negative symptoms), and it has been discussed whether or not SD might have a therapeutic value in certain contexts—for example, when treating schizophrenia (Gibby, Adams, and Carrera 1977; Grassian and Friedman 1986, p. 60; Andersen 1992).

A limited number of studies have been carried out with volunteers in individual social isolation, but under conditions that did not amount to sensory and perceptual deprivation. According to psychologist Duane P. Schultz, individual social isolation produces more "serious consequences" than small group social isolation, and generally evidence points toward significant "individual differences in tolerance" (Schultz 1965, pp. 164–67).

Generally speaking, SD and PD studies revealed that isolating people and severely restricting sensory stimulation can provoke a number of quite drastic reactions and symptoms—even after short durations of isolation (hours or days)—including, for example, hallucinations, confusion, lethargy, anxiety, panic, time distortions, impaired memory, and psychotic behavior (Zuckerman et al. 1962; Brownfield 1965; Schultz 1965; Vernon 1965; Rasmussen 1973; Zubek 1973; Andersen 1992; Haney and Lynch 1997).

In 1965 Schultz concluded that sensory restriction could result in "gross disturbances of functioning" and affect perception, cognition, and learning (1965, p. 169). In 1973 Zubek concluded that the literature revealed that SD and PD produced "widespread behavioral and physiological impairments" (1973, p. 64). According to Haney and Lynch, SD studies therefore "emphasize the importance of sensory stimulation in human experience and the dramatic effects that can be produced when such stimulation is significantly curtailed" (1997, p. 502).

II. Modern Research

A few post–World War II studies of solitary confinement in prisons report no or minor health effects, but the vast majority report substantial health effects. Different opinions on the effects of solitary confinement exist, and some have referred to research into this area as "complex" (Coid et al. 2003*b*, p. 336). I have found only two studies of solitary confinement in prisons that did not use volunteers and did not conclude that there were substantial negative health effects (Suedfeld et al. 1982; Zinger and Wichmann 1999).

One of these (Zinger and Wichmann 1999) is a longitudinal control group study of sixty inmates of whom twenty-three remained for sixty days in administrative segregation; but it represents quite limited evidence in this context since only ten inmates in the final sample were subjected to involuntary isolation (p. 39). The initial testing of the segregated prisoners took place, on average, 3.6 days after their isolation, whereby the initial probably very difficult period of adjustment and possible deterioration was lost to the study. A very high attrition rate (out of fifty-five originally involuntarily isolated, only ten remained after sixty days) is also an obvious problem. That those in segregation had significant previous segregation experience (on average twelve previous segregation experiences) also is clearly important (Roberts and Gebotys 2001; Jackson 2004). The authors were well aware of some of the study's limitations and considered their findings "somewhat irrelevant to current segregation practices in the United States where offenders can be segregated for years for disciplinary infractions with virtually no distractions, human contacts, services or programs" (Zinger and Wichmann 1999, p. 64). But perhaps the most significant problem was the *limited* confidentiality that participants were offered. The researchers told the inmates that any information obtained during interviews that in any way related to their own safety or that of the institution would be disclosed (p. 81). As Palys and Lowman have pointed out, the researchers in the Zinger study thereby effectively told the inmates that they wanted to know about the effects of solitary confinement, but if they revealed any, for example, irrational anger or suicidal tendencies, they would probably report them, a report which could clearly influence the prisoner's possibilities of getting out of segregation (according to Jackson [2004]).

The Suedfeld et al. (1982) study reported numerous adverse health effects (difficulty to adapt, difficulty in concentrating, sleeping disturbances, dizziness, distortion of the sense of time, anger, apathy, impaired memory) in a pilot study but refused to treat these symptoms reported by prisoners as objective negative health effects of solitary confinement.[16]

The Suedfeld et al. study along with some experimental studies led two Canadian authors, Bonta and Gendreau, to conclude that solitary confinement actually had no adverse health effects (Gendreau and Bonta 1984; Bonta and Gendreau 1990 [reprinted in Flanagan (1995)]).[17]

The configuration and content of a specific study will shape its results, and some studies may—owing to their methodology—not have been able to penetrate the psychology of the imprisoned individuals. Different conditions in prisons, and especially the differences between laboratory research using volunteers and involuntary isolation in real prisons, can explain some variations in results. This would go a long way to explain why some researchers have been unable to find negative effects of solitary confinement in experimental settings.[18]

Many researchers have reported that it can be difficult to learn about symptoms suffered by isolated inmates since many hide their condition (Koch 1982, p. 378; Grassian 1983, p. 1451; Jackson 1983, p. 65; Toch 1992, p. 52). This is perhaps especially true concerning male prisoners (Jensen 1988, p. 16). Inability of prisoners to cope with solitary confinement might be perceived as a weakness by prison guards—a weakness many prisoners will try hard not to reveal (Fellner and Mariner 1997, pp. 62–63). Even if prisoners reveal such weaknesses, they may often be interpreted by prison staff (doctors, guards, etc.) as conscious attempts at manipulating the authorities in order to get special treatment (Grassian 1999, p. 20; Kupers 1999, p. 5; Conover 2001, p. 139). A Human Rights Watch report describes how staff (at Attica Prison) were preoccupied with not being "conned" or manipulated by prisoners (Grassian 1999). Even self-mutilation can be interpreted in that way.

Several observers report that it is often extremely difficult, traumatic,

[16] Concerning the symptoms mentioned, see Suedfeld et al. (1982, pp. 316, 331). The authors were apparently unaware of the historical material reporting negative health effects of solitary confinement (p. 312). See also Haney and Lynch (1997, p. 520).

[17] Gendreau and Bonta display the same historical unawareness that characterized Suedfeld et al. (1982) since they claim that the pioneering study of solitary confinement is from 1963 (Gendreau and Bonta 1984, p. 469).

[18] One of the articles sometimes drawn forward as a study that does not document adverse effects is Walters, Callagan, and Newman (1963). This study deals with an experimental situation, although it takes place in a prison (twenty volunteers were selected for experimental solitary confinement). Furthermore, isolation lasted only four days, and adverse effects were reported: an increase in anxiety among isolated individuals (p. 772).

and painful for formerly isolated individuals to talk about—and thereby relive—their experience of solitary confinement (Koch 1982, p. 379; Jackson 1983, p. 65). A few studies seem to explain the fact that some inmates do not complain and seem to adapt more or less peacefully to solitary confinement as a sign of a healthy coping strategy; others explain this as an unhealthy sign of social withdrawal typically accompanied by severe psychological problems. Such problems often will be discovered only by personal in-depth interviews in a positive (therapeutic) atmosphere (Koch 1982, pp. 376, 379; Toch 1992, chap. 1). An illustrative symptom of apparent adjustment to solitary confinement is the way that long-term isolated prisoners will sometimes try to avoid (the already minimal) contact (Koch 1982, p. 376).

Another phenomenon often encountered in prisons is that prison staff sometimes become accustomed and numb to the behavior of isolated inmates (Koch 1982, p. 379; Jensen 1988, p. 17; Kupers 1999, p. 5). In some institutions—such as supermax prisons—a "callous and cynical" attitude may develop (Toch 2001, p. 383). According to Toch, "supermax work degrades the workers" (p. 383).

Another problem in describing the effects of solitary confinement is that a relatively high percentage of inmates, especially in disciplinary/administrative segregation, special housing units (SHU), and supermax prisons, are mentally ill from the outset (Hodgins and Coté 1991; Fellner and Mariner 1997, p. 70; Bresnihan 2002; Abramsky and Fellner 2003; Coid et al. 2003b). These prisoners will typically experience a deterioration of their health in solitary confinement. However, the problem of inmates being mentally ill from the outset is less significant in connection with isolation of remand prisoners. Several studies cited below have a longitudinal element, which makes it possible to address the effect of isolation even on mentally ill prisoners.

Finally, research suggests that people can react very differently to solitary confinement. According to Danish psychiatrist Henrik Steen Andersen, there is "a great individual difference, ranging from no reaction to being in solitary confinement for a year to serious reaction to a short period of solitary confinement, so the individual constitution is important—not surprisingly" (Thelle and Traeholt 2003, p. 769; Grassian 1993, p. 13). Some clearly manage to adapt more successfully than others (Toch 1992, p. 48; concerning coping activities in solitary confinement, see Melvin [n.d.] and Deaton, Berg, and Richlin [1977]), and one study reports a few cases of positive behavioral change in disruptive inmates through the use of isolation (Suedfeld and Roy 1975). For some actively psychotic prison inmates or psychiatric hospital patients, according to some studies, solitary confinement can be used as a beneficial treatment (Gibby, Adams, and Carrera 1977; Grassian and Friedman 1986, p. 60), although many will be affected negatively. Some experts therefore discourage the use of seclusion in psychiatric hospitals or suggest less use of seclusion (Farrel and Dares 1996).

A few mentally healthy people can apparently also turn the experience of solitary confinement into something positive. Ludovick S. Mwijage, who was incarcerated in several African prisons, claims in his memoirs that once "solitary confinement had sharpened my mind," although he also reported a negative effect such as insomnia (1996, pp. 86, 95). The vast majority of memoir writers who have experienced solitary confinement—for example, former hostages—have a much more disturbing recollection of their imprisonment and describe many adverse symptoms (concerning hostages, see, e.g., Siegel [1984] and Turnbull [1997]). According to Jack Abbot, for example, who wrote about his many years in American prisons, solitary confinement could "alter the ontological makeup of a stone," and from his numerous experiences of isolation he described how time descended in his cell "like the lid of a coffin." The primary goal was to go on "without losing my mind" (Haney and Lynch 1997, p. 511).

Despite the methodological difficulties outlined here, research on effects of solitary confinement has produced a massive body of data documenting serious adverse health effects. Haney and Lynch—whose review covers a broader range of topics (seclusion in hospitals, studies of torture victims) than this one but significantly fewer studies of solitary confinement in actual prisons—stressed that "a very clear and consistent message [documenting the negative health effects of solitary confinement] emerges from the examination of studies conducted over a vast array of isolated and restricted conditions for subjects who differed greatly in background and the duration of their confinement" (1997, p. 499).

A systematic summary and classification (according to the discussion of health effects) of the studies discussed here is provided in the Appendix.

A. Major Studies and Their Overall Conclusions

Solitary confinement produces a higher rate of psychiatric and psychological health problems than "normal" imprisonment. This has been shown especially convincingly in studies with randomly selected samples and control groups of nonisolated prisoners.

In a study of 203 male patients in a psychiatric clinic in Zurich, of whom 102 were committed from a prison (every tenth patient in the clinic came from a prison), 76 percent came directly from solitary confinement (although the vast majority of Swiss prisoners of course are not isolated). For 71 percent of the 102 prisoners, it was their first hospitalization for psychiatric reasons. The study was based on medical records, criminal records, and a limited number of interviews. The authors concluded that "Untersuchungs-Einzelhäftlinge [werden] proportional viel häufiger psychiatrisch hospitalisierungsbedürftig als Gemeinschaftshäftlinge des Strafvollzugs" (Remand prisoners in solitary confinement are proportionally much more often in need of psychiatric hospitalization compared with prisoners not in solitary confinement [trans. by the author]) (Volkart, Rothenfluth, et al. 1983, p. 374). Remand prisoners in solitary confinement were, in other words, much more often hospitalized for psychiatric reasons than prisoners who came from communal prison conditions. Those who were hospitalized from solitary confinement had experienced, on average, eighty-six days of imprisonment prior to their hospitalization, as opposed to 173 days experienced by those who came from communal imprisonment (p. 373).

Volkart and colleagues published another study in 1983 comparing thirty prisoners in solitary confinement (twenty remand prisoners and ten in disciplinary segregation) with a control group of twenty-eight prisoners in communal imprisonment. The study was cross-sectional, incorporated no longitudinal data, and was not interview-based. According to Andersen, the participants were tested for "few pre-prison factors" (Andersen 2004, p. 39). Isolated inmates had spent an average of ninety-one days in solitary confinement (minimum thirty days), whereas the control group had spent, on average, 326 days imprisoned. All participants had normal intelligence. Their health and personalities were then assessed through psychiatric questionnaires. The group of isolated inmates "showed considerably more psychopathological symptoms than the control group . . . [and these] effects were mainly caused by solitary confinement; age, schooling, duration of detention and personality turned out to be of subordinate importance" (Volkart, Dittrich et al. 1983, p. 44).

Two Norwegian studies of remand prisoners have also documented health risks involved in using solitary confinement. A 1993 longitudinal study of sixty-three isolated remand prisoners, which excluded inmates with obvious withdrawal symptoms and those deemed at risk of suffering from a psychosis, found a development of widespread health problems after four weeks of solitary confinement, including depression, anxiety, stomach and muscle pains, and inability to concentrate (Gamman 2001, pp. 44–45). A follow-up in 1995 with a sample of fifty-four remand prisoners included a control group (twenty-seven inmates in each group) and had a longitudinal design. Those in solitary confinement suffered significantly more both physically and psychologically than the prisoners in the control group (sleeplessness, concentration problems, anxiety, depressions, etc.). The isolated prisoners were given and used much more medication than the control group (Gamman 1995, 2001, p. 45). Gamman's 1995 study has been criticized for not using standardized instruments besides the Montgomery-Åsbergs Depression Rating Scale (Andersen 2004, p. 39). Gamman points out that the control group in his 1995 study was slightly different from his isolation group, and the latter contained more detainees charged with drug offenses and had a five-year higher average age. Most important, though, the isolation group was healthier (both physically and mentally) than the control group (Gamman 1995, p. 2245; 2001, p. 45). The 1995 study also excluded inmates with a known intolerance for solitary confinement. Eleven remand prisoners were thus excluded, of whom six were in solitary confinement. All six developed a psychosis during the imprisonment in isolation, and of the five others only one became in need of psychiatric treatment (Gamman 1995, p. 2245).

A large-scale Danish longitudinal study from 1994—involving 367 pretrial detainees—reported a significantly higher rate of psychiatric problems among isolated than among a control group of nonisolated prisoners. A higher incidence of psychiatric morbidity—mainly adjustment disorders—was found among those in solitary confinement (28 percent) than among those not in isolation (15 percent). The rate of psychiatric morbidity was highest (43 percent) among a third group (which did not overlap with the above-mentioned groups) of remand prisoners who had been in long-term solitary confinement (more than two months) (Andersen et al. 1994, p. 114). A number of standardized instruments were used to measure health quantitatively. The scores for those in solitary (as a group) were unchanged throughout the isolation period, and those not in isolation "had a gradual improvement on most quantitative mental health scores during this early phase of imprisonment" (Andersen 2004, p. 39). Those in solitary confinement experienced an improvement in health scores when the solitary confinement conditions were relieved (p. 39). The researchers concluded that the differences between the isolated remand prisoners and the control group were caused "mainly by different conditions of SC and non-SC" (p. 39). Finally, it was concluded that pretrial detention in isolation compared with pretrial detention without isolation involved strain and risk of damaging the mental health of the imprisoned individuals (Andersen et al. 1994, vol. 1, pp. 114, 165).

The 1994 study is (methodologically speaking) perhaps the best-designed scientific quantitative study on the effects of solitary confinement so far. Still an important methodological issue should be addressed. The very thoroughness of the study caused the research itself to constitute a very significant intrusion into the lives of the isolated (and nonisolated) prisoners, something that Andersen and colleagues have themselves discussed (Andersen et al. 1994; Andersen 2004, pp. 40–41). Initially remand prisoners included in the sample were interviewed by one of the researchers—typically for three hours; afterward the inmate had to fill out questionnaires, and his or her pulse and blood sample were taken. One to three days later, one or two days of psychological testing and a further interview followed—typically lasting two hours each day (or four hours one day). The psychological testing and interview would then be repeated after three weeks of confinement, after two months, and then after each additional month for those still in pretrial detention. This meant that the imprisoned individuals— including those in so-called isolation—received extensive attention from doctors and psychologists during the study period. During the first approximately three weeks of imprisonment, those in isolation were typically subjected to four or five days of intense interviews and testing of around two (sometimes three or four) hours each day—not counting filling out questionnaires, having blood samples taken, and so forth. In other words, these remand prisoners were effectively *not* in solitary confinement during those four or five days. This constituted around 20–25 percent of the period between the first test and the end of the second test round after approximately three weeks. This leveled out some of the differences between the solitary confinement and non-solitary conditions and must almost certainly have significantly downgraded the measured differences between the isolated prisoners and the control group. This would be especially true since the interviews constituted meaningful social contact in which the well-being and innermost thoughts of the imprisoned individual were in focus, precisely the kind of contact that isolated prisoners normally lack.

This methodological issue might help explain why the second part of the 1994 study—a survey of hospitalization among remand prisoners—could be interpreted as giving even more clear-cut results. A sample of 124 remand prisoners who had been transferred to a prison hospital revealed that if "a person remained in SC [solitary confinement] for four weeks the likelihood of being admitted to the prison hospital for a psychiatric reason was about twenty times as high as for a person remanded in nSC [non–solitary confinement] for the same period of time" (Sestoft et al. 1998, p. 103). A sample of thirty-seven remand prisoners admitted to a specific prison hospital also revealed that among those who came directly from isolation, 63.7 percent were admitted purely for psychiatric reasons and 18.2 percent purely for somatic reasons. Among those who came from nonisolation, 42.3 percent were admitted for purely psychiatric reasons and 53.8 percent purely for somatic reasons (p. 101).

The authors concluded that "individuals detained in SC are forced into an environment that increases their risk of hospitalization to the prison hospital for psychiatric reasons. These findings reflect the national [Danish] legislation, and hence those responsible must consider methods of achieving an acceptable standard for law and order and public security either without SC or with major modifications" (Sestoft et al. 1998, pp. 105–6).

A 1997 follow-up of the 1994 study was based on reports (questionnaires) from former participants in the original study. Almost half the original participants (excluding those in the survey of hospitalization among remand prisoners) completed questionnaires (between 41 and 49 percent from the three different groups of isolated, nonisolated, and long-term isolated remand prisoners). The dropout rate was caused by individuals leaving the country, dying, disappearing, and not wanting to participate (Andersen, Lillebæk, and Sestoft 1997). Analysis of the dropout rate revealed that three factors could explain it: the higher the subject's intelligence, the likelier that the participant would answer the follow-up questionnaires; participants suffering from schizophrenia (or related disorders) were less likely to answer; and the longer the imprisonment, the greater the chance of answering (p. 24).

The 1997 follow-up highlights how some remand prisoners remember their imprisonment. Former remand prisoners having been imprisoned under an isolation regime found their incarceration significantly more straining than remand prisoners who had been imprisoned under "normal" conditions. Thirty-eight percent of those in solitary confinement and 36 percent of those in long-term solitary found their remand imprisonment extraordinarily straining, as opposed to 12 percent of those not in solitary (Andersen, Lillebæk, and Sestoft 1997, p. 31). More formerly isolated remand prisoners also reported having suffered strong psychological reactions while being imprisoned than those who were not isolated: 23 percent of those in solitary confinement and 27 percent of those in long-term solitary reported that they experienced severe psychological reactions after their remand imprisonment, as opposed to 9 percent of those not in solitary (p. 38). The basic conclusion from the 1994 study was supported but also strengthened since the authors recommended that both "medically and psychologically" solitary confinement should not be used during pretrial confinement (p. 59).

In the early 1990s, psychologist Craig Haney assessed the psychological health of 100 inmates in California's Pelican Bay SHU and has produced the most thorough research on the effects of the supermax variant of solitary confinement. Haney's original study was conducted as part of the *Madrid vs. Gomez* case. The sample of 100 inmates was randomly selected, and inmates were then individually assessed in two different face-to-face interviews. The data were considered representative of the entire group of prisoners at this specific supermax facility (Haney 2003, pp. 132–33). Considerable and severe effects of solitary confinement were found with very high prevalence rates. For example, 91 percent suffered from anxiety and nervousness, and 70 percent "felt themselves on the verge of an emotional breakdown" (p. 133). Seventy-seven percent were in a state of chronic depression, and two-thirds suffered from many different symptoms (pp. 133–34).

Some obvious methodological problems worth noting are that there was no control group, and no longitudinal data were available. Nevertheless the extremely high prevalence rates clearly exceed base expectancy rates for mental health problems even among prisoners generally found in disciplinary or administrative segregation. Compared with the studies of Swiss, Danish, and Norwegian solitary confinement conditions, the Californian supermax conditions would probably be considered more inhumane by most observers. According to Haney, the Pelican Bay SHU is "the most lifeless environment in . . . [California's]—or any—correctional system" (Haney 1993, p. 3).

Stuart Grassian's 1983 study of a group of inmates in solitary confinement includes only fifteen inmates but is one of the most cited on the effects of solitary confinement (possibly together with Suedfeld et al. [1982]). Like Haney's, it was carried out in connection with a court case; fifteen inmates from a prison in Massachusetts were plaintiffs (and fourteen were interviewed and studied). Grassian described numerous and severe symptoms suffered by the inmates and asserted that these symptoms formed "a major, clinically distinguishable psychiatric syndrome" (1983, p. 1459). The study is methodologically problematic because of the small sample size, the lack of a control group, and the obvious selection bias. Grassian produced a qualitative analysis, however, that was consistent with nineteenth-century German literature and clearly caught the attention of others interested in the field.

While both Haney's and Grassian's studies were carried out as parts of ongoing court cases, that was not the case with the Swiss, Danish, and Norwegian studies. The Danish 1994 and 1997 studies, though, were requested by the Danish Ministry of Justice, which was represented in a reference group, under whose auspices the study was carried out (the researchers themselves were independent). The Danish study setup could therefore potentially create bias in favor of the state and its existing practice. But being affiliated with plaintiffs in court cases could also possibly bias researchers against or in favor of in-state practices of solitary confinement.

B. Other Studies and Literature Reviews

Other studies on the effects of solitary confinement on prisoners are briefly described below, together with conclusions from some of the most important literature reviews.

Clare et al. (2001) evaluated the English Close Supervision Centers (CSC) in 2001, dealing with many issues related to the practice of segregating prisoners. Psychiatric assessments of prisoners in CSCs were made and interviews were conducted with twenty-three inmates. A high rate of mental illness was found. A study of the effects of solitary confinement was not made, however, but interviews with four prisoners who had been isolated for twenty-three hours a day reported briefly on possible effects of solitary confinement. Severe symptoms, including hallucinations, were reported, but these could have been caused by prior illnesses such as schizophrenia.

The Human Rights Watch report *Cold Storage* is based on studies of inmates in two supermax facilities in Indiana in 1995, 1996, and 1997. In both facilities, the research team had short conversations with around forty inmates and extended interviews in private rooms with approximately ten inmates in 1995 and 1996. In 1997, two psychiatrists conducted structured interviews with and assessed the health of forty-one inmates while using a rating scale "widely accepted in the psychiatric field" (Fellner and Mariner 1997, p. 4). The psychiatrists identified many prisoners "who were suffering from serious mental disorders." It appeared that most "had previous histories of mental disorder," so the researchers could not conclude that isolation had caused mental illness; but they concluded that "their condition was exacerbated by confinement at the MCF and SHU" and thereby proposed a causal link between segregation in solitary confinement and adverse health effects (p. 70).

In 1988, psychologists Stanley Brodsky and Forrest Scogin presented three studies of the effects of protective custody in three different U.S. prisons. In all three studies, Brodsky had acted as an outside expert brought in by attorneys for inmate plaintiffs or the state in a class action law suit against prison/protective custody conditions. In the first study, several prisoners were in solitary confinement (twenty-three hours in cell time), but some were double-celled. No control group was established, but the sample was apparently randomly selected. A standardized procedure using the Omnibus Stress questionnaire and an isolation effects checklist was used. In the second study, an Isolation Sentence-Completion Test was devised and used. Forty-five prisoners were interviewed in the first two studies, and a very high prevalence of psychological (and physical) symptoms was found including nervousness (84 percent), hallucinations and delusions (42 percent), and suicidal thoughts/depression (77 percent) in the first study and physical symptoms (79 percent), anxiety (45 percent), and depression (36 percent) in the second. The authors were not able to assert the cause of these symptoms, since many of those in protective custody could have had preexisting pathologies. But a third study in another prison showed that inmates in protective custody, with spacious two-man cells and access to program activities, had no complaints. The authors concluded that protective custody was not necessarily harmful, but it had "strong potential for harmful effects" (Brodsky and Scogin 1988, p. 279) and pointed to social isolation as a possible cause. While conditions never amounted to sensory deprivation, protective custody could "deprive the inmates of the opportunity to engage in the behaviors that allow us to define who we are" (p. 279). The authors therefore recommended that "sufficient stimulation and activities" were provided "to ensure the psychological well-being of the prisoners" (p. 280). Brodsky and Scogin's material is importantly different from the other studies cited here since a significant proportion of their inmates had chosen protective custody themselves, and not all of those in such custody were in solitary confinement. A qualitative Norwegian study also deals with the effects of isolation among inmates who have chosen isolation themselves (Hammerlin and Larsen 2000).

In 1987 Foster and colleagues published a study of South African detention practices, which included an empirical study of remand prisoners and dealt with the effects of solitary confinement. The study sample consisted of 175 cases of detention involving 158 individuals, and 79 percent of the detentions involved solitary confinement. Most also involved beatings or other forms of abuse. Information was gathered through semistructured interviews. Remand prisoners described the experience of solitary confinement in very negative terms, including such effects as anxiety, talking to oneself, and fears of going insane. The authors conclude that "there can be little doubt that solitary confinement under these circumstances [in South Africa] should in itself be regarded as a form of torture" (Foster, Davis, and Sandler 1987, p. 136).

Hinkle and Wolf's 1956 report on "Communist Interrogation and Indoctrination of 'Enemies of the States'" is a special study seen in the present context, primarily because it rests on information "obtained from a number of sources . . . from experts in the area, who for security reasons must remain anonymous" (1956, p. 116). In other words, it is a product of the Cold War—written in the days when "brainwashing" became a commonly known term—and should of course be seen in that light. Knowledge of "prisoners' reactions to their experiences," according to the authors, was thus "obtained by the direct observation of persons recently released from Communist prisons. Some of these observations continued for weeks and were supplemented by follow-up observations over periods of months" (p. 116). The subject was not solely solitary confinement; nevertheless, it was concluded that an isolation regimen could produce anxiety, depression, illusory experiences, visual hallucinations, and in some cases psychosis. Insanity was normally avoided by breaking the routine of total isolation, and the "lesser" effects were "usually sufficient to make the prisoner eager to talk to his interrogator and to seek some method to escape from a situation which had become intolerable" (p. 129).

Jackson's (1983) *Prisoners of Isolation*, about the use of solitary confinement in Canada, was based primarily on his work on a court case concerning a group of prisoners isolated in British Columbia Penitentiary. Seven plaintiffs were interviewed. They described severe effects of their imprisonment in solitary confinement. Their claims were assessed by several experts. The case was won, and conditions in the special correctional unit at British Columbia Penitentiary were described as cruel and unusual punishment.

A number of Danish studies concerned with the effects of solitary confinement were published during the early 1980s. They were made by the so-called isolation group, which campaigned for reduction or abolishment in the practice of solitary confinement during pretrial isolation. Much of their material was based on case studies of forty-six remand prisoners in solitary confinement. The studies were strictly qualitative (there were no control groups or standardized instruments, and typically relatively brief analyses of the symptoms registered were offered by psychiatrists and psychologists [Jensen et al. 1980*a*; Jørgensen 1981]). Finn Jørgensen claimed to identify both an acute and a chronic isolation syndrome (Jørgensen 1990). The most detailed analysis was delivered by psychologist Ida Koch, who concluded that nearly "all prisoners isolated [to avoid collusion] suffer after days or a few weeks of nervous symptoms like concentration and memory difficulties, lack of ability to sleep, psychosomatic symptoms etc. After a few weeks many isolated prisoners suffer from depersonalization, lack of emotional control, anxiety, hallucination and paranoia. Those severe symptoms continue often after isolation when the prisoners again can relate to others. Many feel very handicapped in social contexts and 'choose' to continue their lives alone" (1982, p. 382; see also Koch 1983).

In 1975, Benjamin and Lux wrote about the effects of solitary confinement as experienced by prisoners in the segregation unit at Maine State Prison. The authors concluded that the use of "forced isolation" at Maine State Prison caused "a severe deterioration of psychological functioning" (1975, p. 89). Interviews with two prisoners were quoted at length, but the number of inmates studied is unclear.

Psychologist Richard Korn has written two reports on the effects of confinement in a high-security unit for administrative segregation at Lexington, Kentucky. The reports are based on two visits to the unit in July and November 1987 by Korn and attorneys from the National Prison Project. The staff was interviewed, and on both occasions the same five women inmates were also interviewed and their psychological situation was assessed. Korn reported serious psychological and psychosomatic effects including severe depressions, hallucinations, anxiety, apathy, loss of weight, and dizziness, which he described as effects of their confinement (Korn 1988*a*, 1988*b*). Confinement conditions, apart from creating "extreme isolation" (1988*a*, p. 10), were also exacerbated by staff hostility (1988*b*, p. 28).

Criminologist Joane Martel produced a qualitative in-depth study based on interviews with twelve women who had experienced segregation in Canadian prisons. No standardized measures or a control group were used. The study covers the conditions of segregation, the prisoners' experiences of segregation, and their life after segregation. Segregation conditions generally meant twenty-two hours in cell time (Martel 1999, p. 41). The segregation experiences of ten of the studied women "suggest that segregation produces substantial and sometimes lasting, debilitating outcomes for them" (p. 101). Martel also described how "fears of 'going crazy' or of 'losing their minds' appear to be recurrent in conditions of segregation" (p. 103). She concluded that "the effects of these conditions are damaging and reach far beyond the original intent of segregation policies" (p. 104).

Lorna Rhodes (2004) has recently conducted an anthropological study of a supermax prison in Washington State. The primary aim was not to assess the possible effects of solitary confinement, but the subject was unavoidable. The relevant material consisted primarily of the medical records of 122 inmates and interviews with eighty-seven inmates. Rhodes describes effects of solitary confinement, including hallucinations, anger, and uncontrolled thought processes and illustrates how prison mental health workers are charged with easing symptoms of "paranoia, depression, and delusion." According to Rhodes, these staff members are in a sense charged to protect prisoners "from the prison itself" (2004, p. 110).

A Norwegian psychiatric study of punitive and administrative segregation in Oslo Prison was conducted in 2000 and 2001. Thirty inmates in segregation were studied and compared with a control group of thirty inmates who had been referred to psychiatric treatment and had not been in segregation. The method was psychiatric interviews and a protocol that three investigators (two psychiatrists and one psychologist) agree on the diagnosis; no standardized instruments were used. The study did not assess the effects of solitary confinement as such but reported extensive and severe mental problems during imprisonment in segregation, including depressions and hallucinations (Stang et al. 2003).

Psychologist Hans Toch's *Mosaic of Despair: Human Breakdown in Prisons* (1992) is based on hundreds of in-depth interviews with inmates in New York state prisons, with an unknown number of them being in segregation. Toch identifies damaging effects connected especially with solitary confinement (versus other forms of imprisonment). He uses the term "isolation panic" and describes a range of symptoms including panic, rage, loss of control, and complete breakdown. According to Toch, "isolation removes even the coping resources ordinarily available in prisons" and can "dramatize the pains of imprisonment per se." Isolation panic can therefore mark "a dichotomy in the minds of inmates—a distinction between imprisonment, which is tolerable, and isolation, which is not" (1992, pp. 48–54).

I undertook a study of the effects of solitary confinement in a Danish nineteenth-century penitentiary based on archival material. This included medical reports, journals, and prisoner journals from the prison archive, as well as official statistics and publications from the Danish Prison Service and other experts. Most of the data were longitudinal, and the study had both qualitative and quantitative aspects. Conclusions were based on a sample of 300 inmates, and in some cases on statistics covering more than 3,000 inmates. A third (33 percent) of the inmates suffered from symptoms caused mainly by isolation. In comparisons of data with modern research, a significant number of methodological issues, of course, arise. The study, for example, lacks a control group, and the definition of mental illness was different in the nineteenth century. It nevertheless clearly shows that the prison administration itself came to perceive the use of solitary confinement as a huge health problem (they condemned the practice). Symptoms such as lethargy, anxiety, and hallucinations were treated by allowing extra out-of-cell time and limited social contact for certain inmates (Smith 2003, 2004a).

All the studies just mentioned report significant adverse effects experienced during solitary confinement, and some go a long way toward identifying these as a product of isolation. Most earlier reviews dealing broadly with the literature on solitary confinement have also concluded that isolation of prisoners can be a very harmful practice (Bonta and Gendreau's [1990] study is the most obvious exception). In 1986, for example, psychiatrist Stuart Grassian and psychologist Nancy Friedman concluded that "late nineteenth and early twentieth-century German clinicians . . . contributed altogether thousands of descriptions of psychosis associated with solitary confinement" while the "more recent literature on this subject has also nearly uniformly described or speculated that solitary confinement has serious psychopathological consequences" (Grassian and Friedman 1986, p. 53).

Three years earlier in another review of the literature concerning the effects of solitary confinement, Reto Volkart concluded that "über den Verlauf der Auswirkungen sind sich die Autoren weitgehend einig, dass massive Einzelhafteffekte sehr rasch (in den ersten Tagen und Stunden) auftreten können. Aber auch sehr langer Einzelhaft wurden besondere Wirkungen zugeschrieben" (Researchers widely agree that massive effects of solitary confinement can set in very quickly—during the initial days or hours. But particular effects are also attributed to very long periods of solitary confinement. [trans. by the author]) (Volkart 1983, pp. 18–19).

In 2003 psychologist Craig Haney concluded that "empirical research on solitary and supermax-like confinement has consistently and unequivocally documented the harmful consequences of living in these kinds of environments" (2003, p. 130).

In 2004 psychiatrist Henrik Steen Andersen concluded in a review that solitary confinement of remand prisoners "imposes additional strain and increases the risk of development of psychiatric morbidity," and furthermore noted that when "differences between SC [solitary confinement] and non-SC have been found in studies of sentenced prisoners the trend disfavours SC." Finally Andersen concluded that sensory deprivation "may contribute to the pathogenesis of incident disorders in SC" (2004, p. 40).

III. A Wide Range of Symptoms

A wide range of symptoms are described in the solitary confinement literature. When isolated prisoners are asked, they point to anger, hatred, bitterness, boredom, stress, loss of the sense of reality, suicidal thoughts, trouble sleeping, impaired concentration, confusion, depression, and hallucinations (Jensen, Jørgensen, and Rasmussen 1980*a*; Koch 1982; Jackson 1983, p. 64; Korn 1988*b*, p. 25; Andersen, Lillebæk, and Sestoft 1997; Kupers 1999; Martel 1999; Clare et al. 2001, p. 62; Shalev and Guinea 2003; Rhodes 2004). These symptoms vary in degree as well as their health consequences. Still, there is general agreement among many of those who have studied solitary confinement that this mode of imprisonment can produce severe effects (see, e.g., Gray 1847; Hinkle and Wolff 1956, p. 129; Koch 1982, p. 377; Grassian 1983, p. 1453; Haney and Lynch 1997, p. 531; Gamman 2001, p. 48; Smith 2004*a*, p. 8).

One reason symptoms vary is the different conditions under which solitary confinement is carried out. There are huge differences among isolation in nineteenth-century penitentiaries, in U.S. supermax prisons, and in Scandinavian remand prisons. One important lesson nevertheless is that a significant percentage of prisoners subjected to solitary confinement suffer from a similar range of symptoms irrespective of differences in the physical conditions in various prisons and in the treatment of isolated inmates. Solitary confinement has been found to induce everything from different levels of psychological problems to insanity (see also Haney and Lynch 1997, p. 499). The lack of meaningful social contact seems to be a key factor, and access to television, the standard of cell hygiene, and so forth do not constitute social contact, however much these and other prison features may matter for the general health situation and the performance of the prison in question (Liebling 2004).

I have arranged the symptoms of solitary confinement in five categories.[19] These categories necessarily overlap.

A. Physiological Symptoms and Reactions

Severe headaches are a common complaint (Jackson 1983, p. 67; Koch 1982, p. 377; Andersen, Lillebæk, and Sestoft 1997, p. 39; Gam-

---

[19] There exists a variety of categorizations of isolation symptoms, and the one used here is inspired by different studies (see, e.g., Koch 1982; Grassian 1983; Gamman 2001; Haney 2003; Smith 2004*a*).

man 2001, p. 48; Haney 2003, p. 133; Stang et al. 2003, p. 1846; Smith 2004a, p. 12). In one study, 88 percent of the isolated inmates suffered from headaches (Haney 2003, p. 133); in another, 53 percent of long-term isolated remand prisoners (more than two months) complained of headaches (Andersen, Lillebæk, and Sestoft 1997, p. 39). In a Norwegian study, 40 percent of the isolated prisoners suffered from continuous headaches (Stang et al. 2003, p. 1846).

Heart palpitations and increased pulse are also common among isolated inmates (Korn 1988a, p. 16; 1988b, p. 25; Andersen et al. 1994, p. 103; Gamman 2001, p. 48; Haney 2003, p. 133; Smith 2003, p. 223).

Oversensitivity to stimuli is also reported (Grassian 1983, p. 1452; Haney 2003, p. 134).[20] This can apparently result in inability to tolerate otherwise normal stimuli. Some isolated prisoners cannot stand ordinary noises and produce dramatic overreactions (see Grassian 1993, p. 4). This was eerily described in 1851 by Hans Christian Andersen during his visit to a Swedish isolation prison: "In the door to each cell, a glass is fixed, as large as an eye, covered on the outside, and from here, the guard, unobserved by the prisoner, sees everything that occurs; but softly, soundlessly, he must come, for the prisoner's hearing in this solitude is oddly sharpened. I removed the covering very gently and put up my eye to look into the closed room. His glance immediately met mine" (1851, pp. 29–33).

Another physiological reaction reported is pains in the abdomen and muscle pains in the neck and back (Gamman 2001, p. 48; Stang et al. 2003, p. 1846). Pains and pressure in the chest have also been reported (Smith 2004a, p. 12).[21]

Problems with digestion (Gamman 2001, p. 48; Smith 2004a, p. 12) and diarrhea have also been reported (Koch 1982, p. 377). A related symptom is weight loss, which is reported in a number of studies (Koch 1982, p. 377; Korn 1988b, p. 25; Clare et al. 2001, p. 62; Smith 2004a, p. 12). In a nineteenth-century solitary confinement prison, 651 out of 1,596 prisoners, or 41 percent, lost weight during the first three months of their stay (in the 1860s), although the prison doctor was

[20] An experimental study in a Canadian maximum-security prison reported a decline in prisoners' EEG frequency as a result of solitary confinement, which according to the authors possibly represented "an increased readiness to respond to external stimulation as solitary confinement progresses" (Gendreau et al. 1972, p. 58). See also Scott and Gendreau (1969, p. 339).

[21] See also official nineteenth-century reports from the Danish Prison Service; *brystsmerter* ("chest pains") and similar terms were sometimes used to describe diseases suffered by inmates in solitary confinement.

free to change the diet of each inmate. In another sample from the same prison, the typical weight loss was shown to be between five and ten kilograms (Smith 2004*a*, p. 12 [sample size: 300 inmates]). In a sample of five prisoners from a high-security unit in the United States, weight loss likewise varied from five to ten kilograms (Korn 1988*a*, p. 16).

Haney (2003, p. 133) has reported loss of appetite, perspiring hands, dizziness, and fainting among a significant number of isolated inmates. Dizziness and loss of appetite have also been noted as a symptom of isolation by others (Korn 1988*a*, p. 16; 1988*b*, p. 25). The term dizziness was also used in official reports from the Danish Prison Service in descriptions of illnesses suffered in the isolation prison Vridsløselille.

B. Confusion and Impaired Concentration

Isolated inmates often observe that they frequently experience severe problems with their ability to concentrate (Koch 1982, p. 375; Grassian 1983, p. 1453; Jackson 1983, p. 66; Korn 1988*b*, p. 25; Lærum 1990; Andersen, Lillebæk, and Sestoft 1997, p. 40; Gamman 2001, p. 48).[22] As a result, isolated prisoners are sometimes apparently unable to read and cannot even watch television, although that may be one of the very few ways to pass the time (see, e.g., Koch 1982, p. 376). Prisoners who experience these problems apparently become unable to focus and concentrate enough on specific issues or activities in order to comprehend what is going on.

A state of confusion is a related and an often-reported symptom (Grassian 1983, p. 1452; Gamman 2001, p. 48; Smith 2004*a*, p. 13). A number of observers use the term "confused thought process" (Haney 2003, p. 134), and others write of "disturbances of thought content" in the form of paranoia and violent fantasies (see below) (Grassian 1983, p. 1453). Korn (1988*b*, p. 25) describes how isolated prisoners have "difficulty in communicating with individuals from outside" and notes a "decreasing ability by prisoners to direct the flow of their own ideation."

Loss of memory is another reported experience (Koch 1982, p. 375; Grassian 1983, p. 1452; Gamman 2001, p. 48).

---

[22] In Andersen et al. (1994), prisoners also reported problems with concentration, but these did not show up in cognitive tests.

C. Hallucinations, Illusions, and Paranoid Ideas

Andersen and colleagues reported some—but few—hallucinatory symptoms and changes in perception among isolated Danish remand prisoners (Andersen et al. 1994, p. 116). In Haney's SHU sample, 41 percent experienced hallucinations and 44 percent perceptual distortions (Haney 2003, p. 134). Grassian also reported hallucinations and illusions in his 1983 study, including wavering cell walls, movements, and even the experience of entire visits in the cell (Grassian 1983, p. 1452). The same disturbing effects were reported by isolated prisoners elsewhere in the United States and in Canada (Jackson 1983, p. 66; Korn 1988a, p. 16; 1988b, p. 26). In a Norwegian study, 20 percent of those in solitary confinement experienced perceptual distortions (Stang et al. 2003, p. 1846). Hallucinations have also been reported by isolated prisoners in Northern Ireland and the former Soviet Union (Hinkle and Wolff 1956, p. 128; Shallice 1972, p. 390), as well as by isolated hostages (see, e.g., Siegel 1984).

Hallucinations and illusions can be connected with paranoia, which in itself is an often-reported symptom of solitary confinement (Koch 1982, p. 377; Grassian 1983, p. 1453; Smith 2004a, p. 13). Stang et al. (2003, p. 1846) describe strong feelings of suspicion as a symptom. Cases of paranoia can in isolation apparently deteriorate into "overt psychosis" (Grassian 1993, p. 5). An English case study reports how a twenty-seven-year-old man developed monosymptomatic hypochondriacal psychosis—psychoses with hypochondriacal delusions—in prison segregation (consisting of twenty-three hours or more a day for more than a year). According to the authors, solitary confinement "played a significant part in the development of the illness" (Humphreys and Burnett 1994, p. 345).

Another form of perceptual distortion reported by isolated prisoners is the experience of hearing voices (Grassian 1983, p. 1452; Lærum 1990). Many isolated prisoners also begin talking to themselves (63 percent according to Haney [2003, p. 134]; see also Foster, Davis, and Sandler [1987, p. 139] and Lærum [1990]).

Finally, studies report that isolated individuals fantasize to a great extent (Koch 1982; p. 375). Often these fantasies become violent and aggressive (Grassian 1983, p. 1453; Haney 2003, p. 134).

D. Emotional Reactions and Impulsive Actions

Depression and anxiety show up in most studies (Hinkle and Wolff 1956, p. 128; Jørgensen 1981, p. 3346; Grassian 1983, p. 1452; Foster, Davis, and Sandler 1987, p. 137; Korn 1988*b*, p. 25; Andersen et al. 1994; Clare et al. 2001, p. 62; Gamman 2001, p. 48; Haney 2003, p. 133; Stang et al. 2003, p. 1846). Andersen and colleagues reported some cases of depression and anxiety and a significant rate of "adjust-ment disorder" among isolated prisoners (Andersen et al. 1994, p. 115). Grassian reported "massive free-floating anxiety" among 71 percent of the inmates in his sample, and 91 percent of the prisoners suffered from anxiety in Haney's study (Grassian 1983, p. 1452; Haney 2003, p. 133). Toch focuses on panic and despair in his description of isolated prisoners in punitive segregation and concludes that "irrespective of dominant concerns, the reaction to isolation is a panic state" (Toch 1992, p. 52).

Problems with impulse control, violent reactions, and self-mutilation are reported with alarming frequency (Koch 1982, p. 376; Grassian 1983, p. 1453; Korn 1988*b*, p. 26; Martel 1999, p. 58; Gamman 2001, p. 48). Toch (1992, p. 52) gives an example of a prisoner banging his body into the walls. Actions of self-mutilation can take the form of suicide attempts, which are treated below.

E. Lethargy and Debilitation

Lethargy and chronic tiredness are common symptoms of solitary confinement, which are often described by prisoners as a feeling of how everything comes to a complete standstill (Grassian 1983, p. 1453; Jackson 1983, p. 67; Martel 1999, pp. 57, 73; Haney 2003, p. 133; Smith 2004*a*). In an experimental study of sensory deprivation using volunteers in a Canadian maximum-security prison, a slowing of EEG, alpha frequency, was recorded among socially isolated inmates, which "correlated with apathetic, lethargic behavior" (Scott and Gendreau 1969, p. 340; see also Gendreau et al. 1972, p. 57).

This lethargic condition has been described by researchers in con-nection with a complete breakdown or disintegration of the identity of the isolated individual. This can be described as a simultaneous attack of several symptoms that effectively erase the personality of the isolated individual: they experience problems talking and understanding others, hallucinate (hear and see things), have constant headaches, are troubled by anxiety, lose control (cry, become lethargic, have fits of rage, etc.), and reach a condition that resembles (or is) psychosis (Jørgensen 1981, p. 3347; Koch 1982, p. 377). Grassian uses the term "a clinically distinguishable syndrome" when describing the suffering of these multiple isolation symptoms (Grassian 1983, p. 1453). In the words of a South African remand prisoner, "I think your whole personality is transformed" (Foster, Davis, and Sandler 1987, p. 140).

Haney uses the term "impending nervous breakdown" (which 70 percent of his sample suffered) and "overall deterioration" (which 67 percent suffered) (Haney 2003, p. 133).

Another frequent symptom is trouble sleeping (Korn 1988b, p. 25; Lærum 1990; Andersen, Lillebæk, and Sestoft 1997, p. 40; Gamman 2001, p. 48; Haney 2003, p. 133), which often comes with loss of the sense of time, and chronic tiredness and lethargy.

Finally, the question of suicidal tendencies. The literature suggests that "physical and social isolation appears strongly related to suicide" (Coid et al. 2003b, p. 321). This is supported by reported thoughts of suicide among isolated inmates and self-mutilations (Jørgensen 1981, p. 3347; Gamman 2001, p. 48; Haney 2003, p. 134). Rates and frequencies of suicides during pretrial isolation are discussed below.

F. How Many Are Affected by Solitary Confinement?

A multitude of pathological reactions are possible, and they can vary greatly. Some suffer from all or most of the symptoms described, some suffer from one or two, and others exhibit no visible ill effects. The prevalence of symptoms also depends on specific prison conditions. It is therefore difficult to give a precise evaluation of the rate of adverse symptoms due to solitary confinement in general.

In supermax prisons in the United States, many adverse symptoms are reported with dramatic prevalence rates. Among "Pelican Bay" SHU prisoners, the following symptoms were in each case suffered by between 83 and 91 percent of the inmates: anxiety, headaches, lethargy, irrational anger, confused thought processes, and social withdrawal. Hallucinations and perceptual distortions were each suffered by more than 40 percent of the studied inmates (Haney 2003, p. 133). Many other authors also report alarming rates of psychological problems and mental disease in supermax prisons (see, e.g., Fellner and Mariner 1997; Kupers 1999). It has to be remembered, of course, that many supermax and SHU prisoners may be mentally ill on arrival. This group of mentally ill prisoners will presumably—like the healthy ones—generally experience a significant deterioration of their condition during their time in solitary confinement (Fellner and Mariner 1997, p. 70; Kupers 1999; Abramsky and Fellner 2003, p. 149).

Psychiatrist Terry Kupers has visited numerous control units and segregation units in the United States and concludes that "in all the super-maximum security units I have toured, between one-third and half of the prisoners suffer from a serious mental disorder" (1999, p. xviii). Generally speaking, the supermax prisons have been termed as producing "extreme states of mind" (Rhodes 2004, p. 29).

At least 33 percent (and most likely many more) suffered adverse symptoms in a nineteenth-century Danish prison constructed on the Pennsylvania model (samples taken during the period 1859–73). All these prisoners were categorized as both physically and mentally healthy when they arrived in the prison (Smith 2004a).

In a study of Norwegian remand prisoners in solitary confinement, 94 percent suffered from adverse symptoms after four weeks; many suffered from serious symptoms such as depression and anxiety (more than half), and 13 percent had mutilated themselves (Gamman 2001, p. 44). In another Norwegian study, more than 43 percent of the isolated prisoners suffered adverse symptoms (Stang et al. 2003, p. 1846).[23]

Some studies do not provide specific percentages of the overall number of inmates who are affected negatively by solitary confinement. Many conclude that solitary confinement constitutes a significant health risk compared to imprisonment without isolation (see, e.g., Andersen et al. 1994; Andersen, Lillebæk, and Sestoft 1997; Sestoft et al. 1998).

G. The Duration of Solitary Confinement and the Associated Health Effects

Several studies show that serious symptoms can occur in healthy individuals after only a few days in isolation. A Swiss study reported that 36 percent of those sent directly from solitary confinement to a psychiatric clinic were hospitalized during the first one to five days of their confinement in isolation (Volkart, Rothenfluth, et al. 1983). A Danish study of remand prisoners described how symptoms could materialize after a few days but typically did so after two weeks. So-called

---

[23] Stang et al. report only the prevalence of specific symptoms and do not tell us how many suffered from one symptom or the other. Therefore, more than 43 percent must have suffered from some kind of symptom, and most likely many more.

chronic symptoms were reported after one or two months (Jørgensen 1981). A Danish prison chaplain who had in-depth conversations with many isolated remand prisoners reported serious symptoms after three to six weeks (Manzano 1980, p. 18).

A Norwegian study of remand prisoners found serious and widespread health effects (including anxiety, depression, and self-mutilations) after four weeks of isolation. The author furthermore concluded that the amount of time spent in isolation increased the damaging effects (Gamman 2001, p. 45).

Andersen and colleagues originally reported no specific connection between the duration of solitary confinement and the health of the isolated prisoners (Andersen et al. 1994, p. 165). But since solitary confinement constituted a significant health risk compared to "normal" imprisonment, each day in isolation was likely to constitute a risk that is heightened the longer the isolation continues. This was later confirmed by Sestoft and colleagues in a study of hospitalization of prisoners: "the relative risk of hospitalization in the prison hospital [owing to a psychiatric reason] increased markedly across time spent in SC [solitary confinement]" (Sestoft et al. 1998, p. 105). Still Andersen concluded in an interview that "the reactions [to solitary confinement] often set in very quickly" (Thelle and Traeholt 2003, p. 769).

The overall conclusion must therefore be that, though reactions vary between individuals, negative (sometimes severe) health effects can occur after only a few days of solitary confinement. The health risk rises for each additional day in solitary confinement.

H. Will Symptoms Recede after the Termination of Solitary Confinement?

A number of studies note that people quickly recover when solitary confinement is terminated (Grassian 1983, p. 1453; Andersen et al. 1994, p. 164; 2003, p. 175; Kupers 1999, p. 62). These tendencies toward "psychological regeneration" could indicate that the health effects of solitary confinement are not chronic. But other studies report serious postisolation effects (e.g., Martel 1999) and a chronic isolation syndrome (Koch 1982; Jørgensen 1990).

The Danish longitudinal follow-up study from 1997 did not report any chronic pathologies or isolation syndromes (Andersen, Lillebæk, and Sestoft 1997, pp. 56, 59), but the data suggested that prisoners who had been in solitary confinement experienced less "psychological compensation" after their release than prisoners who had not been isolated. The pains of imprisonment were in that sense more intensive among the isolated prisoners during their isolation and afterward (pp. 55, 59).

That is supported by descriptions of how prisoners experience serious trouble returning to society (or imprisonment under "normal" conditions) after having adapted to solitary confinement (Rhodes 2004, p. 34). (Concerning medical and social retrieval of hostages who have experienced solitary confinement, see Turnbull [1997].) This type of reaction has also been found in Denmark (Koch 1982, p. 378). Some apparently experience great anxiety when confronted by social situations after being released from solitary confinement, and some voluntarily continue to prolong their isolation. Many have trouble engaging in social behavior and fear emotional contact. According to Haney, supermax "confinement creates its own set of psychological pressures that, in some instances, uniquely disable prisoners for freeworld reintegration" (2001, p. 11). Martel reports "agoraphobia or panic disorder" in formerly segregated women. Half the sample in Martel's study experienced "difficulties being in crowded or noisy rooms," and some felt "utter hate of being around people" (1999, pp. 85–86). Many women therefore "chose to seclude themselves" from the rest of the prison population after being released from segregation (p. 86). Canadian, Danish, and American research thus shows severe signs of social disablement after having experienced solitary confinement (Koch 1982, p. 378; Martel 1999, p. 83; Rhodes 2004, p. 34).

On postsegregation effects in general, Martel concludes that "invalidating stigmas, relived abuse, uncontrollable paranoia or anxiety, self-imposed seclusion, difficulties with sexual intimacy or banal human interactions are all long lasting predicaments that the women have had to struggle with after being detained in segregation. In sum, the aftermath of segregation generally translates into overpowering feelings of inadequacy. Moreover, these feelings appear to be interiorized in a particularly reconstructed or reshaped self-image. Living after segregation often means grappling on a daily basis with such an 'altered' self-image" (1999, p. 87).

A Danish study of how parents in prison and their families on the outside cope also touches upon the issue of postisolation effects—not only for the isolated prisoner but also for his or her family. A mother who was arrested and subjected to solitary confinement (according to standard Danish pretrial practice), for example, described how they came in police cars and took me to prison. I can't let it go. They handcuffed me. I wasn't allowed to see my husband, two months passed before I saw him . . . they told me that the kids were at an institution. They said that they could keep me as long as they pleased. I was in pre-trial solitary for one month, and after that, one month where I was allowed to have visits, except from my husband. . . . Then they told me I was free to go, and that the kids would come home . . . My brother picked me up . . . he took me home where the kids were. . . . The youngest, who was two years old, wouldn't have anything to do with me. In two months time he had forgotten me. It was a very cold feeling. A week went by where he wouldn't have anything to do with me, and it wasn't until after one or two months before he wanted contact with me. . . . When we came home the whole thing was a mess . . . they had searched the house . . . I broke down. I couldn't cope with anything. I think I didn't do anything but sit and cry for half a year. In the end my kids told me, that it had to stop, that I had to do something. . . . But I still cry easily. (Christensen 1999, p. 45; translated by the author)

According to Christensen, the "psychological message is, that the person subjected to solitary confinement risks losing her self and disappearing into a non-existence" (p. 45; translated by the author).

The overall conclusion must therefore be that symptoms generally recede and people generally get better when they get out of solitary confinement. Several studies have suggested this, and some can therefore—upon the termination of isolation—be considered cured in the sense that they exhibit no pathological signs. Some, however, carry with them the negative health effects after the termination of solitary confinement and experience serious social disablement. More research is needed in this area to identify the scope and extent of this problem. Little is likewise known about the suffering experienced by children, partners, and close relatives when their parent or partner is subjected to solitary confinement.

IV. Special Issues Concerning Solitary Confinement and Remand Prisoners

Isolation of remand prisoners raises a number of policy issues, which are especially relevant in the pretrial context, most notably relating to suicide and to processing of criminal cases.

A. The Intense Feeling of Uncertainty

Solitary confinement during pretrial isolation can be worse than some forms of administrative and disciplinary segregation or isolation because of the overwhelming feeling of uncertainty: when will the isolation end, and how will my case end? (Hinkle and Wolff 1956, p. 129; Jørgensen 1981, p. 3346). A similar feeling of uncertainty can be experienced by individuals in isolation without time limit and has been experienced by POWs subjected to solitary confinement (Deaton, Berg, and Richlin 1977, p. 241).

B. Solitary Confinement during Pretrial Isolation and the Rate of Suicides

The initial move from freedom to imprisonment is very stressful. Prisons (or jails) holding remand prisoners face special problems. The initial phase of imprisonment—often pretrial detention—carries with it special psychological hardships. English data clearly identify remand prison populations as a suicide risk group (Liebling 1994, pp. 12–13, 31). According to Andersen and colleagues, the "early phase of imprisonment on remand . . . seems to be a vulnerable phase with changes in symptom scores and emergence and disappearance of psychiatric disorders" (Andersen et al. 2003, p. 175; see also Benjaminsen and Erichsen 2002). Harvey (2004) concludes that the "initial transition into prison was a difficult experience for prisoners." Problems could be eased by social contact, such as cellmate ties, and "outside social support." Harvey also concludes that the way that "prisoners formed and maintained social attachment was central to their adaptation."

The most fatal consequence of the stressful character of the first fourteen days of incarceration is the elevated rate of suicides during this period. A U.S. national study of jail suicides, for example, documented that more than half of suicide victims "were dead within the first twenty-four hours of incarceration" (Hayes 1983, p. 471). In Denmark, around half of all prison suicides are committed during the first two weeks and by remand prisoners (Benjaminsen and Erichsen 2002, p. 17). The suicide rate in the Danish remand prisons is twelve times that of the suicide rate in the general population (p. 16). Danish researchers have argued that isolation constitutes an additional suicide risk factor (Jørgensen 1981, p. 3347; Koch 1982, p. 376). A Danish study reported a disproportionately high rate of suicides among remand prisoners in isolation, but the sample was small, and the author hesitated to draw conclusions (Christiansen 1991, p. 176).

Liebling (1992, p. 51) concludes that a "disproportionate number of suicides occur in special locations, such as prison hospitals, the punishment block and other areas of seclusion." An American study of 419 suicides in county jails and local jails in the United States during 1979 documented that 68 percent of victims had been "held in isolation at the time of their suicide" (Hayes 1983, p. 471). This use of isolation was not used to avoid collusion as in Scandinavia but was "purportedly intended for inmates who are a danger to themselves and others" (p. 471). Hayes concluded that "the use of isolation enhances the chance of suicide, and it should, therefore, be prohibited" (p. 480). The findings were confirmed seven years later in a study that reported that 67 percent "had been held in isolation prior to their suicides" (Hayes 1989, p. 20). Likewise, a Massachusetts commission concluded in 1984 that "most experts on the subject of inmate suicide agree that placing the detainee in isolation greatly increases the chances of him or her attempting or committing suicide" (quoted from Liebling [1992, p. 150]). A study of suicides in Bavarian prisons (in Germany) between 1945 and 1974 produced similar results: "A much higher risk of suicide was found for the first day of imprisonment . . . [and the] most common method was by hanging in solitary confinement" (Spann, Liebhardt, and Seifert 1979, p. 315). In Finland, "almost one third of the [prison] suicides [1969–92] were committed in isolation rooms" (Joukumaa 1997, p. 167). Research also points toward a connection between isolation and self-mutilation: "An analysis of the 902 self-mutilation incidents in the North Carolina Department of Corrections occurring between 1958 and 1966 revealed that nearly half occurred in segregation units" (Haney and Lynch 1997, p. 525). In 2002, Toch concluded that "segregation increases despondency and self-destructive motives" and pointed out that "suicidologists recommend contact and communication as requisites for suicide prevention" (2002a, p. 10).

Still, the rate of suicides (and self-mutilations) among prisoners in different kinds of segregation units could "be an artefact of allocation procedures, which direct suicide risks away from lower security or open establishments" (Liebling 1992, p. 52). But figures concerning suicide rates among Norwegian remand prisoners in solitary confinement more clearly suggest causality (because, as mentioned earlier, Norwegian data show that these prisoners are mentally healthier upon imprisonment than their colleagues in nonisolation). In Norway between 1956 and 1991, three-quarters of all prison suicides were committed by remand prisoners (Hammerlin 2000, p. 29), and remand prisoners constituted a much smaller proportion of the national prison population—in recent years around one-quarter (Hammerlin 2001, p. 11; Danielsen and Hansen 2002, p. 9). Furthermore, 40 percent had committed suicide during the first three weeks (Hammerlin 2000, p. 29). In 1999, 40 percent of all Norwegian remand prisoners started their imprisonment with restrictions (Hammerlin 2001, p. 11)—meaning none or very little access to communal activities—and according to psychiatrist Tor Gamman, "more than half of all suicides in Norwegian prisons are committed during periods of isolation" (2001, p. 42).

The evidence strongly suggests that use of solitary confinement during the early phases of imprisonment increases the suicide risk and most likely also raises the likelihood of incidents of self-mutilation.

C. Practice of Solitary Confinement as Extortion

It is illegal, according to Danish law, to use solitary confinement and pretrial detention as extortion to coerce suspects into confessing or pleading guilty. It has nevertheless often been claimed that the element of extortion often is very real—both as a motive (for the authorities) and as a reality (for the imprisoned). In 1980, the later Danish minister of justice and then defense attorney and member of the Conservative people's party, Erik Ninn-Hansen, for example, stated "that solitary confinement today is used less to avoid detainees from communicating with others and more to squeeze out a confession." Ninn-Hansen observed that "solitary confinement is a commodity" and remand prisoners could free themselves from isolation at the price of a confession (*Politiken* 1980, p. 3; translated by the author).

Many other defense attorneys have claimed the same thing: that pretrial detention—and especially isolation—in reality is (sometimes or often) used as extortion (Petersen 1998, p. 34; Stagetorn 2003, p. 38).[24] In 2000, for example, the Danish defense attorney Manfred Petersen asserted that "solitary confinement is a form of pressure in order to obtain information and/or a confession" (quoted from Thelle and Traeholt [2003, p. 772]).

Professor Rod Morgan, who has assisted the CPT, has pointed to an unfortunate relationship between prisoner confessions and the ter-

[24] Another Danish defense attorney (the fourth quoted for this viewpoint here) stated the same in a radio interview recently (DR [Danmarks radio], in the program "Lige lovligt," May 6, 2004).

mination of their isolation (according to Gamman [2001, p. 43]). Morgan has written critically of the "Scandinavian way"—the isolation of remand prisoners—which he describes as "reckless" and allowing the police "extreme powers to exploit" (Morgan 1999, p. 204). He concludes that pretrial isolation can be "severely painful" but also seeks to know whether or not "it is purposefully imposed with a view to eliciting confessions, intelligence and other evidence? It is at this point that legal casuistry comes into play. The answer must technically be no—but in practice, the answer is sometimes almost certainly yes" (p. 202).

In other parts of the world, the use of pretrial solitary confinement has long been a well-known extortion technique to inflict psychological pain on remand prisoners in order to force out a confession. This was, for example, the case in the Soviet Union and in South Africa during apartheid (Hinkle and Wolff 1956; Riekert 1985; West 1985; Foster, Davis, and Sandler 1987; Veriava 1989). Communist methods have been analyzed as follows: "When the initial period of imprisonment is one of total isolation, such as used by the KGB, the complete separation of the prisoner from the companionship and support of others, his utter loneliness, and his prolonged uncertainty have a further disorganizing effect upon him. . . . He becomes malleable . . . and in some instances he may confabulate. The interrogator [then] exploits the prisoner's need for companionship" (Hinkle and Wolf 1956, p. 173). It was for similar reasons—that is, "the effectiveness of indefinite detention and solitary confinement in provoking anxiety and psychiatric instability—that the CIA included [these methods] . . . among its principal techniques of coercion in now repudiated manuals on interrogation from the 1960's" (Brief of Amici Curiae Human Rights First et al., *Hamadan v. Rumsfeld*, 546 U.S. 05-184 [2005], p. 5). As described from the inmate's point of view by a South African remand prisoner, "One morning you get up and say to yourself, I'm not going to stand for this any more. I am going to tell them, I'm going to give evidence, providing they just let me out. You're prepared to do anything to get out of that condition of solitary confinement" (Foster, Davis, and Sandler 1987, p. 140; see also Dr. Louis West's report "Effects of Isolation on the Evidence of Detainees" in Bell and Mackie [1985, p. 69]).

In 1910, the same (pretrial) effect of solitary confinement was clearly described by the Washington Supreme Court: "The effect of solitary confinement on the mind of a person charged with a crime may be imagined. It is a well-known psychological fact that men and women have frequently confessed to crimes which they did not commit. They have done it sometimes to escape present punishment which had become torture to them; sometimes through other motives" (*State v. Miller*, 61 Wash. 125, 111 Pac. 1053 [1910]; here quoted from Haney and Lynch [1997, p. 486]).

According to Professor Don Foster and colleagues, "there seems little doubt that solitary confinement for purposes of interrogation, indoctrination or information extraction does have aversive effects and should be regarded as a form of torture" (Foster, Davis, and Sandler 1987, p. 68).

D. Remand Prisoners' Inability to Defend Themselves Legally

An obvious problem connected with the isolation of pretrial detainees is that solitary confinement hampers their ability to function properly and thereby defend themselves. When remand prisoners suffer some of the above-mentioned health effects, they are less able to speak coherently and thereby to assist their lawyers in preparing a sensible defense.[25] This, of course, constitutes a direct attack on their most basic legal rights.

V. Conclusion

Solitary confinement can have serious psychological, psychiatric, and sometimes physiological effects on many prison inmates. A long list of possible symptoms from insomnia and confusion to hallucinations and outright insanity has been documented. A number of studies identify a distinguishable isolation syndrome, but there is no general agreement on this. Research suggests that between one-third and more than 90 percent experience adverse symptoms in solitary confinement, and a significant amount of this suffering is caused or worsened by solitary confinement. The conditions of solitary confinement very likely influence the level of distress suffered. The U.S. supermax prisons could be one of the most harmful isolation practices currently in operation.

---

[25] This has been pointed out by several defense attorneys (see, e.g., Stagetorn 2003, p. 39). In a recent radio interview, a Danish defense attorney explained how isolated remand prisoners in his experience often changed their personality and became more difficult to speak with after around four weeks (DR [Danmarks radio] in the program "Lige lovligt," May 6, 2004). See also Koch (1982, p. 376) and Korn (1988*b*, p. 25). In an English study, prisoners (not remand) found it "hard to talk after long periods of isolation" (Clare et al. 2001, p. 62).

The allocation of mentally ill inmates to supermax prisons (and sometimes to other places of punitive or administrative segregation) is likely to be high, but the prevalence of adverse psychological symptoms in some supermax prisons is clearly significantly higher than even high base expectancy rates for mental illness.

Very different individual reactions to solitary confinement are clearly possible. Some people cope much better than others in isolation. According to some researchers, some inmates can handle even prolonged solitary confinement without displaying any serious adverse symptoms.

Still, the overall conclusion must be that solitary confinement—regardless of specific conditions and regardless of time and place—causes serious health problems for a significant number of inmates. The central harmful feature is that it reduces meaningful social contact to an absolute minimum: a level of social and psychological stimulus that many individuals will experience as insufficient to remain reasonably healthy and relatively well functioning. Prisoners in general prison populations suffer from a high rate of psychiatric morbidity and health problems (inside and outside of prisons), but solitary confinement creates significant additional strain and additional health problems. This was the case in the nineteenth century where Pennsylvania model prisons experienced serious problems with the health of inmates—problems not experienced in the same manner or with the same intensity in Auburn model prisons. The same difference has been documented in contemporary prisons by studies conducted throughout the last approximately thirty years.

Use of solitary confinement in remand prisons can in some ways be considered even worse than the practice of isolating sentenced prisoners. The psychologically stressful and dangerous first two weeks of imprisonment and the disturbing suicide rates in remand prisons illustrate this. The element of effective coercion of guilty pleas from the isolated prisoners is another. The coercion problem, which Rod Morgan compares to "moderate psychological pressure," makes isolation of remand prisoners a dubious practice (1999, pp. 201–4). Use of solitary confinement in remand prisons can damage the health of citizens who have not been condemned and are still—until the sentence is pronounced—to be considered not guilty.

When one is studying the relationship between time spent in solitary confinement and health effects, negative (sometimes severe) health effects can occur after only a few days of solitary confinement. The health risk appears to rise for each additional day.

Our knowledge is much more tentative concerning what happens upon release from solitary confinement. Several studies suggest that most negative effects wear off relatively quickly. Other studies identify more or less chronic health effects. Most studies do not address the question of postisolation effects, and more research is clearly needed. Still a number of studies describe how formerly isolated inmates experience significant problems clearly related to their isolation experience—such as difficulties handling social situations and close social and emotional contacts. The only large-scale follow-up study identified less postimprisonment "psychological compensation" among formerly isolated prisoners than among formerly nonisolated prisoners.

A. Policy Implications

Solitary confinement harms prisoners who were not mentally ill on admission to prison and worsens the mental health of those who were. The use of solitary confinement in prisons should be kept at a minimum. In some prison systems, there is a clear and significant overuse. This is especially apparent in the case of the U.S. supermax prisons. But the use of solitary confinement is problematic elsewhere. While things have improved in Scandinavia in recent years, it is difficult to justify a practice of subjecting pretrial detainees to solitary confinement to avoid collusion, when other Western nations can do without such measures or use this kind of solitary confinement much less. The basic advice must be to avoid using solitary confinement in order to protect ongoing investigations. The police must be able to instigate control measures in order to avoid detainee collusion, but twenty-two to twenty-four hours of isolation should be avoided.

Isolation is simply "not good practice" (Coyle 2002, p. 73). When addressing the most extreme conditions of solitary confinement being used against disruptive prisoners, where inmates have nothing to do, only an hour of outdoor solitary recreation, and are being strip-searched and shackled every time they leave their cell, Coyle concludes that "this method of dealing with prisoners . . . often arises from an absence of proper management techniques" (p. 73).

But regardless of the specific circumstances, and whether solitary confinement is used in connection with disciplinary or administrative segregation or to prevent collusion in remand prisons, effort must be made to raise the level of meaningful social contacts for inmates. This can be done in a number of ways, such as raising the level of prison staff–inmate contact, allowing access to social activities with other inmates, allowing more visits, and allowing and arranging in-depth talks with prison chaplains, psychologists, psychiatrists, and volunteers from the local community. In Denmark, a prison chaplain has drafted a proposal for revising the restrictions in remand prisons that would disallow strict solitary confinement but rationalize and improve an option of limited isolation. Remand prisoners who were considered likely to engage in collusion would be allowed contact with a selected number of fellow inmates, while being cut off from contact with others. Visits and correspondence would also be strictly controlled. A certain level of meaningful social contact should thereby be secured for all inmates being subjected to limited isolation (Rasmussen 2000, pp. 24–26). A proposal for a Model Segregation Code regulating administrative and punitive segregation of sentenced prisoners has also been drafted (Jackson 1983, pp. 245–50). Prisoners in segregation would be allowed to participate in "programs, services, and activities . . . for no less than six hours per day, which shall include not less than one hour of outside exercise" (p. 249).

It is of course difficult—and most likely impossible—to identify some sort of breaking point: *the* minimum level of social contact needed to avoid the effects of solitary confinement. Research tells us that such a breaking point would be very individual. But it seems fair to conclude that one or two hours of out-of-cell time (even including some social contact) is not enough. Whether three, four, five, or six hours would suffice to eliminate the differences between isolation and nonisolation is not known, but even three hours of out-of-cell time including social contact would most likely create much better and mentally healthier conditions.

B. What We Need to Know

One important issue, mentioned only briefly, is how staff cultures affect the effects of solitary confinement. Quite a lot of research has been done on prisons and staff cultures, but studies and experiments focusing specifically on the effects of isolation have generally not taken that subject into account. Research dealing more broadly with super-max regimes or other forms of maximum-security confinement have dealt with prison and staff cultures (Clare et al. 2001; Toch 2001,

2002*b*; Rhodes 2004), and it has been argued that the effects of segregation can be ameliorated by influencing staff culture (see, e.g., Toch 2002*b*). Since isolated inmates have little contact with the outside world and meet only staff (and then infrequently), it seems relevant to speculate that the staff culture encountered by an isolated inmate is likely to have a strong effect.

More research into the more dramatic effects of solitary confinement (e.g., hallucinations, major depressions, and psychosis) would be welcome, since the effects of isolation are apparently not only a matter of a higher prevalence of the effects of imprisonment. Isolation appears to be a qualitatively different situation, which can have specific effects of its own. Research in this area would help us specify the exact differences between the effects of imprisonment and the effects of solitary confinement and might also help us identify whether "isolation syndrome" is a relevant diagnosis.

More research into the connection between solitary confinement and suicides and self-mutilations would also be useful. Longitudinal studies with designs that would enable us to analyze the degree and importance of causal connections between solitary confinement and suicidal behavior and self-mutilations would be highly relevant. Base expectancy rates for mental illness would have to be taken into account and control groups used, so that it could be identified to what degree the higher rate of suicides in segregation or isolation is a result of allocation procedures.

One important area left more or less open for future research is the subject of post–solitary confinement effects. While many effects disappear upon termination of solitary confinement, research suggests that there might also be serious postisolation effects, but evidence is relatively scarce. It would also be useful to look for social aftereffects of isolation—such as the possible loss of job and friends, relations with relatives, and so forth—instead of concentrating solely on mental health and outright pathologies. Adrian Grounds (2005) has made a strong argument for rethinking the debate over, and research on, prison effects. Grounds suggests that there might be special effects of long-term imprisonment and argues that "forms of adaptation that are functional in the prison context may be dysfunctional in the postrelease social and family context" (2005, p. 3). He points to the need to take into account the released "individual's preprison social world and life prospects" and how the outside world has changed during the duration of the imprisonment (p. 4). These are clearly factors that could be even more important in cases of release from long-term solitary confinement since that kind of isolation arguably removes the imprisoned even further from the outside world. Adaptation to solitary confinement requires an even more intensive and inward psychological process than adaptation to communal imprisonment. The literature on adaptation to isolation under different circumstances—which addresses psychological methods of keeping sane—seems to suggest this (see, e.g., Deaton, Berg, and Richlin 1977). Adaptation to (especially long-term) solitary confinement will in other words *perhaps* tend to create personalities who are more inward and have more difficulty adjusting to social life in the free world than other prisoners. This would be very useful to study not least in the United States, where prisoners are sometimes released directly onto the street from years of supermax imprisonment.

This finally leaves the question of how families are affected by having a parent in long-term solitary confinement. This would clearly be a very relevant subject for research in the United States, where supermax confinement seems likely to have a potentially strong effect on family members of the isolated individual—arguably during as well as after confinement. But this perspective is also relevant in Scandinavia, where arrest and pretrial isolation can cut bonds abruptly and for several months between parents and very young children.

APPENDIX

A Quantitative Classification of Studies Based on
Nonexperimental Data Discussing Solitary Confinement and
Health Effects

Only studies based on original research (i.e., new empirical evidence) in prisons are listed in table A1. Furthermore, only studies using real prisoners in real prisons are included in the list. Where authors have presented the same empirical material in different publications, only the first publication (or alternatively the most important study) has been included. A few exceptions exist (as mentioned in the footnotes) in which different authors have published different interpretations of the same corpus of otherwise original data.

The studies have been labeled according to research method:

   i. study based on quantitative data including a control group,

TABLE A1
Studies Reporting Health Effects

Study	Methodology	Sample Size	Involuntarily Isolated	Study Type No. 1	Study Type No. 2	Study Type No. 3	Conclusions
A. Studies Reporting None or Minor Negative Health Effects							
1. Suedfeld et al. 1982	i	115[a]	71		X		According to the authors, the data "do not support the view that SC in prisons is universally damaging, aversive, or intolerable" (p. 303)
2. Zinger and Wichmann 1999	i	60	10		X		According to the authors, "this research revealed no evidence that administrative segregation for periods of up to 60 days was damaging" (p. 65)
B. Studies Reporting Serious Negative Health Effects							
1. Andersen et al. 1994	i	367	173			X	Pretrial detention in SC (to avoid collusion) compared with pretrial detention without SC was found to impose additional strain and increase the risk for disturbing the mental health of the imprisoned individuals
2. Andersen, Lillebæk, and Sestoft 1997	i	104	70			X	The 1994 conclusion was supported, and it was recommended, from a medical and psychological viewpoint, not to use SC to avoid collusion during pretrial detention

Study						Findings
3. Benjamin and Lux 1975	iv	2 (?)[b]	2 (?)		X	The use of "forced isolation" at Maine State Prison was found to cause "a severe deterioration of psychological functioning" (p. 89)
4. Brodsky and Scogin 1988[c]	ii–iv	69	?		X	Protective custody was found to have "strong potential for harmful effects" and could "deprive the inmates of the opportunity to engage in the behaviors that allow us to define who we are." Therefore, "sufficient stimulation and activities" should be provided "to ensure the psychological well-being of the prisoners" (pp. 279–80)
5. Fellner and Mariner 1997	iv	41 (121)	41 (121)[d]		X	Many prisoners in the sample suffered from serious mental disorders, but most "had previous histories of mental disorder." Still, it was concluded that the condition of these prisoners "was exacerbated by confinement at the MCF and SHU" and a causal link between isolation and adverse effects was thereby proposed (p. 70)
6. Foster, Davis, and Sandler 1987	iv	158	125[e]	X[f]	X	The authors concluded that "there can be little doubt that solitary confinement under these circumstances [in South Africa] should in itself be regarded as a form of torture" (p. 136)

TABLE A1 (*Continued*)

Study	Methodology	Sample Size	Involuntarily Isolated	Study Type No. 1	Study Type No. 2	Study Type No. 3	Conclusions
7. Gamman 2001 (1993)[g]	ii	63	63			X	Widespread health problems were found after four weeks of SC, including depressions, anxiety, stomach and muscle pains, lack of ability to concentrate, etc. (inmates with obvious withdrawal symptoms and those deemed in risk of suffering from a psychosis had been excluded from the sample)
8. Gamman 1995	i	54	27			X	"The results showed that secluded prisoners had more health problems than prisoners serving less restrictive prison sentences did. The most usual complaints were headache, pain in the neck, stomach and shoulders, anxiety and depression" (p. 2243). SC inmates were also given and used much more medication than the control group
9. Grassian 1983	iv	14	14		X		The author found that severe symptoms were caused by SC and asserted "that these symptoms form a major, clinically distinguishable psychiatric syndrome" (p. 1450)

10. Gray 1847	i + iv[h]	4,000+	4,000+[i]	X	The author concluded "that from the experience of our own country hitherto, it appears that the system of constant separation [SC according to the Pennsylvania model] as established here, even when administered with the utmost humanity, produces so many cases of insanity and of death as to indicate most clearly, that its general tendency is to enfeeble the body and the mind" (p. 181)
11. Haney 2003[j]	ii	100	100	X	Considerable and severe effects of SC were found with very high prevalence rates. For example, 91 percent suffered from anxiety and nervousness, and 70 percent "felt themselves on the verge of an emotional breakdown" (p. 133). 77 percent were in a state of chronic depression and two-thirds of the inmates suffered from many different symptoms at once
12. Hinkle and Wolff 1956	iv	Classified	Classified[k]	X	An isolation regimen was found to produce anxiety, depression, illusory experiences, visual hallucinations, and in some cases psychosis. Insanity was normally avoided by breaking the routine of total isolation, and the lesser effects were "usually sufficient to make the prisoner eager to talk to his interrogator and to seek some method to escape from a situation which had become intolerable" (p. 129)

TABLE A1 (*Continued*)

Study	Methodology	Sample Size	Involuntarily Isolated	Study Type No. 1	Study Type No. 2	Study Type No. 3	Conclusions
13. Jackson 1983	iv	7	7		X		Severe effects of long-term SC were found including anger, violence, hallucinations, and insanity
14. Jensen et al 1980a	iv	46	46			X	The authors agreed that the collected data described "very serious mental and social effects of pre-trial isolation" (p. 5; translated by the author)
15. Jorgensen 1981[l]	iv	46	46			X	The author found SC to cause severe symptoms including anxiety, depressions, hallucinations, and insanity, and claimed to identify both an acute and a chronic isolation syndrome
16. Koch 1982[m]	iv	50	50[n]			X	The author identified short-term effects of SC such as "concentration and memory difficulties, lack of ability to sleep, psychosomatic symptoms etc." and long-term effects (after a few weeks) such as "depersonalization, lack of emotional control, anxiety, hallucination and paranoia" (p. 382)

17. Korn 1988*a*	iv	5	5	X	The author reported serious psychological and psychosomatic effects caused by the confinement including severe depressions, hallucinations, anxiety, apathy, loss of weight, and dizziness
18. Korn 1988*b*	iv	5	5	X	The author reported serious psychological and psychosomatic effects caused by the confinement including severe depressions, hallucinations, anxiety, apathy, loss of weight, and dizziness
19. Martel 1999	iv	12	12	X	According to the author, the experiences reported "suggest that segregation produces substantial and sometimes lasting, debilitating outcomes for" inmates (p. 101) and "the effects of these conditions are damaging and reach far beyond the original intent of segregation policies" (p. 104)
20. Rhodes 2004	iv	122/87	122/87°	X	The author describes effects of SC, including hallucinations, anger, and uncontrolled thought processes and relates how prison staff are in a sense to protect prisoners "from the prison itself" (p. 110)

TABLE A1 (Continued)

Study	Methodology	Sample Size	Involuntarily Isolated	Study Type No. 1	Study Type No. 2	Study Type No. 3	Conclusions
21. Sestoft et al.1998[p]	i	345	152			X	If "a person remained in SC for 4 weeks the proportionality of being admitted to the prison hospital for a psychiatric reason was about 20 times as high as for a person remanded in nSC [non-solitary confinement] for the same period of time" (p. 103)
22. Smith 2004a[q]	ii + iv	300/3,000+	300/3,000+[r]		X		At least around a third of the inmates suffered from symptoms such as, e.g., lethargy, anxiety, and hallucinations, which were found to be caused mainly by SC. These symptoms were being treated by allowing, e.g., extra out-of-cell time and limited social contact for certain inmates
23. Stang et al. 2003	i	60	30	X			The study did not assess the effects of solitary confinement as such, but reported extensive and severe mental health problems during imprisonment in segregation, such as depressions and hallucinations

Study		Total	Solitary confinement		Notes
24. Toch 1992	i + iii	600	An unknown number of these were in solitary confinement	X	Toch use the term "isolation panic" and describes a range of symptoms including panic, rage, loss of control, and complete breakdown. According to Toch, "isolation removes even the coping resources ordinarily available in prisons" and can "dramatize the pains of imprisonment per se." Isolation panic can therefore mark "a dichotomy in the minds of inmates—a distinction between imprisonment, which is tolerable, and isolation, which is not" (pp. 48–54)
25. Volkart, Rothenfluth, et al. 1983	i	203	78	X	"Remand prisoners in solitary confinement are proportionally much more often in need of psychiatric hospitalization compared to sentenced prisoners not in solitary confinement" (p. 374; translated by the author)[a]
26. Volkart, Dittrich, et al. 1983	i	58	30	X	The group of isolated inmates "showed considerably more psychopathological symptoms than the control group . . . [and these] effects were mainly caused by solitary confinement; age, schooling, duration of detention and personality turned out to be of subordinate importance" (p. 44)

[a] This study could also be listed among the studies reporting substantial health effects—because it does report substantial health effects (pp. 316, 331)—but the authors claim that these effects are not objective and not caused by solitary confinement.

TABLE A1 (Continued)

Study	Methodology	Sample Size	Involuntarily Isolated	Study Type No. 1	Study Type No. 2	Study Type No. 3	Conclusions

[b] The total number of inmates studied is not mentioned in Benjamin and Lux (1975), but two prisoners from the segregation unit are quoted at length.

[c] A study of protective custody, which therefore could be difficult to compare with the other studies mentioned here.

[d] According to the report, researchers met approximately forty prisoners in one facility in 1995 and approximately forty prisoners in another facility in 1996 (out of whom twenty participated in extended interviews). But only forty-one inmates (in the two facilities in 1997) were subjected to structured psychiatric assessment. Most of the inmates in this Human Rights Watch study were mentally ill prior to their isolation (in disciplinary or administrative segregation), and the authors were therefore not able to establish whether solitary confinement produced mental disorders. But as explained in the table, they concluded that "their condition was exacerbated by confinement at the MCF and the SHU" and described cases of panic attacks, sleeplessness, anger, paranoia, confusion etc. (Fellner et al. 1997, p. 35).

[e] The sample made by Foster (professor in psychology) and colleagues consists of 175 cases of detention involving 158 individuals. 79 percent of the detentions involved solitary confinement, so I have applied this percentage to the number of individuals (158). My result (125) is of course not likely to be completely correct.

[f] This study deals only with remand prisoners but deals with many other issues than just solitary confinement and is therefore—in the terminology used here—both a prison study and a study of the effects of solitary confinement on remand prisoners.

[g] Gamman's (1993) study (and the 1995 study) is described in Gamman (2001).

[h] Parts of Gray's study—like his statistics on death rates and insanity—are quantitative and with control groups; other parts of his study are qualitative.

[i] Gray deals with isolated prisoners from many Pennsylvania-type prisons. The total number of prisoners is unknown but exceeds 4,000.

[j] Haney's own sample (100 SHU prisoners) is from an earlier study, but the data are further analyzed and compared with other studies in Haney (2003).

[k] The material used was confidential but included, among other things, systematic and longitudinal observations of prisoners after their release.

[l] This study is based on analysis of documentation (cases) presented in Jensen, Jorgensen, and Rasmussen (1980a, 1980b).

516

[m] This study is partly based on analysis of documentation (cases) presented in Jensen, Jørgensen, and Rasmussen (1980a, 1980b), but also on forty-seven interviews with women remand prisoners, many of whom were isolated (Koch 1982, p. 374).

[n] According to Koch, her material consists of "more than fifty cases." She also states that she has interviewed remand prisoners who were not in solitary confinement, and her study can in that sense perhaps claim to have a control group element.

[o] The medical records of 122 inmates were used, and eighty-seven were interviewed (Rhodes 2004, p. 229).

[p] This study was originally part of Andersen et al. (1994). But a somewhat stronger conclusion was reached, and a more direct criticism of the use of SC was communicated.

[q] The main study is in fact Smith (2003), but since my 2004b article gives an account of the health effects of solitary confinement in English, I have chosen to cite that one.

[r] Different calculations are based on different samples in this study. Some illness rates are based on a sample of 300 prisoners and another on a sample of 1,596 prisoners. In all more than 3,000 prisoners passed through the prison in the period in which all available medical reports etc. were read.

[s] "Untersuchungs-Einzelhäftlinge [werden] proportional viel häufiger psychiatrisch hospitalisierungsbedürftig als Gemeinschaftshäftlinge des Strafvollzugs."

   ii. study based on quantitative data without control group,

   iii. qualitative study (e.g., based on in-depth interviews) with control group, and

   iv. qualitative study (e.g., based on in-depth interviews) without control group.

Some studies can of course be termed both quantitative and qualitative. Finally, the number of participants in the study, the number of involuntarily isolated prisoners, and the type of study (or subject) are noted. Three different types/subjects are acknowledged: (1) prison studies that deal with several issues but also report on the effects of solitary confinement, (2) studies that deal primarily or solely with the effects of solitary confinement in prisons, and (3) studies that deal primarily or solely with the effects of solitary confinement in remand prisons.

REFERENCES

Abramsky, Sasha, and Jamie Fellner. 2003. *Ill-Equipped: U.S. Prisons and Offenders with Mental Illness.* New York: Human Rights Watch.

Amnesty International. 2003. "Turkey: Solitary Confinement of Abdullah Ocalan." Public statement, January 31. http://web.amnesty.org/library/Index/ENGEUR440052003?open&of=ENG-360.

Andersen, Hans Christian. 1851. *I Sverrig.* Copenhagen: C. A. Reitzel.

Andersen, Henrik Steen. 1992. "Sensorisk deprivation." *Ugeskrift for Læger* 154:2665–70.

———. 2004. "Mental Health in Prison Populations: A Review—with Special Emphasis on a Study of Danish Prisoners on Remand." *Acta Psychiatrica Scandinavica Supplementum* 110(424):5–59.

Andersen, Henrik Steen, Tommy Lillebæk, and Dorte Sestoft. 1997. *Efterundersøgelsen—en opfølgningsundersøgelse af danske varetægtsarrestanter.* Copenhagen: Schultz.

Andersen, Henrik Steen, Tommy Lillebæk, Dorte Sestoft, and Gorm Gabrielsen. 1994. *Isolationsundersøgelsen. Varetægtsfængsling og psykisk helbred.* Vols. 1–2. Copenhagen: Schultz.

Andersen, Henrik Steen, Dorte Sestoft, Tommy Lillebæk, Gorm Gabrielsen, and R. Hemmingsen. 2003. "A Longitudinal Study of Prisoners on Remand: Repeated Measures of Psychopathology in the Initial Phase of Solitary versus Nonsolitary Confinement." *International Journal of Law and Psychiatry* 26: 165–77.

Bell, A. N., and R. D. A. Mackie, eds. 1985. *Detention and Security Legislation in South Africa: Proceedings of a Conference Held at the University of Natal, September 1982.* Durban: University of Natal.

Benjamin, Thomas B., and Kenneth Lux. 1975. "Constitutional and Psychological Implications of the Use of Solitary Confinement: Experience at the Maine State Prison." *Clearingshouse Review* 9 (June): 83–90.

Benjaminsen, Sigurd, and Birgit Erichsen. 2002. *Selvmordsadfærd Blandt Indsatte.* Copenhagen: Direktoratet for kriminalforsorgen.

Beretninger fra Kontoret for Fængselsvæsenet, Straffeanstalternes Tilstand, 1. april 1878 til 31. marts 1883. 1885. Copenhagen.

Beretning fra Overinspektionen for Fængselsvæsenet, Straffeanstalterne i Danmark, 1. april 1886 til 31. marts 1891. 1898. Copenhagen.

Beretning om Straffeanstalterne i Danmark, Finansaaret 1911–12. 1913. Copenhagen.

Beretning om Straffeanstalterne i Danmark, Finansaaret 1912–13. 1914. Copenhagen.

Beretning om Straffeanstalterne i Danmark, Finansaaret 1913–14. 1915. Copenhagen.

Beretning om Straffeanstalterne i Danmark, Finansaaret 1914–15. 1916. Copenhagen.

Beretning om Straffeanstalterne i Danmark, Finansaaret 1930–31. 1932. Copenhagen.

Beretning om Straffeanstalterne i Danmark, Finansaaret 1931–32. 1934. Copenhagen.

Beretning om Straffeanstalterne i Danmark, Finansaaret 1933–37. 1939. Copenhagen.

Berggrav, Eivind. 1928. *Fangens sjel—og vår egen. Erfaringer og iakttagelser fra botsfengslet i Oslo.* Oslo.

Bonta, James, and Paul Gendreau. 1990. "Reexamining the Cruel and Unusual Punishment of Prison Life." *Law and Human Behavior* 14:347–72.

———. 1995. "Reexamining the Cruel and Unusual Punishment of Prison Life." In *Long-Term Imprisonment: Policy, Science, and Correctional Practice,* edited by Timothy J. Flanagan. Thousand Oaks, CA: Sage.

Boston, John. 2000. "The Constitutional Law of Isolated Confinement: A Quick and Dirty Review." Paper presented at a conference at the International Centre for Prison Studies at Kings College, London, February 23–24.

Bresnihan, Valerie. 2002. "Out of Mind, out of Sound: Solitary Confinement of Mentally Ill/Dysfunctional Prisoners in Irish Prisons." *European Journal of Health Law* 9:111–20.

Briggs, Chad S., Jody L. Sundt, and Thomas C. Castellano. 2003. "The Effect of Supermaximum Security Prisons on Aggregate Levels of Institutional Violence." *Criminology* 41:1341–76.

Brodsky, Stanley L., and Forrest R. Scogin. 1988. "Inmates in Protective Custody: First Data on Emotional Effects." *Forensic Reports* 1:267–80.

Brownfield, Charles. 1965. *Isolation: Clinical and Experimental Approaches.* New York: Random House.

Bruun, Frederik. 1867. *Om fuldbyrdelse af Strafarbeide.* Copenhagen: F. H. Sibes Forlag.

Christensen, Else. 1999. *Forældre i fængsel—en undersøgelse af børns og forældres erfaringer.* Report no. 99/5. Copenhagen: Socialforskningsinstituttet.

Christiansen, W. Frees. 1991. "Selvmord i danske fængsler og arresthuse: En undersøgelse som dækker 10-året 1.4.1977–31.3.1987." *Nordisk Tidsskrift for kriminalvidenskab* 78(3):164–79.

Clare, Emma, Keith Bottomley, Adrian Grounds, Christopher J. Hammond, Alison Liebling, and Caecilia Taylor. 2001. *Evaluation of Close Supervision Centres.* London: Home Office Research Studies.

Coid, Jeremy, Ann Petruckevitch, Paul Bebbinton, Rachel Jenkins, Traolach Brugha, Glyn Lewis, Michael Farrel, and Nicola Singleton. 2003a. "Psychiatric Morbidity in Prisoners and Solitary Cellular Confinement, I: Disciplinary Segregation." *Journal of Forensic Psychiatry and Psychology* 14: 298–319.

———. 2003b. "Psychiatric Morbidity in Prisoners and Solitary Cellular Confinement, II: Special ('Strip') Cells." *Journal of Forensic Psychiatry and Psychology* 14:320–40.

Committee against Torture. 1997. "Concluding Observations." Denmark. 01/05/97. A/52/44, paras.171–88. http://www.unhchr.ch/tbs/doc.nsf/0/14e23179777ab903802565a30053abee?Opendocument.

Conover, Ted. 2001. *Holding the Key.* London: Scribner.

Coyle, Andrew. 2002. *A Human Rights Approach to Prison Management: Handbook for Prison Staff.* London: International Centre for Prison Studies.

Danielsen, Trond, and Wilhelm Meek Hansen. 2002. *Kvalitet i varetektsarbeidet: En undersøgelse fra Oslo fengsel om varetektsinsatte med restriksjoner.* Oslo: KRUS.

Danish Ministry of Justice. 1983. *Betænkning om Isolation af varetægtsarrestanter.* Betænkning Nr. 975. Copenhagen: Stougaard Jensen.

Deaton, John, William Berg, and Milton Richlin. 1977. "Coping Activities in Solitary Confinement of U.S. Navy POWs in Vietnam." *Journal of Applied Social Psychology* 7:239–57.

Dickens, Charles. 1985. *American Notes.* London: Penguin. (Originally published 1842.)

European Committee for the Prevention of Torture and Inhuman or Degrading Treatment or Punishment. 1991. *Report to the Danish Government on the Visit to Denmark Carried out from 2 to 8 December 1990.* http://www.cpt.coe.int/documents/dnk/1991-12-inf-eng.pdf.

———. 1997. *Report to the Danish Government on the Visit to Denmark Carried out from 29 September to 9 October 1996.* http://www.cpt.coe.int/documents/dnk/1997-04-inf-eng.pdf.

———. 2002. *Report to the Government of Denmark on the Visit to Denmark from 28 January to 4 February 2002.* http://www.cpt.coe.int/documents/dnk/2002-18-inf-eng.pdf.

Evans, Malcolm D., and Rod Morgan. 1998. *Preventing Torture: A Study of the European Convention for the Prevention of Torture and Inhuman or Degrading Treatment or Punishment.* Oxford: Clarendon.

Farrel, Gerald A., and Gerry Dares. 1996. "Seclusion or Solitary Confinement: Therapeutic or Punitive Treatment?" *Australian and New Zealand Journal of Mental Health Nursing* 5:171–79.

Fazel, Seena, and John Danesh. 2002. "Serious Mental Disorder in 23,000 Prisoners: A Systematic Review of 62 Surveys." *Lancet* 359:545–50.

Fellner, Jamie, and Joanne Mariner. 1997. *Cold Storage: Super–Maximum Security Confinement in Indiana.* New York: Human Rights Watch.

Flanagan, Timothy J., ed. 1995. *Long-Term Imprisonment: Policy, Science, and Correctional Practice.* London: Sage.

Forsythe, Bill. 2004. "Loneliness and Cellular Confinement in English Prisons 1878–1921." *British Journal of Criminology* 44:759–70.

Foster, Don, Dennis Davis, and Diane Sandler. 1987. *Detention and Torture in South Africa: Psychological, Legal and Historical Studies.* Cape Town and Johannesburg: David Phillip.

Foucault, Michel. 1995. *Discipline and Punish: The Birth of the Prison.* New York: Vintage.

Franke, Herman. 1992. "The Rise and Decline of Solitary Confinement." *British Journal of Criminology* 32:125–43.

Gamman, Tor. 1995. "Uheldige helsemessige effekter av isolasjon. En klinisk studie av to grupper av varetektsinnsatte." *Tidsskrift for den norske Lægeforening* 115:2243–46.

———. 2001. "Om bruk av isolasjon under varetektsfengsling." *Nordisk Tidsskrift for Kriminalvidenskab* 88:42–50.

Gamman, Tor, and Olav M. Linaker. 2000. "Screening for psykiatrisk lidelse blant fengselsinnsatte." *Tidsskrift for den Norske Lægeforening* 120:2151–53.

Gendreau, Paul, and James Bonta. 1984. "Solitary Confinement Is Not Cruel and Unusual Punishment: People Sometimes Are!" *Canadian Journal of Criminology* 26:467–78.

Gendreau, Paul, N. L. Freedman, J. S. Wilde, and G. D. Scott. 1972. "Changes in EEG Alpha Frequency and Evoked Response Latency during Solitary Confinement." *Journal of Abnormal Psychology* 79:54–59.

Gibby, Robert, Henry B. Adams, and Richard N. Carrera. 1977. "Therapeutic Changes in Psychiatric Patients Following Partial Sensory Deprivation." In *Sensory Isolation and Personality Change*, edited by Mark Kammerman. Springfield, IL: Thomas Books.

Gould, Stephen Jay. 2003. *The Hedgehog, the Fox, and the Magister's Pox: Mending and Minding the Misconceived Gap between Science and the Humanities.* London: Jonathan Cape.

Grassian, Stuart. 1983. "Psychopathological Effects of Solitary Confinement." *American Journal of Psychiatry* 140:1450–54.

———. 1993. "Psychiatric Effects of Solitary Confinement." Court statement submitted in September 1993 in *Madrid v. Gomez*, 889F.Supp.1146. London: King's College, International Centre for Prison Studies.

———. 1999. "Overview: Summary of Substantive Findings." Report from a January 1999 visit to the Attica Special Housing Unit. http://www.hrw.org/reports/2003/usa1003/Grassian_Report_Eng_Site_Visit_One.pdf.

Grassian, Stuart, and Nancy Friedman. 1986. "Effects of Sensory Deprivation in Psychiatric Seclusion and Solitary Confinement." *International Journal of Law and Psychiatry* 8:49–65.

Gray, Francis C. 1847. *Prison Discipline in America*. Boston: Little, Brown.

Greenberg, Karen J., and Joshua L. Dratel. 2005. *The Torture Papers: The Road to Abu Ghraib*. Cambridge: Cambridge University Press.

Grounds, Adrian. 2005. "Understanding the Effects of Wrongful Imprisonment." In *Crime and Justice: A Review of Research*, vol. 32, edited by Michael Tonry. Chicago: Chicago University Press.

Hammerlin, Yngve. 2000. "Selvmord i norske fengsler: del 1." *Suicidologi* 5(1): 29–31. http://www.med.uio.no/ipsy/ssff/0001Hammerlin.htm.

———. 2001. "Varetekt—et haleheng i kriminalforsorgen?" *Tidskrift för Kriminalvård*. 56(3):11–21.

Hammerlin, Yngve, and Egil Larsen. 2000. *Tungtsonende*. Oslo: KRUS.

Haney, Craig. 1993. "'Infamous Punishment': The Psychological Consequences of Isolation." *National Prison Project Journal* 8 (Spring): 3–7.

———. 2001. "The Psychological Impact of Incarceration: Implications for Post-prison Adjustment." Paper presented at the National Policy Conference "From Prison to Home: The Effect of Incarceration and Reentry on Children, Families, and Communities," Washington, DC, January 30–31, 2002. http://www.aspe.hhs.gov/hsp/prison2home02/index.htm.

———. 2003. "Mental Health Issues in Long-Term Solitary and 'Supermax' Confinement." *Crime and Delinquency* 49(1):124–56.

Haney, Craig, and Mona Lynch. 1997. "Regulating Prisons of the Future: A Psychological Analysis of Supermax and Solitary Confinement." *Review of Law and Social Change* 23:477–570.

Harvey, Joel. 2004. "Transition and Adaptation to Prison Life: A Study of Young Adults Aged 18 to 21." Unpublished summary of PhD thesis, University of Cambridge, Institute of Criminology.

Hayes, Lindsay M. 1983. "And Darkness Closes In . . . a National Study of Jail Suicides." *Criminal Justice and Behavior* 10:461–84.

———. 1989. "National Study of Jail Suicides: Seven Years Later." *Psychiatric Quarterly* 60:7–29.

Henriques, U. R. Q. 1972. "The Rise and Decline of the Separate System of Prison Discipline." *Past and Present* (54):61–93.

Hess, Albert G. 1972. "Foreword." In *Reports of the Prison Discipline Society of Boston: The Twenty-nine Annual Reports of the Board of Managers 1826–1854 with a Memoir of Louis Dwight*. Montclair, NJ: Patterson Smith. (Originally published 1855. Boston: T. R. Marvin.)

Hinkle, Lawrence E., and Harold G. Wolff. 1956. "Communist Interrogation and Indoctrination of 'Enemies of the State.'" *AMA Archives of Neurology and Psychiatry* 76:115–74.

Hodgins, Sheilagh, and Gilles Côté. 1991. "The Mental Health of Penitentiary Inmates in Isolation." *Canadian Journal of Criminology* 33:177–82.

Howe, Samuel Gridley. 1846. *An Essay on Separate and Congregate Systems of Prison Discipline; Being a Report Made to the Boston Prison Discipline Society*. Boston: Ticknor.

Human Rights Watch. 2001. "Turkey: Isolation of Prisoners Condemned."

Human Rights News (April 5). http://hrw.org/english/docs/2001/04/05/turkey246.htm.

————. 2004*a*. "Iran: Briefing to the 60th Session of the UN Commission on Human Rights." *Human Rights News* (January). http://hrw.org/english/docs/2004/01/29/iran7129.htm.

————. 2004*b*. "Tunisia: Long-Term Solitary Confinement of Political Prisoners." *Human Rights Watch Index* 16:3(E), July. http://hrw.org/reports/2004/tunisia0704/.

Humphreys, Martin, and Frances Burnett. 1994. "Monosymptomatic Hypochondriacal Psychosis and Prolonged Solitary Confinement." *Medicine, Science and the Law* 34:343–46.

Ignatieff, Michael. 1978. *A Just Measure of Pain: Penitentiaries in the Industrial Revolution, 1780–1850*. New York: Macmillan.

Immarigeon, Russ. 1992. "The Marionization of American Prisons." *National Prison Project Journal* 7(4):1–5.

Jackson, Michael. 1983. *Prisoners of Isolation: Solitary Confinement in Canada*. Toronto: University of Toronto Press.

————. 2002. *Justice behind the Walls: Human Rights in Canadian Prisons*. Vancouver: Douglas & McIntyre. http://www.justicebehindthewalls.net/.

Jensen, Jørgen Pauli. 1988. "Report on Solitary Confinement in Danish Prisons." Amnesty International Research Project on Solitary Confinement in Prisons. Reports from Europe and Canada. International Rehabilitation Council for Torture Victims (IRCT), Documentation Centre. Article no. 8210. Copenhagen.

Jensen, Jørgen P., Finn Jørgensen, and Jørgen W. Rasmussen. 1980*a*. *Testimony on the Mental and Social Consequences of Imprisonment in Isolation in Denmark*. Haarby, Denmark: Forlaget i Haarby.

————. 1980*b*. *Vidnesbyrd om de psykiske og social følger ag dansk isolationsfængsling*. Haarby, Denmark: Forlaget i Haarby.

Johnston, Norman. 2000. *Forms of Constraint: A History of Prison Architecture*. Chicago: University of Illinois Press.

Jørgensen, Finn. 1981. "De psykiske følger af isolation." *Ugeskrift for Læger* 143:3346–47.

————. 1990. "Isolationssyndromer." *Ugeskrift for Læger* 152(24):1755.

Joukumaa, Matti. 1997. "Prison Suicide in Finland, 1969–1992." *Forensic Science International* 89:167–74.

King, Roy. 1999. "The Rise and Rise of Supermax: An American Solution in Search of a Problem?" *Punishment and Society* 1:163–86.

Koch, Ida E. 1982. "Isolationens psykiske og sociale følgevirkninger." *Månedsskrift for Praktisk Lægegerning* 60(June):369–32.

————. 1983. "Isolationens psykiske og social følgevirkninger." In *Umenneskelighedens ansigter: Temabog om tortur, dødsstraf, isolationsfængsling og Amnesty Internationals lægegrupper*, edited by Søren Ganes et al. Copenhagen: Amnesty International Dansk Forlag.

Koch, Ida E., and Manfred Petersen. 1988. "Isolation af varetægtsfængslede."

In *Retspolitisk Status: Festskrift i anledning af Dansk Retspolitisk Forenings 10 års jubilæum*. Copenhagen: Jurist- og Økonomforbundets forlag.

Koch, Ida, Bent Sørensen, Manfred Petersen, Jørgen Worsaae Rasmussen, and Henning Glahn. 2003. "Isolation—en plet på det danske retssystem." In *Retspolitiske udfordringer*, edited by Jørgen Jepsen and Jens Lyhne. Copenhagen: Gads Forlag.

Køppe, Simo. 2004. *Neurosens opståen og udvikling i 1800-tallet*. Copenhagen: Frydenlund.

Korn, Richard. 1988a. "The Effects of Confinement in the High Security Unit at Lexington." *Social Justice* 15:8–19.

————. 1988b. "Follow-up Report on the Effects of Confinement in the High Security Unit at Lexington." *Social Justice* 15:20–29.

Kramp, Peter. 1993. "The 1992 Survey of Psychiatric Morbidity in the Danish Prison Population." Unpublished paper. Copenhagen: Danish Prison Service.

Kupers, Terry. 1999. *Prison Madness*. San Francisco: Jossey-Bass.

Kurki, Leena, and Norval Morris. 2001. "The Purposes, Practices, and Problems of Supermax Prisons." In *Crime and Justice: A Review of Research*, vol. 28, edited by Michael Tonry. Chicago: University of Chicago Press.

Kyvsgaard, Britta. 1999. *Klientundersøgelsen*. Copenhagen: Direktoratet for Kriminalforsorgen.

Lærum, Haakon. 1990. "Ulvens ansigt. Isolationsfængsling." *Ugeskrift for læger* 152(24):1755–57.

Laurie, Peter. 1846. *"Killing No Murder;" or, The Effects of Separate Confinement on the Bodily and Mental Condition of Prisoners in the Government Prisons and Other Gaols in Great Britain and America*. London: John Murray.

Liebling, Alison. 1992. *Suicides in Prison*. London: Routledge.

————. 1994. "Introduction." In *Deaths in Custody: International Perspectives*, edited by Alison Liebling and Tony Ward. Bournemouth, U.K.: Bourne Press.

————. 2004. *Prisons and Their Moral Performance: A Study of Values, Quality, and Prison Life*. Oxford: Oxford University Press.

Lipke, Richard L. 2004. "Against Supermax." *Journal of Applied Philosophy* 21: 109–24.

Luise, Maria A. 1989. "Solitary Confinement: Legal and Psychological Considerations." *New England Journal on Criminal and Civil Confinement* 15: 302–24.

Manzano, Jorge. 1980. "Om isolation i varetaegtsarrest." In *Vidnesbyrd om de psykiske og social følger ag dansk isolationsfængsling*, edited by Jørgen Jensen, Finn Jørgensen, and Jørgen Rasmussen. Haarby: Forlaget i Haarby.

Martel, Joane. 1999. *Solitude and Cold Storage: Women's Journeys of Endurance in Segregation*. Edmonton, Canada: ACI Communication.

Melvin, Marcie A. n.d. "Counteracting the Effects of Solitary Confinement." Article no. 04192. Copenhagen: International Rehabilitation Council for Torture Victims (IRTC), Documentation Centre.

Miller, Holly A., and Glenn R. Young. 1997. "Prison Segregation: Administrative Detention Remedy or Mental Health Problem." *Criminal Behavior and Mental Health* 7:85–94.

Morgan, Rod. 1999. "Moderate Psychological Pressure: The Scandinavian Way?" *Kritisk Juss* 26(3):201–4.

Morris, Norval, and Leena Kurki. 2001. "The Purposes, Practices, and Problems of Supermax Prisons." In *Crime and Justice: A Review of Research*, vol. 28, edited by Michael Tonry. Chicago: University of Chicago Press.

Morris, Norval, and David Rothman, eds. 1998. *The Oxford History of the Prison*. Oxford: Oxford University Press.

Mwijage, Ludovick S. 1996. *The Dark Side of Nyerere's Legacy*. Copenhagen: Olduvai Publishers.

Nilsson, Roddy. 1999. *En välbyggd maskin, en mardröm för själen*. Lund: Lunds University Press.

———. 2003. "The Swedish Prison System in Historical Perspective: A Story of Successful Failure?" *Journal of Scandinavian Studies in Criminology and Crime Prevention* 4:1–20.

Nitsche, Paul, and Karl Wilmanns. 1912. *The History of the Prison Psychoses*. Nervous and Mental Disease Monograph Series, no. 13. New York: Journal of Nervous and Mental Disease Publishing Co.

Peters, Edward M. 1998. "Prison before the Prison." In *The Oxford History of the Prison*, edited by Norval Morris and David J. Rothman. Oxford: Oxford University Press.

Petersen, Manfred W. 1998. "Isolation—en illusion?" *Retspolitik* 16(2):31–34.

Pizarro, Jesenia, and Vanja M. K. Stenius. 2004. "Supermax Prisons: Their Rise, Current Practices, and Effect on Inmates." *Prison Journal* 84(2):248–64.

Politiken. 1980. "Politisk enighed: Færre i isolation." January 8, sec. 1, p. 3.

Porporino, Frank. 2002. "Foreword." In *Living in Prison: The Ecology of Survival*, by Hans Toch. Washington: American Psychological Association.

Potter, Harry. 1993. *Hanging in Judgment: Religion and the Death Penalty in England*. London: SCM Press.

Rasmussen, John E., ed. 1973. *Man in Isolation and Confinement*. Chicago: Aldine.

Rasmussen, Jørgen Worsaae. 2000. "Der er alternativer til total isolationsfængsling." *Amnesty* (2):24–26.

Reports of the Prison Discipline Society of Boston: The Twenty-nine Annual Reports of the Board of Managers 1826–1854 with a Memoir of Louis Dwight. 1972. Montclair, NJ: Patterson Smith. (Originally published 1855. Boston: T.R. Marvin.).

Rhodes, Lorna. 2004. *Total Confinement: Madness and Reason in the Maximum Security Prison*. Los Angeles: University of California Press.

Riekert, J. G. 1985. "The DDD Syndrome: Solitary Confinement and a South African Security Law Trial." In *Detention and Security Legislation in South Africa*, edited by A. N. Bell and R. D. A. Mackie. Durban: University of Natal, Centre for Adult Education.

Riveland, Chase. 1999. *Supermax Prisons: Overview and General Considerations*.

Washington, DC: National Institute of Corrections. http://www.nicic.org/pubs/1999/014937.pdf.

Roberts, Julian V., and Robert J. Gebotys. 2001. "Prisoners of Isolation: Research on the Effects of Administrative Segregation." *Canadian Journal of Criminology and Criminal Justice* 43:85–98.

Rossi, Michael. 1969. "General Methodological Considerations." In *Sensory Deprivation: Fifteen Years of Research*, edited by John P. Zubek. New York: Appleton-Century-Crofts.

Rothman, David J. 1971. *The Discovery of the Asylum*. Boston: Little, Brown.

———. 1998. "Perfecting the Prison: United States, 1789–1865." In *The Oxford History of the Prison. The Practice of Punishment in Western Society*. Oxford: Oxford University Press.

Salvatore, Ricardo, and Carlos Aguirre. 1996. *The Birth of the Penitentiary in Latin America*. Austin: University of Texas Press.

Schlesinger, James R., Harold Brown, Tillie K. Fowler, Charles A. Homer, and James A. Blackwell. 2004. *Final Report of the Independent Panel to Review DoD Detention Operations*. Washington, DC: U.S. Department of Defense.

Schultz, Duane P. 1965. *Sensory Restriction: Effects on Behavior*. New York: Academic Press.

Scott, George, and Paul Gendreau. 1969. "Psychiatric Implications of Sensory Deprivation in a Maximum Security Prison." *Canadian Psychiatric Association Journal* 14:337–41.

Sestoft, Dorte Maria, Henrik Steen Andersen, Tommy Lillebæk, and Gorm Gabrielsen. 1998. "Impact of Solitary Confinement on Hospitalization among Danish Prisoners in Custody." *International Journal of Law and Psychiatry* 21:99–108.

Shalev, Sharon, and Daniel Guinea. 2003. "La Détention en isolement au Royaume Uni." In *La détention en isolement dans les prisons européennes: Les régimes spéciaux de détention en Italie et en Espagne et les mesures administratives en France et au Royaum Uni*, edited by Malena Zingoni-Fernandez and Nicola Giovannini. Brussels: Bruyant.

Shallice, T. 1972. "The Ulster Depth Interrogation Techniques and Their Relation to Sensory Deprivation Research." *Cognition* 1:385–405.

Siegel, Ronald K. 1984. "Hostage Hallucinations: Visual Imagery Induced by Isolation and Life-Threatening Stress." *Journal of Nervous and Mental Disease* 172:264–72.

Smith, Peter Scharff. 2003. *Moralske hospitaler. Det moderne fængselsvæsens gennembrud 1770–1870*. Copenhagen: Forum.

———. 2004a. "Isolation and Mental Illness in Vridsløselille 1859–1873: A New Perspective on the Breakthrough of the Modern Penitentiary." *Scandinavian Journal of History* 29(1):1–25.

———. 2004b. "A Religious Technology of the Self: Rationality and Religion in the Rise of the Modern Penitentiary." *Punishment and Society* 6:195–220.

———. 2005. "Varetægtsfængsling i isolation: En besynderlig skandinavisk tradition?" *Social Kritik* 99:4–17.

Spann, W., E. Liebhardt, and S. Seifert. 1979. "Suizide in bayrischen Vollzug-sanstalten." *Münchener medizinische Wochenschrift* 121:315–16.

Spierenburg, Pieter. 1996. "Four Centuries of Prison History." In *Institutions of Confinement*, edited by Norbert Finzsch and Robert Jütte. Cambridge: Cambridge University Press.

Spitz, René A. 1952. "Authority and Masturbation: Some Remarks on a Bibliographical Investigation." *Psychoanalytic Quarterly* 21:490–527.

Stagetorn, Merethe. 2003. *Forsvarsadvokaten: Hverdag i retssale og fængsler.* Copenhagen: Nørhaven.

Stang, Jan, Jens Moe, Inge Arne Teigset, Bjørn Østberg, and Tron Anders Moger. 2003. "Fanger i sikkerhetscelle—en utfordring." *Tidsskrift for Den norske Lægeforening* 123(13–14):1844–46.

Suedfeld, Peter. 1969. "Introduction and Historical Background." In *Sensory Deprivation: Fifteen Years of Research*, edited by John P. Zubek. New York: Appleton-Century-Crofts.

Suedfeld, Peter, and Chunilal Roy. 1975. "Using Social Isolation to Change the Behavior of Disruptive Inmates." *International Journal of Offender Therapy and Comparative Criminology* 19:90–99.

Suedfeld, Peter, Carmenza Ramirez, John Deaton, and Gloria Baker-Brown. 1982. "Reactions and Attributes of Prisoners in Solitary Confinement." *Criminal Justice and Behaviour* 9:303–40.

Teeters, Negley K. 1944. *World Penal Systems: A Survey*. Philadelphia: Pennsylvania Prison Society.

———. 1949. *Deliberations of the International Penal and Penitentiary Congresses: Questions and Answers, 1872–1935*. Philadelphia: Temple University Book Store.

Thelle, Hatla, and Anne-Marie Traeholt. 2003. "Protection of Suspects' Rights versus Investigation Needs: The Use of Solitary Confinement in Denmark." In *How to Eradicate Torture: A Sino-Danish Joint Research on the Prevention of Torture*, edited by Morten Kjærum, Xia Yong, Hatla Thelle, and Bixiaoqing. Beijing: Social Sciences Documentation Publishing House.

Toch, Hans. 1992. *Mosaic of Despair: Human Breakdowns in Prison*. Lawrenceville, NJ: Princeton University Press.

———. 2001. "The Future of Supermax Confinement." *Prison Journal* 81(3): 376–88.

———. 2002a. *Living in Prison: The Ecology of Survival*. Washington, DC: American Psychological Association.

———. 2002b. "Opening Pandora's Box: Ameliorating the Effects of Long-Term Segregation Conditions." *Prison Service Journal* 82(November):15–21.

———. 2003. "The Contemporary Relevance of Early Experiments with Supermax Reform." *Prison Journal* 83:221–28.

Tryde, Chr. 1871. *Cellestraffens Indvirkning paa Forbrydernes mentelle Sundhedstilstand*. Copenhagen: Schultz.

Turnbull, Gordon. 1997. "Hostage Retrieval." *Journal of the Royal Society of Medicine* 90:478–83.

Veriava, Yosuf. 1989. "Torture and the Medical Profession in South Africa—Complicity or Concern?" *Critical Health* 26:39–52.

Vernon, Jack A. 1965. *Inside the Black Room.* London: Souvenir Press.

Volkart, Reto. 1983. "Einzelhaft: Eine Literaturübersicht." *Schweizerische Zeitschrift für Psychologie und ihre Anwendungen* 42:1–24.

Volkart, Reto, A. Dittrich, T. Rothenfluth, and W. Paul. 1983. "Eine kontrollierte Untersuchung über psychopathologische Effekte der Einzelhaft." *Schweizerische Zeitschrift für Psychologie und ihre Anwendungen* 42:25–46.

Volkart, Reto, Thomas Rothenfluth, Erner Kobelt, Adolf Dittrich, and Klaus Ernst. 1983. "Einzelhaft als Risikofaktor für psychiatrische Hospitalisierung." *Psychiatrica Clinica* 16:365–77.

Vyvyan, Richard. 1845. *A Letter from Sir Richard Vyvyan, Bt., M.P., to the Magistrates of Berkshire, upon Their Newly Established Practice of Consigning Prisoners to Solitary Confinement before Trial, and Ordering That They Be Disguised by Masks Whenever They Are Taken out of Their Cells.* London: Ridgway.

Walters, Richard, John Callagan, and Albert Newman. 1963. "Effect of Solitary Confinement on Prisoners." *American Journal of Psychiatry* 119:771–73.

Wessely, Simon. 1995. "Neurasthenia and Fatigue Syndromes: Clinical Section." In *A History of Clinical Psychiatry*, edited by German Berrios and Roy Porter. London: Athlone.

West, Louis J. 1985. "Effects of Isolation on the Evidence of Detainees." In *Detention and Security Legislation in South Africa: Proceedings of a Conference Held at the University of Natal, September 1982*, edited by A. N. Bell and R. D. A. Mackie. Durban: University of Natal.

Wilson, J. G., and M. J. Pescor. 1939. *Problems in Prison Psychiatry.* Caldwell, ID: Caxton.

Zinger, Ivan, and Cherami Wichmann. 1999. *The Psychological Effects of 60 Days in Administrative Segregation.* Ottawa: Correctional Services of Canada, Research Branch.

Zubek, John P. 1973. "Behavioral and Physiological Effects of Prolonged Sensory and Perceptual Deprivation: A Review." In *Man in Isolation and Confinement*, edited by John E. Rasmussen. Chicago: Aldine.

Zuckerman, Marvin. 1969a. "Hallucinations, Reported Sensations, and Images." In *Sensory Deprivation: Fifteen Years of Research*, edited by John P. Zubek. New York: Appleton-Century-Crofts.

———. 1969b. "Variables Affecting Deprivation Results." In *Sensory Deprivation: Fifteen Years of Research*, edited by John P. Zubek. New York: Appleton-Century-Crofts.

Zuckerman, Marvin, Richard J. Albright, Clifford S. Marks, and Gerald L. Miller. 1962. "Stress and Hallucinatory Effects of Perceptual Isolation and Confinement." *Psychological Monographs: General and Applied* 76(30):1–15.